MASTERING COMMUNICATION
Second Edition

DENNIS S. GOURAN
The Pennsylvania State University

WILLIAM E. WIETHOFF
Indiana University at Bloomington

JOEL A. DOELGER
University of Arkansas

The only text
that shows students
the link between
communication,
leadership and persuasion,
and
social responsibility!

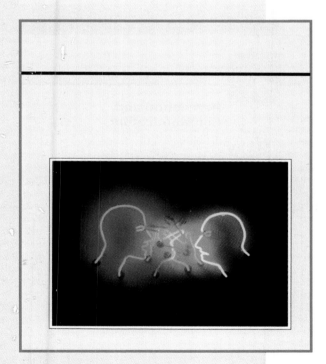

The new Second Edition offers

- The best informed authorship

- Top-flight research

- Accessible pedagogy

- An Innovative teaching
  package including:
  - An Annotated Instructor's Edition
  - CNN video
  - An extensive video library and
  - A computerized test bank

ALLYN & BACON

A hybrid text with an interactive, skill-building format

MASTERING COMMUNICATION's interactive format and motivating skill-building pedagogy stresses the development of basic communication skills that span the full spectrum of communication issues. This Second Edition addresses the growing concerns over communication in the workplace and family and across intercultural relationships. In this new edition you will find

■ A well-balanced presentation of theory and practice in Interpersonal, Group, and Public Communication — with an emphasis on communication research

■ A unifying model of communication that applies to a full spectrum of real-world social contexts — emphasizing communication's role in leadership and social responsibility

■ New sections that focus on contemporary issues of intercultural, family, and organizational communication

■ Exceptional reviews of the important aspects of the production and reception of messages (Chs. 2-4)

■ A unifying model of communication that applies to all social contexts — more closely resembling real-life situations of communication than other pedagogical approaches

■ Opportunities in every chapter for students to assess their own communications skills and to practice building new skills

---

involved, the way they conduct themselves, communicatively speaking, may vary considerably from their conduct on a less significant occasion. If you were paying tribute to your favorite teacher on his or her retirement, you undoubtedly would be much more concerned about your "message" than you would be if a friend were to ask you for your reactions to a movie you have just seen.

Physical conditions, communicative context, and occasion are just a few of the aspects of the situations in which messages are exchanged that influence their content and consequences. In mentioning these, we are attempting to show you that even though the same general model applies to all instances of communication, the way in which the process occurs depends heavily on the surrounding circumstances.

Generalizations About Communication

From our discussion of communication, several generalizations emerge. The foundation for these will be more clearly apparent as you become more familiar with the information presented in the remaining chapters. The generalizations, however, will help you to integrate the material to which you will be introduced, so bear them in mind as you move forward with your study of communication:

1. Communication is symbolic.
2. Communication aims at the creation of shared meanings and influence.
3. Communication occurs in stages.
4. Communication is affected by characteristics of the participants and situations in which they exchange messages.

■ THE RELATIONSHIP OF COMMUNICATION TO LEADERSHIP

Depending on your own experience and interests, you may admire a famous mayor, consumer advocate, manager, or preacher. You may also admire less well-known leaders who nonetheless speak fluently and confidently about intercultural affairs, politics, society, business, or religion. Surprisingly, however, many people do not recognize the connections between communication and leadership.

Leaders of every type place communication skills at the foundation of their activity. During the early 1980s, for example, Sam Harris founded RESULTS, an international organization that keeps the pressure on politicians to support ways of reducing world hunger. At the local level, RESULTS "partners" study relevant facts and figures, practice expressing their thoughts about world hunger, and then communicate their ideas in three ways. They talk with each other in weekly meetings as well as with their political representatives, newspaper editors, and other influential people. The partners discuss world hunger at monthly meetings of local RESULTS groups. They also accept invitations to address interested classes, organizations, and other people. The underlying

---

Perception and Communication

Chapter objectives

After reading this chapter you should be able to:

1. distinguish perception from sensation
2. understand that perception is a process that involves the interpretation of sensory experience
3. realize that perceptions vary considerably in accuracy
4. recognize that perceptions are tentative, learned, and selective
5. identify factors that affect perception, especially beliefs, motives, and attitudes
6. appreciate how perceptions influence communication
7. develop sensitivity to the ways that communication shapes perceptions of others and self

Key terms and concepts

perception
metaperception
empathy
anxiety
sign
symbol
stereotype
cultural stereotype
belief
motive
attitude
fundamental attribution error
relational message
ego-involvement
assimilation effect
contrast effect
deliberate ambiguity
labeling

21

New features that make this edition better than ever!

Two new chapters

Ch. 6 Intercultural Communication

The Importance of Intercultural Communication
Cultural Differences and Their Effect on Communication
Factors That Influence Interaction between Cultures
Individual Approaches to Crossing Cultural Boundaries
Training and Developing Competency in Intercultural
Communication and Awareness

Ch. 9 Family Communication

Functions of the Family
Family Decision Making
Family Power Structures
Mastering Communication Skills with the Family
Primary Role Relationships
Satisfaction in Marital Relationships
Satisfaction in Family Relationships

Expanded coverage that keeps up with current research and pedagogy

Ch. 3 Critical Thinking and Listening
What Critical Thinking Is
Effects of Deficiencies in Critical Thinking
Improving Critical Thinking
Questions Reflective of Critical Thinking

Outstanding learning aids in every chapter help students develop, test, and master basic communication skills —

and explore the theme of leadership and communication.

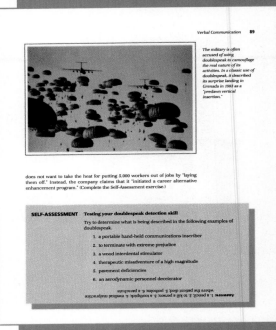

Clearly written and well-organized, every chapter of MASTERING COMMUNICATION is packed with features to help your students study more effectively and improve their communication skills, including...

- ■ **Self-Assessment Boxes** in every chapter guide your students through an evaluation of their own communication competencies, preconceptions, and skills.

- ■ **Mastering Communication Skill Boxes** helps students enhance their existing skills and encourage students to build valuable new skills.

- ■ **Focus on Leadership Boxes** in every chapter draw from the worlds of government, business, civics, and our daily lives to focus on the vital link between communication, influence, and leadership.

- ■ **Chapter Objectives** begin each chapter with a description of the information students will be able to apply once they learn the chapter material.

- ■ **Key Terms and Concepts** are listed in each chapter opener and are boldfaced throughout the text.

- ■ **In-Chapter, End-of-Chapter, and Experiential Exercises** involve students in fascinating activities to highlight the real-world application of text concepts and explore a wide range of basic and complex communication principles .

- ■ **Chapter Introductions, Related Readings, Case Studies, Annotated Bibliography, and Chapter Summaries.**

- ■ **A full color design** including captivating color photographs, fine art reproductions, and exciting figures that add visual impact to the study of communication.

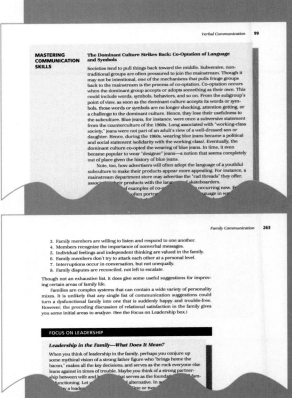

Figure 2.2
Functions of
Perception in
Communications.

1	2	3	4
Perceptions influence what one says (content) to others.	Perceptions influence how one communicates (manner) with others.	Perceptions influence the meanings assigned to messages.	Perceptions influence how people respond to messages.

messages are misperceived, they are unlikely to have the effect one intends. At least, they are not likely to have the desired consequences so long as the target of influence sees him- or herself as having the ability to withstand the perceived threat.

We have seen how perception influences what message producers say and how they say it. We also have considered the ways in which perceptions affect message reception in respect to the assignment of meaning and receiver reactions. Figure 2.2 provides a summary of the main points. While this is a large part of the story about communication and perception, it is not the whole story. Just as perception influences communication, communication influences perception. The relationship is reciprocal.

HOW COMMUNICATION CAN INFLUENCE PERCEPTION

Since humans cannot attend to all of the features of an object of perception, their interpretations of what they experience are necessarily limited. The properties of the object themselves have a significant impact on what we attend to and how we categorize it. Intensity (for example, brightness and loudness) helps focus attention. Movement is another such factor. Still another is contrast. You are more likely, for instance, to notice the first tree that changes color in the fall than the ones surrounding it.

Teaching Objective 2–7
Convey the reciprocal influence of communication on perception in the areas of focused attention, provision of categories for interpretation, and the creation of associations among categories.

As important as qualities such as these are, they do not fully account for what we perceive at any given time. Important for our purposes are three roles that communication plays: (1) focusing attention; (2) providing categories for the interpretation of experience; and (3) creating associations among categories.

Focusing Attention

If you have had training in public speaking prior to the course you are now taking, you might recall your instructor's urging you to become more animated, to use more gestures, to vary your pitch and rate more, or to regulate and adjust your volume. Why do you think he or she made these suggestions? You were probably not doing enough to establish yourself as a focus of attention. After all,

---

begun to cast doubt on the value of eyewitness testimony in criminal proceedings because it is so frequently inaccurate (Loftus, 1979).

Because perceptions are selective and observers tend to focus on only a few features of an object of perception at any given time, two objects having those particular features in common can be easily confused. More than one person has spent time in prison because of misidentification by an eyewitness who noticed only some prominent features of the actual criminal that were highly similar to those of the unfortunate suspect. The Alfred Hitchcock movie *The Wrong Man* explores the true story of a musician to whom this very thing happened.

FACTORS AFFECTING PERCEPTION

Because perceptions are learned, it follows that factors affecting learning also indirectly affect perceptions. The most significant of these are beliefs, motives, and attitudes. The term **belief** refers to a person's feelings about what is true. A **motive** is the reason behind an action that causes an individual to behave in a particular way. Finally, an **attitude** is the inclination a person has to evaluate objects of perception favorably or unfavorably. Beliefs, motives, and attitudes all affect interpretations of what we experience (Fishbein and Ajzen, 1975). A few illustrations may serve to show how such factors indirectly influence perceptions.

Teaching Objective 2–5
Explain the influence of the factors of belief, motive, and attitude on perception.

Beliefs

In 1989, the issue of flag burning received considerable attention. President George Bush went on record in support of a constitutional amendment pro-

Our beliefs, motives, and attitudes influence our perceptions. If we believe that the flag is the embodiment of our country's values, we may well react negatively to its destruction.

The Annotated Instructor's Edition

Provides easy access to the entire integrated teaching package — right at your fingertips!

The Annotated Instructor's Edition (AIE) —

contains valuable information and ideas that help supplement and enhance your classroom presentations. Time-saving blue annotations, printed in the margins, quickly alert you to appropriate supplements and pedagogical features and offer additional examples for your lectures.

The following annotations appear throughout the text ...

Teaching Objective describes the teaching objective of the corresponding text material.

Discussion Question suggests questions related to the specific material to facilitate better understanding.

Cross-Reference relates topics to other sections in the book for more information.

Current Research provides up-to-date findings on the topic.

Leadership Note cites additional studies and surveys, and link communication to leadership and the exercise of influence.

An in-text Instructor's Section

Written and prepared by Jeanne Tessier Barone,
Indiana University — Purdue University at Fort Wayne

Bound into the front of each Annotated Instructor's Edition, this convenient teaching tool provides

- chapter outlines
- chapter summaries
- teaching objectives keyed to the learning objectives in the text
- discussion questions
- skills exercises
- and a list of key terms.

Innovative new materials to help you teach in the classroom!

A wealth of powerful teaching tools helps you pull it all together. You'll have everything you need to make learning more accessible and exciting for your students and easier for you!

Annotated Instructor's Edition

Computerized Test Bank
Contains 1,000 multiple choice, true/false, and essay questions for use on IBM or Macintosh systems.

Cable New Network (CNN)
Communication Leadership Video
Presents public speaking at its finest with powerful speeches delivered by General Norman Schwarzkopf, President Clinton, Rosa Parks, Jesse Jackson, and many others.

The Allyn & Bacon Communication Video Library *
Qualified adopters may select from several videos including:

- *Perception and Self Awareness*
- *Non-Verbal Communication — Paralanguage and Proxemics*
- *Non-Verbal Communication — Eye Contact and Kenesics*
- *Defensive/Supportive Communication*
- *The Listening Process*
- *Critical Thinking*

* Some restrictions may apply. See your Allyn & Bacon representative for details. All information is accurate as of date of printing. Subject to change without notice.

ANNOTATED INSTRUCTOR'S EDITION

MASTERING COMMUNICATION

SECOND EDITION

Dennis S. Gouran
THE PENNSYLVANIA STATE UNIVERSITY

William E. Wiethoff
INDIANA UNIVERSITY

Joel A. Doelger
UNIVERSITY OF ARKANSAS

Instructor's Section and Annotations Prepared by
Jeanne Tessier Barone
INDIANA UNIVERSITY–PURDUE UNIVERSITY AT FORT WAYNE

ALLYN and BACON
Boston London Toronto Sydney Tokyo Singapore

Senior Editor: Stephen Hull
Editor in Chief; Humanities: Joe Opiela
Editorial Assistant: Brenda Conaway
Editorial-Production Administrator: Rowena Dores
Cover Administrator: Linda Dickinson
Text Designer: Rita Naughton
Composition Buyer: Linda Cox
Manufacturing Buyer: Louise Richardson
Editorial-Production Service: Progressive Typographers

ISBN 0–205–15509–X

Printed in the United Stated of America
10 9 8 7 6 5 4 3 2 1   97 96 95 94

Brief Contents

Contents of Instructor's Section

Contents of Student Text

The complete table of contents begins on page v of the student text.

CHAPTER **1**

AN INTRODUCTION TO COMMUNICATION

CHAPTER SYNOPSIS

Ours is an age of increasing technological development and social complexity, expanding knowledge, and rapid change. The need for competent communicators and skilled leaders has never been greater. The overarching purpose and theme of this text is to explore and develop the integral relationship between communication and leadership and to offer students the knowledge and opportunities for practice needed to hone their communication and leadership skills.

The pervasive need for and importance of communication skill is emphasized. The nature of communication is defined "as the purposeful production and transmission of a message" from one person to another. The primary objectives of communication are explained in terms of the need or desire for sharing meaning with and exerting influence over another.

The process of communication is explored sequentially, from the initial stimulation which prompts a desire or motivation to communicate, to the generation of an idea, its symbolic formation and transmission to another, and the reception, interpretation and reaction to the communication on the part of the receiver of the message. A graphic model of the circular or transactional nature of the communication process is presented.

The factors influencing communication are defined in terms of two broad categories: personal characteristics of the communicators and situational factors influencing communication events. Personal characteristics include an individual's communication skill and knowledge, cultural background, and point of view and seem to have the greatest impact on communication in message recipients who are experiencing an attempt on the part of a message producer to influence them. Situational influences include the physical environment and any noise which interferes with the communica-tion, the occasion of the communication, and the context in which it occurs. Communicative context is divided into three categories: interpersonal, group, and public settings. The unique qualities of these three contexts are described.

Four foundational generalizations about communication are offered: first, that communication is symbolic; second, that communication involves shared meaning and influence: third, that communication is sequential; and, fourth, that the personal qualities of the communicators and the situations in which communication occurs affect the outcome of the event.

The need for leadership in every kind of communication context and the integral relationship between leadership and communicative skill is explored through examples. The issue of ethics in communication is discussed, with emphasis on the inevitable long-term failure of unethical communication practices.

Students are offered a self-assessment exercise, which also introduces in summary form the communication skills which will be covered in later chapters of the text. An overview of the text is then provided, with a numbered list of skills to be addressed in the areas of interpersonal, group, and public communication contexts. Students are encouraged to make full use of the activities and exercises included in the book in order to develop their personal communicative skills.

CHAPTER OUTLINE

The Importance of Communication Skill
The Nature of Communication
    Definition of Communication
    Objectives of Communication
        • Fidelity—The Creation of Shared Meanings
        • The Exertion of Influence

Stages in the Communication Sequence
- •Stimulation—Arousal
- •Motivation—Desire
- •Generation—Idea
- •Formation—Encoding the Message
- •Transmission—The Choice of Medium
- •Reception—Message Received
- •Interpretation—Message Decoded
- •Reaction—Receiver Response
- •Feedback—A Message Returned

Factors Affecting Communication
Personal Characteristics
- •Types of Characteristics
- •Impact of Characteristics

Situational Influences
- •The Impact of Physical Environment
- •The Impact of Noise
- •The Impact of Communication Context
- •The Impact of Occasion

Generalizations About Communication
Communication as Symbolic
Communication as Purposeful
Communication as Sequential
Communication as Affected by Persons and Contexts
Communication and Leadership
Communication and Ethics
What the Student Will Learn
Interpersonal Communication Skills
Group Communication Skills
Public Communication Skills
Summary
Exercises
Suggested Readings
References

TEACHING OBJECTIVES

1-1. To emphasize the importance of communication skill to personal success, leadership strength, and the solution of social problems.

1-2. To present a definition of communication as purposeful and sequential.

1-3. To explore the objectives or purposes of communication as shared meaning and influence.

1-4. To describe, with relevant examples, the stages of the communication process, and emphasize the ongoing nature of communication.

1-5. To explain the factors which influence communication.

1-6. To introduce the concept of communication as symbolic.

1-7. To explore the nature of leadership and the importance of communication to the skillful exercise of leadership.

1-8. To raise the question of ethics in communication.

1-9. To provide students with a broad overview of the purpose and content of the course.

DISCUSSION QUESTIONS

1-1. What are the most pressing problems facing the world and/or our society today? In what ways does a lack of successful communication contribute to these problems? In what ways could improved communication contribute to the solution of these problems?

1-2. What communication event have you observed on television or in "real life" in the last few days? Was the purpose of this event to share meaning or to influence? How do you know?

1-3. What are the qualities you possess which affect your creation and reception of communication?

1-4. How would you describe the kinds of noise which affect communication in your classroom?

1-5. Who are the most important leaders in the world community today? How would you describe their communication skills?

1-6. When, if ever, is dishonest or deceit "the right thing to do" in communication? Is it always more ethical to tell the truth?

SKILL MASTERY EXERCISES

1-1. Select and describe in as much detail as possible a real or fictionalized but realistic communication event; allow students to ask for more details as needed. In small groups, have the students analyze the communication event and decide the following: What are the objectives of the communicators: How would you rate the fidelity of the messages received? What feedback is provided? What personal characteristics and situational influences seem to affect this communication? What is the context? What is the occasion?

1-2. Discuss the nature of models, using the model in Figure 1.1 and others as examples. Have your students divide into groups of five or six, provide them with a posterboard or blank overhead transparency and markers, and ask them to create a visual model of communication which includes and describes a message producer, a message recipient, a message, noise, personal characteristics, context, and occasion. Have each group then explain its model to the rest of the class.

1-3. Using the following examples, ask your students to decide the most ethical approach to communication for the given situation:

(1) Ten-year-old Kevin's parents have just been informed that Kevin has a terminal illness and has at most another year to live. Kevin asks them, "What is wrong with me? How soon will I be well?"

(2) You have just learned through a classmate that your best friend's spouse is having an affair. After class, you meet your best friend for lunch as previously planned and, in the course of your conversation, your friend says, "I know my spouse would never deceive or betray me."

(3) A friend of yours has just graduated from medical school and has applied for a job with your uncle's thriving medical practice. Your friend brags to you that she is sure to get the job because she graduated with top honors. You respond, "Wow, that's terrific! How'd you do it?" And your friend laughs and replies, "Well, don't tell your uncle I said this, but to tell you the truth, I cheated my way through."

1-4. In small groups or as a whole class, ask each member to take several minutes to decide what leadership qualities she/he possesses and then ask each member to attempt to influence her/his group to elect her/him leader. After each student has had an opportunity to speak, have the group vote for the best leadership candidate. Once the vote is completed, ask for discussion about what qualities they considered most important in their decision making.

KEY TERMS AND CONCEPTS

leadership (p. 4)
communication (p. 6)
objective (p. 6)
fidelity (p. 6)
influence (p. 7)
stimulation (p. 7)
motivation (p. 8)
generation (p. 8)
formation (encoding) (p. 8)
transmission (p. 9)
medium (p. 9)
reception (p. 9)
interpretation (decoding) (p. 9)
reaction (p. 9)
feedback (p. 10)
noise (p. 11)
ethical communication (p. 13)

CHAPTER 2

PERCEPTION AND COMMUNICATION

CHAPTER SYNOPSIS

Perception is the process of determining and interpreting experience. Perceptions vary greatly and affect every aspect of the communication process. Perceptions are affected by the amount of information available. Sometimes the word *perception* is reserved for directly observable experience and the term *metaperception* is used to describe the process of inferring what another is experiencing.

Much misperception can be attributed to making judgments about another's experience from one's own and substantially different frame of reference. Empathy is the ability to understand another's behavior from his or her own frame of reference. Empathy is invaluable as an aid to framing messages effectively and communicating successfully, especially with those from different cultural backgrounds.

The perception process involves four stages: sensation, or the reception of sensory data; awareness, or recognition of the sensation; categorization, or the association of the stimulus to existing categories of information; and interpretation, or a decision about what has been perceived.

There are three essential characteristics of perceptions. First, perceptions are tentative, or based on incomplete information. When a perception is so tentative as to defy categorization, it can result in an internal state known as anxiety, or arousal from an uncertain cause. Situational factors influence our interpretation of perceptions.

Second, perceptions are learned. We attach meanings to events, objects, and feelings on the basis of prior experience and conditioning. Meanings are attached to both signs and symbols and become stable over time. A sign is anything that represents something else. A symbol is a sign intentionally chosen to represent something else. Perceptions that become resistant to change result in the formation of stereotypes, or fixed views about the characteristics of objects in a class of objects, views which ignore individual differences. Cultural stereotypes are fixed views of a group of people who share some characteristics in common which disregard differences among the members. Stereotypes impede effective communication. The connections between signs and what they signify may be either arbitrary, or conventional, or nonarbitrary, involving some natural or obvious relationship.

Third, perceptions are selective. We focus our attention only on aspects of a thing and not on the whole. Because we focus only on a few characteristics of objects, people, or events, it is easy to misperceive on the basis of a few shared characteristics.

Factors affecting how and what we learn also affect our perceptions. Beliefs, motives, and attitudes are the three most significant factors affecting perception. Beliefs are one's feelings about what is true. Motives are the reasons behind actions; motives arise from needs and focus on the reduction of needs. Attitudes are tendencies to view perceived objects favorably or unfavorably. Beliefs, motives, and attitudes all affect our interpretations of experience.

Perception affects the messages we produce, both in terms of their content and how they are framed, or expressed. The content of messages is sometimes influenced by the tendency to assign motives and intentions to the actions of others and then to respond accordingly. The tendency to misassign intentions to others' behavior is known as fundamental attribution error. The framing of messages is likewise influenced by our perceptions; for example, the framing of a message is often relational, i.e., it reveals something about our feelings for the other.

In addition, perception influences the meanings we assign to the messages we receive. For example, we respond to messages differently depending on the degree of ego-involvement, or personal investment, we have in the subject of the message. We also tend to have distorted perceptions of the messages of others as a result of our ego-involvement. If we view a position expressed in a message as closer to our own beliefs than it actually is, this is known as an assimilation effect. If, on the other hand, we view an expressed position as more distant from our own than it actually is, this is known as a contrast effect. Assimilation is more likely when ego-involvement in a subject is low, and contrast is more likely when ego-involvement is high.

Finally, perception also affects our reactions to the messages of others. If, for example, we perceive that another will react negatively to our point of view, we might choose to reach with a vague message rather than a clear one; this strategy is called deliberate ambiguity. Our reactions will reflect and be tempered by our interpretations of the messages and meanings of the other.

Just as perception influences communication, so also does communication affect or influence perception. First, communication focuses our attention and the attention of others by calling attention to specific aspects of an object or event. Second, communication provides and shares categories for the interpretation of experience. *Labeling* is the term used to describe the process by which individuals develop self-concepts on the basis of terms or categories applied to them by others. And, third, communication creates direct and indirect associations among categories or labels for experience. Direct associations are those provided by the message producer; indirect associations are those linked by past experience in the mind of the message receiver.

The relationship between perception and communication is reciprocal. Understanding the influence of perception on communication and vice versa is important for successful communication and leadership.

CHAPTER OUTLINE

The Nature of Perception
    Perception

TEACHING OBJECTIVES

2-1. To provide a basic understanding of perception and to emphasize the central importance of perception to communication.

2-2. To emphasize the sequential nature of the perception process.

2-3. To describe the tentative, learned, and selective nature of perception.

2-4. To provide an understanding of the negative impact of stereotyping on effective interaction.

2-5. To explain the influence of the factors of belief, motive, and attitude on perception.

2-6. To describe the impact of perception on the production, reception, and interpretation of messages.

2-7. To convey the reciprocal influence of communication on perception in the areas of focused attention, provision of categories for interpretation, and the creation of associations among categories.

DISCUSSION QUESTIONS

2-1. What is the difference between empathy and sympathy?

2-2. What experiences have you had in other cultures or with people from other cultures in which your frame of reference was different and a misperception resulted?

2-3. How do the stages in the perception process coincide with or parallel the stages in the communication process?

2-4. What are your perceptions about the differences between men and women? Which of these perceptions can be categorized as cultural stereotypes?

2-5. How might the selective nature of perception be a factor in cases of date rape?

2-6. In what ways or situations do your moral beliefs affect how you judge the actions of others?

2-7. Imagine that in one day your parent, your lover or significant other, and your neighbor's five-year-old child all told you they loved you. How would you interpret the meaning of these messages?

2-8. When would be an appropriate occasion to utilize the strategy of deliberate ambiguity?

2-9. How many words do you know to describe a promiscuous man? And to describe a promiscuous woman? How are these "categories for the interpretation of experience" different and/or the same?

SKILL MASTERY EXERCISES

2-1. Select a series of photographs, drawings, or paintings in which are contained several images of persons engaged in actions (good sources of images are collections of copyright-free art, such as those published by Dover Publications). Show the images for brief intervals (ten–fifteen seconds) to your students and ask them individually to jot down what they saw in the pictures and what they think was going on. After all the images have been shown and responses recorded, ask the students to share their observations and interpretations about the pictures in the order in which they were shown. Emphasize that there are no right or wrong answers, only various perceptions. After each image is discussed, show it again and talk about the various elements of the images and how differences in focus and categorization might lead to differences in interpretation.

2-2. Show the students several objects or artifacts which are familiar and ask them to briefly describe them in writing. Share some of their descriptions and discuss the influence of familiarity on the similarity of perceptions or interpretations. Then show them several objects or artifacts which are likely to be unfamiliar (specialized tools, for example, or possibly familiar objects disguised by their only being able to see or touch part of it) and ask for their written descriptions. Again then, share these and discuss them in terms of the limited information available to form perceptions and the anxiety which may have resulted from the lack of complete information.

2-3. Using the familiar poem "The Blind Men and the Elephant" by John Godfrey Saxe as a stimulus, ask your students to form small groups and to create a similar example of vastly different perceptions of the same event or object using contemporary experiences, such as witnesses to the beating of a black man by police officers, responses to a Madonna videotape, etc. (The films *Blowup* (1966) and *The Elephant Man* (1980) are also excellent vehicles for launching a discussion of perception.)

2-4. A. Prepare a list of words which describe personal qualities attributable to people, for example, *careful, gracious, greedy, loving, desperate, simple-minded, strong, wise, slow-moving,* etc. Provide your students with a copy of the list of fifty or more words and ask them to separate the words into two columns, "good" and "bad" or "desirable" and "undesirable."

B. Next, provide them with three or four other descriptive terms, one at a time, and ask them to quickly jot down four or five other qualities they associate with the one you mentioned. When they have finished, compare lists via discussion and ask for further discussion about how and when they learned these terms and developed their perceptions of them.

C. Finally, provide them with a description of a person consisting of nothing more than four or five of the qualities earlier listed for them; be careful to select a mixture of qualities from both the "good" and "bad" categories. Ask them to decide whether or not they would like this person and why, and then discuss this.

KEY TERMS AND CONCEPTS

perception (p. 22)
metaperception (p. 23)
empathy (p. 24)
anxiety (p. 27)
sign (p. 27)
symbol (p. 28)
stereotype (p. 28)
cultural stereotype (p. 28)
belief (p. 31)
motive (p. 32)
attitude (p. 32)
fundamental attribution error (p. 33)
relational message (p. 35)
ego-involvement (p. 36)
assimilation effect (p. 36)
contrast effect (p. 36)
deliberate ambiguity (p. 37)
labeling (p. 40)

CHAPTER 3

LISTENING AND CRITICAL THINKING

CHAPTER SYNOPSIS

Listening is an important but often overlooked part of the communication process. It may be the most widely used of all communication skills. It is also a skill in great demand in the professional world. Listening involves a complex set of skills which can be improved.

Listening involves attention to sound and speech patterns, identification of signs and symbols, and comprehension. It differs from hearing, the physiological process of receiving sounds, because listening involves the cognitive process of assigning meaning.

Listening, too, is a sequential process. It begins with hearing, or the correct and complete reception of aural stimuli. Hearing is affected by various factors and can be enhanced through the use of the following suggestions: Repeat the message to confirm it has been heard correctly; eliminate environmental noise, or external interferences; avoid mental distractions, or internal interference; fight physical fatigue, which interferes both with hearing and with listening. Additional safeguards include requesting message repetition, note taking, and even postponing the event until a better time.

The second stage of the listening process involves attending to the message. Factors which affect this stage include an inability to focus on the message, either because of competing stimuli or an inability to pay attention. Two suggestions for enhancing one's ability to attend to the message are, first to focus on the message, not the speaker, which helps avoid prejudgment and, second, to focus on the speaker's thoughts, not one's own, which helps prevent anticipatory responses.

The third stage of the listening process involves interpretation, or the assigning of meaning to the message, a complex process which requires assessment and filtering of information at many levels. Effective interpretation of messages involves attention to (1) context, or the history, relationships, and physical setting in which the communication occurs; (2) the speaker's purpose, which may include phatic communication, or small talk, cathartic communication, or seeking emotional support,

informative communication, and persuasive or influential communication; and (3), the organization and arrangement of the message.

There are four types of listening. Listening for enjoyment seeks the pleasure of sensory stimulation or entertainment and is the easiest type of listening. Listening for information requires more focus and effort and has as its goals understanding and retention. This type of listening requires that the listener seek clarification of information not clearly understood. Evaluative listening involves the need to make a judgment or decision on the basis of what is learned and depends on the employment of critical thinking on the part of the listener; it is a more demanding and difficult type of listening than either of those above. Reflective listening, sometimes called therapeutic or supportive listening, involves listening for the purpose of helping the other. This type of listening moves beyond message interpretation to concern with feedback and support.

Common listening problems include the following: misuse of the time advantage gained by being able to absorb information faster than it can be spoken, faking attention, allowing distractions to interfere, listening only to easy material, becoming overstimulated (involved in one thought or idea to the exclusion of those which follow), selective listening (ignoring opposing views), and egocentric (self-centered, judgmental, or interruptive) listening.

Successful communication is the joint accomplishment of speaker and listener. A checklist of positive listening behaviors includes: preparing to listen at the appropriate level, providing nonverbal reinforcers, using the "thought speed" advantage, and structuring the environment to eliminate distractions.

Reflective listening involves mastery of some additional skills. Reflective listening involves both cognitive attention and appropriate response, or sustained feedback; it is listening empathically. Particular obstacles to reflective listening include inattentiveness, evaluative feedback or judgment, and asserting control or attempting to offer solutions rather than support. Important reflective listening tools include paraphrasing or restatement, which guards against judgment, and careful attention to the emotional content of the messages received.

Our responsibilities as listeners go beyond understanding and empathy. Effective listeners must also be able to utilize critical thinking to judge the credibility of what is heard.

Critical thinking is a process of making inferences about the credibility of message content. Critical thinking is an important response to the ongoing attempts on the part of others to influence our actions and beliefs. Failure to employ critical thinking to assess messages received can have unfortunate and even dangerous consequences.

Critical thinking skills can be improved through the systematic use of questions to assess messages received. These questions are: Is the message plausible? Is the message consistent? Is the source of the message reliable? Are the facts in the message verifiable? Plausibility, consistence, reliability, and verifiability are defined. While the use of these questions to assess messages aids listeners in improving their critical thinking skills, even assessments made through use of these questions are not infallible in judging the credibility of messages.

Listening is a complex and active process which is critical to successful communication. Critical thinking is the important ability to assess the believability of the messages to which we listen.

CHAPTER OUTLINE

The Importance of Listening
    An Overlooked Skill
    A Widely Used Skill
    A Skill in Great Demand
    A Skill That Can Be Improved
The Listening Process
    Hearing versus Listening
    Hearing the Message
        • Repeat Message
        • Eliminate Environmental Noise
        • Avoid Mental Distraction
        • Fight Physical Fatigue
        • Take Corrective Steps
    Attending to the Message
        • Focus on Message, Not Speaker
        • Focus on Other, Not Self
    Interpreting the Message
        • Context

        • Speaker's Purpose
        • Organization and Arrangement
Types of Listening
    For Enjoyment
    For Information
    Evaluative Listening
    Reflective Listening
Common Listening Problems
    Misuse of "Thought Speed" Advantage
    Faking Attention
    Allowing Distractions to Interfere
    Listening Only to Easy Material
    Becoming Overstimulated
    Selective Listening
    Egocentric Listening
Positive Listening Behaviors
    Listening at Appropriate Level
    Providing Nonverbal Reinforcers
    Using "Thought Speed" Advantage
    Structuring Environment to Eliminate Distractions
Reflective Listening Skills
    Defining Reflective Listening
    Obstacles
        • Inattention
        • Evaluation
        • Control
    Enhancements
        • Paraphrasing
        • Attention to Emotions
Critical Thinking
    Definition
    Effects of Deficiencies
    Improving Critical Thinking
    Questions for Critical Thinking
    A Note of Caution
Summary
Exercises
Related Readings
References

TEACHING OBJECTIVES

3-1. To emphasize the importance of listening as an overlooked, much-needed, teachable skill which is critical to successful communication.

3-2. To clarify the difference between hearing and listening.

3-3. To examine and describe the sequential nature of the listening process: hearing, attending to the message, and interpretation of the message.

3-4. To further explore the concept of context.

3-5. To describe the varieties of speaker purposes: phatic, cathartic, informative, and persuasive communication.

3-6. To examine the types of listening—for enjoyment, for information, evaluative, and reflective—and delineate the differing needs and goals of the four types.

3-7. To develop recognition of common listening problems.

3-8. To emphasize positive listening behaviors.

3-9. To distinguish and teach reflective listening skills.

3-10. To distinguish critical thinking from listening.

3-11. To develop critical thinking skills for assessing the credibility of messages.

DISCUSSION QUESTIONS

3-1. How much of your time was spent in listening yesterday? How much training in listening have you received?

3-2. How many conversations have you heard or over-heard today that you didn't really listen to?

3-3. How many different sounds or noises are you aware of hearing right now?

3-4. How many different things have you thought about since you sat down?

3-5. When was the last time you gave another person your full and undivided attention as they were talking to you?

3-6. A man walks up to you on the street today and says, "Soon you will die." How will you interpret this message? What cues will you look for and attend to in helping you decide what this person meant?

3-7. When was the last time you thought in advance about what kind of listening would be needed for an event you were attending? How would you plan for the next communication event you are about to engage in?

3-8. How many of these common listening problems do you recognize as a frequent part of your own listening habits?

3-9. How could we structure or restructure this classroom environment so as to eliminate distractions?

3-10. How would you rate yourself as an empathic listener?

3-11. How would you assess your critical thinking skills?

3-12. What sources of information do you tend to believe without question? What other sources of information do you tend to *disbelieve* without question?

SKILL MASTERY EXERCISES

3-1. As a way of beginning discussion of listening as a necessary and underdeveloped skill, divide students into small groups and ask each of them to share a brief statement or illustrative story about the kind of person he or she is. Allow enough time for all to share. When all have spoken, ask each student to write down in summary form the essential information or quality which each of their group members shared. Have the individual storytellers then read the summaries and correct or clarify the meaning of their stories for each of the listeners.

3-2. As each student enters class, hand her or him an index card on which one of the following messages is written:

"Today's lecture is for your enjoyment; relax and receive."

"Please listen and be ready to describe the three main points in today's lecture."

"There will be a quiz at the end of class on today's lecture material. Pay close attention to the material."

"Please help me decide, on the basis of today's lecture, which information on listening is essential and which is unnecessary and should be eliminated."

Proceed to present some standard lecture material for ten–fifteen minutes and then ask students to record what they heard on the index cards they were given at the start of class. Use these to generate discussion about selective perception and the types of listening.

3-3. Have students divide into small groups and discuss how they would reflectively listen to the person described in one of the following vignettes:

A. Your best female friend has just discovered she is pregnant. You are the first person she has told. She does not know whether to tell the man involved (she's not married). She doesn't know whether she could or should have the baby. She is not sure the child would be whole and healthy, as she has been using drugs regularly for several months. She's not sure she's capable of parenting effectively. She does not know how she feels about abortion or adoption as options. She also doesn't know what to expect from her parents if she were to confide in them about her situation. She has asked you to help her think about and talk through the realities and possibilities of her dilemma.

B. A childhood friend of yours is just completing her senior year of high school in the small town in central Indiana where you both grew up. She is graduating at the top of her class, is a National Merit Scholar, and has won many awards for scholastic and athletic endeavors in her high school career. She has been offered all-expenses-paid scholarships to three different colleges or universities and has asked you to help her come to a clear decision about which offer she wants to accept. Each opportunity is different—small school or large, close to home or far away, athletic or scholastic requirements, etc.

If one or two groups discussed vignette A and the others used vignette B, there would be additional opportunity to discuss not only what is involved in reflective or empathic listening but also the degree to which our own beliefs and attitudes impinge upon our ability to listen.

KEY TERMS AND CONCEPTS

listening (p. 52)
hearing (p. 52)
phatic communication (p. 57)
cathartic communication (p. 57)
informative communication (p. 57)
persuasive communication (p. 57)
evaluative listening (p. 59)
reflective listening (p. 60)
selective listening (p. 63)
egocentric listening (p. 63)
paraphrasing (p. 70)
critical thinking (p. 71)
message credibility (p. 73)
plausibility (p. 73)
consistency (p. 73)
source reliability (p. 74)
verifiability (p. 75)

CHAPTER **4**

VERBAL COMMUNICATION

CHAPTER SYNOPSIS

Verbal communication can be used for various purposes and has a significant impact, including sometimes dictating a particular response. The use and impact of symbolic language involves much more than the words themselves.

Language is an arbitrary set of symbols with commonly accepted meanings and standard rules for usage. Language is conveyed on a channel, or medium, such as the voice or the written word. Verbal communication refers to any use of symbolic language to convey a message, whatever the channel.

We study verbal communication for several reasons: to more fully appreciate the complexity of language use, to understand the impact of language on social structure and personal experience, and to gain new respect for the power of language to aid us in understanding, predicting, and controlling our experiences in the world. Language emerges out of lived experience; we create words to fit and define the reality we perceive. At the same time, language provides the framework for our experience; the words we have, in other words, tend to limit and define what we see. The Sapir-Whorf hypothesis suggests that language determines how we think.

Language is representational, that is, words "stand for" or represent objects, people or events. Verbal communication serves many functions, but these functions can be broadly categorized into four areas. First, language has an instrumental function; it is a tool we use to get what we want or need. Second, language has a regulatory function; it is used to direct and control actions and events. Third, there is a social function of language; through our communication with others, we define ourselves and create and maintain our social networks. Fourth, language has a problem-solving function; we use language to structure thought and to seek and process the information needed for understanding. Most of the time, verbal communication is multifunctional.

Much of the time, language is used to share understanding, but language can be used to obscure reality as well as to clarify it. Two ways in which language is used to obscure reality are euphemisms and doublespeak. Euphemisms are mild or inoffensive words used to mask harsher or emotionally laden subjects or words or to give a more appealing appearance to reality; for example, we "put animals to sleep" instead of killing them, or we describe an aged politician as an "elder statesman." Doublespeak is the intentional and insidious use of language to distort or mask reality, as in the labeling of civilian deaths in wartime "collateral damage."

Meanings reside not in the words themselves but in the people who use them; there is no inherent meaning in the arbitrary symbol we use to describe a referent, or given reality. Words have two sets of meanings. Denotative meanings are the official, socially accepted or dictionary meanings. Connotative meanings are the individual and personal associations, memories, and experiences which language users attach to words they use. Misunderstandings frequently occur when people agree on the denotative meaning of a word but do not share the same connotative meanings.

Language is dynamic and changing. New words are created to describe new experiences and old words take on new meanings or fall out of use altogether. When a word falls out of common use, the denotative meaning may remain, but the rich store of connotative meanings will diminish.

The meaning in words is also tied to the particular context in which the words are spoken. Both the physical setting and the relational context of the language users have an impact on the meanings derived from the language used. Meaning is also tied to the intent of the user and to the communication sequence in which the words occur; sometimes our words do not actually express what it is we want or mean. Adjacency pairs are recognized communication sequences, such as question-answer and invitation-response, which provide meaning cues.

Language use has a social impact. First, language use helps define group membership; this is particularly evident in the area of sublanguage or "slang." Sublanguages serve as private codes; their use allows members to claim group identification and also serves to exclude nonmembers.

Second, language use defines rights and responsibilities. In the area of titles or forms of address, for example, the use or avoidance of certain forms defines and communicates important information about the roles and privileges of those engaged in the communication.

Third, language use reveals how others see the world. The language choices others make provide clues as to their interests, knowledge, and perceptions, including their sense of causal relationships.

There are, however, inherent problems involved in language use; some of these are polarization, intentional orientation, bypassing, fact-inference confusion, and static evaluation. *Polarization* refers to the tendency of our language to dichotomize experience into black and white, good and bad, etc. *Intentional orientation* refers to the tendency of language users to treat words or labels as real rather than as representational. *Bypassing* occurs when communicators do not share the same meanings for a symbol they are using; a good safeguard against bypassing is paraphrasing. *Fact-inference confusion* refers to the frequent tendency for communicators to make inferences on the basis of limited observations and then to discuss or report those inferences as facts. And, lastly, *static evaluation* describes the tendency of words to capture or convey their referents at a particular moment in time, much as we tend to remember old friends as they were the last time we saw them, however many years ago that may have been.

Sexist and racist language are two particular types of language use which are offensive and personally damaging and which limit the aspirations and expectations of those who are affected by their use. Sexist language demeans or offends members of a specific gender through the creation of fixed expectations and qualifications and through the defining of limited roles. Racist language has the same effect applied to members of a specific cultural group. Both racist and sexist language are dehumanizing, are used by dominant groups as a means of social control, and have detrimental effects on individuals, groups, communication, and society.

CHAPTER OUTLINE

What Is Verbal Communication?
    Language, an Arbitrary Symbol System
    Conveyed on a Channel
Why Study Verbal Communication?
    Language and Complex Purposes
    Language and Experience
    Language and Perception
The Functions of Verbal Communication
    Language Represents
    Language Is Instrumental
    Language Is Regulatory
    Language Has Social Value
    Language Has Problem-Solving Utility
    Language Can Obscure Reality
        • Euphemisms
        • Doublespeak
The Relationship Between Language and Meaning
    Meaning Is Tied to People
    Meaning Is Multilayered
        • Denotative Meanings
        • Connotative Meanings
    Meanings Change
    Meaning Is Tied to Context
        • Physical Setting
        • Relational Context
    Meaning Is Tied to Intent
    Meaning Is Tied to Sequencing
        • Language as Rule-Governed
        • Adjacency Pairs as Sequences
The Social Effects of Language Use
    Language Use Defines Membership
        • Sublanguages as Private Codes
        • Sublanguages as Group Identifiers
        • Sublanguages as Exclusionary
    Language Use Defines Rights and Responsibilities
    Language Use Reveals How We See the World
Problems Caused by Language Use
    Polarization—Dichotomizing
    Intentional Orientation—Literalizing
    Bypassing—Unshared Meanings
    Fact-Inference Confusion
    Static Evaluation—Time-Stopping
    Sexist and Racist Language
        • Dehumanize
        • Limit Expectations
        • Limit Roles
        • Maintain Social Divisions
        • Insult and Offend

TEACHING OBJECTIVES

4-1. Define language and channels and verbal communication as the use of language on any channel.

4-2. Emphasize the importance of language to social life and personal identity and survival.

4-3. Describe the reciprocal relationship between language and experience.

4-4. Explain the representational nature of language and the various functions it serves.

4-5. Depict the power of language to obscure as well as to clarify.

4-6. Emphasize that the meanings of words reside in those who use them.

4-7. Explain that words have many meanings, both denotative (or socially defined) and connotative (or personal associations) and that meanings change over time.

4-8. Describe the ways in which meanings are interpreted on the basis of context, sequence, and perceived intent as well as through the words themselves.

4-9. Stress the social implications of language—its power to include and exclude (i.e., racist and sexist language), to define roles and privileges, to describe how individuals and cultures perceive their world.

4-10. Demonstrate some of the problems or limitations inherent in language use, and in particular the problems of polarization, intentional orientation, bypassing, fact-inference confusion, and static evaluation.

DISCUSSION QUESTIONS

4-1. What are your preferred channels of communication? Speech? Song? The written word? Would you rather talk on the phone or in person? Would you rather show or tell? Are you more of an aural person or a visual person? Do the people closest to you prefer the same channels or different ones?

4-2. Can you remember or imagine a time before you had words to define and/or explain your experience? What would you think of a nightmare if you didn't know what it was? How would you respond to an animal you'd never seen or heard of the first time you came upon one?

4-3. What experiences have you had that your parents have not, and do you have words to describe them? Do these words have meaning to your parents?

4-4. Consider the power of advertising and other slogans to change how we think, what we feel or believe, and what we do. What is the social and/or personal impact of Nike's "Just Do It"? How about "Kleenex says 'Bless You'"? And what about "Carpe Diem? Seize the Day!"?

4-5. Take a few minutes to list all the euphemisms for death in our language. What can they teach us about how our society views death and feels about it?

4-6. Consider the word *touch.* What denotative meanings does it have? What connotative meanings does it have for you? What connotative meanings might it have for a blind person, or for a survivor of physical abuse?

4-7. What causes words to change their meanings over time?

4-8. What are some examples of ways in which context and sequencing have affected the meanings you attributed to another's words?

4-9. What are the racist and sexist terms you learned as a child? What impact have they had on how you feel about yourself? What impact have they had on how you relate to other people?

SKILL MASTERY EXERCISES

4-1. Divide the class into small groups and provide each group with a paperback dictionary. Ask each group to develop a list of the ten most important words in the American culture, and to provide a denotative definition that satisfies all group members as well as a list of all the connotative meanings and associations the members have to these words. Later, compare their lists and talk about why these words are important and what they mean to the culture.

4-2. Ask the class to help you generate a variety of single-sentence statements of any kind (censoring as needed), such as "Do the dishes," "Want to go to a movie?", etc. Write the statements on the board, leaving room between them to add later comments.

Then ask what functions these statements serve. Record their choices by the statements along with whatever comments or suggestions are made about such factors as context, intent, or sequencing to an understanding of function.

Perhaps you could close the discussion by asking if they can think of any statement, word, or term which has a universal meaning unchanged by circumstance or speaker.

4-3. Again in small groups, ask the class to decide (or recall from an earlier discussion—see Chapter 1) what are some of the most pressing problems facing the world today. Then tell them to imagine they have been given the money and power to develop a massive public service campaign to address whichever of those problems they feel is most pressing. Ask them to focus on one problem of their choice and to develop a series of simple slogans for an ad campaign to change the way people see the world or this problem or themselves in relation to the problem. They must use words but can combine a slogan with a visual image if they so choose.

Sample problem: World Hunger
Symbolic message: "We are the human family. Your brothers and sisters are starving."
Sample problem: War
Symbolic message: (with a drawing of the earth blown to bits) "It's either peace, or we pick up the pieces."

4-4. Divide the class into males and females and ask each gender group to discuss and develop a list of sexist statements or attitudes which bother them about the way members of the other gender think of them, describe them, or treat them.

When they've finished, have the two groups stand or sit so that they face each other across the room and have group members take turns, first one gender and then the other, back and forth, making statements such as, "It bothers us when some of you . . . ," "We feel angry when we hear some of you say . . . ," etc. Emphasize that the statements must be (1) inclusive on the part of the gender group speaking—we feel, it hurts us, etc.; (2) noninclusive in references to the other gender group—always qualifying the statements by saying "some of you"; and (3) descriptive rather than accusatory—"we feel" instead of "you made me feel" etc. Allow each gender group to share its full list, even if one is longer than the other.

Process this experience with discussion or written comments afterward about what individual members learned or discovered as a result of the experience.

KEY TERMS AND CONCEPTS

verbal communication (p. 83)
Sapir-Whorf hypothesis (p. 86)
euphemism (p. 88)
doublespeak (p. 88)
denotative meaning (p. 91)
connotative meaning (p. 91)
sequencing (p. 95)
polarization (p. 100)
intensional orientation (p. 101)
bypassing (p. 102)
paraphrasing (p. 102)
fact-inference confusion (p. 103)
static evaluation (p. 104)
sexist language (p. 105)
racist language (p. 106)

CHAPTER 5

NONVERBAL COMMUNICATION

CHAPTER SYNOPSIS

Leaders must be able to obtain accurate information in order to make effective decisions. Obtaining accurate information requires skilled listening to obtain verbal messages and skilled observation and interpretation in order to "hear" the nonverbal messages that form an essential part of any communication event and are crucial to understanding of meanings.

Nonverbal communication is characterized as messages sent on channels other than words. Nonverbal communication can be vocal but involves vocal characteristics and meanings other than the voicing of words. Whereas verbal communication is usually symbolic, involving an arbitrary connection between the words and their referents, nonverbal communication is usually nonarbitrary, characterized by more or less obvious connections between the expressions and their referents. Essentially, nonverbal communication involves communication via signals other than words.

There is debate within the field over whether nonverbal communication includes both intentional and nonintentional messages. A solution to this debate is to

view the communication from a perspective known as message orientation, which includes in the study of nonverbal communication all behaviors that are viewed as meaningful by most members of society, whether they are intentional or not. A second limitation of value is to restrict attention to what can be manipulated by the communicators, head nodding, for example, as opposed to eye color.

Estimates of the importance of nonverbal communication to meaning in a given communication event vary, but in general there is agreement that most of the meaning to any communication event is carried on the nonverbal channels. The importance of nonverbal communication can easily be seen in the area of first impressions, in which judgments are formed primarily on the basis of nonverbal information. Leaders must be able to accurately assess people and their abilities; in order to do so, they must be aware of the impact of nonverbal impressions and messages.

In contrasting nonverbal and verbal communication, several distinctions can be said to apply. First, nonverbal communication tends to be more ambiguous, more open to interpretation. Second, there is usually a less arbitrary connection between symbol and referent in nonverbal communication. The distinction between arbitrary and nonarbitrary is best understood by means of a continuum, with arbitrarily coded messages (no connection between symbol and referent) at one end, iconic coding (some resemblance between symbol and referent) in the middle, and intrinsic coding (a clear connection between symbol and referent) at the other end. In general, verbal communication occurs at the arbitrarily coded end of the continuum and nonverbal communication occurs at the intrinsically coded end.

A third contrast is that nonverbal communication tends to be more biologically determined. Whereas language systems differ widely across culture, there is evidence that certain nonverbal behaviors, particularly facial expressions, have universal meanings across cultures. However, many nonverbal actions are culturally based. A fourth contrast between the two communication channels is that in general nonverbal communication seems to be less consciously controlled; as a result, we tend to view nonverbal messages as more credible.

There are various ways in which nonverbal messages can change or modify a verbal message. A nonverbal message can repeat, delivering the same message on both channels simultaneously, as when we say "Yes" at the same time we are nodding. It can complement, modifying or elaborating on a message, as when a warm verbal greeting is accompanied by a hug. A nonverbal message can accent, providing additional emphasis, as when we point at someone while scolding. A nonverbal message can substitute for a verbal message, as when we flash the "thumbs up" sign at someone whose actions we approve of. Likewise, a nonverbal message can contradict the verbal meaning, as when we say "Love that hat!" in a tone of voice which clearly indicates we hate it. When a nonverbal message unintentionally contradicts the verbal one, it is known as leakage. And, finally, a nonverbal message can regulate the flow of conversation through a variety of signals, including head movements, eye contact, and vocal tones, which communicate when we are finished speaking or ready to speak and when we wish for another speaker to take a turn or remain silent.

Nonverbal communication has numerous social functions. First, it communicates identity, primarily through our choices of dress and other bodily artifacts. Second, it communicates relationships status via such means as who interrupts who, how touch is used to express intimacy or distance, etc. Nonverbal communication also serves to express emotions, to exert influence

through dress, speaking style, and other means, to achieve or communicate understanding through head nods and backchannels ("uh huh," "yeah," "I see," etc.), and to manage interaction through regulation of the flow of the communication.

There are various dimensions or types of nonverbal communication. *Kinesics* refers to the use of body movement or body language to communicate. Several categories of kinesic behavior have been distinguished. Emblems are gestures that readily translate to verbal statements, such as head nodding and raising fingers to describe numbers. Illustrators are gestures which emphasize the verbal message, such as gestures describing the size of an object. Affect displays are gestures and expressions which convey emotion. Regulators are nonverbal cues which regulate the flow of interaction. Adaptors are nonverbal behaviors used to manage tensions or anxieties, such as hand wringing and finger drumming. There are cross-cultural differences in kinesic communication.

Proxemics refers to the use of space to communicate, typically divided into the categories of personal space and territorial space. *Personal space* refers to the area of space around our bodies which we consider our own, and which, when entered without our permission or desire, threatens our sense of safety and security. Space contains various dimensions or zones: intimate distance (touching to about eighteen inches), personal distance (eighteen inches to four feet—this is what is traditionally known as personal space), social distance (four to twelve feet, distances maintained for impersonal interactions), and public distance (twelve to twenty-five feet, used for public speaking and ceremonial events). The distance we keep from others expresses our evaluation of the type of relationship we have with them.

Territoriality refers to our sense of control over space. Primary territory is space over which we have or claim exclusive control, such as a desk, bed, or office. Secondary territory is space not exclusively ours but which we tend to view as ours, such as a specific desk in a classroom which hosts many classes each day and in which no actual seat assignments are made. Public territories, such as restaurant tables or parks benches, are open to all but we may temporarily claim them as private territory by placing markers (personal possessions) on them.

Sometimes territorial encroachment occurs. *Violation* refers to the use of one's private territory without permission. *Invasion* refers to someone taking control of one's territory. *Contamination* describes acts whereby the unapproved use of one's territory leaves it unclean. There are cultural differences in the use of space.

Haptics refers to the use of touch to communicate. *Functional-professional touching* describes the touch employed by those whose work involves people's bodies, such as physicians and barbers and masseuses. *Social-polite touch* describes such things as handshakes and other forms of haptic greetings. *Friendship-warmth touch* refers to the touch used to display nonintimate closeness and is sometimes open to misinterpretation. *Love-intimacy touch* describes touch at a closer level of bonding, such as between lovers or parents and children. Sexual arousal is physically stimulating touch which usually leads to sexual intercourse. There are also cultural differences in the uses of touch.

Paralanguage is any vocal cue other than that contained in the content of the words spoken. Paralanguage includes vocal qualities such as rate, pitch, and volume, vocal characterizers such as yawns and groans, and vocal segregates, also known as vocal fillers, such as "um" and "ah." Sometimes such things as dialect and accent are also included under paralanguage.

Paralanguage has several regulatory functions. Vocal fillers sometimes serve as turn-maintaining cues. There are also turn-yielding cues and turn-requesting cues. In addition, paralanguage cues express emotion, exert influence, and can be used to contradict the verbal message, as in the case of sarcasm. Paralinguistic cues can act as leakage. Paralanguage contributes to impression formation. Silence is also a form of paralinguistic communication and can serve several functions: punctuation or accenting, evaluation, revelation, emotion (the "silent treatment"), and mental activity.

Physical appearance is an important dimension in nonverbal communication, as we all make judgments of people on the basis of appearance. Judgments made on the basis of appearance can become a self-fulfilling prophecy or prediction of future reality because we act according to our judgments and the other person responds on the basis of our actions. We make appearance judgments of others on the basis of attractiveness, body size and shape, and clothing.

Chronemics refers to the ways we use and structure time as a means of communication. We express time orientations, focusing more heavily on the past, present, or future. We also make distinctions between formal time and informal time in ways which are culturally based.

CHAPTER OUTLINE

Defining Nonverbal Communication
    Vocal versus Nonvocal
    Arbitrary vs. Nonarbitrary Symbol Use
    Intentionality versus Nonintentionality
    Message Orientation
    Ability to Manipulate
Importance of Nonverbal Communication
Nonverbal Communication and Leadership
Comparing Nonverbal to Verbal Communication
    Greater Ambiguity
    Less Arbitrary Symbol-Referent Connection
        •Arbitrary Coding
        •Iconic Coding
        •Intrinsic Coding
    More Biologically Determined
    Less Overtly Controlled
Interaction Between Nonverbal and Verbal
    Repeat
    Complement
    Accent
    Substitute
    Contradict
    Regulate
Social Functions of Nonverbal Communication
    Communicating Identity
    Communicating Relationship Status
    Communicating Emotions
    Exerting Influence
    Achieving Understanding
    Managing Interaction
Dimensions of Nonverbal Behavior
    Kinesics
        •Emblems
        •Illustrators
        •Affect Displays
        •Regulators
        •Adaptors
        •Cultural Differences
    Proxemics
        •Personal Space
        •Territoritality
        •Cultural Differences
    Haptics
        •Types of Touch
        •Cultural Differences

Paralanguage
- Types of Paralanguage
- Functions of Paralanguage
- Effects of Paralinguistic Cues
- Silence as Paralinguistic Communication

Physical Appearance
- Physical Attraction
- Body Size and Shape
- Clothing

Chronemics
- Psychological Time Orientations
- Cultural Time Orientations

Improving Nonverbal Communication Skills
  Improving Ability to Interpret Nonverbal Messages
  Improving Ability to Use Nonverbal Messages
Summary
References
Suggested Readings
Exercises
Key Terms

TEACHING OBJECTIVES

5-1. Define nonverbal communication as manipulated signals other than words which are conventionally recognized as meaningful and intentional.

5-2. Emphasize the primary importance of nonverbal communication as the carrier of meaning in communication events.

5-3. Further clarify the difference between nonverbal and verbal communication by contrasting them in terms of their relative ambiguity, arbitrariness, biological connection, and overt control.

5-4. Explain the various types of relationship between verbal and nonverbal communication within a communication event.

5-5. Describe the social functions of nonverbal communication and offer examples of each.

5-6. Articulate the various aspects of kinesic communication, emphasizing the cultural basis of these behaviors.

5-7. Define proxemics and depict the importance of and relationship between the concepts of space and territoriality; explore cultural differences.

5-8. Depict the use of haptic communication as relationship-governed and culturally influenced.

5-9. Explore the varieties of paralanguage, its meaning, functions, and effects, as well as silence as a form of paralanguage.

5-10. Examine the domain of physical appearance as a form of nonverbal communication, attending to the variables of attractiveness, body size and shape, and clothing.

5-11. Describe the uses of time as a form of nonverbal communication, exploring cultural differences.

DISCUSSION QUESTIONS

5-1. What are some situations which leaders in particular face or encounter in which accurate assessment of nonverbal meanings is vital?

5-2. Do you agree that nonverbal communication is generally more ambiguous? Can you think of circumstances in which this isn't so? If the meaning of a verbal statement such as "Very funny" is determined by the nonverbal accompaniments, which is more ambiguous?

5-3. Are there situations or contexts in which leakage is more likely to occur?

5-4. What are the primary ways that people in this culture communicate their identities nonverbally?

5-5. How might a person of high status communicate distance or separation from people of lower status nonverbally?

5-6. How do men and women differ in their abilities and methods of communicating emotion in this culture?

5-7. How might a person use kinesic behavior to control or intimidate another? How might this same person use proxemics for the same purpose?

5-8. Should there be another haptic category for touch which is used as an instrument of control?

5-9. What conclusions do you draw or assumptions do you make about people on the basis of their vocal qualities?

5-10. Which dimension of nonverbal communication is the most important or most valued in this culture? Why do you think so? What does this say about the culture?

SKILL MASTERY EXERCISES

5-1. A useful exercise which requires preplanning involves obtaining your students' first impressions of you on the first day of class, as soon as you have entered the classroom. Hand out a preprinted form which asks for first impressions in some specific and some general ways. Don't talk until the students have completed writing. (Sample handout below; feel free to adapt as seems appropriate.)

If you're already well into the class, this exercise can also be used by having a cooperative stranger (stranger to your students, perhaps a friend of yours) come in unannounced, standing silent at the front of the room while first impressions are recorded. Ideally, the friendly stranger would be willing to stay and share information about her/his real self in relation to the perceived selves recorded by the students. This can be a good way to informally test the validity of first impressions and lead into a more thorough discussion of nonverbal cues and how we interpret them. It is useful to talk about differences in what we attend to as well as how we interpret.

Sample First Impression Handout:
1. How old do you think this person is?
2. Male or female?
3. Married or single?
4. Heterosexual or homosexual?
5. What would you guess is this person's occupation?
6. What are your thoughts or observations about this person as to her/his personality, likes, dislikes, habits, etc.?

5-2. Using videotapes of films you own or have available through your media center or library, select and show brief segments of interaction between two or more individuals, sound off, so that only their non-vocal nonverbal behavior is observable. Seek film segments which are not likely to have been seen by your students and ask those who recognize the film and know the content of the interaction to disqualify themselves from commenting.

Play five or so segments, thirty to sixty seconds each, one at a time; ask your students to record their decisions about the nature and content of this communication after each segment. Use their recorded impressions then as a basis for discussion about how we decide what another person is feeling or saying and how we decide or make judgments about the nature of relationships between people on the basis of their nonverbal communication.

An additional option is to provide printed transcripts of video interactions after they have been viewed and comments recorded but before playing them again with sound. Ask students to match the dialogue to the particular video segment.

5-3. Divide the class into three or more groups and assign as their task that they are to devise an in-class experiment to demonstrate or test the concepts of personal space and territoriality. See what they come up with and let them try their experiments out on one another (presuming none are too manipulative or damaging of other people).

5-4. Consult an intercultural communication text, such as Hall's *The Silent Language* (see References at the end of the chapter), and pull from it any number of nonverbal communication behaviors which are common to another culture but uncommon in our own, for example, greeting a person by kissing her on both cheeks, same-sex friends holding hands, etc. For each behavior, write a brief description on an index card and distribute these among your students. Announce to the class as a whole that we are going to engage in a brief comparative study of nonverbal communication in other cultures and instruct the students who received index cards to find a convenient moment and person with whom to engage in the nonverbal behavior described. Having the whole class seated in a circle would make this exercise easier to engage in and to observe. Discuss the responses of not only the participants but those who watched.

A good way to conclude this exercise, emphasizing that all cultural behaviors have a tendency to appear strange or nonsensical to an outsider, is to ask the class to consider what behaviors or habits common to our culture might appear strange or unacceptable to visitors from other cultures. You could of course ask international students in the class to think back to their own early experiences of the culture and what they found most puzzling or strange, but don't expect them to share much unless the rest of the class clearly indicates a willingness to look at its own culture's behaviors from another's point of view.

KEY TERMS AND CONCEPTS

nonverbal communication (p. 117)
kinesics (p. 128)
emblems (p. 128)
illustrators (p. 128)

CHAPTER **6**

INTERCULTURAL COMMUNICATION

CHAPTER SYNOPSIS

Intercultural communication is a difficult process, involving differences in understanding that extend far beyond language differences. Intercultural communication is increasingly important as the influence of mass media and a global economy bring us more frequently in contact with members of other cultures. Even within U.S. culture, subcultural differences create a need for greater understanding of intercultural communication principles.

Intercultural communication is defined as communication between individuals or groups from different cultural or subcultural backgrounds that focuses on cultural facets of interpersonal communication and the effect of cultural differences on patterns of communication. Studies of intercultural communication may be interactive, focusing on communication between cultures, or comparative, focusing on cultural differences.

Intercultural communication is distinguished from other related studies as follows: Intercultural communication focuses on interpersonal interaction between members of different cultures or subcultures. Cross-cultural communication compares interpersonal interaction patterns of members of different cultures. International communication studies mass media within different cultures.

Culture is defined as a pattern of thinking, consisting of beliefs, values, and practices, shared by a group of people. Culture is also the shared set of categories contained in language and the shared standards of behavior of cultural members. The shared values of cultures are expressed and revealed through the language system of the culture.

Cultural differences are not always clearly distinguishable. Cultural characteristics, for example, frequently cross national and ethnic boundaries. Ultimately, the boundaries of a culture are defined by the sense of personal belonging of the members. Individuals may hold membership in more than one culture. Identification with a smaller culture within a culture marks membership in a subculture. When the cumulative knowledge of interactants is different and affects understanding, intercultural communication is occurring.

Cultural communication differs in a number of ways. Language variations include many differences that are untranslatable, reflecting deep cultural differences and values. Beyond language differences, verbal style differences may be direct or indirect, elaborate or succinct, personal or contextual, instrumental or affective. Cultures may differ considerably in their verbal styles. Even men and women within cultures may differ considerably in their verbal styles.

In addition to language and verbal style differences, scholars have differentiated broad cultural dimensions or values which express basic cultural differences.

These dimensions include: individualism to collectivism, masculinity to femininity, degree of uncertainty avoidance, and a dimension of power distance. Individualism-collectivism expresses the basic self or group orientation of cultural members. The masculinity-femininity dimension expresses the cultural emphasis on power, assertiveness and other traditional male values versus an emphasis on feminine relational and interdependence issues. The uncertainty avoidance dimension registers the culture's degree of tolerance of differences and change. Power distance is a dimension which expresses the degree of acceptance by members of a culture of the differential distribution of power within the culture. Cultures vary along other dimensions as well, including family and social structure.

Culture shock is the term used to describe an inability to adapt to life in another culture and to successfully accomplish basic necessary social tasks. Symptoms of culture shock include: psychological strain, feelings of loss, deprivation, and rejection, feelings of confusion, anxiety, and disgust in regard to the new culture, and feelings of impotence to cope with the new culture.

Adjustment to a new culture usually is accomplished by movement through these stages of response: fascination even though barriers are encountered, frustration and feelings of superiority about one's own culture, adjustment with humor, and, finally, biculturalism, or comfortable adaptation to the new culture.

Four basic individual approaches to encountering new cultures are described: acculturation, or the attempt of the individual to merge completely into the new culture and leave her/his old culture behind; chauvinism, or clinging to the conviction that one's own culture is superior; marginalism, or living on the outer edges of both old and new cultures without assuming full membership in either; and mediation, or synthesizing elements of both cultures while maintaining the essential differences and features of each.

Members of different cultures are likely to have difficult encounters when those encounters are forced, competitive, involve opposing viewpoints, express racial or ethnic inequalities, and include power or status differences. Intercultural encounters are more likely to be successful when the members meet with an understanding of power or status equality, interaction is in-depth, common goals which unite them are identified, and the context for the encounter is pleasant and rewarding.

Several principles which promote intercultural communication competence are identified. First, individuals need to avoid ethnocentric values and views which treat other cultural beliefs and values as inferior. Rather, differences should be celebrated. Second, communicative flexibility is desirable, including a tolerance for ambiguity, responsiveness to change, and willingness to try new behaviors or attitudes. Third, intercultural communicators should develop different expectations of communicative effectiveness, anticipating difficulties and misunderstandings and accepting their inevitability.

Various types of intercultural communication training currently exist. Information or fact-oriented training uses a classroom approach to deliver information about the other culture in order to reduce the impact of culture shock when differences are first encountered. Attribution training offers students descriptions of intercultural encounters and experience with interpreting the intentions of the members of the new culture. Cultural awareness training attempts to enhance student understanding of their own cultures and cultures in general, to foster an appreciation of cultural values and their social consequences. Cognitive-behavior modification training teaches students to identify what aspects of culture they find rewarding or punishing and provides strategies for seeking or avoiding these aspects in the new culture.

Experiential learning immerses trainees in interactive learning situations involving simulations and role playing. These approaches allow individuals to obtain actual practice with necessary social skills. Interaction training brings trainees together with members of or those knowledgeable in host cultures for interaction and discussion.

Intercultural communication, while difficult, offers many rewards of a business, social, and personal nature. Intercultural communication involves risk but offers enriched understanding of the nature and impact of culture.

CHAPTER OUTLINE

The Importance of Intercultural Communication
    Economic Importance
    Societal Importance
    Personal Importance
Defining Intercultural Communication
    Conceptual Definitions
    Differences From Other Studies
Defining Culture
    Shared Values and Beliefs
    Shared Pattern of Thinking

Shared Language System
Defining Boundaries Between Cultures
  Beyond Nationality
  Beyond Ethnicity
  Sense of Belonging
Cultural Differences and Their Effect on
  Communication
    Language Variations
      •Idioms
      •Untranslatables
    Verbal Style Differences
      •Direct vs. Indirect
      •Elaborate vs. Succinct
      •Personal vs. Contextual
      •Instrumental vs. Affective
    Dimensions of Cultural Variability
      •Individualism–Collectivism
      •Masculinity–Femininity
      •Uncertainty Avoidance
      •Power Distance
Reactions to Dealing with Other Cultures
  Culture Shock
  Cultural Adjustment
Individual Approaches to Crossing Cultural Boundaries
  Acculturation
  Chauvinism
  Marginalism
  Mediation
Factors that Help or Hinder Interaction Between
  Cultures
    Hindering Factors
    Helpful Factors
Intercultural Communication Competence
  Different is Good
  Flexibility Helps
  Change Your Expectations of Effectiveness
Intercultural Communication Training
  Information or Fact-oriented Training
  Attribution Training
  Cultural Awareness
  Cognitive Behavior Modification
  Experiential Learning
  Interaction Approach
Summary
Exercises
Related Readings

TEACHING OBJECTIVES

6-1. Emphasize the increasing importance of intercultural communication competence.

6-2. Provide a clear definition of intercultural communication which synthesizes the definitions provided.
6-3. Define the various common elements of cultures.
6-4. Explore the impact of language variations on intercultural understanding.
6-5. Discuss verbal style differences within and between cultures.
6-6. Consider these and other dimensions of cultural differences.
6-7. Define culture shock and cultural adjustment.
6-8. Emphasize factors which aid intercultural encounters.
6-9. Summarize the elements of intercultural communication competence.
6-10. Explore the various forms of intercultural communication training.

DISCUSSION QUESTIONS

6-1. How many individuals from other cultures or subcultures have you encountered in the past week? Did you seek or seek to avoid these encounters?
6-2. What would you say are the distinguishing features of U.S. culture?
6-3. To how many cultures and subcultures do you belong?
6-4. What are some of the idiomatic or untranslatable aspects of American English?
6-5. How would you describe your own verbal style? How does it compare to the verbal style of your culture?
6-6. Have you ever experienced a kind of culture shock in a new situation within your own culture?
6-7. How might members of subcultures within your own culture be brought together to develop greater intercultural understanding?
6-8. Which approach to intercultural communication training do you think you would find most helpful and effective? Why?

SKILL MASTERY EXERCISES

6-1. Divide the class into groups of 4-5 persons each. Instruct each group member to generate a list of each of the cultures and subcultures of which s/he is a member. Have group members then discuss and compare their "culture lists," seeking overlapping memberships.

Have each group develop a visual model, showing overlap and differences, of the cultural and subcultural groupings represented in their groups. As the groups share their models, encourage discussion of potential areas of misunderstanding within the groups where lack of shared experiences are greatest.

6-2. If the human resources are available, invite to your two or three native representatives of diverse non-U.S. cultures—for example, a member of an Arab nation, a Chinese or Japanese person, and a European or Indian native. Have students prepare questions in advance to ask these cultural representatives about aspects of the language, values, nonverbal communication, etc. which distinguish the various cultures. Explore the notion, with students and guests, that various behavioral aspects of cultures reflect the values and beliefs of those cultures—for example, that the bowing greeting of Japanese culture reflects that culture's emphasis on power distance, formality, and respect, whereas the handshake of U.S. culture reflects the direct, familiar, and egalitarian values of the culture.

6-3. *Japanese Cultural Encounters and How to Handle Them* by Hiroko C. Kataoka and Tetsuya Kusumoto (Lincolnwood IL: Passport Books, 1991), available in paperback, contains numerous short vignettes describing intercultural encounters between Americans and Japanese. Readers are asked to chose from among various possible interpretations of the Japanese responses in the stories. Correct responses are provided which also contain valuable lessons about beliefs and behavior in Japanese culture. If you can purchase or obtain this book from the library, select and present a series of the vignettes to the class orally, offering the options for interpretation and allowing discussion, as a way of exploring the various language, style and variability differences of cultures.

KEY TERMS

intercultural communication (p. 149)
culture (p. 151)
subculture (p. 152)
verbal style (p. 156)
individualism-collectivism p. 159)
masculinity-feminity (p 160)
uncertainty avoidance (p. 160)
power distance (p. 161)
culture shock (p. 162)
acculturation (p. 164)
chauvinistic (p. 164)
marginal (p. 164)
mediating (p. 165)
ethnocentrism (p. 168)
information training (p. 171)
attribution training (p. 172)
cultural awareness (p. 172)
cognitive behavior modification (p. 173)
experiential learning (p. 173)
interaction approach (p. 174)

CHAPTER **7**

INTERPERSONAL COMMUNICATION

CHAPTER SYNOPSIS

Theorists are divided into two camps on the question of how interpersonal communication should be defined. The contextual definition of interpersonal communication distinguishes interpersonal communication from other communication contexts on the basis of 1) the number of communicators (few), 2) the physical proximity of the participants (close), 3) the available sensory channels for the communication (many), and 4) the immediacy of the feedback (immediate). According to this definition, interpersonal communication stands at the opposite end of the contextual continuum from mass communication, where the numbers are many, proximity is distant, sensory channels are limited, and feedback is delayed.

The developmental definition of interpersonal communication, on the other hand, measures the communication shared on a continuum of level of knowledge of the other, from impersonal to interpersonal. Cultural-level knowledge is shared knowledge the members of a culture possess; for example, greeting rituals or formalized communication between individuals with carefully defined roles constitute cultural-level knowledge. Sociological-level knowledge is knowledge about the groups to which an individual belongs; this knowledge allows for some degree of prediction about who the other is. Psychological-level knowledge is knowledge based on knowing the other as a unique individual. According to the developmental definition, communication is only truly interpersonal when it involves or is based on the psychological-level knowledge of the other. Both views have value: The contextual view offers understanding of the unique context of interpersonal communication, and the developmental view acknowledges the depth of knowledge and understanding involved in interpersonal relationships.

There are three recognized functions of interpersonal communication. The first is the acquisition of social knowledge; social knowledge is that knowledge which allows some measure of predictability in our encounters with others in our world. Some theorists suggest that we communicate primarily to reduce uncertainty. Interpersonal communication allows us to acquire the kind of broad social knowledge about how people act and interact that can reduce uncertainty and guide our interaction with others.

One way of looking at the process of social knowledge acquisition is called social penetration theory, also known as the "onion model," developed by Altman and Taylor. This model acknowledges the breadth and depth of the human personality and views the process of relationship-building as one of gradually "peeling away" the outer layers of a person's attitudes and beliefs in order to discover her or his inner core of beliefs and feelings.

There are several groups or types of strategies we use to gather information about others. Passive strategies are those through which we simply observe others in social situations in order to learn how they react to others (reactivity searching) and/or how they "naturally" behave in informal settings (disinhibition searching).

Active strategies for acquiring social knowledge include asking others about the "target" person and environmental structuring, which involves staging incidents or situations in order to determine how the other will react. Interactive strategies involving direct encounters with the other include interrogation (asking) and self-disclosure.

Self-disclosure, the voluntary sharing of information not likely to be available from other sources (i.e., psychological-level knowledge), is a much-studied area of communication. Self-disclosure can be seen both as an information-gathering strategy and as a measure of the depth or quality of a relationship. Self-disclosure always involves risk.

Self-disclosure is useful as a strategy for gaining information because of an unspoken expectation within the culture that one person's self-disclosure is an encouragement to the other to also self-disclose; this is known as the norm of reciprocity. Self-disclosure helps to build trust.

Self-disclosure is also a means of obtaining social validation, or acceptance; the more you have shared about yourself, the more fully accepted or validated you will feel. Self-disclosure also allows for self-discovery; sometimes we have to express who we are or what we feel in order to come to a deeper understanding of ourselves.

As stated before, however, self-disclosure involves risks. We can meet with rejection because of what we have chosen to disclose. We give the other power over us if what we disclose is not something we want other people to know. Also, if what is disclosed is burdensome or threatening to the other, the relationship can be jeopardized.

The following guidelines for appropriate self-disclosure are offered. First, start slow and increase self-disclosure in small increments. Second, be sure the other is comfortable receiving the disclosure, keeping in mind the norm of reciprocity. Third, make sure the disclosure is important to the ongoing relationship.

The second function of interpersonal communication is creation of a context of understanding. Relational contexts are what help us to understand the meanings in each other's messages. There are several types of messages exchanged in interpersonal communication, all of which help to define and refine the context of understanding. Content messages are the literal messages exchanged. Relationship messages, often unspoken, are indirect accompaniments to content messages which offer aids to interpretation.

Metacommunication is direct talk about the relationship itself. Episodic-level metacommunication is a response to a specific communication episode, such as, for example, saying "I was just teasing you when I said that." Relationship-level metacommunication refers to broad discussions of the entire relationship, for example, talking with your mate about how you argue together.

A third function of interpersonal communication is that it involves the creation, maintenance, and alteration of our social identities. Our social identities are composite, consisting of both roles and face. Roles are social categories which designate rights and responsibilities and provide guidelines for behavior. Roles tend to be formalized, numerous, and often overlapping. Our roles exert influence on our interactions.

Face refers to the sense of self-worth or ideal self-image which we present to the world and strive to maintain; face is the personal image of competence and value for which and of which we seek affirmation and acceptance from others. Roles are given or won. Face is a conscious creation which we struggle to maintain. The face we present as a conscious part of our social identity can be either accepted or rejected by those we meet.

Our identities, in other words, are subject to negotiation. Identity management is interactional and involves two primary components. The first aspect or component is the self-presentation of the individual, the person's attempt to claim an identity. The second component of identity management is known as altercasting; it is the attempt on the part of the other to offer or force an alternate identity or image.

Interpersonal communication involves the ongoing negotiation of social identities, frequently through the vehicles of confirming, disconfirming, and rejecting responses. A confirming response acknowledges the value of the other as a person and affirms or upholds her or his self-presentation. A disconfirming response is the opposite; it represents a complete refusal to acknowledge the worth of the other as a person. A rejection response denies the request of the other without altercasting.

Interpersonal communication competence is the ability to communicate in a personally effective and socially appropriate manner. Effectiveness refers to the attainment of goals (obtaining what was desired from the interaction). Appropriateness has to do with the attainment of goals in socially acceptable ways, preferably in ways that do not do damage to the relationship.

Communication competence can also be described in terms of knowledge and performance. *Knowledge* refers to the ability to distinguish which skill is appropriate to what occasion. *Performance* refers to the mastery of the necessary interaction skills.

Conversational competence refers to the specific ability to manage the initiation, flow, and conclusion of conversation. A conversation is a spontaneous creation which involves topic choices and flow, or turn taking among interactants.

The initiation of conversations involves a signaled transition from no interaction to interaction, indications about the relationship between the interactants, and accessibility for further conversation. Forms of initiation include verbal salute, personal acknowledgement of the other; reference to the other, acknowledging some portion of the other's identity or face; personal inquiry, a request for information; and external reference, allusion to some feature of the surrounding environment.

A conversational device known as a demand ticket is another useful strategy for initiating a conversation; this involves the use of a question to engage the other and return immediate control of the conversation to the initiator. Nonverbal signals also figure prominently in the initiation of conversations.

Strategies for concluding conversations include signaling future inaccessibility, supporting the other, and summarization of the encounter and may involve showing appreciation, giving an external reason for leaving, etc. Nonverbal cues are also provided. Typically, conversations are successfully concluded when participants agree to end them, positively evaluate the encounter, and propose a future meeting.

Topic change and turn exchange are the central elements of the body of a conversation. Conversational coherence is desirable and occurs at two levels: sequential coherence, connecting one utterance to the next, and global coherence, an underlying framework or connectedness to the whole conversation. Coherence is an ideal not always attainable, particularly when encountering egocentric speakers.

Turn taking refers to the smooth exchange of talk from one interactant to the other. Effective turn taking maintains the comfort of the interactants and promotes mutual participation. Speaker transition points (pauses or breaks) occur regularly in conversations; at each transition, the speaker can select the next speaker, the next speaker can self-select, or the original speaker can choose to continue. Problems arise when one interactant either refuses to self-select or refuses to surrender a turn.

CHAPTER OUTLINE

Defining Interpersonal Communication
    Contextual Definition
        • Few Communicators
        • Close Proximity

- Many Sensory Channels
- Immediate Feedback

Developmental Definition
- Cultural-Level Knowledge (impersonal)
- Sociological-Level Knowledge (quasi-personal)
- Psychological-Level Knowledge (interpersonal)

Functions of Interpersonal Communication

Social Knowledge Acquisition
- Social Penetration Theory
- Social Information-Gathering Strategies
- Self-Disclosure

Building a Context of Understanding
- Content and Relationship Messages
- Metacommunication

Establish and Negotiate Identity
- Role and Face
- Identity Management
- Confirming, Rejecting, and Disconfirming Responses

Interpersonal Communication Competence

Defining Interpersonal Competence
- Effectiveness and Appropriateness
- Knowledge and Performance

Conversational Competence
- Initiations
- Conclusions
- Topic Changes
- Turn Taking

Summary

Exercises

Suggested Readings

References

TEACHING OBJECTIVES

7-1. Explain the contextual and developmental definitions of interpersonal communication.

7-2. Suggest the contribution of both the contextual and the developmental views to an understanding of interpersonal communication as bounded by context and offering interactants the potential for mutual knowledge at the psychological level.

7-3. Describe the social knowledge acquisition function of interpersonal communication, discussing social penetration theory, information-gathering strategies, and self-disclosure as methods of social knowledge acquisition.

7-4. Discuss the second function of interpersonal communication as the creation of contexts in which to communicate and through the existence of which the interpretation of messages is made easier; draw parallels to earlier discussions of context.

7-5. Emphasize the importance of establishing and maintaining identity as the third basic function of interpersonal communication; attempt to create an appreciation for the importance of roles and face to identity negotiation and management.

7-6. Analyze the ways we affirm and disconfirm or altercast the self-presentations of others and the impact of these actions.

7-7. Define communication competence, describe some of the tools for measuring competence (effectiveness, appropriateness, etc.), and encourage attention to the complexities of and value in conversation.

DISCUSSION QUESTIONS

7-1. In a sense, the contextual versus developmental debate regarding interpersonal communication is about how we communicate versus how much we know or have the potential of discovering about the other. Looking at your own relationships—acquaintances, friends, family—which matters more? Or is it that the context is necessary in order for the knowledge to unfold?

7-2. What about this idea that we communicate in order to reduce uncertainty? What experiences have you had with being in situations where you were uncertain? How did you communicate?

7-3. Who knows you better than anyone else? How long have you known each other? How long did you know each other before you shared some of your deeper layers?

7-4. How would you evaluate the various social information-gathering strategies in regards to the following: directness, manipulative quality, potential for obtaining the most reliable information?

7-5. Think about your closest relationship. How much of your communication would you estimate is metacommunication? How about with your newest friend? What do you think is the relationship between the depth of your knowledge of another person and the amount of time you spend metacommunicating?

7-6. Are you bothered by the concept of having a "face" you present to the world? Is having a "face identity" a kind of phoniness? Are there ever times when you're with other people and not wearing a "face"? How about when you're alone?

7-7. Who of all the people you know altercasts you the most? How does she/he do it? Why do you think she/he does it? And who do you altercast most often?

7-8. What would be the best way to find out if you are a competent communicator? Who would you ask? How would you ask? What would you ask? Could you find out without asking others?

SKILL MASTERY EXERCISES

7-1. Provide four enlarged copies of the "blank" onion model to each student. After discussing the model and what it represents, give them these instructions:

1. Take a copy of the onion model and write your name at the top of the page.
2. Below your name, write the first name of a person you feel close to, someone who lives nearby and who you will see sometime before the next class.
3. Take a second copy of the onion model and do the same thing, writing the name of a person you feel close to who lives nearby and who you will see sometime before the next class.
4. Now use a pen or pencil to color in portions of the onion to represent how much of yourself at various levels you feel this person you have named knows about you. Do this with both of the people you have named on the two pages you have labeled.

When the students have finished, collect these two copies; promise to return them at the next class.

Now ask them to take the other two copies home with them. Ask them to explain the model to the friends they have named and to ask each friend to fill in the onion to represent how much they feel they know about your student at various levels. Have the students bring these copies with them to the next class. Make sure their friends sign the model.

At the next class, return to each student the models they filled out and ask them to get into small groups and to share with each other their own and their friends' versions of the onion model and to talk about how and why they are the same or different.

End with a general discussion about whether we tend to over- or underestimate how well someone else knows us. You can use the students' own "findings" as a basis for this discussion.

7-2. Have your students form small groups for discussion, separated by gender. Provide each group with the following list and ask them to discuss and decide which disclosure they would be willing to share and with whom (see below). After discussion, ask for results and compare male and female groups to discover differences, if any.

How many would disclose	To a parent	Significant other	Best friend
a nightmare			
suicidal thoughts			
early sexual experiences			
career ambitions			
most embarrassing experience			
proudest accomplishment			
that you cry			
others you love			
someone you hate			
greatest fear			

7-3. Have students self-select into pairs and "metacommunicate" about how each of them individually communicates with a parent, a sibling, or a significant other. (Each pair can select which type of relationship to metacommunicate about, but both in the pair should talk about the same type of relationship, i.e., both should talk about parent or both should talk about sibling communication.)

Suggest that they include in their metacommunication discussion concerning how they greet their parent or sibling or significant other, how they argue, how they ask for what they want, how and when they use manipulation to get what they want, and how they part company.

Afterward, invite those who are willing to share what they learned from their metacommunication.

KEY TERMS AND CONCEPTS

interpersonal communication (contextual definition) (p. 181)

interpersonal communication (developmental definition) (p. 182)

cultural-level knowledge (p. 182)

sociological-level knowledge (p. 183)

psychological-level knowledge (p. 183)

self-disclosure (p. 189)

social validation (p. 190)

metacommunication (p. 193)

role (p. 194)

face (p. 195)

self-presentation (p. 196)

altercasting (p. 196)

confirming response (p. 197)

disconfirming response (p. 197)

communication competence (p. 199)

communicative effectiveness (p. 200)

communicative appropriateness (p. 200)

CHAPTER **8**

COMMUNICATION IN RELATIONSHIPS

CHAPTER SYNOPSIS

Relationships are central to human life and are often the source of life's greatest joys. Such importance merits understanding, although there is sometimes resistance to the notion of submitting relationships to scientific investigation. Common criticisms of the scientific study of relationships include the assertions that, given the unique nature of each relationship, generalization is impossible and that scientific analysis ruins relationships and provides only trivial results.

Social science researchers have dispelled some common fallacies about relationships. Contrary to popular opinion, relationships are not a matter of matching individual personality traits of the individuals, but have more to do with how personalities are communicated to one another. A second fallacy about relationships is that more communication will solve any relational problem. A third fallacy is that effective relationships are self-regulating, or stable and resistant to change, when in fact relationships require continual input, adaptation, and meshing of needs.

The key features of interpersonal relationships are interdependence and duration. Interdependence involves mutual reliance to achieve common goals and mutual influence, the actions of one having impact on the other. Duration refers to the existence of relation-

ships over time and the development of a relational history.

Relationships can be classified according to standard role labels (friend, sibling, etc.) or on the basis of key features such as intimacy and control. Wish and Kaplan offer a dimensional classification system which evaluates and classifies relationships on five scales: from cooperative and friendly to competitive and hostile, from intense to superficial, from equality to dominance, from formal and cautious to informal and open, and from task oriented to non-task oriented. Measuring the shift of relationships along these dimensions over time illustrates their ongoing, processual nature. Communication is the lifeblood of relationships at all stages and levels and is the primary tool with which we form, change, and end relationships.

Relationships go through phases of initiation and termination. Relationship initiation refers to the process of building a relationship and the movement from initial interaction to greater levels of intimacy. The formation of relationships involves a filtering process whereby we gather information and make decisions about the level of knowledge and intimacy we desire with the other. We begin with incidental or sociological cues concerning the availability of the other for interaction and proceed to other preinteraction cues, such as the appearance, dress, and apparent status of the other.

Eventually, if there is sufficient interest, we move to interaction cues, those gained by conversation, and through these to cognitive cues about the personality and attitudes of the other. Wilmot suggests that the filtering process continues as we make decisions about moving into greater degrees of intimacy with the other. In any case, relationships begin with small talk, or phatic communication, which is characterized as superficial, noncontroversial, and broad in topical nature.

Relationship maintenance is the process of sustaining a relationship and fulfilling relationship expectations. Maintaining relationships requires skill and effort. The first requirement for relationship maintenance is the ability to balance the competing needs for independence and interdependence in the individual members of the relationship. This balancing of independence-interdependence needs is ongoing.

Maintaining relationships also involves meeting the relational expectations of the parties involved. This task is made difficult by the differing and sometimes conflicting expectations of the individuals. Clarification of expectations is essential to successfully maintaining relationships.

Relationship termination is the process of moving from greater to diminishing levels of intimacy. Relationship termination is not just the reversal of the initiation process. Termination can be primarily accomplished by one person and does not necessarily involve a loss of information. Termination can also be accomplished abruptly, whereas initiation is usually a gradual process. The termination of a relationship has social repercussions far beyond the immediate individuals. Strategies for terminating relationships vary in their degree of directness and their concern for the feelings of the other.

Knapp's theory of relational change views relationships as processual at both initiation and termination. He characterizes the stages of relationship development as initiation, or agreement to explore; experimentation, or small talk; intensification, involving frequent self-disclosure; integration, the formation of a merged identity; and bonding, the announcement of commitment.

The termination of relationships involves these stages: differentiating, or reassertion of independence; circumscribing, reduction in amount and depth of communication; stagnating, refusal to discuss the relationship and increasing silences; avoiding, the movement toward separate physical space; and terminating, the clear statement of the end of the relationship by one or both partners.

Movement through relational stages is systematic and sequential, although partners may move back and forth through the stages. Movement may take place even within stages as those involved adapt to change. Relationships continue to change for as long as they continue to exist.

Managing conflict in relationships is essential to their survival. Conflict in relationships is normal and necessary to continued growth. Conflict is defined as an expressed struggle between interdependent people who perceive the existence of incompatible goals, insufficient resources, or interference in their relationship with each other.

Common problems in our approaches to conflict include avoidance, or the refusal to admit or engage in conflict. Avoidance can lead to gunnysacking, or the storing up of unsettled resentments until a chaotic explosion of conflicts results.

A second problematic tendency in conflict situations is blaming the other. This problem has its root in a tendency to judge the actions of others as stemming from their personalities while assuming our own actions are the result of the necessities of external circumstances; this tendency is known as the actor-observer difference in causal attributions. There is also a related tendency for people to generalize immediate problems into broader problems, using words such as *always* and *never* to label the behavior of the other. These problems can be resolved by emphasizing shared responsibility for conflicts, by empathizing with the situation of the other, and by using language which accepts responsibility for one's own feelings and avoids blame.

A third problem in conflict management is the tendency to view conflict as a win-lose situation; as a result, we refuse to give in and obstruct the other's attempts to attain his or her objectives. This attitude causes conflicts to escalate. Resolutions must be sought which allow both parties to attain their objectives, as much as that is possible, through use of problem-solving strategies.

CHAPTER OUTLINE

The Importance of Studying Relationships
    Criticisms of the Study of Relationships
        • Inability to Generalize
        • Scientific Analysis Damaging
        • Trivial Results
    Fallacies Commonly Held Regarding Relationships
        • Relationships Involve Careful Matching

TEACHING OBJECTIVES

8-1. Delineate the key features of interpersonal relationships as interdependence and duration.

8-2. Explore various methods of classifying interpersonal relationships, especially Wish and Kaplan's dimensional scales.

8-3. Describe the stages of relationship initiation, maintenance, and termination and the unique needs of each of these stages.

8-4. Explicate Knapp's theory of relational change from escalation to termination, emphasizing the dynamic nature of relationships and the various possibilities for movement between phases.

8-5. Explore the nature of conflict in interpersonal relationships, illustrating common problems in handling conflict as well as strategies for resolving conflicts.

DISCUSSION QUESTIONS

8-1. What other dimensions or scales might be useful in classifying relationships?

8-2. How would you describe the filters or distinctions you draw between the various categories of relationships in which you are involved?

8-3. What do you think is the most common strategy or process whereby relationships are ended? Are the strategies different for teenagers than for adults or people of other ages? Are the strategies different for friends than for intimates?

8-4. Can one member of a relationship terminate a relationship without the consent or agreement of the other? What if the other party does not want the relationship to end?

8-5. What would you say are the most common markers of friendship identities among your peers?

8-6. What would you say is the most common human response to conflict? How do most people tend to handle conflict in their everyday lives?

SKILL MASTERY EXERCISES

8-1. Assign students the task of viewing a "realistic," readily rentable film depicting human relationships. (This can be a group or individual assignment.) After viewing the film, have them write a three–five page paper analyzing one of the relation-ships portrayed, using the concept of filtering in the development of relationships, the theory of relational change, or the discussion of common problems in conflict management.

8-2. As a class or in small groups, explore the notion that, like individual relationships, each stage of chronological life encompasses some struggle or adjustment in the balance between dependence and independence for the individual. Is it possible to chart a cycle or rhythm of movement from dependence to independence and back again?

8-3. Divide the class into groups of four or five. Have each group create and write a description of a con-flict in an interpersonal relationship, giving as much detail as is necessary to provide someone unfamiliar with the situation some understanding of the nature of the problem.

When this task is finished, have the groups trade problems and assign them the task of discussing and developing a means of solving the problem that allows both parties to win.

If time permits, have the various groups share their conflicts and solutions with the whole class.

KEY TERMS AND CONCEPTS

relationship initiation (p. 219)
relationship maintenance (p. 221)
relationship termination (p. 222)
conflict (p. 230)
gunnysacking (p. 231)
actor-observer difference (p. 232)

CHAPTER **9**

FAMILY COMMUNICATION

CHAPTER SYNOPSIS

The ideal family, where no problems exist, is a myth. Defining a family is not as easy as it would seem; cer-tainly, biological ties alone are insufficient to determine family boundaries. Three approaches to defining family are presented: the "family structure" approach, the "task" approach, and the "transactional process" approach.

The family structure approach employs a combina-tion of biological and legal ties to define family. All per-sons bound by genetic, marital or adoptive ties are considered "extended" family. All extended family mem-bers who share the same household are considered "nuclear" family. This definition would include even persons who do not feel like members of a family. The task approach defines family on the basis of who fulfills basic family obligations such as the care and nurturing of children. The transactional process approach defines families on the basis of the quality of their interaction with one another, suggesting that families are those who see themselves as family and interact accordingly. Other approaches attempt to combine these definitional qualities.

In any case, definitions of family need to be broad and inclusive. Interaction is more important than biol-ogy. The American family is changing. Communication is a vital tool for negotiating family change.

Families fulfill certain basic and essential func-tions. Family members are interdependent. Not all fam-ilies fulfill all family functions equally or well, but successful fulfillment of family functions depends upon effective family communication. Basic functions of fami-lies include: providing affection and support, nurturing and socializing children, and providing economic sup-port.

Certain processes are a part of all family structures and histories. These processes include family decision-making, distributions of power, and family evolution. Families display decision-making styles that can remain constant or change over time. Three basic decision-making styles are: *consensus,* or unanimous agreement by all family members; *accommodation,* or concession by some family members to the decisions of other members, as in "majority rule" decisions; and *de facto,* when disagreements prevent family members from reaching decisions, and unilateral decision-making sometimes results.

Power is not distributed equally within families. Family power is defined as the ability of family members to influence other members; family power, in other words, is relational. Sources of power within families include: punishment (coercive) power, reward power, expertise, legitimacy (role power), identification (admiration), and persuasion.

Families evolve, whether because of external factors such as economic changes or because of the aging and changing roles of family members. Families progress through stages of development as well as encounter unexpected changes. All change is a source of stress. Change also alters the roles of family members. Communication helps negotiate change effectively. Divorce is a common and multi-staged source of ongoing role and relationship changes among family members.

Certain role relationships predominate in family structures. Husband-wife relationships involve many shared concerns, including the central concern of maintaining a balance between independence and interdependence. There are both shared and personal identities in most husband-wife relationships, but the balance between these shared and personal aspects can vary considerably. Sometimes the life cycles of families are characterized on the basis of the evolving relationships between husbands and wives, those stages being courtship and early marriage, raising young children, raising adolescents, launching young adults, and the post-parenting couple.

Parent-child relationships can be characterized as consisting of messages that communicate either support or control. Research suggests that supportive messages enhance the self-esteem of children and produce children with low levels of aggressiveness, while control messages create dependency and aggressiveness in children.

Sibling relationships significantly affect life in families. Sibling relationships tend to be more egalitarian than parent-child relationships. Siblings allow children to develop negotiation and friendship-building skills, as well as more aggressive strategies. Siblings can serve as role models and teachers and provide a mutual support system, but sibling relationships can also be characterized as competitive and rivalrous.

The success of a family is generally measured on the basis of the individual perceptions of relational satisfaction of the members. In general, satisfying marital relationships are characterized by effective communication with high levels of self-disclosure and supportive messages as well as responses to conflict that keep the conflicts from escalating and do not include personal attacks. Dissatisfied couples tend to focus their perceptions on and remember negative experiences more than satisfied couples.

In general, family relationships are more satisfying if families are spontaneous and adaptable, yet with a clear sense of boundaries and power structure. Some communication qualities of successful families include: close relationships, good listening and response skills, valuing of individual thoughts and feelings, and reconciliation. The ongoing complexity and evolution of family life makes clear prescriptions for success difficult, but some of the behaviors described in this chapter at least offer guidelines for family communication.

CHAPTER OUTLINE

TEACHING OBJECTIVES

9-1. Introduce the concept of family as broader, more fluid, and more inclusive than traditional conceptions and myths.

9-2. Explore the various definitions of family and seek commonalities between them.

9-3. Describe the basic functions of family life.

9-4. Emphasize the importance of decision-making patterns, power distribution, and relationship evolution to the structure of family life.

9-5. Characterize the boundaries and structure of husband-wife, parent-child, and sibling relationships within the family.

9-6. Explore the qualities that typify marital and familial satisfaction in relationships.

DISCUSSION QUESTIONS

9-1. What are the characteristics of the most atypical family you know?

9-2. Where would you draw the line concerning family boundaries—a homosexual couple with an adopted child? a homosexual couple without children? the residents of a group home for mentally handicapped adults? a heterosexual couple cohabitating?

9-3. Which of these approaches seems to be the most accurate? Which seems to be most adaptable to the changing nature of families?

9-4. Are there other functions that you believe are a part of family life? Must there be children to be nurtured and socialized for a family to exist?

9-5. How would you characterize family decision-making in most of the families you have known, including your own? Do these categories include a place for the decision-making patterns you have observed?

9-6. Which power do you think is employed most often by parents in families? Which power is used most often by children with their parents? Which power is used most often by siblings with one another?

9-7. What do you think are the biggest changes that affect the structure and evolution of families?

9-8. Which husband-wife role relationship do you think would provide the best parent-to-child relationships as well?

9-9. Which kinds of parental messages are more common in your experience—support or control messages?

9-10. What qualities or characteristics would you say describe the best relationships in which you are involved?

SKILL MASTERY EXERCISES

9-1. Divide the class into groups of 4-6. Give each group the following three-part task:

    (1) Create a list that describes the dominant communication and relational qualities of *real* American families.

    (2) Now create a list of communication and/or relational qualities that would describe the *ideal* American family, that is, the family that would most successfully nurture and care for its members.

    (3) Now discuss and develop some suggestions for how real American families could be taught to communicate with and nurture one another more successfully.

9-2. In smaller groups or as a whole class, engage students in a discussion of television portraits of American family life. Encourage them to critically consider the following questions:

    (1) Which show presents the most positive view of an American family?

    (2) Which show presents the most negative view of an American family?

    (3) Which show presents the most realistic view of an American family?

    (4) Considering all the current "family" shows together as a portrait of American society, how would you assess the health or condition of the American family?

9-3. Consider introducing students to *Walden Two,* psychologist B. F. Skinner's futuristic portrait of ideal human communities in which the nurturing *and* socialization of children is taken out of the hands of individual parents and placed in community child care centers where children spend their days and nights with occasional visits from their biological parents. Lead students, then, in a discussion of whether some social agency or local community might better provide a consistent pattern of care and nurturing of children. (Be prepared for a high-intensity discussion!)

KEY TERMS

family (p. 244)
extended family (p. 244)

nuclear family (p. 244)
consensus decision making (p. 248)
accommodation decision making (p. 248)
de facto decision making (p. 249)
power (p. 250)
punishment (p. 250)
reward power (p. 250)
expertise (p. 250)
legitimacy (p. 250)
identification (p. 250)
persuasion (p. 251)
independent marital types (p. 256)
separate marital types (p. 256)
traditional marital types (p. 256)
support (p. 259)
control (p. 259)

CHAPTER 10

INTERVIEWING

CHAPTER SYNOPSIS

Interviewing is a process of communication with a predetermined purpose involving two parties in the asking and answering of questions. The interviewer is the person or persons conducting the interview and asking most of the questions. The interviewee is the person responding to the questions. The specific purpose which brings the parties together can vary.

Interviews may be directive (strongly controlled by the interviewer) or nondirective (minimally controlled by the interviewer). In directive interviews, the interviewer's role involves maintaining control; in the nondirective interview, the interviewer introduces broad topics for discussion and encourages the interviewee to answer them. In either case, the interviewer should do less talking then the interviewee.

Interviews may have various purposes. They may be job-related, including employment, promotion, or exit interviews, as well as performance appraisal and grievance interviews. Interviews may have an information-gathering purpose, as in the case of journalistic

interviews, surveys, research interviews, and opinion polls. There are also helping interviews, such as counseling and social work interviews.

Questions are the primary tool of the interviewer. Primary questions introduce a new topic area. Secondary questions follow up answers to primary questions by seeking further details. An effective interviewer prepares a set of primary questions for the interview as well as a repertoire of possible secondary questions. Two noteworthy types of secondary questions are probe and mirror questions. Probes are brief words or phrases such as "I see" or "uh huh" which encourage the interviewee to go on. Mirror questions restate an interviewee's previous response in the form of a question to check the correctness of interpretation and/or encourage elaboration.

Questions vary in the degree to which they limit the response options of the interviewee. Closed questions limit response options, whereas open questions allow the respondent free rein to answer in any way she or he chooses. Bipolar questions are a special type of closed question asking the respondent to choose from two answer options. Open questions allow creativity, elaboration, and detail. Closed questions are faster, more directive, and get at specific information the interviewer desires.

Leading questions hint at the answer desired and thereby limit the interviewee's ability to answer honestly. Neutral questions give no indication of the answer desired. Loaded questions are strongly leading questions characterized by unproven presumptions, inflammatory language, and/or a forced choice between opposite extremes.

Prior to conducting an interview, the interviewer needs to set goals by considering the appropriateness of the interview to the purpose and by determining what desired information the prospective interviewee may possess. Then the interviewer should develop a list of primary questions designed to obtain the needed information.

During the interview, the interviewer should explain the purpose of the interview, provide transitions between questions, and provide closure by paraphrasing or summarizing findings. It is the interviewer's responsibility to maintain control of the interview process. The key to avoiding undue digressions and gaining the necessary information is careful listening. Leading questions should be employed with caution.

To be an effective interviewee in an employment interview, preparation is vital. A job candidate should do research about the company prior to the interview, both to demonstrate interest and to ask intelligent questions. The interviewee should also have examined his or her own needs and skills to determine her/his long- and short-term goals and to prepare suitable answers to likely questions. Finally, the interviewee should understand the interview process itself.

During the interview, the interviewee needs to be aware of impressions given, especially early in the interview, answer questions appropriately, and effectively handle unexpected questions. It is important for the interviewee to emphasize his or her own positive qualities and to avoid negative comments about others. The interviewee must attempt to know the purpose of the interviewer's questions in order to answer them effectively. When an interviewee is uncertain about the meaning of a question, she or he can either ask that it be rephrased or offer his/her interpretation of the meaning of the question as she or he answers it.

CHAPTER OUTLINE

The Nature of the Interview Process
    Defining the Interview
    Roles of the Interviewer and Interviewee
        • Directive
        • Nondirective
    Types of Interviews
        • Job-Related Interviews
        • Information-Gathering Interviews
        • Helping Interviews
    Questions in the Interview
        • Primary versus Secondary Questions
        • Open versus Closed Questions
        • Neutral versus Leading Questions
Conducting an Information-Gathering Interview
    Steps Prior to the Interview
        • Developing Goals
        • Developing Primary Questions
    During the Interview
        • Providing Organization
        • Maintaining Control
Participating in an Employment Interview
    Preparation
    Performance
Summary
Exercises
References

TEACHING OBJECTIVES

10-1. Define the unique nature of interviews as involving two parties, with a pretermined and serious purpose and involving the asking and answering of questions.

10-2. Describe the roles and purposes of the interviewer and interviewee.

10-3. Explain the varieties and diverse purposes of interviews.

10-4. Illustrate the differences between primary versus secondary, open versus closed, and leading versus neutral questions.

10-5. Emphasize the importance of interviewer preparation to the successful conduct of an interview.

10-6. Describe the value of organization and control to the interviewer's effective completion of an interview.

10-7. Stress the importance of interviewee preparation and careful impression management to the successful completion of an employment interview.

DISCUSSION QUESTIONS

10-1. What kinds of interviews have you been involved in thus far? What was hard about them? What was surprising or unexpected?

10-2. Who do you think is the best of the TV news or talk show interviewers? Why? How does he or she relate to the interviewees? What kinds of questions does she or he ask?

10-3. Which of the various job-related interviews are or have been used at your places of work? How effective are they? What do interviewers and interviewees stand to gain from each of these forms of interview?

10-4. What would you say are the major differences between job-related, information-gathering, and helping interviews? Would different interviewer skills be required? Would there be differences in interviewer-interviewee relationships? Which type of interviewing do you think would be the most difficult? Why?

10-5. As an interviewee, would you have different emotional responses to open versus closed questions? Would you be likely to have different responses to the interview and interviewer if questions were more often open or more often closed? How would you tend to feel about leading or loaded questions?

10-6. Who is the one person you would most like to interview? Why? What would you want to ask? What would you want to know?

10-7. How would you rank-order the factors involved in determining who gets chosen for a job? For example, is appearance more important than accomplishments? Is a personal connection (who you know) more important than the knowledge you possess?

SKILL MASTERY EXERCISES

10-1. Provide your class with a list of five or six names of famous people, choosing them from a range of careers including, perhaps, a legislator, a musician, a movie star, a sports figure, etc., people you believe would be of interest to your students. Have your students then form into small groups on the basis of their interest in the named person. (Note: This is a multistage assignment. Feel free to have your students do as much or as little of the assignment as your own scheduling and emphasis on interviewing allows.)

1. Assign each group the task of interviewing the person selected. Have them begin by discussing in their groups how and where they would conduct research about this person prior to the actual interview and what they would want or need to know about the interviewee before planning the interview itself. Depending on how much time you want to devote to this assignment, you can have the groups actually conduct this research and possibly even seek an interview.

2. Have each group then develop a list of primary questions for the interviewee and organize them in a way that seems appropriate to the purpose of the interview and the needs of the interview process. Have them also include secondary questions where these seem likely to be needed or appropriate.

3. Have the groups then exchange their lists of questions and analyze each other's lists, evaluating and labeling the questions on the open/closed and leading/neutral continua.

4. If you use "locally famous" people, you can expand this exercise to include actually seeking and conducting interviews and comparing the effectiveness of the interviews on the basis of the information obtained, cooperativeness of the interviewee, etc.

10-2. Select a videotape of an interview, either from actual interviews conducted on television or in another classroom or from a film source. Possibilities include the 1988 Bush-Rather interview, the admission interview of the Jack Nicholson character in the film *One Flew over the Cuckoo's Nest*, the initial counseling interview portrayed by Judd Hirsch and Timothy Hutton in the film *Ordinary People*, the exit interview and subsequent job interview portrayed by Dustin Hoffman in the film *Kramer Versus Kramer*, etc.

Show the interview clip in class and ask for discussion of the success or failure of the interview from the point of view of both interviewer and interviewee. The Bush-Rather interview is particularly effective in this regard because of the conflicting purposes of the two participants.

Depending on the interview selected, you may also want to ask the class, individually or in small groups, to evaluate the questions used by the interviewer and to "rewrite" the interview to include questions, responses, or clarifications which might have added to its effectiveness. For these discussions, a transcript of the interview would be useful.

10-3. After discussion of impression management in job interviews, assign your students the task of "dressing for success" at your next class meeting. Have the students identify in advance the jobs for which they will be hypothetically interviewing, and then tell them to present themselves at the next class as though they were arriving for a real interview for that position.

At the "dress class," provide index cards to students and have them observe and record observations about each jobseeker, evaluating the effectiveness of appearance of the candidate for the job sought and rendering a "hire" or "don't hire" decision on the basis of appearance alone.

KEY TERMS AND CONCEPTS

interview (p. 270)
directive interview (p. 271)
nondirective interview (p. 271)
employment (job-entry) interview (p. 273)
promotion interview (p. 273)
exit interview (p. 273)
performance appraisal interview (p. 273)
grievance interview (p. 273)
information-gathering interviews (p. 273)
primary question (p. 275)
secondary question (p. 275)
probe question (p. 278)
mirror question (p. 278)
closed question (p. 278)
open question (p. 278)
bipolar question (p. 278)
leading question (p. 279)
neutral question (p. 279)
loaded question (p. 279)

CHAPTER **11**

GROUP PROBLEM SOLVING AND DECISION MAKING

CHAPTER SYNOPSIS

Problem-solving and decision-making groups are a part of everyday life in American culture, forming the basis of conference gatherings and the committee life of organizations as well as assuming increasing importance in the workplace. Leaders in particular spend much of their time working in groups, but all of us are likely to have numerous group involvements in our lives. As a result, understanding what groups are, how they work, and how we can contribute to them effectively is vitally important.

Groups can be defined as a collection of two or more people, usually five–seven members, who share information and exchange ideas to achieve a common goal. Groups are characterized by their possession of goals, norms, positions, roles, and structure. A goal is the end a group hopes to achieve by its performance of a task or tasks. A task is the set of activities performed to achieve a goal, or the means to the end. Goals vary in their clarity and attainability, among other things, and the nature of the goal impacts on group interaction and performance.

Norms are the standards of behavior or rules, usually unspoken, which govern the interaction, performance, and relationships of group members; norms are often unnoticed and unverbalized until violated. The violation of important norms could result in expulsion of a member from a group. Norms govern conduct.

Positions are the designated assignments or titles of group members. Positions may be formal and specialized, such as chair, secretary, etc., or they may be informal and undifferentiated, such as member or facilitator. Roles are the behaviors or expectations associated with given positions. Roles may be designated (specified) or emergent (developing out of group and/or position needs), but in either case, roles evolve and change over time. Roles within a group may be either loosely or narrowly defined.

Conflict can develop within groups in relation to roles. One source of conflict has to do with a group member enacting a role differently than other group members believe it should be enacted. A second source of conflict has to do with one member crossing role boundaries to perform actions which are perceived to be in another member's proper domain. Role conflicts can hamper group effectiveness as well as intergroup relationships.

The pattern of relationships among the positions and roles within a group is known as its structure. Some groups, known as centralized, are highly structured; others are more loosely defined, with authority and power shared among the members, and are known as decentralized. Status refers to the relative importance of group members to one another; in centralized groups, status is differentiated, whereas in decentralized groups, members have relatively equal status. A group's structure and status affects who speaks to whom in what manner as well as who exercises the greatest influence.

Groups have great value in the areas of problem solving and decision making. *Problem solving* refers to a set of activities performed to reduce or eliminate a felt difficulty. *Decision making* refers to the act of choosing among alternatives. While different tasks, problem solving and decision making are frequently utilized in tandem by groups.

Groups are useful to problem solving and decision making for several reasons. First, they represent the essence of the democratic tradition in this culture, where sharing of responsibility and decision making is valued. Second, groups encourage the involvement of persons with different areas of expertise, all contributing jointly to solutions and decision; this combined expertise is a strength. Third, group involvement in problem solving and decision making means that more collective knowledge is brought to bear on the problem at hand and the likelihood of decisions based on misinformation is reduced. Fourth, there is evidence that involvement in group problem solving and decision making results in higher morale, productivity, and satisfaction among the members. And, fifth, we as individuals tend to place more confidence in group decisions and the actions that result.

There are two general approaches to problem solving. Conventional problem solving utilizes a set of steps for group members to follow in order to arrive at a solution: first, identify the problem; second, establish the criteria for evaluating solutions; third, generate possible solutions; fourth, evaluate each solution, using the established criteria; and, fifth, select the solution that best satisfies the criteria. Criteria are the factors to be considered in making judgments.

Creative problem solving is useful when the problem is clear and the focus is on solutions. Creative problem solving involves the use of brainstorming, a process of generating as many ideas as possible as quickly as possible without stopping to evaluate them. Brainstorming is based upon the premise that the best solution is more likely to be voiced in circumstances which encourage all ideas and avoid evaluation until after the ideas are generated.

Brainstorming is not in itself a problem-solving process; the use of analytical and evaluative skills would need to be employed once the creative work was done in order to decide on the best solution. A variation on brainstorming is known as the Nominal Group Technique and involves the generation of ideas and solutions in writing by individual members, whose ideas are then later compiled and shared for group use. Advocates of the Nominal Group Technique claims it better guards against evaluative comments, assures authorship of ideas, and eliminates the reluctance of lower-status members to contribute while in the presence of high-status members.

Decision making is required in situations where the need faced by a group has to do with questions of fact, conjecture, value, or policy. A question of fact pertains to the need to decide what is true in a given situation and usually takes one of two forms: 1) deciding whether a particular condition exists, or 2) identifying the causes or underlying reasons for a condition. A question of conjecture involves deciding what is likely to happen under certain conditions, such as the likely impact of a price hike or plant closing. A question of value pertains to decisions about what is acceptable, desirable, justifiable, or right; usually questions of value concern making judgments about actions after the fact. Questions of policy are those concerning what should be done in a certain case, determining a course of action.

In order for a group to effectively make a decision, it must first define any ambiguous or problematic aspects of the question at hand. Next, the group must recognize what type of information is necessary in order to make the best decision. Third, the group needs to assess what the available information suggests about the answer to the question. Fourth, the group should consider whether there are grounds for doubt concerning the apparent answer. And fifth, of course, the group should make a choice, even if the choice is that a decision can't be arrived at.

Group decision making and group problem solving are closely related and often work hand in hand toward the attainment of a group goal.

There are five steps group members can take to prepare for profitable discussion of problems or needed decisions: (1) become informed; (2) determine the need for an agenda (a formalized list of topics to be covered in the order desired); (3) consider the likely behavior and impact of other group members; (4) prepare an advantageous physical setting; and, (5) withhold judgment and seek to enter the process with an open mind.

CHAPTER OUTLINE

The Nature of Groups
    What Groups Are
    Group Characteristics
        • Goals
        • Norms
        • Positions
        • Roles
        • Conflict
        • Structure
        • Status
The Value of Group Problem Solving and
    Decision Making
    Problem Solving versus Decision Making
    Reasons for Group Problem Solving and
        Decision Making
        • Democratic Tradition
        • Multiple Expertise
        • More Information
        • Better Productivity and Satisfaction
        • Better Acceptance of Decisions
Problem-Solving and Decision-Making Discussions
    Group Problem Solving

        • Conventional Problem Solving
        • Creative Problem Solving
Decision Making
        • Types of Questions
             Fact
             Conjecture
             Value
             Policy
        • Requirements of Group Decision Making
             Define Terms
             Recognize Information Needed
             Determine What Information Suggests
             Consider Doubts About Apparent Answer
             Make Choice
The Relationship of Decision Making to Problem Solving
Preparing for Problem Solving and Decision Making
    Discussions
        Inform Yourself
        Determine Need for Agenda
        Consider Group Characteristics
        Prepare Physical Setting
        Withhold Judgment
Summary
Exercises
Suggested Readings

TEACHING OBJECTIVES

11-1. Emphasize the presence and importance of groups in every aspect of modern life, beginning with the family and moving into the workplace and beyond.

11-2. Define groups and describe their primary characteristics; depict the nature and likelihood of conflict.

11-3. Describe the difference between problem solving and decision making, but acknowledge that they are often both utilized in group processes.

11-4. Accentuate the benefits of group approaches to problem solving and decision making.

11-5. Explain conventional and creative approaches to problem solving and that both are often utilized by one group at various stages of the problem-solving process.

11-6. Discuss the questions of fact, value, policy, and conjecture; distinguish these types of questions from one another.

11-7. Distinguish among the stages or requirements of group decision making.

11-8. Emphasize the need for preparation in order to

make effective use of group process, and explore the various facets of preparation and their benefits.

DISCUSSION QUESTIONS

11-1. Are group and interpersonal contexts one and the same? (See Chapter 7)

11-2. What are the norms that govern classroom behaviors? How do the norms of this class differ from those of other classes in which you've been a student (or teacher)?

11-3. How many groups are you a member of at this moment in time? Are these groups formal of informal? What is your position and/or roles in each? In how many of these groups do you play multiple roles?

11-4. Are there other sources of conflict in groups than conflicts over roles?

11-5. In a sense, family life is our first and central experience of group membership; it was where we first learned how to be group members and what to expect from group involvement. How would you describe the status and authority structure of that first group experience of yours? What did you learn from that experience about being a group member?

11-6. What particular skills, talents and abilities do you bring to the groups of which you are a member?

11-7. How do you make decisions when faced with them? Have you ever used a systematic approach? Have you ever made a snap decision? Have you ever thought about how you make decisions?

11-8. Take a close look at the room you're in. How well or poorly suited is it for a group process? What is needed? How should the space, seating and other aspects be arranged? Design a "group communication room."

SKILL MASTERY EXERCISES

11-1. In a roundtable discussion, whole class or smaller groups, seek consensus on ten (or fifteen or twenty) norms which govern life in American culture. Emphasize that all must agree that the norm is a felt part of their existence, which does not, of course, mean that the norm isn't sometimes (or often) violated.

Example: "While riding in elevators, face the door and remain silent unless riding with someone you know." An interesting secondary discussion, then, if you're so inclined, is to ask for discussion about what this agreed-upon set of norms says about who we are as a people.

11-2. In small groups, ask your students to decide what role choices are available to students on your campus. Ask them to describe and define those roles in as much detail as possible, including some sense of the privileges and responsibilities that go with the role. Perhaps, then, they could also rank-order the roles from high to low status. Finally, discuss how one wins or is given these roles and how many of the roles they feel are available to them.

11-3. This is a lengthy exercise. Begin by dividing the class into two (or four) groups. Ask both groups to generate a list of ten specific social problems that exist on your campus; have one group use the brainstorming method and the other use the Nominal Group Technique. Compare lists and ask for discussion and evaluation of the process when the task is completed.

Next ask the same groups to decide which of the problems they generated is the most pressing, or most in need of solution, using the requirements of group decision making discussed in the text. When a decision on one problem has been reached, ask for discussion on how the choices were made.

Finally, ask the groups to find a solution to the problem, with one group using conventional problem solving and the other using creative problem solving. With the whole class, discuss first the solutions decided and then the process used to arrive at the solutions.

These three portions of the exercise would likely consume three class periods. They could, if you chose, serve as the basis for a semester-long group project, if you went on to assign the real enactment of their proposed solutions by semester's end and tied the assignment into your continuing study of leadership and group process. (There are professionals in the field who use a similar process to combine a group process and peace studies approach.)

KEY TERMS AND CONCEPTS

group (p. 294)
goal (p. 295)
task (p. 295)
norm (p. 295)
position (p. 295)
role (p. 296)
role conflict (p. 297)
structure (p. 297)
status (p. 297)
problem solving (p. 299)

decision making (p. 299)
quality circle (p. 301)
conventional problem solving (p. 302)
creative problem solving (p. 302)
criterion (p. 302)
brainstorming (p. 304)
Nominal Group Technique (p. 306)
question of fact (p. 307)
question of conjecture (p. 307)
question of value (p. 307)
question of policy (p. 308)

CHAPTER 12

LEADERSHIP IN PROBLEM-SOLVING AND DECISION-MAKING GROUPS

CHAPTER SYNOPSIS

Leadership refers to any action that exerts positive influence toward the accomplishment of a problem-solving or decision-making task. A leader is any group member who performs such acts. The exertion of leadership does not require extraordinary skills.

There are four standard perspectives on leadership. The first, generally unsubstantiated by research, is that leaders possess certain inherent traits which are the source or cause of their leadership ability. A trait is an identifiable characteristic. Some evidence exists that leaders may acquire or develop certain traits or exercise the use of certain traits to a greater degree than other members.

The second perspective, known as stylistic, describes basic approaches to leadership. A style is a characteristic way of behaving. Leadership style describes a characteristic way of leading. In general, leadership style can be categorized as either group-centered or leader-centered. Group-centered style invites participation, guides discussion, asks for reactions, accepts majority decisions, and seeks consensus. Leader-centered style is associated with control, direc-

tion, unilateral decisions, and assumption of responsibility for determining solutions. The important issue with regard to leadership style is the appropriateness of the style for the particular circumstances and the unique characteristics of the group.

The third, or situational, perspective emphasizes that different leadership qualities are needed to fit specific conditions and are particularly influenced by the nature of the task, the power of the designated leader, and the relationships of the members. Also known as contingency theory, this approach calls for leaders capable of adapting to immediate circumstances.

The fourth perspective on the nature of leadership is known as the functional perspective. This approach argues that there are certain acts or tasks which must be performed in order for a group to be effective and that leadership resides in and with those who perform the essential acts or functions. Leaders, in other words, are those who facilitate progress toward accomplishment of the group goal.

Leaders may be either designated or emergent. Designated leaders are those who have been officially appointed or chosen for the leadership role. Emergent leaders are those who, while not in official leadership positions, nonetheless are instrumental in moving the group forward toward the accomplishment of a goal. Emergent leaders frequently become designated leaders at some future point.

Group members who do not actively participate because of a perceived sense of their own unimportance limit, as a result, their opportunities for future leadership roles, thus engaging in a type of self-fulfilling prophecy which limits future possibilities because of restricted present beliefs or predictions. On the other hand, group members who engage in leadership actions despite their lack of designated or recognized status or power can frequently become unsung heroines or heroes because of their positive influence.

Whatever one's official status, the performance of the leadership role is vital to success. The role of leadership involves (1) assuring that he necessary steps are taken so that the group's goal is attained and (2) creating and maintaining a climate in which attainment of the goal is possible. Climate refers to the psychological atmosphere of the group. While many types of interferences–physical, practical, and psychological–can detract from or weaken the climate of a group, there is much the leader can do both before and during group meetings to create a favorable climate.

The responsibilities of leadership begin before a group ever meets and extend beyond the accomplishment of the group's task. A leader's prediscussion responsibilities include such items as calling the meeting, arranging suitable space, providing necessary background information, etc. Prediscussion responsibilities do much to create the proper climate for the successful completion of the task. In-process leadership responsibilities include initiating the meeting effectively, regulating interaction, handling the interpersonal needs of the members, clarifying issues, seeking consensus, etc. Postdiscussion responsibilities will vary according to the task and decision, but generally include the need to represent the group and its decision to appropriate people and to see to it that necessary follow-up actions are taken. Persons considering taking on leadership positions should be aware that their responsibilities frequently extend far beyond influence exerted at the meetings themselves.

There are certain personal qualities or approaches to group action which contribute to the effective completion of the designated task. These include commitment to group goals, personal responsibility, understanding of task needs, interpersonal sensitivity, ability to manage conflicts, verbal ability, listening skill, openness, adaptability, and fairness.

CHAPTER OUTLINE

The Nature of Leadership
    Definition of Leadership
    Perspectives on Leadership
        • Trait Perspective
        • Stylistic Perspective
        • Situational Perspective
        • Functional Perspective
    Designated Versus Emergent Leadership
The Role of Leadership in Problem-Solving and
    Decision-Making Groups
        Ensuring Task Requirements Are Satisfied
        Creating Climate Which Encourages or
            Allows Success
Responsibilities of Leadership
    Prediscussion Responsibilities May Include:
        • Set Meeting Time
        • Find Suitable Location
        • Notify Members
        • Identify Question
        • Prepare Agenda
        • Provide Relevant Information
        • Indicate Preparation Needes
        • Other Tasks as Needed
    In-Process Responsibilities May Include:
        • Introduce Members—Call Meeting to Order
        • Review Task or Question
        • Ensure Understanding
        • Indicate Problem Areas
        • Review Agenda
        • Secure Procedural Agreement
        • Introduce Relevant Information
        • Initiate Interaction
        • Regulate Interaction
        • Respond to Interpersonal Needs
        • Raise Appropriate Questions
        • Clarify Issues
        • Assure Progress Toward Goal
        • Identify Solutions Obtained
    Postdiscussion Responsibilities May Include:
        • Review Outcome
        • Determine Others' Perceptions/Conclusions
        • Inform Responsible Parties
        • Report Accomplishment
        • Represent Group to Others
        • Set Next Meeting Time

I
N
S
T
R
U
C
T
O
R
'
S

S
E
C
T
I
O
N

• Prepare and Distribute Minutes
• Implement Solutions
Qualities That Promote Effective Leadership
    Commitment to Group Goals
    Sense of Responsibility
    Understanding of Task Requirements
    Interpersonal Sensitivity
    Ability to Manage Conflicts
    Verbal Ability
    Skill in Listening
    Openness to Diverse Views and Opinions
    Adaptability
    Fairness
Summary
Exercises
Related Readings

TEACHING OBJECTIVES

12-1. Define leadership as actions influential toward the accomplishment of goals and leaders as those who exert such actions. Seek real leaders, familiar to the audience, to use as examples.

12-2. Examine the four perspectives on leadership and seek to emphasize areas of commonality, compatibility, and overlap among them, aiming toward a unifying outlook.

12-3. Explore the notions of role and climate as they apply to group interaction. Seek parallels to individual social roles and the notions of situational and relational context.

12-4. Emphasize the notion of leadership as extending beyond the specific boundaries of actual group meetings to the preparatory and follow-up work which is inevitable and essential to the successful completion of group tasks.

12-5. Describe and examine the qualities that promote effective leadership and how these qualities match or fit with the trait, stylistic, situations, and functional approaches to leadership.

12-6. Suggest that effective group leadership (exerting positive influence toward the accomplishment of group goals) is the shared responsibility of all group members.

DISCUSSION QUESTIONS

12-1. Name some leadership acts which you have witnessed or performed in any setting. Is it possible to group these examples of leadership in any way? Do they have any recognizable distinguishing characteristics?

12-2. What traits do you think of when you think of leaders and leadership? How are they similar to or different from the traits you find in the people you most admire?

12-3. Imagine and describe a variety of situations in which some kind of leadership would be needed. For each of these situations, would a group-centered or leader-centered style of leadership be more appropriate? Why?

12-4. Which is more important: (1) what a leader needs to do or what a leader needs to be; (2) skill at handling tasks or skill at handling people; (3) the kind of person you are or the power you have been given?

12-5. Where in your own life do you find evidence or examples of the impact of a self-fulfilling prophecy on what you did or did not accomplish?

12-6. How would you go about creating a positive psychological climate for a meeting or gathering?

12-7. What is the difference between situational influences, context, and climate? What is the same about them? How much is overlap?

12-8. In groups you have been a part of in the past, which of these qualities did you find sufficiently represented most of the time? Which were least often present or represented? Which of these qualities do you think our culture has most successfully taught? And which have been least successfully transmitted?

SKILL MASTERY EXERCISES

12-1. Divide the class into three groups. To one group, hand an index card announcing or appointing a designated leader, choosing a student who seems to you to demonstrate some leadership ability. In the second group, provide the members with an index card which instructs them to begin by electing a group leader. To the third group, hand an index card which provides no leadership appointments or instructions. On all three cards, provide this assignment:

"Decide and make a recommendation as to the best way for this instructor to determine the mastery of communication by the students in this class. One recommendation per group. The instructor promises to give fair consideration to recommendations received."

Allow twenty–thirty minutes for the exercise; use remaining class time to ask for group members' feedback on their experiences of leadership, seeking input on their satisfaction with group process and assessment of the group's leadership. Seek meaningful responses concerning differences in the experiences of the three groups. Share your own observations about how the three groups seemed to approach and process their assignment and whatever perceptions you had of group interactions.

12-2. This is a risky exercise, but could prove of great interest and value. After an appropriate introduction of the concept of climate, divide the class into three or four groups and give them the assignment of being responsible for creating the appropriate climate for learning within your classroom on days of your choice (each group, in other words, gets a day to itself). Let them know the topic for the assigned day and provide a preview of the kinds of information that will be presented or covered. Emphasize that the climate they create should enhance the likelihood that the given subject matter will be absorbed and retained. Draw whatever limits or guidelines around the assignment which you deem necessary. Some you might consider are:

The classroom cannot be changed or damaged in any permanent fashion, i.e., no paint, no objects or artwork affixed to any wall or furniture which cannot be removed without damaging the surface when the class is over.

No weapons, no flames, nothing that violates university regulations, no "cheap tricks" or special effects which would interfere with rather than enhance the learning experience.

Possible changes include rearrangement of existing furniture, the temporary removal of existing furniture and its replacement with items available through the school's physical plant or which students themselves might provide, the introduction of auxiliary lighting or art objects, music or background sounds, and suggestions as to how the day's subject matter might be presented.

It would be wise to have the topic of the last assigned day be the creation of climate. Seek summary evaluation on the part of the students as to the effect of the various climates on their reception and absorption of the various days' presentations.

This discussion could also serve to reemphasize the overall importance of nonverbal communication to human interaction.

12-3. Invite a colleague or acquaintance form the community to come speak to your class on the subject of leadership from the perspective of her or his own leadership experiences. Emphasize that you're seeking personal leadership stories to augment your students' academic understanding of the subject and that the presentation should be ten minutes in length. At the same time, let her know that her presence will fulfill a dual role because you will also be using her appearance in the class as a way of exploring the power of self-fulfilling prophecies. Share the details of the following informal experiment and ask for her participation.

On the given class day, tell the class you will be hearing a guest speaker today who will be sharing some of her or his personal leadership experiences and stories. Say that you have prepared a handout which will provide background information on the speaker and that you will ask for their responses to the speaker and experiences related. Emphasize that the speaker will not see the written feedback and that it will be used for discussion purposes only once the speaker is gone. Make this announcement and distribute the handouts, giving the students a few minutes to read them before the guest speaker enters the classroom and begins. When the speaker enters, introduce him by name only; provide no additional information.

"Randomly" distribute handouts which are the same in regard to the questions asked and which visually appear to be identical but which differ slightly in the background information provided at the top of the page. Have these read as follows:

Form 1: _____ _____ is an acknowledged leader in the academic community [substitute accurate information about your particular speaker]. He [she] has had some successful leadership experiences over the years in the areas of [supply appropriate information]. I know you will find his [her] experiences of interest and value.

Form 2: _____ _____ is a reputed leader in the academic community [substitute accurate information about your particular speaker]. He [she] has had some successful leadership experiences over the years in the areas of [supply appropriate information]. I hope you will find his [her] experiences of interest and value.

Form 3: _____ _____ is supposedly a leader in the academic community [substitute accurate information about your particular speaker]. He [she] claims successful leadership experiences over the years in the areas of [supply appropriate information]. I hope you will find his [her] experiences of some limited value.

Below the background information on all handouts provide these questions, leaving space for them to be briefly answered. Make sure the spacing on all three sets of handouts is the same.

1. In your opinion, which was the best example of leadership provided by this speaker?
2. In your opinion, which was the most questionable example of leadership provided by this speaker?
3. What qualities associated with leadership did you observe in this speaker?
4. On a scale of one to ten, with ten being the best, how would you rate this speaker as a leader on the basis of what you have seen and heard here today?

When the speech is finished, thank your speaker and walk him or her to the door. Ask your students to take a few minutes to complete their evaluation forms without talking before you begin to discuss the presentation.

When the speaker is gone and the forms have been completed, collect and sort them. Have the class, divided into three groups, summarize the findings with each group responsible for one set of forms. When the findings are summarized, compare them for differences. Ask for responses to the background information provided; hopefully, your findings will give credence to the power of the self-fulfilling prophecy. If they do not, seek to explain the lack of impact of the background information on the basis of the overriding strengths of the speaker's stories or whatever other variables seem important and relevant.

KEY TERMS AND CONCEPTS

leadership (p. 318)
leader (p. 319)
trait (p. 320)
acquired traits (p. 320)
leadership style (p. 320)
group-centered style (p. 320)
leader-centered style (p. 320)
contingency theory (p. 323)
function (p. 323)
designated leader (p. 325)
emergent leader (p. 325)
unsung hero (p. 326)
climate (p. 327)
interpersonal sensitivity (p. 332)

CHAPTER **13**

ANALYZING AUDIENCES TO CHOOSE SUBJECT, PURPOSE, AND THEME

CHAPTER SYNOPSIS

All types of communication involve analytical skills, the ability to listen to and learn from those encountered. This is particularly true in public speaking situations, where effective and ultimately successful speakers pay careful attention to the beliefs, motives, and attitudes of those they will be addressing. Audience analysis involves seeking information in a number of specific areas in order to develop a basic understanding of the audience one is about to meet.

The best speeches always involve an adjustment of the speaker's ideas and values to the intended audience. Adjustment of ideas to people is the central need of the successful speaker, who must learn what the audience already knows and believes in order to discover the best avenue to create receptiveness to his own ideas. An annotated sample speech is presented to provide a sense of the kinds of adaptations which effective speakers make when addressing an audience they have successfully analyzed.

Audience analysis involves the investigation of an audience's basic characteristics, including demographic information and other data which provide clues as to values, attitudes, and beliefs. Some information, such as age and gender, can be obtained with fair accuracy by means of direct observation. Other information, however, such as educational level, income, memberships, and attitudes involves the asking of specific questions. Ideally, both methods of information collection are employed for effective audience analysis.

There are several standard factors or variables which are considered important to effective audience analysis; the projected size of an audience is the first of these. The size of an audience influences the formality of the presentation and style of delivery. Generally, an audience of twenty or fewer members is considered a small audience. The larger the audience, the more impersonal a presentation usually becomes; large audiences expect a formal, impersonal style of presentation. Large audiences also necessitate speaking with more general rather than specific information and examples, because the larger the audience, the harder it is to accurately move all of the members with the same kinds of arguments and analysis. The speaker must attempt to identify relevant subgroups in the audience and address specific examples and illustrations to each of them.

Age is another important distinguishing variable of people and audiences. The age factor allows for some important inferences about the experiences and cultures of an audience. The form of speeches must generally be tailored to address the dominant age of the audience, perhaps, for example, presenting a more formal, polished presentation to an older audience and a more casual, informal style of delivery to a younger one. While ages alone do not provide enough information to allow intelligent decision making about speech content and form, audience age does reveal something about the background experiences and different sources of knowledge of the persons who will be addressed.

Gender is another meaningful variable or factor in audience analysis, although, like age, it does not provide sufficient information to make intelligent judgments, especially because our social roles exert as much influence over our values and interests as our sexual identity, and the social roles of men and women are much less distinct and predictable now than they were in earlier decades. Speeches must adapt to current gender roles, including, for example, those of both female executives and male homemakers.

A fourth basic factor in audience analysis involves understanding the educational level of the audience, keeping in mind that education takes place in many settings other than academic institutions. While one's education is not a measure of a person's intelligence, it does give a sense of the areas of knowledge to which a person may have been exposed. In general, well-educated audiences will be receptive to a variety of styles of public speaking presentation because they will have been exposed to many styles previously. Well-educated audiences may also be more receptive to topics or concerns which are more removed from their own everyday lives. Speakers must be careful to avoid both underestimating an audience's intelligence and overestimating its ability to infer meaning from the language and ideas expressed. Speakers need to speak clearly, define their terms and present the needed information to convey their messages.

Income level is a fifth factor generally considered in audience analysis, especially when the topic involves money in some fashion or degree. It is by no means a clear indicator, however, about lifestyles or choices an audience might select.

Occupation is a sixth factor or variable in audience analysis, important (as was earlier stated) because of the influence of social roles on beliefs, motives, and attitudes as well as because of the information it can provide about the experiences and interests of the members. Occupational information may influence speaker choices about level of knowledge and details to include as well as the types of illustrations and evidence which would likely be effective. Speakers must structure their messages in terms that appeal to the orientations of their listeners.

The memberships of audience members are a seventh variable to consider when conducting an audience analysis. Membership can be voluntary (clubs, political parties, etc.) or involuntary (family of origin, country of origin, etc.). One's memberships both reflect and influence one's beliefs. An effective speaker needs to ascertain the loyalties and values of the groups to which her or his audience belongs and include content which acknowledges group norms and expectations, particularly if the audience addressed is a specific group. Adjustment to one's audience does not mean compromising or masking one's own beliefs.

Culture is another variable to be considered in audience analysis. Culture refers to the shared values, customs, and beliefs of a society, nation, or other large social grouping. One's cultural background provides valuable information. Culture provides clues as to religious beliefs and values, relationships and even local interests, such as the importance of basketball to the local culture of Indiana. Culture may even influence how long a speech should be and norms for audience response, such as heckling or applause. Public speakers need to be curious about people and able to adapt their messages to what they learn about who will be listening.

Even the place where a speech will be given and the time of day of the presentation are important factors to consider when preparing a speech. Time of day will affect audience receptivity, depending in particular on the habits of the individual members. Seasons and holidays may call for adaptations or acknowledgment in presentations. Recognition of and attention to the expected time limit of a presentation is also important.

The setting of a presentation is important in order to determine the "mood of the place" as well as whatever constraints the place puts on the style of presentation. The larger setting of a city or locale may also be important in order to incorporate local references into a presentation.

Intermember relationships, or the social dynamics of a group of listeners, are also important for a speaker to know and understand. Sometimes important information about factions or differences within a group can be inferred by seating and conversational patterns of the audience members. A divided audience might require a speaker to address each group individually or to take special precautions to keep peace between them.

All of these variables together are useful as ways of attempting to tap into or ascertain vital information about the belief systems of audience members. Beliefs are opinions, feelings, or viewpoints about what is true, good, and desirable and what is not. All of the variables discussed so far influence the formation of beliefs, but to truly determine the belief system of an audience or individual, underlying values, attitudes, and motives need to be examined.

Attitudes are judgments that a given object is good, bad, or neutral. Values are attitudes of a general nature that individuals consistently maintain. That which is valued is desired. Values indicate what is important to a person or group. An effective speaker must recognize and address the relevant values of an audience.

Most public opinion polls measure attitudes, which teach us what the polled individuals like and dislike. An attitude is a specific judgment, as opposed to a general belief or value; for example, a person who believes human life is a precious gift might have a negative attitude toward the necessity of killing in wartime. Many attitudes remain fixed over a lifetime, while others change or diminish. Attitudes are especially important to audience analysis because they provide specific responses to objects and ideas.

Attitudes and values can be tapped or discovered through self-designed opinion polls or written surveys. Such polls or surveys should be brief and aimed at the specific information needed for a given presentation. If a survey is not possible, talking to members of the group to be addressed can help ascertain the needed information. Seek to ask accurate, specific, unbiased questions of several different types (open and closed, simple yes/no answers or more detailed responses).

Motives are inner drives which influence actions. Motives "move" us toward a goal in a direction consistent with our values. Since all speeches seek to inform or influence, it is useful to know what moves or drives those who will be addressed. The best way to ascertain audience motives is to listen carefully

The choice of an appropriate subject is a strategic decision for a speaker. Sometimes the subject is dictated by the invitation or the occasion. At other times, the speaker is free to choose. A way to begin to define broad subject areas is to survey your own knowledge and interests, and to look at what is around you and/or what is being discussed in the news media.

Targeting subject matter involves seeking the "bull's-eye" of a perfect fit between your own interest and knowledge and those of the audience, based on a survey of your knowledge and interests and your audience analysis. First, a subject should be chosen about which the speaker already has some knowledge, so that the bulk of his or her time does not have to be consumed with background research. The speaker should have previous, if limited, knowledge of the subject matter. Likewise, the audience should have some rudimentary knowledge of the subject matter or the bulk of the speaker's time will be spent in defining terms and providing background information.

Hitting the interest bull's-eye means finding a subject about which both the speaker and the audience have some genuine interest and enthusiasm. Interest and enthusiasm can be seen in careful preparation, the use of personal experiences to enhance discussion of the subject matter, and fluency in speaking about the subject matter. Audience interest will be determined or inferred from careful audience analysis. There must be a good fit between the speaker's interest and a relevant interest on the part of the audience.

The choice of subject matter must then be limited to fit the time available for speaking. Limits on subject matter can be established in several ways. "Time" limits involve selecting a portion of the subject on the basis of time factors, such as confining one's presentation to only newer or older approaches to a subject or models of an object, by looking only at a specific time period in the development of a subject, focusing on a decade or century.

Size can be used as a limiting factor by focusing on only the larger or smaller types or aspects of a topic or problem, looking only at the largest cathedrals or the smallest airplanes, for example. Place can also be used as a limiting factor by focusing only on local problems or situations or, by contrast, looking only at those same problems or situations as they can be seen at a distant locale. Utility is one more way of narrowing subjects, by focusing on the most practical or essential information about the subject.

Speaking to inform involves the speaker's attempt to improve awareness, understanding, or memory about a subject. Speaking to persuade involves a more direct goal of influencing the audience to change in some way, either in what they believe or in how they behave. Persuasion also involves degree of change, seeking only a slight change in awareness or behavior or a more radical alteration of action or belief. Again, knowledge of the audience is the best aid to understanding the degree of change that is likely or possible.

Addressing a special occasion involves speaking for a specific and often ritualistic purpose, such as commemorating a person or event or honoring or introducing a guest. On these occasions, there is no subject or purpose to be dealt with beyond the occasion itself. Most of the time, speakers have multiple purposes; for example, one can hardly persuade someone to believe differently without also informing him or her as to why change is needed. Leaders often have multiple purposes to their presentation.

Once subject and purpose are clear, effective speakers go on to choose a unique and appropriate theme or perspective on their subject, one which aids the audience's ability to focus on and remember the speaker's material. To be effective, a theme, much like an advertiser's slogan, must be distinctive.

Ideally, themes express foresight, skill, and industry. Foresight involves the anticipation of future needs or events, leading the audience to connect your subject with future possibilities. Skill requires tying your subject to a particular area of personal expertise, providing thereby a unique analogy or metaphor for the subject at hand. Industry involves incorporating themes which reveal the extent of your research and preparation.

Themes call for a precise response from the audience, a response which mirrors the purpose of the speech. Themes provide a focal point, a magnet or center for the audience's attention. Expressed early and repeated within the speech, themes create recognition of purpose and remainder of desired response; themes can serve as frameworks or building blocks on which speeches are erected. Ideally, themes become the essence of what the audience remembers, the distinctive perspective of the speaker which continues to resonate in the audience long after the speech is done. In summary, an effective theme offers a unique perspective, a desired response, a clear focus, and a memorable idea.

CHAPTER OUTLINE

Analyzing Audiences
Analyzing a Specific Audience
    Size
    Age
    Gender
    Education
    Income
    Occupation
    Memberships
    Culture
    Time
    Place
    Intermember Relationships
    Belief System
        Values
        Attitudes
        Motives
Choosing An Appropriate Subject
    Targeting Subject Matter
        Knowledge Bull's-Eye
        Interest Bull's-Eye
    Limiting Subject Matter

TEACHING OBJECTIVES

13-1. Foster an appreciation of the important of audience analysis to effective public speaking.

13-2. Emphasize the importance of finding a balance between one's own ideas and adjustments or adaptations to the needs and belief systems of the audience in order to effectively communicate one's ideas.

13-3. Provide meaningful examples of what it means for a speaker to adapt to his or her audience.

13-4. Develop the concept of audience analysis as the need to know what is important to know about those whom we are addressing.

13-5. Examine the idea that there are some things we can try to ascertain about others through direct observation.

13-6. Describe the various standard demographic variables and why they are useful and describe what kinds of information can be learned and what can be inferred from this type of knowledge, emphasizing again why it is important for a speaker to know these things in order to adapt to the realities of the audience.

13-7. Accentuate the value to a speaker of understanding the occasion of a presentation–the size of the audience, the time and place of the gathering, the expectations of the audience as to length of presentation, etc.

13-8. Explore the notion of intermember relationships and its relevance to a speaker's presentation.

13-9. Discuss the concept of belief systems and the elements of values, attitudes, and motives which together comprise such a system, clarifying the differences among these elements.

13-10. Define an appropriate subject as one which represents a good fit between personal knowledge and interest and audience knowledge and interest.

13-11. Emphasize the need to limit subject matter to what can effectively and appropriately be covered in the given time period, offering the time, size, place, and utility factors as possible ways of determining limitations.

13-12. Explain the importance of clarity of purpose and provide the general purpose categories of informing, persuading, celebrating an occasion, and combining multiple purposes.

13-13. Describe the nature and utility of themes as a way of creating a distinctive, focused, purpose-centered, and memorable perspective or framework with which to bolster one's presentation.

DISCUSSION QUESTIONS

13-1. What is the difference between adjustment or adaptation to an audience and "selling out," or telling an audience what it wants to hear? Where and how do we draw the line?

13-2. What are the tools we normally use to "investigate our audience" when we are meeting a person for the first time at a party or other social gathering?

13-3. How can we discover and use information such as the age and gender of our audience without stereotyping?

13-4. Do you consider yourself well educated or less educated? What kinds of presentations and presenters are you most receptive to? What kinds of teachers are able to move you to openness about their subject matter?

13-5. What kinds of inferences do we normally draw about people on the basis of their work? How could we test the accuracy of our inferences?

13-6. In how many groups do you hold voluntary memberships? What do you think those memberships say about you?

13-7. Which of the various factors considered in audience analysis exerts the greatest influence on what an audience believes? Why?

13-8. What are the major values, attitudes, and motives in your belief system? Which have changed over time? Which have remained the same?

13-9. What are the subjects you know something about?

Which of these are of most interest to you? Which of these receive interested responses from others when you mention them?

13-10. What are the most important issues in the news this week—local as well as national and worldwide? Which of these issues or subjects are likely to still be of interest two weeks or a month or more from now? How important is timeliness to the choice of subject matter for a presentation?

13-11. Do you think a speech always needs to tell an audience what it can do for them or have some direct usefulness?

13-12. Which is easier—to inform or to persuade? Some people say all speeches are persuasive; what do you think?

13-13. How many speeches have you heard or do you know of that actually brought about change in an audience or part of an audience?

SKILL MASTERY EXERCISES

13-1. Select several magazine or television advertisements which seem to be targeted at a particular audience. Have your students discuss one or more of the ads in small groups, with the goal of deciding, on the basis of the content of the ads, what assumptions these "speakers" have made about their targeted audiences.

13-2. In small groups, have students generate a list of controversial topics of interest to your local academic or geographic community. Have each group select one of the topics generated and create a one-page survey or opinion poll to determine the attitudes and values of the classroom audience concerning this issue.

In the follow-up class, have the surveys administered to the remaining class members and then discuss together the effectiveness and findings of the various surveys.

13-3. Select an existing example of public speaking (Martin Luther King's "I have a Dream" or John F. Kennedy's inaugural address are useful possibilities) that contains vivid illustrations of adaptations to audience. Provide each student with a printed copy of the address. In small groups or within the class as a whole, ask for discussion and examples of adaptations and adjustments within the speech

13-4. Have your class use the Nominal Group Technique described in Chapter 9 to generate a list of possible speech topics.

On one class day, perhaps at the end of class and without much discussion, ask each student to write on an index card five–ten subjects she/he knows something about and has an interest in. Collect these and prepare a handout for the next class which simply lists all subjects students generated.

At the next class, distribute the handouts and ask your students, in small groups, to survey the list and decide which are the subjects of greatest interest to them. (You can ask for a particular number of choices if you like and you can suggest that subjects included in their "class interest list" should meet with the approval of the majority of their group members.)

In discussion later, combine the finings of these lists and suggest ways your students could use this information as a guide as they begin to develop their own topics and purposes.

13-5. Give all students the same subject of your choice–something local and timely–and, in small groups, have them develop an appropriate purpose and theme for the assigned subject, with the class as the target audience. Afterward, discuss and compare the themes; have the class vote on which is most effective and most likely to be memorable.

KEY TERMS AND CONCEPTS

audience analysis (p. 342)
audience size (p. 343)
age factor (p. 344)
gender (p. 345)
level of education (p. 345)
income (p. 346)
occupation (p. 347)
membership (p. 347)
culture (p. 348)
time (p. 348)
intermember relationships (p. 349)
beliefs (p. 350)
values (p. 351)
attitudes (p. 351)
motives (p. 353)
appropriate subjects (p. 354)
knowledge bull's-eye (p. 356)
interest bull's-eye (p. 356)

CHAPTER **14**

DISCOVERING SPEECH MATERIAL AND SPEECH CONFIDENCE

CHAPTER SYNOPSIS

True leaders have substance; their lives reveal their values. Effective speakers also have substance; theirs comes in part from careful research, the gathering of needed information to flesh out and substantiate their goals. In this chapter methods of discovering speech substance and speaking with confidence are explored.

A speech contains both facts and opinions. A fact is an occurrence whose accuracy can be confirmed. An opinion is a belief or judgment, the validity of which is decided, at least in part, on the basis of the credibility of the speaker. Both facts and opinions contribute to the substance of a speech; both are used by effective public speakers.

Material to substantiate one's arguments or beliefs can be obtained from many sources, including other people. We can learn much from others through conversation, informal talk with no set time limits and no scripted preparation. Conversation, while unplanned and unfocused, can be a rich source of stories or insights useful to a speaker. A speaker's diary, a daily record or account of noteworthy statements by others, is a useful tool for recording and preserving materials obtained through conversation.

Interviews are a more formal method of obtaining valuable information from other people. Interviews are preplanned or scripted, time-limited, and directed toward obtaining specific information for specific purposes. Interviews may be conducted in person or over the telephone.

Certain guidelines for interviewing are proposed. First, obtain clear agreement to the interview from the interviewee, including permission in advance to record the interview in taped or written form, with a clear explanation of the purpose for which the material is being gathered. Set a definite time limit and attempt to accommodate the interviewee with appropriate dress and language for the setting and occasion. Use clear language, free of unnecessary jargon.

Begin by establishing rapport. Identify yourself and clarify your purpose. Describe the type and scope of information needed. Seek to create an interview environment which is free of distractions and intrusions and which offers privacy to the interviewee.

Use prepared questions. These allow for a clear focus on the area of interest, they save time, and they may even be organized in the same general order as the main points of your speech, thus saving organization time later. Read from your scripted questions to avoid missing an important one and also to keep the phrasing of the questions as clear as when scripted. At the same time, use unscripted follow-up questions as needed to clarify what you have heard and clear up any misunderstandings.

Be careful not to allow your own opinions to intrude on the interview process. This wastes time and also is likely to result in the interviewee's speaking less freely or honestly as he or she attempts to accommodate to the opinions you have expressed.

Make a written record of the interview, organizing the interviewee's responses into categories relevant to the speech subject. Be careful to record the interviewee's comments accurately.

Along with other people, the library is an important source of information for speech preparation. Making effective use of a library's material begins with talking to library staff and receiving an orientation to its layout and resources. Library research generally begins in the reference section, containing books which identify more detailed resources as well as other general reference works. Dictionaries and encyclopedias, general and specialized, are contained in reference sections, as well as indexes to serials and periodicals which provide information, organized by subject or topic areas, as to when articles on a given subject were published in various newspapers and journals or magazines. There are both general and specialized periodical indexes as well. In addition, yearbooks offer annual summaries of important facts and events, statistical abstracts offer census information, and other specialized yearbooks exist as well. There are also numerous works containing brief biographies of important individuals, living and dead.

The card catalog of a library contains listings, by author, title, and subject area, of the individual books in the library's collection. The card catalog is divided into two sections, one listing books by subject area and the other containing combined author/title listings. Every book listed will have a call number, which will help you to locate the book itself on the shelves of the library. The vertical file, another valuable resource, is a collection of pamphlets, brochures, and newspaper and magazine clippings categorized by subject area and maintained by library staff.

Government documents can also be useful. These can be obtained at a local or law library and sometimes at more specialized locations. There is also a *Monthly Catalog of United States Government Publications*, which lists inexpensive or free pamphlets, brochures, and books on specialized topics published by government sources.

Electronic data bases are also now available at many libraries to assist researchers in locating information. These include reference data bases, which access encyclopedias, dictionaries, etc., and source data bases, which function much like card catalogs to allow access to books and other printed materials. Access to some electronic data bases can be costly, whereas most other library resources are free.

Whatever sources of information are used, they are only as helpful as the quality of notes taken by the researcher to collect, organize, and substantiate materials. Notes must be complete so that sources can be properly credited; to use uncredited facts and opinions taken from other sources is plagiarism, which is both unethical and illegal. Notes must be accurate and not misuse information taken out of context.

For ease of use, notes should be recorded on notecards, which are easy to organize and use. The notecards should have headings indicating the subject or significance of the material. They should contain accurate quotations and data. The source of the material should be fully recorded on the notecard, including author or editor, article and/or book or publication title, publisher where appropriate, volume number where needed, and relevant page numbers. Others should be able to find the material easily from the information recorded on notecards.

Communication apprehension, extreme nervousness which inhibits a speaker's ability to express ideas, may have several causes, including fear of the unknown, fear of judgment, or even basic shyness. The best way to boost speech confidence is to prepare thoroughly at every stage of the presentation. Before the speech, audience analysis and familiarity with the setting are essential, as well as oral rehearsal of the presentation, ideally in the actual setting. Obviously, careful preparation of speech materials and organization are also vital.

At the time of the speech, just before beginning speakers can stretch and relax hands and feet and rotate shoulders and head to release excess energy. At the start of a speech, it is sometimes helpful to begin with either a quotation or a visual aid which engages audience attention while drawing direct focus away from the speaker. During the speech, keeping physically active is helpful while taking care to avoid nervous pacing. Movement and gestures also help to release excess energy. Being careful to conclude slowly without racing to the finish is important.

After the speech, speakers should begin to build confidence for their next presentations by listening closely to feedback from the audience, especially that feedback which indicates the message was received. Speakers should plan whatever adjustments are needed for next time and recognize and retain those adaptations and methods which were effective.

CHAPTER OUTLINE

Discovering Material Through Other People
    Conversation
        • Unscripted Talk
        • Speaker's Diary
    Interviews
        • Obtain Agreements
        • Introduce Yourself and Your Purpose
        • Maintain a Quiet or Private Setting
        • Use Prepared Questions
        • Use Follow-Up Questions
        • Avoid Expressing Your Opinions
        • Record Responses

TEACHING OBJECTIVES

14-1. Explore the notions of substance and substantiation and meanings and differences in meaning of fact and opinion.

14-2. Emphasize the value of other people as sources of ideas, insights, and information.

14-3. Define conversation, and depict a speaker's diary as a means of preserving the serendipitous knowledge and benefits of conversation.

14-4. Explain the nature and potential benefits of interviews. Describe the stages of the interview process and their importance to the success of the process.

14-5. Enhance awareness of the rich treasures a library provides.

14-6. Describe the various resources of libraries and how they may be accessed.

14-7. Introduce the art of note taking as essential to the completion of accurate and effective research.

14-8. Offer a reminder of what constitutes plagiarism and why it is both illegal and unethical.

14-9. Discuss the reality of communication apprehension; emphasize the importance of preparation at every stage and level of the speaking process to building confidence and assuring success.

DISCUSSION QUESTIONS

14-1. What do we mean when we call someone "a person of substance"? How does the notion of substance compare to that of substantiating our ideas?

14-2. When was the last time you learned something of real insight or value from a conversation? Sometimes, these serendipitous moments are called "aha" experiences, when we suddenly see or hear something in a new and startling way. When has this happened to you? Did you tell someone else about it? Did you write it down?

14-3. Have you ever interviewed someone? Have you ever been interviewed? Where and when have you seen interviews conducted and what did you learn from them?

14-4. How many times have you used a library for research in your lifetime? How many of the materials described here have you ever used? How many materials are you sure you could find if you walked into your local library?

14-5. What exactly constitutes plagiarism? How is it different from paraphrasing? Why is it important? Martin Luther King's "I Have A Dream" speech contains many lines and phrases borrowed from Bible verses, the sources of which are not cited in his speech. Is this plagiarism?

14-6. How would you rate your own level of communication apprehension on a scale of one to ten? Is it different in different situations? Has it gotten better or worse over the years?

14-7. What was the worst public speaking or similar experience of your life? What happened? How did it end?

SKILL MASTERY EXERCISES

14-1 In order to introduce students to the full range of information sources available to them, and to encourage detailed research, careful note taking, and cooperation, it would be useful to introduce this chapter's information early in the semester and have their first speaking assignment be a group project on a topic of your or their choice. Together, the students could hone their research skills and discuss and learn the basic elements of effective speech structure and content, thus laying the groundwork for their individual presentations.

The terms of the assignment should be that the research work should be shared, a consistent format for recording and organizing information should be followed, the group as a whole should evaluate the information received and decide what should be included and what excluded from the final product, and the speech should be organized, prepared, and practiced by the group as a whole, with one member of their choice delivering the final product.

Grading of the presentation should be on the research done and notecards prepared, the records of meetings and group discussions maintained, and the strength of the final product, with all relevant material submitted for the grading process.

While there is always merit in allowing students to make their own topic choices, there would be great interest and value here in assigning the same topic to all three or four of your class's groups and then allowing them, as well as you, to compare the quality, quantity, and use made of information obtained.

14-2. Ask the students, in groups or individually, to rent and view the movie *My Dinner with Andre*, directed by Louis Malle (1981). The film depicts a lengthy conversation over dinner between two old friends who haven't seen each other in years; it contains many interesting and insightful statements and ideas.

Ask each group or student to keep a "speaker's diary" of the conversation. Assign a deadline for watching the film and a day to bring the speaker's diaries to class.

Then use the diaries as a basis for discussion of diaries as tools and, on the basis of differences in wordings of statements recorded, the importance of recording accurately. The different focuses and observations of the students could also serve as a useful means of reminding the class about perceptual differences and their impact on what we see and hear; this discussion, in turn, can be tied to the nature of interviewing and the importance of recording and clarifying what we think we heard.

14-3. If your university library offers its orientation programs to introduce students to its services, particularly any electronic data systems in use, assign students to complete the orientation process and provide proof of having done so.

14-4. Seek to identify students who perceive themselves as highly apprehensive about public speaking and ask for volunteers from among them who would be willing to acknowledge and talk about their apprehensiveness with a small group of their peers. If you have volunteers, divide the class into small groups with one or two of the apprehensive students in each group. Ask the groups to develop plans to build speaking confidence with the apprehensive students in their group, using suggestions from the text and elsewhere and possibly even making plans to rehearse together. This exercise should be employed sufficiently in advance of the next speech assignment to allow planning and preparation time.

KEY TERMS AND CONCEPTS

fact (p. 374)
opinion (p. 374)
conversation (p. 375)
speaker's diary (p. 375)
card catalog (p. 382)
vertical file (p. 384)
government documents (p. 384)
electronic data bases (p. 384)

CHAPTER 15

DEVELOPING SPEECH ORGANIZATION

CHAPTER SYNOPSIS

Successful leaders are successful organizers, in both their work and their speeches. The basic principles of organization are unity, coordination, and subordination.

Unity is accomplished when the speech as a whole deals only with the subject at hand and when its various elements or parts contain only related ideas or use only one type of supporting material. Coordination is accomplished when the parts of a speech are equal and parallel in importance and receive similar amounts of speaking time and vocal emphasis. Subordination is effectively attained within a speech when the main points or ideas are supported well with subpoints and specific details. A speech by Julie Graef is presented in both manuscript and outline form to illustrate these principles.

There are five major patterns of organization for speeches. Each pattern corresponds in some way to natural patterns of perception in human beings. The conventional pattern is used to describe the basic elements or parts of a subject; the order in which the elements are presented is not important. When the goal is to emphasize the similarity among parts or functions, a comparative order may be used. When the goal is to emphasize differences, a contrasting order may be used. The conventional pattern satisfies common expectations and reflects common divisions of a subject; however, it adds nothing distinctive to a presentation.

The spatial pattern adds clarity to a speech by organizing the parts or elements on the basis of their relationship in physical space. The speech must be organized in such a way that the spatial movement is in one direction, from outside to in, for example, or from bottom to top; the order of points is crucial to the successful use of this pattern. The spatial pattern is useful only with subjects which involve physical space.

The temporal pattern of discussing a subject follows a natural chronological order, such as from past to

present or from the present into the past. Here, too, following a one-directional order is vital to the successful use of this pattern. Depending on the subject, only one order, from start to finish, would be effective. The temporal pattern requires vividness and drama to avoid being boring.

With the problem-solving pattern, the speaker addresses a need of the audience and explains a way of satisfying that need. If a problem has multiple possible solutions, a speaker can use this method to define criteria for the best solution and test the various solutions against the criteria to find the best one. The "motivated sequence" is another form of the problem-solving pattern; it involves getting the audience's attention, demonstrating the need, identifying the satisfaction of the need, visualizing the results, and requesting a response. The problem-solving pattern is effective and has few drawbacks as long as it is appropriate to the subject matter; failure to gain agreement on the existence of a problem is the only risk involved in the use of this pattern.

The causal pattern is appealing because people are innately curious to know what causes events and phenomena. Causal relationships are difficult to prove, but audiences are receptive to evidence. The use of the causal pattern involves being able to identify the relevant stimuli and responses in a given situation; the speech must provide accurate and sufficient evidence of causality. Each of these five patterns involve building links or relationships among the various parts or elements of a subject.

Introductions and conclusions are also vital elements of successful speeches. Both seek to establish and maintain connections between the speaker and the subject, occasion, and audience. The introduction also involves getting the audience's attention, while a conclusion requires a summary or restatement of main points.

The relationships between speaker and subject can be established in an introduction by revealing personal knowledge of or experience with the subject and/or by expressing a sincere interest or concern. The relationship between speaker and occasion is established by answering in the introduction the question, Why is this speaker addressing this subject here and now? The relationship between speaker and audience is established by the speaker's development of personal credibility and by creating a sense of kinship or connectedness through either language or reference to items of mutual interest. Few introductions establish all three relationships equally.

Speech conclusions seek to maintain or remind the audience of relationships established in the introduction. Sometimes this can be done quite directly using the technique known as mirroring, which involves referring directly back to the material with which one began. In any case, the conclusion seeks in some way to reinforce the links between the speaker and the subject, occasion, and audience. In this way, both introductions and conclusions support the body of the speech by enhancing receptiveness to the speaker and the message.

Effective outlining assures clear organization of the speech and aids the speaker in delivering the speech as planned. The traditional use of symbols (Roman numerals for main points, uppercase letters for subpoints, etc.) in outlining is explained. Spacing and indentation are used to visually reinforce the distinctions between main points and subpoints; the relative importance of the ideas can then be seen in relation to their proximity to the left side of a page.

There are three methods of wording or phrasing speech outlines. The substantial quotations method essentially places the entire content of the speech, word for word, in outline form. The full sentence outline words all main and subordinate points in whole sentences. A key word outline uses single words or brief phrases to express the essence of main and subordinate points. Whichever method is used, parallel phrasing, using the same pattern to express similar points or ideas, is beneficial because it emphasizes the equal importance or coordinate status of the parallel ideas.

CHAPTER OUTLINE

Recognizing the Principles of Organization
    Unity
    Coordination
    Subordination
Using Organizational Patterns
    Conventional Pattern
    Spatial Pattern

    Temporal Pattern
    Problem-Solving Pattern
    Causal Pattern
Using Introductions and Conclusions
    Introductions
        • Relationship Between Speaker and Subject
        • Relationship Between Speaker and Occasion
        • Relationship Between Speaker and Audience
    Conclusions
        • Relationship Between Speaker and Subject
        • Relationship Between Speaker and Occasion
        • Relationship Between Speaker and Audience
Using Outlines
    Symbols
        • Roman Numerals–Main Points
        • Uppercase Letters–Subpoints
        • Arabic Numerals–Supporting Material
        • Lowercase Letters–Additional Support
    Spacing
    Phrasing
        • Substantial Quotations
        • Full Sentences
        • Key Words
Sample Outline
Summary
Exercises
Related Readings

TEACHING OBJECTIVES

15-1. Explain the principles of unity, coordination, and subordination and their importance to the organization of an effective oral presentation.

15-2. Define the five traditional patterns of organization, describing the usefulness, drawbacks, and necessary qualities of each, and emphasizing the relationship between each pattern and basic patterns in human perception.

15-3. Emphasize the importance of effective introductions and conclusions to the success of a speech; define them in terms of relationships between the speaker and the subject, occasion, and audience.

15-4. Review with the students the principles of outlining, including traditional symbol usage and spacing and the phrasing options of substantial quotations, full sentence, and key word outlining.

DISCUSSION QUESTIONS

15-1. Could these same principles of unity, coordination, and subordination be used to evaluate the organization of any work of art? Can a speech be a work of art?

15-2. Are the problems discussed by Ms. Graef regarding rap music reflective of racist or of free speech issues?

15-3. Each of us, when approaching a new problem or experience, perceives it differently, some wanting to know first what it's made up of (conventional pattern), others wanting to know what came first (temporal) or what caused this thing to occur (causal). Of the five patterns your test explains, which best describes your basic or general approach to new experiences or problems? What is it you first want to know?

15-4. When you need to ask someone you know for assistance, how much thought do you give to how you will begin? For example, how would you introduce the subject of wanting to borrow a large sum of money from your mom or dad?

15-5. How do you go about attempting to present yourself as believable and trustworthy in your everyday life?

15-6. How would you outline the pattern of your life?

SKILL MASTERY EXERCISES

15-1. Provide students with a copy of Susan B. Anthony's "On Woman's Right to Suffrage." In small groups or individually, ask them to examine the content of the speech for evidence of its unity, coordination, and subordination. Afterward, lead them in a discussion of the effectiveness of the speech; such a discussion will be more successful if some background information on the speaker and her times are provided.

SUSAN B. ANTHONY, WOMEN'S ADVOCATE

[1820—1906]

Susan B. Anthony, temperance advocate, opponent of slavery and proponent of women's suffrage, was arrested in 1872 for casting a vote in a presidential election. She was fined $100, which she never paid. The following speech was delivered in 1873.

ON WOMAN'S RIGHT TO SUFFERAGE

Friends and fellow citizens:—I stand before you tonight under indictment for the alleged crime of having voted at the last presidential election, without having a lawful right to vote. It shall be my work this evening to prove to you that in thus voting, I not only committed no crime, but, instead, simply exercised my *citizen's rights*, guaranteed to me and all United States citizens by the National Constitution, beyond the power of any State to deny.

The preamble of the Federal Constitution says:

"We, the people of the United States, in order to form a more perfect union, establish justice, insure *domestic* tranquility, provide for the common defense, promote the general welfare, and secure the blessings of liberty to ourselves and our posterity, do ordain and establish this Constitution for the United States of America"

It was we, the people; not we, the white male citizens; nor yet we, the male citizens; but we, the whole people, who formed the Union. and we formed it, not to give the blessings of liberty, but to secure them; not to the half of ourselves and the half of our posterity, but to the whole people—women as well as men. And it is downright mockery to talk to women of their enjoyment of the blessings of liberty while they are denied the use of the only means of securing them provided by this democratic-republican government—the ballot.

For any State to make sex a qualification that must ever result in the disfranchisement of one entire half of the people is to pass a bill of attainder, or an *ex post facto* law, and is therefore a violation of the supreme law of the land. By it the blessings of liberty are for ever withheld from women and their female posterity. To them this government has no just powers derived from the consent of the governed. To them this government is not a democracy. It is not a republic. It is an odious aristocracy; a hateful oligarchy of sex; the most hateful aristocracy ever established on the face of the globe. An oligarchy of wealth, where the rich govern the poor; an oligarchy of learning, where the educated govern the ignorant; or even an oligarchy of race, where the Saxon rules the African, might be endured; but this oligarchy of sex, which makes father, brothers, husband, sons, the oligarchs over the mother and sisters, the wife and daughters of every household–which ordains all men sovereigns, all women subjects, carries dissension, discord and rebellion into every home of the nation.

Webster, Worcester and Bouvier all define a citizen to be a person in the United States, entitled to vote and hold office.

The only question left to be settled now is: Are women persons? And I hardly believe any of our opponents will have the hardihood to say they are not. Being persons, then, women are citizens; and no State has a right to make any law, or to enforce any old law, that shall abridge their privileges or immunities. Hence, every discrimination against women in the constitutions and laws of the several States is to-day null and void, precisely as in every one against negroes. (*World's Greatest Speeches*, Dover Press.)

15-2. Provide students with a copy of the speech known as "Reply to Mr. Cram," delivered by a Native American known as Red Jacket (tribal name Sagoyewatha) in 1805. In groups, have them discuss and describe the speaker's introduction, pattern of organization, and conclusion. Encourage them to talk about the ways in which the speaker attempts to establish and maintain a relationship with his or her audience. Ask each group to prepare an outline of the speech. When they've finished, have them write them on the chalkboard or overhead projector for comparison. Did each group recognize the same main and subordinate points? Discuss together the question of the effectiveness of the speech, its introduction, and its conclusion.

SAGOYEWATHA: RED JACKET, NATIVE AMERICAN ORATOR

The following speech was delivered by Red Jacket in 1805 at a council of chiefs of the Six Nations after a white missionary had addressed them.

Reply to Mr. Cram

Friend and Brother:—It was the will of the Great Spirit that we should meet together this day. He orders all things and has given us a fine day for our council. He has taken His garment from before the sun and caused it to shine with brightness upon us. Our eyes are opened that we see clearly; our ears are unstopped that we have been able to hear distinctly the words you have spoken. For all these favors we thank the Great Spirit, the Him only.

Brother, this council fire was kindled by you. It was at your request that we came together at this time. We have listened with attention to what you have said. You requested us to speak our minds freely. This gives us great joy; for we now consider that we stand upright before you and can speak what we think. All have heard your voice and all speak to you now as one man. Our minds are agreed.

Brother, you say you want an answer to your talk before you leave this place. It is right you should have one, as you are a great distance from home and we do not wish to detain you. But first we will look back a little and tell you what our fathers have told us and what we have heard from the white people.

Brother, listen to what we say. There was a time when our forefathers owned this great island. Their seats extended from the rising to the setting sun. The Great Spirit had made it for the use of Indians. He had created the buffalo, the deer, and other animals for food. He had made the bear and the beaver. Their skins served us for clothing. He had scattered them over the country and taught us how to take them. He had caused the earth to produce corn for bread. All this He had done for His red children because He loved them. If we had some disputes about our hunting-ground they were generally settled without the shedding of much blood.

But an evil day came upon us. Your forefathers crossed the great water and landed on this island. Their numbers were small. They found friends and not enemies. They told us they had fled from their own country for fear of wicked men and had come here to enjoy their religion. They asked for a small seat. We took pity on them, granted their request, and they sat down among us. We gave them corn and meat; they gave us poison in return.

The white people, brother, had now found our country. Tidings were carried back and more came among us. Yet we did not fear them. We took them to be friends. They called us brothers. We believed them and gave them a larger seat. At length their numbers had greatly increased. They wanted more land; they wanted our country. Our eyes were opened and our minds became uneasy. Wars took place. Indians were hired to fight against Indians, and many of our people were destroyed. They also brought strong liquor among us. It was strong and powerful, and has slain thousands.

Brother, our seats were once large and yours were small. You have now become a great people, and we have scarcely a place left to spread our blankets. You have got our country, but are not satisfied; you want to force your religion upon us.

Brother, continue to listen. You say that you are sent to instruct us how to worship the Great Spirit agreeably to His mind; and, if we do not take hold of the religion which you white people teach we shall be unhappy hereafter. You say that you are right and we are lost. How do we know this to be true? We understand that your religion is written in a Book. If it was intended for us, as well as you, why has not the Great Spirit given to us, and not only to us, but why did He not give to our forefathers the knowledge of that Book, with the means of understanding it rightly. We only know what you tell us about it. How shall we know when to believe, being so often deceived by the white people?

Brother, you say there is but one way to worship and serve the Great Spirit. If there is but one religion, why do you white people differ so much about it? Why not all agreed, as you can all read the Book?

Brother, we do not understand these things. We are told that your religion was given to your forefathers and has been handed down from father to son. We also have a religion which was given to our forefathers and has been handed down to us, their children. We worship in that way. It teaches us to be thankful for all the favors we receive, to love each other, and to be united. We never quarrel about religion.

Brother, the Great Spirit has made us all, but He has made a great difference between His white and His red children. He has given us different complexions and different customs. To you He has given the arts. To these He has not opened our eyes. We know these things to be true. Since He has made so great a difference between us in other things, why may we not conclude that He has given us a different religion according to our understanding? The Great Spirit does right. He knows what is best for His children; we are satisfied.

Brother, we do not wish to destroy your religion or take it from you. We only want to enjoy our own.

Brother, you say you have not come to get our land or our money, but to enlighten our minds. I will now tell you that I have been at your meetings and saw you collect money from the meeting. I can not tell what this money was intended for, but suppose that it was for your minister; and, if we should conform to your way to thinking, perhaps you may want some from us.

Brother, we are told that you have been preaching to the white people in this place. These people are our neighbors. We are acquainted with them. We will wait a little while and see what effect your preaching has upon them. If we find it does them good, makes them honest, and less disposed to cheat Indians, we will then consider again of what you have said.

Brother, you have now heard our answer to your talk, and this is all we have to say at present. As we are going to part, we will come and take you by the hand, and hope the Great Spirit will protect you on your journey and return you safe to your friends. (*World's Greatest Speeches*, Dover Press.)

15-3. Provide your students with the outline of a speech, perhaps one a student in a previous class of yours submitted, or one of your making which speaks to a subject of suitable interest to this audience. Ask half of them to write an introduction for this speech and the other half to write a conclusion. Present this assignment as a competition, saying the whole class will vote for the best effort in each category and that the winner in each category will be rewarded somehow, perhaps by being given first pick of when he or she will deliver her/his next speech or being offered bonus points to be added to the assignment of his/her choice. Allow ten–twenty minutes for their creative efforts, depending on how soon they seem to be finished. Have them write their completed efforts on large index cards, with their names written on the back or bottom. In order to avoid embarrassment to those who write the worst efforts, do not announce the authors of the entries.

In order to eliminate the impact of various delivery styles on the judging, you could read all entries yourself or have one or two of your best speakers read the entries aloud. Have the students vote for each entry on a scale of zero–ten, tallying the votes on the board, the winners being those with the highest numerical averages. Announce the names of the authors of the winning entries with applause or other fanfare as desired; then talk about what made the entries effective or ineffective.

This exercise allows for an entertaining and enlightening class period, combining exposure to a wide variety of introductions and conclusions with discussion of what made them fail or succeed.

KEY TERMS AND CONCEPTS

unity (p. 398)
coordination (p. 399)
subordination (p. 399)
conventional pattern of organization (p. 406)
spatial pattern of organization (p. 407)
temporal pattern of organization (p. 408)
problem-solving pattern of organization (p. 409)
causal pattern of organization (p. 411)
substantial quotations outline (p. 421)
full sentence outline (p. 422)
key words outline (p. 422)

CHAPTER 16

USING ORAL LANGUAGE AND SKILLFUL DELIVERY

CHAPTER SYNOPSIS

Effective speakers choose their words carefully. Oral language and written language are not the same. This chapter discusses four desirable features of oral language and basic delivery skills.

The requirements of oral language, in order to be effective, include the use of simple diction. Listeners, unlike readers, have only one opportunity to catch the meaning in the message. Speakers should choose words which are familiar and easily pronounced.

Effective oral communicators also make use of personal references, pronouns such as *I* and *you,* to establish a relationship with the audience. The use of personal references can emphasize the speaker's foresight, skill, and industry and enhance the response desired from the listeners.

Public speaking also involves the use of flexible grammar; the speaker should seek to more nearly duplicate the informal language which we speak rather than more formal written rules. Sentence fragments, for example, can be used appropriately within the oral style.

The use of the active voice in public speaking is also preferred, avoiding the passive voice conjugated with the verb *to be.* The use of the active voice renders spoken language more lively and dynamic.

Lastly, the public speaker should speak primarily in short, relatively simple sentences, which are easier for the listening audience to grasp. Public speaking is measured in terms of statements rather than sentences. A statement is the total number of words which can be spoken in one breath. Not all statements need to be whole sentences.

In their use of oral language, speakers should incorporate certain stylistic features to enrich and strengthen their presentations. Clear language allows the audience to easily grasp the speaker's meaning. Emphatic language emphasizes important ideas. Vivid language makes speeches memorable, and appropriate language prevents offending or alienating the audience.

Clarity is achieved through the use of specific rather than abstract or general words; specific words make meanings precise and offer concrete images. Transitional words also add to clarity by providing connections between ideas and reminding the audience of the order and progression of the presentation.

Emphasis is attained through the skillful use of repetition, or restatement. Schemes, figures of speech which emphasize ideas through use of unusual pattern or structure, are also useful for creating emphasis. Schemes include parallelism, a form of repetition which either begins successive statements with the same language (anaphora) or ends them with the same language (epistrophe), and antithesis, a form of contrast which expresses differences by using parallel structure.

Vividness in language is established through careful and detailed description which draws on the sensory abilities of the audience. Vividness also is enhanced through the use of tropes. Tropes are figures of speech which assign unusual meanings to words and include metaphor, simile, alliteration, euphuism, and onomatopoeia. Metaphors are figures of speech which indirectly compare two ideas or objects not normally associated. Similes are explicit comparisons of two ideas using the word *like* or *as*. Alliteration involves the use of a series of words which begin with the same consonant sound. Euphuism is a similar device, linking a series of words with the same vowel sound. Onomatopoeia involves the use of the sounds of words to duplicate or suggest the sound of the object being described.

Appropriateness of language use is assured by careful restriction of the use of jargon, dialect, profanity, and malapropisms. Jargon is technical or professional language of a given profession that is not likely to be understood by those outside the profession; it can confuse an unfamiliar audience. Dialect is regional language use; dialect is also likely to confuse the uninitiated. Profanity is irreverant or coarse language which profanes what others hold dear. Vulgarity involves reference to ideas or objects considered offensive. Malapropism involves the misuse of words which have similar sounds by replacing an appropriate word with a similar-sounding word of totally different meaning, an error likely to make the speaker appear foolish to the audience. Sexist language limits, offends, or excludes by using gender terms which are not inclusive or by expressing a perception of lower status for one gender.

A portion of a speech by Frederick Douglass is provided as a means of allowing students to locate the various stylistic language devices which have been presented.

Delivery is a crucial element in public speaking. Effective leaders are skillful at delivering their messages. There are four main types of delivery: impromptu, extemporaneous, manuscript, and memorized.

Impromptu delivery involves the spontaneous adaptation of preselected subject matter and purpose to an occasion for which exact planning of speech length and structure is not possible in advance. This form of delivery requires command of a broad range of subject matter and the ability to organize ideas quickly. This method is not suitable for beginning speakers or those with communication apprehension.

Extemporaneous delivery requires extensive planning and preparation and the use of a prepared outline, but with flexibility in wording and timing to adapt to the needs of the occasion and audience. The purpose and structure of the extemporaneous presentation does not change, but the speaker may restate or rephrase information as needed to adapt to audience response.

Manuscript delivery involves creation of a word-for-word speech script which the speaker then reads aloud. This type of delivery is appropriate when mistakes in wording could be disastrous, for example, on formal occasions or in times of crisis. Manuscript delivery is difficult. Ability to adapt to the occasion and audience is severely diminished, physical movement is restricted because of the need to remain close to the manuscript; sustaining sufficient energy, variety, and activity to prevent audience boredom is harder; and greater care must be taken to assure that the physical setting provides a lectern which does not form a physical barrier between speaker and audience.

Memorized delivery requires composition of a manuscript which is then committed to memory before presentation. This involves extensive preparation, but prohibits adaptation to the audience or flexibility in presentation. Problems arise if a speaker forgets some words and then loses whole segments of the speech. Mnemonic devices, formulas or codes to aid the memory, are sometimes useful in this form of preparation. Acronyms, words formed from the initial letters of a phrase or title, are one form of mnemonic device.

Speech delivery is comparable to musical performance in the need to develop richness and variety in the use of the voice and body to create an effective presentation. The various aspects of vocal delivery are volume, rate, pitch, quality, and pronunciation.

Volume refers to vocal force. Volume must be adapted to the setting and the audience, with electronic equipment if necessary, so that all can hear without straining. Volume also must be adjusted to correct for competing noises or distractions. Effective speakers maintain emphatic volume by planning variations in volume to emphasize significant ideas and by taking care to prevent drop-offs in volume at the end of sentences.

Rate refers to the basic tempo or pace at which words and statements are uttered. Nervous speakers often speak at unnaturally fast rates. Rate should be varied within speeches, slowing for complex or serious ideas and speeding up to express excitement, anger, or energy. Pausing is integral to the pacing of speeches. Pauses are useful to define shifts in subject or ideas and also give audiences time to consider one idea before moving on to the next. Pausing is sometimes difficult for public speakers; many tend to fill the silences with vocal filler such as "um" or "ah." Speakers should practice varying both rate and volume to enhance their oral style.

Vocal pitch has to do with the rate of vibration of vocal chords which causes a voice to sound high or low. Recognition of one's own pitch and practiced variations in pitch to add emphasis are important. One's natural pitch range is difficult to adjust, but certain pitch changes are essential to express questions (a raise in pitch at the end), express serious ideas (lowered pitch), etc. Repeated practice is necessary to develop sufficient pitch range to avoid monotonous delivery.

Vocal quality is subjectively assessed and varies from listener to listener, but the term basically describes the pleasure with which a voice will be received. Distinctive delivery involves careful and expressive articulation. Attractive delivery avoids extreme nasality, hoarseness, or breathiness.

Correct pronunciation is essential to maintaining speaker credibility. Errors in pronunciation suggest ignorance and unpreparedness and can be offensive to audience members.

Physical delivery is also important to effective speaking. Facial expressiveness and eye contact are particularly vital. Speakers should smile, frown, and appear quizzical as needed to enhance the meaning of their words. Eye contact need not be continuous, but it must be frequent, direct, and, at moments at least, sustained.

Gestures, the expressive use of movements of head, hands, and arms, are important for interest and emphasis. Variety in gestural expression is needed. Gestures can be used to emphasize, enumerate, or describe. Gestures should sustain interest in and attention to the speaker and should be timed to correspond to verbal messages.

Movement refers to major physical expressions or adaptations within a speech. Stepping forward or backward, for example, can express intensity or reservations. Slower movements are generally desirable to avoid startling the audience.

CHAPTER OUTLINE

Using Oral Language
  Clarity
    • Specific Words
    • Transitional Words
  Emphasis
    • Repetition
    • Schemes
        Parallelism
        Anaphora
        Epistrophe
        Antithesia
  Vividness
    • Description
    • Tropes
        Metaphor
        Simile
        Alliteration
        Euphuism
        Onomatopoeia
  Appropriateness
    • Jargon
    • Dialect
    • Profanity
    • Malapropism
    • Sexism
Using Skillful Delivery
  Impromptu Delivery
  Extemporaneous Delivery
  Manuscript Delivery
  Memorized Delivery
  Using Vocal Delivery
    • Volume
    • Rate
    • Pitch
    • Quality
    • Pronunciation
  Using Physical Delivery
    • Facial and Eye Control
    • Gesture
    • Movement
Summary
Exercises
Related Readings

TEACHING OBJECTIVES

16-1. Emphasize the differences between written and oral language and the need for oral language to be appropriate to the needs of listeners rather than readers.

16-2. Explain the primary adaptations of oral language through use of simple diction, personal references, flexible grammar, active voice, and short, simple statements.

16-3. Introduce the notion of clarity in language, and develop an appreciation for the use of specific and transitional language to achieve oral clarity.

16-4. Describe the value of emphasis to oral expression, providing definitions and examples of repetition, parallelism (anaphora and epistrophe), and antithesis.

16-5. Introduce the figures of speech known as tropes and, through definitions and examples, seek to enhance appreciation of the power of metaphor, simile, alliteration, euphuism, and onomatopoeia.

16-6. Raise the issue of appropriateness in language use for various settings and audiences and offer examples of the use and potential impact of jargon, dialect, profanity, vulgarity, malapropisms, and sexist language.

16-7. Describe the four basic types of delivery and the advantages and disadvantages of each, stressing the importance of preparation to each type.

16-8. Stress the importance of vocal delivery to effective speaking, making sure students understand the elements and impact of volume, rate, pitch, quality, and pronunciation.

16-9. Examine the necessity and impact of physical delivery in effective speaking, particularly in the areas of facial expressions and eye contract, gestures, and movement.

DISCUSSION QUESTIONS

16-1. How must oral language differ from conversation?

16-2. Who are the best storytellers you know among your friends and family. What is it about the way they tell their stories which makes them interesting?

16-3. How might the power of Mr. Florence's words have very different kinds of impact on white versus black audiences? How about a mixed audience?

16-4. Many who heard, or heard about, Malcolm X's "The Ballot or the Bullet" speech around the time it was delivered thought he was advocating violence. On the basis of the segment of the speech your text provides, what do you think?

16-5. What are some of the elements of the regional dialect which is native to you? Could we say that college or university campuses have their own dialects as well?

16-6. Who is the most effective speaker you have ever seen, in person or on film? What was it about her or his presentation that made her or him so effective?

16-7. What are your emotional and physiological responses when someone shouts at you, or speaks so loudly given the space and situation you're in that it feels like shouting? How about, at the other end of the spectrum, when you have to strain to hear?

16-8. All of us can describe certain kinds of voices which we find it difficult to listen to—what are the ones that get to you? Why? What is it about them that bothers you?

16-9. Have you ever had someone mispronounce your name? How did you feel? How did you respond?

16-10. Different cultures can have different gestural repertoires or habits. How would you describe the gestural habits of your family or ethnic background?

SKILL MASTERY EXERCISES

16-1. Find passages of a paragraph or two in length which are written in a complex or even florid style–passages readily available in classic writings such as Jane Austen's *Pride and Prejudice*, Charlotte Bronte's *Wuthering Heights*, and Nathaniel Hawthorne's *The Scarlet Letter*. Divide the class into small groups and distribute copies of one excerpt to each group member. To begin have one group member read the excerpt aloud to get a sense of the unsuitability of written language for oral use. Then have the groups write an "oral language style" version of their excerpts, simplifying the diction, shortening the statements, and incorporating personal references, flexible grammar, and the active voice as suitable. Share efforts with the whole class, if time permits, when the groups have completed their task.

16-2. Give your students the assignment of describing an entire day or experience by its smells alone. (You could assign other senses as well for variety, but the sense of smell is generally the least noted and discussed, so it is likely to provide a greater language challenge. Have the descriptions presented orally.

16-3. It is possible to combine experience with impromptu speaking and course review by assigning each student a particular and limited subject area covered in the textbook (kinesics, reflective listening, etc.) and asking each to thoroughly review the material for discussion at the next class. At the next meeting, then, have one student at a time come forward, ask a specific question pertaining to the subject area she/he was to have studied, and allow one minute to prepare and one or two minutes to deliver an organized response. This exercise is more likely to be effective if a point value is attached to successful completion of the assignment; it can also be expected to produce at least one or two vivid "proofs" of the necessity of preparation to successful impromptu speaking.

16-4. Divide the class into small groups and give each group one of the quotations drawn from *Bartlett's Familiar Quotations* (Little Brown, Boston, 1968) below:

"Here are your waters and your watering place. Drink and be whole again beyond confusion." (Robert Frost)

"Those comfortably padded lunatic asylums which are known, euphemistically, as the stately homes of England." (Virginia Woolf)

"That island of England breeds very valiant creatures: their mastiffs are of unmatchable courage." (Shakespeare)

"If wishes were horses, beggars would ride." (John Ray)

"Go from me. Yet I feel that I shall stand henceforward in their shadow." (Elizabeth Barrett Browning)

"We are not amused." (Queen Victoria)

Feel free to choose other statements more to your liking. Ask each group to develop two to three different oral readings of the assigned line, incorporating changes in pitch, rate, volume, quality, etc.,

as needed, which through variations in vocal delivery communicate different meanings for the messages.

When finished, ask for presentations of the various vocal experiments.

KEY TERMS AND CONCEPTS

clear language (p. 431)
emphatic language (p. 431)
vivid language (p. 431)
appropriate language (p. 431)
transitional language (p. 435)
repetition (p. 436)
scheme (p. 437)
parallelism (p. 437)
anaphora (p. 437)
epistrophe (p. 437)
antithesis (p. 437)
trope (p. 439)
metaphor (p. 439)
mixed metaphor (p. 439)
simile (p. 440)
alliteration (p. 440)
euphuism (p. 440)
onomatopoeia (p. 440)
jargon (p. 441)
dialect (p. 441)
profanity (p. 442)
malapropism (p. 442)
sexist language (p. 442)
impromptu delivery (p. 444)
extemporaneous delivery (p. 445)
manuscript delivery (p. 446)
memorized delivery (p. 447)
mnemonic device (p. 448)
volume (p. 449)
rate (p. 450)
pitch (p. 451)
quality (p. 452)
pronunciation (p. 453)
facial expressions (p. 454)
gesture (p. 456)
movement (p. 457))

CHAPTER **17**

SPEAKING TO INFORM

CHAPTER SYNOPSIS

Information is a process of recognition, understanding, and retention in which both speakers and audiences play active roles. Recognition occurs when listeners are exposed to facts or figures previously unknown to them. Understanding occurs when the significance of data is explained. False impressions are unclear or wrong understandings about the significance of data which a speaker must seek to correct. Retention involves remembering what has been recognized and understood.

Public speakers attempt to accomplish one or more of the following goals: interpretation, description, and demonstration. Interpretation, also known as explanation, makes subject matter clear and familiar to audiences. Description provides listeners with clear mental images of the subject. Demonstration shows an audience how to engage in or accomplish some task or activity.

Public speakers use a variety of supporting materials. Definitions and explanations reveal the meaning of the subject or the category to which it belongs. Unusual, technical, or ambiguous information must be clarified. Quotations are word-for-word statements by others used as support, whereas paraphrases are the findings of others described in the speaker's own words. Comparisons reveal similarities among objects, qualities, or actions of the same general type, whereas contrasts point out differences. Analogy involves the comparison of basically dissimilar objects, qualities, or actions and is especially useful for explaining unfamiliar ideas by relating them to those which are familiar.

Examples are brief references to an actual or hypothetical case, used to make subject matter concrete and real to the audience. Illustrations are longer, more detailed examples. Anecdotes are long and often either humorous or poignant illustrations.

Numbers are simple measures of how much, how many, or how long which add precision to speeches; numbers are abstract and difficult to visualize or compare. Statistics are explanations of numbers which connect their meanings in understandable ways, offering relationships such as mean, median, and mode. An annotated sample speech with supporting materials is provided.

Audio-visual materials allow the speaker to present information to several of the senses simultaneously, thus increasing its memorability. Types of visual aids include: objects and models, which reduce the need to provide verbal description; pictures and drawings, which enhance the audience's ability to grasp specific information or explanations and can also serve as evidence; charts and graphs, which allow the audience to visualize the relationships among numbers and statistics; and film, video, and sound recordings, which can create atmosphere, add drama, and enhance interest. Audio-visual materials are valuable when used to amplify supporting material but should not themselves become the focal point of the speech.

The following guidelines for the use of audio-visual aids are offered: 1) Preparation and practice are essential, because anything that can go wrong with audio-visual material will be sure to do so. 2) The speaker must ensure that the whole audience can see or hear the audio-visual material, and the material should be located close to the speaker. 3) The speaker must practice timing in the use of audio-visual materials, just as with gestures, and the material should only be shown when appropriate to what is being said (passing materials around during a speech is always a mistake). 4) While audio-visual materials should be self-contained and self-explanatory to a great degree, the speaker should briefly explain the meaning or significance of each aid as it is presented.

CHAPTER OUTLINE

Understanding the Process of Information
    Recognition
    Understanding
    Retention
Reaching Informative Goals
    Interpretation
    Description
    Demonstration
Building the Speech with Supporting Materials
    Definition and Explanation
    Quotation and Paraphrase
    Comparison and Analogy
    Example and Illustration
    Number and Statistic
Using Audio-Visual Aids
    Types of Audio-Visual Aids
      • Objects and Models
      • Pictures and Drawings
      • Charts and Graphs
      • Film, Video, and Sound Recordings
    Guidelines on Use of Visual Aids
      • Invest Time in Preparation and Practice
      • Ensure Audience Hearing and Seeing
      • Establish Proper Timing
      • Explain Briefly the Meaning or Significance
Summary
Exercises
Related Readings

TEACHING OBJECTIVES

17-1. Introduce the concept of information not as facts but as the process by which facts, figures, and ideas are shared, a process involving both speaker and listener and one which requires recognition, understanding, and retention of what is conveyed.

17-2. Describe the speech goals of interpretation, description, and demonstration.

17-3. Explain, with relevant examples, the various types of supporting material.

17-4. Describe the various types of audio-visual aids.

17-5. Emphasize the importance of using audio-visual materials well and reinforce the guidelines for use suggested by the authors.

DISCUSSION QUESTIONS

17-1. How does information as a process differ from our normal understanding of this term? Who bears the greater responsibility for the successful completion of this process?

17-2. Which of these three informative speech goals best corresponds to the way you are most likely to recognize, understand, and retain information? Which do you think is the easiest goal for a speaker to attain—explaining, describing, or showing?

17-3. How would you define yourself? How would you explain yourself? What is the difference?

17-4. Suppose you wanted to give a speech on the subject of human beings needing love to survive. How would you go about clarifying what you mean by the ambiguous word *love* in this instance?

17-5. What is your favorite quotation? What is it about the quotation that speaks to you just the way it is? What is the source of its power to move you? Would it lose some of its power if it were paraphrased?

17-6. What would you say is a good analogy to help someone who has never been to college understand what college is like?

17-7. Is a picture really worth a thousand words? When has this been true in your own experience?

SKILL MASTERY EXERCISES

17-1. Select a topic about which most of your students are likely to have some knowledge: dealing with dirty laundry, study skills, simple meals for fast times . . . perhaps they can come up with topics of their own. Find one topic for the whole class and divide the class into three groups. Have the first group develop an explanatory informative speech, the second group develop a descriptive informative speech, and the third group develop an informative speech which demonstrates. Have each group outline its speech plan and later share with the whole class the three plans; discuss which plan the class finds most interesting and/or appealing.

17-2. Assign each student the task of videotaping a television advertisement which they think contains an effective audio-visual message. On the class day the videotapes are due, have the necessary equipment in class and view as many as time and discussion allow, with the student who selected the ad briefly describing why the choice was made and what seems to make this ad effective. Experiment with muting some of the ads to discover how much of the message was conveyed on the visual channel alone.

17-3. Assign your students, in groups or individually (groups allow for fewer projects for later viewing, thus saving class time), the task of creating and presenting a two to four minute "silent speech" on a topic of their choice. Instruct them that they are to incorporate into their speech as many audio-visual materials, gestures, movements, and facial expressions as necessary to convey the desired message and that they are to follow the recommendations for the use of audio-visual material described in the text. After each presentation, ask for analysis from the audience as to what they perceived the point or message of the presentation to be and compare these with the intent of the speaker.

KEY TERMS AND CONCEPTS

information (p. 466)
recognition (p. 466)
understanding (p. 467)
false impressions (p. 468)
retention (p. 469)
interpretation (p. 470)
description (p. 470)
demonstration (p. 470)
definition (p. 471)
explanation (p. 471)
quotation (p. 472))
paraphrase (p. 472)
comparison (p. 473)
contrast (p. 473)
analogy (p. 473)
example (p. 474)
illustration (p. 474)
anecdote (p. 474)
number (p. 474)
statistic (p. 474)
audio-visual aid (p. 478)

CHAPTER **18**

SPEAKING TO PERSUADE

CHAPTER SYNOPSIS

Leaders are often agents of change. The goal of persuasive speaking is to seek change in the beliefs, attitudes, or behaviors of the audience. Change refers to any measurable difference in thought or action. Change can be brought about by coercion, the denial of choice by the one seeking change, or by compliance, the surrender of choice by the one who changes, but most public speakers seek a free and conscious decision to change on the part of the audience.

Like informative speaking, persuasion involves a joint effort on the part of speaker and audience.

Remember that attitudes are judgments based on beliefs and are tied to motives, the driving force behind behavior. Behavior involves action and response as well as judgment. Changes in attitude lead to changes in behavior.

The themes of persuasion are related to the questions of fact, conjecture, value, and policy discussed in Chapter 9. Persuasive speakers ask listeners to reach a decision about one or more of these questions.

Questions of fact refer to decisions as to whether or not something exists or does not exist or is true or false. Conventional, spatial, and temporal patterns of organization are most useful for this theme, as is the use of concrete, specific words. The persuasive speaker seeks belief as well as understanding.

Questions of conjecture involve seeking the audience's change of belief regarding the past or future likelihood of some reality or event and, as a result, can only be answered tentatively. Here, too, conventional, spatial, and temporal patterns are useful; in addition, the causal pattern may be of value. Conjectural themes require vivid language. Themes of conjecture also seek to effect a change in belief in the audience.

Values, enduring interpretations of reality, are difficult to change. In persuasion, the speaker asks listeners to change their judgment of a particular subject, usually pertaining to the rightness or wrongness of an action or event. Here, too, change is sought. All major patterns of organization are useful. Language which clearly expresses judgment is required. Like themes of fact and conjecture, the persuasive theme of value seeks a change in attitude or belief, in this case a judgment of rightness or acceptability.

Persuasive themes of policy seek to answer the question, What should be done? As such, a change in the actual actions or behaviors of the audience is sought. An audience might already share a belief with the speaker, but acting on belief may not yet have occurred. The problem-solving pattern of organization is best suited to themes of policy, although other patterns can be used to develop subordinate points within the speech. Emphatic language is essential to move people to act.

Persuasive speakers must prove the necessity or desirability of change. Three types of appeals are used in combination for effective persuasion: credibility appeals, emotional appeals, and rational appeals. Credibility appeals have to do with assuring the audience that the speaker is believable, ethical, and trustworthy. The perception of or belief in a speaker's credibility is based on several factors and is greatly enhanced during a speech by the dynamism, or perceived energy, attractiveness, and enthusiasm, of the speaker. One factor in speaker credibility is evidence of the speaker's knowledge, experience, or ability, which may include borrowed credibility, established on the basis of information cited from reputable experts, whose credentials are presented to the audience prior to citing them.

Character is the second factor in speaker credibility; character is a judgment on the part of the audience members as to the integrity of the speaker and his or her similarity to them. To enhance this aspect of credibility, speakers often emphasize the similarity of their backgrounds and concerns to those of the audience, sometimes through analogy. Judgments of integrity involve perceptions of consistency between the speaker's past and present words and actions.

Good will is the third factor or element of speaker credibility. Good will is the audience's perception of the speaker's sincere interest in the audience's welfare. Also known as altruism or benevolence, good will depends on the perceived sincerity of the speaker.

Emotional appeals are attempts on the part of speakers to trigger feelings in their audiences through the evidence presented. Effective speakers predict an audience's emotional responses after careful audience analysis. This is harder to do with very large audiences, where the possible range of emotional responses is vast. Emotional appeals are seldom appropriate when addressing themes of fact or conjecture and should be used cautiously when addressing themes of value, where the feelings of the audience will already be aroused. Emotional appeals are effective and often necessary when seeking changes in policy; people must be moved to act.

Maslow's hierarchy of needs suggests that there are five ascending categories of need which drive human behavior: physiological needs, or the most basic survival needs; safety needs, which involve to a basic sense of security about one's life and are fulfilled after physiological needs have been met; belonging or love needs, those met by group membership and interpersonal bonds; self-esteem needs, met through acceptance and accomplishment in the world; and self-actualization needs, met through attainment of personal wholeness. Maslow estimated that these various levels of need are met to varying degrees in most humans, with the physiological needs most fully met and the self-actualization needs least met. Maslow also posited that human beings would not respond to appeals to the higher-level needs until lower-level needs had been met, and that change in thought or action may result from a person's desire to fulfill several categories of need. Emotional appeals are likely to be most effective when tied to one or more of these levels of human need.

Rational appeals are reasons or arguments, supported by evidence. Reasoning takes two forms: deductive reasoning and inductive reasoning. Deductive reasoning moves from a general point on which audience and speaker agree to a specific point on which the speaker is seeking agreement. Variations in deductive reasoning include arguments from generalization, which begin with a generally accepted principle and ask acceptance of a specific subject, and arguments from cause, which begin with an observable influence and ask the audience to accept a previously unrecognized effect.

Inductive reasoning moves from the specific point on which there is agreement to an equally specific or more general point on which agreement is sought. Variations in this form of reasoning are these: arguments from specific instance, moving from a specific instance to seek acceptance of a general principle; arguments from effect, moving from observable effect to probable cause; arguments from sign, moving from observable evidence to possible conditions; and arguments from analogy, which seek to find links to one case from another unrelated event or experience. In induction, the speaker begins with a specific fact or conjecture, and then the audience is asked to make a decision on a similar or related matter that reflects the desirability of the initial fact or conjecture.

Evidence is the substance by which proof is provided. Evidence consists of the same kinds of supporting materials used in and discussed in regard to informative speaking: definition/explanation, used to seek agreement or establish connections; comparison/analogy, used to argue similarity; example/illustration, used as evidence that a proposed change is realistic; quotation/paraphrase, used both as evidence and to build credibility; and number/statistic, used as proof. Sample arguments employing various types of reasoning and evidence are provided.

CHAPTER OUTLINE

Understanding the Process of Persuasion
    Change
    The Relationship Between Attitude and Behavior
Themes of Persuasion
    Fact
    Conjecture
    Value
    Policy
Using Persuasive Appeals
    Credibility Appeals
      • Knowledge
      • Character
      • Good Will
    Emotional Appeal
      • Matching Emotional Appeals to Persuassive
        Themes
      • Matching Emotional Appeals to Human Needs

Rational Appeals
      • Types of Reasoning
      • Types of Evidence
Summary
Exercises
Related Readings

TEACHING OBJECTIVES

18-1. Explore the relationship between leadership skills and persuasive skills.

18-2. Examine the relationships among attitudes, motives, and behavior.

18-3. Reexamine the questions of fact, conjecture, value, and policy as themes in persuasion and consider the differences among them in terms of patterns of organization and what is expected of the audience.

18-4. Emphasize the importance of credibility and describe the factors contributing to an audience's perception of speaker credibility.

18-5. Explore the premises and levels of Maslow's hierarchy of needs and examine ways that emotional appeals can be tied to these levels of need.

18-6. Describe what is meant by rational appeals and the nature of evidence. Contrast deductive versus inductive reasoning.

DISCUSSION QUESTIONS

18-1. Must one be a skilled persuader to be a leader? Are leadership and persuasive power synonymous?

18-2. Which is easier to change—attitudes or behavior? Are both basically habits, one of thought and the other of action? Can they be changed all at once or must they be gradually unlearned?

18-3. How much direction and degree of change is it realistic for a persuasive speaker to expect from one persuasive effort?

18-4. Which is easier—to convince someone of facts, probabilities, judgments, or needed actions?

18-5. How could we measure the impact of a persuasive effort? When should we measure it? Would it make a difference?

18-6. How would you rate your own credibility on the basis of your knowledge, character, general good will, and dynamism? Do you think we tend to assume that most people are credible or that they are not?

18-7. Which gender do you think would have higher credibility as a rule in this country? Why?

18-8. Are emotional appeals by their nature manipulative?

18-9. Do you agree with Maslow's percentages? How would you assign them?

18-10. Which type of reasoning do you find more powerful or convincing–moving from a general to a specific point of agreement, or vice versa?

18-11. Which of these types of evidence do you believe is the most convincing?

SKILL MASTERY EXERCISES

18-1. In small groups, ask each group to develop an ad campaign (for an existing product of its choice) which incorporates appeals to all five levels of need described by Maslow. Share, explain, and discuss.

18-2. Assign a persuasive research topic of your choice to the entire class and have each student find and bring to class on a given day one strong piece of persuasive evidence pertaining to the topic of one of the types described on pages 32–35. In class, then, have students present their pieces of evidence, discuss which type of evidence each is, and seek discussion and evaluation of the strength or persuasive power of each.

18-3. As a class, devise a questionnaire to ask audiences to register their responses to various persuasive appeals. Stress simplicity and general applicability as well as accuracy. Administer the questionnaires during your next round of persuasive speeches. Share the results with the individual speakers, but also compile the results on an ongoing basis as an in-class experiment to measure response to persuasive appeals.

KEY TERMS AND CONCEPTS

persuasive change (p. 488)
attitude (p. 490)
behavior (p. 490)
motives (p. 490)
credibility appeal (p. 496)
dynamism (p. 496)
knowledge (p. 497)
character (p. 498)
good will (p. 498)
emotional appeal (p. 499)
physiological needs (p. 501)
safety needs (p. 501)
belongingness needs (p. 502)
self-esteem needs (p. 502)
self-actualization needs (p. 502)
rational appeal (p. 504)
deductive reasoning (p. 504)
inductive reasoning (p. 504)
evidence (p. 505)

MASTERING COMMUNICATION

SECOND EDITION

MASTERING COMMUNICATION

Dennis S. Gouran
THE PENNSYLVANIA STATE UNIVERSITY

William E. Wiethoff
INDIANA UNIVERSITY

Joel A. Doelger
UNIVERSITY OF ARKANSAS

ALLYN and BACON
Boston   London   Toronto   Sydney   Tokyo   Singapore

Senior Editor: Stephen Hull
Editor in Cheif; Humanities: Joe Opiela
Editorial Assistant: Brenda Conaway
Editorial-Production Administrator: Rowena Dores
Cover Administrator: Linda Dickinson
Text Designer: Rita Naughton
Compostion Buyer: Linda Cox
Manufacturing Buyer: Louise Richardson
Editorial-Production Service: Progressive Typographers

Copyright © 1994, 1992 by Allyn and Bacon

A Division of Paramount Publishing
160 Gould Street
Needham Heights, MA 02194

Library of Congress Cataloging-in-Publication Data
Gouran, Dennis S.,
    Mastering communication / Dennis S. Gouran, William E. Wiethoff,
Joel A. Doelger.—2nd ed.
      p.   cm.
    Includes bibliographical references and index.
    ISBN 0–205–15508–1
    1. Communication.   I. Wiethoff, William E.,
II. Doelger, Joel A.   III. Title.
P90.G63   1994
302.2—dc20
                             93-21229
                             CIP

Printed in the United States of America
10 9 8 7 6 5 4 3 2 1 97 96 95 94

Continued on page 542, which constitutes an extension of the copyright page.

Contents

Preface

The twentieth century has been a time of remarkable achievement, but also a period in which we have experienced a substantial number of economic, political, and social problems that deny us full access to the benefits of our expanding knowledge. To bring people's well-being into greater harmony with the possibilities our advances have created will require increasing numbers of well-educated citizens. It will also require that they be able to use their intellectual skills and personal resources in ways that enable them to manage their relationships with others effectively, address significant issues, make important decisions, and influence the thinking and behavior of others. This new edition of *Mastering Communication* is designed to assist you in understanding and developing the communicative skills necessary for performing these functions.

Themes of the Book

Several distinct but related themes informed the writing of this book. Our hope is that each of them, working together, will contribute materially to the goals outlined above.

Communication Skill Building. One of the principal goals of the Introduction to Speech Communication course, and, indeed, one of the principal motivations for you in taking the course, is the acquisition of basic skills across the spectrum of communication settings. *Mastering Communication* introduces and reiterates skill assessment and skill building continually throughout the book so that you finish a particular chapter with a strong sense of your own competencies in a specific area of communication.

Leadership and Social Responsibility. Throughout the text you will see repeated emphasis on the dual themes of leadership and social responsibility. Much of your education focuses on career preparation, but other important aspects of it involve equipping you for broader concerns of social and professional life. The quality of our personal and collective lives depends on our ability to bring leadership to the tasks and situations we continually confront, and to do so in a socially responsible manner. We exercise such leadership through communication.

Cross-cultural Differences in Communication. While communication is a universal fact of life, the forms it takes vary from one society to another, and, within societies, from one group to another. Ethnocentrism—the automatic belief that one's own culture and patterns of behavior are superior to other cultures and patterns of behavior—is a worldview that few of us can, or would wish to maintain. Thus in this text you will discover some interesting surprises about ways in which communication both varies and remains stable throughout cultures.

Features and Pedagogy

In carrying out our goals and the themes of the book, we have created several special features and pedagogical devices which, we hope, will significantly reinforce and enhance your understanding of the material.

Self-Assessment Boxes. Each chapter includes a special boxed feature designed to test your skills in a particular area of communication competence by identifying strengths and weaknesses, and testing comprehension of chapter material. For example, chapter 4's "Testing your doublespeak detection skill," or chapter 5's "Nonverbal skills assessment."

Mastering Communication Skills Boxes. As a follow up to the self-assessment box, Mastering Communication Skills boxes focus on a key aspect of the communication process presented in the chapter and provide a skill-building exercise designed to give you greater confidence as a communicator. For example, chapter 8's "Utilizing conflict management skills," and Chapter 10's "Building your secondary question repertoire."

Focus on Leadership Boxes. Most of us know that an effective leader must be an adept communicator. But how important is listening to leadership? What kinds of verbal and nonverbal communication skills are crucial to successful leadership? How can you best exercise leadership in group settings? It is to these, and related questions that the *Focus on Leadership* feature is addressed. Found in each chapter, this special boxed feature explores such issues as the need for leaders to be sensitive to sex differences when sending and receiving verbal and nonverbal communication; the role of perception in leadership; and the role of ethics and social responsibility in leadership.

Mastering Communication has a number of other features that will help you in studying, understanding, and applying the material presented.

Chapter Objectives identify goals you should master by carefully reading the chapter and completing the exercises. These objectives give you a roadmap to what in the chapter you should understand and be able to do upon completion, as well as another basis for self-assessment.

Key Terms and Concepts are identified at the beginning of each chapter to give you a preview of vocabulary that is likely to be new to you. Each of these terms is bold-faced in the text where it first appears.

Chapter Summaries restate the major ideas presented in the chapter. In some cases you may find it valuable to read the summaries first in order to focus attention on the central ideas and enable you to think ahead as they read the full text of the chapter.

Chapter Exercises provide yet another opportunity for basic skill building. Each chapter concludes with several exercises that you may carry out by yourself, or in groups.

Related Readings are a valuable resource for you in exploring a given topic further. All entries are annotated to give you a brief description of the work cited.

The **Glossary,** found at the end of the text, pulls together all the key terms from every chapter of the book and provides succinct definitions for study and review.

Plan of the Book

Mastering Communication, Second Edition, is divided into four major parts. Part I focuses on general principles of communication and the critical elements involved. The six chapters comprising this section of the volume address matters related to the nature of communication and its connection to leadership (Chapter 1), perception and communication (Chapter 2), listening and critical thinking (Chapter 3), verbal aspects of communication (Chapter 4), nonverbal aspects of communication (Chapter 5), and intercultural differences (Chapter 6).

In Part II, you will begin to learn how the principles of communication to which you have been introduced apply in the context of interpersonal interaction. Interpersonal communication, interpersonal relationships, communication in families, and interviewing are the topics examined in Chapters 7, 8, 9, and 10, respectively.

Part III moves to the arena of group communication, with special attention to problem-solving and decision-making discussion. Chapter 11 introduces you to the subject of group process and then relates it specifically to problem solving and decision making. In Chapter 12, you will learn about the role of leadership in problem-solving and decision-making groups and how you can influence their performance.

The final six chapters constitute Part IV and focus on communicating formally in public situations. In studying the materials included, you will learn about audience analysis, how to limit subject matter, and choosing a specific purpose (Chapter 13), how to develop appropriate material and improve self-confidence (Chapter 14), how best to organize your thoughts (Chapte 15), how to use language and become more adept in presenting a speech (Chapter 16), what are the best ways of preparing a speech to inform (Chapter 17), and how to approach the speaking situation when your purpose is to persuade (Chapter 18).

Changes from the Original Edition

In preparing the current edition, we have retained the general organizational structure of the original. However, we have made numerous changes throughout. In making these changes, we have been sensitive to the feedback and comments of reviewers and instructors who used the original edition in their courses.

In addition to updating material, we have included in the chapter on listening (Chapter 3) a section dealing with critical thinking, a skill that is increasingly important in determining suitable grounds for belief, choices among competing messages, and social action. Chapter 14, on the development of speech material, now includes a section on speaking with confidence as linked to more general aspects of preparation.

We have added an entirely new chapter on intercultural communication (Chapter 6) designed to sensitize the reader to the ways in which differences in cultural background affect the process of human interaction. We have also continued mention of such influences throughout the volume. Chapter 9, "Family Communication," is also new. The family represents a fundamental social unit in which much of our communication occurs and in which many of our habits, beliefs, attitudes, and characteristic patterns of interaction take shape.

The material on public communication has undergone substantial reorganization. In Chapter 13, we have condensed and combined subjects previously covered in separate chapters on audience analysis and choosing a speech topic. In similar fashion, Chapter 16 combines previously separate discussions of the uses of language and delivery. These changes bring greater coherence to related aspects of presentation in public speaking.

Acknowledgements

Our efforts in preparing the revised edition of *Mastering Communication* have been aided by a number of people. We are grateful to Stephen Hull, Senior Editor, and Branda Conaway, both of Allyn & Bacon. Also instrumental in the process of completing the design and production features of this edition were Rowena Dores, Editorial-Production Administrator, and Shanna Weidner. We are most appreciative of the assistance each provided. Special thanks are again due to Judy Meyer, without whose clerical and typing skills the project would not have been completed on schedule. We would like to thank the following colleagues who advised us on the first edition of *Mastering Communication:* Martha Atkins, Iowa State University, David Berube, University of Vermont; Carl Burgchardt, Colorado State University; Robert Dixon, St. Louis Community College at Meramec; Joel Doelger, University of Arkansas; Charles Fleischman, Hofstra University; Carol Jablonski, University of South Florida; Frank O'Mara, State University of New York at Oneonta; Donald Rubin, University of Georgia; Donna Spaulding, St. Louis Community College at Florissant Valley; David Switzer, Indiana Univeersity-Purdue University at Fort Wayne; Dudley Turner, University of Akron; Beth Waggenspack, Virginia Polytechnic Institute and State University; Leonard Worthman, California State University at Northridge. Professional colleagues who provided comments leading to the changes described above include: Kathleen M. Galvin, Northwestern University; Lorraine D. Jackson, California Polytechnic State University; Anita L. Vangelisti, University of Texas. All of the individuals mentioned above in one way or another played a crucial role in the development and completion of what we hope is an improved and useful introduction to the study of human communication.

MASTERING COMMUNICATION

MASTERING COMMUNICATION ESSENTIALS

An Introduction to Communication

Chapter objectives

After reading this chapter you should be able to:

1. see the importance of being able to communicate well

2. define communication

3. identify the major reasons for communicating

4. understand how communication works

5. point out personal and situational factors that influence communication in interpersonal, group, and public contexts

6. recognize that communication contributes to effective leadership

7. appreciate the value of exercising leadership through ethically responsible communication

Key terms and concepts

leadership
communication
objective
fidelity
stimulation
motivation
generation
encoding
transmission
medium
reception
decoding
reaction
feedback
noise
ethical communication

Our world stands at the threshold of the twenty-first century confronted by unsurpassed challenges and opportunities. Technological development has reached remarkable heights in such areas as space exploration, transportation, communications, education, and medicine, but our shrinking world faces any number of political, economic, and social problems that threaten its very survival. In many respects, our mushrooming knowledge has outpaced our ability to use it in the pursuit of productive, humane ends.

As a person preparing for the future, you can play an important role in identifying the ends toward which knowledge should be applied and in creating the conditions that will contribute to realizing those ends. Never before in human history has there been a greater need for well-educated, socially conscious, and responsible people who are capable of communicating effectively in different private and public contexts and of influencing the processes by which we individually and collectively seek to achieve desired goals. An important aim of this book is to help you develop skills that will enable you to become this kind of person.

Throughout this book, you will find a continual interweaving of the theme of leadership with the aspects of communication being discussed. Since leadership is exercised through communication, the two subjects are inseparable. The type of influence that leadership represents, moreover, occurs in every type of communicative situation. Whether one is persuading an audience, managing a conflict, dealing with a family problem, or assisting the members of a group to achieve their objectives, some degree of leadership is present. How effective the leadership will be depends heavily on the communicative ability of the person exercising it.

In focusing on the communication-leadership relationship, we do not wish to leave the impression that this book is a how-to discussion or manual for achieving positions of prominence in politics, business, and other professions. Our concern, rather, is acquainting you with basic principles and communicative practices that can assist you in functioning more effectively in situations that require leadership. These situations, you will discover, include a broad range of social contexts and relationships. You will also discover that leadership is not restricted to the behavior of people whom we call leaders. **Leadership** is influence directed toward the achievement of desired ends. It differs from other forms of social influence in its focus on the achievement of collectively shared goals. Leadership may be easier to exercise in some positions than in others, but your position in a relationship, group, organization, or society is not what will enable you to exert it. Rather, it is your skill in communication that is crucial.

■ THE IMPORTANCE OF BEING ABLE TO COMMUNICATE WELL

How often in your interactions with others have you found yourself frustrated by an inability to be as effective as you would have liked or to have the sort of

Teaching Objective 1–1
Emphasize the importance of communication skill to personal success, leadership skill, and the solution of social problems.

Leadership Note 1–1
The ability to communicate was rated an essential leadership trait for 21st century executives in a poll of Fortune 500 CEO's. (*Fortune*, April 24, 1989)

Cross-reference 1–1
Leadership in the areas of problem-solving and decision-making will be explored more fully in Chapter 12.

Current Research 1–1
In *Thriving on Chaos* (1987), Tom Peters argues that the most successful organizations are those with employees who function as leaders at all levels of the organization.

matter how clear your thoughts may be to you, if you cannot represent them in ways that those to whom your messages are directed can interpret accurately, you will have little success.

Transmission.   **Transmission** is the process by which a message is conveyed from the sender to the person or persons for whom it is intended. We transmit messages by various means. **Medium** is the term we use for a particular means of communication. Voice is a medium by which we convey a great many of our messages. We also use writing, sound, and visual images as media. Increasingly, we have come to rely on electronic means for transmitting messages. Whatever the medium, if the messages we send do not "arrive," there can be no communication.

Reception.   Up to this point, we have been talking about communication largely in terms of the message producer. Once communication has passed the transmission stage, however, those to whom a message is directed become the focus of concern. **Reception** occurs when an individual is aware of a message and recognizes it as such. The last part of this definition is very important. Not everything we become aware of is a message (King, 1988). When you hear the rain falling outside your window, you do not think of it as a message. Nor would most of us consider the sight of a speeding car as a message, even though we might react to it. In speaking of communication, then, we are concerned with only those situations in which one becomes aware of something that he or she recognizes as a message.

Interpretation (Decoding).   Since messages are representations of the sender's thoughts, reception alone is not sufficient for completion of the process of communication. If you received the message @%+#*)*!, it probably would not mean anything to you, even if the source of the message had something very important in mind to say to you. For this message to make sense, you would have to have some basis for knowing what the characters represent as thoughts. In short, you would have to be able to interpret, or decode, them. **Decoding** is a mental process by which one assigns meanings to messages and determines what the message producer presumably intends to say.

Reaction.   After the recipient interprets the message, he or she typically reacts in some way. **Reaction** refers to what an individual understands, believes, feels, or does as a result of his or her interpretation of a message. Usually, the recipient has more than one reaction. For instance, after listening to a persuasive speech on environmental hazards, you may (1) feel that you know much more about the issues addressed and (2) want to do something about the problem. Or, after listening to an acquaintance tell you about "what your problem is," you may (1) have hurt feelings, (2) change your attitude toward the person, and (3) say something in response that you later wish you had not. The reactions we have to messages are often the source of stimulation for forming our own messages, which we then transmit (either directly or indirectly) to the original

Cross-reference 1–5
The importance of feedback to effective listening will be discussed in Chapter 3.

message producer. We often refer to this type of message as feedback. **Feedback** is a special type of message revealing a person's reactions to what another person has said.

Because we do react to messages, at this stage, the process of communication begins anew. The message recipient becomes a message producer who generates, forms, and transmits new messages. The original message producer becomes a message recipient. Figure 1.1 shows this ongoing quality of communication.

Factors Affecting Communication

Teaching Objective 1–5
Explain the personal and situational factors which influence communication.

How well the communication process we just described functions is a product of numerous factors. We can divide these into two general categories: personal characteristics and situational influences.

Discussion Question 1–3
What personal qualities do you possess which impact on your creation and reception of communication?

Personal Characteristics.   As we have said, the content of messages consists of representations of thoughts and feelings. How "content" develops depends on a message producer's ability to translate thoughts and feelings into forms that others can receive, interpret, and react to appropriately. Your level of knowledge, familiarity with the means of communication available to you, point of view, cultural background, and the like are all personal qualities that enter into the messages you produce. The same sorts of characteristics also affect the ways in which recipients interpret and react to messages.

Figure 1.1
A Model of the Process of Communication.

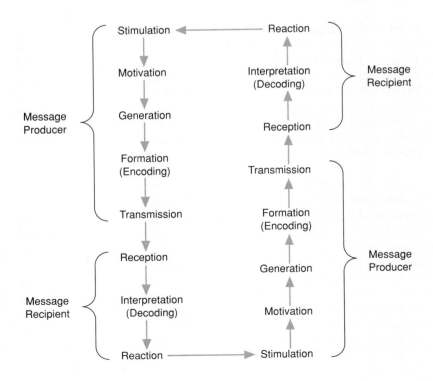

Personal qualities can affect reactions to messages on many different levels. If you were urging an audience to adopt an antiabortion or prochoice stance on the issue of abortion, for instance, you might succeed in making your position clear, but be unsuccessful in convincing those who disagree with you to change their views. Although personal factors can affect communication at any stage, they appear to have the greatest impact in the reaction stage in those situations in which one is attempting to exercise influence. This does not mean that you should ignore such factors at any point, however.

Even the simple act of responding to a request for directions can fail if a communicator neglects such considerations as the person's probable familiarity with the surroundings, how many separate instructions he or she can keep straight, and how precise the language has to be to make the message clear. Have you ever asked for directions to some location and been told something like "Go up here a ways, turn right at the cornfield, and take the curvy road for several miles. You can't miss it." From the producer's point of view, the message has been very helpful, but from your perspective, you are no better off than you would have been if you had not bothered to ask for directions. Communication often fails because we do not sufficiently consider what those with whom we interact know or are capable of understanding (Berlo, 1960).

Situational Influences.   In addition to the effect that personal factors can have on communication, there are various aspects of the situations in which messages are produced and transmitted that affect their content, transmission, reception, and interpretation. The physical environment, of course, has an important bearing on communicative transactions. Aspects of the environment such as lighting, acoustics, room temperature, and various competing external stimuli all can influence how carefully an individual attends to a message and thus how he or she reacts to it. Some individuals refer to any such type of competition as "noise" (see, e.g., Pierce, 1961). As a factor in the process of communication, **noise** is any source of interference that limits reception of a message.

In addition to physical conditions that affect communication, the social context in which it occurs exerts an important influence on the production and reception of messages. In this book, we are primarily concerned with interpersonal, group, and public contexts. In *interpersonal contexts*, communication tends to be loosely structured, and much of what we have to say is a direct result of what other parties are saying (Keltner, 1970). The typical conversation is a good example of what we are suggesting here. *Communication in groups* resembles that in interpersonal exchanges in many respects, but there tends to be more influence resulting from the task that a group is performing (Poole and Doelger, 1986). The task, in part, dictates the sorts of messages that members of groups produce. In *public contexts*, messages tend to be of relatively long duration. The message producer engages in extended elaboration of an idea or set of ideas. The message recipient, on the other hand, typically has little opportunity to participate, except by means of nonverbal feedback.

Another situational influence affecting communication is the occasion that marks a communicative event. If the occasion is important to the parties

Leadership Note 1–2
According to Warren Bennis in *On Becoming a Leader* (Addison- Wesley, Reading, Mass., 1989), the personal characteristics of leaders are a guiding vision, passion, integrity, trust, curiosity and daring.

Cross-reference 1–6
Knowing your audience is as important to interpersonal communication as it is to public speakers. Audience analysis as a specific tool for public speakers will be discussed in Chapter 13.

Discussion Question 1–4
What kinds of noise are affecting communication in your classroom right now?

involved, the way they conduct themselves, communicatively speaking, may vary considerably from their conduct on a less significant occasion. If you were paying tribute to your favorite teacher on his or her retirement, you undoubtedly would be much more concerned about your "message" than you would be if a friend were to ask you for your reactions to a movie you have just seen.

Physical conditions, communicative context, and occasion are just a few of the aspects of the situations in which messages are exchanged that influence their content and consequences. In mentioning these, we are attempting to show you that even though the same general model applies to all instances of communication, the way in which the process occurs depends heavily on the surrounding circumstances.

Generalizations About Communication

From our discussion of communication, several generalizations emerge. The foundation for these will be more clearly apparent as you become more familiar with the information presented in the remaining chapters. The generalizations, however, will help you to integrate the material to which you will be introduced, so bear them in mind as you move forward with your study of communication:

Teaching Objective 1–6
Explore with examples the symbolic nature of both verbal and nonverbal communication.

1. Communication is symbolic.
2. Communication aims at the creation of shared meanings and influence.
3. Communication occurs in stages.
4. Communication is affected by characteristics of the participants and situations in which they exchange messages.

◼ THE RELATIONSHIP OF COMMUNICATION TO LEADERSHIP

Teaching Objective 1–7
Using an example familiar to your classroom audience, explore the nature of leadership and the importance of skillful communication to leadership success.

Depending on your own experience and interests, you may admire a famous mayor, consumer advocate, manager, or preacher. You may also admire less well-known leaders who nonetheless speak fluently and confidently about intercultural affairs, politics, society, business, or religion. Surprisingly, however, many people do not recognize the connections between communication and leadership.

Leaders of every type place communication skills at the foundation of their activity. During the early 1980s, for example, Sam Harris founded RESULTS, an international organization that keeps the pressure on politicians to support ways of reducing world hunger. At the local level, RESULTS "partners" study relevant facts and figures, practice expressing their thoughts about world hunger, and then communicate their ideas in three ways. They talk with each other in weekly meetings as well as with their political representatives, newspaper editors, and other influential people. The partners discuss world hunger at monthly meetings of local RESULTS groups. They also accept invitations to address interested classes, organizations, and other people. The underlying

Discussion Question 1–5
Who are the most important leaders in the world today? How would you describe their communication skills?

principle is that no one can successfully solve the problem of world hunger without analyzing it carefully and communicating skillfully to those in positions to do something about it. The case of RESULTS is an excellent illustration of the diversity of situations in which people in positions of leadership must depend on their communicative skills to perform important tasks.

You may not think of yourself as a potential leader, but sooner or later, you will face situations that invite you to play a leadership role by using communication skills. The Student Conservation Association (SCA), for example, is a nonprofit, educational organization that provides high school and college students—and persons who are out of school—with the opportunity to volunteer their services. Suppose you wanted to be one of the SCA volunteers who gains work experience in the management and conservation of our nation's parks, public lands, and natural resources. According to SCA brochures, communication training would come in handy. If you were interested in helping visitors appreciate Wyoming's Fort Laramie National Historic Site, good communication skills would be required. If you wanted to work in Maine's Acadia National Park, proficiency in public speaking would be desirable.

In the future, you will face situations that challenge your communication skills. You may need to take some initiative to preserve a deteriorating personal relationship. You may need to help other civic-minded people discuss available methods of controlling crime in your neighborhood or city. You may need to report on new technology to your staff or deliver a brief speech at the retirement dinner of a co-worker. In each situation, you would provide the services of a leader.

As the preceding examples suggest, leadership occurs in virtually every type of social context. In addition, the successful exercise of leadership is inextricably bound to how skillfully one communicates. In situations involving interpersonal communication, leadership may take the form of helping another person to build self-confidence, managing disputes, creating trust, and developing and improving friendships. In groups, leadership consists of such activities as establishing commitment to a task, encouraging participation, questioning poor judgment, clarifying issues, building cohesiveness, keeping members on track, and forging consensus. In the public realm, leadership frequently entails such uses of communication as proposing imaginative solutions to social problems, setting an agenda, charting a course for the future, defending causes, and mobilizing collective action.

Leadership Note 1–3
" . . . leadership: liberating people to do what is required of them in the most effective and humane way possible." (DePree, Max, *Leadership Is an Art*, Doubleday, New York, 1989, p. 1)

Ethical Communication

Because the type of influence that leadership represents can adversely affect others—often large numbers of others—it is important that we try to become ethically responsible communicators. According to Richard L. Johannesen (1990), "Ethical issues arise in human behavior whenever that behavior could have significant impact on other persons, when the behavior involves conscious choice of means and ends, and when the behavior can be judged by standards of right and wrong" (p. 1). **Ethical communication** involves the display of

Teaching Objective 1–8
Introduce the question of ethics as an integral issue in human communication.

In the Watergate scandal, former President Richard Nixon undermined his presidency and lost the trust of the nation by condoning unethical campaign tactics and then attempting to cover up the incidents.

appropriate sensitivity to the well-being of those to whom messages are directed. The ethical communicator respects the rights of others, speaks truthfully, and consciously attempts to avoid causing personal injury.

Upholding ethical standards of communication may mean that you will sometimes fail in your efforts to exercise leadership. There are occasions when such tactics as deception, damaging others' self-esteem, and using threats to gain compliance enable a communicator to have more influence than he or she would by employing ethical means. Effectiveness under these conditions, however, is usually short lived. Leaders who use communication unethically to achieve certain ends can succeed for only so long. In the end, they lose credibility, severely limit their possibilities for future influence, and sometimes destroy themselves.

The irony in unethical communication is that it is unnecessary. Enough is known about the factors that contribute to effective communication that those who use it ethically will succeed at least as often in achieving their objectives as those who resort to unethical practices. In short, unethical communication does nothing to improve the odds of successful leadership. And as many a fallen leader could testify, over time, it probably reduces them by a substantial margin. Former President Nixon is a case in point.

Discussion Question 1–6
Is it always more ethical to tell the truth? When, if ever, is dishonesty or deceit the "right thing to do" in human communication? For a succinct and interesting answer to this question, see Peck, M. Scott, *The Road Less Travelled,* Simon and Schuster, New York, 1978, pp. 62–63.

◼ WHAT YOU WILL LEARN

Take stock of your level of knowledge and skills in communication by rating yourself on each of the items in the Self- Assessment exercise. If you find yourself disagreeing or unsure (a score of 3 or less) in your responses to a third or more of the items in the exercise, you probably feel that you still have much to learn about communication. Even if you express considerable agreement (a score of 4 or 5) with most, if not all, of the items in the exercise, you will find

SELF-ASSESSMENT   **Assessing your communication knowledge and skills**

For each of the following items, choose the number between 1 and 5 that best represents your level of agreement with the statement. A *1* means that you strongly disagree with the statement; a *2* means that you disagree somewhat; a *3* means that you neither agree or disagree or are unsure; a *4* means that you agree somewhat; and a *5* means that you strongly agree.

_____ 1. I am aware of the factors that influence perception.

_____ 2. I am a good listener and seldom miss what others with whom I am communicating say.

_____ 3. I understand what language is and how it influences the process of communication.

_____ 4. I am easily able to read others' nonverbal behavior.

_____ 5. I have little trouble making and keeping friends.

_____ 6. I usually manage my conflicts with others without much difficulty.

_____ 7. I am comfortable in groups.

_____ 8. I understand the differences between problem solving and decision making in groups and believe that I know how to contribute effectively to both types of activities.

_____ 9. In a position of leadership in a group, I believe that I would know how to deal with most problems that interfere with members' ability to complete their tasks and achieve their goals.

_____ 10. I think that I am a good judge of audiences and know what will influence them.

_____ 11. I seldom have difficulty choosing subjects to talk about or identifying what it is I seek to accomplish through communication.

_____ 12. I have little difficulty finding material to help me develop my ideas.

_____ 13. I know how to organize ideas in ways that bring them clearly together.

_____ 14. My command of language is good, and I usually am able to find appropriate words for expressing my ideas.

_____ 15. I know how to use my voice, body movement, and other visual means to hold attention and to maintain interest in what I am saying.

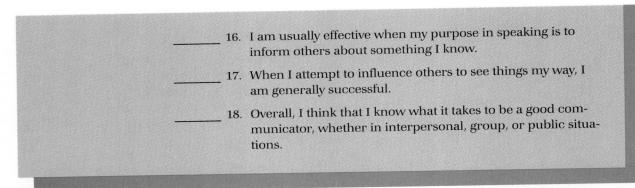

_____ 16. I am usually effective when my purpose in speaking is to inform others about something I know.

_____ 17. When I attempt to influence others to see things my way, I am generally successful.

_____ 18. Overall, I think that I know what it takes to be a good communicator, whether in interpersonal, group, or public situations.

that your self-confidence can become even greater as a result of your study of the material and completion of the exercises presented in the following chapters. No one ever succeeds in perfecting the art of communication, but all of us, no matter how skillful and knowledgeable we may presently be, can improve. The principal goal of this book is to help you achieve greater proficiency in communication, whatever your starting point.

In equipping yourself to exercise leadership through communication, there are many aspects of the activity with which you need to become familiar. In this book, we examine communication in interpersonal, group, and public contexts. You will learn how communication functions in each context and how to adjust your behavior to the requirements of various social situations in which you may find yourself.

As your study progresses, you will learn about processes that affect the production and reception of messages in formal and informal social contexts. You will become more knowledgeable about the subjects of perception, listening, and critical thinking and will develop a greater appreciation of their role in the interpretation of messages and the reactions people have to them. You will learn that communication is a symbolic process in which producers of messages use verbal and nonverbal codes to represent their ideas, thoughts, and feelings and will see how differences in codes can affect the possibilities for creating shared meanings and exercising influence. You will also learn how such factors as attitudes, motives, beliefs, values, and cultural background enter into the process.

Teaching Objective 1–9
Introduce your students to an overview of the purpose and content of the course, emphasizing connections among the areas of study wherever possible.

In addition to enlarging your understanding of communication in general, the material and activities to which you will be exposed introduce you to specific types of communicative situations and provide you with insights into how best to address the problems you are likely to encounter.

Your study of interpersonal communication will enable you to

1. be more aware of the role that personal characteristics and cultural differences play in shaping your interactions with others;
2. devise strategies for forming, building, and improving personal and professional relationships;
3. acquire information for use in making personal and professional decisions;

4. avoid and manage conflict;
5. get along with others;
6. develop sensitivity to others' concerns and needs; and
7. become more interpersonally competent.

As you move to the arena of group communication, you will

1. learn about the characteristics of groups that influence the interaction of members;
2. acquire a better understanding of how to solve problems and make decisions;
3. know what type of preparation is necessary and how to respond to difficulties that prevent groups from achieving their goals; and
4. understand the requirements of leadership in groups—in respect to both formal responsibilities and needs that arise in the process.

In your exploration of public communication, you will learn how to

1. analyze audiences;
2. prepare speeches having different purposes and for different occasions;
3. organize ideas in ways that are consistent with the purpose of a speech;
4. locate relevant information;
5. use ethical, logical, and emotional appeals appropriately;
6. develop and amplify ideas;
7. choose language that makes your ideas clear, understandable, and interesting; and
8. present speeches in a manner that holds attention and enhances your credibility.

The activities and exercises included throughout this book enable you to put into practice many of the principles discussed in the various chapters. They offer a good way to build your skills as a communicator. Knowledge of principles is important for becoming an effective communicator, but so is practice. The ultimate test of your skill in communication is not what you know, but how well you can apply what you know. We strongly encourage you, therefore, to do the exercises and to take advantage of other opportunities to develop your communication skills. Through practice based on sound principles, you will be better prepared for the realities of communication and the challenges of leadership.

■ **Summary**

Skill in communication is becoming increasingly important in an age of advanced technology and ever-increasing social problems. At every level of society, there is a corresponding need for well-educated, socially conscious, and responsible individuals who are capable of providing effective leadership. Leadership is influence exerted through communication. Being able to communicate well has implications not only for individuals' personal agendas, therefore, but also for larger social concerns.

Communication is the purposeful production and transmission of a message by a person to one or more other persons. The objectives of communication are to create shared meanings and to influence what others think, feel, believe, and do. There are several stages of communication: stimulation, motivation, generation, formation, transmission, reception, interpretation, and reaction. Message recipients reveal reactions by means of feedback. Feedback reverses the role of message producer and recipient, and thereby starts the process anew.

Communication is affected by the personal and cultural characteristics of the message producer and message recipient. Knowledge, point of view, and cultural background are among these characteristics. Situational influences also affect communication. Physical factors, the social context (interpersonal, group, and public), and the occasion contribute to the content of messages and their consequences.

Four generalizations derived from accumulated knowledge that help to integrate an understanding of communication are that it (1) is symbolic; (2) aims at the creation of shared meanings and the exercise of influence; (3) occurs in stages; and (4) is affected by the characteristics of the participants and situations in which they exchange messages.

Communication is essential to leadership. Leaders of every type place communication at the foundation of their activities. Leadership is required in interpersonal, group, and public contexts. Whether leaders succeed in their objectives depends heavily on how skillfully they use communication. Effective leadership also depends on how ethically one communicates. Ethical communication involves appropriate sensitivity to the well-being of others. The ethical communicator respects the rights of others, speaks truthfully, and consciously attempts to avoid causing personal injury. To be effective in exercising influence, prospective leaders can profit from the formal study of communication. Such study provides a set of principles that guides practice and thereby prepares one better for the realities of interacting with others and the challenges of leadership.

■ Exercises

1. Think of the worst time you can recall trying to communicate with someone else. On the basis of the information presented in this chapter, develop an explanation. Come to class prepared to discuss the incident and your account of it.

2. Think of an individual whom you admire for his or her leadership. Write down everything you can recall about the individual as a communicator. How many of these characteristics appear to account for the person's skill in leadership?

3. What is your professional goal? For the kind of position you are preparing for, identify the ways in which you may have to use communication to be successful. How many different ways were you able to identify?

4. Can you think of anyone whose communication you would consider to be unethical? In what respects was it unethical? Did anything happen to the individual because of his or her disregard of ethics?

5. If someone were to explain how communication works, what would you say? Use your answer to develop a model like the one in Figure 1.1. Be prepared to discuss your model and how it compares with and differs from the one presented in the figure.

Bramson, R. M. (1981). *Coping with difficult people.* Garden City, N.Y.: Anchor Press/Doubleday.

Bramson provides an interesting and entertaining discussion of how people in positions of leadership must often use communication to deal with "problem" people.

De Pree, M. (1990). *Leadership is an art.* New York: Dell Paperbacks.

This popular handbook illustrates, in general terms, that leadership is a role that can be learned and played by many different people.

Hackman, M. Z., and Johnson, C. E. (1991). *Leadership: A communication perspective.* Prospect Heights, IL: Waveland.

This book emphasizes communication and leadership in business organizations. However, it also includes examples of communication and leadership in other settings, such as small groups, politics, social movements, education, and the military.

Jaksa, J. A., and Pritchard, M. A. (1988). *Communication ethics: Methods of analysis.* Belmont, CA: Wadsworth.

This brief book offers a survey of leading issues in communication ethics. The authors also provide a related bibliography and thought-provoking exercises.

■ **Related Readings**

Perception and Communication

Chapter objectives

After reading this chapter you should be able to:

1. distinguish perception from sensation

2. understand that perception is a process that involves the interpretation of sensory experience

3. realize that perceptions vary considerably in accuracy

4. recognize that perceptions are tentative, learned, and selective

5. identify factors that affect perception, especially beliefs, motives, and attitudes

6. appreciate how perceptions influence communication

7. develop sensitivity to the ways that communication shapes perceptions of others and self

Key terms and concepts

perception

metaperception

empathy

anxiety

sign

symbol

stereotype

cultural stereotype

belief

motive

attitude

fundamental attribution
   error

relational message

ego-involvement

assimilation effect

contrast effect

deliberate ambiguity

labeling

Has anyone ever responded to you by saying, "We're just not communicating"? What do you think people mean when they make such a statement? Are they trying to convey the notion that you fail to see things clearly or accurately? Are they expressing the feeling that you do not understand something in a way that they believe it should be understood? Do they mean that you have neglected to notice something that most others usually do notice? Depending on the circumstances, the answer to all of these questions could be yes. When someone says, "We're not communicating," the problem often is a result of differences in perception.

Teaching Objective 2–1
Provide a basic understanding of perception and use examples to emphasize the importance of perception to communication.

As perceivers, humans vary a great deal. The fact that they do vary so much makes this aspect of human behavior a compelling subject for anyone who wishes to be an effective communicator. **Perception** is the process of determining and interpreting what we experience. As such, perception is central to the ways in which we form, comprehend, and react to messages. Whether you are speaking in public, participating in a group, or simply exchanging views with a friend, your own perceptions and those of others will affect how well you succeed. By understanding what perception is and how it relates to communication, you will be better able to avoid unnecessary problems in your interactions with others. You will also find that the ability to create favorable perceptions is a valuable asset to the exercise of leadership. The account of Chrysler President Lee Iacocca given in the Focus on Leadership box illustrates the point.

◼ THE NATURE OF PERCEPTION

Humans are perceiving beings. We make interpretations of what we experience (Gregg, 1984). On the basis of what we see, hear, touch, smell, or taste, we are able to categorize sensations (that is, what we are feeling or experiencing). Usually, the more of one's senses that are involved, the easier it is to make an appropriate interpretation. For example, if you hear a quacking sound, you are likely to believe that a duck is nearby, but not be completely certain. On the other hand, if the sound is accompanied by a visual sighting of an animal with webbed feet, a bill, and feathers, you would almost certainly interpret what you are experiencing as a duck. This suggests an important point about the nature of perception. It is a process that is affected in important ways by the amount of available information. The more information we have, the easier it is to determine what we and others are experiencing.

Possibly the most difficult types of interpretations to make with confidence in their accuracy are those involving what others are thinking, feeling, or experiencing. The nature of those decisions was of special interest to the well-known psychiatrist R. D. Laing (1967, 1969). Laing felt that a great many of the

FOCUS ON LEADERSHIP

Perception and Leadership

One of the consequences of the electronic age has been the increased importance of image. As a society, we are perhaps more image conscious than at any other time in history. Images rest, in part, on perceptions people form from visual, and other types of, information. For those who aspire to positions of leadership, image can be an important source of influence. Although leadership is much more than a matter of perception, you should not underestimate the extent to which others' perceptions can affect your opportunities to exercise it.

An excellent example of the value of favorable perceptions in leadership is the case of Lee Iacocca, former president of the Chrysler Corporation. Chrysler was on the verge of collapse at the time Iacocca took charge in 1978. To prevent this, he sought assistance from the federal government. Many legislators were reluctant to set a precedent that might bring other organizations to the public coffers. Yet Chrysler was a major corporation, and the well-being of millions of people was at stake. Assistance was eventually provided, which in no small part was attributable to the positive impression Iacocca created in testifying before Congress.

In addition, following what many people, in less than complimentary terms, referred to as the bailout of Chrysler, its dynamic president began an aggressive campaign to improve the corporation's financial position and to restore public trust. He appeared in a number of commercials and soon became something of a media celebrity. His famous "If you can find a better car, buy it" challenge to consumers conveyed the image of a person having considerable confidence in his product and his company. Iacocca's facility in speaking and his ability to describe innovations in production that Chrysler was implementing further conveyed an impression of competence. As a result of Iacocca's campaign, the organization acquired new life, and the automobile-buying public began turning attention to this company, which only months earlier had been facing financial ruin. Iacocca later used his persuasive skills shortly before his retirement in 1992 to convince consumers that Chrysler's modernization program had resulted in the production of genuinely superior automobiles. The corporation's substantial gain in market share through the first half of 1993 reflected his success.

Cross-reference 2–1
To some extent audience analysis can be understood as inferring what another is or will be experiencing on the basis of known information (Chapter 13). Metaperceptions are usually formed in response to perceived feedback (Chapter 3).

problems individuals have in their interpersonal relationships are the direct result of inaccurate perceptions of others' inner states. He used the term *metaperception* to refer to this class of decisions and reserved the term *perception* for directly observable behavior. More specifically, **metaperception** refers to

Cross-reference 2–2
Empathy is related to and develops through effective listening (Chapter 3).

Discussion Question 2–1
What is the difference between empathy and sympathy? Can the ability to empathize really be taught?

Leadership Note 2–1
Stephen R. Covey, in *The 7 Habits of Highly Effective People* (Simon and Schuster, New York, 1989), describes empathic listening as an essential tool of effective leaders (pp. 239–243).

Discussion Question 2–2
What experiences have you had with people from other cultures? What misperceptions resulted from differences in your frames of reference?

the process of inferring what another person is experiencing. You can think of this as one person's perceptions of another person's perceptions. As an illustration of Laing's basic point, have you ever had anyone ask you what you were angry about when you were not angry? If the other person persisted in asking, you may have become angry out of sheer frustration from having to repeat the denial.

What has occurred here is that the other person interpreted the cues your behavior provided from his or her own frame of reference and not yours. This is a frequent source of misperception. Our own frames of reference are often inadequate for making accurate interpretations of what others are experiencing. As a result, we may misjudge their intentions, their feelings, and the causes of their behavior.

Those who are skilled in perceiving another's frame of reference and in using those perceptions to interpret that person's behavior are empathic. **Empathy** refers to the ability to understand another person's behavior from that person's perspective (Miller and Steinberg, 1992). Efforts to develop empathy can do much to prevent breakdown in communication. For example, a public speaker who is attempting to persuade an audience to support or oppose restrictions on the production and distribution of pornography might be more successful if he or she has some appreciation of how those favoring restrictions feel about the depiction of women in such material. Similarly, a person urging a family member to seek psychological counseling might have less difficulty if he or she understands the implications seeking help has from the family member's perspective.

People's perceptions vary widely depending upon the culture in which they live. Empathy is thus an essential skill when communicating with others of different cultural backgrounds.

Current Research 2–1
For purposes of improving communicaton, it is useful to view those who are disabled or otherwise significantly different from ourselves as members of another culture with unique communicative qualities. [Braithwaite, Dawn, Viewing persons with disabilities as a culture, in Samovar and Porter, *International Communication:* A Reader (pp. 136–142). Wadsworth, Belmont , Calif., 1991.]

Efforts to be empathic are also valuable when communicating with others of different cultural backgrounds (Asuncion-Lande, 1990). For instance, in American culture, being on time is seen as a virtue. In some Latin countries, however, timeliness is treated more casually. As a result, a person from the United States might interpret a Latino's lateness for a meeting as an act of rudeness or contempt, when, in fact, the other party was simply behaving as he or she ordinarily would. It would be unfortunate if the misperception led to some insensitive comment.

This difference in perception of time is also characteristic of some cultures in the near Middle East. One of the authors recently experienced difficulty in meeting deadlines for a collaborative project with representatives of a Turkish university. In this case, patience proved to be a virtue and the deadlines were met, though a little too closely for the author's comfort.

THE STAGES OF PERCEPTION

Suppose you awake in the middle of the night aware of an object close to your bed. At first, you think it is another person, but you are not sure. The object does not move, nor does it make any noise. This leads you to conclude that what you think is there is something else. When you start to get up, it becomes apparent that the object is nothing more than a pile of clothes that the moonlight has accented in ways that create the appearance of a hunched-over person. This movement from uncertainty to certainty is typical of the way in which perception occurs. Bruner (1957) suggests that perception is a progression that has several distinctive stages. Perception proceeds, in general, from sensation to awareness to categorization to interpretation. What happens at each stage affects the remaining stages.

Sensation

In this stage, the perceiver is stimulated by sensory data. Our eyes capture some movement, an aroma activates our sense of smell, the wind picks up and blows hard against our face, and the like. For perception to occur, there must be some stimulus that activates one of our five senses.

Awareness

Reception of sensory data alone is insufficient for perception to occur. At some point, the perceiver becomes aware of a sensation. If someone were to blow a dog whistle in your presence, you would not hear the sound even though a dog might soon appear on the scene. The reason for this is that the pitch is beyond the range of the human ear to detect. Even though you would be receiving sound, you nonetheless would not be aware of the fact. For all practical purposes, then, you would perceive nothing. If the person were to blow a referee's whistle, however, you would undoubtedly be aware of the sound unless you have a hearing impairment.

Teaching Objective 2–2
Emphasize the sequential nature of the perception process.

Cross-reference 2–3
There are parallels between the stages of perception and the sequential stages of the communication process as described in Chapter 1.

Discussion Question 2–3
How do stages in the perception process coincide with the stages in the communication process?

Categorization

Once a person becomes aware of sensory data (that is, is experiencing a sensation), he or she begins to categorize the information. If you see an object at a distance, you may begin to use such categories as shape, color, and size to begin determining what it is. Such categories are often as helpful in determining what something is not as in determining what it is. If you touch something that is hot, for example, you will know that it is not ice.

Interpretation

When we have categorized the information our senses take in, at some point we are able to decide what we are experiencing. The process of perception is complete at this point (see Figure 2.1). This is not to say, however, that the interpretation will be accurate. We frequently make interpretations on the basis of insufficient information or miscategorization of it. Such deficiencies are the base of many misunderstandings and failures in communication.

In many instances, the process of perception is almost instantaneous. The greater a person's familiarity with the relevant objects, the more rapidly he or she may complete the process. We have little trouble, for example, recognizing our children, parents, and close acquaintances or distinguishing them from other people. In contrast, a person whom you have met only casually and on one previous occasion could be difficult to recognize at some future point. At least, you would be more hesitant in deciding whether you "know that person."

■ CHARACTERISTICS OF PERCEPTION

The interpretations we make of sensory experience have measurable characteristics. Three characteristics of perception especially important in communication are that they are tentative, learned, and selective.

Perceptions Are Tentative

Figure 2.1
Stages of perception.

Some perceptions are formed easily. Common physical objects seldom present us with much difficulty once we have learned what they are. Few, if any, people

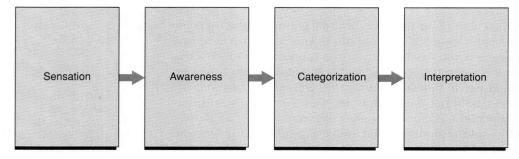

| Sensation | → | Awareness | → | Categorization | → | Interpretation |

in American culture, for instance, would be unable to recognize an automobile, football, house, or the like, unless, of course, they have some type of sensory incapacity or neurological impairment. On the other hand, a person handling a foreign currency for the first time might be very uncertain about how much money he or she has. This actually happened to an acquaintance of one of the authors. In the rush of getting from a currency exchange to an airport, the person in question was not sure whether she had given the taxi driver a $4 or a $40 tip.

As another illustration, did you ever spot an individual you thought you knew and came close to saying something like "Hi, Bob," only to hold off because you were not sure it was that person? This common experience usually occurs when we are unable to get a good look at the person. We are unable to fill all of the categories necessary for deciding who the person is. In short, we lack adequate information and, as a result, are hesitant.

Still more complicated are perceptions involving inner experiences. Up to this point, we have been talking about experiences with phenomena that are external to the perceiver—in other words, about things "out there." Not everything we experience, however, is external. Our bodies react to all sorts of internal sensations, but we do not always know the source of the stimulation. When this happens, interpretations of what we are "feeling" are hard to make. Our bodies are talking to us, but we do not always understand what they are saying.

The type of physiological arousal that experts in perception and related branches of psychology refer to as "visceral" often is of nonspecific origin. When a person has no basis for knowing what is causing a particular physical sensation, he or she may be frustrated in attempting to categorize it. **Anxiety** is the term frequently applied to arousal of uncertain cause. Of course, not all feelings we experience without understanding their cause or origin fall into the category of anxiety. A great many do not. If you have pain, for instance, you can recognize what it is without knowing why you have it.

Because we usually lack completely satisfactory information for interpreting experience, most of our perceptions are tentative to some degree. Fortunately, situational factors often assist us in determining what an internal stimulus may be telling us (Zillmann, 1978). If your heartbeat begins to escalate and your fingers are trembling in the presence of someone who is saying threatening things, you will likely interpret these physiological characteristics as symptoms of fear. If the comments are merely hostile, the symptoms may reflect anger. Immediately prior to, or during, a sexual encounter, on the other hand, a person might interpret the very same physical sensations as symptoms of pleasure.

Perceptions Are Learned

The interpretations of experience we make, especially of others' inner states, are not innate, but learned. Whether by conditioning or through repeated experience, people begin to attach particular meanings to certain signs and groups of signs. A **sign** is anything that represents something else (Eco, 1976, 1984). For instance, a tipped-over trashcan may be taken as a sign that a dog is loose in the

Teaching Objective 2–3
Describe the tentative, learned, and selective nature of perception.

Leadership Note 2–2
Robert Kriegel and Louis Patler have developed a new vision of leadership which is based upon challenging or contradicting the traditional perceptions or conventional wisdom of business. (See Kriegel and Patler, *If It Ain't Broke . . . Break It!*, Warner, New York, 1991.)

neighborhood or that some vandal has been around. It could be a sign of many other things as well, such as a strong wind, a careless driver, or the fact that the person putting out the trashcan placed it on too steep a slope for it to remain upright.

Cross-reference 2–4
The symbolic nature of language and its relationship to perception is explored in greater detail in Chapter 4.

Combinations of signs make it easier for us to determine what may be true in a given case. A lot of uprooted trees in the vicinity of the trashcan would rule out the dog and vandal theories, unless one had in mind either a very big dog or a very strong vandal. The point is that connections between signs and the things they represent are learned over time. The individual inquiring about the reasons for your anger has probably learned that some types of physical characteristics, such as tone of voice, gaze, and various facial configurations, are signs of anger. As the illustration of the trashcan suggests, however, the same signs are often indicative of more than one thing.

Teaching Objective 2–4
Explore the negative impact of stereotyping on effective interaction.

A special type of sign that is central to communication is the symbol. A **symbol** is anything we intentionally choose to represent something else. The connection between a symbol and what it represents is usually arbitrary. There is no necessary relationship between the word *chair*, for instance, and the particular object we identify by that name.

Discussion Question 2–4
What are your perceptions about the differences between women and men? Which of these perceptions are cultural stereotypes?

Once we have learned a particular connection, it becomes increasingly difficult to entertain other possibilities. Perceptions become stable. This is one of the reasons people frequently can appear to be so certain that they know what is going on in one another's minds. The same observable quality is uniformly taken as a sign of the same thing, whether appropriately or not. This type of learning, like other kinds, is difficult to undo, and some individuals become almost impervious to the possibility that their perceptions can be in error. No doubt, you have encountered a person who tells you what you are thinking or feeling and persists in his or her interpretation even though you repeatedly deny it.

Current Research 2–2
Date rape and sexual harassment are influenced by cultural stereotypes. The frequency of positive results of forced kissing in television broadcasts is explored in Larson, Stephanie Greco, Television's mixed messages: sexual content on *All My Children*, *Communication Quarterly*, Spring 1991, pp. 160–161.

Stereotypes.   Perceptions that are resistant to realistic change often result in the formation of stereotypes. A **stereotype** is a fixed view of the common characteristics of the objects in a class of objects that ignores individual differences. A **cultural stereotype** is a fixed view of a group of people, united by some common characteristics, that disregards differences among the members. Cultural stereotypes are frequently unfavorable. One of the more insidious aspects of cultural stereotypes is that information about a single individual is often generalized to entire groups of people. Racism and sexism are examples of the result. Symptomatic of cultural stereotyping is the flurry of Japan-bashing by some government officials and representatives of the automobile industry that occurred over trade practices in the early 1990s.

Discussion Question 2–5
How might the selective nature of perception be a factor in cases of date rape or sexual harassment?

Cultural stereotypes can affect people's self-image and concept. Others' perceptions of us can begin to affect the ways in which we view ourselves. If a person is consistently treated as if he or she possesses some undesirable set of characteristics, that person may, over time, begin to exhibit those characteristics. (See Chapter 4 for a discussion of the harmful effects of racist and sexist language.)

MASTERING COMMUNICATION SKILLS

Combating Cultural Stereotypes and Other Misperceptions

At one time or another, nearly every one of us has been guilty of misunderstanding or hurting others because the perceptions we formed were false. Similarly, at some point we have all used a cultural stereotype to describe a group of people. (Recall that cultural stereotypes result from the tendency to see all members of a particular group of people as having the same characteristics.) Misperceptions of all kinds, including cultural stereotypes, result from the nature of perception itself—the fact that perceptions are tentative, learned, and selective. But we cannot leave it at that. The following are ways that you can improve your ability to form accurate—and fair—perceptions:

1. *Consider whether you have enough information to form an accurate perception.* Have you formed an impression of others based solely on one or two sources of information? Does your perception need to be changed on the basis of additional information or changing conditions?

2. *Check the accuracy of your interpretation of the signs and symbols used to form your perception.* Could these signs and symbols signify meanings other than the ones you have assigned to them?

3. *Consider your focus of attention.* Has your perception been formed on the basis of only a few features of an object, person, or idea? What might you have missed that could alter your perception?

As constructive communicators, one of our major tasks is to overcome the damage done by stereotyping. This task is particularly crucial for those in positions of leadership. A school administrator, for instance, may have to break down certain perceptions of school board members about the conscientiousness of teachers before he or she can convince them of the need for a proposed salary increase. The coach at a school with a history of losing may have to overcome a defeatist attitude in order to get the members of an athletic team to perform to their potential. In the United States, a great deal of the emphasis in the civil rights and women's movements has been on the breaking down of cultural stereotypes and on convincing members of these groups that they need to alter the concepts of self that stereotypic portrayals have frequently contributed. (See the Mastering Communication Skills box.)

Current Research 2–3
Likewise, if people are consistently treated in positive ways, positive changes in self-image and behavior can result: " . . . it is fundamental that leaders endorse a concept of persons. This begins with an understanding of the diversity of people's gifts and talents and skills." (DePree, Max, *Leadership Is an Art,* Doubleday, New York, 1989, p. 7)

Arbitrary Versus Nonarbitrary Learning.   In some types of learning, connections between signs and what they signify are nonarbitrary. In other words, there is some natural or obvious relationship between a sign and what it represents. If we almost always hear a barking sound come out of a dog's mouth, the barking sound alone eventually becomes a sign for a dog. When we hear a bark, then, we have good reason to believe that it is a dog producing it, although the reality might be that some person is imitating a dog. Nevertheless, when the learning of signs involves nonarbitrary connections to what they signify, a person's perceptions are likely to be reasonably accurate a good percentage of the time.

In other instances, the connection between a sign and what it signifies is arbitrary. By convention, we learn to take some things as signs of other things to which they have no necessary or natural relationship. It is the learning of these types of signs that we find particularly problematic for perceptions involving others' inner states and, in many instances, even our own. The discussion of stereotypes is a case in point. Problems such as the formation of stereotypes are more likely when the learned connections among signs and groups of signs are arbitrary.

Even when the signs we use in forming perceptions appear reliable, they can nevertheless lead to the wrong interpretations. This possibility is well illustrated in Walter Van Tilburg Clark's classic novel, *The Ox-Bow Incident* (1940), in which three innocent people are hanged as a result of erroneous conclusions drawn from several seemingly indisputable signs of criminal activity.

Perceptions Are Selective

None of us can attend to everything about an object of perception simultaneously. Some characteristics stand out more than others. As a result, what we perceive, in large part, is determined by our focus of attention. If you doubt this, try the following exercise. Ask several of your friends to identify whose picture is on the face of a one-dollar bill. We predict that most will say, "George Washington," and they will be correct. Then ask what color the face of a dollar bill is. We predict that most will say, "Green," but they will be wrong. The face of a dollar bill is gray and beige. Money is so frequently described as green, or "green stuff," that the color of the face of a dollar bill is not something on which most of us focus. We do focus on the picture of the person who appears on the face, however, because, among other things, we want to avoid giving someone the wrong denomination. We attend to the numbers on bills for the same reason, but since the numbers designating value appear several times, they are less an object of focus.

Again, if you want to test this assertion, ask your friends how many times the number *1* appears on a dollar bill and where it appears. If your experience is consistent with ours, you will find very few who say, "Eight times, once in each corner on the front and back sides," which is the correct answer.

If there is such inattentiveness to something as common and simple in appearance as a dollar bill, you can imagine how much we miss when the object of perception is considerably more complex and less familiar. How much does one fail to notice, for example, in watching a person give a thirty-minute speech, gossiping about a common acquaintance, or while being robbed? In the latter case, you might find it interesting that more and more evidence has begun to cast doubt on the value of eyewitness testimony in criminal proceedings because it is so frequently inaccurate (Loftus, 1979).

Because perceptions are selective and observers tend to focus on only a few features of an object of perception at any given time, two objects having those particular features in common can be easily confused. More than one person has spent time in prison because of misidentification by an eyewitness who noticed only some prominent features of the actual criminal that were highly similar to those of the unfortunate suspect. The Alfred Hitchcock movie *The Wrong Man* explores the true story of a musician to whom this very thing happened.

FACTORS AFFECTING PERCEPTION

Because perceptions are learned, it follows that factors affecting learning also indirectly affect perceptions. The most significant of these are beliefs, motives, and attitudes. The term **belief** refers to a person's feelings about what is true. A **motive** is the reason behind an action that causes an individual to behave in a particular way. Finally, an **attitude** is the inclination a person has to evaluate objects of perception favorably or unfavorably. Beliefs, motives, and attitudes all affect interpretations of what we experience (Fishbein and Ajzen, 1975). A few illustrations may serve to show how such factors indirectly influence perceptions.

Teaching Objective 2–5
Explain the influence of the factors of belief, motive, and attitude on perception.

Beliefs

In 1989, the issue of flag burning received considerable attention. President George Bush went on record in support of a constitutional amendment pro-

Our beliefs, motives, and attitudes influence our perceptions. If we believe that the flag is the embodiment of our country's values, we may well react negatively to its destruction.

Discussion Question 2–6
In what specific ways and situations do your moral beliefs affect how you perceive and judge the actions of others?

hibiting this and other acts he considered forms of desecration. A person with strong beliefs about what it means to be patriotic might perceive an act of flag burning, or more specifically, the person performing it, in a highly negative manner—as evil, hateful, undesirable, contemptuous, and the like. On the other hand, a person who believes that the flag is only a symbol, that the material from which it is made has no special significance in itself, or that its destruction does nothing to what the flag symbolizes, more than likely would perceive the act differently. He or she might see a flag burner as foolish, lacking in understanding, or possibly pathetic. Some would even see the person as heroic.

Motives

Cross-reference 2–5
Misperceptions resulting from differences in beliefs, motives, and attitudes are a common cause of communication difficulty in intercultural communication. See Chapter 6.

Like beliefs, motives influence perceptions. A new car may somehow appear better when we are in need of one than when we are only looking. Food smells and tastes better when we are hungry than when we have just eaten. A superior can seem more threatening to an employee seeking advancement in an organization than might be true if the employee is well satisfied with his or her present position. A quiet roommate appears to be much nicer if a student needs to study for an examination than if he or she wants to talk about a personal problem. We could continue listing examples, but these are sufficient for our purposes. Motives arise from needs and focus on the reduction of these needs or their satisfaction. Depending on the motivational state, a person's judgment of the very same object can vary considerably.

Attitudes

Finally, attitudes may affect perceptions. If you dislike a person—that is, evaluate him or her largely in unfavorable terms—you are more likely to see that person's behavior differently than would someone who has a favorable attitude. You might see a person you like as competent, considerate, intelligent, thought-

Table 2.1
Key Aspects of Perception

1. Perception is more than sensation.

2. Perception involves the interpretation of experience.

3. Perception occurs in stages and progresses from sensation to awareness to categorization to interpretation.

4. Perception varies in accuracy.

5. Perception is tentative.

6. Perception is learned.

7. Perception is selective and moves toward stability.

ful, and outgoing. On the other hand, if you dislike the person, you might view exactly the same behavior as reflecting incompetence, inconsiderateness, dullness, lack of thoughtfulness, and aloofness. Teachers have sometimes received evaluations from students in the same class that have ranged from highly favorable to highly unfavorable, even though all the students, objectively speaking, were exposed to the same behavior.

The preceding discussion has introduced you to many facets of the complex phenomenon of perception. Table 2.1 summarizes the key ideas.

HOW PERCEPTION INFLUENCES COMMUNICATION

Perception influences both the production and reception of messages. In the first case, it affects what message producers say and how they say it. In the second case, perception affects how those who receive messages assign meaning and react to them.

Influences on Message Production

Suppose that you are sitting in your dorm room preparing for an examination, and you hear a knocking sound coming from the direction of the door. The knock invites a number of responses, such as "Yes," "What?", or "Come in." Now suppose that the knocking is very loud. This might irritate you and lead to your framing one of the responses in a hostile manner. Even though the person doing the knocking may simply have been trying to ensure that you have heard him or her, a previously learned interpretation of loud knocking as the sign of a person who is offensive or obnoxious leads you to respond in a way that reveals your irritation.

Influences on What Is Said. The situation described above, or one like it, is something most of us have experienced at one time or another. Such experiences serve to illustrate an important point: The reality we perceive is the one on which we act. Perceptual reality strongly influences the messages we produce. Nowhere is this effect more evident than in the motives and intentions we assign to other people (Heider, 1958). The tendency to misassign intentions to others' behavior is what some scholars refer to as the **fundamental attribution error** (Nisbett and Ross, 1980). In the example of the person knocking on your door, the loudness of the knocking would lead many of us to think the person responsible was trying to be obnoxious.

Other examples may reinforce the point. A teacher sees a student yawn during a lecture and feels compelled to ask, "Are you bored or something?" An employee receives a lower raise than expected and complains to his or her boss, "I know you don't like me, but I find this raise insulting." A person impatient to have dinner says to a date, "Do you want us to get there just in time for closing?" A corporate executive blames low productivity on deliberate indiffer-

Cross-reference 2–6
The importance of an understanding of beliefs, motives, and attitudes is essential to audience analysis, i.e., to predicting how and what an audience will perceive (see Chapter 13).

Teaching Objective 2–6
Describe the impact of perception on the production, reception, and interpretation of messages.

Cross-reference 2–7
Fundamental attribution errors are common in intercultural communication situations (see Chapter 6).

Current Research 2–4
Common rhetorical devices within Arab culture include exaggeration and overassertion. American cultural standards could result in misperceiving these standard communication practices as excessive boasting and intentional deceit. (Samovar and Porter, *Communication Between Cultures,* Wadsworth, Belmont, Calif., 1991, pp. 156–157.)

Current Research 2–5
"Koreans in intercultural situations often come across as seemingly agreeing with their foreign communicators when in reality they are merely showing sympathy for the foreigner's position. A statement such as 'I understand the position you are in, and I'll do my best,' while accepted by the foreigner as a commitment, often is a polite way of saying 'I cannot do it.'" Park, Myung-Seok and Kim, Moon-Soo, Communication practices in Korea, *Communication Quarterly*, Fall 1992, p. 400.

ence of employees and sends out a strongly worded memorandum about disloyalty to the company. Finally, a person who has just been insulted by a friend responds, "I know you didn't mean that."

In each of these cases, perception of the other party's intention or motive could very well be inaccurate. Once the perception has formed, however, the person assumes that it is correct. Reactions in the first four cases could do much to injure relationships. They might even escalate to the point of conflict. In the final case, since the misperception isn't a disparaging one, it might not further damage the relationship, but the failure to recognize that the insult is deliberate could make the target appear naive, foolish, or even stupid.

These kinds of perceptions are not the only ones that affect the production of messages, however. The perception that something is threatening may cause you to express fear. The perception that you have benefitted from another's behavior may lead you to express appreciation. The presence of some particularly noticeable feature of an object may result in your commenting on it. (Children are particularly apt to announce in public something they have noticed about another person or object at times when their parents would prefer that they not share their perceptions.) These are but a few of the ways in which perceptions can affect the content of messages communicators produce.

Influences on How Messages Are Framed.   In using the expression *how a message is framed,* we are not exclusively, or even primarily, concerned with such qualities as tone of voice or fluency. Framing also has to do with one's choice of language. For example, the words *Yah* and *Hello* both have the same content when one is answering the telephone. *Yah,* however, is a more likely

Our perceptions influence how we receive messages. If we admire Sugar Ray Leonard, for instance, we are more likely to endow the product he endorses with positive qualities.

choice when one finds the ring bothersome than would probably be true if he or she were eagerly awaiting an important call.

As a more extensive illustration, suppose that you perceive one of your superiors as a very self-important, directive person—the type who is used to getting his or her own way. Suppose further that as a subordinate you are aware that you are expected to comply with your superior's requests, so long as they are appropriate to the professional relationship, of course. Suppose still further that the superior is in a position to make noncompliance punishing. Finally, suppose that the superior has made a request; for instance, "Would you run downstairs and get last month's sales report, please?" Despite the inclusion of "please," you nevertheless interpret the request as an order. Somewhat resentful, you still manage an acceptable response, for example, "Yes, sir," or "Yes, ma'am." If your perception of the person and the request were different, your response might be more casual: "Sure, why not," "I'll be glad to," or "Gotcha."

All four of the ways of indicating compliance in our example have the same content. What distinguishes them as messages is the manner in which they are framed. The responses convey what some writers (e.g., Fisher, 1979; Millar and Rogers, 1976) refer to as relational messages. A **relational message** is one that reveals something about how a communicator feels about the person with whom he or she is interacting. In the first instance, the message suggests obedience to authority, whereas the last three suggest a cooperative relationship.

Perceptions, thus, are important both to what we say and how we say it. There is yet another side to the perception-communication coin, which has to do with how perceptions influence the reception of messages.

Influences on Message Reception

Communication involves the transmission of symbols. As communicators, we choose symbols (usually words and specific nonverbal indicators) to represent our thoughts and feelings (Burke, 1966). These symbols are taken as signs of what the message producer means to say. In a very real sense, the message in a communicative transaction is always one the receiver constructs from his or her interpretation of the symbols that a message producer transmits. Depending on how the receiver assigns meaning, his or her reactions will differ. Clearly, perception has a great deal to do with this process. Specifically, perception affects the assignment of meaning and the reactions that follow.

Influences on the Assignment of Meaning.   Have you ever wondered why celebrities so frequently appear in advertisements and commercials? For some reason, the association of the celebrity with a product we are being urged to purchase makes the product, perceptually speaking, different from what it is when associated with someone else.

Many years ago, the psychologist Solomon Asch (1948) attempted to account for the apparent power of prestigious sources in changing attitudes. After studying the problem, he came to the conclusion that it is not attitudes that change. Instead, it is the object of perception that changes. In other words, when a well-

Discussion Question 2–7
Imagine that in one day your parent, your significant other and your neighbor's five-year-old child all told you they loved you. How would these differing "sources" of the same message affect your interpretation of their meaning?

known athlete urges us to eat a particular brand of cereal, for instance, we see the cereal as more attractive, nourishing, etc. From the perceiver's point of view, the cereal the athlete is promoting is not the same one someone else is selling. Because we view the celebrity's cereal in more favorable terms, we assign a different meaning to the message urging us to purchase it. In short, the product is a good thing to buy. Because the source of a message affects perceptions of it, the celebrity's characteristics may have a great deal to do with the effects of the message.

The assignment of meaning to messages is also affected by characteristics of receivers. One of the most important of these factors is called **ego-involvement**. When we say that a person is ego-involved, most of us mean that he or she has a strong interest in something or firm beliefs about it. If you think the president of the United States is either an effective leader or a failure and cannot see merit in any position other than your own, you would be highly ego-involved (Sherif, Sherif, and Nebergall, 1965). At least you would be highly ego-involved insofar as matters relating to the president are concerned. If you view either of the previously mentioned positions as your own, but do not feel terribly committed to it (that is, you accept less extreme positions), you are probably not ego-involved.

In their research on the subject, Sherif, Sherif, and Nebergall identified two ways in which ego-involvement may lead to distortions in perception. They used the labels *assimilation effect* and *contrast effect* to refer to these types of distortion. An **assimilation effect** occurs when we view a position in a message as closer to our own than it actually is. If you like auto racing and report that a friend of yours doesn't think racing is much fun to watch when, in fact, what the person has actually said is, "I hate racing," the type of distortion the report reflects is assimilation. A **contrast effect** occurs when we view the position in a message concerning some matter as more distant from our own than it actually is. Interpreting the statement "Racing is not much fun to watch" as "She hates racing," is an example of a contrast effect.

Cross-reference 2–6
Reflective listening is the best protection against distorted meanings. See Chapter 3.

Assimilation occurs more frequently among those who are low in ego-involvement, whereas contrast is more characteristic of those having high ego-involvement. In either case, the message to which one assigns meaning is distorted, and depending on the degree of distortion, the message receiver's reactions will vary.

Influences on Reactions. Whether distortion in perception of a message comes about as a result of producer or receiver characteristics with which it is linked, people's reactions can be affected in important ways. Try to recall the last argument you had. Did you find yourself saying things like "That's not what I meant," "What I am trying to say is . . . ," or "Why are you always putting words in my mouth?" The argument might have started from something as innocent as your saying, "Why don't we watch television?" From your point of view, you have simply made a suggestion about how to spend time. From the respondent's perspective, the comment represents a decision, which may prompt a response, such as "Why do we always have to do what you want to do?"

Distorted perceptions may sometimes work to the message producer's advantage. To use two of our previous examples, when people see the cereal promoted by an athlete as being better than it actually is, or perceive a speaker's views about the president as closer to their own than they actually are, the advertiser or speaker is in a stronger position to influence their judgment and behavior. Since ambiguity increases the scope for assignment—and misassignment—of meaning, a tendency to be vague when clarity might elicit a negative reaction is sometimes recommended as a communication strategy. The strategy is called **deliberate ambiguity.** Deliberate ambiguity is frequently evident in the public statements of elected officials on such issues as abortion and tax increases. In general, however, there is little evidence suggesting that distorted perceptions aid effective communication. More likely, they work to the communicator's disadvantage. If your purpose is to be understood, misperception does not help. If your purpose is to influence, you may succeed, but not necessarily in the way you would like. For example, former President Ronald Reagan's vagueness on his involvement in the Iran-Contra affair did much to tarnish his public image in the 1980s (Mayer and McMannus, 1988).

Discussion Question 2–8
When would be an appropriate occasion to utilize the strategy of deliberate ambiguity?

When another person misperceives what you are saying or what you are urging him or her to think, feel, believe, or do, you may succeed only in irritating the person, creating antagonism, encouraging conflict, building resistance, or even driving him or her in a direction other than the one you intend.

In an article entitled "The Abilene Paradox: The Management of Agreement," J. B. Harvey (1974) tells the story of a family who took a long, uncomfortable trip to Abilene one Sunday afternoon only to discover later that no one had wanted to go. How can something like this happen? Apparently, one member of the family asked if anyone was interested in going to the city. The others interpreted the question as reflecting a wish to make the trip and one another's silence as agreement. Consequently, all took part in an action of which none individually approved.

In another illustration of how misperception can influence receiver reactions, a parent expressing concern about a child's performance in school may be seen as badgering. Rather than recognizing the real motive, the child feels put upon and chooses to show resentment by performing even more poorly. Similarly, the way in which concern about the responsible use of alcohol is expressed by college administrators might be viewed as an attack on the rights of students. Rather than listening, some might be apt simply to dismiss the concern as one more symptom of "old-fogeyism."

The type of situation our last two examples represent can be explained in terms of Brehm's (1966) theory of psychological reactance. According to Brehm, when an individual perceives his or her freedom of action to be threatened, that person will take steps to preserve it. Resistance may take the form of changes in attitude and behavior opposite to those sought by the source of attempted influence. When this occurs, we say that a message has boomeranged. Requests, expressions of hope, and stated wishes often have the appearance of threats to a message receiver's freedom—for example, the statement "I wish you wouldn't do that" can be taken as a not-so-disguised command. When these kinds of

Figure 2.2
Functons of
Perception in
Communications.

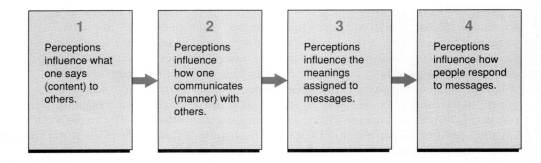

1	2	3	4
Perceptions influence what one says (content) to others.	Perceptions influence how one communicates (manner) with others.	Perceptions influence the meanings assigned to messages.	Perceptions influence how people respond to messages.

messages are misperceived, they are unlikely to have the effect one intends. At least, they are not likely to have the desired consequences so long as the target of influence sees him- or herself as having the ability to withstand the perceived threat.

We have seen how perception influences what message producers say and how they say it. We also have considered the ways in which perceptions affect message reception in respect to the assignment of meaning and receiver reactions. Figure 2.2 provides a summary of the main points. While this is a large part of the story about communication and perception, it is not the whole story. Just as perception influences communication, communication influences perception. The relationship is reciprocal.

HOW COMMUNICATION CAN INFLUENCE PERCEPTION

Since humans cannot attend to all of the features of an object of perception, their interpretations of what they experience are necessarily limited. The properties of the object themselves have a significant impact on what we attend to and how we categorize it. Intensity (for example, brightness and loudness) helps focus attention. Movement is another such factor. Still another is contrast. You are more likely, for instance, to notice the first tree that changes color in the fall than the ones surrounding it.

As important as qualities such as these are, they do not fully account for what we perceive at any given time. Important for our purposes are three roles that communication plays: (1) focusing attention; (2) providing categories for the interpretation of experience; and (3) creating associations among categories.

Teaching Objective 2–7
Convey the reciprocal influence of communication on perception in the areas of focused attention, provision of categories for interpretation, and the creation of associations among categories.

Focusing Attention

If you have had training in public speaking prior to the course you are now taking, you might recall your instructor's urging you to become more animated, to use more gestures, to vary your pitch and rate more, or to regulate and adjust your volume. Why do you think he or she made these suggestions? You were probably not doing enough to establish yourself as a focus of attention. After all, in any speaking situation, we compete for attention with a host of other elements; for instance, others in the vicinity, the thoughts they are experiencing, external noise, and the like. Your instructor was offering advice about how to use nonverbal behavior to secure and hold your audience's attention.

At a verbal level, we also influence perceptions by leading others to focus on particular aspects of an object of perception. If you and an acquaintance were visiting a zoo, and your friend, in passing the elephant's cage, said, "Would you look at the honker on that beast!", you would probably focus on the elephant's trunk, rather than, say, its size, color, or odor. Of course, you might come to notice the other attributes, but for the moment you would be perceiving the elephant disproportionately in terms of only one of its features.

So far, we have been speaking of cases in which the object of perception is present. Remember, however, that humans are symbol users and contribute to the creation of perceptions on the basis of the symbols they choose. How one person describes another you have never seen, for example, leaves you with an image of that person. How accurate the image may be will be determined in large part by how selective the person providing the description has been and how closely his or her meanings correspond to yours. Note that we are assuming that the message producer is not deliberately trying to mislead. If he or she were, then the test of accuracy is not the correspondence of the perception with the actual characteristics of the object in question, but with the perception the message producer would like the receiver to have. Ironically, perceptions in cases involving intentional misrepresentation may be more accurate in this sense than those stemming from efforts to be realistic.

Providing Categories for the Interpretation of Experience

Another important way in which communication affects perception is by providing the categories with which people interpret sensory and cognitive experience. You may have been in a situation in which you observed someone behaving in a manner that you interpreted as friendly, but of which others appeared to have a different impression. They might have regarded the behavior as "phony." If so, then you had learned to use a different set of categories for interpreting what it was that the person's overt behavior signified. It is also likely that you acquired these categories from other people, who in one way or another told you what friendliness is and what the signs of it are. Similarly, those who had a different perception probably learned through their interactions with others that behavior of the kind they observed reveals something other than friendliness.

By what criteria do you determine whether someone is friendly? You probably make the judgment from observations of what the person does or says in particular sets of circumstances. Perhaps the person smiles when he or she is speaking. He or she may make inquiries about others' and your well-being, such as "How have you been," "How's the family," or, "Hey, what's happening?" Possibly, the person always answers questions that you and others raise,

Leadership Note 2–3
A vital leadership responsibility, as discussed by Peters, DePree, and others, is the need for leaders to articulate a vision of the mission and goals of a business, in effect focusing the attention of their people on a direction and aim.

whether they be casual or somewhat personal. When you observe such signs, or combinations of them, you refer them to several categories and select the category that fits best. In this case, the category is called friendliness. You were not born with such a category lodged in your mind, however. Rather, you learned it. You probably learned it from hearing others label as friendly people who say and do the sorts of things mentioned above.

When different categories are used for labeling the same characteristics of an object, perceptions vary. If smiling, asking about others, and being responsive to questions are behaviors to which people of your acquaintance typically assign the label "phony," all other things being equal, you too would probably begin to interpret such behavior as signs of phoniness.

If the process we have been describing amounted to nothing more than attaching labels to what we perceive, it would not matter a great deal what categories we use. Perceptions, in effect, would be the same. Unfortunately, our categories do make a difference. A "friendly" person strikes us as different from a "phony," and we interact differently with each type as a result. Similarly, we like people, including ourselves, better if we see them as "curious" rather than as "nosy." Communication provides the categories people use in perceiving themselves, others, and the world in which they reside. In this way, we literally "construct" much of our reality (Berger and Luckman, 1966).

As with stereotypes, how someone is labeled can affect his or her self-concept. **Labeling** is the process by which individuals develop a self-concept from the terms others use to describe them. The old adage that "names can never hurt you" is simply not true. If others consistently refer to you in unfavorable terms, the labels may begin to stick. In anger, a parent may refer to a youngster as "good for nothing" and, thereby affect his or her sense of self-worth. Adolescents can be particularly cruel in applying such labels as "nerd," "dweeb," "weenie," and "jerk" to acquaintances. In so doing, they not only hurt the target's feelings, but may also damage his or her self-concept.

Creating Associations Among Categories

Closely related to creating categories for our perceptions is a third role that communication plays in the process of perception. That role has to do with the ways in which messages link categories to shape larger perceptions.

In the past few years, the United States's relationship with the countries comprising the former Soviet Union has undergone substantial change. Whereas early in the 1980s our image of the Soviet Union was generally unfavorable, by 1990 the image was quite different. And with its subsequent breakup, our image has changed even more dramatically. Gestures by the constituent nations indicating a desire to become part of the world community have been largely responsible for this change in perception. Communication affects perceptions either directly or indirectly by associating categories we use to interpret information we receive about objects of perception.

Direct Associations.   All objects of perception have numerous properties. In talking about them, however, we seldom have occasion to mention more than a

Discussion Question 2–9
How many words do you know to describe a promiscuous man? To describe a promiscuous woman? How are these "categories for the interpretation of experience" different and/or the same?

Current Research 2–6
The impact of labeling on stepmother/stepchild relationships has been documented by several sources described in "The Power of Personal Narrative: Stepmothers and Stepdaughters" by Pamela Cooper, presented at the Central States Communication Association Convention in Chicago in April 1991.

few. A friend of yours, for example, may be (1) abrasive, (2) hard working, (3) unfriendly, (4) skillful, (5) aloof, (6) prompt, (7) inconsiderate, and (8) energetic. Notice that we have listed these characteristics in a pattern. Beginning with the first one, every other attribute refers to a quality most people would be apt to consider as negative. Beginning with the second one, every other quality appears to be positive. In talking about your friend, if you referred only to his or her negative qualities (the odd-numbered items) or only to his or her positive qualities (the even-numbered items), others' perceptions of the person obviously would differ according to the subset you chose. In fact, a person you exposed to only one subset would probably conceive of an entirely different individual from the one envisioned by someone who'd been exposed to only the other subset.

It is this type of selectivity that occasionally results in surprise when we actually encounter a person or thing someone else has described, even if the descriptors chosen have been completely accurate. Only rarely do we have the experience of recognizing immediately someone or something another has described to us. Our perceptions, then, are strongly influenced by those characteristics of an object of perception that a message producer has selected and linked in particular configurations.

In the example above, suppose you describe your friend as abrasive and hard working. In this case, you have selected one positive and one negative attribute. Had the positive attribute been "prompt" instead of "hard working," it seems likely that the message receiver's perception of your friend would be less favorable. In other words, "abrasiveness" has greater weight in determining a message receiver's perception when linked to some attributes than when linked to others. It strikes us that an abrasive, hard-working individual will be viewed more favorably than one who is abrasive and prompt because hard work is more highly valued than promptness. We could be wrong in our assumptions, of course, but if we are correct, these examples serve to illustrate our point concerning the direct influence of communication on perception through the linkages among attributes and characteristics of objects of perception it establishes.

This knowledge can be important to a person who is trying to exercise influence. If you were leading a group discussion in which a proposal being considered was not popular, for example, you might have a better chance of changing other members' perceptions if you were to link the proposal to qualities they valued. A proposal that is "beneficial," for instance, would be more appealing than one that will merely "work."

Indirect Associations.   The second way in which communication affects perceptions by linking categories involves associations that are already in the minds of message receivers. Particularly instructive in this respect has been the scholarship of Robert S. Wyer, Jr. and Donald E. Carlston (1979). These theorists have called attention to the fact that people have existing associations among words they use. For instance, the adjective *good* tends to be associated with others that have favorable connotations, such as *desirable, worthwhile, effective, moral,* and *dependable.* If someone were referred to as a "good person," the

Table 2.2
Effects of Communication on Perception

1. Communication helps focus the attention of perceivers.
2. Communication provides categories for the interpretation of experience.
3. Communication creates *direct* and *indirect* associations among categories.

adjectives in the preceding list that probably would have the most relevance are *moral* and *dependable*.

From Wyer and Carlston's perspective, mention of the term *good* in speaking of a person would likely evoke the other two adjectives we generally associate with a person's being good even though the source of the message does not mention them. To describe Mary, for instance, as a good person is also to project an image of her as moral and dependable. It could be the case, however, that the message producer does not regard Mary as an especially dependable person. Despite this fact, he or she has nonetheless contributed indirectly to the message receiver's perceiving her as precisely that.

Perception thus has a tremendous amount to do with how messages are understood and acted upon (Table 2.2 summarizes the principal types of influence). Awareness of this fact will help you function more effectively as both a message producer and a message receiver. Remember too that in important ways, functioning effectively in different communicative contexts is what leadership is all about. To this end, how your communicative behavior affects perceptions can have an important bearing on how well you can function as a leader.

Check your understanding of the concepts introduced in this chapter by completing the Self-Assessment exercise.

Summary

Perception is the process by which we determine and interpret what we experience. Accuracy of perception depends heavily on the amount and type of information the perceiver has available. Some perceptions form more easily than others. Particularly problematic for communication are perceptions of what others are experiencing. Metaperception is the process by which one infers others' inner states and is frequently a source of communication breakdown. Empathy is a quality characteristic of individuals who are capable of viewing and interpreting others' behavior from the perspective of the person observed.

The process of perception occurs in stages and generally progresses from sensation to awareness to categorization to interpretation. Three aspects of perceptions that are important for communicators to know are that they are tentative, learned, and selective. Perceptions are tentative because we usually lack sufficient information for achieving certainty about what we are experiencing, especially in the case of internal sources of arousal, such as anxiety. In addition, we determine and interpret what we experience on the basis of combinations of

SELF-ASSESSMENT   **Self-test of key concepts**

Write the letter of the term in the top list that best fits each description in the list below.

    A. anxiety

    B. assimilation effect

    C. contrast effect

    D. deliberate ambiguity

    E. ego-involvement

    F. empathy

    G. fundamental attribution error

    H. labeling

    I. metaperception

    J. perception

    K. perceptiveness

    L. relational message

    M. sign

    N. symbol

_____ a state of arousal of uncertain origin

_____ a tendency to see another's position as further from one's own than it actually is

_____ the ability to understand another person's behavior from his or her own perspective

_____ the tendency to believe that the consequences of others' behavior are always intentional

_____ a thing that is intentionally chosen to represent something else to which it has no necessary connection

_____ the interpretation of what another person is experiencing

_____ the process by which individuals develop a self-concept from the terms others use to describe them

Answers: A, C, F, G, N, I, H

signs and symbols and associations among them. Associations are learned and over time become resistant to change. Learned aspects of perception can give rise to the sort of misjudgments represented by stereotypes, which, in turn, can affect the self-concepts of those to whom they apply. Finally, limits on the perceiver's ability to attend to all aspects of an object of perception simultaneously make perception necessarily selective. Selectivity can affect the accuracy of interpretations of what one is experiencing.

Perceptions are also influenced by beliefs, motives, and attitudes. How one interprets what he or she experiences can be strongly affected by previously formed feelings about what is true, the motivational state that exists at the moment of stimulation, and prior tendencies to evaluate objects of perception in favorable or unfavorable terms. In each case, distorted perception may be the result.

The relationship between communication and perception is reciprocal. Perception enters into both the production and the reception of messages. It affects what we choose to say (content), the way in which we frame it (manner), the meanings we assign to messages, and our reactions to them. The characteristics of both the message producer (for example, prestige) and the message receiver (for example, ego-involvement) affect perception of messages and how receivers therefore react to them. Common types of perceptual distortion include the misassignment of intentions to others' behavior (fundamental attribution error) and the tendencies to see the positions in messages as closer to (assimilation effect) or further from (contrast effect) one's own than they actually are. Misperception is a root cause of misunderstanding—and when messages have effects other than the ones intended, some type of misperception is usually involved.

Communication influences perception by focusing attention on certain aspects of objects of perception, by providing categories for the interpretation of experience, and by creating direct and indirect associations among these categories. As a result of these influences, perceptions are frequently distorted and limit a communicator's potential to achieve desired outcomes. These same influences, however, can shape perceptions in ways that are consistent with a communicator's intent.

The effects of perception on communication and of communication on perception have implications for the level of understanding communicators achieve, their possibilities for exercising influence, and the quality of relationships they develop. Awareness of the basic aspects of perception and the ways in which they relate to communication is important for successful interaction with others, as well as for the exercise of leadership.

Exercises

1. Ask a friend to describe what someone you both know looks like. How many different categories does he or she use in providing the description? What are they? Are there any you would have included that your friend neglected to use? Do you think someone hearing the description would be able to recognize the person in question from a photograph? Why or why not?

2. Have several of your acquaintances draw a picture of the American flag from memory. How many include the correct number of stars and stripes? Of those who do, how many make the correct placement of the stars and stripes?

3. Try to recall a situation in which someone has accused you of deliberately doing something that you considered to be accidental; for example, running a stop sign. Did the other person accept your explanation, or did he or she persist in the feeling that your behavior was deliberate? Come to class prepared to share the experience.

4. Think of a person you met for the first time and discovered was not at all like what you had expected. Write a short essay in which you attempt to account for the discrepancy between your expectations and your experience.

5. Ask several people to draw the outline of a one-dollar bill to exact size without looking at one. Ask several others to do the same with a twenty-dollar bill. Compare the two sets of drawings. Are there any noticeable differences in size? Are the dimensions close to the standard size of an actual bill? If you find differences between the sets or in comparisons with an actual bill, how do you account for them?

Related Readings

Harvey, J. H., and Weary, G. (1981). *Perspectives on attribution processes.* Dubuque, IA: William C. Brown.

> Harvey and Weary provide a useful discussion of the factors that influence judgments of the causes of observed behavior. The material provides a basis for understanding important sources of misperception.

Kleinke, C. L. (1975). *First impressions: The psychology of encountering others.* Englewood Cliffs, NJ: Prentice Hall/Spectrum.

> The author discusses characteristics of the perceiver and person perceived that are central to the formation of impressions.

Littlejohn, S. W. (1989). *Theories of human communication* (3rd ed., chs. 3, 6, 9, 10). Belmont, CA: Wadsworth.

> Littlejohn reviews a number of different theories of perception and the role communication plays in shaping perceptions, especially of other people.

Raven, B., and Rubin, J. Z. (1983). *Social psychology* (2nd ed., ch. 3). New York: Wiley.

> Raven and Rubin present an excellent overview of the nature of perception as both a physiological and a cognitive phenomenon.

Schneider, D. J., Hastorf, A. H., and Ellsworth, P. C. (1979). *Person perception.* Reading, MA: Addison-Wesley.

> The authors explore the personal and social factors that affect perceptions of others and impression formation.

Listening and Critical Thinking

Chapter objectives

After reading this chapter you should be able to:

1. describe why listening is a crucial component of the communication process

2. differentiate listening from hearing

3. explain the three steps in the listening process

4. describe several steps listeners can take to improve message reception and retention

5. list the different types of listening and their purposes

6. explain several listening problems and describe the positive listening behaviors that can be used to overcome them

7. explain the nature of reflective listening and describe several skills that can be used to enhance your reflective listening ability

8. distinguish critical thinking from listening

9. apply critical thinking skills in assessing the credibility of messages

Key terms and concepts

listening

hearing

phatic communication

cathartic communication

informative
   communication

persuasive
   communication

evaluative listening

reflective listening

selective listening

egocentric listening

paraphrasing

critical thinking

message credibility

plausibility

consistency

source reliability

verifiability

It's Thursday night, and the last episode of a TV miniseries is wrapping up six hours of tightly woven plot and characters. It's been some of the best TV you've seen in quite a while. The murderer is about to be uncovered, and her motives revealed. You hear a knock at your door.

"Come on in. It's open," you shout. "Hi Gail, have a seat." She enters and sits, while your eyes jump from her to the TV.

"Hi, how are ya?" asks Gail.

"Fine."

"Anything good on TV?"

"Oh, it's just that miniseries, 'Evil Intentions.'"

Though he had fallen in love with her, Inspector Benton knew that Carol was the only one who could have tipped off the mob. She also must have been the one who killed the sergeant and his wife.

"Is it any good?"

"Yeah, it's not bad."

Benton knew she was in the office, and he also knew she had a gun. There was no doubt she knew how to use it.

"Hey, I'm sorry for interrupting, but I was wondering if I could get your advice on something?"

"Yeah, sure. What is it?"

Carol had feelings for Benton. He could tell that. The question was, would her instincts for self-preservation dominate her affection? She had the gun, but could she pull the trigger when he was on the receiving end of that deadly .38?

"It's me and Craig. It seems like we're always arguing. I don't know what the problem is."

"Uh huh."

Carol had to kill Sergeant Taylor. He was blackmailing her, threatening to turn her in. But why kill Taylor's wife? Was it just to lead the investigation in another direction? Could she be that cold blooded?

"It's at the point where I'm just thinking of breaking it off. I mean, what's the point of being in a relationship if we're just going to make each other unhappy?"

"Yeah, uh huh."

Benton opens the door. Carol is behind the desk, in the shadows. Her hands are in her lap. He's sure they're not empty. But he enters anyway. He needs an explanation.

"Does Craig ever talk to you? I don't know what he's feeling."

"Huh."

"Oh hell. I don't know why I bother. I'll just tell him it's over. It's probably what he's thinking anyhow."

"Yeah, sure. Whatever you think is best."

"Look, I gotta go. I'll see you later."

She'll give Benton an explanation. She owes him that. Meantime, she can decide what to do. She hasn't decided yet.

"Okay, see you later. Bye now."

"Mind if I sit?" asks Benton. "I think we have some things to talk about." . . .

The plot line of "Evil Intentions" is certainly predictable, but the story behind the skill of listening may be a bit more surprising. We're not suggesting that TV is more important to you than your friends, but, more than likely, you have found yourself in situations like this, in which competing demands are put on your listening abilities. Listening is a vital communication skill. As the example illustrates, there is also a difference between hearing and listening. No doubt, you heard what Gail was saying to you about her relational problems, but the scenario suggests that you may not have been listening. The miniseries you were watching intently was hindering your ability to listen carefully. A number of factors can enhance or hinder listening ability. In addition, there are several common problems associated with inappropriate listening. We tried to display the problem of pretending to listen in the example above. Listening is a skill, and, like other skills, there are techniques available to improve your listening ability. Later in this chapter we discuss "reflective listening," a type of listening that is done quite poorly in the preceding example.

In this chapter, we begin by noting the importance of listening as part of communication and as a practical skill. The final section of the chapter introduces the subject of critical thinking. To participate effectively in the process of communication, you must not only be able to interpret messages and assign meanings to them but also be able to determine whether the claims are credible. Critical thinking is a skill that enables you to make such determinations. In our treatment of it, we discuss what critical thinking is, why it is important, the consequences of deficiencies in it, and how to use it more effectively. Coupled with what you will learn in this chapter about listening, your understanding of critical thinking will prepare you for judging how best to respond to messages you receive in a variety of communicative situations.

THE IMPORTANCE OF LISTENING

Listening is an often-overlooked part of communication. Many scholars would argue that communication is, by nature, a social event. In other words, communication is what happens between people. It is not merely what one person does. By this definition, a person talking by him- or herself in a room would not be communicating, since the message would not be received by anyone. Thus, without the act of listening, communicating does not occur.

Obviously, there are other ways to be a communication "receiver." You can read a letter, or watch someone use hand signals and still be a receiver. People who are deaf communicate by means other than listening. For those with hearing, however, listening is the dominant means of receiving messages. Listening is a widely used skill, perhaps the most widely used of all our communication skills. According to Ross (1987), 75 percent of the waking time in most individu-

Teaching Objective 3–1
Emphasize the importance of listening as an overlooked, much-needed, teachable skill which is critical to successful communication.

Discussion Question 3–1
How much of your time was spent listening yesterday? How much training in listening have you received for all you do?

Figure 3.1
Percentage of
Communication Time
Spent Listening. (After
R. S. Ross, *Speech
Communication,* 7th ed.
(Englewood Cliffs, NJ:
Prentice-Hall, 1986.)

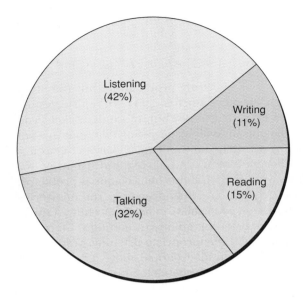

Listening
(42%)

Writing
(11%)

Reading
(15%)

Talking
(32%)

Leadership Note 3–1
"In short, the true leader is
a listener. The leader listens
to the ideas, needs, aspirations, and wishes of [oth-
ers] and then . . . responds
to these in an appropriate
fashion." (James O'Toole in
DePre, May, *Leadership
Is an Art.* New York:
Doubleday, 1989, p. xix)

*Recognizing the link between
listening and productivity,
many companies include
listening training in their
formal employee training
programs.*

als' lives is spent communicating. As shown in Figure 3.1, we spend most of that
time engaged in listening (42 percent of all time engaged in communicative
behavior is spent listening, compared to 32 percent for talking, 15 percent for
reading, and 11 percent for writing).

Another reason for studying listening is that it is a skill in great demand in
the professional world. Research indicates that on average listeners work at
only 25 percent listening efficiency (Wolvin and Coakly, 1982). This low level of

FOCUS ON LEADERSHIP

Listening and Leadership

Some people mistakenly assume that when it comes to leadership, communication flows in one direction—leaders just give orders, and subordinates follow them blindly. Not only doesn't this fit reality, it also falls short of what is desirable and effective. Effective leaders must be skillful listeners. The goal of the effective leader is not simply to dictate whims and preferences to others. The effective leader must coordinate resources, react to changing situations, and respond to the needs of subordinates. None of this is possible without the crucial ingredient of effective listening skills.

Leaders must often work in a dynamic, constantly changing environment. The resources at his or her disposal (economic, personnel, material, etc.) are constantly changing. Leaders can't be everywhere, so it is necessary that others provide feedback on the status of various resources and goal attainment. The leader must therefore listen to know what is going on.

Leaders cannot simply call themselves good listeners and then ignore the information coming from followers. Nor should information providers be held responsible for giving bad news. Sherman Okun (1975) suggests three features of a good listening environment. He suggests that followers must

1. know what their leaders need to hear;
2. be given the chance to provide the information; and
3. feel assured that the leaders can accept the information in a way that will not discourage disclosure of even bad news.

In addition, leaders must deal with followers as human beings and not just as resources or sources of information. This involves reflective listening, which we discuss later in the chapter. There really is no such thing as an effective leader who is not a good listener.

Current Research 3–1
Much corporate communication training is focused on listening. Beliefs held by many corporate personnel include that listening is important to organizations, that listening skills are deficient, and that training improves listening skills. (Wolvin, Andrew D., and Coakley, Carolyn Gwynn. A survey of the status of listening training in some Fortune 500 corporations. *Communication Education,* April, 1991, pp. 152–154.)

Current Research 3–2
Research by Wheeless, *et. al.,* found a relationship between behavioral receptivity (good listening skills) and communication satisfaction and attraction. Good listeners, in other words, are well-liked and allow others to feel satisfaction in the interpersonal relationships they share. (Wheeless, Frymier, and Thompson, A Comparison of Verbal Output and Receptivity in relation to attraction and communication satisfaction in interpersonal relationships. *Communication Quarterly,* Spring 1992, pp. 102–115.)

listening efficiency can lead to inefficiency, waste, and even dangerous working conditions. As a result, effective listening has become a highly prized skill in the business world. Its importance has encouraged a number of top corporations to include listening training in their formal employee training programs. (See the Focus on Leadership box.)

Later in this chapter we will discuss specific ways in which you can improve your listening behavior. First, however, we define the nature of listening, particularly the difference between listening and hearing.

THE LISTENING PROCESS

Cross-reference 3–1
The complex realities involved in understanding verbal messages will be explored more fully in Chapter 4.

As with many aspects of communication, listening is taken for granted. Unless a problem arises, we seldom look closely at it. Upon investigation, however, you'll see that listening is a fairly complex process, which should not be mistaken for the process of hearing alone. Listening is an *active* process. When you are listening, you are not just acting as an audio sponge, soaking up the information that comes to you. Instead, you actively seek some audio stimuli, while ignoring others. Furthermore, listening involves the active process of interpretation, through which you assign meaning to aural stimuli. We can consider **listening** as attention to sounds and speech patterns, identification of signals and symbols, and comprehension of aural messages.

HEARING VERSUS LISTENING

Teaching Objective 3–2
Clarify the difference between hearing and listening with questions and examples.

Discussion Question 3–2
How many conversations have you heard or overheard today that you didn't really listen to?

In everyday conversation, people often confuse hearing with listening. Although they are closely related, an important distinction emerges: **Hearing** is a physiological process—a process of the brain's awareness of outside acoustical energy, which is picked up and transmitted by the ear to the brain. Listening, however, is defined as a cognitive (thought) process—one that begins with attention to stimuli, usually sounds or speech patterns. Listening involves identification and processing of signals and symbols and ends with comprehension (Heinich, Molenda, and Russell, 1989). That is, some assignment of meaning is involved. As Timm (1983) has stated, "The 'cocktail party effect' provides a good example of the difference between hearing and listening. At a cocktail party, there are usually several conversations going on simultaneously in the same room. Everyone present at the party is aware of these conversations in that they can be heard. On the other hand, we usually have to make a conscious effort to listen" (p. 258).

According to Timm, listening is different from hearing because it is a higher-order thinking process that allows us to *attach meaning* to the acoustic signals and symbolic patterns presented to our minds. One process is entirely physiological (hearing), whereas the other (listening) is entirely cognitive or mental. Interestingly, the mental or cognitive aspects of listening will not occur without hearing, yet the ability to hear in no way ensures that one has the ability to listen. Thus, if someone were speaking a language with which we were completely unfamiliar, we could hear what the speaker said, but we would be unable to listen since we would not be able to assign meaning to the symbolic patterns in the unfamiliar language.

STEPS IN THE LISTENING PROCESS

Teaching Objective 3–3
Describe and examine the three steps in the hearing process.

Listening occurs through a sequential process that involves three steps: *hearing, attending to the message,* and *interpreting*. A number of problems or shortcomings can occur at any of these stages that can prevent accurate listening from

critic may write, "*The Teenage Blood Fiends* is a poor excuse for contemporary entertainment. The editing and directing are crude, the sets are obviously cheap, and the acting is stiff, at best. The only redeeming feature of this movie is the promising acting of Sally Tatum as the mad scientist's daughter." Of course, the movie publicist will drop the negative aspects of the review and highlight in the movie's ads that "critics hail Sally Tatum as a promising new star"!

Other components of context include, but are certainly not limited to, the relationship between the interactants, the past history between them, and the physical setting in which the message is sent and received. As a listener, you must be aware of the larger picture, or context, because it will often aid your interpretation.

Cross-reference 3–3
Compare the discussion of context here with that presented in Chapter 1.

Understand the Speaker's Purpose.

Imagine that you've met your friend Pat, who asks you, "So, what are you doing this weekend?" Your reply will probably depend on how you perceive Pat's purpose. Why is the question being asked? Is Pat going to ask you for a date? Is help needed at a local candidate's campaign office? Perhaps Pat is just making conversation to find out how you are. Your interpretation of Pat's question will depend on your perceptions of her purpose.

Understanding the speaker's purpose is necessary for effective listening. Though it would be impossible to list every possible speaker purpose, we can provide a group of broad categories that illustrates the range of purposes. **Phatic communication** involves the sharing of emotions and communicating to socialize. "Small talk" is often cited as a prime example of phatic communication. If Pat was just asking about your plans for the weekend to touch bases and see how you've been, this would be phatic communication. Sometimes we share information in order to elicit emotional support and understanding, a purpose known as **cathartic communication**. Imagine that your friend Diane approaches you with her complaints about her biology class. If she were seeking your support regarding the difficult time she's having in her class, she would be engaged in cathartic communication. Sometimes we simply exchange information, by either providing or requesting information. This is referred to as **informative communication**. Finally, we also try to influence others, suggesting a course of action for others to follow. This we call **persuasive communication** (Floyd, 1987).

Teaching Objective 3–5
Describe and give examples of the range of speaker purposes.

Discussion Question 3–7
How much of your day-to-day communication would you estimate is: phatic, cathartic, informative, and persuasive?

Focus on the Organization and Arrangement of the Message.

Message interpretation can be aided if you can assume that the speaker has arranged or organized the message according to a standard pattern. You might not be able to make this assumption in everyday conversation, but when you listen to a speech or formal presentation, it is likely that the message will follow a recognizable pattern. Focusing on the language cues or organizational patterns through which a speaker arranges messages gives listeners insight into the message's key points. These organizational patterns include climactic arrangements (those that build to a conclusion) versus anticlimactic arrangements (those where the conclusion is stated or already known at the beginning of the

Cross-reference 3–4
Patterns of message organization will be discussed fully in Chapter 15.

Teaching Objective 3–6
Describe the types of listening and delineate the different needs and goals of each.

message), general to specific, problem to solution, number to number, space to space, and pictorial visualization. By recognizing the pattern, the listener can anticipate the main points, get a clearer sense of the whole picture being presented, and generally listen more effectively.

The processes of hearing, attending to, and interpreting collectively form the process of listening. A breakdown at any of these three junctures hinders listening. In addition to investigating these three processes, it may be useful to recognize that there are different types of listening, and that each type may require various skills in order for the listener to be effective.

▣ TYPES OF LISTENING

Few people are surprised to hear that there are different types of listening. Listening to a comedy routine is different from listening to a lecture, which are both different from listening to a political debate, and all these are different from listening to a friend who needs to discuss a personal problem. They primarily differ in the amount of cognitive effort you have to bring to the listening situation. Some listening requires more effort and concentration.

Listening for Enjoyment

This is probably the easiest type of listening. In most instances, watching a movie, viewing a TV show, going to a concert, hearing a comedy routine, or taking in a good storyteller all involve listening for enjoyment. You listen to gain appreciation, or just for the pleasure of sensory stimulation. Your focus is not necessarily on remembering the information. Instead, you are trying to enjoy the moment. Listening for enjoyment is pleasurable and does not generally put great demands on your attention.

Listening for Information

Listening to a lecture in a college course is an example of listening for information. Your primary goals in this type of listening are understanding and retention. This requires more focus and effort than listening for enjoyment. Key terms need to be understood, and it may also be useful to take notes to aid retention. Notice how difficult it can be to understand a lecture and retain the information if you are tired, restless, or unprepared to put some effort into your listening.

Though the college lecture provides a clear example, there are many other instances in which listening for information is vital. If the clerk at the hardware store begins to explain how you should connect the washer you are buying into your faucet at home, you must understand and retain the instructions in order to use that information effectively at home. This type of listening also places a burden of clarification on the listener, a burden that is less important in listening for enjoyment—that is, if the explanation of how to connect a washer or the lecture on speech introductions is not clear, there is a burden on the listener to ask for clarification. You cannot be an effective listener in these situations if you fake understanding when something is not clear.

Evaluative Listening

Imagine that you're planning to vote in a statewide election next week, but you haven't decided which candidate would make the best governor. You decide to listen to the televised debate between the candidates. Tuning in, you quickly realize that this type of listening is not easy. **Evaluative listening** is listening that depends on critical thinking. You have to comprehend what the debaters are talking about, judge their ability to construct effective arguments with clear claims and evidence, and then balance their stances against your personal beliefs about what makes a good governor.

Evaluative listening is more difficult than the preceding types mentioned because of the need to think critically. In addition, you also must apply a personal set of standards to make a judgment. If candidate Jones argues that the state government needs to lure more businesses to the state, and provides fig-

---

← *Listening for enjoyment is the least demanding of the four different types of listening we perform. Viewing a TV show such as "America's Funniest Home Videos" is an example of listening for enjoyment—if you like the program!*

SELF-ASSESSMENT   **Adapting your listening approach**

Not all listening is the same. Test this proposition. Select a class in which the instructor lectures most of the time. Over a three-class period, enter the class with different listening goals. On the first day, listen for enjoyment (you might want to have a friend take particularly good notes that day so that you can pick up any information that will later be on an exam). Minimize your note-taking, and listen as though you were hearing someone tell a story. On the second day, listen for information. This is the type of listening you would normally engage in during a lecture. Take notes. Listen for comprehension. Define key terms. Ask for clarification when necessary. On the third day, listen for evaluation. Go to class with a set of evaluative criteria for what makes a clear, well-organized lecture (for example, transitions, examples, etc.). As you listen to the lecture, ask yourself whether the instructor is meeting the criteria. After you've listened to all three lectures, sit down and determine whether you picked up different types of information as a result of the different approaches you took to listening.

ures to support this claim, you must weigh the arguments. In addition, knowing that business is sometimes lured by relaxing environmental protection standards, you may also apply a personal standard that protection of the environment is of primary importance. Hence, while you may believe that Jones argues her points well, you might vote for the other candidate because he takes a stronger environmental stand.

There are numerous situations where you will engage in listening for evaluation. Product advertisements and sales pitches are constantly being sent your way. One way to deal with them is to ignore them. Another is to listen critically. If you are shopping for an expensive item, such as a car or computer, you may take the time to listen critically to the arguments of salespersons. Evaluative listening requires effort and concentration. Complete the Self-Assessment exercise.

Current Research 3–5
It is important to learn to set goals for listening as we often do for speaking; goals set should specify the desired end, the specific conditions, and the way results will be measured. (Roach, Carol, and Wyatt, Nancy. *Successful Listening*. New York: Harper & Row, 1988, pp. 39–44.)

Reflective Listening

Sometimes referred to as "supportive listening," "listening to help," or "therapeutic listening," reflective listening requires considerable personal investment. **Reflective listening** is listening to help others deal with personal problems or concerns. Restating what the other person said, to give him or her a sense of support and understanding, is a typical part of the reflective listening process. The experience of discussing a personal problem with a friend is quite different from listening for enjoyment, information, or evaluation. To be an effective reflective listener, you must hear the other person out and provide emotional

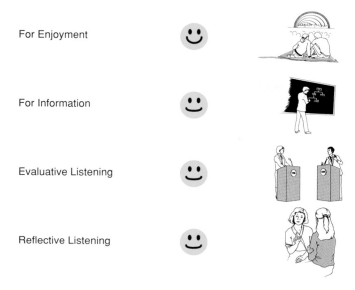

For Enjoyment

For Information

Evaluative Listening

Reflective Listening

Figure 3.2
Types of Listening.

support. While the previous three types of listening focused mainly on message interpretation (a process that takes place within an individual), reflective listening is also concerned with the feedback and support that the listener gives to the speaker (a process that occurs between people). Figure 3.2 summarizes the different types of listening.

RECOGNIZING COMMON LISTENING PROBLEMS

Letting "Thought Speed" Outrace Listening Speed

Communicators speak on the average of between 100 to 150 words per minute. Listeners, however, can comfortably absorb spoken information at the rate of 400 words per minute. Because we can listen with such speed, two universal problems occur. First, we often don't use the excess time available to us productively. Instead, we daydream or allow ourselves to be distracted. The second common problem is that we take no mental or written notes. Characteristically, poor listeners suffer both of these problems.

Teaching Objective 3–7
Develop student awareness of common listening problems.

Faking Attention

This listening error manifests itself as several different, yet related, listening disorders. One problem involves faking attention. We do that when we use the appropriate verbal reinforcers, such as "I see" or "Yeah, that's interesting." Our minds, however, are elsewhere. By the time most students enter eighth grade, they are virtual experts at displaying behaviors that suggest that they are paying attention to the teacher, when, in fact, their minds are occupied by other things.

Discussion Question 3–8
How many of these listening problems do you recognize as a frequent part of your own listening habits?

Allowing distractions to interfere is a common listening problem among children and adults alike.

Allowing Distractions to Interfere

Another listening problem occurs when we allow distractions to prevail. Examples include giving in to the conversation across the hall, focusing on the weather, being distracted by the speaker's dress and appearance—anything except focusing on the message.

Listening Only to Easy Material

Giving up on "boring" or "difficult" material is the listening disorder of "tuning out" speakers and their messages for fear that they will be "too tough" or "too dull." This behavior, of course, limits our opportunity to gain insight from what might have been an important message. It's a mistake to assess too early the merit of the material before thoroughly listening to it.

Becoming Overstimulated

Another type of listening problem comes when listeners are *too involved* in the speaker's message. This phenomenon is known as *overstimulation*—reaching a "fed up" point while the speaker is still presenting material, thereby dismissing the rest of the message. If a professional career counselor visited a high school English class to discuss career opportunities and after discussing TV broadcast journalism, found that a third of the class could not recall any of the other career paths mentioned, he or she might conclude that they were overstimulated by the thought of becoming network anchorpersons—with the result that a substantial portion of the class simply ignored the rest of the career opportunity message. Information that triggers a listener to become deeply involved in the subject at hand presents a danger of absorbing all the available mental energy, leaving none for listening. Be alert to the tendency to get sidetracked into your own thoughts by something the speaker mentions.

Selective Listening

Similarly, some listeners fill in the gaps. That is, they mistakenly believe they know enough about the speaker's subject to "add what's missing" or finish the thought on their own. Listeners who indulge in mentally inserting their own information in place of the speaker's often come away with a message that is vastly different from the one presented (see Figure 3.3). **Selective listening** refers to the tendency to rationalize or support your own existing beliefs by ignoring opposing positions. We may ignore some points made by a speaker instead of postponing judgment in an effort to better understand the opposition's views.

Egocentric Listening

Another listening problem comes not from under- or overstimulation, but from an egotistical point of view. **Egocentric listening** occurs when the message receiver concentrates more on him- or herself than on the incoming message. This self-centeredness allows the listener to believe that other people have nothing important to say. This is also referred to as the "me-first phenomenon." This type of egocentric listener is not interested in what others have to say. He or she is not interested in dialogue. Rather, this "listener" only wants an audience to provide him or her with the required undivided attention.

A second type of egocentric listener can be characterized as "the Judge." She or he listens only for details and facts, rather than the communicator's main ideas. Furthermore, this type of listener is quick to judge the individual facts with no attention to the broader arguments made. She or he might try to

Cross-reference 3–5
The egocentric listener corresponds to the conversational narcissist referred to in *Current Research* note 3–4.

Figure 3.3
Selective Listening.

Skilled listeners understand the value of providing speakers with nonverbal reinforcers such as eye contact and responsive facial expressions.

help explain the speaker's information with "what you should have done . . . " or "what your data really mean . . . ," even though the speaker was not asking for assistance.

The third variety of the egocentric listener is the "insensitive listener." This person just can't wait to express his or her ideas. When you're faced with an insensitive listener, it's important to avoid any hesitation between sentences. The insensitive listener takes any pause as a cue to interrupt the speaker. Rather than wait his or her turn, this type of listener cuts the speaker off and either fails to remember or ignores the basic courtesy of acknowledging the worth of the speaker's words.

■ POSITIVE LISTENING BEHAVIORS

Teaching Objective 3–8
Emphasize positive listening behaviors and how they can be developed.

One effective way for responsible communicators to improve listening skills is to compare the listening problems discussed in the sections above with the following checklist of positive listening behaviors. Generally, positive behaviors are the direct opposites of the problems mentioned. But even more important, notice how the basic tenet of *active listening* differs from the comparatively passive approach that is associated with many of the listening problems.

A Checklist of Positive Listening Behaviors

The checklist that follows offers a series of characteristics displayed by successful, active listeners. Each suggestion can help you enhance your listening skills. You must recognize, however, that listening behaviors are resistant to change. If you really want to improve your listening ability, these suggestions should be practiced frequently and deliberately.

Prepare to Listen at the Appropriate Level.   We mentioned earlier that there are different types of listening, and that they differ in the amount of effort required by the listener. This can be very useful knowledge. It suggests that you need to prepare to listen at the appropriate level. Being the easiest, listening for enjoyment does not require excessive preparation. However, if you know that a situation requires listening for understanding, you will need to be prepared accordingly. It will be useful to be rested, alert, and focused, and it might also be helpful to have a pencil and paper to take notes to ensure later recall of the information. Listening for evaluation requires the same level of alertness and focus as listening for information. In addition, it is useful to have your standards of judgment or evaluative criteria in mind. You can be sure that when your teacher for this class listens to your speeches, he or she is thinking of the areas you are evaluated in (for example, eye contact, quality of introduction, etc.) and a standard for distinguishing relative effectiveness in these areas. Listening for evaluation requires that these judgmental standards be considered ahead of time.

Think ahead and consider the type of listening that is expected of you. If you cannot be properly prepared, try to compensate in other ways. If you've been up all night studying for a big exam, it's unlikely that you'll be able to listen for information very effectively the following day. You might compensate by having a friend take very thorough notes on a class that you know you won't be able to listen effectively in.

Provide Nonverbal Reinforcers.   Another way you can be a more effective listener is to provide useful nonverbal reinforcers to the speaker. Most speakers tend to be at ease and can communicate more effectively when they are treated and received courteously. Give the speaker reasonably sustained eye contact, provide responsive facial expressions (such as head nodding and smiling when appropriate), offer supportive silence while the speaker collects his thoughts, and occasionally give verbal reinforcers, such as "yes . . . uh huh . . . I see," to give the speaker a sense of confidence. Even if you are actively listening, avoid excessive slouching, shifting, or other distracting nonverbal behaviors. Signal to the speaker that you are attentive through your nonverbal cues.

Use "Thought-Speed" Advantage.   We mentioned earlier that you can listen at a rate much faster than the rate at which the average person can speak. As a result, you have spare time available with which to organize what you are hearing. You can improve your listening ability if you use that spare time to your advantage. For instance, in a public speaking situation, in which you can presume that the message is organized according to a recognizable organizational pattern, you can try to identify the pattern and make a mental outline of the message. Be able to identify and repeat the speaker's main ideas.

Whether you are in a formal speaking situation or in ordinary conversation, you can take some further steps. Try to paraphrase the speaker's points. Also, listen for the emotions as well as the words. If someone says, "I was asked if I'd like to take an early retirement," did the speaker sound bitter, happy, or uncertain, or was another emotion present behind the message?

Leadership Note 3–2
Leaders must create listening environments that offer a safe forum, well-equipped listening places, feedback, listening training, and frequent opportunities to listen. Peters, Tom, *Thriving on Chaos,* New York: Harper & Row, 1987. pp. 366–370.

Leadership Note 3–3
"Effective meeting leaders are active, attentive listeners." (Hackman, Michael Z. and Johnson, Craig E., *Leadership: A Communication Perspective.* Prospect Heights IL: Waveland Press, Inc., 1991. p. 129)

Figure 3.4
Positive Listening
Behaviors.

Positive Listening Behaviors

LISTEN AT THE APPROPRIATE LEVEL	Identify the type of listening and respond accordingly
PROVIDE REINFORCERS	Provide eye contact, responsive facial expressions, and verbal reinforcers
USE "THOUGHT-SPEED" ADVANTAGE	Identify and organize speaker's main ideas
STRUCTURE THE ENVIRONMENT TO ELIMINATE DISTRACTIONS	Focus on speaker; minimize physical barriers

With the spare time, you can also try to think more critically. Be flexible as you begin to process and retain the speaker's message. Take a few notes. Ask yourself if the speaker has any hidden agenda or unspoken motives. How does one thought connect to another in the message? Can you generate a personal response to the speaker that differs from that of the rest of the audience? Adopt the perspective of a detective. Try to learn as much about the speaker, subject, and situation as you can. Avoid focusing on nonessential details. Look for the big picture. What is really important to the speaker?

Discussion Question 3–9
How could we structure or restructure this classroom environment to eliminate distractions?

Structure the Environment to Eliminate Distractions. Remember that listening is a highly demanding activity, so make the environment work for you. Control or eliminate distractions as much as possible. Focusing on the speaker, giving eye contact rather than staring out a window, is an example of a necessary first step. Try to minimize physical barriers if possible. Many students recognize that a good way to maximize listening focus, particularly in a class that is difficult to pay attention to, is to sit in the front row of the classroom. It can also be useful to contemplate the information in the message after you can separate yourself from possible distractions. Set aside some time and, if possible, a place to reflect on the message after the fact.

All these positive listening behaviors (summarized in Figure 3.4) will help you to process, comprehend, and retain information more effectively. There is another type of listening, called reflective listening; it requires attention to social skills that go beyond the processing of information.

■ REFLECTIVE LISTENING SKILLS

Although the skills required for appreciative, informative, and evaluative listening are useful here, reflective listening is somewhat distinct and requires mastery of additional skills. Think back to the opening example in this chapter. You were watching a TV miniseries, and your friend, Gail, came to talk to you about some relational problems she was having. In this situation, she was looking for a friend to engage in reflective listening. No doubt, you have an intuitive sense of what reflective listening is by now, and we briefly defined it earlier by distinguishing it from listening for enjoyment, information, and evaluation.

Defining Reflective Listening

Your main purpose as a reflective listener is to hear the other person out—to act as a sounding board. A friend needs to talk about relational troubles. A co-worker is having trouble dealing with the boss. Your mother is having trouble relating to your brother or sister. When you engage in reflective listening, you attempt to help someone you know work through a personal problem by listening and providing feedback.

This basic listening process has been called by several different names. For instance, it has been referred to as *active listening* (Rogers and Farson, 1977). We have argued that all listening is essentially "active" in the sense that a listener has to be mentally active to interpret messages. The difference here is that a reflective listener has to be socially active (by providing supportive feedback) as well as mentally active. Another term used to describe this listening behavior is *therapeutic listening* (Wovin and Coakley, 1982), since it resembles the type of listening that a therapist might use in a counseling session. Other terms used include *listening to help*, since you are trying to help a person with his or her problems, and *empathic listening*, since it is useful to empathize, or put yourself in the other person's place, in order to engage in this type of listening effectively.

Regardless of what it is called, the need for reflective listening arises when a person needs to talk to someone else about a personal problem. No doubt, you realize that some people are better listeners than others. Consider your own life. When you have a personal problem that you want to talk to someone about, whom do you turn to? What type of listening skills does that person use? What about the other people or friends whom you may consider close, but would not seek out for this type of listening? What do they lack, or what do they do, that would make them undesirable as reflective listeners? Not everyone is equally adept at this skill. We can suggest some of the common problems associated with bad reflective listening, and provide some correctives to these problems.

Reflective Listening Problems and Correctives

The following list of problems associated with reflective listening should not be viewed as comprehensive, but rather as an attempt to capture the more prevalent problems in this area.

Being Inattentive. We attempted to capture this problem in the opening example of the chapter: A friend wants to discuss a relational problem, but

Leadership Note 3–4
Female leaders in Helgessen's research used listening both as a tool to gather information that had bearing on managerial decisions, and as a way of making the people in their organizations feel that their ideas and beliefs were of value. Helgessen describes one female leader, Frances Hesselbein, who "viewed listening as a discipline that lay at the very heart of her kind of leadership." (Helgessen, *The Female Advantage: Women's Ways of Leadership.* New York: Doubleday Currency, 1990, pp. 242–243)

you're too wrapped up in a TV show. This inattentiveness is a fairly common problem associated with reflective listening. It is a problem for a number of reasons. Inattentiveness is a hindrance to any type of communication, but could be a more serious problem here. When people want to discuss a personal problem, they are revealing themselves and making themselves vulnerable to rejection. Not receiving attention could be considered an even more severe rejection than being disagreed with. When we are inattentive, we are indirectly saying that "your problem isn't worthy of time or consideration." Inattentiveness is also a problem because personal problems are often emotionally charged. In order to deal with the problem at the emotional level and provide effective support and feedback, we have to listen carefully to what is said.

The key to improving in this area is to make a conscious effort to provide effective verbal and nonverbal feedback. As we'll suggest in a moment, your task as a reflective listener is not to solve the other person's problems, but rather to hear the person out. Thus your feedback should consist primarily of prompting, encouraging moves, not evaluative statements. To prompt and encourage the other person to talk and express him- or herself, you use simple verbal and nonverbal cues. It is surprising how much can be accomplished with a head nod, a simple "uh huh," or a rephrasing of what the other person said. In addition to such prompts, you also want to use verbal and nonverbal cues to show that you are paying ongoing attention. Maintaining reasonable eye contact is crucial for you to indicate attentiveness. Again, you begin the process by indicating that you're paying attention, and that you're willing to hear the other person out.

Evaluative Feedback.   Your ultimate goal as a reflective listener is to get the person with the problem to solve it for him- or herself. You do this by encouraging the person to talk through the problem, exploring it thoroughly. There's a natural tendency in conversation to share evaluative comments. "How'd you like the movie?" "It was pretty good, but I didn't like the ending." "Yeah, I know what you mean." Everyday conversation is largely based on such evaluative statements. Unfortunately, this strategy will hinder the other's self-exploration of a problem when the goal is to talk through a personal problem. Evaluative feedback leads to "telling the other what to do," which, as we will see momentarily, is a further hindrance to effective reflective listening. Instead of helping the other to explore the problem, the two of you may get caught up in arguing back and forth about the facts of the problem. That's fine in a debate, but it is not desirable when a personal problem is at stake.

What you should try to do instead is listen with empathy. In other words, try to put yourself in the other person's position as you listen. Don't play "devil's advocate," or try to counterargue every point. Instead, provide support, encourage the person to express him- or herself, and put yourself in his or her position as much as possible.

Asserting Control.   We live in a "can do" society. If there's a problem, our natural tendency is to offer a solution. Thus when a friend comes to us with a problem, we assume that he or she wants us to solve it. As a result, we jump to take control of the situation. This automatic tendency may be counterproductive in the long run when it comes to solving personal problems. Instead of solving the friend's problem, an effective reflective listener should help the friend work through the problem and come to a solution him- or herself. Rather than taking control of the other's problems, just help him or her through the solution process. There are several reasons to take this approach. First, the person with the problem probably has more relevant information on the problem than anyone else does. As a result, he or she is the most qualified to deal with the problem. A second reason is that the advice or solution you give may not be effective. We have a tendency to give bold advice when we don't have to face the consequences of a choice ourselves. If the advice we give is bad, it could threaten the relationship with that friend. There's a final reason why we should not try to provide a solution for another person. Ultimately, it could make him or her less capable of solving personal problems in the future. He or she may become more dependent on our advice, rather than more self-sufficient.

Instead of offering solutions, the best strategy is to help your friend work out the problems him- or herself. You do this not by abandoning him or her, but by lending an ear as he or she talks through the situation. Offer support and interpretations. He or she will often have the solution already, but need to talk his or her way to it. If necessary, help your friend explore the various options available, but let the person with the problem provide the evaluative statements. The listener should just encourage the exploration. (See the Mastering Communication Skills box.)

Additional Reflective Listening Skills

Now that you know some of the do's and don'ts of reflective listening, there are some additional skills worth utilizing.

MASTERING COMMUNICATION SKILLS

Recognizing Effective Reflective Listeners

Some people are better reflective listeners than others. Develop two lists to help you distinguish effective from ineffective reflective listeners. On one list, put down the names of one or two friends whom you consider good reflective listeners, people whom you would turn to if you had a personal problem you wanted to talk about. On the other list, jot down the names of friends whom, though you might like them in general, you would not go to to talk about a personal problem. On each list, describe their reflective listening styles. What listening behaviors do they exhibit that would make you approach or avoid them?

Paraphrasing.   One of the best ways to avoid evaluative statements, show that you are being attentive, and leave the other in control is to use **paraphrasing.** With paraphrasing you reflect back what the other said to you. For example, suppose your coworker complains, "I just can't seem to get along with the boss. Every time I do something he's all over my case. I never hear a word of praise out of his mouth." A paraphrase would acknowledge what you heard and encourage your co-worker to continue talking about the problem. For instance, you could say, "So you think the boss is too hard on you, and you feel unappreciated." Rather than agreeing or disagreeing, you encourage your co-worker to explore the problem further while showing that you're paying attention.

Discussion Question 3–10
How would you rate yourself as an empathic listener?

Attend to the Message at the Emotional Level.   When a person wants to talk about a problem, he or she is often as concerned about the associated emotions as with the "facts" of the situation. For that reason, it is important to attend to the message at the emotional level. What feelings are being expressed as the person talks about the problem? The listener needs to attend to the emotional level of the message and provide feedback showing that it was understood. If Gail complains that her relationship with Craig is in trouble right now because of their constant fights, you might want to give reflective feedback regarding the emotional content of her message: "You sound pretty upset and worried about this right now." In the world of human affairs, our emotional reactions to situations are as important to us as the facts of any situation. When engaging in reflective listening, help the other to explore the facts that he or she is facing.

As you can see, reflective listening involves several different skills when compared to the other types of listening. The key is to encourage the other to explore the problem, but ultimately to let him or her to solve the problem him- or herself. Be attentive, provide verbal and nonverbal feedback, but don't take control of the other person's problems.

◼ CRITICAL THINKING

As we have suggested throughout this chapter, listening is not simply a receptive activity. To be a good listener requires effort and a certain amount of ability. When you are listening well, you will achieve a much better grasp of the messages that others are transmitting to, and exchanging with, you. For good communication, all of us can profit from greater attention to this matter. Understanding what others say to us is not the full story, however.

Our responsibility as listeners further entails attempts to determine the credibility of what we hear. To do this, a listener must be able to engage in *critical thinking.* What critical thinking is and why it is important will become clear in the discussion that follows.

Critical Thinking Defined

Suppose that a friend approaches you in an excited state and tells you that little green people from Mars just landed. You might think your friend is trying to pull your leg, hallucinating, or spreading a rumor that he or she is gullible enough to accept. Whatever your suspicion, you probably will not believe the story even though you fully understand what your friend is telling you. Why? Because your experience, knowledge, and judgment suggest that such an event has a very low probability of being true. When you draw on knowledge and experience to reason in this way, you are exercising the skill of critical thinking.

Although related, critical thinking is different from listening. Whereas listening involves the interpretation and assignment of meaning to aural symbols, **critical thinking** is a process by which one makes inferences about the believability of message content. A significant problem in communication occurs because many people fail to use critical thinking skills enough of the time.

Teaching Objective 3–10
Help students to distinguish between listening and critical thinking.

Importance of Critical Thinking

When you are in the receiver role, those to whom you listen are usually attempting to influence you in some way. They want you to agree with them, accept what they are saying, behave in a particular manner, or in some other sense be compliant. Doing what others wish can prove to be costly, however, as anyone who ever has been the victim of a "get-rich-quick" scheme or has purchased a worthless product, for instance, can readily testify. Therefore, we need means for discriminating among messages in terms of the confidence we can place in their contents.

Because what others communicate to us provides bases for many of our personal decisions, as well as for what we think, feel, and do, responding to messages uncritically is not a good practice. As an illustration, suppose that you are interviewing for a job with a large firm. The interviewer appears to be very interested in you and, as a means of convincing you that you should accept employment with the firm, says that the company "has no unhappy employees." If true, that certainly would make the job more attractive, but is such a strong claim likely to be very accurate? If you were to accept the position on the basis of this claim, you might later discover that you had acted unwisely and, as a result, had forgone other employment opportunities.

Effects of Deficiencies in Critical Thinking

As the preceding example suggests, a failure to use critical thinking in responding to the influence attempts of others can have unfortunate consequences. These can directly affect the well-being of the message receiver or indirectly affect others as a result of the message receiver's actions. For example, if you were to purchase a defective automobile through uncritical acceptance of what a salesperson had told you about it, you might later find yourself burdened with a lot of unanticipated expenses. Even worse, you could become involved in an accident in which you or other parties receive serious injury.

In a book dealing with foreign policy disasters, Irving Janis (1982) found that top-level decision makers repeatedly accepted advice from other uncritically, often because such advice supported actions toward which they were already inclined. In at least two of these cases, the United States became involved in major wars that possibly could have been avoided. Not all lapses in critical thinking have consequences on this scale of severity, of course. However, that is no excuse for permitting ourselves to be placed in situations in which we take unnecessary risks with what we think, feel, and do when we have at our disposal appropriate means of prevention.

Improving Critical Thinking

Discussion Question 3–11
How would you assess your critical thinking skills?

Although there is little question that people vary in the extent to which they display critical thinking, the reasons for such variation are not altogether clear. To some extent, it may be attributable to natural ability, but our experience suggests that, more often than not, differences in critical thinking are linked to prior learning. In short, many individuals simply have not been taught what questions to ask about the messages they receive or have had insufficient opportunities to apply such questions even though they may be aware of them.

Our natural tendency as consumers of information is to believe what we hear or are told unless we have obvious reasons not to do so. Many aspects of our education and social organization reinforce this tendency. Teachers and parents, for instance, are authority figures. We learn early in life not to question what they say unless they encourage us to do so. This early tendency later generalizes to other domains. We believe a story because it appeared in a newspaper or was on television. We listen to our superiors and follow their advice because they are presumably more knowledgeable than we. If we disbelieve such sources, it is more likely to be a result of our attitudes toward them than of careful assessment of what they say. As with any skill, becoming proficient in critical thinking requires practice and discipline. With disuse, the skill will diminish. The familiar expression, "Use it, or lose it," clearly applies here. From our perspective, critical thinking is a skill that can be acquired and nurtured. Even though the capacity for critical thinking may be inherited, each of us possesses that capacity in some degree and can learn to employ that skill to maximum advantage. For significant improvement to occur, however, one must have appropriate tools with which to work. For our purposes, these tools consist of particular questions you should be prepared to ask about the messages you receive. The answers to these questions provide the bases for making inferences about the believability of the messages we receive.

Questions Reflective of Critical Thinking

Teaching Objective 3–11
Provide examples of messages to assist students in testing messages with the help of these questions.

For any message you receive, there are numerous questions you can raise. Four general ones, however, are especially useful for determining whether you should believe the message:

1. Is the message plausible?
2. Is the message consistent?
3. Is the source of the message reliable?
4. Are the factual claims in the message verifiable?

How you answer these questions has implications for your decisions concerning **message credibility**, or the apparent degree of truth in a communicator's utterances. Let us now examine each of these "tools" of critical thinking.

Plausibility.   The term **plausibility** refers to the extent to which a message, on its face value, rings true. In our earlier example of the little green people from Mars, you would be unlikely to believe the story because it is implausible. In 1938, however, a Halloween Mercury Theatre radio broadcast of H. G. Wells's *War of the Worlds* led thousands of listeners to panic (Cantril, 1941). The perpetrator was the late screen actor and director Orson Wells, who was greatly surprised by the public response to a fictitious radio drama. The program, however, was presented in the format of a breaking news event and, therefore, was highly plausible, especially to those who tuned in after the broadcast was underway.

Plausibility, then, is not always easy to access. Nevertheless, we need to develop the habit of asking questions about whether what we hear or are told makes reasonable sense when taken at face value. Skepticism can go a long way in preventing us from acting unwisely on the basis of information we receive from others. Beware the individual who sends messages containing claims that strike you as having a low probability of being true. There is an excellent chance that they are not.

Consistency.   The **consistency** of a message refers to how free of contradictions it is. Messages can be examined in terms of both their internal consistency and their consistency with other known information. An internally consistent message is one in which the claims advanced are compatible; for example, "We are going to reduce the national debt. To do so, we will have to reduce spending and probably increase taxes." An example of a message that is consistent with known information would be: "Smoking increases the risk of heart disease, stroke, cancer, and other serious illnesses."

When messages are lacking evidence of these types of consistencies, they are not highly believable. Former President George Bush's denials about his involvement in the Iran-Contra scandal became increasingly less convincing as a result of his contradictions over time about what meetings he had or had not attended and what his own records and memoranda subsequently revealed.

Inconsistencies in messages are not always obvious; one must be attentive in order to pick up on them. Because contradictory claims frequently occur at different points in a speech, one might not focus on the fact, for example, that a speaker suggesting at one point that a problem is extremely complicated is at another point recommending a very simple solution to it. A person who is attentive and accustomed to looking for inconsistencies would be more apt than others to notice this and, in light of the severity of the problem, to doubt the efficacy of the solution, or vice versa.

Reliability of the Source.   Because of the nature of some subject matter, listeners are not always able to assess the plausibility or consistency of messages.

Discussion Question 3–12
What sources of information do you tend to believe without question? What other sources of information do you tend to *disbelieve* without question?

This does not mean, however, that they are helpless. Critical thinkers, under such circumstances, will raise questions about the reliability of sources. Thus **source reliability** is the source's reputation for accuracy and truthfulness. You might think of it as a person's "track record" as a producer of messages.

Some sources are highly reliable; others are notoriously unreliable. The greater your familiarity with those with whom you communicate, the easier it is to form judgments about the believability of their messages. If an inveterate gossip tells you a rumor and has a history of spreading rumors that seldom prove to have any substance, you will have little reason to believe that individual. On the other hand, if an acquaintance in whom you have always been able to confide pledges to keep a secret you have shared, the assurance will be quite believable.

Not all sources with whom we interact are well known to us. Thus, when possible, the critical thinker reserves judgment about the believability of a message until he or she can acquire more information about its source. This is preferable to the extreme position that some people take in such instances, which is to distrust what anyone they do not know is saying. This posture is not symptomatic of good judgment; rather, it represents an escape from the responsibility of having to exercise it. In this sense, the uncritical skeptic is no better than an extremely gullible individual in distinguishing those messages to which one should be responsive from those to which one should not be responsive.

Verifiability.   Even if one cannot determine the reliability of a source, the critical thinker still has at least one more avenue open for assessing the believability of a message. If a claim is true, in principle, there will be in most instances some means for verifying it. The assertion that SAT scores are lower than they

SELF-ASSESSMENT   Testing Your Understanding

For each of the claims that follows, first determine how you might go about verifying it. Then indicate the limitations, if any, of the means of verification you identified.

1. When Ronald Reagan was shot by John Hinckley, the president came within five minutes of dying.

2. The first person to lose his life in the American War of Independence was an African American named Crispus Attucks.

3. The classic film, *Citizen Kane,* is based on the life of William Randolph Hearst.

4. Retired Supreme Court Justice Thurgood Marshall died on January 24, 1993.

5. Overeating is the leading cause of heart disease.

were twenty years ago is one that can be checked for factual accuracy. So can the announcement that someone you know has been hospitalized. In both instances, you can easily verify what you have been told by consulting independent sources. **Verifiability**, then, is a characteristic of messages relating to the possibility of establishing the authenticity of the factual claims they embody. (See if you can apply this notion by identifying the appropriate way to verify each of the claims in the preceding Self-Assessment exercise.)

If the source of a message makes claims for which there are no apparent means of verification, you have far less reason to believe the message than one for which such means are available. Questions concerning the verifiability of claims advanced by the producers of messages are especially important when those claims are out of the ordinary. The popular astronomer Carl Sagan is fond of saying, "Extraordinary claims require extraordinary evidence." We would all do well to remember this comment when reacting to what others tell us.

A Note of Caution

It should now be clear to you why it is important to raise questions about plausibility, consistency, source reliability, and verifiability when you are listening to messages. For ease of memory, we have restated these questions in Table 3.2. Important as they are, raising these questions, you must remember, will not guarantee error-free assessments of the believability of messages. They can help you to become a more discriminating consumer of them, and to sort out more effectively what you reasonably can believe and what you probably should not believe. Those who have achieved some level of sophistication in critical thinking understand this principle and, in general, do a better job of responding appropriately to the messages they receive—particularly those having potentially important consequences.

Table 3.2
Questions Critical Thinkers Ask About Messages

Focus	*Question*
Plausibility	Does the claim being advanced by a source, on its face value, ring true?
Consistency	Is the claim being advanced by a source free of contradiction with other claims in the message and other known evidence?
Source reliability	Does the person making the claim have a reputation for accuracy and truthfulness?
Verifiability	Is the claim being advanced by a source whose authenticity can be established?

◼ Summary

Listening is a complex process that is critical for effective communication. Without listening, communication cannot take place. Listening is an important skill that is in great demand in the business world as well as in everyday life. Certainly, to be an effective leader, a person must be a good listener.

Listening is best thought of as an active process. One of the more common problems we have as listeners is the tendency to assume that listening is passive in nature and requires little effort. While that may be true of the physiological process of hearing, the cognitive process of listening requires focused attention and interpretative skills, thereby necessitating an active approach.

Listening involves at least three steps: hearing, attending to the message, and interpreting the message. At any stage of this process, problems can arise that will prevent us from being effective listeners. By planning ahead and by taking the necessary steps, many of these listening pitfalls can be avoided.

One of the points about listening that is most often overlooked is that there are different types of listening. Listening for enjoyment, listening for information, listening for evaluation, and reflective listening are different from one another. Listening for enjoyment, for information, and for evaluation vary from the least to the most demanding. Listening for evaluation requires that you use a set of evaluative standards or judging criteria.

Regardless of the type of listening in which you are engaged, there are some common pitfalls of listening, such as allowing distractions to interfere, being overstimulated, selective listening, and egocentric listening. However, if you are aware of these problems, and can recognize when you fall victim to them, you are capable of taking the necessary precautions. For instance, you can use your spare listening time wisely, you can try to block out distractions, and you can take an empathic approach to listening. You can also make sure you try to practice the listening behaviors that characterize effective listeners. These would include preparing to listen at the appropriate level, using effective verbal and nonverbal reinforcers, and structuring your environment to eliminate distractions.

In this chapter, you also learned more about reflective listening skills. Reflective listening is used when you are called upon to provide support and understanding to a person you know with a personal problem. Contrary to our natural instincts, you should not try to solve the other person's problems. Instead, you should act as a sounding board. You should hear the other out, encouraging him or her with simple verbal and nonverbal cues, as well as through the use of paraphrasing. Keep in mind the need to deal with the emotional side of the problem as well as with the facts of the case. Usually, people can work out their own problems if they have the support and understanding that is provided through the use of reflective listening.

Finally, you have been introduced to the subject of critical thinking—the process by which one makes inferences about the believability of message content. Critical thinking is important, and deficiencies in it can lead to changes in thoughts and behavior that a message receiver may later come to regret. Although individuals vary in their capacities for critical thinking, everyone can become better in assessing the credibility of messages by learning to ask appropriate questions about their plausibility, consistency, source reliability, and verifiability.

---

1. Make a conscious attempt to use your thought-speed advantage in a listening situation. A lecture class would be ideal for this exercise. Rather than letting your mind drift, use the thinking-talking speed differential to your advantage. As we recommended in the chapter, try to (a) determine the type of organization the speaker is following; (b) keep track of the speaker's main points and key ideas; (c) connect the ideas being addressed at the moment to those that preceded them; (d) identify the "big picture" that the speaker is trying to capture; (e) identify any hidden motives that the speaker might have; and (f) identify any emotional connection that the speaker might have to any of the ideas. It takes a substantial amount of effort to maintain focused listening over a whole class period. How well were you able to do it? Did it change your listening experience? Were you able to understand and retain more information as a result?

2. Effective reflective listeners are able to use paraphrasing skillfully. In this exercise, try to develop this skill. Pair off with another person in class. Talk about the adjustments you had to make when you started college life. After the first person starts it off, the other partner cannot add new comments or information until he or she first paraphrases what the other person said. From there on in, each person in the pair should begin with a paraphrase of what the other said. Notice the effects of this on the ongoing conversation.

3. Learn how to specify your evaluative criteria for an evaluative listening situation. Too often, in listening situations, we take the easy way out, just forming a global impression of the speaker, and evaluating everything he or she said on the basis of that global impression. A more effective approach is to have a set of evaluative criteria beforehand and apply those criteria or standards as you listen. Plan to attend a public speaking event on campus or somewhere in your community. Before attending, specify the criteria of evaluation you'll use to judge the presentation. It will be helpful to divide your list into delivery and content-related areas. For instance, in the delivery area, you may feel that an effective speaker should give the audience eye contact and be able to speak with confidence. In the content area, you might feel that a speaker should have a clear set of main points and should be able to provide vivid examples as evidence. Try to have four delivery and four content criteria before you go. As you listen to the speech, use your criteria to evaluate the presentation. Listen critically to judge the speaker's strengths and weaknesses. Has your listening experience changed as a result of applying these criteria? In what way? Did you generate any additional criteria as a result of listening to the presentation? What were they?

4. We have noted that people aren't very effective listeners, certainly not as effective as they should be. As a public speaker, that could pose some poten-

■ **Exercises**

tial problems for you. Given what you now know about listening, develop a strategy you can put to use to make sure that your audience maximizes their effectiveness as listeners while you're speaking. For instance, one of the problems for audiences is the use of numbers and statistics. If you rely on statistics in your speech, what can you do to make sure that the audience pays attention to them and interprets them in the way you want? What other verbal and nonverbal techniques can you use to help the audience pay attention while you speak?

5. How do you know when something you hear is true? Write a brief essay in which you answer this question. Then compare the way in which you make such determinations with the four questions in Table 3.2. What similarities do you note? Have you identified any ways of determining probable truth that are not covered by the four questions? If so, how do these additional items assist you in judging whether to believe what you have heard? Come to class prepared to discuss your answer.

Capaldi, N. (1979). *The art of deception* (2nd ed.). Buffalo, NY: Prometheus.

Capaldi introduces the reader to basic principles of reasoning and common tests of evidence. A familiarity with the material covered can be very helpful in the development of critical thinking ability.

Friedman, P. G. (1986). *Listening processes: Attention, understanding, evaluation.* Washington, DC: National Education Association.

Friedman compiled a brief research-based booklet that is geared to the needs of teachers and future teachers. He describes the special listening needs of the classroom for both teachers and students.

Keefe, W. F. (1971). *Listen, management! Creative listening for better management.* New York: McGraw-Hill.

Keefe addresses the listening needs of managers. He asserts that people in leadership positions have special listening needs, and he provides numerous suggestions for listening improvement in managers.

Nichols, R. G., and Stevens, L. A. (1957). *Are you listening?* New York: McGraw-Hill.

This remains one of the classic texts on listening. Nichols and Stevens emphasize the importance of listening, cover factors that hinder effective listening, and describe how listening can be improved in a variety of contexts.

■ Related Readings

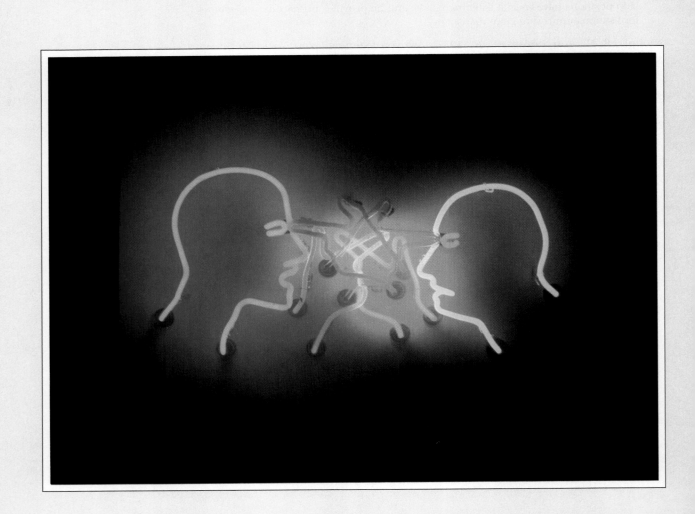

Verbal Communication

Chapter objectives

After reading this chapter you should be able to:

1. distinguish verbal communication from other forms of human communication

2. identify at least four reasons why verbal communication is important to study

3. describe how language helps us understand, predict, and control the world around us

4. describe the relationship between experience and language development

5. describe several functions of verbal communication

6. identify language tools used to clarify and obscure meaning, including euphemism and doublespeak

7. differentiate between denotative and connotative meanings

8. understand the dynamic nature of language

9. identify the destructive effects of sexist and racist language

Key terms and concepts

verbal communication
Sapir-Whorf hypothesis
euphemism
doublespeak
denotative meaning
connotative meaning
sequencing
polarization
intensional orientation
bypassing
paraphrasing
fact-inference confusion
static evaluation
sexist language
racist language

Imagine that you walk into a music store one afternoon, and you happen to see two friends browsing through the latest CDs. You go over to say hello and one of them says, "Hey, I really like that sweater you're wearing." You thank your friend for the compliment and begin discussing other things.

Now consider how your friend's statement would be taken differently if he had rolled his eyes and jabbed the other friend with an elbow while commenting on your sweater. Some compliment, eh? Or, what if your friend had avoided the obnoxious nonverbal modifiers, but you happened to be wearing a sweater that was clearly old and tattered?

These examples suggest the limitations of looking at words alone when trying to understand communication. In each case, the words did not change, but many other things did, including the communicative act being performed by the speaker, the effect on you (the listener), and the effect on the interpersonal relationship. Thus, *communication* is *not* synonymous with *language*. While language can be roughly understood as comprised of semantics (the words we use) and syntactics (the rules of grammar for properly ordering and arranging words in sequence), communication encompasses far more than language. As we saw in Chapter 2, for instance, perceptions play a major role in all forms of communication. In addition, as we will see in Chapter 5, nonverbal behavior also plays a key role in communication.

Consider communication to be a richly woven fabric, in which language constitutes some of the thread. Nonetheless, language use, or verbal communication, represents an extremely important part of what we know as communication. Verbal communication itself is rich and complex.

In this chapter we define verbal communication and explain why we need to study it. We discuss the functions served by language use, the relationship between language and meaning, the social impact of language, and some of the barriers or problems caused by our use of language. The chapter concludes with a discussion of how to overcome these problems.

■ WHAT IS VERBAL COMMUNICATION?

What does the term *verbal communication* mean? On the surface, providing a definition appears straightforward. After all, isn't verbal communication what people do when they talk to one another? There are potentially confounding examples. What about writing a letter to someone, or the exchange between deaf individuals using American Sign Language? In each case, symbolic language is being used even though no words are spoken. Are these examples of verbal communication? Most communication scholars would agree that they are. We must recognize a distinction between the symbolic nature of the message and the channel used to send the message.

The channel is the medium used to transfer information. Some communication channels or messages are vocal (radio broadcasts, telephone conversations), some are visual (newspapers, letters, sign language), some are tactile (signing for the visually impaired, braille), and some are exchanged through an olfactory channel (that is, through smell). Most face-to-face interactions involve the exchange of information through multiple channels simultaneously. Independent of the channel used, however, is the question of whether the message is symbolic.

Language *is* symbolic. This means there is an arbitrary connection between the symbols used and what they refer to. It also means that the people using the language must agree on the meaning of the symbols if the language is to work effectively. A message exchange is considered verbal if it involves the use of language, regardless of the channel used. Therefore, spoken, written, and signed words are all considered forms of verbal communication. Nonsymbolic messages are considered nonverbal communication, regardless of whether they are transmitted vocally (grunts, laughter), visually (a wink, a smile), or tactilely (a push, a hug).

The communication scholar Michael Nolan (1975) has advanced a useful scheme to help distinguish verbal and nonverbal dimensions of communication across vocal and nonvocal message channels. This scheme, in slightly modified form, is presented in Figure 4.1. The figure displays a total of four cells. Each cell represents an aspect of communication that shares at least two qualities, as noted by the respective row and column headings. For example, row 1 (cells 1 and 2) represents all language systems, where *language system* refers to any arbitrary, human symbolic arrangement of sounds or structures to represent ideas and feelings. Verbal communication, as defined here, is represented by cells 1 and 2. We now finally have our definition! The key distinguishing feature of **verbal communication** is the use of language, an arbitrary system of symbols, to facilitate message exchange. Verbal communication is synonymous with all systems of arbitrary, symbolic interaction.

Discussion Question 4–1
What are your preferred channels of communication? Speech? Song? The written word? Would you rather talk on the phone or in person? Would you rather show, or tell? Are you primarily an aural or a visual person? Do the people you're closest to prefer the same channels or different ones?

Leadership Note 4–1
T. Boone Pickens, founder, president, and chairman of the board of Mesa Petroleum and member of the National Petroleum Council, has this to say about communication channels for business leaders: "Talking is the natural way to do business. Writing is great for keeping records and putting down details, but talk generates ideas." (Safire, William, and Safir, Leonard. *Leadership*, New York: Simon & Schuster, 1990, p. 46)

Distinguishing Verbal and NonVerbal Communication

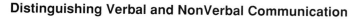

	Vocal	Nonvocal
VERBAL	Spoken language Cell 1	Written language Finger-spelling Braille Cell 2
NONVERBAL	Vocal qualities (rate, pitch, etc.) Response cries Cell 3	Emotional displays Kinesics Gestures Body types Cell 4

Figure 4.1
Distinguishing Verbal and Nonverbal Communication. (After M. J. Nolan, The relationship between verbal and nonverbal communication, in G. J. Hanneman and W. J. McEwen (Eds,), *Communication and Behavior*. (Reading, MA.: Addison-Wesley, 1975.)

Teaching Objective 4–1
Define language and chan-
nels. Define verbal communication as the use of any
language on any channel.

Cells 3 and 4 of the figure categorize various message elements that are primarily nonsymbolic or nonverbal, regardless of the vocal or nonvocal channel
through which the information is presented. These types of messages or behaviors (discussed in Chapter 5 on nonverbal communication) include vocal qualities, response cries, and a variety of other classifications traditionally considered to be part of the nonverbal domain.

■ WHY STUDY VERBAL COMMUNICATION?

Teaching Objective 4–2
Emphasize the importance
of language to social life as
well as to one's identity and
survival.

Verbal interaction constitutes a significant part of our communicative behavior.
A closer look will help us gain a greater appreciation of the complexity of our
language use. We tend to take communication in general, and verbal interaction, in particular, for granted. There is an old saying that the fish would be the
last to discover water. Water is such a basic part of the fish's environment that it
could not picture a world without it. The same may be said for our use of language. Once we learn our native tongue, we pretty much take language use for
granted—that is, until we try to learn another language, or until we have problems communicating with another person. Thus, to truly understand language
use, we must look closely at it.

Another reason we look at language use is that, in spite of our taking it for
granted most of the time, communication problems often arise. Every one of us
has misinterpreted someone else's words or felt that our own words were misunderstood at one time or another. Hence, we look at verbal communication to
come to grips with misunderstandings that are rooted in our language use and
to suggest ways to avoid or overcome these misunderstandings.

Current Research 4–1
Some scholars suggest that
our very sense of self is
developed through commu-
nication, on the basis of
feedback we receive from
others. Recent research by
Renee Edwards affirms the
importance of verbal feedback to self-image.
(Edwards, Renee, Sensitivity
to feedback and the development of the self.
Communication Quarterly
38(2), 1990, pp. 101–111.)

A final reason to explore language use (discussed in Chapter 2) is that communication—or, more specifically, language—provides us with the essential
categories for interpreting our experiences. The world has been described as a
booming, bustling confusion of sensory input. Yet we don't experience the
world as chaotic and random (except while going through class registration or
those couple of days before tax returns are due!). We order our experience by
categorizing it. Words—our language—provide us with the categories we use to
order our experience. To a large degree, we make sense of our experiences
through our language. There are two implications of this that are worth exploring further. One is how language allows us to encounter our world in a meaningful way. The second is that by changing the category system (or language),
we can also change how a person experiences the world.

Language allows us to encounter our world in a meaningful way because it
is the primary tool we use to generalize and see similarities, as well as to draw
distinctions between the objects and events we encounter in our lives. Walking
down the street, for instance, you may notice a four-legged animal that has a
tail, a fairly long nose, and floppy ears. You may also notice that it makes a barking noise when you approach the yard it is in. Of course, you have a name or
word that helps categorize this animal. We call it a dog. Since you are in possession of that word, *dog*, and you can use it to properly categorize components in

your environment, you demonstrate your understanding of the concept of "dog-ness." You can see the doglike qualities in similar animals, and you can distinguish dogs from other animals, objects, or named events.

Because you are aware of the word *dog*, you are better able to *understand*, *predict*, and *control* the world around you. The term *dog* helps you to generalize across similar animals. Each encounter with a four-legged, barking, floppy-eared animal does not have to be treated as an entirely new experience. That way, you can better *understand* the present animal's behavior, on the basis of your comparison to other animals that fit into the same category. For instance, if the present animal is showing its teeth and raising its hackles as you walk by the yard, you might understand that the dog is protecting its territory (as dogs tend to do).

Language also helps you to *predict* better. Such a hostile display by the dog would suggest that entering that yard could lead to some painful consequences.

Finally, your categorization allows you to *control* the situation better. Presumably, you would avoid entering that yard. This is not to suggest that animals without language cannot generalize or categorize differences. However, the fact that we do these things by using language is part of what makes us human. It allows us to think at higher levels of abstraction than other animals can. It also suggests that we experience our world through our language. Thus if you change the language, you'll change how a person experiences the world. A useful comparison is to think of language as a template or a pair of eyeglasses through which we observe our world. A different pair of glasses would let us see the world differently.

Consider how a person could describe and experience different types of wine. One person may have a very basic understanding of wine. He may take a sip and be able to distinguish between a dry and a sweet taste. Now consider how a person with a more refined palate for wine may describe it. She may take a sip from the same glass tasted by the first person and distinguish whether the wine is dry, sweet, oaken, tannic, fruity, bold, full bodied, assertive, or any other number of adjectives. (We recommend, however, that you maintain a healthy suspicion of anyone who describes a wine as "sincere" or "impertinent"). The point is not just that she can describe the wine in more detail than he can. It is easy to argue that she probably experiences the taste of the wine differently than he does. Her experience is richer and more detailed *because* she has the language to make those fine distinctions. It is worth noting that her wine vocabulary probably did not pop out of thin air. She probably had to taste a number of wines and have someone help her learn the distinctions. Once she knows the distinctions or categories, however, she can apply them to wines she had never tasted before.

LANGUAGE AND EXPERIENCE

The new words that a person learns are often the result of the need to make important distinctions. An example often given is the Eskimo language, which

Discussion Question 4–2
Can you remember or imagine a time before you had words to define or share your experience? What would you think about a nightmare if you didn't know what it was? How would you respond to an animal you'd never seem or heard of the first time you met it face-to-face?

Current Research 4–2
Recent research by Bell and Roloff suggests a direct relationship between loneliness and an inability to communicate effectively, which suggests that verbal communication is central even to control of our own emotional states. (Bell, Robert A., and Roloff, Michael E. Making a love connection: loneliness and communication competence in the dating marketplace. *Communication Quarterly, 39*(1), 1991, pp. 58–74.)

Teaching Objective 4–3
Describe the reciprocal relationship between language and experience.

Cross-reference 4–1
The relationship between language and experience was also discussed within the context of perception in Chapter 2.

Discussion Question 4–3
What experiences have you had that your parents have not, and do you have new words to describe them? Do these words have meaning to your parents?

Discussion Question 4–4
Consider the power of advertising and other slogans to change how we think, what we feel or believe, and what we do. What is the social and/or personal impact of Nike's "Just Do It"? How about "Kleenex says 'Bless You'"? And what about "Carpe Diem! Seize the Day!"?

has dozens of words for snow. By comparison, our language has relatively few, including *snow* and *slush*. Skiers have added *powder* and *corn*. Perhaps you know several more. Still, we have nowhere near the number of words for *snow* that exists in the Eskimo language. That difference is the result of the vastly different environments in which we live. To the Eskimo culture, snow is very important and much more pervasive. Since the Eskimos have to travel over it more, it is useful to have one word for snow that can be safely crossed and a different word for snow that may be dangerous to cross. The traditional housing unit, or igloo, was made of snow, so it is not surprising that a term developed specifically for snow that can be used as a building material, as opposed to blowing or drifting snow.

Language thus emerges from the need to make useful distinctions. Further, experience (the world around a person or culture) influences the language that develops. In turn, language use influences how people experience the world around them. Figure 4.2 shows this process.

Language and Perception

The extent to which language use influences our perceptions is an issue of some enduring debate. Some theorists have taken an extreme position, arguing that we cannot think of things for which we have no words. This view is influenced by the theory of the linguist Benjamin Lee Whorf and his colleague Edward Sapir, whose **Sapir-Whorf hypothesis** suggests that language *determines* how we think (Whorf 1956). A more moderate view suggests that language *influences* or *channels* how we think. In support of this moderate view, communication theorists argue that anyone from a non-Eskimo culture could easily learn to distinguish between igloo-building snow and snow that couldn't be used for igloos (particularly if the differences were pointed out) even if that person didn't learn the words for these different types of snow.

■ THE FUNCTIONS OF VERBAL COMMUNICATION

It would be difficult to come up with a complete listing of every function served by verbal communication. A useful way to begin thinking about this may simply

Figure 4.2
The Reciprocal Relationship Between Language and Experience.

be to develop a broad category scheme of functions (Brooks, Schafe, and Siler 1980). When considering this category system, keep in mind that language is "representational." In other words, the words or linguistic symbols we use serve to *represent* other things, such as physical realities (for example, a bicycle), abstract ideas (for example, freedom), emotional states (for example, rage), or complex relationships (for example, causality). Don't restrict your thinking, as though words only served to represent concrete objects.

Given that general characterization, we can say that language serves several other functions (see Figure 4.3). First, language serves as an instrument through which we can satisfy our personal drives, needs, and wants. Language is said to have an *instrumental function* because it is a tool for helping us to achieve goals and fulfill our needs. Simply ordering a pizza would be an example of language serving an instrumental function. You have a need (hunger), and you use language as a tool to achieve a goal (get something to eat). Conversely, language also has a *regulatory function;* that is, we use language to control and influence the actions and conduct of others with whom we associate. We do that through the messages we send. If you persuade a friend to order a pizza with anchovies on it, in spite of her initial reluctance, you would be trying to influence her actions. Hence, this would be an example of the regulatory use of language.

Aside from the instrumental and regulative functions, a great volume of communication activity falls into what can be thought of as a *social function*. It is largely through the process of verbal message exchanges over long periods of time that we develop our sense of individual identity and personhood. We engage in dialogue and discourse for social purposes whenever we are motivated by an interest in sharing for the sake of mutual benefit, discussion, and fellowship. Sitting around and just chatting with friends is typically fulfilling the social function. Lastly, we use language in an effort to accomplish a *problem-solving function*. We ask questions and process information in an effort to develop our understanding of the social and physical environment. In fact, language serves to

Current Research 4–3
"Anyone sensitive to the ways in which language shapes perception will recognize the powerful but covert influence [our male-oriented language use] customs must have on our thinking about men and women." (Haiman, Franklyn S. *Communication Education* 40, 1991, p. 5)

Teaching Objective 4–4
Explain the representational nature of language and the various functions it serves.

Current Research 4–4
Even within everyday conversations, use of language has a regulatory function. Palmer found that both time spent talking and the initiation of topic shifts were linked with interpersonal dominance and control. (Palmer, Mark T. Controlling conversations: turns, topics and interpersonal control. *Communication Monographs, 56*(1), 1989, pp. 1–17.)

The Functions of Verbal Communication

REPRESENTATIONAL	Verbal communication represents such things as physical objects, abstract ideas, emotional states, and complex relationships
INSTRUMENTAL	Verbal communication helps us achieve goals and fulfill needs
REGULATORY	Verbal communication helps us manage our interactions with others and influence them
SOCIAL	Verbal communication helps us develop our sense of individual identity and personhood
PROBLEM-SOLVING	Verbal communication allows us to understand and master our environment

Figure 4.3
The Functions of Verbal Communication.

structure thought. Thus, as facility with language develops, so does sophistication of the thought processes. This point was made earlier when we discussed how an elaborate vocabulary on wine leads to a more fully developed understanding of it.

While only four functions have been advanced, the reality of language usage is highly complex. It is very seldom that only one function is associated with a communication event. Most often, language activity is multifunctional; that is, several different functions are served simultaneously.

Language Is Used to Clarify and Obscure

Teaching Objective 4–5
Depict language as capable of obscuring as well as clarifying experience.

Discussion Question 4–5
Take a few minutes to list all the euphemisms for death in our language. What can they teach us about how our society views death and feels about it?

Language is used by people to share understanding. Whether you are clarifying a goal, a restriction, or an attempt to share information, when used skillfully, language allows people to share understanding. On the other hand, language can also be used to obscure or hide meaning.

One of the more or less harmless ways we can use language to obscure is through the use of euphemisms. A **euphemism** is an inoffensive word or phrase that is used in place of a term that people may find too explicit or tactless. Euphemisms may be used to avoid taboo subjects and unwanted negative emotional associations that some words carry, or to put a better light on a term or subject and thereby make it less controversial. Euphemisms also allow us to avoid words that have very strong emotional impact, particularly if that emotion is negative. For example, if your elderly dog can no longer see, hear, or control its bodily functions, you might consider having him "put to sleep." You would never talk about this as "having the dog executed" or "taking him in to be killed." Talking about it as having him put to sleep helps us to deal with this difficult decision.

We sometimes use euphemisms to enhance, or brighten, a drab term or title. Being a secretary doesn't sound glamorous or important, so a company can enhance the status of this position by calling people who type, file, and schedule "administrative assistants." Similarly, the term "garbageman" is hardly impressive. "Sanitation engineer," on the other hand, conveys a distinctly different impression.

While euphemisms can obscure meaning, they do not entirely distort reality. William Lutz, a professor at Rutgers University, has spent considerable time tracking word use that is intended to distort through deliberate misuse of language. He calls this practice **doublespeak** (Lutz 1989). For example, instead of referring to dropping bombs on enemy soldiers and territory, a military spokesperson will talk of "delivering ordinance." During the Persian Gulf crisis, the U.S. military referred to deaths suffered by Iraqi civilians as "collateral damage." Everyone knows that it is nearly political suicide for an elected official to advocate raising taxes nowadays. Instead, the politician may suggest that the government pursue certain types of "revenue enhancement."

Leadership Note 4–2
"The very essence of leadership is [that] you have to have a vision. It's got to be a vision you articulate clearly and forcefully on every occasion." (No room for doublespeak here.) (Theodore Hesburgh, in Safire, William, and Safir, Leonard. *Leadership*. New York: Simon & Schuster, 1990, p. 240)

Professor Lutz and others argue that doublespeak becomes particularly dangerous when it obscures meaning by making bad things seem good or inoffensive, or by making negative things seem positive. Doublespeak typically misleads by shifting the blame or responsibility for an act or policy. A company

The military is often accused of using doublespeak to camouflage the real nature of its activities. In a classic use of doublespeak, it described its surprise landing in Grenada in 1983 as a "predawn vertical insertion."

does not want to take the heat for putting 5,000 workers out of jobs by "laying them off." Instead, the company claims that it "initiated a career alternative enhancement program." (Complete the Self-Assessment exercise.)

SELF-ASSESSMENT   **Testing your doublespeak detection skill**

Try to determine what is being described in the following examples of doublespeak.

1. a portable hand-held communications inscriber

2. to terminate with extreme prejudice

3. a wood interdental stimulator

4. therapeutic misadventure of a high magnitude

5. pavement deficiencies

6. an aerodynamic personnel decelerator

Answers: 1. a pencil; 2. to kill a person; 3. a toothpick; 4. medical malpractice where the patient died; 5. potholes; 6. a parachute

■ THE RELATIONSHIP BETWEEN LANGUAGE AND MEANING

Because communication often proceeds so smoothly, it can be terribly frustrating when misunderstandings occur. Think for a moment of the last time you were misunderstood by a friend or family member. Were you able to explain how the misunderstanding occurred? The easiest answer, and the one we rely on too often, is that it's the other person's fault. He or she misunderstood you because of stupidity or narrow-mindedness. More likely, however, the two of you simply failed to share understanding because of the inherent complexity of communicating through language. The same features that make language use interesting, fun, and playful, also make misunderstandings possible.

Meaning Is Tied to People

Teaching Objective 4–6
Emphasize that the meanings of words reside in those who use them.

The first mistake that most people make is believing that meaning is in words themselves. In actuality, there is no inherent link between a word and its *referent* (what it stands for). This is what we mean when we say that language is symbolic. We develop symbols to stand for or represent things, ideas, emotions, and the like. But the link between a word and its referent is an arbitrary one.

By common agreement within our language culture, we call the furry animal that purrs when petted and scratches when teased a cat. Yet there's nothing very catlike about the letter combination C-A-T. The word itself bears no resemblance to the animal. Furthermore, if everyone suddenly decided to call that type of animal a "vanilla wafer" tomorrow, we would probably no longer refer to it as a cat.

Now, it is unlikely that we will stop referring to our feline friends as cats, but let us present a simple example of the arbitrariness of language. Consider the case of a couple whose young daughter, while developing her language skills, was not able to say the words *potato chip*. In spite of not being able to pronounce the words, she would occasionally desire those crisp, lightly salted, tasty morsels. As a result, when requesting them, she would refer to a potato chip as an "ebu" (that's pronounced: e'-boo). It didn't take long for everyone in the family to start referring to that snack as ebus (the plural of ebu, of course). The new word worked perfectly well, as long as there was an agreement among the language users (here, an individual family) about what the word referred to.

Figure 4.4 provides a reconceptualized way to think about the relationship between words and meaning. The connection between a symbol and its referent is indirect. What links them is the shared agreement among the people who use the language. As soon as we recognize the role of people in linking meaning to words, we can begin to understand some of the more interesting and dynamic features of language.

Denotative and Connotative Meaning

Since the meaning of words depends on consensual user agreement, there is a need to provide some stability to language. Language users can develop an "offi-

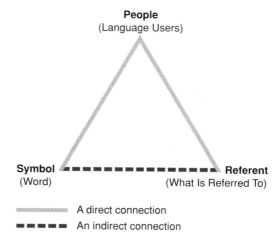

People
(Language Users)

Symbol ◂ ▪ ▪ ▪ ▪ ▪ ▪ ▪ ▪ ▪ ▪ ▪ ▪ ▸ **Referent**
(Word)   (What Is Referred To)

▬▬▬ A direct connection

▪ ▪ ▪ ▪ ▪ An indirect connection

Figure 4.4
The Symbol-Referent
Relationship.

cial document" regarding the meaning of words. This official meaning of words—the meaning that appears in a dictionary—is called the **denotative meaning**.

The funny thing about language is that the words are like magnets. They pick up all sorts of examples, emotions, and associations as we use them. If asked to define the word *friend* for someone who doesn't understand the term, you might talk about what friends do together or the good feeling associated with friendship, or describe a display of friendship, or show that person a picture of your friend. These are not part of a dictionary definition of *friend*, but they may be useful in providing a working definition. To give the straight denotative meaning of friend, "someone you know well and like; an ally," doesn't exactly provide a full picture. The **connotative meaning** of a word, then, is the rich personal definition you bring to a word, which includes all the examples, emotions, and associations that you attach.

Misunderstandings can occur when two people agree on the denotative meaning of a word, but disagree on its connotative meaning. Take the term *Indian summer*. Denotatively, it could be defined as a period of summer heat that lingers into autumn. If you live in the northern United States, *Indian summer* probably has wonderful associations: Temperatures in October that linger in the mid-seventies. Warm fall afternoons. Ahhh! On the other hand, if you are from the South, it can mean a sustained hot spell. Just when you thought you could turn off the air conditioner, now you have to put up with an extra week of hot, muggy temperatures. Imagine the northerner who speaks longingly to the southerner about the chances of an Indian summer this year. The southerner will think the northerner is either kidding or crazy.

Language Is Dynamic

Since meaning is not in words but the result of the users' agreement about what a word means, language has a dynamic quality—that is, it has the *potential to change*. As a result, new words emerge in our language, and old words take

Teaching Objective 4–7
Explain that words have many meanings, both denotative and connotative, and that meanings change over time.

Discussion Question 4–6
Consider the word "touch." What denotative meanings does it have? what connotative meanings does it have for you? What connotative meanings might it have for a blind person, or for a survivor of physical abuse?

on new meaning, while other old words fall out of use and seemingly lose their meaning. One of the more interesting things about language is the tendency for new words to emerge. These words may be necessary to describe recently developed objects or processes. (Twenty years ago, it would have been silly to have the term *laptop computer* since no such object existed.) Or new terms may emerge that describe existing objects, processes, and such in novel, often colorful ways.

Discussion Question 4–7
What causes words to change their meanings over time?

Linguists and other scholars often monitor the changing nature of language use, and track the incorporation of new words into our culture (Munro 1991; Bernstein 1988). For instance, you may be familiar with some of the following terms being used on college campuses today: To *chill* is to stand someone up for a date ("She *chilled* on me, so I guess I'm staying home tonight"); to *box tonsils* or to *play tonsil hockey* is to kiss passionately; having *beer goggles* is a temporary loss of judgment due to alcohol intake ("Boy, I must have been wearing *beer goggles* when I agreed to go on a date with him"); a *McPaper* is a quickly written paper that isn't very good; and a *granola* is a person with a dated, 1960s outlook and personal style.

Another dynamic feature of language is the tendency of old, commonly used words to take on new meaning, that is, to be associated with new referents. For instance, in 1934, Fred Astaire starred in a movie entitled *The Gay Divorcee*. The title had nothing to do with the sexual orientation of any of the characters. At the time, *gay* was simply a reference to a person's emotional state. Only later did the term come to refer to a person's sexual preferences. Old words take on new meaning.

If words fall out of use, the strength of the association between a word and its referent tends to weaken. The denotative meaning of the word may remain logged somewhere in a dictionary. However, the rich associations that are connected to the word, its connotative meaning, seem to fade. Take, for example, the distinctive language that emerged during the 1960s. Such terms as *pig, put-on, bad vibes,* and *soul* were part of everyday conversation. Notice how difficult it is to generate precise definitions for some of these terms, even if you lived through that era. Near the end of the decade, *Newsweek* magazine printed a short "dictionary" of the terms of this era. *Put-on* was defined as "*n.* a subtly untrue statement made to mislead someone for humorous effect. *put-on, v.* Making such a statement (You'd say I'm putting you on. But it's no joke—Beatles, 'I'm So Tired')," while *soul* was characterized as, "*n.* In Am. Negro parlance, omnibus term for courage, sensitivity, humor, style, arrogance, and grace. Cf. Span. *duenede. adj.* E.g., soul music" ("The Freaks Had a Word for It" 1969, p. 18). Note how stiff and awkward these definitions seem. Do you think these definitions give you a really clear picture of how the words were used at the time? A denotative definition fails to capture the richness of a term's meaning, so the meaning is diluted as the word falls out of use.

Meaning Is Tied to Context

We have already pointed out that misunderstandings occur when meaning is assumed to be in the words themselves. A related mistaken belief is that the meaning of a word is constant, regardless of the context. Sociologist Kenneth Leiter (1980) provides an illuminating illustration: "The book is in the pen." Depending on the physical setting in which this sentence is uttered and the relationship between the persons interacting, this simple sentence can take on a number of different meanings. Imagine that two spies are discussing the location of a hidden microfilmed document, or that a hog farmer's wife is telling her husband where his recently purchased novel turned up. Perhaps an English teacher is telling students to relax when they are writing—speaking metaphorically about the writing process. In each of these cases, "the book is in the pen" takes on completely different meaning. This shows that language use has to be sensitive to the context in which it is used.

For the sake of examining this example, we can break the context down into the *physical setting* and the *relational context*. The physical setting consists of the actual physical environment in which a communication event occurs. The physical setting provides cues regarding what is topically relevant to the interaction. For example, the hog farmer knows what his wife is referring to because a pigpen is one of the physical features on a hog farm.

Meaning is also linked to the *relational context*. The relational context is the nature of the relationship between the interactants: their past history with each other, the rights and responsibilities implicit between them, and any emotional connections as well. If you had a parent, a sibling, a friend, and a romantic partner in a room, and you said, "I love you," to each of them, the same words would take on different meaning for each. To a large degree, that would be due to the different relationship you had with each of them.

Misunderstandings can occur when interactants hear the same words, but have different interpretations of the context in which the words were spoken. Many a TV sitcom plot is based on the notion that one person interprets the other's behavior as an indication of romantic interest, while the other saw no romantic relationship existing.

Meaning Is Tied to Intent

We can't rely on just words themselves to contain meaning. If we could, the following misunderstanding would not have occurred:

> LaSalle basketball coach, Speedy Morris, tells the following story: "When I first got the job at LaSalle, the phone rang and my wife told me it was *Sports Illustrated*. I cut myself shaving and fell down the steps in my rush to get the phone. And when I got there, a voice on the other end said, 'For just 75 cents an issue . . . .' "

Consider the nature of the misunderstanding. Coach Morris assumed that a reporter from *Sports Illustrated* wanted to interview him about his new job, when, in fact, the call was just an ordinary sales pitch, such as you and I would get. How could any misunderstanding occur? Did he not understand what his wife had said when she claimed *Sports Illustrated* was on the phone? That's unlikely. The key to this misunderstanding was that there was confusion regarding the *intent* of the telephone message. In order to understand a com-

Teaching Objective 4–8
Describe the ways in which meanings are interpreted on the basis of context, sequence, and perceived intent as well as through the words themselves.

Cross-reference 4–2
Sensitivity to context is essential to communication at all levels. Context affects perceptions (Chapter 2), the meanings of nonverbal communication (Chapter 5), and interpersonal relationships (Chapter 7). Also, an understanding of context is vital to effective audience analysis (Chapter 13).

munication event, we sometimes have to separate *what is said* from *what is done*. By looking at what is being done we are isolating the intent of the other person.

Take the example of everyday greetings. You see a friend on the street, and he or she says, "Hi, how are ya doing?" How do you respond? Do you tell your friend about the slightly scratchy feeling you've had in the back of your throat since morning? Do you reply that your energy level is much higher than it usually is at this time of the day? Probably not. If you do, you'll probably find that your friends will consider using a new greeting for you. Your friend is not really asking about your physical and/or emotional state. While the greeting sounds like a request for information, if you separate what is being said from what is being done, you'll realize that he or she is simply offering a greeting, the proper response to which is a greeting in return (for example, "Pretty good. How 'bout you?").

You might wonder at this point why language use evolved this way. Wouldn't it be easier if we were just literal all the time? Instead of asking how a person is doing when we greet him or her, we could just say, "Hello, I greet you, my friend." If we were to try this, however, we would not only sound funny, but would also lose much of the richness and subtlety of language use. Because of the way we presently use language, a speaker can actually *mean more than he or she says*. Through limited words, we can get a listener to fill in the gaps or the implications of what we say. Imagine, for example, that your roommate has cranked up his or her stereo while you are trying to study. You could scream, "Turn it down!" Or you could make the observation, "That stereo is kinda loud." Either way, you are requesting your roommate to turn the music down. The difference is that the second approach asks him or her *indirectly*. This indirectness is possible because our language use is not strictly literal. In this instance, it also has the advantage of being more tactful. People often respond to the form of language used. If you scream at your roommate, it's likely that he or she will do the same in return. However, if you "state a fact" or "make an observation," the other person is less likely to feel personally threatened.

The potential downside of indirectness is that the other person may not accurately perceive your intent. If you tell your roommate that the music sure is loud, and he or she replies, "Yeah, isn't this a great tape when it's cranked up?", you know you'll have to try a more direct approach. Ultimately, the fact that we search for intent in verbal messages is not only inevitable; it also makes language use much more interesting.

Meaning Is Tied to Sequencing

As you can see by now, we rely on all sorts of outside knowledge in order to connect meaning to words. We rely on knowledge of the denotative and connotative meanings of words, knowledge of the relationship between interactants, and even knowledge (or a best guess) of the intent of the speaker. Another type of knowledge we rely on is our understanding of how language is typically used. There are all sorts of patterns and conventions we follow when using language.

Not only do these conventions provide the rules for *constructing* verbal communication; they also are *resources,* or rules of interpretation, for understanding language use. Consider the way we use **sequencing**, for instance. Sequencing is necessary in verbal interaction. Everyone cannot talk at once and hope to be understood. Thus, one person talks and finishes, and then the next person talks and finishes (generally). This is a mundane feature of language on the surface, but this simple feature allows us to do some creative things with language. Consider an example. You bump into a friend between classes and the following exchange takes place:

> You: You going to the party Friday night?
> Friend: Is the Pope Catholic?

On the surface, your friend's reply looks pretty goofy. As noted in the previous section, you have to separate what is being said by your friend from what is being done. Your friend is obviously going to the party, but how do you know that? You asked a question and you got a question in return. How do you make sense of that?

To make sense of your friend's reply, you're relying on two implicit rules about how we use language. The first rule is that people should stay on topic; in other words, their contributions should be relevant to what came before. Hence, you assume (until proven otherwise) that your friend's reply is relevant to your question. The second rule is more directly tied to sequencing. This rule is that some types of language use come in pairs, in which one person performs the first part of the pair, and the other person is expected to perform the second part of the pair. Examples of these *adjacency pairs* include a greeting (followed by another greeting), a compliment (followed by an acceptance or rejection of it), and an invitation (again, followed by an acceptance or a rejection). One of the basic forms of these adjacency pairs is the question-answer pair.

In the example above, you asked a question and expected an answer. You also assumed that your friend would respond in a relevant manner. When your friend replied with a question about the Pope's religious affiliation, you were forced to look deeper into the reply. No doubt, you quickly surmised that your friend's answer to your question was not just yes, but "obviously yes."

Discussion Question 4–8
What are some examples of ways in which context and sequencing have affected the meanings you attributed to another's words?

Teaching Objective 4–9
Stress the social implications of language: its power to include and exclude (especially with regard to racist and sexist language), to define roles and privileges, and to describe how individuals and cultures perceive their world.

THE SOCIAL EFFECTS OF LANGUAGE USE

Until now we've discussed the functions of language use and how we come to understand it as meaningful. We now turn to the social impact of language. Some of the social consequences of language use are predictable and intentional, while others are simply the natural consequences of that use.

Language Use Defines Membership

We noted earlier that word usage changes. New words come into play, and old words take on new meaning. As new usage occurs, it doesn't just pop up and spread to every member of the language community overnight. New word usage is a gradual process, typically beginning in some subpopulation of the language community, and sometimes never spreading to the whole culture. One result of this is that language use helps identify group membership. People who have similar needs, or who want to be identified with a particular group, adopt the unique words that are characteristic of that group. Specialized language that differs from what is generally used in the population is often referred to as a *sublanguage*. In everyday terms, we often refer to this as *slang* or *jargon*.

Table 4.1 presents just a few sublanguages. Can you think of other groups that use a sublanguage? Consider the jargon of certain professional groups, such as doctors, lawyers, and economists. Have you heard unique terms used by different racial or ethnic groups? How about the specialized language used by people with a focused common interest, such as computer users, hunters, or gardeners?

There are some clear social consequences that result when people rely on sublanguage vocabulary—consequences for both the people who understand the sublanguage and those who don't. One consequence is *the establishment of a private code*. A second consequence is *group identification*. A third, related consequence is *the alienation of nonusers*.

By establishing a private code, a sublanguage allows the users to hide information from nonusers. Consider how the language of the underworld, or *argot*, would benefit prison inmates whose world is closely watched. Or consider the medical profession, in which doctors, nurses, and technicians can speak openly about a patient's condition in front of the patient or family with impunity. We

Doctors share a sublanguage consisting of medical jargon. This specialized language fosters group identification and ensures technical precision. Some people complain that it also often confuses patients.

Table 4.1
Terms from Various Sublanguages

In his book *Slang!*, Paul Dickson has compiled these examples of terms from selected sublanguages.

The language used in prison or in the criminal world is often referred to as argot:

> *All day and night*—A life sentence
> *The dance hall*—The execution chamber
> *Gladiator school*—A maximum security prison
> *Shank*—A knife, or to stab with a knife
> *Strapped*—A gang term for armed

Special terms have developed in the real estate business to reflect its concerns:

> *Birdbath*—A paved area that holds water, though it is not meant to
> *Crank*—To refinance an existing mortgage
> *Handyman's special*—A house badly in need of repair
> *Kennel*—A substandard house
> *Monkey*—The mortgage

Auctioneers have come up with terms useful for their profession:

> *Boat anchor* or *Hernia special*—A heavy item with little appeal
> *Early*—A descriptive term used for anything old, pre-Sputnik
> *Lookers*—People who don't bid on any merchandise
> *Puffer*—A bidder in league with the auctioneer to raise prices
> *Turnpike cruiser* or *New York tureen*—A bedpan

The world of automotive sales has some unique terms as well.

> *Bagel*—A poorly maintained car
> *Barefoot pilgrim*—A naive, overly trusting car buyer
> *Cement mixer*—A car that makes loud noises
> *Flea*—A car buyer out to get a great bargain
> *Roach*—A car buyer with no credit, or with bad credit

Source: Paul Dickson, *Slang!* (New York: Pocket Books, 1990).

are not suggesting that members of the medical community are particularly deceptive or sneaky, or that medical jargon was developed to keep patients in the dark. Medical jargon, as a sublanguage, developed from a need for technical precision. That this sublanguage allows doctors and nurses a private code is simply a by-product. However, this ability to use a private code is probably recognized and occasionally used.

A second consequence, one alluded to earlier in the chapter, is that use of a sublanguage allows a user to claim group identification. You might have noticed this in your own communicative behavior. Does your word choice change depending on whom you're with? This suggests that we not only try to adapt to our audience, but also try to establish that we're like the listener when we do this. A common pattern, for instance, is using one kind of language for relatives and another for friends. When we're with older relatives, we try to be polite and pleasant (because families like to think of themselves as groups of "nice people"). But when we're with our friends, we might try to use language that reflects how the group of friends sees itself. That could be language that is more contemporary, more vulgar, more "cool," more sophisticated, or more cynical, depending on the group.

A sublanguage can also set a group apart by challenging the values of the larger culture. In this sense, some sublanguages are seen as "subversive." For example, in the 1960s, members of the counterculture (that is, "hippies") used the term *pigs* to refer to police. This clearly challenged the view of the dominant culture that police, whose stated purpose was to protect and serve, warranted respect. The counterculture was never a formal club with dues and identity cards; one way for people to portray themselves as members of the counterculture was simply to adopt the language. If you wanted to claim membership in that group, all you had to do was to call police "pigs" and use other terms and symbols of the counterculture (for example, wear bell-bottomed blue jeans, wear peace symbols, etc.). Can you think of any ways people claim membership in subculture groups nowadays? (See the Mastering Communication Skills box.)

Language Use Defines Rights and Responsibilities

Another social consequence of our language use is that it helps to define our rights and responsibilities. Our rights (that is, what we are allowed to do) and our responsibilities (that is, what we are expected to do) are seldom spelled out explicitly in our everyday behavior. There are laws that govern some of your behavior as a citizen, and a job description may define some of your rights and responsibilities in the workplace, but what guides your behavior as a family member? When you meet a person for the first time, how do you know the level of formality at which the conversation will be conducted? We certainly rely on roles, past experience, and other social knowledge, but we also rely on language use. Language use helps us to negotiate and define the rights and responsibilities of people as they interact.

For instance, consider the use of titles or forms of address, sometimes referred to as *membership categorization devices* (MCDs) (Sacks 1972). An MCD places the person being referred to in a category, such as Misters, Madams, officers, reverends, or captains. Along with these MCDs, there are certain expectations of the rights and responsibilities accorded the person being addressed. To take a simple example, imagine that you meet a friend of a friend, and he is introduced to you as Bob Jones. You might say, "Pleased to meet you, Mr. Jones." You have accorded a level of formality to the conversation because of the MCD you have used. If he were to say, "You can just call me Bob," he would be lowering the level of formality, and he might also be adjusting the rights and responsibilities he is claiming for himself.

MASTERING COMMUNICATION SKILLS

The Dominant Culture Strikes Back: Co-Optation of Language and Symbols

Societies tend to pull things back toward the middle. Subversive, non-traditional groups are often pressured to join the mainstream. Though it may not be intentional, one of the mechanisms that pulls fringe groups back to the mainstream is the process of co-optation. Co-optation occurs when the dominant group accepts or adopts something as their own. This could include words, symbols, behaviors, and so on. From the subgroup's point of view, as soon as the dominant culture accepts its words or symbols, those words or symbols are no longer shocking, attention getting, or a challenge to the dominant culture. Hence, they lose their usefulness to the subculture. Blue jeans, for instance, were once a subversive statement from the counterculture of the 1960s. Long associated with "working-class society," jeans were not part of an adult's view of a well-dressed son or daughter. Hence, during the 1960s, wearing blue jeans became a political and social statement (solidarity with the working class). Eventually, the dominant culture co-opted the wearing of blue jeans. In time, it even became popular to wear "designer" jeans—a notion that seems completely out of place given the history of blue jeans.

Note, too, how advertisers will often adopt the language of a youthful subculture to make their products appear more appealing. For instance, a mainstream department store may advertise the "rad threads" they offer, associating their products with the language of skateboarders.

Try to think of examples of co-optation that are occurring now. For example, rap music often portrays values and uses language in ways that are not in agreement with the dominant culture. But what happens when rap star Hammer starts appearing in Pepsi and KFC commercials? As institutions of the dominant culture adopt spokespersons from subculture groups, is the subculture's ability to be subversive weakened? Can you think of other examples?

MCDs may be used strategically to highlight roles and the rights and responsibilities associated with them. Consider the teacher-student relationship. You may have some teachers who insist on being addressed more formally, with "doctor," or "professor." Others may invite you to call them by a first name. Does this have any effect on how you deal with them? Get a teacher mad, and it's a good way to get her to address you more formally (for example, Mr., Ms., or whatever). By addressing you formally, the teacher can attempt to heighten your responsibilities (for example, punctuality, class manners, etc.) in the teacher-student relationship. In general, language helps us define our rights and responsibilities, a point that will be extended when we discuss sexist and racist language later in the chapter.

Language Use Reveals How Others See the World

We have seen that the language you use influences how you see the world around you. The flip side of this principle is that by paying attention to how other people use language we can gain considerable insight into how they see the world around them. At a basic level, we can get some indication of a person's interests and knowledge by their language use. Going back to the wine example, a person who can speak eloquently about the characteristics of wine is probably interested in and knowledgeable about it.

We can observe how others use language to gain insight into their perceptions of social events, including how they perceive causal relationships. The next time two of your friends get into a fight with each other, pay close attention to how each describes the conflict. It is likely that both will repeat essentially the same "facts" of the incident, but listen closely to how their descriptions vary when they tell you the cause of the conflict and the intent of the other person. It is quite likely that each person will describe him- or herself as having had to react to the other's outrageous behavior. Furthermore, each will probably infer that the other is to blame for the conflict.

■ PROBLEMS CAUSED BY LANGUAGE USE

Teaching Objective 4–10
Demonstrate some of the problems or limitations inherent in language use.

Language is an incredible tool that allows us to think in complex ways, and it also allows us to share those thoughts with others. Unfortunately, language is not without its problems. It can influence our thought processes in undesirable ways. Furthermore, it is not a foolproof way of sharing thoughts with others. Here we mention just some of the perceptual and social problems that are connected to language use. (See Figure 4.5 for a summary.)

Polarization

Have you ever noticed how our language often splits the world into opposing dichotomies: into categories that represent extreme opposites? A person is described as tall or short. A painting is beautiful or dreadful. A class is exciting or boring. A room may be described as warm and relaxing, or cold and sterile. Language leads to extremes of opposition. This is not to say that we can't talk and think about things that are "in-between." However, notice how it tends to take about twice as many words to describe a person who is neither tall nor short, or a painting that is neither beautiful nor dreadful. This tendency of language to force us to think or talk about extremes is known as **polarization**. Polarization can be detrimental if it prevents us from recognizing and considering all the gray areas between the black and the white. For example, it is currently popular to pigeonhole politicians as being either conservative or liberal. Yet this may not capture a politician's actual record. Representative Smith may take a conservative stand on monetary issues, while having a more liberal

Problems Caused by the Connection Between Language & Perception

POLARIZATION	The tendency of language to force us to think or talk about extremes
INTENSIONAL ORIENTATION	The tendency to treat labels or words as real
BYPASSING	A language-related problem that occurs when people fail to share the same connection between a word and what it stands for (its referent)
FACT-INFERENCE CONFUSION	A language-related problem that occurs because we cannot determine from language alone whether a speaker is describing a direct experience or an inference drawn from assorted information
STATIC EVALUATION	The tendency to allow words to capture an object, event, or feeling at a particular point in time, regardless of intervening events

Figure 4.5
Problems Caused by the Connection Between Language and Perception.

approach to social issues. Simply calling Representative Smith a liberal does not do justice to his or her overall political views.

Because of the way we use language to think about the world we encounter, and because of the way language channels us to think in terms of opposites, language can be a barrier to effective thinking and effective communication. What can be done to avoid this problem, or minimize its detrimental effects? Certainly, the first step is awareness of the problem. Recognize when language is being used to force you to choose between "guns and butter" (a reference to the never-ending political decision of whether to make national defense or social programs the top priority). Take the time to consider the gray area in between. Finally, be willing to explore the gray area if a middle ground can be reached (for example, "I want both a strong defense *and* adequate social programs—and give them to me in moderation, please.").

Intensional Orientation

Another perceptually-based language problem is the **intensional orientation**. This is the tendency to treat labels or words as real. One of the best illustrations of this phenomenon was reported by the linguist Benjamin Lee Whorf (Whorf, 1956). Working as an insurance investigator at one point in his life, Whorf looked into the case of an industrial explosion. Apparently, several workers were on break, smoking around some gasoline drums that were labeled "Empty." The workers were reacting to the term *empty*, inferring that *empty* meant *safe*. In other words, they were thinking of the reality of words, instead of the reality of the physical world. Most people who handle gasoline know that the fumes of the gasoline are extremely dangerous. Although the drums had no liquid gasoline in them (in that sense, they were "empty"), they still were filled with explosive fumes. It was the fumes that exploded in this case.

Advertisers are well aware that people react to words, often without thinking about what is behind them. That's why packages are covered with all sorts of puffery, such as, "new," "improved," "new formula," "extra," and "imported." If a merchant advertises shirts that are made of "100% imported cotton," should that make a difference? Does "domestic" have such a bad ring to it? Is imported cotton any better than American cotton? Such advertising ploys assume that the consumer will react to the words without considering the reality behind them.

In many ways, language is a two-edged sword. On the one hand, it allows us to think abstractly, to transcend the present by talking about the past and the future, and to share meaning with others. These are powerful features of language. On the other hand, language can impose blinders on us by limiting what we can think of and perceive. We can also distance ourselves too much from the concrete world of the here and now. The result of this is that we may react to abstract symbols (words) rather than to the physical realities of our world. This is the problem we face with the intensional orientation.

Bypassing

Two friends were talking, and the topic turned to a mutual acquaintance, Dan. For some time, each related stories about Dan, and what he had been up to recently. It was only after about ten minutes of conversation that the friends realized that each had been referring to a different person named Dan. In our terms, there had been no common referent throughout their discussion of Dan. This is an example of one form of bypassing.

Bypassing is a language-related problem that occurs when people fail to share the same symbol-referent associations. It is the result of the arbitrary connection between symbols and referents in language that we discussed earlier in this chapter.

Bypassing takes two forms: (1) As in the "Dan" example above, two people may use the same term, but refer to different things. (2) The second form of bypassing occurs when people use different words to refer to the same thing, but don't realize they have a common referent. This makes their actual agreement appear to be a disagreement. Imagine that Amie and Beth are shopping for a watch for their father. Amie insists that they find something that is "manly," while Beth is sure he needs a watch that is "elegant." They argue back and forth for a while, only to realize that Amie's view of a manly watch is about the same as Beth's vision of an elegant watch. Using different terms to refer to the same thing, without realizing it, is a type of bypassing.

There is one clear technique that can be used to avoid or prevent bypassing: You can paraphrase what the other says. As we saw in Chapter 3, **paraphrasing** is simply restating what the other says as a means of providing feedback about your interpretation. In the example above, if Beth had said, "By 'manly,' do you mean uncluttered features, three or fewer metallic tones, and a brushed finish?" Beth and Amie could have recognized their underlying agreement much earlier.

Obviously, we can't constantly paraphrase every time someone talks to us. It would take an enormous amount of time, and conversations would inch forward at a snail's pace. But it is a useful technique when key terms need to be identified.

The Fact-Inference Confusion

We gain a significant amount of information by talking to other people. In other words, we use social networks to gather information. We often have to make decisions based on the information we receive through social networks. But how do we know whether such social network information is factual—based on another's direct observation—or a conclusion drawn by the speaker based on limited information? The problem is that we can't tell the difference, at least not on the basis of language alone. The way we use language does not reveal whether a person is describing a direct experience or an inference, and therein lies the crux of the **fact-inference confusion**. The problem is that we may take what the other person says as accurate or factual, when that person may simply have arrived at a poor conclusion based on the information available. Let's look briefly at the difference between facts and inferences, and then at an example of this problem.

For the sake of this discussion, we can consider what a person directly experiences through her sensory apparatus as "factual." If I ask you about the weather outside, and you see a perfectly blue sky when you check, then your subsequent report about clear weather would be based on direct experience or observation. If you taste the soup, and tell me it's too salty, that is based on direct experience as well. However, if I ask you how the stock market will be doing next year, there's no way you can give me an answer based on direct experience. You have to make an inference, based on other information. You may check the money flow through the banking system, the likelihood of improvements in the real estate market, and numerous other indicators to provide you with an educated guess, but you could never give an answer based on direct experience.

The problem arises when a person is physically capable of providing information based on direct experience but may not be doing so. The language used (for example, word choice, sentence structure, etc.) will not provide any clues. For example, you might ask me about the weather outside. I come back and tell you it's warm and sunny. You would probably assume that I went outside and checked personally. What if, instead of sticking my head out of the building, I just looked in the hallway and observed how people were dressed? I didn't see any heavy coats or umbrellas, so I inferred that it was warm and sunny out. From my report to you, it is impossible for you to tell whether I have passed on directly experienced (factual) information, or if I have merely passed along an inference. Now, there's little difficulty involved if all you have to do is go back indoors and grab a jacket, but imagine the following scenario. You've wanted to ask Pat out for some time. The problem is, you don't know if Pat is interested in you. You ask your friend Tonya to help out. Tonya reports back that Pat will go out with you; all you have to do is ask. Would you leave it at that, and just take Tonya's word? Or would you find out how Tonya got her information? It would probably make a difference to you whether Tonya got a direct reply from Pat, or if Tonya just mentioned your name among a group of friends and looked to see if Pat grimaced when you were mentioned. The former approach would be more closely based on direct experience, while the latter approach would yield an inference that Tonya had drawn. Too often, we assume that information from such a social network is based on direct observation, when, in fact, it might be based on an inference.

One way to avoid this problem is to find out whether the information was directly experienced. Two difficulties arise here. First, the information may have passed through several people before it got to you. As the information gets passed along, each person in the network may filter the information and draw various inferences. Ultimately, you can't tell what was directly observed and what was inferred. A second problem is that it is somewhat rude to question whether a reported event was directly observed. You can do it, but if you question the accuracy of reports all the time, you won't have many friends for long. What you can do is ask yourself whether the person reporting the information has been the source of reliable information in the past, and whether he or she was in a position to directly observe what is being reported.

Static Evaluation

A final problem associated with language use is static evaluation. **Static evaluation** is the tendency of words to capture an object, event, or feeling at a particular point in time, regardless of intervening events. The way we use language is not always sensitive to the changes that occur around us. Sometimes when we capture something in words, we fail to see how it changes subsequently.

As the Persian Gulf war against Iraq heated up, some antiwar protesters began to surface, questioning our participation in that war. Counterprotesters soon hit the streets, voicing their outrage at the antiwar protesters for failing to support the men and women serving in the military. Interestingly, the antiwar protesters had tried to voice their support for the servicemen and -women, while questioning the policy of the decision makers in Washington. In other words, the antiwar protesters wanted to avoid the abuse that had been inflicted on the soldiers who returned from the Vietnam War twenty-five years earlier. Many others, however, had developed a static evaluation of the term *antiwar protester*. To these people, the only way to think about war protesters was to think of the 1960s variety: loud, often obscene, long haired, questioning everything sacred, calling returning soldiers "baby killers." Their vision of a war protester was twenty-five years old, though the contemporary protesters were voicing other concerns.

One way to minimize the effects of a static evaluation is to index comments; that is, to situate them in time. In the example above, you might talk about contemporary war protesters, as opposed to 1960s protesters.

Sexist and Racist Language

In addition to causing perceptual and social problems, some language patterns can also result in offending others. Here we briefly want to mention the problems of sexist and racist language. Our point here is not simply that these forms of language use are not "polite." While this is true, far more important is the fact that these language forms are often used to deny power to certain individuals by restricting their rights and burdening them with excessive responsibilities.

Sexist Language. It has been said that both the structure of the English language and the way it is typically used discriminate against women. For instance, the English language does not have a non–gender-specific pronoun to refer to both men and women. As a result, users of the language have tended to use male pronouns (for example, *he, his, him*) even when the referent could be either male or female. This becomes a problem because the language then tends to ignore the role of women. Language shapes expectations, particularly in children. When children recognize that the "doers," the active characters in story and reference, are mostly "he," they develop expectations and aspirations accordingly. Language use alone suggests to children that boys grow up to do important things, while girls grow up to fade into the background. **Sexist language** is language usage that has the effect of demeaning or otherwise offending a specific gender.

Not only does the language structure discriminate against women, but we often make matters worse by the way we use language. For example, we tend to qualify our language use when we acknowledge women in positions of authority. Have you ever heard someone say, "I went to see my doctor, who's a woman . . . ," or "My cousin is a female pilot"? You wouldn't expect to hear someone talk about their Irish doctor, or the Catholic pilot. Yet, for some reason, many find it necessary to qualify and thereby diminish the role of a woman in a position of responsibility. Any variation from a role expectation is noted (the term "male nurse" is equally bad).

A third, related problem is the tendency to place women in limited roles, such as the supporter role or sex object role, through our terms of reference. We discussed the importance of membership categorization devices earlier in the chapter. These can be used to restrict people's rights and expectations. When women are referred to as "chicks," "babes," "broads," and the like, it is an attempt to place them in a role as sex object, offering them few rights, and limiting what they are to be acknowledged and rewarded for. The "supporter" role is equally limiting, as it devalues the actual accomplishments of women. Author D. W. Cross (1979) wondered how men would feel if their work were acknowledged in the same manner as women's efforts often are when she wrote:

> Yesterday, State Senator Thomas Friedmann and Lieutenant Governor Richard Terris attended the festive benefit launching the new statewide muscular dystrophy drive.
>
> Blue-eyed Senator Friedmann, the husband of Mrs. Thomas Friedmann, wore a flattering tweed vest set off by a daring green ascot. A for-

Discussion Question 4–9
What are the racist and sexist terms you learned as a child? What impact have they had on how you feel about yourself? What impact have they had on how you relate to other people?

Current Research 4–5
Eleven-year-olds are unable to recognize "man" as a generic term most of the time; this finding supports the likelihood that women are not perceived as equally present and active in literature. (Wolff, Struckman-Johnson, and Flanagin. Generic 'man': grammatical distribution and perception. In Pearson, Turner, and Todd-Mancillas, *Gender and Communication*. Dubuque: William C. Brown, 1991, p. 83)

Current Research 4–6
In a paper presented at the Central States Communication Association convention in April of 1991, Jo Young Switzer reported: "Even in 1990, women Assistant Secretaries in the Department of Veteran's Affairs [in Washington] are routinely called 'Little Miss Coffeemaker' and 'Angel' by Ed Derwinski, Secretary of the Department." (Switzer, Jo Young. Political women speak: communicative adaptations in a 'man's world,' submitted version, p. 4)

mer redhead, Senator Friedmann was constantly surrounded by crowds of admirers.

Richard Terris, the pert father of four, also drew admiring glances with his tight-fitting turtleneck sweater, which clung provocatively to his trim, muscular 40-32-36 frame. Dick, who previously served as the Undersecretary of State, was voted "Best-looking Senior" by his high-school class. (pp. 137–138)

Sex bias in language is simply unnecessary. Sexist terms, such as "babe," and "chick" can simply be avoided. Although a non–gender-specific pronoun has not been adopted or widely accepted, we can often avoid making gender-specific references. The "chairman" can be referred to as the "chairperson," or simply as the "chair." "Authors" of the female persuasion do not have to be called "authoresses," as the original term is nonspecific. Or alternative terms can be substituted, such as "writer." There are a number of fine guides that can help you to avoid these terms (see, for example, Maggio 1987). The Focus on Leadership box discusses sex differences in the use of language.

Racist Language.   Racist language is more than just rude; it has broader individual and social consequences. **Racist language** is a language usage that has the effect of demeaning or otherwise offending a specific group or groups. In his book, *The Language of Ethnic Conflict: Social Organization and Lexical Culture,* I. L. Allen (1983) lists six different types of ethnic slurs:

1. proper names of groups that are changed into derisive adjectives;
2. ethnic derogation through metaphors—"Italian perfume" for garlic, "Jewish flag" for a dollar bill, "Mexican carwash" for leaving the car out in the rain;
3. names changed to derisive verb forms—to "welsh", to "jew", to "dutch";
4. "ethnicons"—"turk" for a cruel person, "welsher" for a reneger, "polock" for a dumb person;
5. slurs as proverbs, as in certain children's rhymes; and
6. ethnic slurs, as in stories or jokes.

Current Research 4–7
Interviews with Afro-Americans on interethnic conversation indicated recurrent issues of negative stereotyping and felt powerlessness. (Hecht, Ribeau, and Alberts. An Afro-American perspective on interethnic communication. *Communication Monographs, 56,* 1989, pp. 385-408)

One of the disturbing things that racist language does is to justify different treatment for those who are not part of the dominant social class. Ethnic slurs allow a group to distinguish between "humans" and "nonhumans." A group that is labeled with racist language is somehow less human. In the eyes of the group using the racist language, this allows the labeled group to be treated differently. It justifies the opinion that "nonhumans" don't deserve the same rights as everyone else. And if inequalities exist between the groups, the ethnic slurs somehow suggest that those inequalities are reasonable.

By separating groups and creating a hierarchy of "good" and "bad" groups, racist language also helps those on top to maintain control of the social order. The dominant group will control the preferred social values. Hence, diversity will be ridiculed with further ethnic slurs, and other groups will not be allowed to influence the dominant values of the culture.

Finally, racist language is used to insult and injure others. A side effect of

FOCUS ON LEADERSHIP

Sex Differences in Language Use

In general, leaders must be flexible to maximize their effectiveness. Specifically, sometimes leaders need to adapt their language style to communicate effectively, particularly when interacting with members of the opposite sex or when settling disputes between male and female subordinates.

Linguistics professor Deborah Tannen (1990) wrote about the different ways men and women use language. Tannen notes the differences in the male and female language styles and traces these differences to some inevitable conflicts. Tannen argues that men use language to create social hierarchy. A man will also attempt to use language to claim a higher status in that hierarchy than that of the person he is talking to. By contrast, women use language to establish and maintain a network of social connections. Rather than using language to dominate another person, a woman will use it to establish closeness and support. As a result of these differences, men and women appear to play the same game of communication with different sets of rules. Men challenge one another verbally and expect to be challenged in return. Women provide support and expect social connections to be tended. When men and women interact, the clash of their typical styles causes problems.

In a corporate or work setting, a man may use his typical style and verbally challenge and assert authority when interacting with others. If he is interacting with a woman, she may take this as a personal attack and become defensive. In the same setting, a woman may spend time establishing rapport and engaging in small talk to develop a personal connection. If she is interacting with a man, he may feel that such small talk is just a waste of time, and that control needs to be asserted in the conversation (by him).

Orders from the boss are another area of conflict and concern. A female boss will often phrase a directive as a request (for example, "Can you get that Jones file done by tomorrow?"), rather than an order (for example, "Be sure that Jones file is on my desk by tomorrow."). To a man, the request sounds optional, or at least of low priority. If the work isn't done on time, the female boss feels that she isn't being taken seriously, and her expressed displeasure makes the male subordinate feel manipulated.

As a leader, it's vital that you recognize the verbal sparring style that men use, and the verbal support style that women use. Though these are generalizations that don't hold true for every individual, they still demonstrate the need to adapt your verbal style, particularly when working with subordinates of the opposite sex.

this is that people who are the object of racist language may come to hate the group of which they are a part. Racist language forces a false negative self-image on people who are the target of this language. This can lead to self-loathing and alienation as well.

As you can see, sexist and racist language are worse than just rude. They also have detrimental social effects.

Summary

In this chapter we defined verbal communication as any communication that uses language. We defined language as an organized system of arbitrary symbols used to exchange messages. Language gives us categories for understanding the world around us. Hence, language influences perception.

Verbal communication serves several functions, including an instrumental function that allows us to achieve our goals; a regulatory function that allows us to control and influence our interactions; a social function that allows us to develop our individual identity and sense of personhood; and a problem-solving function that allows us to understand and master our environment.

Perhaps the most complex aspect of verbal communication is the link between language and meaning. Meaning is not found in words themselves. Instead, it is created by the shared understanding of the people who use the language. Words possess both denotative and connotative meanings. Since the connection between meaning and language is created by people, language is dynamic. Words change meaning, and new words come into use. As users of language, we must look beyond ourselves to uncover meaning. We can discern meaning by investigating context, perceived intent, and linguistic cues such as sequencing.

The problems associated with language use demonstrate that communication does not always proceed smoothly. Because language influences perception of our experiences (and experiences similarly influence our use of language), language can hinder or enhance the way we see our world. Polarization forces us to think in extremes. An intensional orientation is the tendency to treat labels as real. Bypassing occurs when we fail to share agreed-upon meaning with others.

Just as language can empower us, it can also disempower us. Racist and sexist language demeans its victims and restricts the rights of those who are its targets. Such language practices should be avoided at all costs.

Exercises

1. Expanded language development can give the user a greater appreciation of differences and distinctions. This was pointed out with the example of wine in the chapter. Think of two areas where your vocabulary has expanded in the last year or two. List some of the new terms you became familiar with. In what way (if at all) has this given you a different appreciation of those subjects?

2. People often try to hide behind words by using euphemisms and double-speak. Follow the next public scandal in the news (watch TV news, read newspaper and newsmagazine articles on the subject) and take note of how public figures use language for damage control or to fend off blame. For example, during the 1990–1992 Gulf War against Iraq, members of the press uncovered several incidents in which U.S. troops accidentally fired upon allied soldiers, with tragic results. When asked to explain these incidents, U.S. military spokespersons claimed that losses due to "friendly fire" were the unfortunate result of the confusion on the battlefield. Why would the spokesperson use the term friendly fire, instead of allied attacks, or fratricide? Compile a list of other examples which soften the hard edge of reality, or shift blame.

3. Use this exercise to distinguish the denotative from the connotative meaning of words. Pair up with another member of the class. Individually, develop denotative (dictionary-type) definitions of five or six words. Then provide a connotative definition for each. After you're done, compare your definitions with those of your fellow class member. Which are more similar, the denotative or connotative definitions? When the definitions vary widely, try to explain how these differences occur.

4. New words emerge constantly, and old words are often used in novel ways. Develop a list of the new words and novel word use that you hear on campus. What subject matter do they tend to cover? Do you, or have you heard anyone else, use this language to claim group membership?

Ellis, D. G., and Donohue, W. A. (Eds.) (1986). *Contemporary issues in language and discourse processes.* Hillsdale, NJ: Lawrence Erlbaum.

■ **Related Readings**

This scholarly book brings together the writings of many of the notable researchers who study language and discourse processes. The chapters cover a wide range of theoretical and research concerns. Much is revealed about the connection between language use and meaning.

Enkvist, N. E. (1980). Categories of situational context from the perspective of stylistics. *Language teaching and linguistics: Abstracts, 13*(2): 75–95.

What does it mean when we say that language has to be understood in context? Enkvist addresses this question by categorizing the different senses of *context*. He explores the areas of linguistic context, compositional context, temporal context, relational context, and more.

Haney, W. V. (1973). *Communication and organizational behavior: Text and cases* (3rd ed.). Homewood, IL: R. D. Irwin.

The analysis of such language problems as polarization and bypassing can be traced to Haney. In addition to covering these problems in great depth, the author provides numerous examples from organizational settings. Haney also manages to suggest a wide range of techniques for coping with these problems.

Maggio, R. (1987). *The nonsexist word finder: A dictionary of gender-free usage.* Phoenix, AZ: Oryx Press.

This book is a treasure for any writer. In addition to identifying sexist language, the author provides alternatives, gives suggestions for how to alter gender-specific terms, and indicates when certain gender-specific terms must be understood in their historical context.

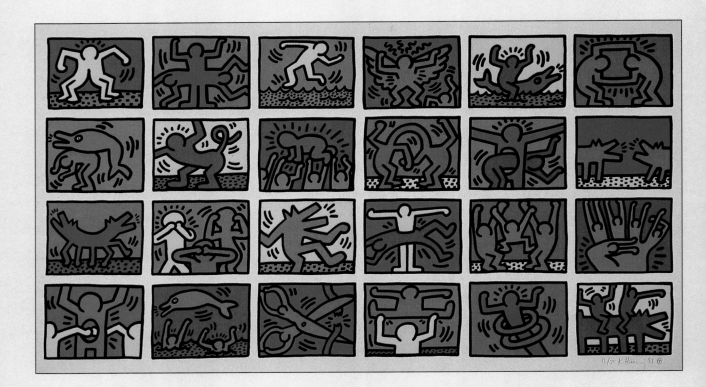

CHAPTER 5

Nonverbal Communication

Chapter objectives

After reading this chapter you should be able to:

1. define nonverbal communication and describe how it differs from verbal communication

2. explain why skill in nonverbal communication is essential for leaders

3. describe how nonverbal communication can change or modify a verbal message

4. discuss the social functions of nonverbal communication

5. describe cross-cultural differences in nonverbal behaviors, including body movement ("kinesics"), the use of space ("proxemics"), and touching behavior ("haptics")

6. explain the role of paralanguage in nonverbal communication

Key terms and concepts

nonverbal communication
kinesics
emblems
illustrators
affect displays
regulators
adaptors
proxemics
personal space
territoriality
intimate distance
personal distance
social distance
public distance
haptics
vocalics
paralanguage
chronemics

One of the primary responsibilities of a leader is decision making. Successful decision making, in turn, requires accurate information. As we saw in Chapter 3, to acquire accurate information, a leader must be an effective listener. Getting accurate information also requires that a leader be able to accurately interpret verbal messages and be able to deal with the problems that occur in the verbal realm. In this chapter, we show that leaders must also be sensitive to and acute observers of nonverbal communication.

Because nonverbal messages can have such a profound influence on our understanding of a communication event, we seldom consider the verbal message alone. Consider the opening example in Chapter 4, in which a friend comments on your sweater. The statement "Hey, I really like that sweater you're wearing" was transformed from a compliment to a sarcastic comment when your friend rolled his eyes and jabbed another friend with an elbow as he said it. To accurately interpret this, or any communication event, the nonverbal messages must be weighed in conjunction with the accompanying verbal messages. As a leader, you must be able to interpret messages accurately in order to have the necessary information to make effective decisions. Understanding nonverbal communication is crucial for accurate message interpretation.

In this chapter we provide an overview of nonverbal communication, beginning with a discussion of the controversy surrounding how *nonverbal* should be defined. We compare nonverbal communication to verbal communication and illustrate how each mode influences the other. We also explore the different channels through which nonverbal communication is expressed. At the end of the chapter suggestions are provided to improve your ability to use and interpret nonverbal messages.

DEFINING NONVERBAL COMMUNICATION

In the preceding chapter we saw that defining verbal communication is somewhat more complex than you might have anticipated. Similarly, defining nonverbal communication can also be difficult. One way to begin is to look at how others have defined *nonverbal* in the past. These definitions can provide an initial sense of direction:

> *Nonverbal communication* [can] be defined as *all messages (or communications) which are not coded in words.* The major distinction between verbal and nonverbal communicative behavior is that verbal behavior is organized by language systems, whereas nonverbal behavior is not. (Lewis 1975, p. 151)

> . . . Nonverbal communication can be defined as communication involving signals "other than words" as long as it is understood that the

distinction between words and "other" signals is sometimes unclear and overlapping. (Knapp 1990, pp. 54–55)

Vocal Versus Nonvocal

As these definitions and the definition of verbal communication in the preceding chapter suggest, the verbal-nonverbal distinction cannot be based on whether the message is spoken or not. As we noted in Chapter 4, written messages and American Sign Language are both considered verbal, though neither is spoken. Similarly, though accents, vocal "fillers" (for example, "um," "uh," etc.), and vocal characteristics (for example, tone, pitch, etc.) are produced by the voice, they are all considered part of the nonverbal domain.

Arbitrary Symbol Use

A more useful distinction can be made between "symbolic" and "nonsymbolic" message systems. In the last chapter we pointed out that verbal communication is symbolic. In other words, there is an arbitrary connection between a word or

Current Research 5–1
Hickson and Stacks define nonverbal communication in this way: "a process whereby people, through the intentional or unintentional manipulation of normative actions and expectations (other than words themselves) express experiences, feelings, and attitudes in order to relate to and control themselves, others, and their environments." (Hickson, Mark L. III, and Stacks, Don W. *Nonverbal Communication* Dubuque: William C. Brown, 1989, p. 11)

In general, there is a closer connection between messages and the symbols used to convey these messages in nonverbal versus verbal communication. This is not always the case, however. This coach is using an arbitrary symbol to communicate nonverbally to other officials at a basketball game.

symbol and its referent (the object to which it refers). Generally, nonverbal communication is characterized by a closer connection between a given message and its referent. For example, if someone asks you if you like Italian food, and you reply by licking your lips, rubbing your stomach, and making a "yummy" sound, your nonverbal messages have a natural connection to the physical result of a pleasurable eating experience. There is a physiological link between those nonverbal behaviors and eating.

While this "arbitrary symbol" distinction is useful, it doesn't always distinguish the verbal from the nonverbal. For example, some verbal communication is not arbitrarily connected to its referent. There are numerous examples of onomatopoetic words (words that imitate the sounds with which they are associated), such as *clang* and *whisper*, in which the word *does* resemble its referent. Similarly, there are quite a few nonverbal messages that are arbitrary. Take the example of sporting events, where a coach may try to communicate to a player on the field. Arbitrary hand signals are developed, such as those sent from a baseball coach to a baserunner. These signals have to be arbitrary; otherwise, the opposing team would know what play or strategy is going to be used.

Ultimately, it's useful to remember the caveat that Knapp put in his definition above, that "nonverbal communication can be defined as communication involving signals 'other than words' as long as it is understood that the distinction between words and 'other' signals is sometimes unclear and overlapping" (Knapp 1990, pp. 54–55).

Intentionality

There is debate over whether the study of nonverbal communication should include both intentional and unintentional behaviors. Should we limit our analysis to intended messages, such as the extended thumb of the hitchhiker and the hand clapping of the appreciative crowd? This provides clear limits, but eliminates such unintended but highly expressive behavior as the unconscious finger drumming of the anxious job applicant or the unintended sour look on the face of the friend who questions your choice of movies. The problem is that if we study every unintended "message," we risk burdening the field with inconsequential behavior, such as accidentally tripping on a crack in the sidewalk. We go too far if we have to account for every behavior on which some idiosyncratic interpretation can be placed.

Burgoon (1985) proposes a useful alternative to these two choices. Instead of defining nonverbal communication from the sender's perspective (in which only intended messages are communication), or from the receiver's perspective (in which all behavior is potentially communication), she suggests that we look at the message itself. This third view is referred to as a *message orientation:*

> What qualifies as communication are those behaviors that form a socially shared coding system; that is, they are behaviors that are typically sent with intent, used with regularity among members of a social

community, are typically interpreted as intentional, and have consensually recognizable interpretations. (p. 348)

To paraphrase Burgoon, if a behavior is viewed as meaningful by most members of society, then it should be examined. We don't, however, have to focus on behaviors that are generally unintentional and void of shared meaning, such as wearing an unmatched pair of socks.

The Ability to Manipulate

Burgoon (1985) also makes a significant contribution to limiting the study of nonverbal communication when she suggests that we restrict our attention to what can be manipulated. If something can't be manipulated or changed, then it can't be seen as having intended meaning. As she points out, a rash, body shape, or natural body odor cannot be manipulated, and therefore should not be seen as expressive or communicative. It's useful to remember that *information* is not the same as *communication*. You might see the rising sun and use that information to get out of bed, but it would be silly to suggest that the sun communicated with you and told you to get up.

In sum, our analysis of **nonverbal communication** will focus on manipulated signals other than words (recognizing that the distinction between words and "other signals" isn't always clear) that are normally recognized as meaningful and intentional by a member of the culture.

Teaching Objective 5–1
Define nonverbal communication as manipulated signals other than words that are conventionally recognized as meaningful and intentional.

THE IMPORTANCE OF NONVERBAL COMMUNICATION

Just how important is nonverbal communication? Some researchers have actually tried to quantify its importance in comparison to verbal communication. Mehrabian and Ferris (1967) estimated that in face-to-face interaction a full 93 percent of the meaning of a communication event is dependent on the nonverbal code. Burgoon, Buller, and Woodall (1989) criticized this estimate as being based on faulty methodology, and suggested that Birdwhistell's (1955) estimate of around 65 percent is probably more accurate. For our purposes, it's not really necessary to argue that one code is more important than the other. A communication event is a unified whole. To understand it, we have to understand both the verbal and nonverbal components. By understanding nonverbal codes, we get a better understanding of communication as a whole.

Teaching Objective 5–2
Emphasize the primary importance of nonverbal communication as the carrier of meaning in communication events.

Nonverbal Communication and Leadership

It would be nice to be able to report that leaders possess an inherent wisdom, that they gather information fairly and accurately, and that they always make intelligent decisions based on this information. Unfortunately, that's not always the case. Leaders are human. They fall victim to the same interpretative mis-

Discussion Question 5–1
What are some situations that leaders in particular face or encounter in which the accurate assessment of nonverbal meanings is vital?

Cross-reference 5–1
The importance of our perceptual framework to our formation of first impressions cannot be overemphasized. See Chapter 2.

Leadership Note 5–1
"Never hire anyone who is going to report directly to you who you do not intuitively just plain like from first impressions. . . . If your instincts tell you you're going to have a hard time working with someone, pass." (Fred Charette, as quoted in Safire, William, and Safir, Leonard, *Leadership,* Simon and Schuster, New York, 1990, p. 43)

Leadership Note 5–3
"If you want to succeed, you'd better look as if you mean business." (Jeanne Holm, as quoted in Safire, William, and Safir, Leonard, *Leadership.* New York: Simon and Schuster; 1990, p. 85)

Teaching Objective 5–3
Further clarify the difference between nonverbal and verbal communication by contrasting them in terms of their relative ambiguity, arbitrariness, biological connection, and overt control.

takes as everyone else. In order to improve the accuracy of their interpretations, leaders must understand how their interpretations are formed.

As it happens, a surprising amount of our impressions and interpretations are based on our reading of nonverbal cues. Consider first impressions. When you initially meet someone, you typically go through a routine of trading broad demographic information ("Where are you from?" "What do you do?"). Normally, this won't give you too much deep insight into the other person. Nonetheless, you still form a fairly well-developed first impression. Given that you know very few intimate details about this person, where does this global impression come from? A considerable amount of our first impressions is based on an analysis of nonverbal characteristics: How does she dress? Does she have an accent? Did she engage in eye contact? All these features (and more) go into our first impression. Obviously, some people are better at forming accurate first impressions of people than are others, just as some people are better at creating positive first impressions. Accuracy in impression formation is likely associated with awareness of what those impressions are based on. To improve your interpretative abilities, you have to be more conscious of how you draw conclusions about first impressions.

The effective leader must be able to assess people and their abilities. First impressions play a significant role in this assessment. Therefore, the ability to form accurate first impressions is important to the art of leadership.

An effective leader should also be knowledgeable about the nonverbal mode of expression because of the types of messages that are typically sent nonverbally. For example, we tend to express emotion more powerfully and continuously through our nonverbal than through our verbal code. As a leader, it is important to be able to interpret the emotional state of others. We also use the nonverbal code to send messages that cannot or should not be sent verbally. When questioned about their ability to work together, two co-workers might say to the supervisor that they get along just fine. But by saying it through clenched teeth they send an altogether different message. To ensure effective teamwork, that supervisor would have to be able to pick up on the message behind the message.

Leaders need to appreciate subtlety in messages. Nuance and small differences can make a big difference when it comes to planning and decision making. One way people express subtlety and nuance is through the use of the nonverbal messages that accompany the verbal messages.

COMPARING NONVERBAL TO VERBAL COMMUNICATION

Nonverbal Communication Is More Ambiguous

We can learn a good deal about nonverbal communication by comparing it to the general features of verbal communication. One of the features that distinguishes nonverbal from verbal communication is that nonverbal communication is more ambiguous. While not ignoring the richness of verbal com-

Nonverbal communication is more ambiguous than verbal communication. This woman's expression is difficult to interpret. Is she signalling boredom, apprehension, or something else entirely?

munication, nonverbal messages lend themselves to a wider variety of interpretations. Words tend to have more discrete meanings. By comparison, what does a smile mean? Happiness, agreement, disbelief, resignation, not to mention the difference between the smile of happiness and that of sinister glee—these diverse messages are all part of the same limited facial feature.

At first, you might think this is a disadvantage of the nonverbal code. In actuality, it can be quite a benefit. This ambiguity allows us to soften messages that might otherwise hurt a person's feelings. Rather than telling someone you don't like him or her, you can send the message nonverbally by making less eye contact, adjusting body orientation away from him or her, and showing a lack of interest in vocal tone. This may still feel awkward and painful to the other person, but the verbal alternative would be worse. Another potential advantage of the ambiguity of nonverbal messages is that they are deniable. If the boss tells you to make sure your subordinates don't slack off on a pleasant spring afternoon, and then winks at you, the potential message could be, "Here's the company line, but let's be realistic here." The message was sent, but the boss doesn't have to worry about not espousing the company's rules. Such deniability is not always desirable (the boss could have been flirting with you, and didn't want to be held to it), but is potentially beneficial.

A number of popular mass market books published in the 1970s suggested that it was possible to "read a person like a book" if you only knew what the particular nonverbal signals meant (e.g., Nierenberg and Calero, 1973). Given the inherent ambiguity of the nonverbal code, this claim to understanding human psychology through nonverbal signs was clearly overstated. Statements such as "If you see someone at a party with her arms crossed over her chest, it means

Discussion Question 5–2
Do you agree that nonverbal communication is generally more ambiguous? Can you think of circumstances in which this isn't so? If the meaning of a verbal statement such as "very funny" is determined by the nonverbal accompaniments, which is more ambiguous?

that she is 'closed' and does not want to be talked to" assume too much. Perhaps she thought the room was too chilly, or her shoulders were tight from the previous night's aerobic workout and needed to be tensed and relaxed. Thus to suggest that nonverbal cues always have direct, unambiguous meaning is unrealistic.

A Less Arbitrary Connection Between Symbol and Referent

When compared to the verbal code, in which the connection between a symbol and its referent is arbitrary, there tends to be a more natural connection between symbol and referent in the nonverbal code. Rather than thinking about codes as being arbitrary or not, however, it may be more helpful to think about this distinction along a continuum, as illustrated in Figure 5.1 (Ekman and Friesen 1969). With an *arbitrarily coded message*, there is no inherent connection between the symbol used and the referent. As we pointed out in the last chapter, the fact that the word *cat* is used to refer to that small clawed animal is purely arbitrary. In *iconic coding*, the symbol bears a resemblance to the referent. In a warm classroom, you might indicate how uncomfortable you are to a friend by hanging your tongue out of your mouth and fanning your hand near your face. This is called iconic coding because the nonverbal messages you're sending bears a resemblance to a person's normal physical reaction to heat. With *intrinsic coding*, the connection between symbol and referent is even stronger, so that message and referent are essentially the same. For example, when a person asks you for directions to the nearest mailbox, and you point in the direction, your pointing is giving the direction. Or when an adult wants to send a message of reassurance or protection to a child, an act such as wrapping the child in his or her arms not only signifies protection, it also provides or *is* physical protection.

Although there are some arbitrary nonverbal messages, such as many commonly used hand gestures, the nonverbal code generally fills the left side of this continuum. By contrast, the verbal code tends to fill the right side of this continuum, though there are some words that are not arbitrarily connected to their referents (such as onomatopoetic words, mentioned earlier).

Nonverbal Communication Is More Biologically Determined

The closer connection between symbols and referents in the nonverbal code suggests that there is a biological basis or link in the nonverbal domain. Indeed,

Figure 5.1
A Continuum of Symbol-Referent Similarity.

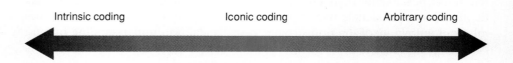

Intrinsic coding   Iconic coding   Arbitrary coding

there is evidence that some nonverbal messages are culturally universal. Ekman (1973, 1982) found that the facial expressions used to display fear, surprise, anger, happiness, and disgust were strikingly similar, regardless of the culture in which a person was raised. This even held true for cultures that had been isolated from contact with modern cultures.

Other evidence of the biological link behind some nonverbal messages was provided by Eibl-Eibesfeldt (1973). He compared the facial expressions of children who were blind from birth with those of children who did not face such limitations and found them to be quite similar. Obviously, the blind children could not have learned the facial expressions by modeling what they saw.

In spite of such similarities, it would be wrong to label the nonverbal code a "universal language." Although there is evidence of a cross-cultural, biological basis for some nonverbal messages, other nonverbal messages, such as hand gestures, are learned within individual cultures (just as words are). Perhaps it is our expectation of cross-cultural similarity in nonverbal messages that leads to trouble. We expect a gesture, or direct eye contact, or a head nod to mean the same thing, no matter what culture it is used in. We will point out later in this chapter that such an expectation may be quite unfounded.

Less Overt Control in the Nonverbal Domain

While sometimes we may regret what we said, or, conversely, feel that a sudden outburst was provoked, generally we have pretty clear control over our verbal expressions. This is not as true for nonverbal messages. Because of their links to emotions, and because of their ties to our biological nature, nonverbal messages may be less subject to our conscious control. We've all probably heard someone tell us, "No, I'm not upset," in short, clipped syllables, with a tense jaw and a cold unblinking stare. The verbal message denies being upset, but all the nonverbal ones contradict this. We tend to believe the nonverbal messages, presuming that people have less control over them than over the verbal message.

Thus, there are clear differences between the verbal and nonverbal codes. These differences tend to balance out the shortcomings of each type of communication, which is why the two codes work so well together. Table 5.1 summarizes the differences between verbal and nonverbal communication.

Table 5.1
Comparing Nonverbal to Verbal Communication

Nonverbal Communication is:

- more ambiguous than verbal communication
- more closely connected to its referent than verbal communication
- more biologically determined than verbal communication
- less subject to conscious control than verbal communication

THE INTERACTION BETWEEN NONVERBAL AND VERBAL COMMUNICATION

Teaching Objective 5–4
Explain the various types of relationship between verbal and nonverbal communication within a communication event.

Discussing verbal communication in one chapter and nonverbal communication in another may be a useful teaching tool, but it also creates an artificial distinction. The two work hand in hand, and influence each other. In this section, we discuss how nonverbal messages can change or modify a verbal message. According to Knapp (1978), the nonverbal code can serve to repeat, complement, accent, substitute, contradict, or regulate the verbal.

Repeat

When you send a verbal message, you can simultaneously send a nonverbal message that is virtually identical. If you were asked if you'd seen any movies lately, and you replied by saying no, while shaking your head at the same time, your nonverbal message would be repeating your verbal message. Shaking your head means virtually the same thing as no.

Complement

It is somewhat different when you send a nonverbal message that slightly modifies or elaborates on the verbal message. This is *complementing*. For instance, imagine that a close friend comes back to visit you after living in another state for two years. You give your friend a hug and say, "Hey, it's really good to see you." The hug provides elaboration for your verbal message. While greetings are sometimes accompanied by hugs, a hug doesn't literally translate into "I greet you," in the same sense that shaking your head literally translates into no in the example above. This lack of a direct translation provides the essential difference between the repeating relationship and the complementing relationship.

Accent

Slightly different from the previous two is the accenting relationship between nonverbal and verbal messages. A nonverbal message can accent a verbal message by providing additional emphasis, as though the nonverbal message were serving to "underline" the verbal message or make it bolder. In an impassioned speech, a speaker may pound the podium to add emphasis to a particular passage. Imagine a boss is scolding a subordinate for not doing something right. While telling the subordinate to shape up or else, the boss shakes his finger and even pokes the subordinate in the chest to drive home the point. The nonverbal message is clearly providing additional emphasis to the verbal message.

Substitute

Often a nonverbal message can be used instead of a verbal one. If you ask for directions while visiting a city for the first time, you might say nothing and respond simply by lifting your palms up, shrugging your shoulders, and flashing your eyebrows. This gesture combination sends the message "I don't know," without the need for any additional verbal message.

Contradict

You can send a nonverbal message that contradicts the verbal message. This can be done intentionally to create irony or sarcasm: "Oh, I really like your sweater," said while rolling your eyes and overemphasizing the word "really." There are also instances where the contradiction of the verbal by the nonverbal is unintentional. When confronted about the broken lamp, the little girl shuffles her feet and looks down at the floor while muttering, "I didn't do it." Her verbal message professes innocence, but her nonverbal messages signal guilt, or at least indicate that the verbal message isn't necessarily to be trusted. When a nonverbal message contradicts a verbal one, thereby revealing specific hidden information, it is known as *leakage*.

Discussion Question 5–3
Are there situations or contexts in which leakage is more likely to occur?

Regulate

The flow of conversation usually seems orderly and smooth. However, have you ever noticed what happens when three or more people try talking over the telephone? There tend to be more conversational overlaps (people talking at the same time), and more empty pauses when no one is talking. That is because we can't rely on the numerous visual nonverbal cues to regulate orderly turn taking while talking on the phone. With just two people, we manage pretty well, but with three or more, we begin to rely much more heavily on these visual cues. Normally the flow of conversation is orderly because we use nonverbal cues to organize the turn taking. Through vocal tone, head movement, and eye contact, you can indicate that you are about to stop talking and let someone else begin. For instance, a dropping vocal tone, a look away from and then back to a listener, and a termination of gesture use indicate that the speaker will let someone else talk.

Speakers can also indicate that they want to keep talking by using "turn suppression cues." Filled pauses (e.g., "uh," "ya know," "and um"), continued gesture use, and inaudible inhalation of breath all indicate that the speaker wants to "keep the floor." It's worth noting that people will often carry these habits over into public speaking situations, where filled pauses reflect a lack of composure rather than a desire to hold the floor. Students of public speaking sometimes have to unlearn these behaviors, particularly since it's not necessary to prevent others from breaking in while you are giving a speech. The Focus on Leadership box discusses nonverbal cues further.

THE SOCIAL FUNCTIONS OF NONVERBAL COMMUNICATION

Nonverbal messages are used to accomplish a variety of social goals. Knapp (1990) provides a useful scheme for categorizing these functions. We communi-

Teaching Objective 5–5
Describe the social functions of communication and offer examples of each.

FOCUS ON LEADERSHIP

Managing the Flow of Group Discussions with Nonverbal Cues

In small group discussions, leaders must often manage the topic flow so that the discussion does not get mired in unproductive digressions. Burgoon, Buller, and Woodall (1989) note that a leader can monitor the state of the current topic by attending to nonverbal cues of the group members. Furthermore, the leader can help direct topic change through his or her own use of nonverbal cues.

A group may exhaust one topic and flounder before moving to another. This wasted time between topics can be minimized by the leader to make the discussion more productive. Hence, a leader should look for nonverbal cues that indicate that the present topic has been exhausted. Members may signal this by displaying restlessness. They may lean back in their chairs with arms folded across their chests. They may give less eye contact to one another. There may also be extended periods of silence. Recognizing these cues, the leader must move the discussion to a new topic.

Introducing new topics is largely a matter of providing verbal transitions. The leader can enhance the effectiveness of these topic changes by giving the appropriate nonverbal cues. Burgoon, Buller, and Woodall list four nonverbal *boundary markers* that help to signal a topic shift. The *proxemic shift* involves adjusting your physical leaning, either toward or away from the group members. A topic shift can also be signaled by *extrainteractional activities*, such as searching through your briefcase, or lighting a cigarette. *Silences* can also be used to indicate the closing down of one topic before another is initiated. Finally, certain *paralinguistic cues* (coughs, sighs, etc.) can signal the shift to a new topic.

cate who we are, what our relationship is to others, and what our emotional state is at the moment. We also use nonverbal messages to influence others, to share understanding, and to manage interaction.

Communicating Identity

Discussion Question 5–4
What are the primary ways that people in this culture communicate their identities nonverbally?

One of the subtle tasks you face when you interact with others is to communicate who you are. Ultimately, this is important because who you are helps determine your rights and responsibilities. But how do you go about telling people who you are? Do you pass people on the street, saying to them, "I'm fairly liberal, making about $25,000 a year in a lower-level professional position, and my musical tastes lean toward the blues." Well, you probably don't say this verbally, but you might be sending these messages nonverbally. You can send all sorts of messages about yourself by the way you get your hair cut to the types of T-shirts you wear. All these help send messages about who you are.

Among the identity messages you might send are those associated with the groups of which you are a member. These could include income groups, occupation groups, religious groups, and hobby or interest groups. For instance, uniforms often tell others what the wearer's occupation is. On many college campuses, the "Greek letters" on sweatshirts and T-shirts tell of the wearer's fraternity or sorority affiliation.

We can also indicate our preferences and attitudes through certain nonverbal messages. Wearing a T-shirt with a picture of Robert Cray, for instance, would suggest that you like listening to blues music. Political campaign buttons, bumper stickers, and yard signs with an icon of either an elephant or a donkey would send messages about your political preferences.

Communicating Relationship Status

In addition to sending messages about who you are, when you communicate with another person, you also send messages about the nature of the relationship between you and that other person. Again, these messages are conveyed subtly rather than explicitly. You certainly wouldn't say to your boss at work, "You are my superior, and I acknowledge the power you have over me," every time you interacted together. Yet we do send nonverbal messages that convey similar ideas. For instance, when your boss is speaking, you will refrain from interrupting her. However, your boss is more likely to interrupt you when you're talking. There are other ways we indicate power or status relationships as well. The general point is that we often signal status and power differences through nonverbal means.

You have probably also recognized that we use nonverbal messages to indicate the state of our intimate relationships. Typically, after a couple have dated each other for a while, they start engaging in more touching, hand holding in public, and extended eye contact, and they will even begin to match each other in body orientation (for example, they will both lean forward at the same time when talking together). When these nonverbal messages are used to indicate pairing, or "coupleness," behaviors like hand holding are referred to as *tie-signs* (Morris 1977).

Sometimes the norms governing nonverbal behavior come into conflict with one another. This can lead to confusion, or worse. For example, the general norms suggest that it is perfectly acceptable for a boss (superior) to initiate touching behavior with a worker (subordinate). The boss may put his arm around a member of the sales staff to accompany a compliment: "Great job on that Texlax account, Johnson (*pat, pat*)." In our culture, however, touching is also associated with relational intimacy, or attraction. What happens if Johnson is a female, and the boss is male? Is there a potential confusion of messages, power differentiation, and attraction? Or worse yet, can a lecherous superior

Discussion Question 5–5
How might a person of high status communicate distance or separation from people of lower status nonverbally?

Cross-reference 5–2
Much has been done in American businesses in the past with the use and furnishing of space to communicate status differences among employees. We will talk about proxemics, or the use of space to communicate, later in this chapter.

Current Research 5–2
Status and power cues are most often associated with men because of socialization practices in American culture. These cues include access to a greater expanse of space to move and gesture as well as greater use of breaks in eye contact and the initiation of touch. (Stewart, Stewart, Friedley, and Cooper. *Communication Between the Sexes.* Scottsdale: Gorsuch Scarisbrick, 1990, pp. 103–109)

harass a subordinate under the guise of "just showing support"? Although the ambiguity of nonverbal messages can be beneficial, in cases like this it can also be used for less than admirable purposes.

Communicating Emotions

Discussion Question 5–6
How do men and women differ in their abilities and methods of communicating emotion in this culture?

Think of situations in which people you know expressed extremes of emotion. Regardless of whether the emotion was anger, joy, disgust, elation, or sorrow, it's likely that you remember as much about the nonverbal displays as the verbal expressions. Nonverbal displays give us a powerful outlet for expressing emotion and mood. Consider how facial expressions, vocal characteristics, posture, and movement could be used to differentiate nervousness, depression, and joyful excitement. A nervous person may have a wrinkled brow, a breaking voice, and a tendency to drum his or her fingers. You might be able to tell when a friend is depressed by a dull, lifeless voice, slouching posture, and slow, labored movement. By contrast, an excited friend may have a smile on his or her face, and use a fast, higher-pitched voice. He or she may also gesture more broadly. In general, we use nonverbal messages to express our emotional state and to read the emotional states of others.

Exerting Influence

When we interact with other people, we often try to influence or persuade them. Nonverbal messages can be used to enhance our persuasive abilities by exhibiting expertise, power, or similarities. If a person or audience perceives you to be knowledgeable, or an expert in an area, they are more likely to be persuaded by you. You can enhance these perceptions of expertise if you use nonverbal messages effectively. For instance, experts often dress the part. In TV advertisements you'll sometimes see spokespersons dressed in lab coats to give them the look of scientific rigor. We presume that anyone who pauses often, says "um uh" too often, and looks at the floor too much is not knowledgeable or believable. By contrast, speakers who maintain eye contact and are fluent in conversation are more likely to be seen as experts.

Cross-reference 5–3
The use of oral skills to exert influence is discussed in detail in Chapter 18.

We are also more likely to be persuaded by people who are powerful or who have authority. Uniforms, such as police uniforms, serve as a display of power and authority. Finally, we are sometimes persuaded by people we perceive to be similar to us. During the next presidential election, notice how the candidates change their appearance to match the environment in which they campaign. In a factory, the candidate will have rolled-up sleeves. In an agricultural area, you'll see plaid shirts and open collars. At the banker's convention, the candidate's conservative suit will match all the other conservative suits in the room. It's presumed that similarity breeds respect.

Achieving Understanding

We've already pointed out that there is a rich relationship between verbal and nonverbal messages. The nonverbal message can repeat, complement, accentuate, contrast, substitute, and regulate verbal communication. Each one of these functions helps interactants share understanding more effectively. In addition, we also use nonverbal cues to let other speakers know that they are being understood. Head nods and vocalized *backchannels* (for example, "uh huh," "yeah," "okay," "um") all let speakers know that we're attending to what they're saying and that we understand it.

Managing Interaction

As we've stated, nonverbal cues serve an important function by regulating the flow of conversation. You could almost think of conversation as an elaborate dance that requires the participants to signal their steps and intentions as they go through the movements. In addition to managing the ongoing flow, nonverbal cues also help us to start and stop individual communication episodes. As Knapp (1990) points out:

> We initiate our encounters with others in a variety of ways, but since greetings are primarily designed for making contact and providing a smooth transition to a conversation, many greetings have similar behavior elements. In fact, the eyebrow flash (a rapid up-and-down movement of the eyebrows) has been noted in most cultures throughout the world (Eibl-Eibesfeldt 1975). Making eye contact with the other person is a common method of signaling that the communication channels are open and that the two parties are now obligated to say something to each other (Rutter 1984). (p. 64)

We can also signify leave-taking through nonverbal means. To end a conversation, we look at our watch, gather possessions, decrease eye contact, and begin moving toward the exit (Knapp et al. 1973). Hence, nonverbal messages function to manage the start, middle and end of an interaction (Table 5.2).

Now that we've defined *nonverbal*, seen its relation to the verbal code, and discussed the various functions of nonverbal communication (summarized in Table 5.2), we can begin to categorize the different dimensions of nonverbal behavior.

Table 5.2
The Social Functions of Nonverbal Communication

Nonverbal Communication:

- communicates identity
- communicates relationship status
- communicates emotions
- enhances our persuasive power
- signals understanding
- regulates conversations

■ DIMENSIONS OF NONVERBAL BEHAVIOR

For the sake of analysis, the study of nonverbal communication is often broken down into different dimensions. Although these different dimensions tend to work together, the distinctions are useful in understanding nonverbal behavior. As we discuss the dimensions, we will provide various examples, breaking down the dimensions into subcategories where useful. We'll explain some of the uses of the nonverbal behavior and cover some of the cross-cultural differences in how nonverbal communication is used.

As we have seen, certain nonverbal behaviors translate across cultural boundaries. Equally interesting are the ways cultures *differ* in their nonverbal use. Observing these differences allows us to step back and look at behaviors we take for granted. They also help us appreciate cultural diversity and the complexity of communication. Cross-cultural differences in the use of nonverbal behavior should never be taken as an indication that one culture is better than another. There are many reasons why other cultures may use specific nonverbal behaviors to mean or do different things than in our culture. Though we may be able to discuss some of these reasons in this chapter, many of them will fall outside the scope of our coverage. Typically, the differences have evolved because they were useful in the cultures in which they developed.

Kinesics

Kinesics is the study of body movement, including eye contact, facial expressions, posture, gait, and gestures. In everyday terms, kinesics is sometimes referred to as *body language*. Excluded from this category is all movement related to touching between people. Touching is covered under the separate heading of *haptics*.

As you can imagine, the term *kinesics* covers a wide variety of nonverbal behavior. Ekman and Friesen (1969) developed a system for categorizing kinesic behavior. You may notice that some of these categories overlap with the general functions of nonverbal behavior discussed earlier in this chapter.

Emblems.   Gestures that readily translate to verbal statements are termed **emblems**. There is widespread agreement in a culture about what a given emblem means. You may cross one finger with a finger on the opposite hand in a peeling motion to indicate "shame on you." Shaking your head says no, or "I disagree." Holding your arm out with your thumb extended means you're hitchhiking and want a ride. Note that emblems, like words, are still dependent on the surrounding context for their specific meaning. A finger drawn across the throat could be a threat, "I'm going to kill you." On the other hand, in the context of a rehearsal of a theatrical performance it could also mean "Cut, let's end the scene here."

Illustrators.   When we complement or accentuate verbal messages with body movement, we often use illustrators. Unlike the emblems, illustrators do not have meaning by themselves. Instead, **illustrators** add emphasis or modify the

Teaching Objective 5–6
Articulate the various aspects of kinesic communication, emphasizing the cultural basis of these behaviors.

Cross-reference 5–4
The use and avoidance of eye contact is a vital and much-studied aspect of kinesic behavior; in public speaking settings, increased eye contact on the part of the speaker enhances a perception of credibility. See Chapter 16.

Leadership Note 5–3
"I have known a vast quantity of nonsense talked about bad men not looking you in the face. Don't trust that conventional idea. Dishonesty will stare honesty out of countenance any day in the week if there is anything to be got by it." (Charles Dickens, as quoted in Safire, William, and Safir, Leonard. *Leadership.* New York: Simon and Schuster, 1990, p. 82)

verbal message. If you wanted to emphasize that your next point in a speech was of critical importance, you might say, " . . . and you'll want to be sure to remember this point," while pointing your finger in the air and shaking it slightly. As an angler, you might clarify the tragedy of the one that got away by holding your hands, palms facing, the necessary distance apart while muttering, "Yeah, she would have been trophy size."

Affect Displays.   Face and body movements that reveal an emotional state are called **affect displays**. We use kinesics to display emotional intensity, indicate our present mood, and show attraction or interest. By observing body posture, movement, and facial expression, you can probably tell whether your roommate passed or failed that accounting test. A frown, downturned head, and slouching shoulders probably mean that it didn't go well. We can also tell the intensity of emotions through the amount of body tension and intensity of gesture use.

We also display interest or attraction through kinesics. As mentioned earlier, people who are attracted to each other begin to synchronize their actions, such as body leaning. Pupil dilation is also an indication of attraction or interest. Apparently, the pupils of our eyes dilate (get larger) when we see something we like, and constrict (get smaller) when we see something we don't like. In some interesting research, Hess (1975) showed male students photographs of women's faces and asked them to rate the women's attractiveness. In one set of photos, the women's pupils were retouched to make them look larger. Generally, the women with larger pupils were viewed as having more positive personal attributes than the women with the smaller pupils. As an historical footnote, in the Middle Ages, women would put a substance known as belladonna in their eyes. It had the effect of making their pupils dilate, and hopefully they would then be perceived as more attractive and friendly. It's been reported that jade dealers in Hong Kong use this same basic principle—that pupils dilate to indicate interest. Apparently, they do not put price tags on their merchandise. When a potential customer asks for the price of an item, the jade dealer will look at the customer's eyes. If the pupils are dilated, it suggests that the customer is quite interested, and presumably willing to pay a higher price. If the pupils are constricted, the interest is less, and therefore likely that the announced price will be less.

Regulators.   As we've said before, **regulators** are nonverbal cues that help regulate the flow of interaction. To prevent conversational overlap and extended pauses, we rely on eye contact, gestures, head movements, and the like to indicate when a speaker wants to give up the floor or keep the floor and also to show when a listener wants to put in a request to get the floor next. We can even use gestures and head nods to tell a speaker to slow down or quicken the pace.

Adaptors.   **Adaptors** are nonverbal behaviors used to manage tension or anxiety. Wringing your hands when you're nervous, repetitive clicking of a ballpoint pen to relieve anxiousness, chewing your fingernails to deal with

Current Research 5–3
"Koreans smile when trying to conceal anguish or enmity. Making a circle with the thumb and second finger means 'money' in Korea and OK in the United States. Thumbs up is 'number one,' 'boss,' or 'best' in Korea, in America it signifies OK. Flexing one's arms and raising the hands above the shoulders would be construed as a threat, but in America it is seen as an expression of strength. Raising a finger to the mouth and hissing 'shhhh' means a child wants to perform before the toilet; in America the same sound and gesture means to be quiet." (Park, Myung-Seok and Kim, Moon-Soo, Communication practices in Korea, *Communication Quarterly* 40, 4, 1992, pp. 401–402.)

tension, or continuously running your hand through your hair while giving a speech are all examples of adaptors. These may just be outlets for nervous energy, or they may provide a means to calm ourselves down. Though adaptors are not sent as intended messages, they are often interpreted as telling or meaningful.

Cross-Cultural Differences in Kinesic Use

Current Research 5–4
"According to many observers from other countries, Americans have a characteristic way of walking. It entails long strides, swinging arms, head up, and chest up and out. . . . They move along purposefully and confidently, or arrogantly, depending on one's point of view." (Althen, Gary, The Americans have to say everything. *Communication Quarterly* 40, 4, 1992, p. 419.)

We can gain new insights into our own use of kinesics by observing how they are used in other cultures. History is filled with humorous and tragic examples of what happens when two cultures interact with diverse expectations and norms concerning the use of nonverbal behavior.

A chief difference among cultures lies in their use of emblems. As we pointed out, emblems generally have precise interpretations that correspond to specific verbal translations. Just as different cultures have different words to refer to the same thing, they often have different emblems to refer to the same thing. In our culture, to signify suicide, a person might put a finger to his or her head in a mock handgun gesture. In Japan, the emblem for suicide mimics the plunging of a knife into the stomach. It becomes even more interesting when two cultures use the same emblem, but to refer to different things. Take the example of Richard Nixon in 1958, then vice president under Eisenhower, who managed to insult the population of a Latin American country while on a good will tour. As he got off the airplane in one country, Nixon attempted to greet the crowd and indicate that everything was "a-okay." He made a zero with his thumb and forefinger, and waved it at the crowd. The crowd was shocked and angered. In that culture, the emblem Nixon was using was an obscene gesture. It was the equivalent of the "single finger salute" you might give someone who cuts you off on the highway. Needless to say, Nixon did little to establish good will that day.

In addition to variations in the meanings of emblems, cultures also have different norms that govern the use of kinesic behavior. For example, in our culture, we use head nodding and verbal backchannels ("uh huh") to let the person we're talking to know that we're paying attention and understanding what is said. In Thailand, people do not nod their heads to show understanding and attention in conversation. A Thai student of this author once complained that when she first moved to the United States she found this behavior very distracting. It's also been reported that people in England are more likely to use eye blinking to signal understanding/attention, than vocalized "uh huh" sounds. When the two cultures interact, this difference helps to perpetuate certain cultural stereotypes (Hall, 1966). To the British, Americans seem pushy and abrasive. We're always interrupting with "uh huh" and "yeah." To Americans, the English appear stuffy and aloof. Since we're not trained to notice the eye blinking, and we're not getting the expected vocalized backchannels, we presume that they're not paying attention.

This is just a small sampling of the cross-cultural differences in the use of kinesics. These examples help to show that we can learn a substantial amount about ourselves by observing the nonverbal patterns of other cultures.

Proxemics

Proxemics is the dimension of nonverbal communication that deals with the use of space by humans. Proxemics is typically broken down into the subcategories of *personal space* and *territoriality*. According to Burgoon, Buller, and Woodall (1989, p. 81) they differ in that **personal space** is "an invisible, portable, adjustable bubble of space surrounding an individual that is actively maintained to protect the person from physical and emotional threats," while **territoriality** is "a fixed geographic area that is occupied, controlled, and defended by a person or group as their exclusive domain."

Personal Space.　　This portable, adjustable bubble that separates the user from anyone else can be broken into different zones of use. Generally, we use physical closeness to reflect relational closeness. The different zones of personal space are used to conduct different types of interaction; the closer zones are reserved for more intimate interaction, whereas the more distant zones are used for conducting role-related or impersonal interaction.

According to Hall (1966), the closest zone ranges from touching to about eighteen inches between interactants. This is called **intimate distance**. We let

Discussion Question 5–7
How might a person use kinesic behavior to control or intimidate another? How might this same person use proxemics for the same purpose?

Teaching Objective 5–7
Define proxemics and depict the importance of and relationship between the concepts of space and territoriality; explore cultural differences.

Proxemics, or the use of personal space in communication, varies widely among cultures. In Arab cultures, for instance, people engage in conversations at closer range than do people in the United States.

Current Research 5–5
The personal space bubbles that surround women are usually smaller than those that surround men. Also, women are more bothered by invasions of their personal space from the side, whereas men are more bothered by face-to-face invasions. (Stewart, Stewart, Friedley, and Cooper. *Communication Between the Sexes.* Scottsdale: Gorsuch Scarisbrick, 1990)

Current Research 5–6
The May, 1993 issue of Harper's Index reported that the average distance between two people in conversation considered comfortable by black Americans is 22 inches, while the average distance white Americans considered comfortable is 27 inches. (*Harper's,* May 1993, p. 9.)

people into this zone only if we have close relational ties with them. This zone is reserved for very private conversations and displays of intimate relational connection. From eighteen inches to four feet is the span of the **personal distance** zone. At this distance we tend to conduct conversations with friends and acquaintances. Within this distance, we can still use touching behavior, and we are able to pick up extensive detail of expressive facial cues. The **social distance** zone extends from four to twelve feet. We maintain this distance when engaged in business transactions and impersonal role-related interactions (for example, talking to a salesperson at a store). The final zone is described as **public distance**, spanning twelve to about twenty-five feet. This distance allows many people to see a single individual, and it is used in public speaking and ceremonial events.

By altering the distance between yourself and another person, you can comment on how you view the interaction and the relationship as well. By sitting closer to the person, you create a sense of intimacy and signify that you view the relationship as a close one. If someone sits close to you, and you move to create more distance, you are indicating that his or her initial judgment about the closeness of the relationship was incorrect.

Territoriality.   Territory can be classified according to its importance for the people who use it. According to Altman (1975), we can break it into primary, secondary, and public territory. Any territory that you have exclusive control over is considered *primary territory*. This might include your desk, your bedroom, or if you live alone, your dorm room, apartment, or house. You can claim its exclusivity by keeping the door to your room shut, keeping your apartment locked, or putting a fence around your yard.

Secondary territory is not necessarily your property or exclusive domain, but through repeated use you tend to get associated with it. For example, by the third week of classes, most people will settle into a routine of always sitting at the same desk in a class. The desk then becomes your secondary territory. If someone sits at "your" desk, you might get annoyed or give him or her a dirty look. In the TV show "Cheers," the character Norm always sits at his stool at the end of the bar.

Public territories are open to anyone. These might include a table at a restaurant, a desk at the library, or a bench in a park. Anyone can have access to them, though individuals can claim them temporarily as their own. We claim temporary ownership of public territory by placing a *marker* on it. To save a table at a restaurant while you go to the restroom, you might put your coat over one of the chairs. This signifies that the territory is taken.

Although we make claims on territory, other people sometimes encroach on this space. Lyman and Scott (1967) have listed three different types of territory encroachment with which we are forced to deal. A *violation* occurs when someone uses your territory without your permission. A roommate who uses your desk or borrows a sweater without your permission has violated your territory. If someone were to cross boundaries to take control of your territory, it would be considered an *invasion*. An example might be having someone skip ahead of you in line. Finally, your territory can be *contaminated* if unsanctioned use makes it unclean. Though this may conjure up visions of despicable acts and religious purification, contamination can also be a less dramatic event, such as when someone smokes a bad cigar in your room. (Complete the Self-Assessment exercise.)

Cultural Differences in Proxemic Use

As you can imagine, not all cultures use territory and personal space similarly. Perhaps one of the most significant differences that North Americans find in other parts of the world is the variation in the distance used for conducting a casual conversation. As we mentioned, in our culture we conduct personal conversations in the zone from eighteen inches to four feet. Generally, we keep about an arm's distance between casual interactants. In Arab and Latin American cultures, personal conversations are expected to be conducted at closer distances. For example, in many Arab cultures the sense of smell is very important (Hall 1966). In everyday conversation there is the expectation that the interactants should be able to share each other's breath. That requires that they stand quite close. Needless to say, Americans cringe at the idea of this. We are taught to cover up and be ashamed of our natural body smells. At the distance appropriate for Arab conversation, we would consider the other person to "be in our face" in a way that would be intimidating and uncomfortable. Thus, personal space zones are dictated by the culture, not by any biological demand.

SELF-ASSESSMENT   **Nonverbal Skills Assessment**

It's inevitable that other people will either intentionally or unintentionally encroach on your territory, or invade your personal space. Whether it's a family member looking for a lost item in your primary territory, or a stranger standing close to you at a crowded basketball game, these things happen. Try to identify an example, or series of examples, in which these violations bothered you. Assess the nature of the violation and your response. Was it in any particular setting? Would you consider the area in which it occurred primary, secondary, or public territory? If it was an encroachment, what type was it (*violation, invasion*, or *contamination*)? Was the person who violated your territory trying to send a particular message (for example, intimidation, asserting authority)? Could this affect your reaction? How did you react? Consider the range of responses available to you. You could just get upset and internalize your anger. You could go out of your way to avoid these situations. You could leave the scene where the event was occurring. Another option would be to bring the violation to the attention of the offending party. You could aggressively respond to the violation. We are certainly not advocating one response over another, but we are asking you to analyze your own approach, and to recognize a range of alternatives.

The use of territory is also influenced by culture. Americans are, by nature, a private culture. Though we have public territory, once an American occupies public territory he or she claims it as his or her own, at least temporarily. For instance, if you go to a restaurant, you get seated at *your* table. Regardless of the size of the table, as long as you are in the restaurant, you expect to have private domain over the table. Ask anyone who has traveled through Europe, and you'll find that this expectation is not universal. In Germany, if you and your date are seated at a table for four, don't be surprised if another couple gets seated at the same table. To many cultures, public space means public space. It cannot become the exclusive domain of an individual.

Teaching Objective 5–8
Depict the use of haptic communication as relationship-governed and culturally influenced.

Haptics

Haptics is the use of touching behavior. Although different cultures may vary in their use of touching, there seems to be a general biological need for touching as part of physical and emotional maturation. Touch is used to send a variety of different signals. We use touch to display emotions—anything from anger and hostility to love, support, and appreciation. We signal the beginning and end of interactions with touching behaviors, such as a handshake or a hug. We even use touch to gain someone's attention or to request a chance to talk. Touch has many different uses. Heslin and Alper (1983) developed a scheme to categorize some of the ways we use touch, based on the contexts it is used in and the purposes it serves.

Functional-professional touching includes the sorts of contact that most people will experience with physicians and other health care professionals. The touch tends to be purposeful, businesslike, sometimes probing, and sometimes affectively cold, but usually it is respectfully gentle. The contact with a barber or hairstylist is often of the functional-professional type, although, depending upon the relationship, those who provide personal services regularly may display touch behaviors that cross over onto one or more of the other categories, such as the social-polite or even the friendship-warmth type.

Social-polite touch involves using physical contact to acknowledge another person in ways that are appropriate to both the general culture and the individuals involved. This type of contact is commonly used when people are introduced. A handshake is a good example of this. The purpose of the touch is to be polite and socially appropriate.

The *friendship-warmth* touch is used to display friendship bonds, or closeness. As Malandro, Barker, and Barker (1989) point out, this is the most often misunderstood type of touching. In our society, we try to keep the roles of friendship and sexual intimacy very distinct. Friendship touching is an acknowledgment of the other's uniqueness and value, and therefore this type of touch comes close to the touch we reserve for intimate relationships. As a result, we often restrict the use of friendship-warmth touching to public settings where the surrounding context (for example, a "congratulations" at an awards banquet, or a greeting at an airport) will help define the touching as nonintimate or nonsexual.

Love-intimacy touch includes patterns of physical contact that are highly unique to the intimate pair, whether they are adults who love and care for each other or in a parent-child relationship.

Heslin and Alper's final category, *sexual arousal*, normally involves extensive physical stimulation of the human body leading to sexual intercourse. Clearly, the physical stimulation is exciting and characteristically pleasurable, and it may represent an expression of physical attraction or emotional intimacy, or both.

Heslin and Alper's category scheme progresses from what might be considered more formal and impersonal forms of touch to those that are more intimate, are more personal, and normally transpire with fewer people. It is interesting to note that it is possible to reshuffle the tactile system in curious ways. For example, the retaining of a male or female prostitute can serve to provide a sense of physical intimacy and sexual arousal, but the context is clearly a functional-professional one. Similarly, there are families and interpersonal relationships where very little friendship and warmth are conveyed through touch. In fact, touch may seldom be used except as a display of hostility or aggression. Therefore, while the category scheme is a useful organizing tool for classifying touching behavior, it is important to recognize that human patterns of touch are as complicated as they are communicatively potent.

Cultural Differences in the Use of Haptics

It's been said that we live in a "touch-starved" society. In fact, Knapp (1978) distinguishes between "contact cultures" and "noncontact cultures," and he notes that the United States is considered one of the latter. This is not to say that we never use touch, or that there's anything wrong with using less touch than other cultures do. This is simply a descriptive fact. Sidney Jourard (1968) compared the rates of touching between adults in coffee shops and found the following number of touches per hour: in San Juan, Puerto Rico, 180; in Paris, 110; in Gainesville, Florida, 2; and in London, England, none (see Figure 5.2). Although there are cultures that use even less touching than we do, our culture is accurately described as an noncontact culture.

Discussion Question 5–8
Should there be another haptic category for touch which is used as an instrument of control?

Current Research 5–7
There are also male/female differences in the use of haptics. Women are touched more, men do more touching, and women make more distinctions about kinds of touching than do men. (Pearson, Turner, and Todd-Mancillas. *Gender and Communication.* Dubuque: William C. Brown, 1991, pp. 140–141)

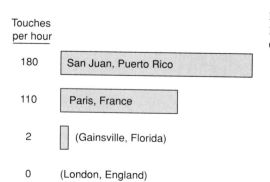

Touches
per hour

180   San Juan, Puerto Rico

110   Paris, France

2   ▯ (Gainsville, Florida)

0   (London, England)

Figure 5.2
Rates of Touching—Cross-Cultural Comparisons.

In addition to using fairly little touch, our culture also has fairly restrictive norms governing its use. For example, we use hand holding as a fairly clear indicator of relational intimacy (with exceptions allowed for children and older adults). By contrast, in many cultures hand holding is simply a sign of friendship. Since it does not carry the sexual overtones that it does in our culture, in many other cultures it is not uncommon to see same-sex friends holding hands while walking down the street. It's worth noting that in spite of the restrictions on touch in our culture, particularly between males, we have ways to circumvent the restrictions. For instance, men can touch each other, but it is typically disguised as aggressive display (for example, punching each other on the arm), or in the context of a sporting event (for example, a pat on the buttocks for a good basketball shot). Again, this just scratches the surface (no pun intended) of the cultural differences in the use of touch. Hopefully, it makes you take notice of the norms you follow every day. Try the experiment described in the Mastering Communication Skills box.

Teaching Objective 5–9
Explore the varieties of paralanguage, its meaning, functions, and effects, as well as silence as a form of paralanguage.

Paralanguage

The nonverbal dimension of **paralanguage** may be defined as "the study of all cues in oral speech other than the content of the words spoken" (Malandro, Barker, and Barker 1989, p. 232). This dimension is sometimes called **vocalics**; it covers any meaning that is stimulated by the sound of the voice. Since we are interested in the nonverbal components that can be manipulated, we might begin by looking at *vocal qualities, vocal characterizers,* and *vocal segregates.*

Discussion Question 5–9
What conclusions do you draw or assumptions do you make about people on the basis of their vocal qualities?

Vocal qualities would include the speaker's speech rate, pitch, volume, articulation, and pronunciation. A yawn, groan, cough, chuckle, gasp, and yelp are all examples of *vocal characterizers*; they are nonsymbolic noises that we make with our vocal apparatus. Finally there are *vocal segregates*, such as "um,"

MASTERING COMMUNICATION SKILLS

Gender Differences in Nonverbal Behavior
Spend an afternoon observing gender differences in nonverbal behavior use on campus (or anywhere). Look for patterns in how men and women differ in the use of the following.

1. body movement
   a. eye contact
   b. posture and gait
   c. gestures

2. personal space and territory

3. touching

Try doing this with an opposite-sex friend. Do the two of you notice different things?

"uh-huh," and "ya know," which are interspersed in conversation without a set wordlike order. They are sometimes referred to as vocal "fillers."

In addition to the abovementioned forms of paralanguage, some researchers would also include dialect, accent, silence, and utterance duration (Knapp, 1978). Paralanguage contains a vast array of cues that we utilize in communication. In fact, it is probably second only to kinesics in terms of overall importance.

Functions of Paralanguage. We use paralanguage strategically to accomplish a number of social goals. Though we mentioned some of these functions earlier when discussing the general functions of nonverbal behavior, you can see here how paralinguistics are used to accomplish these goals.

Several types of paralinguistic cues are used to help *regulate* the flow of interaction. We use *turn-maintaining* cues, such as filling pauses with "um, uh," to signify that we want to continue talking and don't want to be interrupted. *Turn-yielding* cues, such as trailing off the last syllable of a word, are used to let others know that they can take the floor if they want. "W-well" or "b-but" may be used to indicate that you want to begin speaking, and are called *turn-requesting* cues. Paralinguistic cues are used to smooth out the flow of conversation, preventing excessive overlaps and extended pauses.

Paralinguistic cues are also used to display emotion. Excitement, frustration, sorrow, and a wide variety of other emotions, can be characterized by the tone of voice and the rate of speaking. In addition, paralinguistics can be used to modify, influence, or even completely contradict the meaning of the spoken word. For instance, you could modify a statement by adding a tone of concern to your voice. Contradiction occurs whenever you use a sarcastic tone of voice, which indicates that what is being said should be taken as its opposite; "Oh, that was a good suggestion" means the opposite when said sarcastically.

Effects of Paralinguistic Cues. We may use paralinguistics in strategic ways, as seen above. In addition, there are a number of consequences of paralinguistics that may not be intentional but are often interpreted as meaningful. For example, wide variations in vocal tone and excessive pauses may lead a receiver to believe that the speaker is being deceptive. A big brother isn't going to be convinced by the younger sibling who asserts, "I'm not afraid of you," in a hesitating, cracking voice. Hence, paralinguistic cues may provide a form of nonverbal *leakage*.

Have you ever had the chance to talk to someone over the phone a number of times without ever meeting him or her? After a while, you may begin to form an impression of that person, based in part on paralinguistic features. You may begin to picture what the person looks like, and assorted personality features. It's clear that paralinguistics have an effect on *impression formation*.

Silence as Paralinguistic Communication. You may be under the mistaken impression that silence is the absence of information, or is noncommunicative. In fact, silence can convey quite a bit of information, particularly when a reply is expected. Therefore, silence can be very communicative. Knapp (1978, p. 361) notes the following functions of silence:

1. punctuation or accenting—drawing attention to certain words or ideas;
2. evaluating—providing judgments of another's behavior, showing favor or disfavor, agreement or disagreement, attacking (for example, not responding to a comment, greeting, or letter);
3. revelation—making something known or hiding something by being silent;
4. expression of emotions—the silence of disgust, fear, anger, or love; and
5. mental activity—showing thoughtfulness and reflection or ignorance through silence.

The next time your husband or wife or girlfriend or boyfriend says, "I love you," pause just five seconds before replying. You'll find out the hard way that silence can be quite communicative.

Teaching Objective 5–10
Examine the domain of physical appearance as a form of nonverbal communication, attending to the variables of attractiveness, body size and shape, and clothing.

Physical Appearance

Physical appearance is an important part of the nonverbal domain, particularly because of its immediacy. Generally, when you meet someone for the first time, your initial impression is based on what you see—the other's physical appearance. The dimension of physical appearance is concerned with such things as clothes, artifacts (for example, jewelry and glasses), attractiveness, body shape, skin tone, facial features, hair, facial hair, and cosmetics.

This area of nonverbal communication might suggest a change in the old adage. Instead of saying, "You can't judge a book by its cover," we should say, "You're not necessarily going to be accurate when you judge a book by its cover." While it certainly doesn't have the right ring to it, the latter phrase does have some important implications for physical appearance.

The first implication is that we *do* judge people by appearance, and we do this all the time. A substantial amount of research shows that we fall back on old stereotypes when making initial judgments of other people. Even though we do make frequent judgments of people based on appearance, we're not necessarily very accurate in these judgments. Keep in mind, however, that we don't act toward people on the basis of what they are really like. Instead, our behavior is based on our perceptions of them. That is why all this is important for communication. Our expectations and predictions of others will determine whether we choose to interact with them at all, and, if we decide to interact, these expectations will help determine what we decide to talk about.

One other thing to keep in mind here is the phenomenon of the *self-fulfilling prophecy*: Sometimes a situation becomes real because we treat it as real. If you expect attractive people to be warm and personable, you're more likely to initiate a friendly conversation with an attractive person when you meet one. If that attractive person is used to being approached by people who initiate friendly conversations, she or he is likely to view initial interactions as pleasant experiences, and respond in kind. The expectation becomes reality because of the way we act on it.

Physical Attraction.   The perceived attractiveness of a person can have a significant impact on how others interact with him or her. Pointing out only a few of the researched differences, Infante, Rancer, and Womack (1990, p. 254) note that "attractive people are judged more favorably in terms of desirable personality traits, are expected to succeed more, are assumed to be happier, are perceived [as] higher in credibility, and receive less punishment for a wrong-doing in comparison to their less attractive counterparts."

Body Size and Shape.   Along with attraction, these features are not exactly manipulated for communicative value, but they still have an impact on peoples' perceptions. For example, individuals with high body fat content (sometimes referred to as *endomorphs*) are presumed to be easygoing, talkative, and kind. *Mesomorphs*, people with muscular, athletic builds, are judged to be assertive, competitive, and enthusiastic. A thin person, or *ectomorph*, is seen as tense, anxious, cautious, and unsociable. Height also plays a role in perceptions. Tall individuals are evaluated as better leaders, more extroverted, and more attractive.

The important thing to keep in mind here is that these are stereotypes that people hold, not necessarily reflective of any actual association between appearance and personality type. It is important to be familiar with these kinds of stereotypes for two reasons. First, you may hold these stereotypes yourself, and you'll be unable to break them until you are aware of them. Second, others hold these stereotypes, and you can expect them to act upon them. Thus, if you're tall, don't be surprised if others expect you to take a leadership role when you're in a group. If you're heavy, be aware that others may initially expect you to be kind and easygoing, even though that's not the type of person you really are. We're not suggesting here that it's a fair world, but at times it is predictable.

Clothes.   Clothes serve a variety of purposes. They are certainly used to protect us from the elements. In addition, we wear them to make us more attractive. Clothes can be used to establish identity. Teams wear uniforms, and members of a minority culture can maintain their identity by wearing unique clothes. Clothes are also used to differentiate the sexes. Clothes help distinguish roles and status. In a factory, for example, the managers wear suits, the shop supervisor may wear less formal business attire, and the line workers are dressed in utility clothes.

Regardless of whether they lead to accurate conclusions, we often use our perceptions of a person's attire to judge his or her personality, intentions, or professional competence. That is one reason job interviewees are instructed to dress conservatively, and rather formally. The job applicant does not want to give the prospective employer the impression that the interview is not being taken seriously. Even after gaining employment, clothes impact on perceptions. This point has become increasingly important to women as they have expanded their roles in professional careers over the past twenty years. One of the most consistent research findings is that in business professions, women who dress conservatively (wear women's business suits) are more likely to be viewed as credible, and to receive promotions when compared to women who wear more

Current Research 5–8
Physical attractiveness affects every level of social interaction, including proxemics—the personal space of unattractive women is more likely to be violated by pedestrians than that of attractive women. Also, perceptions of attractiveness appear to be becoming universal, at least in regard to women as perceived by men, who prefer large eyes, small noses and chins, and wide cheekbones. (Hickson, Mark L. III, and Stacks, Don W. *Nonverbal Communication.* Dubuque: William C. Brown, 1989, pp. 90–93)

Current Research 5–9
In her interviews with women at high levels of federal government, Jo Young Switzer found that interviewees believed clothing was important, that it affected their perceived credibility, and that their clothing options as women could be advantageous as well as disadvantageous, especially in Congress, where they tended to be more visible by virtue of their wider range of color choices. One congresswoman was quoted as saying that "you don't make points with clothes, but you can lose them." (Switzer, Jo Young, "Political Women Speak: Communicative Adaptations in a 'Man's World,' " presented at the Central States Communication Association convention in Chicago in April 1991, pp. 12–13.)

"feminine" clothes. This is likely a result of stereotypical perceptions, not based on any connection between clothing choice and professional competence. Unfortunately, as long as these stereotypes are held, a woman who prefers to wear more feminine clothes may expect to receive less professional respect. This represents just one example of how clothing influences perceptions, and consequently has consequences for communication.

Teaching Objective 5–11
Describe the uses of time as a form of nonverbal communication, exploring cultural differences.

Chronemics

Pete wanted to ask Amie to the dance, but it was still three weeks away. If he asked now, she might hesitate, not wanting to commit herself too soon. Besides, Pete worries he would look too eager. On the other hand, if he waits too long, someone else might ask her. Then he'll lose his chance. But what if no one else asks her? If he waits too long, the fact that she didn't get a date earlier may make her seem not very popular. She might prefer to stay home rather than admit that, and accept Pete's invitation. As you can see, time and timing can be very communicative.

Chronemics is the study of time, or more precisely, the study of "how humans perceive, structure and use time as communication" (Burgoon, Buller, and Woodall 1989, p. 139). Normally, we don't think of time as something that is "used" in a strategic or communicative way, but it is a changeable, dynamic phenomenon. Time can be communicative because of how we can place behaviors and events in the flow of time to change their meaning. For example, a patriotic speech may simply appear to be a ritual when presented on the Fourth of July, but on August 4, it may appear to be a stronger statement of personal belief by the speaker. As you'll see, people have different orientations to time. Hence, time can also be important because of how it influences communication—what people talk about, and their relational habits with others (a "night person" living with a "morning person"). Let's look first at how individuals experience time differently, and then discuss how whole cultures take different approaches to time.

Psychological Time Orientations.   People take different approaches to time. Some people long for the "good old days." They see time as a cycle wherein events recur. These people are said to follow a *past-time orientation.* You'll hear them telling and retelling old stories. A person with a *present-time orientation* enjoys spontaneity, and lives life to the fullest now. That person will have little regard for the present or future. Someone who maintains a "day-timer" calendar, carefully plans out time, and anticipates future events in light of the present is said to have a *future-time orientation.* Though these are just ways that people orient to time, it's easy to imagine how these orientations affect communication.

Cultural Time Orientations.   Not only do individuals differ in their approaches to time, but whole cultures can differ as well. Each culture teaches its members a sense of *formal time,* the sort of official way that time is measured in the culture. In America we tend to follow a fairly precise sense of chronological time. That is, we have seconds, minutes, hours, days, weeks, months, years, and the like. This is not the only way to chart time flow. Agricultural societies may keep track of time based on the phases of the moon. According to Hall (1973), the Tiv people of Nigeria name the day of the week according to what's being sold in the market that day. Hence, if the trading occurs on a five-day cycle, they will have a five-day week.

Cultures also develop a sense of *informal time*, which is loosely defined, and based on the flow of daily activities. When you ask someone if he or she is ready, and get the reply, "Yeah, in just a minute," this "just a minute" is based on informal time. Does it really mean one minute (sixty seconds)? It probably refers to an indefinite, but short amount of time. Thus five or ten minutes may be acceptable for "just a minute," but thirty minutes certainly would not be. Informal time is made up by such components as *punctuality, duration,* and *urgency.*

Time uses, such as punctuality, are not culturally universal. In our culture, if you arrive within about twenty minutes for a dinner invitation, you are still "on time." In Germany, showing up twenty minutes late for dinner invitation would be a major insult, and a way to make sure that you weren't invited back for another meal. Similarly, duration and the sense of urgency can vary from culture to culture.

We place our behaviors and events in time, and rely on our sense of time, thereby making it a means of communication.

Discussion Question 5–10
Which dimension of nonverbal communication is the most important or most valued in this culture? Why do you think so? What does this say about the culture?

 **Summary**

The nonverbal domain is sometimes overlooked, but it remains a crucial component of the study of communication. It is particularly important that leaders have the ability to interpret nonverbal messages and that they are aware of the nonverbal messages they send.

Nonverbal messages should not be understood in isolation, but in how they interact with one another and with verbal messages as well. Nonverbal behaviors can *repeat, contradict, substitute, complement, accent,* and *regulate* verbal messages. Nonverbal behaviors are also important because of the many social and communicative functions they serve. We use nonverbal codes to communicate identity, comment on the status of relationships, and signify our emotional state. In addition, we also exert influence, enhance understanding, and manage interaction through nonverbal means.

The traditional way of capturing nonverbal communication is by characterizing the assorted codes. *Kinesics* covers all body movement, including eye contact, facial expression, posture, and gestures. However, it does not include touch, which is in the category called *haptics. Proxemics* is the use of space, and is divided into *personal space* and *territoriality. Paralanguage* is the code concerned with all vocal stimuli except the words themselves. Clothing, artifacts, attractiveness, and body size are in the category of *physical appearance.* Finally, *chronemics* is concerned with how we use and orient to time.

We've pointed out that there is widespread diversity in the norms governing nonverbal use among different cultures. This should be taken as a means for gaining insight into our own nonverbal use and not as an indication that one culture is better than another.

■ **Exercises**

1. When we send nonverbal messages to communicate identity, we usually engage in a balancing act. On the one hand, we want to fit in with our peers and establish a similarity to them. On the other hand, we also strive to establish unique identities, somewhat different from those of our friends. Take an inventory of the nonverbal means you use to establish similarity and uniqueness. Consider clothes, artifacts (jewelry, bookbags, etc.), hair styles, gestures, and any other nonverbal means you use to establish either similarity or uniqueness.

2. Talk to a professional salesperson, preferably someone who sells "big ticket items," such as cars or appliances. Find out which nonverbal cues the salesperson looks for, and what the cues mean. Talk to a waiter. Can he or she predict the size of the tip a customer will leave on the basis of the customer's physical appearance? What physical appearance cues does the waiter consider to be telling?

3. Emblems are a widely used form of nonverbal communication. These gestures have a fairly direct literal translation, so it is fairly easy to substitute the emblem for the word or phrase (and vice versa). Test your "emblem literacy." Come up with emblems to match the following statements:

   I promise.
   It's time to take a break.
   I (you) couldn't handle the pressure.
   We're the best.
   That was a tasty meal.
   She's crazy.

Now that you're warmed up, come up with a list of ten additional emblems and their verbal translations.

■ **Related Readings**

Burgoon, J. K., Buller, D. B., and Woodall, W. G. (1989). *Nonverbal communication: The unspoken dialogue.* New York: Harper & Row.

This is the most comprehensive text on nonverbal communication on the market. Burgoon and her colleagues have compiled a book that is both thorough and well supported by research. Virtually all the important research on nonverbal communication has been included in this text. It is very impressive.

Hall, E. T. (1973). *The silent language.* Garden City, NY: Anchor Press/Doubleday.

This is an interesting book, and a classic text on nonverbal behavior, written in a very accessible style. Hall uses various examples and anecdotes to compare the nonverbal behavior of Americans to nonverbal behavior in other cultures.

Henley, N. (1977). *Body politics: Power, sex, and nonverbal communication.* Englewood Cliffs, NJ: Prentice-Hall.

This is a provocative book that takes a strong feminist stand. Henley notes gender differences in nonverbal behavior and traces these differences to power inequities between men and women. Though slightly dated, this book raises many questions and is guaranteed to stir up heated discussions.

Intercultural Communication

Chapter objectives

After reading this chapter, you should be able to:

1. appreciate the growing need to understand intercultural communication

2. differentiate intercultural communication from other forms of cultural studies

3. define culture and recognize when cultural boundaries that can affect communication may be present

4. describe how verbal style can vary among cultures

5. describe how individuals adjust to living in other cultures and to dealing with members of those cultures

6. explain the factors that help members of different cultures deal with each other productively

7. describe the basic principles behind intercultural communication competence

8. select the most appropriate type of intercultural communication for your needs

Key terms and concepts

intercultural communication
culture
subculture
verbal style
individualism-collectivism
masculinity-femininity
uncertainty avoidance
power distance
culture shock
acculturation
chauvinistic
marginal
mediating
ethnocentrism
information based training
attribution training
cultural awareness
cognitive-behavior modification
experential learning
interaction training

Imagine that you recently landed a job as a sales representative for a large company that does a considerable amount of international business. On your first trip abroad you travel to Saudi Arabia with several more experienced colleagues. You soon discover that having a sales pitch and knowing your product are necessary, but not sufficient, skills for your job responsibilities.

Anxious to get started, you look forward to the first sales meeting with your potential Saudi clients. You are happy to find that the Saudis greet you and your colleagues quite warmly at the first meeting. You are also pleased that they all speak English fluently as a result of graduating from prestigious universities in the United States. The clients seem to make a nice group, but after twenty minutes you notice that your colleagues seem only to be engaged in small talk with the Saudis. There will be enough time for socializing later, you think to yourself; it's time for you to show the old-timers just how to make a sale.

"Pardon me for interrupting, but I think you'll really be pleased with the product line we're prepared to bring you and the great service that will back it up." You're about to go into the rest of your sales pitch when you notice the Saudis giving you a strange look. You catch yourself in midsentence as the clients and your colleagues return to a discussion of social pleasantries.

Half an hour passes, and still no one has said a thing about business. You clap your hands together. "Okay, what do you say we get down to business?" The Saudis frown, and you notice your colleagues rolling their eyes in frustration. Perhaps they, too, are tired of beating around the bush and want to deal with the business at hand. Now you really begin to push your sales pitch, only to find the mood going sour. It soon becomes evident that the Saudis are not planning to buy anything from your company at this time. The sales meeting breaks up and you return with your colleagues to your hotel. You are frustrated about the meeting, but you conclude that the Saudis weren't interested in conducting business anyway.

Back at the hotel, your colleagues draw straws to see who gets to throttle you first.

"What were you thinking?" the first one shouts. "You just ruined a great sales prospect."

Taken aback, you manage to stutter, "Bu . . bu . . but . . . what did I do?"

"You just ruined a business relationship that we had been tending and pursuing for weeks," another colleague hisses.

You defend your actions. "But they weren't interested in business. For an hour all they did was conduct a tea party. I thought we were here to make sales, not to socialize."

"Listen kid," the oldest one says, "you're not doing business in New York City. The Saudis play by different rules here. In many Arab countries business is considered part of a personal relationship. They won't conduct business until they know what type of people we are, whether we can be trusted. So we have to plan to spend plenty of time getting to know each other. That's just the way the game is played. When you pushed the business side too quickly, they began to question your character. Since we brought you along, they questioned our character as well."

The preceding scenario demonstrates the difficulties inherent in intercultural communication. It also shows that significant problems can arise in areas you least suspect. Initially, you might think that problems in intercultural communication can be resolved with the help of a competent translator. Achieving shared understanding across cultures, however, involves much more than simply bridging the gap between two languages. Although language is an important part of culture, it is not the sole determining feature. In this chapter, we discuss many of the other ways that cultures can differ, and how these differences can influence communication between members of different cultures. First though, we need to explain why it is important to understand communication that reaches across cultural boundaries.

THE IMPORTANCE OF INTERCULTURAL COMMUNICATION

Intercultural communication is becoming increasingly important to college graduates for a number of reasons. First, our world continues to shrink. Chances are now greater that you will travel to other countries in your lifetime, or that you will meet people visiting our country from other nations. In addition, the pervasiveness of today's mass media brings cultures into contact more

Rather than being a melting pot in which many cultures become one, the United States is more accurately described as a patchwork of many distinct subcultures within the larger culture. Being American does not require that each subculture abandon its unique heritage.

than ever before. Understanding the principles of intercultural communication is a necessary and a desirable skill. Moreover, the growing trend toward internationalization in business is resulting in a more strongly interconnected global economy. Economic growth and successful competition now require an understanding of other cultures and how to communicate with them. Economically, politically, artistically, and socially, cultures have a greater impact on one another now than ever before.

Teaching Objective 6–1
Emphasize the increasing importance of intercultural communication competence.

Even in the United States, Americans could benefit from an appreciation of intercultural communication. The "melting pot" has long been used as a metaphor for the blending of cultures in this country; immigrants came from other lands to become Americans. Yet this may be a more accurate characterization of the blending of European immigrants during the eighteenth and nineteenth centuries than it is of cultural mixing in the United States today. Instead of a "melting pot," many experts now view our society as a "patchwork" of cultures, maintaining their distinct features but striving to work together. As a result, our society is made up of many overlapping subcultures that often have difficulties understanding and dealing with each other. Hence, a greater understanding of intercultural communication principles could greatly benefit our ability to deal with each other in this country.

Finally, by learning about other cultures and how to interact effectively with them, we learn about ourselves. Culture has a pervasive effect on our lives. It influences how we perceive, think, and act; essentially, it helps make us who we are. By gaining insight into the effects that other cultures have on their members, we can better see the impact of our own culture on ourselves.

In this chapter, we discuss several issues related to intercultural communication. We define both intercultural communication and culture. Most of the chapter uncovers the dimensions along which cultures vary, and discusses the impact of these differences on communication attempts between members of different cultures. In addition, we discuss how members of different cultures often react when dealing with one another. Finally, we look into the concept of intercultural communication competence, and discuss some of the training methods used to enhance communication between people from different cultural backgrounds.

◼ DEFINING INTERCULTURAL COMMUNICATION

From our opening example, and from your own intuition, you probably have some preliminary understanding or personal definition of intercultural communication. However, as you already know, there are many "common sense" terms in the social sciences that require more precise, technical definitions in order for us to build a scientific knowledge base. *Intercultural communication* is one such term. The opening scenario to this chapter provides a definition through example. Although this may give you a flavor for the concept of intercultural communication, defining through example does not provide a characterization that is sufficiently precise or that can account for enough variations.

Therefore, we can also define **intercultural communication** both conceptually and through contrast. Consider the following conceptual definitions of intercultural communication from scholars in the field:

> Intercultural communication refers to communication between individuals or groups from different cultures or from different subcultures...of the same sociocultural system. . . . Intercultural communication research might describe how American and Japanese business negotiations are conducted or how Mexican Americans and Oriental Americans communicate with each other. (Infante, Rancer, and Womack 1990, p. 372)

Asuncion-Lande (1990) adds that the study of intercultural communication

> focuses on the cultural aspects of interpersonal communication, and on the effects of cultural differences on communication patterns. . . . Intercultural communication refers to the process of symbolic interaction involving individuals or groups who possess recognized cultural differences in perception and behavior that will significantly affect the manner, the form, and the outcome of the encounter. . . . The cultural frameworks in which the communicators interpret messages may vary from maximal to minimal differences. Some of the differences may be obvious, others may be more subtle. (pp. 211, 213)

These definitions emphasize that in intercultural communication the interactants are influenced by diverse cultural backgrounds, and that the cultural differences can be small or great. The cultural variations can involve people from different nations, or people from different groups (subcultures) within a single culture.

In addition to these conceptual descriptions, it is useful to define intercultural communication through contrast by mentioning similar, though distinct, concepts. Much of the material written about the relationship between communication and culture includes reference to such terms as *cross-cultural communication*, *international communication*, and *comparative mass communication*. Although these concepts may bare some similarity, the distinctions among them help clarify what is covered by the term *intercultural communication*. Noted scholar William Gudykunst (1987; Gudykunst and Ting-Toomey 1988) points out that studies on the relationship between communication and culture may vary according to whether they focus on face-to-face interaction (*interpersonal studies*) or on "one-to-many" communication (*mediated studies*, such as broadcast journalism and political campaigns). (See Figure 6.1.) Studies on communication and culture may also vary, depending on whether the interaction between cultures is the primary focus (for example, how Americans interact with the French), or if there is a comparative focus on the interaction in one culture versus interaction in another (for example, how Americans communicate with one another, versus how the French interact with each other). The former of these are called *interactive studies*, whereas the latter are referred to as *comparative studies*.

According to Gudykunst's two-dimensional scheme shown in Figure 6.1,

Teaching Objective 6–2
Provide a clear definition of intercultural communication which synthesizes the definitions provided.

Discussion Question 6–1
How many individuals from other cultures or subcultures have you encountered in the past week? Did you seek or seek to avoid these encounters?

Figure 6.1
Contrasting Intercultural
Communication with
Other Forms of Cultural
Studies. [Adapted from
W. B. Gudykunst, "Cross-
Cultural Comparisons," in
C. R. Berger and S. H.
Chaffee (Eds.), *Handbook
of Communication Science*
(Newbury Park, CA: Sage,
1987), pp. 847–889.)

	Interpersonal	
Communication Channel	Cross-Cultural Communication	Intercultural Communication
	Comparative Mass Communication	International Communication
	Mediated	
	Comparative	*Interactive*

Point of Focus

intercultural communication—our primary interest in this chapter—is concerned with interpersonal interaction between members of different cultures or subcultures. By contrast, *cross-cultural communication* studies compare interpersonal interaction between members of one culture to interaction between members of another culture (for example, how Americans conduct business meetings with one another, versus how the French conduct business meetings with one another). Hence, the difference between them is that *cross-cultural communication* studies have a *comparative* focus, whereas *intercultural communication* studies have an *interactive* focus.

International communication and comparative mass communication are both concerned with mediated, as opposed to interpersonal, communication phenomena. *International communication* studies deal with mass media within different cultures. One example would be the study of television effects on the rural population of Canada. In even greater contrast to intercultural communication are *comparative mass communication* studies, which compare the mass-media systems of different cultures. Comparing television programming in Canada to that in Senegal would be an example of this type of study. Thus, by contrasting similar terms we can define intercultural communication more precisely.

All of the various definitions of intercultural communication revolve around the notion of culture. But what is culture, and how substantial a difference is necessary before we can say that two people are members of different cultures? These are the questions we turn to next.

■ DEFINING CULTURE

What comes to mind when you hear the term *culture?* Perhaps you initially think of Italian operas, abstract sculptures, and high fashion clothing—things we might refer to as "high culture." Maybe the word *culture* brings to your mind images of dusty museums filled with pottery fragments, arrowheads, and mummies—hence, you may think of culture as a feature of ancient civilizations. Or, culture may make you think of spiked hair, tattoos, and pierced jewelry, drawing up images of a counterculture. Such notions, however, do not quite capture what culture is.

The operas, sculptures and high fashion designs themselves are not culture. It may be more useful to think of culture as the shared set of aesthetic standards that allow a group to find a sculpture visually and tactically pleasing. Arrowheads and pottery fragments are not culture. They are the distant echoes of culture that reverberate through time. Culture is the knowledge passed down from one generation to the next of how to form an arrowhead, or the shared knowledge of how to create a piece of pottery that is both functional and a record of the aesthetic values of its creator. Strange hair styles do not make a culture. But spiked hair and nose jewelry are a display of a shared value system—and, in part, a rejection of the dominant value system held by most people.

Culture can be defined as "a system of shared symbols, beliefs, and practices created by a group of people as an adaptive mechanism for their survival and development and then transmitted to succeeding generations as part of their communicable knowledge" (Asuncion-Lande 1990, p. 211). Similarly, Ting-Toomey (1985) defines culture as "the patterned ways of thinking, acting, feeling, and interpreting that constitute the fundamental webs of culture" (p. 75). Providing a broadly encompassing definition, Porter and Samovar (1976) say that "culture refers to the cumulative deposit of knowledge, experience, meanings, beliefs, values, attitudes, religions, concepts of self, the universe, and self-universe relationships, hierarchies of status, role expectations, spatial relations, and time concepts acquired by a large group of people in the course of generations through individual and group striving" (p. 7).

We can conclude that culture is not the thing itself—not the arrowhead, not the sculpture. Rather, culture is a pattern of thinking shared by a group of people. The pattern of thinking includes standards of what is good or bad, appropriate or inappropriate, important or unimportant. Culture is also the set of shared categories (often crystallized in the words of a verbal language system) that defines the important features of the commonly experienced world (for example, the dozens of terms for snow used by native people of the northern part of North America). Beyond words and values, culture also includes common methods of processing information and shared standards for making the behavior of people meaningful. Thus, while objects may reflect culture, it is sustained and evolves by being shared among people.

It is interesting to note that the shared values of a culture are largely captured in the language system used by members of the culture. Giles and Franklyn-Stokes (1989) give several examples of research studies demonstrating that bilingual speakers express different values depending on the language used. Asked to respond to the same question in different languages, people expressed different values depending on which language they spoke. For instance, the authors cite a study by Ervin (1964) in which American bilingual students developed narrative stories that were noticeably more romantic and

Cross-Reference 6–1
The learned and selective nature of perceptions was discussed in Chapter 2. Here that information can also be tied to a discussion of perceptions as culturally bound or limited.

Leadership Note 6–1
Organizations are now described as possessing cultures with distinctive values, beliefs and vision. Some organizational scholars consider the creation and management of a distinctive organizational culture as the primary role of leaders. (Hackman, Michael and Johnson, Craig, *Leadership: A Communication Perspective.* Prospect Heights IL: Waveland Press, Inc., 1991, p. 148)

Teaching Objective 6–3
Define the various common elements of cultures.

Discussion Question 6–2
What would you say are the distinguishing features of U.S. culture?

emotional when written in French than in English. Clearly, language and culture are intertwined. Language is not just an artifact of a culture. Language captures the values and beliefs of a group of people.

Defining the Boundaries Between Cultures

Where does one culture end and another begin? How great a difference must exist between the backgrounds of two people in order to label their interaction "intercultural"? These are difficult questions to answer. Certainly, we can come up with examples that display clear cultural differences, such as the Aboriginal people of Australia and the inhabitants of Sweden. They come from different countries located in different parts of the world. They have had to adapt to different physical environments. They've developed different languages. Their religions differ. Racially and ethnically, they are different. They have distinct legal and political systems. They have different mythological heroes who personify different heroic ideals. Given these and other differences, we can confidently conclude that native Australians and ethnic Swedes represent two distinct cultures. But this is an extreme example. What can we rely on to separate two cultures, particularly when they are not so radically different?

Unfortunately, we cannot rely solely on geographic or national boundaries for cultural identification for two reasons. First, there may be many distinct cultures within a single country. Second, any given culture may transcend such boundaries. The boundaries of nations often change with little regard for the people who happen to live on one side of a border or the other. Consider the case of what used to be the Soviet Union. That country was a patchwork of different ethnic groups with distinct cultural backgrounds. As a single country, the Soviet Union was made up of many cultures. After the breakup of the Union, many ethnic Russians found themselves within the boundaries of newly declared countries, such as Estonia or Ukraine. Thus, nationality, by itself, cannot define culture.

While national boundaries cannot form the foundation of cultural distinctions alone, neither can ethnicity. Consider the United States, where many people define themselves as Americans, ignoring their ethnic heritage. Still other people may consider themselves Irish-Americans, African-Americans, or Vietnamese-Americans, linking nationality to ethnicity or racial identity. Ultimately, culture may have to be defined through a personal sense of belonging. To the extent that an individual personally identifies with a group, and to the degree that she draws on an accumulated stock of knowledge handed down by that group, we can say that she is a member of that particular culture (whether that group be defined through nationality, ethnicity, race, religious convictions, or other means).

Discussion Question 6–3
To how many cultures and subcultures do you belong?

It is important to note that a person can identify with more than one culture. An African-American may draw on the larger American culture to define part of who he is, but he may also draw on his racial background for cultural features such as family identity, musical tastes, language use, and hero identification. If a person identifies with a smaller culture within a larger culture, it is said that he (or she) belongs to a **subculture**.

In Chapter 1, we mentioned that one of the primary goals of communication is to create shared meaning between people. Many things can either facilitate or hinder the creation of shared meaning. To the extent that the interactants' cumulative deposit of knowledge (that is, culture) is significantly different and affects understanding, we could say that the communication event is intercultural.

With basic differences in what is valued, in how information is processed, and in language, it is hardly surprising that people from different cultures can have difficulty communicating with one another. The specific ways in which cultures differ and the implications for potential communication difficulties are the issues we turn to next.

Cross-Reference 6–2
In a sense, we can view families as subcultures within a larger culture. The culture of the family will be discussed in Chapter 9.

CULTURAL DIFFERENCES AND THEIR EFFECT ON COMMUNICATION

As we shall see, cultures can differ in a number of ways. In this section, we list some of the ways in which cultures can vary and discuss how these variations impact on communication.

Language Variations Across Cultures

Obviously, different cultures often rely on different languages. Less obvious, though, are the implications concerning language variation. As noted earlier, for example, effective intercultural communication requires more than a good word-for-word translator.

Translation difficulties. If you have studied a foreign language you already recognize the limits of using a translating dictionary to interpret language use in a different culture. One limit is that it is difficult for dictionaries to track the idiomatic phrases commonly used, since they change frequently and often do not make literal sense. Imagine that an exchange student from Spain asked what you were talking about while on the phone for a half-hour. You might reply, "Ah nothing, just shooting the breeze." Using an English-Spanish dictionary, your friend would have a difficult time interpreting what you just said.

Not only are idioms troublesome, but there is also the problem of "untranslatable" words. That is, cultures typically have some words for which there is no direct equivalent in another language. That is not to say that the general meaning of the word cannot be explained in English, but that the translation may require an explanation of the cultural characteristics of the people who use the word. Hence, a translation may require a story, a description of human nature from the point of view of that culture, or a global explanation of how that culture views the world—all to translate a single word. In a sense, it may be necessary to first explain a world, prior to explaining a word.

Howard Rheingold (1988) compiled many "untranslatable" words from different cultures in his book titled, *They Have a Word for It.* Some words are able

Cross-Reference 6–3
The relationship between language and perception and between language and meaning was discussed in Chapter 4. In that chapter we learned that meaning is tied to context. Culture is the overarching context for all language use.

to succinctly capture a familiar situation or feeling for which there is no direct English equivalent. Other words require a deeper understanding of their culture of origin. Table 6.1 lists several of both types.

The existence of untranslatable words suggests that language emerge to capture what is important in a culture. Words reflect the culture of their use. This point is also relevant in subcultures. In the United States, ethnic groups, occupational groups (students), and religious groups may all use English, but each have terms used within their subculture to reflect what is important to their members.

Table 6.1
"Untranslatable" Words

---

esprit de l'escalier *(French)* and ***Treppenwitz*** *(German)* [nouns]: The witty remark, or perfect comeback that only comes to mind after it is too late to use it.

razbliuto *(Russian)* [noun]: The emotion or feeling you have for a person you are no longer in love with, but once were.

Katzenjammer *(German)* [noun]: A hangover of monumental proportions. In post–Gulf War terms, "the mother of all hangovers." The literal German translation would be the noise made by a pair of overly amorous cats.

Schimmbesserung *(German)* [noun]: An attempt to fix something that only makes the initial problem worse.

wabi *(Japanese)* [noun]: The slight flaw that adds to the beauty or elegance of an object. The lack of flaws may make something undistinguishable from other "perfect" objects. A slight flaw adds to the distinctiveness and uniqueness of an object, and therefore makes the object special. As an example of this, handmade Persian rugs are woven with a slight deliberate imperfection to distinguish them from cheaper mass-produced rugs.

shibui *(Japanese)* [adjective]: A type of beauty that comes with age. This may seem odd in our culture, where we try to hide or repair the aging process. In other cultures, people learn to develop an aesthetic appreciation of aging rather than fight it. If you doubt the existence of this beauty, look to the work of the great portrait photographers to see how facial lines tell stories and add to the richness of a person's face.

bonga *(Santali, India)* [noun]: The spirits residing in the earth. Ignoring them can come at the cost of stubbing your toe on a rock or falling on the ice covering your sidewalk. The dominant Judeo-Christian religious culture in the United States ascribes little spiritual value to the earth itself, and certainly does not envision spirits living in the earth. Hence, the notion of the earth as a living entity is somewhat difficult to translate.

adjal *(Indonesian)* [noun]: The predestined hour of your death. In cultures where people believe in predestination, it seems natural to have a term for the set time of your death. When it comes, it comes—there is no escaping it. Such a term is unlikely to develop in English, a language built on a Judeo-Christian foundation, since predestination is not a part of this religious tradition.

Source: H. Rheingold, *They Have a Word for It: A Lighthearted Lexicon of Untranslatable Words and Phrases* (Los Angeles: Tarcher, 1988).

The connection of language to culture can pose serious problems in intercultural communication situations. To begin with, when translators are necessary, the difficulty in translating words can disrupt the natural flow of conversation. We expect conversation to have a flow or rhythm, an interactive give-and-take. Pausing for translation can disrupt this flow. In addition, translators may translate words incorrectly. For instance, when former President Jimmy Carter visited Poland and was enthused by the crowds, he commented that he would like to get to know the people of Poland better. Somewhat rusty in his language skills, the interpreter translated to the crowd that the president of the United States wanted to get to know the Polish people carnally (that is, to get to know them in the intimate, physical, "biblical" sense.)

Discussion Question 6–4
What are some of the idiomatic or untranslatable aspects of American English?

Variations in communicative acts. Even with effective word-for-word translation and an understanding of idioms in the other culture, intercultural communication can be difficult. Keep in mind that neither the individual word nor the complete sentence necessarily constitute the unit of meaning in a communication transaction. To be competent, you must also understand how acts, episodes, and relationships are conducted in the other culture. For instance, if your communicative goal was to satisfy your hunger, you might need to know more than just how to say the words, "Chicken please." You would need to know how to order a meal in that culture and how to complete the "eating in a restaurant" script. Do you pay before or after the food is served? Who do you pay—the waiter or a cashier? In other words, you would need to know not only the meaning of the words used, but also what words constitute an act or complete an episode.

Consider, for example, the act of purchasing an object, such as a souvenir. In the United States, you might ask the vendor or salesperson how much the object costs. If you find the price reasonable, you might purchase it; if not, you will likely decline. In a few settings, such as a flea market or garage sale, you might be able to bargain over the price. Tannen (1990) provides an example in which sharing an understanding of the words is not enough to prevent confusion: A tourist visiting Greece was approached by a vendor selling souvenir artifacts. The vendor stood in the tourist's way and thrust an artifact into her hand. She politely stated that she did not want the artifact, only to have another one pushed into her hand. She tried to return them, but he refused to take them back. Deciding she could only get away by buying the objects, she offered half the asking price (in hopes that he would find the offer unacceptable and take the pieces back). The vendor accepted her offer. While paying him for the first two artifacts, he thrust a third one in her hand. Frustrated, she paid him for the third one as well, and left quickly.

Teaching Objective 6–4
Explore the impact of non-verbal differences on intercultural understanding.

Tannen explains that the two people were not playing by the same rules for conducting a transaction. From the vendor's perspective, if the tourist had no interest in a purchase, she should have avoided eye contact with the vendor and walked past him. When she held the artifacts pushed into her hand, she became committed to the bargaining transaction. As long as she held the objects, her "No, I don't want this" was taken as a bargaining position, an attempt to lower the price of the object. To her, simply leaving the objects on the ground and walking on would have been unthinkably rude, but her acceptance of the artifacts and verbal rejections were taken as tough bargaining attempts by the vendor. They shared enough language to interact, but did not share an understanding of how to conduct a financial transaction for mutual satisfaction. Hence, understanding words and understanding acts can be two different things.

Verbal Style Differences

In addition to differences in the structure of languages, cultures may also differ in their verbal styles. **Verbal style** can be thought of as the flavor or tone of spoken language. Gudykunst and Ting-Toomey (1988) note four different dimensions along which verbal styles vary: direct versus indirect, elaborate versus succinct, personal versus contextual, and instrumental versus affective.

Direct versus indirect.   We all know some people who are blunt and to the point and others who are less direct, dropping hints about what is on their minds. Imagine that you are at a social gathering with two friends who are nonsmokers. If someone nearby lights a cigarette, each of your friends might react quite differently. One might cough under his breath a little and wave the smoke away in hopes that the smoker will get the hint. The other friend might speak directly to the person and ask that the cigarette be extinguished. This same sort of variation occurs across cultures. Members of some cultures tend to be *direct*, willing to reveal their intentions quite explicitly. American culture is one example of this style. In *indirect* cultures, members tend to conceal their

Current Research 6–1
Klopf compiled seven comparative studies of Japanese and American communication practices and found that Japanese communicators use emotion less, argue less, are less intimate, less assertive, less responsive, less inclined to talk, and lonelier than Americans. (Klopf, Donald W., Japanese communication practices: recent comparative research. *Communication Quarterly* 39, 2, 1991, pp. 130–143)

Culture shock can lead to anxiety and confusion. Many of the things we take for granted in our culture may be different or missing in other cultures.

intentions so that nobody feels personally threatened. Of course, this style requires other people to be sensitive enough to pick up on indirect intentions. Japanese culture represents this other end of the continuum.

When interacting with each other, direct and indirect cultures face some obstacles. A person from an indirect culture is likely to see the direct style as crude and abrasive or personally threatening. By contrast, a member of the direct culture will have difficulty interpreting the intentions of the indirect culture member. He may get frustrated and want the other to say what is on her mind, rather than "beating around the bush." Each needs to adjust expectations about the level of directness in a conversation.

Elaborate, exacting and succinct.   Another variation in language style runs from elaborate, through exacting, to succinct. The *elaborate* style is rich and expressive, like that of a master storyteller. In contrast, users of the *exacting* style try to provide just as much information as is necessary, no more and no less. The use of understatements, pauses, and silence is characteristic of the *succinct* style (Gudykunst and Ting-Toomey 1988).

Arab cultures tend to exhibit the elaborate style. For instance, an Arab curse might be very imaginative and colorful. By contrast, speakers of English in the United States tend to limit themselves to the same five to seven "swear" or "cuss" words in a very narrow, ritualized version of cursing. This is because many Americans tend to use an exacting style of language, though there are subculture variations. One such variation has been noted in traditional Chinese-American families (Ting-Toomey 1980), and presumably reflects a succinct style in Chinese culture itself. In these families, silence is commonly used as a control strategy. Given that silence plays this important function, it is a more regular part of interaction in this culture. By contrast, English speakers in the United States tend to find silence uncomfortable.

Personal versus contextual.   Conversation among you and your friends is likely informal and on a first-name basis. However, when you talk to your boss at work there is probably more formality involved, reflecting the difference in status (for example, "Good afternoon, Mr. Buckley. Gee, that sure is a nice-looking tie you have on"). At an interpersonal level, this shift from informal to formal parallels what happens at the intercultural level. Some cultures use a contextual verbal style, whereas others are more likely to have a personal style.

People in the United States and northern Europe tend to use the *personal* style. It is informal and presumes an equal power or status relationship between people. It is also person-centered, directed to the unique features of the person being spoken to, rather than role-centered, directed at the status or role of the other. The role-centered approach is more characteristic of the *contextual* style, which is prevalent in Asian cultures (such as in Korea and Japan). It emphasizes hierarchy and power differences. For instance, in the Korean language, completely different vocabularies are used depending on how close the relationship is between the interactants. Not only do forms of address change (for example, "Sir," "Mister," "Bill"), but many other words also vary depending on whether a Korean is speaking to a close friend and acquaintance or a

Cross-Reference 6–4
Cultural differences in non-verbal communication were explored in Chapter 5.

stranger. In this way, the language not only reflects, but also sustains, the status differences present in the society. In cultures based on hierarchical order, this feature of language style makes conversation more orderly and predictable.

Again, communication difficulties can emerge when a person from a culture using a personal style interacts with a person who relies on a contextual verbal style. The personal style presumes that friendly conversations, whether business or social, are based on equal status between participants. By contrast, the contextual style requires that social hierarchy be maintained. Hence, in a verbal interaction a Westerner would likely find an Asian overly formal and stiff, whereas the Asian may feel that the Westerner presumes an uncomfortable level of closeness.

Instrumental versus affective.   The instrumental versus affective style is the final verbal style difference. The *instrumental* style is precise and unequivocal. It is goal-oriented, getting to the point with relatively little regard for the receiver's concerns. By contrast, the *affective* style is process-oriented, nonthreatening to the receiver and the speaker. It is nonthreatening by being imprecise on the surface. The precision of the affective style is contained not in the language itself but in the accompanying subtle nonverbal cues. This style requires the receiver to pay close attention to these cues in order to understand precise meanings. English speakers in North America use the instrumental style, whereas Asian cultures (such as Japan) rely on the affective linguistic style. (Complete the Self-Assessment exercise.)

SELF-ASSESSMENT   **Assessing Your Verbal Style**

In this chapter, we discuss how verbal styles can vary from one culture to another. If you have had a chance to interact with members of several other cultures, differences in verbal style may already be apparent to you. If not, you may still be able to develop a sense of verbal style variation by comparing your style to that of other people you know. Begin by assessing your own typical verbal style on the following scales. Use a unique mark for each person you intend to rank. If you know people from other cultures, rank them along these scales as well. If you have not had encounters with members of other cultures, select a close friend and a person you know well but do not consider a close friend. Rank them on the scales to get a sense of the degree of verbal variation within a single culture.

Direct |-----|-----|-----|-----|-----|-----|-----|-----|-----| **Indirect**

Elaborate |-----|-----|-----|-----|-----|-----|-----|-----|-----| **Succinct**

Personal |-----|-----|-----|-----|-----|-----|-----|-----|-----| **Contextual**

Too often, we think of intercultural communication as something which happens infrequently, even between members of different subcultures. Depending on where the lines between cultures are drawn, intercultural communication may occur quite frequently and display many of the verbal style differences previously discussed. For example, many writers suggest that men and women may constitute distinct language style cultures. In an excellent book on language differences between the sexes, Tannen (1990) points to several examples of instrumental versus affective style differences between men's and women's language use. For example, consistent with an instrumental style, a man may use "yeah" in conversation when he agrees with a person. More typical of the affective style, a woman may use "yeah" to convey, "Okay, I'm with you. I follow what you're saying." Tannen points out that such simple differences in language use can lead to intercultural communication gaps between women and men even when they share the same ethnic, national, and religious culture. The man who hears a woman say "yeah" throughout his turn at talk may be surprised if she disagreed with his points during her turn at talk. He might assume that she was being insincere in her "yeah" saying, even though she was only agreeing to an understanding of the process—understanding (not necessarily agreeing with) the point he was making. Turned around, it is also likely that the woman would misunderstand the man's behavior. If she were making a point that he disagreed with, he may listen silently, withholding any "yeahs" (which would otherwise signal agreement). She might interpret the lack of "yeahs" as a sign of not only his disagreement but of his lack of attention as well.

Hofstede's Dimensions of Cultural Variability

Various anthropologists, sociologists, and other social scientists have developed schemes to differentiate cultures. However, these schemes tend to be general, representing shared beliefs or philosophies within a culture without specifically addressing communication differences. Still, cultural differences inevitably have an impact on intercultural communication attempts. Hofstede's scheme (described in Gudykunst and Ting-Toomey 1988) recognizes four different dimensions along which cultures vary: *individualism–collectivism, masculinity–femininity, uncertainty avoidance*, and *power distance*.

Individualism–Collectivism.   Some cultures emphasize the role of the individual, whereas others focus on the role of the group. This distinction highlights the **individualism–collectivism** dimension of cultural variation. A person raised in an individualistic culture is taught to look after herself, and perhaps her immediate family. In the collectivist culture, a person is taught to work for the best interests of the group first, and to subordinate his own goals or interests. Within an individualistic culture, a person is motivated to improve herself, to find a sense of identity or accomplishment based on what she personally has achieved, and to value personal initiative. In the collectivist culture, a person is motivated to improve the group (or groups) to which he belongs, to find personal identity and accomplishment through groups, and to display group loyalty in return for rewards from the group. Finally, an individualistic culture teaches its members to apply all rules to everyone

Teaching Objective 6–5
Discuss verbal style differences within and between cultures.

Discussion Question 6–5
How would you describe your own verbal style? How does it compare to the verbal style of your culture?

Current Research 6–2
Park and Kim reported compiled research results depicting the following cultural characteristics of Korean communicators as compared to Americans: Koreans are less argumentative, slightly less assertive, more aggressive, less apprehensive, more lonely, and more satisfied with their interpersonal relationships. (Park, Myung-seok and Kim, Moon-soo, Communication practices in Korea. *Communication Quarterly* 40, 4, 1992, pp. 398–404)

equally. In contrast, a member of a collective culture learns to apply a more favorable set of rules or standards to members of his own group than to people who are not in that group.

As you've probably already guessed, English speakers in North America reflect strong individualism, whereas people in Asian cultures (such as Japan) are characteristic of collectivism. It is not difficult to project the potential communication difficulties between these two groups. In trade negotiations, U.S. representatives decry the fact that the Japanese prefer to conduct business with other Japanese even when American merchants can offer better products or prices. To an individualistic culture applying a different set of rules to an outgroup is viewed as unfair. However, to a collectivist culture, it makes sense to buy from one's own group even if one must pay a little more. Hence, trade negotiations between these two groups must recognize that there are two different sets of rules being applied.

Masculinity–femininity. A second set of cultural values varies along the dimension of **masculinity–femininity.** Cultures high in *masculinity* value individuals who exercise power, display assertiveness, and hold many physical possessions. In such cultures, independence and ambition are valued, and men and women typically hold separate roles in society. These cultures also reward personal achievement, and consider work a critical part of a person's life. In contrast, cultures high in *femininity* place less value on things and more value on people and personal relationships. In these cultures, the overall quality of life is considered more important than how many possessions a person owns. The sex roles in feminine cultures are more flexible. For instance, the mother and father may share the responsibility of childrearing. In addition, such cultures place a high value on interdependence and community service (as opposed to personal accomplishment).

Uncertainty avoidance. Along a third dimension, cultures can vary in terms of **uncertainty avoidance.** A culture that is high in uncertainty avoidance typically has members who have a low tolerance for ambiguity or uncertainty. These people prefer a clear system of formal rules and display a lack of tolerance for individuals who "march to a different drummer." They typically resist change, yet avoid conflict rather than address differences. Finally, members of a high uncertainty avoidance culture usually have high levels of anxiety and tend to worry about the future. In contrast is the low uncertainty avoidance culture. Here the need for clarity and formal rules is not as great. Everyone is not expected to fit into the same mold, hence deviance is tolerated. The stress levels in these cultures are lower than in high uncertainty avoidance cultures, and the members are greater risk takers.

Unlike many of the other cultural dimensions, there is no typical North American/European versus Asian split along the uncertainty avoidance dimension. The United States ranks low on uncertainty avoidance, whereas other western European nations, such as Belgium, Portugal, and France, rank quite high. In Asia, Japan and Korea are high in uncertainty avoidance, but Singapore and Malaysia are quite low (Gudykunst and Ting-Toomey 1988).

Current Research 6–3
"Americans place a very high premium on the values of individualism and self-reliance, and usually do not seek deep involvement with other people. In fact, they may seek to avoid such involvement, seeing in it a threat to their independence and freedom of action. Americans emphatically do not seek the sort of deep, mutual interdependence that is typical of social relationships among, say, Koreans, Chinese, and Iranians." (Althen, Gary, The Americans have to say everything. *Communication Quarterly* 40, 4, 1992, p. 416)

Power distance.   The last dimension of Hofstede's scheme is **power distance**—the willingness of less-powerful people in a culture to accept the fact that power is not distributed equally. Thus, people in higher power distance cultures acknowledge that power differences are an inevitable part of society and that people in high-power positions (superiors) are different than people in low-power positions (subordinates). Several expectations follow from this type of value system. For instance, parents strongly expect their children to be obedient. In the workplace, little worker independence is expected and workers rely on close supervision of their work. In these cultures, tactful interaction, proper servitude, and accumulation of money are seen as the means to freedom.

MASTERING COMMUNICATION SKILLS

Discovering Cultural Differences Through a Personal Interview

Too often we assume that other cultures parallel our own, even when profound differences may be present. We often maintain this view simply because we do not have any conflicting information. One way to become more aware of cultural differences is to interview someone from another culture or subculture. The purpose of this experience is to gain a fuller appreciation for the diversity of cultural perspectives.

To begin, you should locate a potential interviewee from a culture different than your own. You may be able to find a likely candidate through your everyday encounters, or you may have to search harder. One potential source for interviewees may be an international student or cultural student organization on campus. Once you have located a potential interviewee, explain the purpose of this task.

Ask the person to identify some of the most noticeable or significant cultural differences. After you obtain some initial information, you might prompt the person further by asking whether she or he has noticed differences in the following areas:

What constitutes rude behavior in this culture, but not in his or her own culture (and vice-versa)?

The typical family structure and family roles.

Forms of family entertainment or entertainment among peers.

Dating rituals.

The social roles of women and men and the characteristic features of feminine and masculine ideals.

The rituals that surround major life events, such as birth, coming of age, marriage, and death.

Finally, take some time to consider how the cultural differences you uncover could impact on communication attempts.

Cultures characterized by low power distance are more egalitarian. Here equality is valued and freedom is achieved through equality and individual respect. Power differences are not viewed as an inevitable, accepted part of the social order. Finally, the exercise of power is not openly used as a means to an end. The U.S. culture ranks fairly low in terms of power distance, whereas Central and South American cultures rank quite high.

Imagine that you accept a job in Guatemala, supervising an operation for a multinational company. You want to give your Guatemalan subordinates considerable autonomy in their work, but you find that they have difficulty dealing with your management style. They expect more oversight than you are used to giving. They treat you with respect, but maintain considerable social distance. In general, you are struggling with your communication skills to develop an appropriate management style. Cultural differences along any of these dimensions of variability can lead to intercultural communication difficulties.

Teaching Objective 6–6
Consider these and other dimensions of cultural differences.

The preceding example does not by any means, exhaust the many differences between cultures. Cultures vary in their views of family structure and in the roles played by social structures (for example, by school, government, and the media). Social rules can also vary among cultures—rules concerning such practices as gift giving, tipping for services, bribery as an institutional lubricant, and celebrations. Any of these can have a profound effect on intercultural communication. Some of these cultural differences, such as in the use of nonverbal behavior, are discussed elsewhere in the text (see Chapter 5). You may also want to read about or directly experience other types of cultural variations (see the Related Readings at the end of this chapter). The differences we have discussed in this section should give you an appreciation for the complexity of intercultural communication attempts. (See the Mastering Communication Skills box.) Now we turn to the consequences of intercultural contact.

■ CULTURES IN CONTACT: REACTIONS TO DEALING WITH OTHER CULTURES

The process of living or dealing with members of another culture can require considerable adjustment. How can people from different cultures best deal with one another? What factors help or hinder the interaction between cultures? We address these two questions in this section.

Dealing with another culture can be traumatic. We begin by discussing the phenomenon of culture shock, an inability to adapt to life in another culture. Then we mention some more successful methods of crossing cultural boundaries. Finally, in this section, we explore some of the social factors and one attitudinal factor that can affect the success of intercultural interaction.

Culture Shock

Have you ever been in a social situation where it soon became evident that you were not exactly sure how to conduct yourself? If so, you probably experienced a small-scale version of culture shock. Broadly speaking, **culture shock** is the failure to adjust to a different culture or the inability to successfully accomplish basic social tasks in an unfamiliar setting. It occurs when you become isolated in a foreign culture and lose your basic routines and social anchors. One of the first definitions of this term described the problem this way:

> Culture shock is precipitated by the anxiety that results from losing all our familiar signs and symbols of social intercourse. These signs or cues include the thousand and one ways in which we orient ourselves to the situations of daily life: when to shake hands and what to say when we meet people, when and how to give tips, how to give orders to servants, how to make purchases, when to accept and when to refuse invitations, when to take statements seriously and when not. Now these cues which may be words, gestures, facial expressions, customs, or norms are acquired by all of us in the course of growing up and are as much a part of our culture as the language we speak or the beliefs we accept. All of us depend for our peace of mind and our efficiency on hundreds of these cues, most of which we are not consciously aware. (Oberg 1960, p. 177)

Symptoms of culture shock. Think about what it would be like to spend time in a foreign culture—one in which there are no air-conditioned hotel rooms and no McDonald's or KFCs. Consider what it would be like to lose the privacy of a bathroom or to have no idea of how public transportation is organized in a large foreign city. How would you deal with the street vendor who forces an item into your hands and demands payment? The characteristic symptoms of culture shock include the following:

Discussion Question 6–6
Have you ever experienced a kind of culture shock in a new situation within your own culture?

1. *Strain* due to the effort required to make necessary psychological adaptations.
2. A *sense of loss* and *feelings of deprivation* in regard to friends, status, profession, and possessions.
3. Being *rejected* by and/or rejecting members of the new culture.
4. *Confusion* in role, role expectations, values, feelings, and self-identity.
5. *Surprise, anxiety,* even *disgust* and *indignation* after becoming aware of cultural differences.
6. *Feelings of impotence* due to not being able to cope with the new environment (Furnham and Bochner 1986, p. 48).

Adjusting to culture shock. While the adjustment to another culture can be difficult, with an awareness of the differences and some training in social skills you can learn to become comfortable in a new culture. Furnham and Bochner (1982, p. 168) describe the adjustment process as follows—from initial involvement to a state of cultural appreciation:

Teaching Objective 6–7
Define culture shock and cultural adjustment.

1. fascination with the new culture, yet being faced with various barriers preventing social interaction with host nationals;
2. hostility and frustration with aspects of the new culture, and a possible emphasis on the superiority of the original culture;

3. improvement and adjustment, with an expression of humor and decreased tension; and

4. biculturalism, where the sojourner [the person traveling through the unfamiliar culture] develops a full understanding of host cultural norms.

Although there is some degree of risk involved when you travel through another culture, worthwhile discoveries are seldom risk-free. Assuming that a person encountering an unfamiliar culture can adapt to the new social settings and rituals, he or she may still choose from several different approaches to that culture.

Individual Approaches to Crossing Cultural Boundaries

If you have regular contact with another culture, you will eventually have to choose the degree to which you want to become a member of that culture. Your individual orientation—your psychological approach to the new culture—may vary from maintaining your separate cultural identity to becoming a member of the culture. Four approaches occur regularly (Bochner 1982).

Acculturation.   **Acculturation**, or "passing," occurs when you try to become a member of the new culture and leave your cultural roots behind. The term *passing* was originally used to describe the attempts of light-colored blacks to integrate themselves into white society by posing as whites. With changes in our culture toward increased pride in African-American culture, and a reduction in the more blatant forms of racism, the term *passing* has fallen out of favor. However, the individual effects of this cultural replacement are similar to those experienced by African-Americans in the 1930s and 1940s for whom the term was coined. There is a loss of ethnic identity that is seldom fully replaced by the new culture. On a larger scale, widespread attempts to acculturate serve to devalue the original culture—to suggest that it is a culture one should avoid being associated with.

Chauvinistic.   A second approach to long-term encounters with a new culture involve a passionate connection to the culture of origin. This is labeled the **chauvinistic** approach, and is the polar opposite of passing. Encountering a new culture, a person may come to value her own culture more than ever. She may go so far as to denigrate the newly encountered culture; for example, viewing it as backward, primitive, or heathen. This approach can result in nationalism or racism and lead to considerable friction with members of the other culture.

Marginal.   A person who adopts the norms of two cultures, in spite of the fact that those norms may be incompatible with each other, is described as **marginal.** This person must often live on the margins of both cultures because the incompatibilities of the two cultures prevents him from being fully integrated into either one. For example, a student from India who wants an education may fit in while going to college in the United States. However, if he were from a strict vegetarian subculture, he may have difficulty eating at a residence hall or going to an American friend's house for dinner. At the same time, trying to work too hard to learn about and fit in with the dominant culture in the United States could result in alienation from his fellow exchange students from India. As a result, he is left on the margins of two cultures, fully integrated in neither one.

Mediating.   Finally, in a few circumstances, a person may be able to synthesize or combine the important features of both cultures without losing what is essential to each. This approach is known as **mediating.** These rare individuals can mediate or translate between members of both cultures. Mediating personalities are truly members of both cultures, and can help to build more harmonious relations between the two cultures.

As you can see, a person's willingness to assimilate into another culture can vary. Regardless of one's intentions, certain factors can make the meeting of two cultures more or less effective.

Factors That Help or Hinder Interaction Between Cultures

Attempts to force contact between different racial or ethnic groups have often lead to increased anger, prejudice, and even violence. In the United States, for example, forced integration of school systems has frequently led to community unrest. One of the underlying beliefs behind school integration was the notion that contact between racial groups would lead to greater understanding and better relations. Unfortunately, contact between the cultures, by itself, does not necessarily reduce tension, prejudice, or hostility between the groups. In fact, forced contact can increase tension, unless certain conditions are present. Bochner (1982) notes several factors that can help or hinder the development of relations between different cultures or subcultures.

Imagine that a skinhead white supremacist and a person of any racial/ethnic minority subculture are locked in a cell together. They are told that only one person will be let out, and it is their task to decide who will go free. Do you think they'd have a civil discussion, make a rational decision, and shake hands at the end? Would they write to each other or meet on visitor's day? It is not exactly a scenario designed to enhance understanding. In fact, it captures most of the features that Bochner says lead to increased tension and prejudice. They are:

1. Forced, involuntary contact between the cultures.
2. An unpleasant situation involving competition between the cultures.
3. Groups with opposing viewpoints.
4. Group norms that condone or espouse racial/ethnic inequality.
5. Groups with unequal power or status.

Discussion Question 6–7
How might members of subcultures within your own culture be brought together to develop greater intercultural understanding?

Teaching Objective 6–8
Emphasize factors which
aid intercultural encounters.

Current Research 6–4
Gudykunst, *et al,* found
that the degree of intimacy
of relationships has a significant positive impact on
reducing uncertainty in
encounters across cultures.
(Gudykunst, Forgas,
Franklyn-Stokes, Schmidt,
and Moylan, The influence
of social identity and intimacy of relationship on
interethnic communication:
an extension of findings
from the United States to
Australia and England.
Communication Reports 5,
2, 1992, pp. 90–98)

Current Research 6–5
"Because two individuals
may not be able to operate
competently or comfortably
according to the norms of
either culture represented
in the dyad, together they
create a somewhat new
and different 'culture' in
which they are both able to
operate. This third culture
is characterized by unique
values and norms that
may not have existed prior
to the dyadic relation-
ship. . . . This third culture
can only develop through
interaction in which participants are willing to open
themselves to new mean-
ings, to engage in genuine
dialogue, and to constantly
respond to the new
demands emanating from
the situation." (Broome,
Benjamin, Building shared
meaning: implications of a
relational approach to
empathy for teaching intercultural communication.
Communication Education
40, July 1991, p. 243)

Fortunately, under certain circumstances, different cultures can meet and develop a greater appreciation for each other. This is likely to happen when:

1. The cultures (or individuals from different cultures) meet on even ground. Neither has more power or status than the other.
2. They have in-depth interaction, rather than just superficial, casual contact.
3. They are able to see superordinate goals; common goals that require the efforts of both groups to be reached.
4. The context of their meeting is pleasant and rewarding.

In all, Bochner suggests that if you intend to successfully bring two or more cultures together, you must carefully prepare the circumstances under which they meet. Increased contact does not necessarily lead to understanding and improved relations. (See the Focus on Leadership box.)

FOCUS ON LEADERSHIP

Seeing Through Racial Differences

"Can't we all just get along?" pleaded Rodney King. Unfortunately, racial harmony cannot be achieved through wishes or good intentions alone. Racial divisiveness remains a serious problem in our nation. It also provides evidence of the difficulties faced when members of two or more groups try to communicate with each other. The social contact can be fraught with distrust, misunderstanding, antagonism, even violence. People in leadership roles are often called upon to heal the wounds, calm the fears, and bring groups together again. To successfully accomplish these tasks, a leader must understand some of the major causes of racial disharmony.

Stereotypes. As we mentioned in Chapter 2, a *cultural stereotype* is a fixed characterization of a group of people who share a common distinguishable feature (for example, skin color, dress, etc.). Such stereotypes are the result of categorizing people into groups. Though categorization is an inevitable part of processing information (including information about people), when we fail to distinguish the individual from the category, stereotyping can have negative effects. Stereotypes can create strong expectations that influence perceptions. For example, if you believe that elderly people are bad drivers, you tend to take note of elderly people who drive poorly (supporting your stereotype), while ignoring or discounting examples of elderly people who drive well (refuting your stereotype). As a result, stereotypes can become "self-sealing" beliefs, resistant to counterexamples.

Given the persistence of stereotypes, what sort of stereotypic beliefs do blacks and whites hold about each other? In one study,

Leonard and Locke (1993) asked blacks and whites to rank a series of descriptive characteristics of members of the other race. The following is a partial list of their results:

Whites saw blacks as:	*Blacks saw whites as:*
1. loud	1. demanding
2. ostentatious	2. manipulative
3. aggressive	3. organized
4. active	4. rude
5. boastful	5. critical
6. alkative	6. aggressive
7. friendly	7. arrogant

Although some of the stereotypes could be considered positive attributes (for example, "friendly" and "organized"), most of the traits are negative. As a result, interracial interactions are likely to get off to a bad start when one person is expected to be loud and ostentatious and the other is initially perceived as demanding and manipulative. Good leaders should be aware of stereotypes and resist the rush to judge people on the basis of stereotypes.

Negative labeling of differences. Because stereotypes can influence perception, members of distinctive racial groups may find that their behaviors are scrutinized and compared against a standard of some mythical "white Anglo-Saxon Protestant" norm. Variations from this norm are not taken as a positive reflection of the wealth of cultural diversity. Too often, such variations are interpreted as an inability to perform at a "white level." Or, variations may be seen as a lack of knowledge of the "proper" way to behave. Schofield (1986) provides a clear example. In a study, she found that white public school teachers often interpreted the wearing of a hat in the classroom as an indicator that a student had an "attitude problem." After all, Anglo-Saxon traditions suggest that wearing a hat indoors is rude. However, the student may come from a black urban background, which does not share the same norms regarding the meaning of wearing a hat indoors. Leaders must be aware that cultural norms vary, and that all behavior cannot be accurately judged by a single standard.

INTERCULTURAL COMMUNICATION COMPETENCE

To this point we have mentioned some of the problems, difficulties, and hazards that pervade intercultural communication attempts. However, there are a number of basic principles that can help to promote intercultural communication effectiveness. In Chapter 7, we develop the notion of interpersonal commu-

Current Research 6–6
Research by Gill and Badzinski confirmed evidence from earlier studies that the accents of speakers affect the perceptions of listeners. Specifically, these researchers found that American listeners viewed speakers with American accents more favorably than those with non-American accents. (Gill, Mary and Badzinski, Diane, The impact of accent and status on information recall and perception formation. *Communication Reports* 5, 2, 1992, pp. 99–106)

Cross-Reference 6–5
In Chapter 7 we will learn the function of interpersonal communication to build a context for understanding. Ethnocentrism blocks the search for a context for understanding.

Current Research 6–7
A study by Martini, Behnke and King found that American audiences saw Asian speakers as having more speech anxiety than American speakers, even though the Asian speakers did not themselves report higher anxiety levels. We need to test our perceptions against the perceptions of those within the cultures we encounter. (Martini, Behnke, and King, The communication of public speaking anxiety: perceptions of Asian and American speakers. *Communication Quarterly* 40, 3, 1992, pp. 279–288)

nication competence. In this chapter, we propose that following certain principles can promote **intercultural communication competence.** Certainly, there are specific communication skills that benefit intercultural interaction; however, the notion of competence raised here primarily suggests changes in perceptions and attitudes (Asuncion-Lande 1990).

Different Is Good

Perhaps the biggest hindrance to satisfactory intercultural exchanges is the belief that cultural differences suggest that the other is somehow wrong, backward, or primitive. To develop intercultural understanding, we want to avoid this ethnocentric view of other cultures. **Ethnocentrism** is the tendency to judge other groups or cultures according to your own cultural values. The ethnocentric person sees his own culture as the pinnacle or height of cultural standards, and all other cultures are judged based on how far down the ladder they stand. Porter and Samovar (1976) elaborate on the nature of ethnocentrism:

> We place ourselves, our racial, ethnic, or social group, at the center of the universe and rate all others accordingly. The greater their similarity to us, the nearer to us we place them; the greater the dissimilarity, the farther away they are. We place one group above another, one segment of society above another, one nation-state above another. We tend to see our own groups, our own country, our own culture as the best, as the most moral. This view also demands our first loyalty and produces a frame of reference that denies the existence of any other frame of reference. It is an absolute position that prohibits any other position from being appropriate for another culture.

The result of ethnocentrism is criticism of cultures that are different than one's own. The differences are not celebrated as interesting variety or novel adaptations to different physical and social circumstances. Rather, they are used to denigrate other cultures. Asuncion-Lande (1990) suggests that instead of hanging on to ethnocentric standards, people should develop a sensitivity to cultural differences and an appreciation of cultural uniqueness.

You can develop a sensitivity to cultural differences by trying to recognize variation in cultural norms when you encounter other cultures. Try to be alert when dealing with people from other cultures. Do you notice differences in how they greet each other? Do they exhibit nonverbal behaviors that you are not familiar with? Do they use words or phrases that you cannot make immediate sense of? Rather than attributing such behavior to the uniqueness of that person, consider the possibility that it represents a cultural difference. Try also to cultivate an appreciation for cultural uniqueness. Attempt to learn what the differences between cultures tell you about your own culture instead of using the differences to insist that other cultures are wrong or weird. In many cultures, people regularly embrace when meeting (including men with other men).

Do not take this as an indication that there is something wrong with such a culture. Ask yourself what it says about the use of touch in your own culture.

Consider another example. Baseball is a very popular sport in Japan, though the rules are somewhat different than those applied in North America. For instance, in Japan, there is a limit placed on the length of baseball games (four hours, or twelve innings in one league and twelve innings in the other league). As a result, a baseball game can end in a tie. To Western fans, this might seem strange; Japanese fans, however, enjoy ties because they result in equal status and produce no loss of face (Whiting 1989). In this case, the difference in the way baseball is played points to some interesting underlying differences between the two cultures. The United States places high value on competition, a fact reflected in its sports. Competition is used to create division, to separate the best from the rest. By contrast, one dominant value of Japanese culture is *wa*, meaning "harmony." To have winners and losers is to create disharmony, hence tie ball games are consistent with Japanese cultural values. By closing yourself to cultural uniqueness, by labeling anything different than your own culture wrong, you would not only fail to recognize the interesting diversity between cultures but you would also learn less about your own culture.

Flexibility Helps

Dogmatic, ethnocentric judgments hinder intercultural communication efforts. Rather than relying on a single set of cultural values, it is important to remain flexible in a variety of judgments. Asuncion-Lande (1990) notes three related points: You need to (1) maintain a tolerance for ambiguities, (2) be responsive to change, and (3) be flexible enough to adopt new alternative behaviors or attitudes.

Intercultural encounters are filled with ambiguities. Confusion and reinterpretations are inevitable. For this reason, it is crucial that you approach intercultural encounters with patience and an open mind. This may also require you to ask for clarification more often than you are used to. Imagine, for instance, that you invite a Chinese international student to a party. She thanks you, and indicates that she will likely attend. On the night of the party, she does not show up, and you are left confused by her acceptance of the invitation. Her cultural values may necessitate that she accept the invitation, because you would have lost face if she had rejected you. This may cause confusion, but it is important that you do not rush to judgment or criticize her for being insincere.

Also important is your willingness to be responsive to change. If a member of another culture is willing to adjust his or her behavior in order to bridge the cultural communication gap, you should recognize that attempt and try to reciprocate. If the Saudi businessman knows that you want to start talking business before an extended personal exchange, he may try to get to the point earlier. It may still not be quick enough for your tastes, but you must be responsive to that change and try to find common ground.

Finally, you must be flexible enough to adopt new alternatives. Consider behavioral options that you had not previously anticipated. Do not be so rigid that you cannot see things from a different perspective. Do not pass up chances to share intercultural understanding simply because you had never used overt praise in a business meeting before, or you never thought the team was more important than the individual. Be willing to explore a variety of alternative behaviors and perspectives.

Change Your Expectations of Communication Effectiveness

It is important to keep in mind that intercultural communication will be more complex and troublesome than communication with members of your own culture. Asuncion-Lande (1990) suggests that you lower your expectations for communication effectiveness. Anticipate that more time and feedback will be necessary to achieve the same level of understanding as with members of your culture. Count on the likelihood of misunderstandings, and be patient when they occur. It is possible that this attitude will make your intercultural encounters even more effective than intracultural encounters. Misunderstandings occur when talking to members of your own culture, but you are less likely to anticipate them. Such misunderstandings will probably go unresolved for longer periods because you won't expect them. If you count on misunderstandings occurring when dealing with people from other cultures, you can recognize and resolve them more quickly.

Teaching Objective 6–9
Summarize the elements of intercultural communication competence.

Intercultural competence is not easily developed, but the basic principles listed in Table 6.2 should help. As Asuncion-Lande (1990) says, "intercultural competence is the ability to demonstrate or use these skills in such a way that other people in the intercultural encounter are able to accept and use them"

Table 6.2
Principles of Intercultural Communication Competence

In order to develop intercultural communication competence, you should maintain:

    1 sensitivity to cultural differences.

    2. an appreciation of cultural uniqueness.

    3. a tolerance for ambiguities.

    4. responsiveness to change.

    5. the flexibility to adopt new alternatives.

    6. lowered expectations for communication effectiveness.

Source: N. C. Asuncion-Lande, "Intercultural Communication," in G. L. Dahnke and G. W. Clatterbuck (Eds.), *Human Communication: Theory and Research* (Belmont, CA: Wadsworth, 1990), pp. 208–226.

(p. 209). These skills must first be understood, then applied in the appropriate situations, if they are to do any good.

INTERCULTURAL COMMUNICATION TRAINING

The opening scenario to this chapter is somewhat unrealistic. It is unlikely that a company doing business in other countries would not have an international sales training program. If such training was not available within the company, then it would likely be provided by an independent consultant or training program. Intercultural communication training, which has gained considerable attention in the business world, is taken quite seriously. In this section, we overview the different types of training programs and highlight some of their strengths and weaknesses.

Although there is a wide variety of programs, models, and theories of intercultural training, the following basic approaches listed by Brislin, Landis, and Brandt (1983) provide a sensible overview of the topic.

Information or Fact-Oriented Training

Information-based international training takes a classroom-style approach to teaching cross-cultural communication. The participants being trained about the new culture (the trainees) are informed through lectures, discussion, and assorted audio or video material. Trainees may learn about the climate, economy, decision-making styles, and some of the language of the host culture (that is, the culture they intend to visit). In addition, the trainees may learn about typ-

Forced interaction between members of different subcultures does not guarantee increased understanding or trust. Equal status, shared goals, and in-depth interaction all help enhance communication efforts.

ical daily routines of the host culture and typical situations the trainees are likely to encounter. These topics are important so that the trainees can avoid culture shock, which is often caused by the trainees' loss of their own routine in a different culture.

The advantage of this approach is that it provides some groundwork for recognizing the cultural differences that the trainee is likely to encounter. However, the approach has also received considerable criticism. Although trainees are informed of cultural differences, they are not trained in how to deal with those differences. The trainees may be told how to adapt to unfamiliar situations, for instance, but the program does not give them opportunities to practice the necessary social or perceptual skills.

Attribution Training

Attribution training is designed to reduce one of the potential problems of intercultural encounters—the misunderstanding of the other person's intentions. Descriptions of intercultural encounters are presented to trainees and they are asked to interpret the host culture's intentions in the event. For example, "Assume that you are working as a female supervisor of several Japanese workers. One morning, you describe a job task to one of the workers, and he stands in front of you scratching his head and saying '*saa.*' Is he doing this because (1) he is unable to take directions from a woman, (2) he doesn't understand your instructions and is displaying embarrassment, or (3) he is waiting for the proper vocal intonation so that he can deal with statement as a command." The trainees would each select an answer and then discuss their interpretations as a group. (By the way, the reaction in the example is a display of embarrassment, so answer 2 would be correct.)

Training in the recognition of critical incidents is useful, and it raises the awareness of trainees to the difficulties in intercultural communication. However, attribution training is not sufficient by itself. It is also important for trainees to practice the social skills they learn about.

Cultural Awareness

Cultural awareness training is an interesting approach that is based on the idea that you learn about other cultures by critically looking at your own culture. Sometimes referred to as a "culture general" approach (Asuncion-Lande 1990; Infante, Rancer, and Womack 1990), it is not directed toward gaining a better understanding of Japanese, or French, or Saudi culture. Instead, it makes the trainee more aware of the effects of culture in general.

Using this approach, the trainee may learn how cultural values, such as independence or rugged individualism, influence various institutions in the United States. Our sporting events, our judicial and legal systems, our business transactions all share common cultural values. The object of this training is to make the trainee aware of values that are typically taken for granted. Such values, and their social consequences, only become a problem when a person must deal with members of a culture who do not share the same values.

The approach is useful because it can be adapted to many different host cultures. Although it raises the trainees' awareness, it does not allow them to practice necessary social skills for the intercultural encounter.

Cognitive-Behavior Modification

Cognitive-behavior modification applies basic learning principles to intercultural encounters. Trainees are asked to identify things they find rewarding or punishing. Then they are told how they might seek these rewards or avoid the punishment in the host culture. Brislin, Landis, and Brandt (1983) elaborate:

> In analyzing rewards, for instance, a trainee might list that he enjoys reading daily newspapers, exercising regularly, meeting new people, and having a pleasant group of co-workers in the office. He would then study written materials about the other culture and contribute to group discussion led by a knowledgeable trainer to determine how these rewarding activities may be obtained. (p. 15)

The same technique would be then used to identify and deal with punishing activities. Recognizing that traffic jams and wasted time are aversive to trainees, a program could be developed to help them cope with these problems in the host culture. They could be informed of the efficient mass-transit system as a way of avoiding traffic jams. If the host culture has a less rigid view of punctuality, trainees could first be made aware that wasted time is more a part of life there. Second, they could be taught how to use waiting time productively.

Though this is a useful training program, it is not widely used because it requires a highly talented trainer with a great deal of knowledge about the host culture. Since all of the trainees generate lists of rewards and punishments, the trainer must know quite a bit about the host culture to suggest solutions. In addition, the approach does not teach trainees how to use the specific social skills necessary for adapting to the host culture.

Experential Learning

The **experential learning** approach is designed to help trainees understand the host culture through experience. Rather than passively hearing about another culture, trainees are guided through interactive situations similar to those in the host culture. A number of different techniques are used, ranging from role playing to cultural immersion.

In role playing, trainees are instructed to act out roles in various scenarios. For instance, a trainee may be told to play the role of an American sales representative working in an eastern European country. The country has little capital to spend, and the sales meeting is with a former Communist official who is resistant to change. The trainee must develop relevant social strategies for the sale and be able to deal with an unreceptive audience. Another trainee might play the former Communist official role to better understand the complexities of the situation. Although this is a useful technique, role playing is less intense and less realistic than the more extreme technique of cultural immersion.

In cultural immersion, there is a greater attempt to place trainees in a simulated version of the host culture, including the details of everyday life. For example, a Peace Corps training program based on this technique was conducted in Hawaii using a re-created Micronesian village. The trainees were being prepared to work in Micronesia, and in this simulated village they had to gather their own food, ration fresh water, protect their skin from the sun without the aid of tanning lotion—in essence, they had to simulate daily life as they would live it in Micronesia. Though the demands of an international sales training program may not require going back to nature, the daily demands of living in the host culture could be re-created.

Regardless of the specific training technique used, all experiential learning approaches have several advantages. Primarily, they allow trainees to practice the social skills necessary to interact in another culture. These programs recognize that a lecture (or any other form of information exchange) about a culture is not the same as interaction within it. In some ways, this approach is even better than direct exposure to the host culture. In experiential learning, a communication attempt can be stopped and dissected at any point. The trainers provide a safety net so that trainees can take risks and try new communication techniques without fear of negative consequences. Another advantage is that a realistic approach, such as cultural immersion, can serve to inoculate trainees to culture shock. Trainees can sample the daily routines of the host culture in smaller doses and become aware of the disorienting effects of leaving their own culture behind.

Unfortunately, experiential learning can be complex and expensive, thereby limiting its use. It can also place substantial stress on trainees. It is not uncommon for trainees to drop out of the program. However, it is better that trainees find out about their difficulties with intercultural encounters before they are faced with one.

The Interaction Approach

Teaching Objective 6–10
Explore the various forms of intercultural communication training.

Discussion Question 6–8
Which approach to intercultural communication training do you think you would find most helpful and effective? Why?

Interaction approach training uses people from the host culture ("host nationals") and people from the trainees' culture who have spent considerable time in the host culture ("old hands"). Trainees are given a chance to interact with host nationals in a relaxed, nonthreatening setting (as opposed to being thrust into the host culture). In this way, trainees can learn to be comfortable around host nationals. Another benefit of this approach is that old hands can pass along advice about how they adjusted to the culture, describing some of the problems they encountered and suggesting solutions.

Like experiential learning, the interaction approach is not just an information-giving program but emphasizes the exercise of social skills as well. It requires cooperative host nationals and insightful old hands to be successful.

As you can see, each of the approaches to intercultural communication training has its own strengths and weaknesses. If you have the opportunity to participate in an intercultural training program, be aware of your own needs and try to match those needs to the appropriate type of training. In general, training that expands your social skills in the other culture is most useful.

Intercultural communication relationships can be very rewarding. They can be financially rewarding by promoting international business ventures. They can be socially rewarding by bringing together members of different cultures and by promoting understanding among members of different subcultures. Finally, these efforts can be personally rewarding. You can learn more about the incredible diversity of human beings and thereby gain a greater appreciation of your own culture.

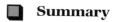 **Summary**

The numerous benefits of successful intercultural communication are not without risks. Intercultural communication can be difficult, fraught with ambiguity, confusion, and misunderstanding. Culture provides an unspoken backdrop of taken-for-granted assumptions to any communication attempt. When the backdrop is not the same for all participants, it is difficult to anticipate all the changes that can occur. This chapter should help you understand the nature of that backdrop, and what you can do to reach a better understanding in intercultural encounters.

In this chapter, we defined culture and described some of its functions. Culture is the knowledge shared within a group to help it adapt to its environment. Although culture influences the development of artifacts, practices, and rituals, it would be incorrect to say that artifacts and the rest are the culture.

We also defined intercultural communication in this chapter. It is generally viewed as interpersonal exchanges between members of different national, ethnic, racial, or social groups or subgroups where the differences in the participants' backgrounds impact on the encounter. This was contrasted with other similar notions, such as cross-cultural communication and international communication.

Much of the chapter explored the dimensions along which cultures vary. Language differences include untranslatable words and difficulties created by various verbal styles. Cultures also differ in terms of their attitudes and values. The value differences include the dimensions of individualism-collectivism, uncertainty avoidance, power distance, and masculinity-femininity. The impact of these differences on communication can be substantial.

When members of different cultures have to deal with one another, the effects on the individuals and the groups are interesting. Culture shocks can occur when an individual is unable to adjust to the daily routines of another culture. Individuals can differ in the degree that they cross the cultural boundaries. Some may try to "pass," rejecting their original culture. Some may reject the new culture and become chauvinistic supporters of their original culture. Others may be caught between two cultures, living on the margins of both without truly identifying with either one. Finally, a few people are able to synthesize two cultures and become mediators between them.

Intercultural communication competence is an important goal that can be broadly defined. To reach a suitable level of competence, one may require intercultural training. Not all approaches to intercultural communication training are alike. Each has its own set of strengths and weaknesses. Ultimately, if you intend to participate in such training to increase your communication competence, you should try to find a training program that will teach you the social skills you will need in the other culture.

Exercises

1. The mediated outlets of expression (such as, movies, TV, magazines, news-papers) often reflect the values of the culture they come from. Look for some international newsmagazines in the library. Even if you cannot understand the language, you can still analyze the products advertised, the pictures used to sell the products, and the general topics covered. Compare a few international magazines to issues of *Time, Newsweek,* or *U.S. News & World Report* for the same week. Be prepared to explain your analysis in class.

2. What is a subculture? When does a group sharing common features become a subculture? For the list of groups that follows, determine which groups are subcultures and which are not. What helps you make the distinction? Be prepared to defend your selections and to explain why the groups you chose are or are not subcultures.

   bikers (members of a motorcycle club)
   bowlers (members of a bowling league)
   computer hackers
   coin collectors
   college students
   auto workers
   Hispanic Americans
   Jewish Americans
   Welsh Americans
   Vietnamese Americans
   students with learning disabilities
   the blind
   the left-handed

3. Different subcultures often distinguish themselves from the larger culture through clothing, artifacts, and other distinctive features. Generate a list of subcultures and describe their distinctive features. Be prepared to explain in class how these features may represent specific values of each subculture.

4. Unlike some other languages (such as Spanish and German), English does not have different pronouns for formal and informal forms of address. In English, the same pronouns are used regardless of whether you are addressing a close friend or a Supreme Court Justice. If English did have formal and informal forms of address, where would you draw the line in their use? Who would you address formally and informally? What would be the consequences if you addressed a person informally who expected a formal mode of address? What does this suggest about our culture? What other verbal and nonverbal means do we use to differentiate levels of formality?

Barnlund, D. C. (1989). *Communicative styles of Japanese and Americans: Images and realities.* Belmont, CA: Wadsworth.

Barnlund does an excellent job exploring communication differences between two cultures. He discusses cultural norms concerning intimacy, commitment, and social space. He uncovers the effects these norms have on the two cultures.

Hall, E. T., and Hall, M. R. (1990). *Hidden differences: Doing business with the Japanese.* New York: Anchor/Doubleday.

With the increased emphasis on international trade, a number of books have been published recently to help American business personnel bridge gaps with other cultures. Edward T. Hall, a prominent scholar, and Mildred Reed Hall wrote this short, readable book to help Americans doing business in Japan. They overview cultural differences, characterize Japanese culture and business, and give practical hints to Americans conducting business in Japan.

Miner, H. (1956). Body ritual among the Nacirema. *American Anthropologist, 58,* 503–507.

A thought-provoking article in which the author focuses with an anthropologist's eye on a strange, primitive culture. The rituals and institutions of this culture appear bizarre, yet oddly familiar. We can learn much about how a description from outside any culture can make it look strange. To recognize the twist in the article, all you have to do is spell Nacirema backwards to realize that the author is describing our own culture. (Try asking a friend to read the article without revealing who it describes. See if your friend picks up on the description. Reveal the twist, and watch for your friend's reaction.)

Whiting, R. (1977). *The chrysanthemum and the bat: Baseball samarai style.* New York: Dodd, Mead & Co.; Whiting, R. (1989). *You gotta have wa: When two cultures collide on the baseball diamond.* New York: Macmillan; and Cromartie, W., with Whiting, R. (1991). *Slugging it out in Japan: An American major leaguer in the Tokyo outfield.* Tokyo: Kodansha.

Robert Whiting wrote two books and assisted with another on the subject of Japanese professional baseball. When "the great American pastime" becomes a Japanese obsession it reveals a surprising amount about both cultures. American ballplayers are hired to play under Japanese managers and alongside Japanese teammates, generating cultural friction. These books are readable, fun, and insightful.

Related Readings

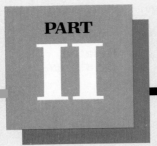

PART
II

MASTERING INTERPERSONAL COMMUNICATION

Interpersonal Communication

Chapter objectives

After reading this chapter you should be able to:

1. discuss interpersonal communication from two perspectives—the *contextual view* and the *developmental view*

2. describe the three types of knowledge we can have of others

3. discuss the specific functions of interpersonal communication, including *gathering social knowledge, building a context of understanding,* and *establishing and negotiating identity*

4. describe how "relational context" influences meaning in interpersonal communication

5. differentiate between content and relationship messages in interpersonal communication

6. explain the importance of "role" and "face" to interpersonal communication

7. differentiate between confirming and disconfirming messages

8. define communication competence and discuss its role in conversations

Key terms and concepts

interpersonal communication (contextual definition)

interpersonal communication (developmental definition)

cultural-level knowledge

sociological-level knowledge

psychological-level knowledge

self-disclosure

social validation

metacommunication

role

face

self-presentation

altercasting

confirming response

disconfirming response

communication competence

communication effectiveness

communication appropriateness

Imagine that you are helping to organize a local community improvement group. A number of neighborhood citizens have banded together to voice their concerns to local municipal officials about inadequate street lights, traffic problems, debris removal from vacant lots, and street repairs. You are helping to delegate responsibilities so that letters get written, local officials get contacted personally, and more members of the community get invited to participate in the group's efforts. Sometimes reluctantly, sometimes willingly, different members are allocated responsibilities.

One member, David, eagerly volunteers to talk personally to elected officials, so you put him on that committee. Several days later, you hear from other committee members that David has an abrasive, argumentative style that is more likely to anger and alienate than to win over the people to whom he's talking. Knowing that eager volunteers are a valuable commodity, you find yourself in a difficult position. Do you pull David off the personal contact committee and risk having him quit the organization? Or, do you let him make the personal calls and risk having him enrage the officials with whom he's supposed to establish contact? Whether you get him to take on different responsibilities or encourage him to adopt a more personable persuasive approach, you will find your interpersonal communication skills will be put to the test.

Effective leadership is not just a matter of setting goals and allocating resources. The effective leader must also be able to work closely with people. This requires that a leader be able to master interpersonal communication skills. In addition to using their critical thinking skills, leaders also must exercise effective social, or people-oriented, skills.

This chapter is designed to help you improve your interpersonal communication skills. We begin by defining interpersonal communication. We next explore some of the common uses, or functions, of interpersonal communication, including gaining knowledge of others, building a context of understanding, and the negotiation of identity. In the third section of the chapter, we explain the general notion of interpersonal communication competence and provide some suggestions for its development.

DEFINING INTERPERSONAL COMMUNICATION

When you think of *interpersonal communication*, you may think of a face-to-face discussion between friends, family members, or co-workers. This is a useful start, but it does not uncover the unique and essential qualities of interpersonal communication. Think, for a moment, about how interpersonal communication differs from other types of human interaction. Seeking a precise answer to this question, theorists and researchers in the field of communication have formed into two camps—at least with respect to how interpersonal communication may be defined. The two definitions that have emerged are the *contextual definition* and the *developmental definition*.

The Contextual Definition

The contextual view defines interpersonal communication by contrasting it with other situations in which communication takes place. Contextual theorists ask, How does interpersonal communication differ from small group, public, and mass communication? Miller (1978) suggested that these different communication contexts can be arranged along at least four continuous scales, involving (1) the number of communicators (ranging from few to many), (2) the physical proximity among participants (from close to distant), (3) the number of available sensory channels (for example, auditory, visual, etc.) that can be used (from many to few), and (4) the immediacy of the feedback (from most immediate to most delayed).

According to the **contextual definition**, interpersonal communication is unique and distinguishable from other communication contexts because (1) there are few participants involved; (2) the interactants are in close proximity to each other; (3) the interactants can see, hear, touch, and smell each other, thereby using many sensory channels; and (4) the feedback can be received immediately, so that a puzzled look can indicate that an interactant didn't understand what was said, or an "uh huh," can provide feedback that agreement is shared.

Compare the characteristics of interpersonal to mass communication, the context at the other end of these scales. In mass communication, such as radio, TV, or print journalism, you will find the following characteristics: (1) There are many participants, sometimes millions involved. (2) The interactants are usually not in close proximity—they can be spread out across the country, or even around the world. (3) Sensory input is limited. For instance, radio can be heard but not seen. Print journalism can be seen but not heard. Even television is limited to just two sensory modalities, sight and sound. (4) The feedback tends to be delayed in mass-mediated communication. If a reader doesn't like a magazine article, he or she may write a letter to the editor. Television and radio programming get periodic popularity feedback through weekly or monthly audience rating systems.

As you can see, within the contextual definition, the interpersonal context has several unique features. In spite of the fact that the contextual view allows us to make these distinctions, however, this definition has had its share of critics. These critics argue that not all face-to-face interactions are equally interpersonal. Out of a dissatisfaction with the contextual definition, the developmental view emerged.

The Developmental View

The waiter arrives at your table, and tells you about the specials of the day. You ask about the type of sauce that is served on one of the pasta dishes. The waiter answers your question and takes your order. According to the contextual view,

Teaching Objective 7–1
Explain the contextual and developmental definitions of interpersonal communication.

Cross-reference 7–1
Later we'll observe how interpersonal communication compares with group communication and is incorporated into it (Chapters 11–12). We will then make a comparison with communication in a public speaking context (Part IV).

Current Research 7–1
Anderson, Lustig, and Anderson (Television and the quality of family life, *Communication Quarterly*, *38*, 4, pp. 312–322) have examined family interpersonal communication in front of the TV in ways which suggest a new "blending" of contextual qualities.

this is an example of an interpersonal interaction. Is it? It certainly involves few interactants who are in close proximity. They are able to use multiple sensory channels in their interaction, and the feedback to the question asked was immediate. Yet, to some this would seem to be *impersonal,* rather than *interpersonal.*

Compare this to a chance encounter with an old friend from high school. She tells you about her new job and the growing responsibilities she's learned to take on. You explain the challenges and triumphs of college life. She mentions her breakup from her long-time boyfriend from high school, and how she was torn apart, but matured from the experience. You both marvel at how a mutual friend got married right out of high school, and now has a pair of twins—instant family. You tell old stories and relive old times before promising to keep in touch, and going your own ways. Is this the same as your encounter with the waiter? Are they both to be categorized as interpersonal communication? Those who share the contextual view would say yes. Those who share the developmental view would disagree.

According to the developmental view, not all face-to-face interactions are interpersonal. This view distinguishes between the *impersonal* and the *interpersonal.* The developmental view suggests there is a qualitative difference between impersonal and interpersonal communication. The **developmental definition** suggests that interpersonal communication occurs when people have interacted with each other over an extended period of time. It is further characterized by an interaction that is adapted to the other as a unique individual, rather than one in which actors play out well-defined roles, such as waiter and customer.

When we interact with others, we make predictions about the likely outcomes of our message strategies. To persuade a reluctant friend to see a movie, you might threaten, plead, bargain, guilt-trip, or use whatever other technique you think might work. Your decision of which strategy to use is based on a prediction of which strategy will most likely be successful. In turn, your predictions of success are based on the kind of knowledge you have about the recipient of the message.

Miller and Steinberg (1975) argue that there are three different types of knowledge that you can possess about another person, ranging from the general to the specific in nature: *cultural-level knowledge, sociological-level knowledge,* and *psychological-level knowledge.* **Cultural-level knowledge** is the shared knowledge members of a culture possess. We assume that anyone raised in our culture shares certain beliefs and information. For instance, we assume that anyone in our culture understands that when they are greeted, we expect them to respond with a greeting in return. Or, we assume that in restaurants there is a typical "script" that is followed: Waiter greets the customers. Drink orders are taken. Drinks arrive, and meal orders are taken. Salad is brought. Main course is delivered. Waiter checks back to see if everything is fine. The check is asked for, and the meal is paid for. There are untold numbers of rituals and interaction procedures that are shared by members of the culture, and everyone is expected to know and follow this information.

Sometimes your choice of a communication strategy may be based on this broad level of shared information. The hypothetical interaction between you

Current Research 7–2
At the framework level of cultural knowledge, cultures differ even in the basic willingness of their members to communicate, with U.S. subjects the most willing to communicate, Swedes reporting the highest overall communication competence, and Micronesians reporting the greatest reticence to communicate in general but the most comfort communicating in groups. (McCroskey, James, and Richmond, Virginia. Willingness to Communicate: Differing Cultural Perspectives, *Southern Communication Journal,* 56(1) 1990, pp. 72–77.)

and the waiter, described earlier, was based on the cultural-level knowledge that you had of the waiter, and that the waiter had of you. You both expected each other to recognize the "restaurant script," which guided your choice of communication strategies. According to the developmental view, this type of interaction is largely determined by the culturally established roles that the interactants play. It is therefore impersonal rather than interpersonal in nature.

In addition to belonging to the larger culture, we are also members of numerous smaller groups. Whether those are voluntary groups, such as labor unions, church groups, political groups, and social groups, or involuntary groups, such as those based on age, gender, race, or weight, we can be categorized by smaller groupings. Groups can be characterized by common beliefs, interests, and values. Therefore, by knowing what groups a person belongs to, we can make predictions about the type of person he or she is. This is known as **sociological-level knowledge** of a person. This knowledge allows us to tailor our messages more closely to the recipient.

Imagine that you didn't like the grade you received on your last English essay, and that your goal was to convince the instructor to raise the grade. You are instinctively aware of many recognizable persuasive strategies at the cultural level. In some contexts, we use begging and pleading to persuade others. However, you know that this strategy will probably not work here. Teachers have probably heard their share of begging and pleading, so they are not likely to be persuaded by such a strategy. Looking beyond the larger culture to the subgroup of teachers, you ask yourself what relevant beliefs or values teachers might hold that you could appeal to here.

You know that teachers usually value hard work and creative risk taking. When you go to talk to the instructor, you take along the rough drafts you had worked through. As you make your case, you point out to the instructor that the multiple drafts stand as evidence of hard work. Furthermore, you verbally explain the creative "angle" you were trying to develop. You agree that the final product may not have captured the style you were hoping for, but that the various drafts display consistent movement toward that goal. We provide no guarantee that this strategy will be successful, but you can see that it is much more sophisticated than begging and pleading. Your message is tailored to the class of people known as teachers. But, alas, according to the developmental view, this is still not interpersonal communication. Although the message is more tailored to the receiver, it is still tailored to a class of people rather than an individual. Your choice of communication strategies is still dictated by the student-teacher roles that are being enacted.

The final type of knowledge we may possess of others is **psychological-level knowledge**. This is based on knowledge of the other as an individual, rather than as a member of a group or the larger culture. Sometimes we can structure our messages on the basis of the knowledge we have of the other's personal preferences, beliefs, or values. Imagine you are trying to persuade a reluctant friend to see a particular movie. You know this friend well enough to tailor the message to him as an individual. Your friend, Doug, has expressed a secret admiration for a mutual friend, Jan. You could persuade Doug to go to the movie by telling him that you overheard Jan talking about going to see it too.

Current Research 7–3
Our communication strategies are always influenced by our cultural framework, even the culturally-specific perceptions of and rules about displaying emotion. (Matsumoto, David. Cultural influences on facial expressions of emotion, *Southern Communication Journal*, 56, 2, 1991, pp. 128–137.)

Cross-Reference 7–2
Sociological-level knowledge is the essence and basis of audience analysis for public speaking. See Chapter 13.

Cross-Reference 7–3
We can infer something about the beliefs of an individual on the basis of her group affiliations or sociological-level knowledge. But psychological-level knowledge is required to know another's attitudes and motives and to therefore understand how she perceives her world. See Chapter 2.

This is not a strategy that would work for anyone in the culture, or for any member of the groups to which Doug belongs. Your strategy is based on your personal knowledge of Doug. According to the developmental view, communication is interpersonal only when your message strategy choice is based on this type of psychological-level knowledge. The developmental view thus has a much stricter definition of interpersonal communication. From a developmental perspective, much of our day-to-day interaction would not be characterized as interpersonal.

Teaching Objective 7–2
Suggest the contribution of both the contextual and the developmental views to an understanding of interpersonal communication as bounded by context as well as offering interactants the potential for mutual knowledge at the psychological level.

For our purposes in this chapter, it is not really necessary to choose between the contextual and developmental view. Each provides a potentially useful view of interpersonal communication. The contextual view makes us reflect upon the unique features of one-to-one interaction. By contrast, the more restrictive developmental view forces us to recognize the constraints that roles place on our interactions. We now turn to the things people accomplish through interpersonal interaction—in other words, the functions of interpersonal communication.

THE FUNCTIONS OF INTERPERSONAL COMMUNICATION

Discussion Question 7–1
In a sense, the contextual vs. developmental debate regarding interpersonal communication is about how we communicate vs. how much we know or have the potential of discovering about the other. Looking at your own relationships—acquaintances, friends, family—which matters more? Or is it that the context is necessary in order for the knowledge to unfold?

When you're engaged in interpersonal communication, you may have an explicit, clearly defined goal in mind, whether it is persuading a friend to go to a movie, or settling a conflict with a boyfriend/girlfriend over how time should be spent together. However, not all interpersonal goals are so immediate and explicit. There are additional results of interpersonal communication that could be considered secondary goals, or even by-products—the natural, inevitable results of engaging in interpersonal communication. These are the functions, or functional consequences, of interpersonal communication. For instance, you probably don't think to yourself, "I think I'll call my brother in order to maintain our relationship and to let him know I care about him." If asked, your primary goal for calling him would probably be to find out what is new in your brother's life. However, a function or natural result of the call will be to maintain the relationship bonds between you and to show that you care about him. Here we discuss three specific functions to interpersonal communication: to *gather social knowledge, build a context of understanding,* and *establish and negotiate identity* (see Table 7.1).

Social Knowledge Acquisition

One of the inevitable results of interacting with people is that you gain information or knowledge about them. This is not just a chance by-product, but a crucial function of interpersonal communication. Social knowledge acquisition allows us to interact more effectively with others. Although there are general rules and guidelines for social interaction, people can be idiosyncratic. Gaining knowledge about a person allows us to interact more effectively with him or her

Table 7.1
Functions of Interpersonal Communication

• Social knowledge acquisition	• To explain, predict, and control interactions
• Builds a context of understanding	• To build and define relationships and their contexts
• Establishes and negotiates identity	• To define ourselves and others

because the knowledge we gain allows us to *explain* and *predict* the other's behavior more accurately. As a result, we can then have a better chance of exercising *control* when we interact with that person.

An old letter to "Dear Abby" comes to mind here. Someone wrote in to complain about a co-worker who took pride in not owning a car, yet mooched rides off everyone at the office, often at considerable inconvenience to the person with the car. Furthermore, the moocher never offered any compensation, even to pay for the gas used. The writer asked Abby what he should do the next time a ride was requested. It was clear that past experience and knowledge of the person allowed the writer of the letter to *explain* and *predict* the moocher's behavioral intent when he said things like, "Say, are you going anywhere near the K-Mart on Green Street on your way home?" What the writer wanted was a useful strategy to help him deal with, or *control*, the situation in a way that didn't make him look bad. We won't keep you in suspense any longer—Abby suggested that the writer should politely but firmly refuse to provide any rides to this person.

The general principle here is that information about the people with whom we interact allows us to deal with them more effectively. Information allows us to structure and control the world around us, including the other people with whom we deal. Berger and Calabrese (1975) even suggested that the search for information is the driving principle behind communication in interpersonal relationships. According to Berger and Calabrese, we communicate in order to reduce uncertainty. They postulated that we are most strongly motivated to reduce uncertainty when (1) the person with whom we are dealing is acting in an unusual or deviant way; (2) we anticipate repeated interaction with this person in the future; and (3) it is likely that the other person can provide us with rewards or punishment.

Social Penetration Theory.   This theory tries to capture the process of social knowledge acquisition. Its developers, Altman and Taylor (1973), suggested that uncovering information about a person is like peeling away the layers of an onion; hence, their pictorial representation of this process has come to be known as the "onion model" (see Figure 7.1).

Teaching Objective 7–3
Describe the social knowledge acquisition function of interpersonal communication, discussing social penetration theory, information-gathering strategies, and self-disclosure as methods of social knowledge acquisition.

Discussion Question 7–2
What about this idea that we communicate in order to reduce uncertainty? What experiences have we had with being in situations where we were uncertain? How did we communicate?

Leadership Note 7–1
Numerous current authors (Peters, DePree, Bennis, and others) writing about leadership emphasize again and again the essential need for the leader to articulate a vision for his or her people. (Peters, *Thriving on Chaos.* New York: Harper and Row, 1987, pp. 488–489) describes that need for a vision as a compass, a source of stability, a beacon and a control, and says that we trust (or feel certain about) those people whose beliefs and actions we can predict.

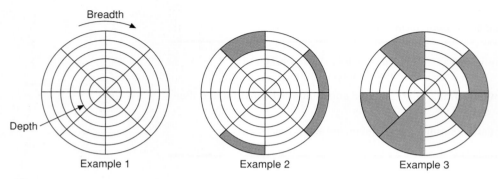

Figure 7.1
The "Onion Model" of Personality Structure.

Visually, the model looks like the cross-section of an onion. Each cross-section represents the features of an individual's personality. Any personality can be characterized in terms of its *breadth* and *depth* (see example 1 in Figure 7.1). Breadth is represented by the various slices or wedges in the onion. Each slice represents a separate area of interest or feature of a person's personality. One slice may represent a person's beliefs and feelings about education; another slice, occupational interests; and yet another slice may capture hobbies or sports. Obviously, any individual may have thousands of such interest areas. For simplicity's sake, the present models only capture eight.

Within any single slice, a person may hold beliefs or feelings that range from the very peripheral (on the outer ring) to the very central or core beliefs (at the center of the "onion"). These various layers represent the *depth* of beliefs that a person may hold. Say, for example, that one of the slices represents your beliefs about career options. On the surface (outer ring), you may believe that it is important to have a career you enjoy. This is "surface" information, which you would be willing to share with anyone. Midway toward the core, you might hold a belief that a good career is one that benefits others, and maintains environmentally sound principles. Note that these are *your* beliefs, and not necessarily everyone's. You may have a friend who believes that making the most money possible is the defining feature of a good occupation. Finally, at the core, you may hold certain beliefs, relevant to career choice, which are closely linked to the type of person you are. Perhaps you believe that a career should put you in the spotlight as an individual, where you succeed or fail on your own skills and efforts. In other words, your view of careers is closely linked to your rugged-individual, non–team player approach to life in general. While these are all your feelings about careers, some of them say more about your core personality, about the type of person you are.

Since, as we said, social information is gathered to help us deal with people more effectively, it is desirable to gain knowledge at the core. Knowing that you're a fierce individualist will help me to explain and predict your behavior more effectively than just knowing that you want a job in which you will be happy. Knowledge of your core personality will carry over into other areas of interest that you have. Because this core information is so revealing, and potentially powerful, we tend to reveal it slowly and reluctantly.

According to Altman and Taylor, social interaction is a process of exploring the depth and breadth of the other's personality. In the course of initial interaction, the participants may reveal several areas of interest (some *breadth*), but little *depth* is exchanged. Depth of personality is only revealed after time has passed and trust has been established. The information you might have about an acquaintance's personality is characterized in example 2 of Figure 7.1. The shaded areas represent those of which you have knowledge. Example 2 shows knowledge of several areas, or domains of interest, but little depth is displayed. You might know where this person grew up and went to high school, his or her college major, various hobbies he or she has, and what his or her job was over the summer. This is surface information, which reveals little about a person's character.

Example 3 of Figure 7.1 might characterize your knowledge of a close friend or family member. It shows an exploration not only of more breadth but also of substantial depth in several of these areas. This is someone you know very well—someone whose behavior you can probably explain and predict fairly effectively. Social penetration theory is useful because it gives us this onion model to pictorially represent the process of social knowledge acquisition. However, we must turn our attention elsewhere to locate the communication tools or strategies used to gather social information.

Discussion Question 7–3
Who knows you better than anyone else? How long have you known each other? How long did you know each other before you shared some of your deeper layers? Have you?

Social Information-Gathering Strategies. By simply talking, you inevitably learn more about a person. You may also set out to gather information intentionally. Berger and Bradac (1982) suggest some of the communication strategies we use to gather information about others. They categorize the strategies into three groups, which they label the *passive, active,* and *interactive* strategies.

Passive strategies involve simply observing a person to gather information. Berger and Bradac list two types of passive strategies. A *reactivity search* occurs when you observe a person interacting in social situations and reacting to the demands of the situation. Some people are very guarded in their actions, however. For instance, it might be difficult to know what a particular movie star is like by observing his or her behavior in public settings. Instead, you might want to observe the star in informal situations when he or she is behaving more naturally. This passive strategy is known as *disinhibition searching*.

Active strategies require the observer to do something to gather information. For instance, you might *ask others about the target person*. If you have a hard time reading one of your classmates—you can't tell from the person's comments in class whether he or she is sarcastic or kind of naive—you might ask a mutual friend what that person is really like. The second active strategy is called *environmental structuring*. According to Trenholm (1986), this strategy "is used whenever we stage incidents in order to gain information about [the] target person's responses. By placing targets in situations where they must make choices, we learn more about how they will behave" (p. 148).

Self-disclosure is a delicate art. Providing too little information about oneself limits effective communication. Providing too much information, and too soon, may contribute to the premature termination of a relationship.

Current Research 7–4
Two longitudinal studies by Vanlear, one of newly formed relationships and the other of intact friendships and romantic relationships, found "clear evidence of recurrent, periodic cycling between openness and closedness, revelation and restraint." Both studies showed apparent cycling both within and across conversations. (Vanlear, C. Arthur, Testing a Cyclical Model of Communicative Openness in Relationship development: two longitudinal studies. *Communication Monographs* 58, 4, December 1991, pp. 337–361.

Interactive strategies involve direct interaction with the target person. The first such strategy is *interrogation,* in which you ask the target direct questions. The second strategy is *self-disclosure,* in which you tell the target person something about yourself in hopes that she or he will reveal some personal information in turn. Much has been written about self-disclosure as an interpersonal communication strategy. We deal with it in more depth below, but first read the Mastering Communication Skills box.

Though not to be taken as an exhaustive list of all the possible social information-gathering strategies, Berger and Bradac's scheme does provide a simple ordering system for investigating this social skill.

Self-Disclosure. This strategy has received a significant amount of attention in the communication field, not only as an information-gathering strategy, but also as a barometer of relationship quality. Though the presence of self-disclosure is no longer viewed as the ultimate yardstick of relationships, it remains a communication strategy worthy of attention.

MASTERING COMMUNICATION SKILLS

When Information Increases Uncertainty

The general principle behind social penetration theory is that new information about others makes them more explainable and predictable (it reduces uncertainty). Although this principle has generally been supported, Planalp and Honeycutt (1985) managed to uncover a number of events in which new information *increased* uncertainty rather than reduced it. They asked college students to generate personal examples in which new information about a person increased their uncertainty about that other. An often-mentioned event was the discovery that a dating partner had been seeing others on the side. New information (about "the cheating") made it more difficult to explain and predict the other's behavior in the relationship.

Have you ever uncovered information that made a friend, dating partner, or family member less explainable and predictable? What effect did this event have on your relationship? How did you acquire this information? Did you use a *passive*, an *active*, or an *interactive* strategy?

The novice may believe that self-disclosure occurs whenever people reveal personal information about themselves, but there is actually more involved. If you were to tell a friend your shoe size, would you consider that self-disclosure? Most communication scholars would not. Self-disclosure involves more than just giving information about yourself to another person. As Pearce and Sharp (1973) state, "**Self-disclosure** occurs when one person voluntarily tells another person things about himself which the other is unlikely to know or discover from other sources" (p. 414). Self-disclosure involves risk and vulnerability on the part of the discloser. It entails revealing personal, private information that you would be reluctant to disclose indiscriminately (Miller, 1990). There was a time when low levels of self-disclosure were considered indicators of a person with a stunted personality, or of a relationship that was deviant and going nowhere (Jourard, 1968). Today, we prefer to view it simply as a useful strategy in the conduct of interpersonal relationships. To that end, it is worth noting the potential rewards and risks of self-disclosure, as well as setting out some guidelines for its use.

We've mentioned already that one reward of self-disclosure is its usefulness in gaining information about another person. There is an underlying *norm of reciprocity*, which dictates that personal disclosure calls for disclosure in turn. Revealing personal information pressures the other person to reveal something also. Obviously, by self-disclosing, the other person also learns about you. By sharing information, you and the other become more explainable and predictable to one another. This helps build the relationship between you. Since self-disclosure provides information that is risky, using this strategy helps to build trust between you and the other. Trust helps strengthen the bonds of interpersonal relationships.

Leadership Note 7–2
Warren Bennis (*On Becoming a Leader*, Addison-Wesley, Reading, Mass., 1989) continually emphasizes the relationship between self- expression (self-disclosure) and leadership. "No leader sets out to be a leader. People set out to live their lives, expressing themselves fully. When that expression is of value, they become leaders." (p. 111)

Social validation occurs when you reveal personal information that is risky, and the other person shows an acceptance of who you are. In other words, you come to feel better about yourself because others accept you, in spite of any flaws or shortcomings you might have. A final reward of self-disclosure is a sense of self-discovery. You can learn about yourself by listening to how you describe your characteristics to another.

You might be wondering, if self-disclosure is so wonderful and provides so many rewards, why don't we use this communicative strategy all the time? As with so many things, the rewards of self-disclosure come at a cost of potential risks. Perhaps the greatest risk, or potential danger, of self-disclosure is that the person to whom you disclose may reject you as a result of the information revealed. In fact, there is evidence that self-disclosure does not necessarily promote liking (Bochner, 1984). If the disclosure is inappropriate (if it is revealed too early in the relationship, or is done outside the bounds of a close relationship), it can lead to negative impressions. If you tell someone you just met that alcoholism runs in your family and that you fear its effects on you, the other person may think you're acting rather strangely. However, the same revelation to a close friend may bring more understanding and closer relational ties. Rejection remains one of the big risks of self-disclosure.

A second risk is that personal revelations can give others power over you. Just the threat that the information could be passed on to others can be intimidating. Another risk is that disclosed information can burden and threaten the relationship. If a close friend tells you he has been having an affair, and you are also close friends with this friend's spouse, this can put you in a very uncomfortable position. The disclosure has jeopardized your ability to remain friends with both the husband and wife without betraying one friendship or the other.

Thus, in spite of the potential rewards, there are also a number of possible risks associated with self-disclosure. If you've ever had a complete stranger dump the messy details of his or her life on your lap regardless of your level of interest in the disclosure, you know that self-disclosure is not always appropriate. Wilmot (1987) suggests a series of guidelines to help you determine whether disclosure is appropriate:

1. *Start slow, and increase your disclosure by relatively small increments.* Don't rush your use of disclosure. Most people prefer that initial interaction between strangers involve little risky self-disclosure (Gilbert, 1976). As trust builds within the relationship, be increasingly willing to use disclosure.
2. *Be sure the other person is comfortable with the disclosure.* Remember that the *norm of reciprocity* is in effect. If you begin disclosing personal details, the person you're talking to will feel compelled to disclose in kind (which he or she may not feel comfortable doing yet), or risk breaking an unwritten conversational rule. Also recall that self-disclosure burdens the other person with certain responsibilities. For instance, he or she is expected not to reveal any of the information presented.
3. *The disclosure should be important to your ongoing relationship with the*

other person. Your intent in using self-disclosure should be to reveal yourself to the other, to encourage the other to reveal him- or herself to you, and to foster trust in the relationship. It should not be used as a means of testing the other, or as a way to manipulate the other with information that he or she may not want or be able to handle.

Self-disclosure is a very useful strategy for gaining information about another person and for strengthening the bonds of an interpersonal relationship. However, the risks involved necessitate that disclosure not be used indiscriminately.

Building a Context of Understanding

A second important function served by interpersonal communication is its use to build a context of understanding. In Chapter 4 on verbal communication, we mentioned that the phrase "I love you" means different things depending on whether the speaker and listener are boyfriend and girlfriend, parent and child, brother and sister, or very close friends. The meaning differs because the *relational context* changes in each situation. Grove (1991, p. 220) also provides an interesting example of this point. Imagine that Ruth says to you, "Please close the door." The meaning of this appears pretty obvious. Grove goes on to weave in details that change the relational context and subsequently the meaning of Ruth's "simple request."

1. Ruth is your supervisor, and you know she is about to urge you to do better work than you have been doing lately.
2. Ruth is sitting closer to the door than you are and has just been advanced to manager of the office where you work.
3. Ruth is your lover and left you a note to meet her in her office at lunchtime.
4. Ruth is your employee, who, rumor has it, is filing a lawsuit against you and your company, charging sex discrimination after she was passed over for advancement.
5. Ruth has been complaining lately about chills, and is wearing a sweater.

Notice how each variation changes the meaning behind Ruth's request. Relational context influences meaning. But where does relational context come from? In part it's made up of past history and events. It is also made up of communication—what has been said between the participants. Let's return to the example of "I love you." The relational context will help determine what this will mean. On the other hand, what is said in the relationship helps define the nature of the relationship. For instance, the first time that one member of a dating couple says this to the other, it changes the relational context. That person has made a bid to redefine the relationship into something more serious. As Figure 7.2 shows, the relational context defines the meaning of a communication event, and the communication event, in turn, helps define the relational context.

Discussion Question 7–4
How would you evaluate the various social information-gathering strategies in regard to the following: directness, manipulative quality, potential for obtaining the most reliable information?

Teaching Objective 7–4
Discuss the second function of interpersonal communication as the creation of contexts in which to communicate and through the existence of which the interpretation of messages is made easier; draw parallels to earlier discussions of context.

Cross-reference 7–4
We have repeatedly emphasized the importance of context: in Chapter 1, as situational influences; in Chapter 2, as cultural influences on perception; in Chapter 3, as aiding or hindering the listening process; in Chapter 4, as essential to the meanings in verbal communication; and in Chapter 5, as in some ways (artifacts, proxemics, etc.) part of the very communication itself. Understanding is impossible without context as the frame.

Figure 7.2
The Reciprocal Relationship Between the Relational Context and Communication Events.

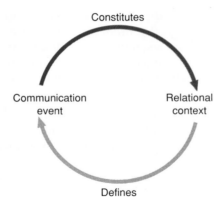

Constitutes

Communication event

Relational context

Defines

Content and Relationship Messages. When you interact, you are actually sending two sets of messages. The raw information that is sent—that is, the message that is apparent on the surface—is referred to as the *content* message. In addition, another message is sent concerning how to interpret the content. This second message is referred to as the *relationship* message (Watzlawick, Beavin, and Jackson, 1967). Recall that in Chapter 4 we mentioned that it is sometimes necessary to distinguish between *what is said* in a communication event and *what is done* in that event. Roughly translated, the content message is what is said, while the relationship message helps define what is done. Imagine that you're out with a friend who starts to cut you down and insult you. You feel hurt and angry as a result. The friend notices the bitter look on your face and says, "Hey, lighten up—I was only teasing you." In this case, the "I was only teasing you" tells you how to interpret the insults—as friendly kidding.

Quite often, the relationship message and the content message are sent simultaneously. Let's return to Ruth's request that you close the door for some examples. In example 5, where Ruth apparently has a chill, the relationship message is obvious. She is simply asking that you close the door so that the room will be more comfortable. Example 2 shows more complexity, and is therefore more interesting. When Ruth, who has recently become your boss, "asks" you to close the door, even though she is closer to it, she seems to be sending an additional message. That message, at the relationship level, could be interpreted as "I'm your boss now, so you better get used to taking orders from me." So the "request" becomes an order, and it is apparent that Ruth is attempting to exert her control over you.

Examples 1 and 4 could both be seen as preludes to confrontation. Ruth has a beef with you, and you'd better be ready to answer her questions. Example 3, in which Ruth is your lover, is interesting because it could indicate several possible relationship messages being sent. On the one hand, this could also be a prelude to a confrontation. Another interpretation could be that the message is a prelude to flirting or romance. Can you think of any other possible relationship messages being sent here?

As you can see, with every content message, you send an accompanying relationship message that aids in interpretation. In addition, the messages and communication episodes shared between interactants help to build a relational context that benefits understanding as well. A relevant communication strategy is worth noting here. It is a strategy that makes the relationship message overt and the subject of discussion. This is known as *metacommunication*.

Metacommunication.   Normally, the relational context serves as a background in which communication events occur, similar to the way a frame draws attention not to itself but to the artwork it surrounds. Our attention is usually drawn to the communication event rather than the relational context. Occasionally, the frame or context itself can be the subject of dispute. When you talk explicitly about the "frame" rather than the content of communication, you are engaging in **metacommunication**. If you argue with your spouse about where to go on vacation, you are communicating. If you argue about how you argue when you make these types of decisions, you are *metacommunicating*.

Wilmot (1987) draws a useful distinction between *episodic-level* and *relationship-level* metacommunication. Anytime you discuss the ongoing process of an individual communication event or episode, you are engaging in *episodic-level* metacommunication. If a friend cuts you down and insults you, and then says, "I was only teasing you," he or she is commenting on the communication episode, and therefore metacommunicating. If you were to say, "I felt real hurt when you insulted me, so stop doing that," you would also be engaging in episodic-level metacommunication.

At other times you may say something that comments on the larger relational context of the interaction between you and another person with whom you are speaking. This would be *relationship-level* metacommunication. If your dating partner says, "I love you," for the first time, the two of you may need to talk about the state of the relationship. This makes your relationship the subject of discussion. As you begin to talk about rules of dating exclusivity, time spent together, and changing levels of commitment, you are engaging in relationship-level metacommunication. The same sort of thing may have happened when you had to tell your parents to start treating you as an adult instead of as a child. The relationship becomes the topic of communication. If you reach a new agreement about the nature of your relationship, it can alter the meaning of future messages in that new relational context. Metacommunicating, therefore, is an overt strategy for helping to build and change the context of communication understanding.

Establishing and Negotiating Identity

A third function of interpersonal communication is that it allows you to establish and negotiate your identity and the identities of the people around you. By identity, we don't mean your name, address, and Social Security number. We're referring, rather, to who you are in relation to the people with whom you interact. You need to establish your rights and responsibilities in relation to the people with whom you have social contact. Your social identity will greatly influence how you interact with others. Furthermore, your identity is largely influenced by how you interact with others. Your social identity is a product of

Discussion Question 7–5
Think about your closest relationship. How much of your communication would you estimate is metacommunication? How about with your newest friend? What do you think is the relationship between the depth of your knowledge of another person and the amount of time you spend metacommunicating?

Teaching Objective 7–5
Emphasize the importance of establishing and maintaining identity as the third basic function of interpersonal communication; attempt to create an appreciation for the importance of roles and face to identity negotiation and management.

The roles of both mother and daughter are sometimes difficult to manage, particularly during adolescence. In this central relationship, each person's sense of identity is profoundly affected by how these roles are carried out.

Cross-reference 7–5
The importance of language as a means of claiming and clarifying social identify was discussed in Chapter 4.

Leadership Note 7–3
"Leaders are self-directed, but learning and understanding are the keys to self-direction, and it is in our relationships with others that we learn about ourselves." (Bennis, Warren. *On Becoming a Leader.* Reading, Mass.: Addison-Wesley, 1989, p. 63.) On the same page, Bennis also quotes Boris Pasternak in DOCTOR ZHIVAGO: "However far back you go in your memory it is always [in] some external manifestation of yourself where you come across your identity. . . ."

your communication efforts. Let's begin by looking at the development of that identity.

Roles and Face.   Your identity is determined, in part, by the roles you play. A **role** is a social category that designates your social rights and responsibilities. It also provides guidelines for behavior, both for how you should conduct yourself and for how others should behave toward you. A role is a somewhat formal category, and each of us plays numerous roles. At different (and sometimes overlapping) times, you may take on the roles of student, employee, child, sibling, friend, citizen, and many more. Each role provides rights, obligations, and guidelines for behavior.

Consider the student and teacher roles. Your responsibilities as a student include performing certain coursework for evaluation. Among your rights in this role is the expectation that the teacher treat and evaluate you in an unbiased manner. When you talk to your teacher, these roles constrain you to show respect to the teacher. Now, imagine that this same teacher joins your municipal league softball team. Even though the same people may be involved, the change in roles can make dramatic differences in your interactions. On the softball diamond, you might tease the teacher, tell jokes together, or go out for a beer after a game. If you're the better player, you might even give him or her pointers on batting technique—the teacher and student reverse roles. Clearly, the roles we play influence our interaction patterns.

Goffman's notion of *face* is similar to the concept of role, in that face is also a component of your social identity. **Face** is the positive sense of social worth that a person claims for him-or herself. It is the public self-image that is presented to others, and it is somewhat less formal than the notion of role. Think of the everyday notion of "losing face," wherein you are embarrassed and unable (at least temporarily) to maintain your positive self-image. This is not the same as losing a role, but reflects your public image that others will or will not accept. Failing a test doesn't disqualify you from the role of student, but it will prevent you from successfully displaying the face (the public image) of "competent student." Hence, friends in your study group are unlikely to take your advice on academic matters until you prove yourself competent again.

Face is an interesting concept because it is largely claimed and upheld through communication behavior. It is not just a category into which you fit. You present a face, and the people you are interacting with accept, modify, or reject that face through their behavior. A person can certainly be unsuccessful in his or her claim of a certain face. For many children, an episode of great embarrassment occurs when one of their parents tries to act like a teenager. The parent will try to do contemporary dance moves, or use language that is typical of a younger generation. Worst of all, the parent will do this in front of *your* friends. As most of us know, few parents can pull this act off. The parent is displaying a face ("Hey, I'm a with-it kind of person who knows what's happening"), but no one is buying it. When a person presents an image that is not supported by others (for example, your friends roll their eyes and emit barely audible groans), the person is said to be *in wrong face*. By contrast, if others accept the image presented and treat it as acceptable, the person is said to be *in face* (Goffman 1967).

As you can see, both roles and face are important components of identity. Furthermore, identity is important because it helps determine your rights and responsibilities in particular interactions. As a result, identity also provides guidelines for behavior. It is equally important to recognize that identity is a social product; through interpersonal communication you establish and negotiate your identity and the identities of the people with whom you interact.

Identity Management.   Your social identity, as well as everyone else's, is subject to negotiation. Identity is a product, the result of your interactions with others. The following is a powerful example of the process of identity negotiation. The interaction is a confrontation between an African-American doctor and a policeman, somewhere in the United States (Coulthard 1977, p. 48).

> Policeman: What's your name, boy?
>   Doctor: Doctor Poussaint. I'm a physician …
> Policeman: What's your first name, boy?
>   Doctor: Alvin.

Discussion Question 7–6
Are you bothered by the concept of having a "face" you present to the world? Is having a "face identity" a kind of phoniness? Are there ever times when you're with other people and not wearing a "face"? How about when you're alone?

If you were to look at this and characterize it merely as several questions and answers, you would be missing quite a bit. What is going on in this short transaction is a battle for identity. In the opening line, the policeman insults the doctor by addressing him as "boy." Not only is this an unacceptable ethnic slur against African-Americans, but it is also a denial of the doctor's adult status. After all, a "boy" is not accorded all the rights and responsibilities of an adult in our culture. A "boy" is expected to show deference to adults.

In reply, the doctor not only answers the question, but he also makes a claim for higher status. By noting that he is a physician, he is making a claim for full adult status, and more. In our culture, doctors are usually accorded high status, and people of lesser status typically show respect to doctors.

By his reply, the policeman indicates that he is still not willing to acknowledge the doctor's adult status, much less recognize him as a person with higher occupational status than a policeman. By asking the question again, the policeman insults the doctor a second time by treating the doctor's response as a failure to answer.

Teaching Objective 7–6
Analyze the ways we affirm and disconfirm or altercast the self-presentations of others and the impact of these actions.

The doctor, probably recognizing that he has been caught in a powerless position, gives in to the policeman's negotiation of his identity by responding with his first name. By doing so, the doctor is forced to surrender his adult status for the duration of this encounter. It's not pretty, but it is an extremely powerful example of identity management at work.

Identity management involves the two processes of self-presentation and altercasting. In an interaction between persons A and B, **self-presentation** would involve A's attempt to establish his or her own identity. In the same interaction, **altercasting** would involve A's attempt to give B or force B into a particular identity. *Self-presentation* involves managing your own identity, while *altercasting* is an attempt to manage the identity of someone else. In the example above, the doctor is engaging in identity management by making claims for his own identity (and consequently his social rights and responsibilities). The policeman is involved in altercasting, forcing the doctor to accept a role that he doesn't particularly want.

Discussion Question 7–7
Who of all the people you know altercasts you the most? How does she/he do it? Why do you think she/he does it? And who do you altercast most often?

Self-presentation and altercasting are communicative strategies used to negotiate identities and the social rights and responsibilities that correspond to them. Sometimes identity is accepted or rejected, whole cloth, rather than being the subject of negotiation. This occurs through the use of confirming and disconfirming messages.

Confirming and Disconfirming Messages. Whenever you talk to someone, you present who you are, as well as any information you are trying to convey. The way the person responds to you will indicate whether he or she accepts or rejects the identity you display. For instance, imagine you are in a large airport, waiting for your connecting flight on a cross-country trip. You look in the airport cafe, and you can't believe your eyes. Standing there in line is Stephen King, one of your favorite authors. You're dumbstruck at first; then you gather up the courage to approach him. "Excuse me, Mr. King, you don't know me, but I'm a big fan of yours. I've read a number of your books. Would you care to join me for a cup of coffee?" Consider his range of possible responses. "Well, I try to keep to myself in public, but for a big fan I suppose I could spare the time for a cup of coffee." Or perhaps he'd say, "I appreciate the invitation, but I'm really in a big hurry. I'm going to grab this coffee and run." As a third alternative, he could look at you for a moment, turn around, and walk away, without ever saying anything to you. The range of responses goes from *confirmation* to *rejection* to *disconfirmation* (Watzlawick, Beavin, and Jackson 1967).

The **confirming response** acknowledges your value as a person. It upholds the sense of identity you sought to portray. The **disconfirming response** is most distressing because it fails to recognize your worth as a person. As a result, the person who receives a disconfirming message is likely to feel confused, unworthy, manipulated, or just devalued (Wilmot 1987). Of less interest is the *rejection response*. Though we sometimes think of rejection as the opposite of confirmation, that is inaccurate. Though it does not show total agreement, even the rejection response acknowledges you as a person worthy of notice. The true polar opposites are confirmation and disconfirmation. To

Table 7.2
Confirming and Disconfirming Messages

Disconfirming Responses	Definition	Example
Impervious	When B fails to acknowledge A's message	A: Could I get your autograph? B: (ignores A, walks by)
Interrupting	When B cuts A's message short	A: I'd like to talk to you about. . . . B: Gotta run, it's getting late.
Irrelevant	When B's response is unrelated to what A had been saying	A: I love you, Pat. B: Looks like rain tonight.
Tangential	B briefly acknowledges A's message, then changes topics	A: I lost my watch. B: Bumer, wanna see a movie?
Impersonal	B responds with a canned speech or series of cliches	A: You charge too much. B: Our prices are based on current market research and they reflect what customers are willing to pay.
Incoherent	B's response is scattered and difficult to follow	A: We need to talk about this. B: Well, uh . . . I don't know, uh it's just that, you know. . . .

Table 7.2 (*continued*)
Confirming and Disconfirming Messages

Disconfirming Responses	Definition	Example
Incongruous	The nonverbal and verbal messages of B are contradicting each other	A: Don't you love me? B: Of course I love you (said angrily through clenched teeth).

Confirming Responses

Direct acknowledgment	B reacts directly to A's message	A: These meetings take too long. B: Let's see if we can deal with that.
Agreement about content	B reinforces A's opinions	A: These meetings take too long. B: I agree. We waste too much time.
Supportive	B reassures A and shows understanding	A: I'm so angry I could scream! B: I know what you mean. You have a right to be upset.
Clarifying	B tries to clarify or elaborate on A's message	A: Our class project should be better. B: You think the group is talented enough to do a better job.
Expression of positive feeling	B shows positive feelings toward A's message	A: It's time to stop talking and act. B: That's what I like to

Source: After S. Trenholm and A. Jensen, *Interpersonal Communication* (Belmont, CA: Wadsworth, 1988), p. 190.

get a better sense of confirming and disconfirming messages, see Table 7.2, (adapted from Trenholm and Jensen 1988, p. 190).

When you interact with others, you certainly want them to use confirming responses, since such responses display positive regard for you. In turn, you should make a point of avoiding disconfirming responses when you interact with others. We all want our identity to be confirmed by the people with whom we interact.

Though interpersonal communication can be used to pursue many ends, in this chapter we have pointed out that it can be used to acquire knowledge of others, to build a context of understanding, and to help you manage and negotiate identities. We turn next to the development of interpersonal communication competence.

INTERPERSONAL COMMUNICATION COMPETENCE

We've all known people who can walk into a room of complete strangers and mingle with extraordinary success. We've also known individuals who are extremely shy, or who have an uncanny ability to insult, annoy, or bore others without even trying. Most of us fall somewhere in the middle of this continuum. What this suggests is that some people display a greater degree of interpersonal communication competence than others. However, while some people may be more socially talented than others, don't be fooled into thinking that interpersonal skill cannot be improved. Communication competence isn't like eye color. You don't inherit a level of competence that you're stuck with for the rest of your life. As you'll see, communication competence is best thought of as a skill, or better yet, as a set of skills. You need to develop the skills and know when to use them.

Cross-reference 7–6
Keep in mind as backdrop to the discussion here that skillful listening is vital to effective communication and in particular to conversational competence. See Chapter 3.

Defining Interpersonal Communication Competence

We all have an intuitive sense of what communication competence is. The following definitions are presented to help you refine and elaborate your existing definition. The first two definitions present broad characterizations of communication competence:

Taken very broadly, communicative competence is the ability to interact well with others. (Spitzberg 1988, p. 68)

Communication competence is *the ability to communicate in a personally effective and socially appropriate manner.* (Trenholm and Jensen 1988, p. 11)

Although these give you a general sense of the concept, the following, more detailed, definitions help us to focus on the critical features of communication competence.

Your level of interpersonal communication competence is the degree to which your behaviors are appropriate to the situation and help you attain personal and relational goals. (Reardon 1987, p. 74)

Competent communication is interaction that is perceived as effective in fulfilling certain rewarding objectives in a way that is also appropriate to the context in which the interaction occurs. (Spitzberg 1988, p. 68)

Teaching objective 7–7
Define communication competence, describe some of the tools for measuring competence (effectiveness, appropriateness, etc.), and encourage attention to its complexities and value in conversation.

Effectiveness and Appropriateness.   The preceding definitions elaborate our understanding by bringing out the two key components of communication competence, *effectiveness* (goal achievement) and *appropriateness.* In many other domains (for example, sports, art) *competence* is defined in terms of your ability to perform or behave in a particular way. A competent volleyball player can set, spike, and dig the ball. A competent painter can master color, form, and brush stroke. But with communication, competence is not so easily defined. To begin with, the competent communicator has to have **communication effectiveness**; that is, the ability to accomplish his or her interactional goals. Hence, competence is not defined merely by one's ability to display a communication skill. You might be able to beg and plead with the best of them, but unless that communication strategy helps you achieve your goals, you have not learned communication competence.

An additional complication is that in any interaction you may have many different goals. An example by Parks (1985) illustrates this point well:

> Consider the case of Jill who has just approached her friend Tom. As she comes nearer, her face brightens as she smiles and says, "Tom, it's so good to see you." Tom returns her greetings and asks her how things have been going. Jill sighs and says, "OK, I guess, but I'm having a hard time getting the fifteen dollars I need for the concert ticket." Tom responds, "I'd like to help you but I'm nearly broke, too." "That's too bad," Jill says, "I was hoping you'd lend it to me, but you're a friend and I'd never want to put you in a bad spot." She pauses and then adds, "Even five dollars would really help." Tom pauses for a moment, but then agrees to loan her five dollars. Jill thanks him profusely and, as she prepares to leave, adds, "Remember, you can always count on me when things are the other way around." (p. 176)

What exactly is Jill's goal in this situation? Actually, she has at least three of them. As an immediate goal, she's trying to borrow some money. Her longer-term goal is to go to the concert. Judging by her approach, it's clear that she also has a third goal—that of maintaining her friendship with Tom. Her effectiveness is determined by her ability to balance and achieve these goals.

You can see that we face multiple levels of goals in any interaction. Achieving some goals at the expense of long-term goals can seriously undermine a person's communicative competence.

Effectiveness at multiple levels, however, is still not enough to capture communication competence. A second component of competence is **communication appropriateness**. According to Grove, "*Appropriateness* refers to the extent to which communicative behavior reflects verbal sensitivity and is suited to the relational and situational context of the interaction" (1991, p. 108). By considering appropriateness, we take into account how your interaction partner viewed your communication use. Appropriateness thereby brings a new dimension to competence, going beyond effectiveness alone. Ultimately, effectiveness has to be judged by how it affects the larger relationship between the participants, not just by how effective one participant felt in achieving his or her goals (Reardon 1987).

Consider the bully who shakes down another child for lunch money every day: "Give me your money or I'll beat you up." On the one hand, the bully may be successful in his or her goal of getting the money, but he or she will not do much to establish a good relationship with the other child. We can't consider this an example of communication competence since the child being threatened would not consider this communication strategy appropriate. See the Focus on Leadership box.

A number of communication strategies can help the user achieve his or her short-term goals, but at a substantial long-term cost to the relationship. Threats, intimidation, blackmail, excessive flattery, and pleading can help the user achieve a goal, but they damage the relationship so that such strategies will not work repeatedly. Communication competence has to be measured in terms of the outcomes for the individual as well as the satisfaction of all parties involved.

Knowledge and Performance. Communication competence can also be broken into the components of *knowledge* and *performance*. In other words, a competent communicator must have mastery of a variety of social skills (performance), and he or she must be able to read situations to know when to

FOCUS ON LEADERSHIP

Leadership and Competent Communication

It is unfortunate, but there is a common stereotype of the leader with a gruff exterior who is never measured by how he or she gets along with co-workers and subordinates. Instead, "getting the job done" is used as the only measure of success. This stereotype is unfortunate because it suggests that for leaders, effectiveness is the sole component of competence. Though leadership positions are not usually popularity contests, and it is sometimes necessary to take an unpopular stance as a leader, effectiveness *and* appropriateness remain the true measures of competence.

Consider the following situation. You are a supervisor at work. One of your subordinates is consistently late, and has been turning out poor-quality work lately. Your willingness to balance effectiveness and appropriateness could have a profound effect on the strategy you employ to deal with the problem and on the eventual outcome. The chart below presents the possible communication strategies resulting from differing attention to effectiveness and appropriateness.

If you utilize a strategy that is designed to be high in effectiveness and high in appropriateness, you will get the desired behavior change and maintain an effective working relationship with your subordinate.

Leadership Note 7–4
"A superior who is known to be argumentative with an affirming communicator style . . . is instrumental to need satisfaction [of employees] because argument encourages free speech and friendly, relaxed, attentive, and verbally nonaggressive supervisory communication nurtures a favorable self-concept for subordinates. The data from this study provided considerable support for these ideas. . . . Dissatisfaction with superiors was strongly related to the extent they were seen by their subordinates as verbally aggressive." (Infante, Dominic and Gorden, William I, How employees see the boss: test of an argumentative and affirming model of supervisor's communicative behavior. *Western Journal of Speech Communication* 55, Summer 1991, pp. 294–304)

	High Effectiveness	Low Effectiveness
HIGH APPROPRIATENESS	Pull your subordinate aside. State your observations clearly. Ask for possible explanations. Clearly state performance expectations.	Stare at watch next time subordinate is late. Tell subordinate, "Your work is okay…could be better." Do nothing.
LOW APPROPRIATENESS	Next time subordinate is late, scream, "If you can't get your butt in here on time, you're history!" Loudly criticize subordinate in front of others about work.	When subordinate is late, act angry, but don't say why. Criticize the quality of work to others, but don't approach your subordinate directly about it.

If you try to maintain a good relationship with your subordinate by using an appropriate strategy, but fail to balance the need for effectiveness (that is, you don't want to offend or confront your subordinate), it is unlikely that your subordinate will change his or her behavior. As a result, you will not have accomplished your interactional goal. A third possibility is that you'll push for the desired change at any cost. Here, you strive for high effectiveness with little or no concern for appropriateness. Threatening, embarrassing, and intimidating your subordinate may initiate the desired behavior response, but it will destroy the larger work relationship between you and your subordinate. You can expect your future decisions and efforts to be undermined by your subordinate whenever possible. Finally, if you have little regard for effectiveness or appropriateness, you will not change the undesired behavior, but you will succeed in creating a bad working relationship. Thus, it is vital that you follow the general guidelines of competent communication when you are in a leadership position. Strive for effectiveness and appropriateness.

apply one skill as opposed to another (knowledge). Being able to self-disclose is not enough for competence. You must also know *when* to self-disclose, and when not to. Conversely, knowing that it's time to introduce yourself, or to bring out a quiet member of a group discussion, are not enough. You also have to know how to accomplish these communicative behaviors. In our next section, we review some of the conversational skills that competent communicators possess.

Developing communication competence is an ongoing process. Communicating appropriately requires that we take into consideration the nature of the relationships and situations in which we find ourselves—and communicate accordingly.

Competence in Conversation

Conversation is the primary—though by no means the only—interactional format used to pursue our interpersonal goals. Interviews, debates, and public presentations, for instance, also allow persons to exchange verbal and nonverbal messages. However, conversation is used more often and with greater regularity than other formats. Some would even argue that conversation is the primary form of interaction from which other forms have evolved (Sacks, Schegloff, and Jefferson 1974). To be a competent interpersonal communicator, you must also be a competent conversationalist.

The gameboard of conversation is difficult to master because there is no rulebook. You learn the rules as you play the game. In addition, the success or failure of a particular "move" isn't always immediately apparent. As a result, feedback on conversational effectiveness isn't necessarily clear (did that person at the party avoid talking to me because he was tired, because he had to go to the bathroom, or because of something I said?). In addition, you only have to recognize the inherent complexity of conversation (in spite of its apparent simplicity), and you'll see why conversation is difficult to master.

What exactly is conversation? To begin with, it is a form of interaction, primarily characterized by its flexibility. Consider, for instance, conversational *topic* and *flow*. Both are said to be *locally managed*—that is, they are not predetermined as you enter a conversation, but instead are managed (changed, maintained, etc.) as you go along. As you enter a conversation, the topic possibilities are wide open. You can talk about a wide range of topics, and you can change the topic as you go. (As you will learn in later chapters, in a public speaking situation, this is not the case.) Often, a speaker is expected to address a particular topic, and deviations from a clear topic are considered ineffective public speaking. Conversational flow (the taking of turns by conversational participants) is also managed as you go. Unlike debates, there is no set time limit on turns or any regular order to turn exchange.

In many ways, several features of conversation seem "up in the air." It is an ongoing, nonscripted product of the participants. Yet in spite of this flexibility, complete strangers regularly engage in perfectly effective conversation. Something as simple as hearing a complete stranger complete one of your sentences is testimony to the highly organized nature of conversation. In spite of its flexibility, however, conversation is orderly. This does not mean that conversation always goes smoothly. Conversational problems can occur. These problems, in turn, can interfere with communication competence.

While we cannot provide a thorough description of all the mechanisms that drive conversation, or list all the possible remedies to all the potential difficulties faced in conversation, we can characterize some of the components of a simple conversational episode. By doing so, we can explain why these components of conversation are structured the way they are, and what you can do if you encounter difficulties in these areas. On the surface, some of this information may appear obvious, but it's what drives the obvious and what leads to the outcomes we expect that is of interest to us. You may already have mastered some of the components of conversation that we'll discuss, but you may not know why you're effective. You may need to improve upon other features of conversation. Either way, it's worthwhile to take a closer look at conversation.

The components of a simple conversational episode include its initiation (or beginning) and its conclusion. To manage a conversation, you must know how to manage both the topic of conversation and turn taking.

Initiating Conversations.   When you initiate a conversation, you are trying to accomplish several things. To begin with, you are trying to gain the other's attention, or if attention is already gained, you and the other are trying to signal acknowledgment of each other. In addition, in the initiation you also try to indicate the purpose of the conversational episode. This purpose may be just small talk ("Hey, how you doing Bill?"), or something more specific ("Say Bill, I wanted to talk to you about that fishing trip"). Krivonos and Knapp (1975) suggest that initiations serve three additional purposes. The initiation signals a transition from a period of no contact to a period of initial access. It also reveals information about the state of the relationship between the interactants (through forms of address, such as "Mister," "Reverend," "Sir," or "Uncle Bob"). Finally, the initiation also signals accessibility for further talk.

Krivonos and Knapp note several ways to initiate a conversation. A *verbal salute* is a personal acknowledgment of the other ("Well, if it isn't Edgar, math student of the year"). The *reference to the other* takes note of some feature of the addressee ("Pardon me, but I really like that hat you're wearing"). A *personal inquiry* requests information about the addressee ("Haven't seen you in a long time. How have you been doing?"). Finally the *external reference* alludes to some event or surrounding feature of the environment ("Hey, good weather for ducks, isn't it?").

Nonverbal signals also accompany the verbal means of initiating conversations. Head nodding, smiling, and the eyebrow flash are all means of acknowledging another person. Mutual gaze is also a powerful means of signaling conversational accessibility. That is why you avoid eye contact when you see a friend to whom you owe money.

Cross-reference 7–7
Nonverbal communication as a means of managing interaction is discussed in Chapter 5.

Conversational initiations don't always go off smoothly. Two potential problems include a lack of response from the addressee, and confusion over the purpose of the episode. Like most of us, you have probably been in situations where you attempt to initiate a conversation but get little or no response. The other person could be signaling a desire for privacy, and sometimes that needs to be respected. At other times, a simple conversational device, known as the *demand ticket*, can be used to draw the person into conversation. The demand ticket is an introductory comment that draws the addressee into the conversation, and then returns conversational control to the person who initiated the interaction (Nofsinger 1975). For example:

A: Guess what.
B: What?
A: I've got a chance for a big promotion.

Or consider a slightly more complex version:

A: I heard something interesting today.
B: What was that?
A: Well, it seems that. . . .

The opening statement in each case is the demand ticket. It forces person B to respond, and thereby acknowledge person A. It also keeps person A in control of the conversation's topic, at least temporarily. It is often one of the first conversational devices children use when they recognize that language can give them some sense of control. Its occasional overuse by children should not be taken as a mark against this opening strategy. It works perfectly well for adults.

Another potential difficulty with conversational initiations arises when the purpose of the episode isn't made clear:

A: What are you doing this afternoon?
B: What business is that of yours?
A: Well, uh . . . it's just that . . . uh. . . .

Persons A and B may get things straightened out, but this conversation is off to a rough start. Part of the problem is that A did not clarify the purpose of this episode. Person B is unwilling to commit to availability, knowing that it could trap her into doing something she didn't want to. To defend against this, B shuts down the conversation as a whole by indicating an unwillingness to talk. Person A could avoid this problem by clarifying the purpose of the episode at the start:

A: Say, we were going to the courthouse to help with the fundraiser this afternoon. Do you have the time to come help us out?

B: Sorry, I can't today. I'm pretty busy with some other projects.

Notice that person A didn't achieve his goal of getting B's help that afternoon, but it was a more effective initiation because the participants were better able to maintain their self-esteem in their short encounter. By clarifying the purpose of the episode, the initiation was more *appropriate*, if not more *effective*. (Complete the Self-Assessment exercise.)

Concluding the Conversation.   The conclusion, or termination, is the second important component of a conversational episode. It indicates communication competence by leaving a lasting impression of the conversation's purpose, and it reinforces the bonds between the interactants. While concluding a conversational episode, you try to (1) signal that you are not accessible for continued conversation, (2) indicate your supportiveness of the other person, and (3) summarize the episode and put it in perspective (Knapp et al. 1973).

A number of verbal and nonverbal cues are typically given to indicate the conclusion of a conversation. Nonverbally, the participants may decrease eye contact, shift body posture, and begin using more paralinguistic fillers ("well, uh . . . ," "huh . . . ," "yeah, uh huh . . . "). Verbally, the participants may use a

SELF-ASSESSMENT   **Evaluating your interpersonal communication competence**

Evaluate your own interpersonal communication competence. Identify five of your greatest communication strengths and five of your communication weaknesses. Try to identify the particular communication skills behind each of your strengths. For example, if people often turn to you with their problems, perhaps your use of empathic listening skills is extremely effective. Now, turn to your weaknesses. For each of them, try to address the following questions: (1) Try to determine whether the weakness is due to a lack of *effectiveness* or a problem with *appropriateness*. In other words, are you unable to achieve your immediate personal goals, or do you fail to satisfy the goals of others with whom you interact? (2) Is this a problem of reading the situation, or an inability to bring the appropriate communication strategy into play (that is, is it a problem of *knowledge* or *performance*)?

variety of strategies: *showing appreciation* ("Thanks for your time"), giving an *external reason for leaving* ("My bus will be here any minute now"), *expressing concern for the other* ("I hope you feel better soon"), or *legitimizing the parting by referring to oneself* ("That's about all I have to add") (Knapp et al. 1973). Frentz and Farrell (1976) note that conversational episodes are typically concluded when the participants fulfill a series of steps: (1) expressing a mutual desire to conclude the episode, (2) expressing satisfaction with the accomplishment of the episode's goals, and (3) proposing future mutual interaction. For example:

A: Look, I really have to get going.
B: Yeah, me too.
A: I'm glad we had the chance to talk about this.
B: Yeah, it really did help clear the air.
A: Maybe we could talk more on Wednesday night?
B: That sounds like a good idea. See you then.

Problems can occur in concluding episodes. The most significant problem is the failure of one interactant to recognize the onset of a conclusion. This is the "person who won't go away" syndrome. Barb may want to end the conversation and do other things, but Molly won't take the cues and cooperate in the disengagement from the conversation.

Barb: I have to go to the mall before it closes.
Molly: Oh yeah, what store are you going to?

Molly's response opens up the conversation again, instead of allowing it to wind down gracefully. This is not an easy problem to overcome. It would be considered impolite for Barb to break away too abruptly. However, if your fellow interactant won't cooperate to conclude the episode, it is sometimes necessary to gradually increase the leave-taking cues, such as decreasing eye contact and moving away from the other person. This becomes a greater problem when you're on your own turf, and the other person refuses to leave.

Topic Change in Conversation.   In addition to managing the parts of a conversational episode, a competent communicator must also manage topic change and turn exchange. Topics vary widely and change frequently in conversation. Still, there remain some general guidelines about the need for coherence in conversation. People who cannot stay on topic are considered rude or incompetent.

Coherence is not always easy to define, however. Broadly, conversation is considered coherent when the individual contributions of the participants are related to prior and subsequent contributions. However, this definition could be too broad. By this definition, the following conversation would be considered coherent:

A: It's a nice day we're having.
B: We're also having pot roast for dinner.
A: I saw a celebrity roast of George Burns today.
B: Burns should be treated or they get infected.

No doubt, you can notice a connection from one sentence to the next, but it would not be accurate to call this coherent. Coherence actually occurs at two levels, *sequential* and *global* (Dascal and Katriel, 1979). The example above displays *sequential coherence*, a connection from one utterance to the next. However, it does not have *global coherence*, an underlying topic connection that runs through the entire sequence. Conversational coherence requires both.

Much has been written about the underlying principles that generate coherence (Craig and Tracy, 1983), the specific linguistic devices that help maintain topic coherence (Planalp, Graham, and Paulson, 1987), and the different ways to change conversational topics appropriately (Planalp and Tracy, 1980). Although we can't discuss all that here, we can point to some of the problems encountered in conversation.

One potential problem is the need to deal with people who have little or no regard for maintaining conversational coherence. Occasionally, you'll interact with someone who drops a comment out of nowhere into the conversation. For example, in an ongoing discussion about the effects of TV violence on children, one of the participants abruptly shifts and begins to talk about the new computer she's thinking of buying. You shake your head, and wonder where that came from. One way to deal with that situation is to frame the computer comment back into the previous topic. By saying something like, "Are you saying that violence in computer games is a lot like what kids see on TV?", you can connect the topics. In this way, coherence can be created after the fact. If nothing else, it serves as a mild reprimand to the person who changed topic. Now she has to expand on your connection or admit that she changed topics recklessly.

The "egocentric speaker" creates other coherence problems. This is the type of person who brings the topic back around to his life or experiences, regardless of what is being discussed. Your story about recent dental work reminds him that his cat needs to get her teeth cleaned. Mentioning a movie reminds him of the time he was an extra on a movie set. Every topic gets brought around full circle to his experience. People do this because they want to gain control, and because of the desire to stay involved in a conversation. For others, it's not much fun. If it's a close friend who does this, you could gently point this habit out. If it's someone you don't know very well, you might need to reintroduce the original topic, in hopes that the person will eventually recognize the world outside his or her individual experience.

Turn Taking in Conversation.   Another conversational skill that needs to be mastered is turn taking, the smooth exchange of talk from one participant to another. This is necessary for two reasons. First, we expect a smooth flow of interaction. Most people feel uncomfortable when conversation is laced with long pauses and frequent occurrences of two people talking at one time. Second, effective turn taking promotes participation and inclusion in the conversation. Conversations don't require that every participant talk for equal lengths of time. Some people are more talkative, while others may be quiet by nature. Yet everyone should feel that he or she can participate if desired. Generally, there is a need for some balance in conversational participation.

Sacks, Schegloff, and Jefferson (1974) note that speaker transition points

Current Research 7–5
The majority of strategies which people seem to employ to cope with conversational narcissists are passive. Rather than confront the narcissist, most choose to show disinterest, leave, or listen, "despite comments that the listening was rarely entertaining or involving for the respondent." (Vangelisti, Knapp, and Daly. Conversational narcissism, *Communication Monographs, 57*(4), 1990, p. 261)

(for example, pauses and hesitations) occur regularly in conversation, and that a set of three rules governs the exchange of turns at these points—(1) the current speaker can construct the message to select the next speaker ("What do you think about it, Kurt?"); (2) a nonspeaker can "self-select" to become the next speaker; or (3) the current speaker can continue to talk. Through this system, turn exchange occurs fairly smoothly, with few extended pauses and little conversational overlap.

Two problems can occur that are worth noting here. One problem is the person who never self-selects. In other words, this is the person who never contributes to the conversation. Sometimes an individual may be reticent and not feel like talking. Or an individual who may regularly converse with gusto may not be in the mood at a particular time. Here, we're more concerned with the individual who wants to participate but lacks the social skill to jump in. Since an effective conversation is the responsibility of all participants, you would do well to help such a person. One way to do this is to select such a person to talk next, as described in the turn-taking rules above. Another way to get a person involved is to use open-ended questions that invite his or her participation.

The opposite problem is the person who completely dominates the conversation, and never lets others participate. On rare occasions you may find an individual who is so interesting and entertaining that you don't mind if he or she takes complete control of the conversation. Unfortunately, the number of people who actually are that interesting are quite rare, particularly when compared to the number of people who think they are that interesting. One strategy for dealing with this type of person is to try to assert control over the topic of conversation. To some degree, topic control can help you maintain turn control. Unfortunately, this doesn't always work. An alternative approach is to leave the scene. Unless you are in an airplane or at a dinner party, you have some control over those with whom you decide to interact. This may be a good time to exercise that control.

Discussion Question 7–8
What would be the best way to find out if you are a competent communicator? Whom would you ask? How would you ask? What would you ask? Could you find out without asking others?

Summary

As a leader, you need to be skilled in interpersonal communication. Dealing with people necessitates these skills. In this chapter we emphasized this need by explaining the rich and complex nature of interpersonal communication. To begin, we defined interpersonal communication by presenting the contrasting contextual and developmental viewpoints. According to the contextual view, we understand interpersonal communication by contrasting it to contexts such as small-group communication and public speaking. By contrast, the developmental view differentiates between interpersonal and impersonal communication. According to this view, we only engage in interpersonal communication when we escape role constraints and tailor our messages to the other as an individual.

We also discussed some of the functions of interpersonal communication. As a result of engaging in interpersonal communication we (1) acquire knowledge of others, (2) build a context for understanding each other, and (3) establish and negotiate the identities of ourselves and any other interactants.

Finally, we discussed the nature of communication competence. Competence involves the ability to read situations (knowledge) and the ability to bring communication strategies into play (skills). In addition, when assessing a person's communication competence, we have to consider the appropriateness of his or her communication use and effectiveness. In the last section, we tried to point out some of the basic components of conversation and what constitutes an effective conversationalist.

An individual conversational episode has a beginning and an end. When initiating a conversation, the competent communicator signals contact and introduces a topic through the strategies of verbal salute, reference to the other, personal inquiry, and external reference. The competent communicator brings the conversation to a close through the strategies of showing appreciation, giving an external reason for leaving, expressing concern for the other, or legitimizing the parting by referring to oneself. When properly accomplished, these closings signal the end of the conversation, leave an impression about the topic of discussion, and reinforce the bonds between the interactants.

Competent communicators also know how to manage topic change in conversations. Interactants must maintain global and sequential coherence. Furthermore, they must be able to bring the contributions of others back to the topic by framing digressions.

Exercises

1. When was the last time that you consciously used self-disclosure in a conversation? Did you have a goal in mind (an anticipated outcome) when you used this strategy? If so, what was the strategy? What was the outcome of the event? What response did you get from the person to whom you self-disclosed? What conclusion(s) can you draw about the nature of self-disclosure? Discuss these questions in two- or three-person groups in class.

2. Have you ever been caught in a confusing situation in which you and another person misunderstood each other because of different understandings of the relational context? A typical example occurs when one party labels an event together as "a date," while the other person sees the same event as "just doing something together." Write a short essay explaining the confusion and how you dealt with it. Address some of the following questions in your essay: How did the confusion become apparent? What did the two of you do to resolve the differing views of the relational context? If you were able to turn back time, would you deal with the situation in a different way?

3. Adolescence is a time of identities in transition in which personality development changes from that of a child to that of an adult. These changes do not magically occur overnight. To a large degree, this identity change is the result of social interaction. Adolescents are forced to hop into the trenches and battle for new identity. Think back to episodes that you survived in making this transition, particularly the interactions with your parents. How did you go about negotiating your adult identity? Who was using self-presentation skills, and who was using altercasting? What rights and responsibilities

became the subject of negotiation? Why did you want these changed? Why did your parents want them to stay the same, or to change in ways that you did not like? In what ways did your behavioral guidelines change in your interaction with your parents (for example, are they now willing and able to listen to your position when you get into a dispute)? In what ways does your interaction remain the same, but with no particular reason (for example, do you still avoid swearing in front of your parents, in spite of your occasional use of vulgarity with friends)?

Goffman, E. (1967). *Interaction ritual: Essays on face-to-face behavior.* Garden City, NY: Doubleday.

Related Readings

Pay particular attention to chapter 2: "On Face-Work: An Analysis of Ritual Elements in Social Interaction." This is not easy reading, but for the dedicated student, Goffman's writings are a veritable gold mine of thought-provoking ideas. He provides valuable insights into our strategies for interacting in the social world.

Knapp, M. L., and Miller, G. R. (eds.) (1985). *Handbook of interpersonal communication.* Beverly Hills, CA: Sage.

This edited volume brings together some of the best researchers and theorists in the area of interpersonal communication. The individual chapters review the key topics in the interpersonal field.

Reardon, K. K. (1987). *Interpersonal communication: Where minds meet.* Belmont, CA: Wadsworth.

In chapter 5 of this textbook, Reardon does an excellent job of discussing interpersonal communication competence. The particular strength of this chapter is her in-depth treatment of the cognitive and behavioral skills that make up communication competence. In chapter 3, she provides a succinct history of the emergence of interpersonal communication as a field of study.

Watzlawick, P. (1976). *How real is real?: Confusion, disinformation, communication.* New York: Vintage Books.

This is a thoroughly enjoyable and thought-provoking paperback. The author illuminates some of the basic principles he helped establish in the classic, *Pragmatics of Human Communication* (Watzlawick, Beavin, and Jackson, 1967). Through an amusing series of anecdotes he covers such topics as communication with animals and extraterrestrials, disinformation in espionage, and the relational binds that hinder our communication effectiveness.

Communication in Relationships

Chapter objectives

After reading this chapter you should be able to:

1. explain the importance of interdependence and length of duration to interpersonal relationships

2. discuss how balancing interdependence and independence and fulfilling expectations contribute to maintaining relationships

3. describe the stages that occur during relationship formation and termination

4. discuss several problems that occur when we encounter conflict and describe strategies to overcome them

Key terms and concepts

relationship initiation
relationship maintenance
relationship termination
conflict
gunnysacking
actor-observer difference

Cross-reference 8–1
This discussion of interpersonal relationships needs to be examined against the backdrop of the more general discussion of interpersonal communication in Chapter 7.

Relationships are vitally important to our lives. Through our relationships, we experience the entire range of human emotions. When asked where their greatest joys come from, people usually indicate that their most rewarding experiences come from relationships with others.

This chapter is designed to show you that the study of human relationships, while still in its infancy, has much to offer. We begin by defining the basic features of relationships, and distinguish between voluntary and involuntary relationships. We also introduce a prominent theory of relationships that describes the development, maintenance, and termination of relationships. Finally, we investigate conflict in relationships—defining it, identifying some of the common mistakes people make in handling conflict, and suggesting some techniques for improving conflict management.

EXPLORING THE FEATURES OF INTERPERSONAL RELATIONSHIPS

We need to take care when using the term *human relationship* because of its loose colloquial use, and because there are so many types of human relationships. We are simply not interested in all types of human relationships. In a sense, there is always a term to describe the relationship between any two people, even if the proper description is "strangers." We are not interested in strangers, or much concerned with acquaintances. The focus in this chapter is on close interpersonal relationships. These are relationships where the participants treat each other as unique individuals, rather than as members of role categories (for example, bank teller–customer, toll booth attendant–driver). In the communication field, there also tends to be a greater interest in relationships that are entered into voluntarily (for example, friendships, marriages), as opposed to relationships that are the result of birth (for example, siblings), other people's marriages (for example, in-laws), or assignment (for example, co-workers). This is because of the field's enduring interest in the factors that bring people together (for example, relational formation processes). However, such involuntary relationships are not ignored completely, and we will refer to them occasionally to demonstrate some of the dynamic properties of relationships.

The Key Features of Interpersonal Relationships

Teaching Objective 8–1
Delineate the key features of interpersonal relationships as interdependence and duration.

Our focus on close interpersonal relationships to the exclusion of acquaintance and role-related relationships is not just an arbitrary distinction. There are key differences between them that make the interpersonal relationships more important from a communication perspective.

Interdependence.   Participants in a relationship are *interdependent* to the extent that they rely on each other to achieve common goals, and to the extent that the behavior of each influences the behavior of the other. In other words, interdependence presumes a connectedness between the participants. As Berscheid (1987, p. 82) says, "[A] relationship's closeness is represented by the extent to which the activities of one person—e.g., his or her thoughts, internal states, and overt behaviors—influence the activities of the other and vice versa." Hinde (1979) refers to this as "mutuality." He says that in close relationships the behavior of one participant influences the behavior choice of the other. To take a simple example, a mother's smile often elicits a matching smile from her child. This is not to say that mutuality is necessarily positive, or always a sign of cooperation. For example, a husband and wife may constantly argue with each other. His complaints about her cooking lead to her complaints about his small paycheck (or vice versa). The repeating cycle may not be a positive one, but the behavior of each (complaining) influences the response of the other (cross-complaining).

The strongest contrasting examples to interdependence are the collective monologues that young children sometimes produce. Two or more children

Interpersonal communication is characterized by interdependence, in which our behavior influences and is influenced by how others feel and act. New to this process, young children often lapse into separate monologues that do not take others into account—a habit some people never outgrow!

can carry on separate and independent "conversations" while in the presence of each other. One child may answer his own questions instead of expecting a response from his playmate. Another may recite her *ABC*s while a playmate is addressing her. The interaction is in the presence of but not in response to each other. Most of us have encountered adults with whom we suffer the same problem, though perhaps not to the same degree. Consider the last time you walked away from a conversation thinking that it had somehow missed—the conversational gears had not meshed. This demonstrates a lack of interdependence. Over time, and with repeated interactions, relational partners are able to closely coordinate their level of behavioral interdependence. The coordinated behaviors are often developed so that the participants can attempt to achieve their mutual goals. Hence, behavioral interdependence is aimed at achieving outcome interdependence.

Lasting Duration.   A second key feature of interpersonal relationships is that they continue over time (Kelley et al. 1983). The participants develop a relational history. One necessary feature for the development of a relational history is continuity between successive interactions. In other words, the present interaction between relational participants is influenced by past interactions (and shaped by the anticipation of future interactions). By contrast, think of the teller at a drive-up bank window and a particular customer, Dawn Smith. They may have interacted dozens of times without realizing it. Dawn may only see a tinted window from twenty feet away and hear a scratchy voice through an over-amplified speaker. The teller may concentrate more on the patron's account number than on her name, and follow a standard routine regardless of the specific customer. There is no continuity between interactions, even though there is repeated contact between them.

Interdependence and lasting duration are the key components of interpersonal relationships. Unfortunately, that still leaves us with a wide range of relationships to sort through and classify.

Classifying Interpersonal Relationships

A number of writers have classified interpersonal relationships. Some have distinguished between the types of relationships we have, such as "friend," "intimate," "sibling," and "marital partner" (Reardon 1987). Others distinguish them by comparing their key features, such as the levels of control, intimacy, and trust that are present in the relationship (Millar and Rogers 1976).

Teaching Objective 8–2
Explore various methods of classifying interpersonal relationships, especially Wish and Kaplan's dimensional scales.

Wish and Kaplan (1977) were concerned with how people characterize relationships on the basis of the communication that is expected to occur. They claim that people classify interpersonal relationships along five independent dimensions or scales (see Figure 8.1).

Apparently, one of the things we key on is how sociable the relational participants are with one another. Along this dimension, relationships vary from being *cooperative and friendly* to being *competitive and hostile*. Independent of its rating on that dimension, a relationship could also differ in the degree to

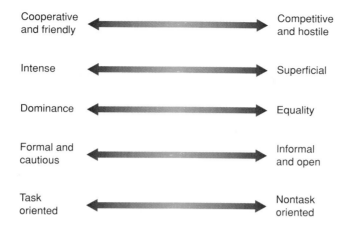

Figure 8.1
Dimensions of
Interpersonal
Relationships.

which it places demands on the participants. Some relationships are very *intense,* whereas others are quite *superficial.* Though some relationships display an equal balance of power between the participants, in others one person may hold predominantly more power. Hence, relationships vary from *equality* to *dominance.* Imagine the relationship between a parolee and his or her parole officer. It would hardly be surprising to have that relationship characterized as *formal and cautious.* However, the person on parole may have a number of strong friendships that would seem much more *informal and open.* Finally, relationships differ on the degree to which they center around getting something done. Some relationships are *task oriented,* and others are *nontask oriented.*

You can take any relationship you are in and characterize it along these independent dimensions. It is important to recognize that these dimensions do not measure the quality of the relationship (how good or bad it is). For instance, you might feel that participants in a relationship should share equal power. That might lead you to believe that *dominance* is bad in relationships whereas *equality* is good. That belief might hold for dating or marital relationships, but in the case of an infant and mother it would lead to disaster. In some relationships, power inequality (*dominance*) is both productive and necessary.

A particular relationship can also change over time. Consider the child-parent relationship again. When the child is an infant, the relationship is likely to be *cooperative* and *intense,* and the parent is likely to exercise *dominance.* During the adolescent years there may be a shift from friendliness to occasional *hostility.* As the child becomes an adult, the *hostility* wanes, power levels become more *equal,* and the relationship may lose some *intensity.* As the parent ages further, the power levels may shift in the opposite direction, with the child controlling the affairs of the parent—the child may come to exert *dominance.* The shifting of a relationship along these dimensions helps to illustrate that it is best to think of relationships as ongoing processes rather than as static states or categories. The Focus on Leadership box discusses the relationship between supervisors and subordinates.

Discussion Question 8–1
What other dimensions or scales might be useful in classifying relationships?

FOCUS ON LEADERSHIP

The Supervisor-Subordinate Relationship

Relationships at work can be as important as our ties with friends, family, and lovers. For instance, the relationship between supervisor and subordinate is vitally important. In fact, Goldhaber (1979) reports that supervisor-subordinate interaction is the most pervasive form of communication in contemporary organizations, and its effectiveness is one of the best indicators of a subordinate's job satisfaction.

When the supervisor-subordinate relationship is sour, the consequences can be detrimental for the organization as a whole. As an example, consider just one problem that occurs when the supervisor-subordinate relationship is bad—*upward distortion*. Upward distortion is the tendency for subordinates to provide supervisors with information that is incomplete, untimely, or inaccurate. It is likely to occur when there is inadequate trust between the supervisor and subordinate. According to Goldhaber (1979), when Bob (the subordinate) distorts information to his supervisor (Mary) he will tend to

1. distort it in a way that pleases Mary
2. tell Mary only what he wants her to know
3. tell Mary what he thinks she wants to hear
4. tell Mary information that reflects favorably on himself, or does not reflect negatively on himself

Obviously, such systematic distortion of information would make it extremely difficult to make decisions as a supervisor. As a supervisor, you could try to unravel the kernel of truth from the pile of distorted information, or you could try to establish good working relationships with your subordinates.

In order to establish effective relationships with subordinates, Goldhaber (1979, p. 205) recommends that a supervisor should

1. praise subordinates when it is deserved
2. make a point of understanding a subordinate's job
3. establish trust with subordinates
4. be warm and friendly
5. be honest with subordinates
6. let subordinates know they can disagree with you without facing retribution

After an exhaustive review of the research, Jablin (1979) uncovered the following five features that distinguish effective from ineffective supervisors:

1. Effective supervisors are more "communication-minded." They

enjoy conversing with subordinates and are not afraid to contribute ideas in meetings.

2. Effective supervisors are more likely to be patient, empathic listeners. They treat all questions seriously, listen to questions and criticisms in a fair-minded manner, and are willing to take action on this feedback.

3. Effective supervisors generally use a softer approach to persuasion. They will "ask" or "reason" with subordinates rather than "ordering" or "demanding."

4. Effective supervisors are able to weigh the emotional and ego concerns of subordinates. For instance, they will reprimand a subordinate in private rather than in public.

5. Effective supervisors are more willing to circulate information. If organizational changes are about to occur, the effective supervisor will notify subordinates and provide the reasons for the changes.

Establishing and maintaining an effective relationship between supervisors (leaders) and subordinates (followers) is not necessarily easy, but its benefits make this a worthwhile effort.

THE DYNAMICS OF RELATIONAL CHANGE

The dynamic, ever-changing nature of relationships is what can make them both fascinating and frustrating. Relationships vary in how dynamic they are. Some settle into a comfortable, predictable routine, whereas others are extremely volatile. Still, all relationships change. Each relationship you currently have originally started as something different, evolved to what it is today, and will undoubtedly change in the future. Here we are interested in the process of relational change. Traditionally, theories of close relations have focused on the dynamic processes of relation *initiation*, *maintenance*, and *termination*.

Teaching Objective 8–3
Describe the stages of relationship initiation, maintenance, and termination and the unique needs of each of these stages.

Relationship Initiation

A Filtering Process.   **Relationship initiation** is the process of building relationships, moving from initial interaction to greater levels of intimacy. All relationships have to begin at some stage. For relationships that we enter into voluntarily, that initial stage is usually referred to as acquaintanceship. Duck (1976, 1985) looks at the development of an acquaintance as an information-gathering process. We don't make acquaintances by instantly matching personality traits to see who fits. Instead, we gather information about others to find individuals who will match or support our personalities, and we do this in stages. Duck claims that there are predictable information-gathering stages that

Discussion Question 8–2
How would you describe the filters or distinctions you draw between the various categories of relationships in which you are involved?

Current Research 8–1
Capella and Palmer support the established interpersonal research finding that attitude similarity among strangers leads to attraction. The authors also found that attitude similarity also affected various nonverbal factors, such as posture and gaze (Capella, Joseph N., and Palmer, Mark T. Attitude similarity, relational history, and attraction: the mediating effects of kinesic and vocal behaviours, *Communication Monographs,* 57, 3, 1990, pp. 161–183.)

Current Research 8–2
Presumably, at every stage of the filtering process in relationship initiation, one party may be more or less willing to proceed to a deeper level of intimacy than the other. The reality of unequal attraction implies the need for human beings to develop refusal skills or messages to indicate a lack of interest in proceeding further in a relationship. Kline and Floyd discuss the relative lack of research on refusal messages. (Kline, Susan L., and Floyd, Cathy Hennen. On the art of saying no: the influence of social cognitive development on messages of refusal, *Western Journal of Speech Communication,* 54, 4, 1990, pp. 454–472.)

we use to find out about others. As we gather information, we make choices about the relationship level we want to pursue with other people. In other words, the information gathered helps us filter out some individuals, and pursue more intense or more demanding relationships with others.

We begin by gathering information from what Duck refers to as *sociological* or *incidental cues.* These are simply the constraints on the opportunities of interacting with another person. Hence, proximity (how close you live or work to another), the frequency of personal contact, and the expectation of future encounters help make up this set of cues.

The next filter is made up of further information gained before actually interacting with the other. These *preinteraction cues* would center on observable cues, such as physical appearance, dress, and other visual indicators of status or personal preferences. Consider how you might use these cues. Imagine that you detest heavy metal music. Between classes you regularly walk the same route as another student, who has bleached hair in an out-of-control cut, black jeans that are intentionally ripped in various places, and a rotating T-shirt wardrobe that spans the range of heavy metal performers. What are the chances that you would cast this person as a likely candidate for your circle of friends?

Eventually, you begin to rely on *interaction cues,* which are gathered while talking to the other person. These cues would include the other's topic choices, his or her conversational pacing, and a variety of nonverbal behavioral cues. Out of a possibly large pool, these cues would help you decide further who to pursue and who to avoid.

Finally, after interacting with the other over a period of time, you get a sense of his or her attitudes and personality. These are referred to as *cognitive cues.* If the other has passed through the previous filters, assessing his or her personality allows you to make a judgment concerning whether that person will match or support your own personality. As you can see, an acquaintance must meet several criteria before we would develop a friendship with him or her. Hence, matching personalities is a concern only after the other has passed several preceding "tests."

Wilmot (1987) extends this notion of filtering to the further development of relationships. He suggests that filters are used to promote a limited number of individuals to progressively more intimate and demanding relational stages. We cannot have a thousand "best friends," or the category would lose its importance. Furthermore, close relationships demand substantial amounts of time and effort, so we have to restrict our relational accessibility to some degree. We filter out most people at various stages and "promote" others who pass our criteria (see Figure 8.2).

Though you may have hundreds of acquaintances, your list of friends is probably substantially smaller. You probably develop increasingly restrictive relational categories and promote individuals to those categories as you get to know them. Furthermore, some people remain acquaintances. You never develop deeper relationships with them. Relationship initiation can be characterized as a process of narrowing a field of potential relational partners on the basis of the information you can acquire.

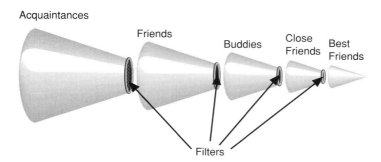

Acquaintances

Friends

Buddies

Close Friends

Best Friends

Filters

Figure 8.2
Relationship Filtering Model.

The Role of Small Talk.   Depending on your outlook, small talk can be either a repugnant social curse or the necessary grease that gets the wheels of social interaction turning. Small talk (sometimes referred to as *phatic communication*) is characterized by its shallow depth, freedom from controversy, and broad topicality. In other words, it doesn't demand much detailed knowledge or a strong opinion to engage in it. When you discuss the weather, the performance of a local sports team, or broad demographic information (such as your hometown or college major) you are engaging in small talk.

Some people detest small talk and view it as a waste of time with little substantial reward. Others find it to be an enjoyable pastime. Many simply find it to be a necessary means to make initial contact with a person. Regardless of your opinion, one point is clear—small talk is a useful means of gathering information about a person and therefore is a regular part of relationship initiation.

Relationship Maintenance

Relationship maintenance is the process of sustaining a relationship and fulfilling relationship expectations. Maintaining a relationship requires skill and effort. There are many important skills that must be mastered. One of them, conflict management, is treated in greater depth in the section that closes this chapter. Here we want to address the need to balance independence and interdependence in the relationship and the need to fulfill relational expectations.

Balancing Independence and Interdependence.   Wilmot (1987) notes that relationships often involve an interplay between opposing forces. Two of the forces he mentions are autonomy and interdependence. In other words, participants in a relationship must balance the opposing needs for independence and interdependence. Each person needs to have a sense of self-worth apart from the relationship—a person may need "breathing space" to grow and gain an independent sense of accomplishment. On the other hand, in order to gain the full benefits of a close relationship, the participants must display a sense of commitment and mutual support. As Wilmot (1987, p. 168) summarizes it, this is "the tension between separateness and connectedness, or between *me* and *we*."

This balance may be difficult to manage if the participants in a close rela-

Current Research 8–3
Bell and Roloff found that lonely people tend to share demographic information but do not move beyond that level of self-disclosure to reveal information about their personalities. (Bell, Robert A., and Roloff, Michael E. Making a love connection: loneliness and communication competence in the dating marketplace, *Communication Quarterly*, 39, 1, 1991, pp. 58–74.)

Leadership Note 8–1
Walter Bennis refers to Erik Erikson's theory that human development involves an essential conflict to be resolved at each stage of life, the second of which is the conflict between independence and dependence and its resolution is personal autonomy. Bennis suggests that these same conflicts recur throughout our lives and that how we resolve them determines how we live. "It is almost never a choice between a right and a wrong." (Bennis, Walter. *On Becoming a Leader*. Reading, Mass.: Addison-Wesley 1989, pp. 119–120).

tionship differ in their needs for independence and interdependence. Furthermore, any person's needs may change over time. The husband or wife who used to demand time to pursue individual accomplishments may suddenly cling to interdependent shared goals.

To manage a relationship over time, the participants need to work out a balance of these forces. This first requires that they recognize the presence of these competing demands. It is also important that they talk about their individual needs and expectations for independence and interdependence. This strategy may not solve all problems in this area. There will be couples who can never agree on the proper balance. However, this approach will help them isolate the problem and may indicate what needs to be done if a resolution is to be reached.

Fulfilling Relational Expectations.   In order to maintain a relationship over time, regardless of whether it is a friendship or romantic relationship, it is necessary for the participants to feel that they are rewarded in it. This sense of reward, or positive outcome, would normally be measured against some level of expectation. Hence, maintaining a relationship is largely a matter of fulfilling each other's expectations. Occasionally, people will stay in abusive or unfulfilling relationships. This can be explained by their belief that even though the present relationship is bad, it may be better than the unknown alternatives.

There can be vast differences in people's expectations for relationships. You may establish friendships in order to simply have *fun* with others. Another person may think of friends primarily as a means of emotional support when things are going badly. If you and this other person were to begin to develop a friendship together, you would probably have difficulty maintaining it. You may get on the phone only to socialize, while your friend may want to talk about problems and difficulties. It would probably not take long to recognize that the two of you were not fulfilling each other's friendship needs.

Though it is not necessarily easy to do, it is sometimes necessary to specify and negotiate your relational expectations with your relational partner. This is particularly true in romantic relationships. Clarify your expectations so that your partner is clearly aware of them. Your partner can then decide whether he or she can reasonably fulfill those expectations. Also, expect to hear his or her expectations in return, and decide whether you are willing to commit yourself to fulfilling his or her expectations.

Relationship Termination

Discussion Question 8–3
What do you think is the most common strategy or process whereby relationships are ended? Are the strategies different from teenagers than adults or other ages? Are the strategies different for friends than for intimates?

Friends move apart. The relationship flickers and ends. Two lovers have a fight and vow to break it off. People die, and we are left only with memories of the relationship. It is inevitable that relationships come to an end. It is useful to understand this process and the communication skills involved in it. **Relationship termination** is the process of moving from greater to diminishing levels of intimacy.

Features of Relationship Termination. For a long time, scholars discussed relationship termination as though it were a mirror image of relationship initiation. More recently, researchers have begun to accentuate the differences between these two processes. Perhaps the main difference between them is that initiating a relationship requires the cooperation of both parties, whereas termination can be accomplished by either person individually (Miller and Parks 1982). The natures of the two processes are also distinct. Relational initiation involves a gradual sharing of personal information. Termination does not involve forgetting or loss of information. Oftentimes a new and surprising bit of information (for example, disclosure of infidelity in a romantic relationship) can instigate the termination of the relationship. A third difference between initiation and termination is the time span of the two processes. Typically, close relationships are built gradually. Although termination can be a drawn-out process, it can also occur quite swiftly. Hence, relationship initiation and termination are quite distinct processes.

Some scholars resist using the label *termination,* instead characterizing this stage as a radical transformation of the relationship. Consider the prototypical example of a husband and wife divorcing. After the divorce, is their relationship "over," or just changed? "Ex," or "ex-spouse" certainly characterizes a type of relationship. It might not necessarily be a positive relationship (though sometimes it is), but ex-spouses often have contact as a result of their children, continued financial obligations, or mutual friends. A relationship still exists, though it might be radically different than it was before the split.

One of the more difficult aspects of relational termination is the question of "who gets the friends." In other words, terminating a relationship can send shock waves through your social network. People who used to be friends with both members of the relationship are often forced to choose sides. Lingering anger or distrust between former friends or lovers may compel a party host to invite only one of them to a social event. Relationship termination has consequences beyond the participants in the immediate relationship.

Strategies for Relationship Termination. Leslie Baxter and her colleagues have investigated the strategies people use to end relationships (Baxter 1982, 1985; Wilmot, Carbaugh, and Baxter 1985). Baxter found that the strategies vary along two dimensions: *directness* (the degree to which the person makes an explicit statement about the end of the relationship), and *concern for the other person* (the degree to which the termination strategy avoids hurting the other person's feelings).

There are direct and indirect relationship termination strategies. *Direct* strategies pull no punches. Picking a fight, confronting the other, or just telling your partner it's over would be examples of direct approaches. The *indirect* strategies are more subtle. With an indirect strategy you are trying to get the other to see that something is wrong with the relationship without spelling it out. Avoidance is one indirect strategy. Not having time to spend with a partner should indicate to him or her that the relationship is "on the rocks." Another

Discussion Question 8–4
Can one member of a relationship terminate a relationship without the consent or agreement of the other? What if the other party does not want the relationship to end?

Current Research 8–4
McCornack and Levine, working with 190 subjects who had recently discovered a lie told by their partners, determined that the importance of the information lied about was the single strongest predictor of the termination of the relationship. (McCornack, Steven A., and Levine, Timothy R. When lies are uncovered: emotional and relational outcomes of discovered deception, *Communication Monographs*, 57, 2, 1990, pp. 131–132.)

Current Research 8–5
Courtright et al. studied married couples in "distressed" relationships who subsequently either repaired or terminated their relationships. They report that couples who ended their marriages employed avoidance, indirectness, and decreased involvement; couples who repaired their relationships were more direct and more involved. (Courtright, Millar, Rogers, and Bagarozzi. Interaction dynamics of relational negotiation: reconciliation versus termination of distressed relationships, *Western Journal of Speech Communication*, 54, 4, 1990, pp. 429–453.)

indirect strategy is withdrawal. Though you may be in the presence of your partner, you can withdraw by limiting your conversational input, or by discussing only trivial topics.

Along the dimension of concern for the other person, there are *other-oriented* and *self-oriented* strategies. Other-oriented strategies maintain a concern for the other's feelings. With this approach you are trying to let the other down easy—to make the breakup as painless as possible. These strategies avoid blame for the end of the relationship. It is not claimed to be someone's fault. Often, an initial move is made to "stay friends." Self-oriented strategies ignore concern for the other's feelings. One such approach is manipulation, in which you get the other to take the initiative to break off the relationship.

When selecting a termination strategy, people can be caught between opposing forces. Most people claim to prefer using the indirect and other-oriented strategies, in order to protect the other's feelings. Unfortunately, these strategies tend to take longer. Though the emotional pain may be lessened, these strategies tend to drag out the termination over a longer period of time. Direct and self-oriented strategies may initially be more painful, but the break tends to be quicker and more complete.

◼ A THEORY OF RELATIONAL CHANGE

Teaching Objective 8–4 Explicate Knapp's theory of relational change from escalation to termination, emphasizing the dynamic nature of relationships and the various possibilities for movement between phases.

Several theories have attempted to explain the dynamics of relational change. Knapp's (1978) theory characterizes these changes as a series of progressive steps. Knapp's theory is particularly useful because it explains the different types of communication that will likely be used at various stages of a relationship. His theory views the development of a relationship as a process involving five steps or stages. Similarly, when a relationship goes through dissolution, it also passes through five steps or stages (as shown in Figure 8.3).

Figure 8.3
Knapp's Relational Stages Model. (Reprinted from M. L. Knapp, *Social Intercourse: From Greeting to Goodbye.* (Boston: Allyn and Bacon, 1978). Used with permission.)

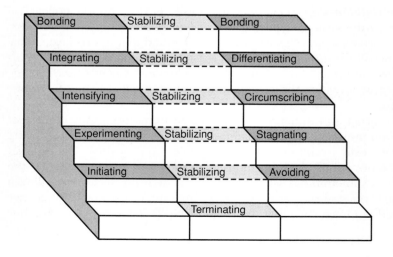

Stages of Relationship Escalation

Initiation. The first stage of relationship escalation is fairly short. Knapp (1978) suggests that *initiation* may last as little as fifteen seconds. During this time the participants are working to form a favorable first impression. It is unlikely that there will be many surprises at this stage—the participants probably follow standard greeting rituals or use standard opening lines.

Experimenting. After fulfilling the necessary greeting rituals, we may begin the process of exchanging information in the *experimenting* phase. It is at this point that small talk is used to gather broad demographic information about each other. Questions are used to uncover information: "Where are you from?" and "What's your major?" As Knapp puts it, you are showing the other person your label in hopes that he or she will be interested in the contents. Once you've progressed into this stage, you would probably consider the other person at least an acquaintance. Many relationships progress no further than this point.

Intensifying. During the *intensifying* phase a number of important communication behaviors begin to occur. You and your partner are likely to begin exchanging more personal information about your beliefs, attitudes, fears, and aspirations. Self-disclosure takes place frequently. As a result, you get to know each other as unique individuals. Forms of address become informal, and you might begin using nicknames for each other. You become more adept at reading each other's nonverbal behaviors and emotional reactions. Verbal expressions of some level of commitment to the relationship may begin to appear (for example, "I'm glad we took the time to go on this camping trip together"). (Complete the Self-Assessment exercise.)

Cross-reference 8–2
Explore how Knapp's theory of the stages of relationship escalation meshes with the penetration theory as discussed in Chapter 7.

Current Research 8–6
Research by Burleson, *et al.* found that people "with similar communication values are more likely to become friends than persons with dissimilar communication values." The authors suggest that people differ in the importance they attach to skills such as providing comfort and ego-support and that they seek friends with similar values. (Burleson, B., Santer, W., and Luccheti, A., Similarity in communication values as a predictor of friendship choices: studies of friends and best friends. *Southern Communication Journal,* 57, 4, 1992, pp. 260–276)

SELF-ASSESSMENT **Personal idioms in close relationships**

Knapp (1978) notes that during the intensifying phase of relationship development the partners may begin to use words, phrases, or gestures that have idiosyncratic meaning for them. These private codes are sometimes referred to as *personal idioms.* For instance, you may have worked out a code with a friend or lover to indicate that you're bored with the social event you're attending and you want to leave. You might use a special phrase, for instance, "They say the fish are biting," or you could use a private gesture, for instance, an "Elvis twitch" on your upper lip. Whatever it is, you two share a private code that is not meaningful to others.

Hopper, Knapp, and Scott (1981) created a category scheme for these personal idioms:

1. *Teasing insults* might include, for example, calling a quiet friend "killer" in playful conversational exchange.

2. *Confrontations* show that you are annoyed by the other's behavior or inform your partner that his or her behavior is out of bounds. A

key phrase, such as "You're delightful when you're psychotic," may be used.

3. *Expressions of affection* may be developed to express love or emotional ties, such as touching index fingers.

4. *Sexual invitations* are idioms that propose sexual behavior. Hopper et al. reported examples, such as "Let's try out the futon."

5. *Sexual reference and euphemisms* are idioms that make reference to sex, sexual behavior, or sex organs without propositioning the partner.

6. *Requests/routines* are behavior that proposes a course of action, such as hinting a desire to leave a party through nonverbal signals.

7. *Partner nicknames* are personal references used for each other, which only the couple would use.

8. *Names or labels for others,* such as calling an unattractive faculty member "the love doctor."

Researchers have found the development of such personal idioms to be fairly common in dating and married couples. Undoubtedly this also occurs to some degree in friendship relationships. Assess your own use of personal idioms, either in a dating-type or friendship relationship. To begin with, do you use such personal idioms? Isolate a relationship in which you use them, and write down a few examples. What effect do they have on the relationship?

Would you say that the use of personal idioms (1) creates relational unity or distance and (2) enhances or hinders relationship development? Mark your answers on the seven-point scales below.

Creates Relational Distance	1	2	3	4	5	6	7	Creates Relational Unity
		-------	-------	-------	-------	-------	-------		

Hinders Development of the Relationship	1	2	3	4	5	6	7	Enhances Development of the Relationship
		-------	-------	-------	-------	-------	-------		

According to Bell, Buerkel-Rothfuss, and Gore (1987), people generally use personal idioms to develop a sense of "we-ness" in the relationship. In other words, personal idioms are generally used to strengthen relational ties and enhance relational unity. In addition, they present an outward display of "coupleness" for others to see. These researchers also found that personal idioms generally help to escalate the relationship. The number and diversity of a couple's idioms (excluding the negative types, such as confrontations) were found to be good predictors of the couple's feelings of love, commitment, and closeness.

Integrating.   During this phase, the relationship begins to take on an identity. The participants begin to surrender some of their individual identity and invest it in their shared relational identity. They begin to search for similarity or common identity. The participants will begin to refer to the relationship as a distinct entity through verbal reference (for example, "*We* should think about joining that wine tasting club"), and by collecting shared items (for example, my music collection and your music collection get combined to form *our* music collection). In addition, outsiders begin to treat the participants as a couple. If only one shows up at a social event, people ask where the partner is. Though independence is not eliminated, interdependence receives emphasis.

Discussion Question 8–5
What would you say are the most common markers of friendship identities among your peers?

Bonding.   The last phase of relational development involves a formal public announcement of commitment. The common example in our culture is marriage. Though same-sex relational partners cannot get married in the United States, several municipalities now allow gay and lesbian couples to declare their shared relational status. Some cultures also have rituals that declare a bond of "best friends." Individuals cooperating in a business venture may announce their partnership. These formal announcements create a relational tie that may carry social, legal, and financial obligations.

Stages of Relationship Termination

Differentiating.   The first step toward relational termination is the mirror image of the integrating stage. Instead of becoming interdependent, the partners begin to reassert their independence. Rather than emphasize "we," the partners begin to be more concerned with "me." Differences become more important than similarities. The partners may seek separate hobbies or activities that the other is not interested in. It is not necessarily a downhill slide from here to the end of the relationship. Differentiating may just be a sign that certain issues need to be renegotiated. This can be a means of instigating relational change. However, some relationships do deteriorate further.

Circumscribing.   This phase is characterized by a reduction in the amount and depth of communication between the partners. Conversation occurs less frequently. Topics that are discussed are less revealing and more superficial. The participants begin to avoid, or "circumscribe," certain issues. Rather than talk about the relational difficulties, a partner may shut down or shift the conversation: "Let's just leave it alone," or "Can we talk about something else?" Surprisingly, friends and family may not be aware that the couple is having any problems. The couple will go out of their way to maintain a facade of normalcy. They will be loose and sociable in the presence of others, but more restrained when alone with each other.

Stagnating.   At this stage the partners begin to cut off even noncontroversial interaction. Discussion of the state of the relationship is strictly taboo. They both feel certain that they know what the other is going to say, so they are willing to endure extended silence in the presence of the other. Also, they

Cross-reference 8–3
Compare these stages of relationship termination to the stages of marriage dissolution described in Chapter 9.

surrender any attempts to reveal aspects of their own identity or to explore the identity of the other. They feel that there is nothing new to be offered. At this point the relationship is going nowhere. The participants are just buying time until the end.

Avoiding.   In previous termination stages, partners created emotional distance between themselves. At this stage they begin to create physical space as well. They may actively avoid being in the same setting at the same time. She may study in the library when she knows he'll be home eating. The participants are shutting down the opportunities to interact. In this sense, this stage is the mirror image of the initiation phase of relationship development. During the initiation phase, people try to open channels of communication through a variety of verbal and nonverbal signals (for example, providing eye contact to someone). Now those channels are being eliminated.

Terminating.   This phase is used to bring the relationship to an end. One or both of the partners will clearly state that the relationship is over. The conversation is likely to be rigid, awkward, hesitant, and carefully measured. Statements will be made about the future after the end of the relationship. These summary statements may reflect a concern for the other's feelings (for example, "I'm sorry that we couldn't make it work, but I want you to keep seeing the kids as much as you'd like"), or they may not ("Get out of here, and I don't ever want to see you again").

Movement Through Knapp's Relational Stages

Knapp's relationship stages model should not be interpreted as a ladder-slide combination. Not every relationship progresses to the bonding stage. Nor do the relationships that do reach bonding inevitably slide down to relational termination. Movement through the stages is dynamic and variable, but it has some predictable patterns.

Movement Is Systematic and Sequential.   There is a tendency for relational partners to move through the stages in sequence. They can skip steps, but doing so is risky to the further progression of the relationship. Consider the whirlwind romance, wherein the participants move quickly from experimenting to bonding. The couple may have to cycle back through the intensifying and integrating stages in order to find out about each other and develop a sense of interdependence. The amount of time spent in any stage is also variable. Some couples may linger in the intensifying stage as good friends for years, only to pursue a closer romantic relationship later.

Movement May Be Forward or Backward.   The relationship can progress forward, toward greater intimacy, or backward, toward less intimacy. You may develop a friendship with a person and invite him or her over for a dinner with some friends but never quite strike the right note. At that point, the relationship may move back to the experimenting stage, and you remain "acquaintances" rather than friends.

Movement Takes Place Within Stages.   Even if a relationship has remained in one stage over a period of time, there is still movement within the stage. A husband and wife may have a very stable relationship and still have occasional arguments. A single episode of conflict does not foreshadow the road of relational dissolution. It simply means that the relationship is alive. Or consider the close friends who are separated by a move. When they see each other it is likely that they will perform a ritualized greeting, engage in small talk, and gather information about what is new before even starting to self-disclose again. In other words, they begin their reunion as though it were a compressed version of the first steps of relationship development.

Movement Is Always to a New Place.   Partners may cycle through relational stages repeatedly, but even movement into a stage that they have been in before opens up new relational possibilities. Many relationships go through the stages of relational decline, only to take on new life and grow again toward greater intimacy. Even though the partners may pass through the integrating stage a dozen times, each time they will bring something new to that stage. Or consider the example of a couple who, after being friends for years, decide to develop a romantic relationship. In this case they decide that it was a mistake to become more than friends, so they try to revert to a friendship relationship. Needless to say, the friendship is never the same as it was before. The friendship becomes a new stage, even though they had a friendship relationship before.

In sum, Knapp's relational stages model is useful because it aids our understanding of relational dynamics. It is not a prescriptive, "how to" list of suggestions for improving your relationships. Instead, this theory describes the communicative behavior that people use as they develop, maintain, and terminate relationships.

MANAGING CONFLICT IN INTERPERSONAL RELATIONSHIPS

Maintaining an effective relationship is not an easy task. Relationships can follow twisted and difficult paths. In order to navigate these paths, we have to master a number of social skills. One of the most difficult skills to master is the ability to manage conflict effectively. In this section we briefly overview the nature of interpersonal conflict, discuss some of the common mistakes people make when dealing with conflict, and suggest some alternative techniques for managing conflict effectively.

Teaching Objective 8–5
Explore the nature of conflict in interpersonal relationships, illustrating common problems in handling conflict as well as strategies for resolving conflicts.

The Nature of Conflict

Conflict is an inevitable part of being in a relationship. We have already mentioned that relationships are characterized by the competing forces of indepen-

Current Research 8–7
"We define argument as communication used to seek convergence on ideas. . . . In short, argument functions in interpersonal encounters as it does in public contexts: as a means of persuasion and as a tool of inquiry." (Canary, Daniel J., Weger, Harry Jr., and Stafford, Laura. Couples' argument sequences and their associations with relational characteristics, *Western Journal of Speech Communication,* 55, 2, 1991, pp. 159–160.)

dence and interdependence. Independence highlights the importance of self-interest, whereas interdependence emphasizes shared interests. With these competing interests, conflict is bound to be a natural part of relationships. It is vitally important to remember that conflict itself is not bad. More often it is the way we attempt to deal with conflict that makes it a frustrating, destructive process. There are many enduring fallacies about conflict that we stubbornly hold on to. Too often we are taught to believe that harmony is normal and conflict is pathological—that it should be avoided whenever possible (Hocker and Wilmot 1991). This attitude makes it more difficult to deal with conflict, and to recognize the important benefits that conflict can bring to a relationship.

By pointing out the functional, or useful, nature of conflict, Coser (1956) made us realize that it is important to manage conflict, rather than avoid it. Conflict is functional because it (1) identifies the need for social change; (2) forces parties to deal with underlying problems; (3) helps clarify important issues; (4) reminds the parties that they have shared, interdependent interests; and (5) can bring the relational participants closer together if the conflict is with an outside party. These positive functions can be realized if the participants take a constructive approach to managing conflict.

According to Hocker and Wilmot (1991, p. 12), **conflict** "is an expressed struggle between at least two interdependent parties who perceive incompatible goals, scarce resources, and interference from the other party in achieving their goals." It is important that conflict involve an *expressed struggle.* You may have a conflict with yourself over which shoes to buy, but such *intra*personal conflict is a matter of individual decision making. *Inter*personal conflict focuses on what occurs between people. Furthermore, we are interested in the expres-

Conflict need not be destructive to relationships. Learning to manage conflicts is probably the single most important task you can assign yourself.

sion of conflict. If you are angry at someone, but all you do is silently fume about the matter, that is of little interest from a communication perspective.

A second important component of the definition above is that it concerns the *perceptions* of incompatible goals, scarce resources, or interference. It is fairly easy to understand why conflict occurs when there is insufficient power, money, food, or affection to fulfill all the demanding parties. Occasionally, conflict will occur when the actual resources are plentiful but the competing parties feel that a shortage is present. This may be more difficult to understand. Keep in mind, however, that people act on their perceptions of events, not necessarily the actual state of affairs. Children sometimes get into fights over who is the best friend of an especially popular playmate. Realistically, that desired status could be allocated relatively equally, but the competing children do not recognize this. As a result, a conflict occurs.

Common Problems in Our Approaches to Conflict

Although conflict can serve a number of important functions, inappropriate management of conflict can be painful and destructive. Here we list three common problems associated with conflict management, their causes, and their consequences. In addition, we offer suggestions for improving your conflict management skills.

Avoidance. When faced with a conflict situation, one of the first choices you have to make is whether to engage in or avoid the conflict. Avoidance can be a useful conflict strategy when (1) you cannot win; (2) one or more of the parties is unwilling to put in the effort to work through the conflict; (3) open communication is not present between the participants and cannot be established; (4) the cost of losing the conflict is too high; or (5) the participants do not know how to engage in constructive conflict management (Hocker and Wilmot 1991). In spite of the fact that some situational factors may make avoidance desirable, it should not be used as a default option—without considering alternative approaches.

Avoidance can have some very damaging consequences when used indiscriminately. Conflict issues that are avoided seldom disappear. Often, the person avoiding the conflict will not dismiss the issues, but will store them away. **Gunnysacking** is the tendency to store up unresolved issues—to set them aside in the back of your mind. Unfortunately, these issues will build up until you cannot contain them any longer. The result is a virtual outpouring, or unloading, of numerous issues in a single megaconflict. This causes serious problems because multiple, unrelated issues are difficult to untangle and resolve. Furthermore, the person who eventually feels the sudden onrush of your wrath will feel "dumped on" and abused. It is likely that he or she will try to strike back with every minor, stored-up grievance that can be found to confront you with. The result is chaos, a spiraling conflict that will be very difficult to resolve, and hurt feelings.

There are variations in how avoidance is carried out. One approach is simply to avoid a topic or to declare the issue off limits. Another way to avoid the

Leadership Note 8–2
"And unless we value the differences in our perceptions, unless we value each other and give credence to the possibility that we're both right, that life is not always a dichotomous either/or, that there are almost always third alternatives, we will never be able to transcend the limits of (our) conditioning." (Covey, Stephen R. *The 7 Habits of Highly Effective People.* New York: Simon and Schuster, 1989, p. 277)

Discussion Question 8–6
What would you say is the most common human response to conflict? How do most people tend to handle conflict in their everyday lives?

Current Research 8–8
Cloven and Roloff found that persons involved in interpersonal relationships tended to perceive problems as more severe and partners as more to blame if they spent considerable time alone thinking about the problems. On the other hand, frequent communication between the partners, especially integrative interaction, lessened perceptions of severity and blame. Avoidance-type interactions did not reduce perceptions of severity or blame. (Cloven, Denise H., and Roloff, Michael E. Sensemaking activities and interpersonal conflict: communicative cures for the mulling blues, *Western Journal of Speech Communication*, 55, 2, 1991, pp. 134–158.)

conflict is to redefine the issue. Imagine that a teenager is confronted by his older sister about the late hours he keeps and how it bothers their parents. His reply is, "You always side with Mom and Dad." Now the issue of whether he keeps late hours is avoided, and the discussion switches to her allegiance to him or their parents. Another variation of avoidance is to dismiss or belittle the original complaint: "I can't believe that you get so upset over leaving the cap off the toothpaste." This leaves the complaining party questioning his original judgment, makes him less willing to approach small conflict issues that should be easy to resolve, and makes it more likely that these small issues will end up in his "gunnysack" until they explode.

These destructive features of avoidance make it worthwhile to consider using alternative conflict management strategies. Hence, one solution to this problem is to deal with conflict issues as they arise, rather than avoiding them. This does not mean that you should always face off in the heat of the moment in order to confront an issue. Much can be said for appropriate timing and the need to cool down before attempting to resolve a problem. However, if you plan to bring up an issue at a later time, follow up on your intentions. Otherwise, it just becomes another item in your gunnysack.

Try to work out a collaborative style from which all parties can gain something as a result of the conflict resolution. When you decide to confront a conflict issue, be direct and specific. Identify the behavior that appears to cause the problem, rather than generalizing about the issues involved: "When you 'ordered' me to get you a beer in front of all your friends, I felt belittled and hurt" is much easier to deal with than "You treat me like dirt—you never show any respect for me or my feelings."

Therapists have suggested using a set format to air grievances in families or groups that have difficulty bringing issues to the surface before they expand. Often facilitated by a third party, these "family meetings" help the parties work through (1) gripe time, (2) agenda building, and (3) problem solving, as a way to break out of destructive conflict cycles (Hocker and Wilmot 1991). As a result, the parties have a system of rules that allows them to air grievances while they are small and easily resolved.

Current Research 8–9
A study by Canary and Spitzberg found support for the reality of attribution biases, in that individuals saw themselves as more globally competent and appropriate in their use of conflict strategies than their partners. (Canary, Daniel J., and Spitzberg, Brian H. Attribution biases and associations between conflict strategies and competence outcomes, *Communication Monographs*, 57, 2, 1990, pp. 146–149.)

Blaming the Other.   One of the perceptual causes of conflict difficulties is the tendency to blame the other person as the cause of the problem. Carrying this tendency even further, we often conclude that the conflict occurred not just because of the other's behavior, but as a result of the type of person she is. Rather than arguing about specific behavior, like the failure to wash her own dishes, you might accuse your roommate of being a slob.

Blaming the other and personalizing the conflict have some interesting causes. One root of this problem is a tendency to perceive different causes of behavior depending upon whether you are evaluating your own behavior or the behavior of someone else. The **actor-observer difference** in causal attributions is the tendency to judge another person's actions as a consequence of her underlying personality, and a corresponding tendency to attribute one's own behavior to external causal forces (Jones and Nisbett 1972). Returning home after a day at school, you notice that your roommate did not clean the bathroom as she was supposed to. You conclude that this behavior (or lack of it) is the result of the type of person your roommate is—generally rather lazy and irresponsible. The following week, when you are supposed to clean the bathroom, it never quite gets done. Judging your own behavior, you conclude that the same failure to clean up was a result of competing time demands at work and the term paper you had to work on. In other words, you attribute your own behavior to these outside pressures or demands. When we get into a conflict situation, we tend to conclude that the other's behavior is the result of her personality traits, such as stubbornness or closed-mindedness, whereas our own behavior is a result of having to react to this stubborn, closed-minded person (an outside force). Meanwhile, the other person views *her* behavior as the result of outside factors, and attributes *your* behavior to your underlying personality traits.

A second cause of this tendency to blame the other is our use of language. We blame the other by the way we tend to frame the problem. When asked to explain the problem, it is likely that an individual would say something like, "*You're* never fulfilling your responsibilities around here. *I* always have to clean up after you." The language casts it as a "me versus you" problem.

The consequence of blaming the other is a deadlocked conflict. Each party blames the other as the cause of the conflict, and each is indignant about being blamed. The resolution of the conflict does not progress because each party feels that he or she is being asked to accept responsibility. To give in would be to lose face, so each decides it's a matter of principle not to give in. After all, cast this way, the resolution of the conflict rests on one person's willingness to change who he or she is. That is a lot to ask. In addition, when the other's personality is viewed as the source of the conflict, there is a tendency to use avoidance as a resolution strategy (Sillars 1980). That becomes another issue that goes into the gunnysack.

In order to resolve this problem, both parties have to share responsibility for the conflict. Recognize that once the problem is aired and the conflict is expressed, it ceases to be "your" problem or "my" problem. It becomes "our" problem. It is a concern for the relationship, not just one party. With attribution differences as a possible cause, it is useful to be aware of the actor-observer difference. This difference can be minimized if each person tries to empathize with the other (Regan and Totten 1975). Put yourself in the other's place, and you might recognize external causal factors and be less likely to attribute his or her behavior to personality alone.

It would also help to use language that accepts responsibility for your own emotions and avoids blaming the other for the conflict. Instead of accusing, "You're a slob," say, "I need to have a cleaner environment to live in or it upsets me." Also, be willing to emphasize your shared relational goals when raising conflict issues. In this case you could say, "We both need a home environment that makes us comfortable and relaxed. When either one of us is upset, it makes life around here miserable for both of us. Right now I have an issue that I have to bring up. . . . " This heightens the shared nature of the problem and the benefits of a resolution.

Figure 8.4

Conflict Resolution Grid. (Adapted from Blake and Mouton's Managerial Conflict Grid, published in R. R. Blake and J. S. Mouton, "The Fifth Achievement," in F. E. Jandt (Ed.), *Conflict Resolution Through Communication*. (New York; Harper and Row, 1973.)

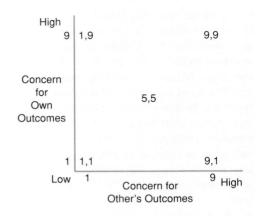

1,1: Avoidance
9,1: Surrender
1,9: Domination
5,5: Compromise
9,9: Problem Solving

Current Research 8–10

In a study of young adult friends, Legge and Rawlins found three modes of managing disputes: (1) *convenience:* addressing specific behaviors, agreeing perceptually about the framework of the dispute, avoiding disagreement and tolerating differences; (2) *cooperation:* each disputant stating her/his position without engaging the other, a frame of friendliness and agreement about the function of argument; and (3) *commitment:* mutual understanding with agreement to disagree. (Legge, Nancy and Rawlins, William, Managing disputes in young adult friendships: modes of convenience, cooperation, and commitment. *Western Journal of Communication*, 56, 3, 1992, pp. 226–247.

Adopting an "I Win, You Lose" Strategy. A third hindrance to effective conflict management is the belief that in order to gain your goals you have to defeat the other person or prevent the other person from attaining his or her goals. Too often we view conflict as a win-or-lose situation. By adopting this view, you try to get the other to give in, or you try to prevent the other from gaining his or her objectives. With this approach, the best you can hope for is a compromise, which won't fully satisfy either party.

The likely result of this strategy is a negative spiral of escalating conflict. As you try to prevent your partner from gaining his or her goals, he or she will recognize your strategy and use it as well. As a result, the original goals get lost as each party sets out to hurt the other. It is not uncommon in divorce proceedings for the ex-spouses to forget their original goals (for example, seeking security for the children), and get wrapped up in hurting the other instead. If a negative spiral continues, the parties may eventually resort to physical violence or aggression.

The solution is to pursue a strategy that maximizes concern for your own and the other's outcomes. Look for a resolution that gives everyone what he or she wants. Figure 8.4 maps some of the possible conflict resolution approaches the parties can take. The *avoidance* strategy has severe drawbacks, as we have already pointed out. The 9,1, or *surrender,* strategy allows the other to have his or her way, without regard for your own interests. This is the martyr scenario. Although it might make your partner happy in the short term, you will end up being so miserable that the relationship will eventually suffer. The 1,9 position is called *domination.* This is also the "I win, you lose" approach. You attempt to resolve the conflict by gaining all your goals while vanquishing your opponent. As we have mentioned, this is unlikely to leave both parties satisfied. If you soften up from this position, it is possible to adopt a 5,5, or *compromise,* strategy. Though we are often taught to compromise, this tends to fall short of an optimum solution. If you give up half of what you want and your partner gives up half of what he or she wants, the best either of you can do is be half-satisfied. Sometimes that is the best you can do. However, to resort to compromise too soon abandons the search for a solution that fits everyone's needs.

The alternative is to adopt a 9,9, or *problem-solving*, strategy. Consider again the case of two roommates who take different approaches to housework. One, we'll call him Felix, is very concerned with maintaining a clean house. Oscar, the other, is a bit more, oh, how shall we say . . . relaxed. It's not that he hates a clean house, but he feels that he has more important things to do with his time. Felix gets upset because Oscar leaves the apartment messy, and Oscar gets annoyed because Felix keeps hounding him. If each adopts an "I win, you lose" strategy, they end up in a deadlock where neither is happy. If they work for a compromise, the best they can hope for is that Oscar may do some cleaning (but it is unlikely that he'd work very hard at it). Meanwhile, Felix won't have to do all the cleaning, but he'll probably be annoyed by the half-hearted job of Oscar that he has to make up for.

An alternative would be to seek out a solution that gives each what he wants. Felix wants a clean apartment, though he's not necessarily crazy about the process of cleaning itself. Oscar wants time to do other things, though he sort of likes having a clean apartment (as long as he doesn't have to do the work). An alternative solution that transcends compromise would be to hire a housecleaner to come in once a month. It would give Oscar his free time, and it would reduce the cleaning load on Felix. They could even weigh the expense so that Oscar payed somewhat more for the service. If they had set out to compromise, they never would have recognized that a mutually satisfying solution was available.

Managing conflict is not easy, but if it is handled constructively it can benefit the relationship. It is important to be committed to resolving the conflicts, to take the perspective of the other person, and to adopt a strategy that offers benefits to all parties. The Mastering Communication Skills box continues the discussion of conflict management skills.

Cross-reference 8–4
Problem-solving skills discussed in Chapters 11 and 12 in relation to group conflicts can also be adapted to the needs of interpersonal relationships.

Current Research 8–11
Vanlear and Zietlow found that flexibility was the key to conflict resolution among married couples. (Vanlear, C. Arthur Jr., and Zietlow, Paul H. Toward a contingency approach to marital interaction: an empirical integration of three approaches, *Communication Monographs,*

MASTERING COMMUNICATION SKILLS

Utilizing Conflict Management Skills

In a study of conflict between college roommates, Sillars (1980) uncovered some interesting features of their conflict management. He was looking for actor-observer differences in the perceptions of conflict causes, and the consequences of these differences for conflict resolution approaches. He found a strong tendency for roommates to blame each other as the cause of conflicts, particularly if the conflict involved what was considered an important issue. When the other person was perceived to be the cause of the conflict (particularly when the conflict was seen as the product of the other's underlying personality), the roommate questioned tended to use a resolution strategy that avoided the issue or blamed the other. The results of these resolution attempts were conflicts that took longer to resolve and in which the person was less satisfied with his or her roommate as a result. One of the ironies of Sillars's findings was that the more important a conflict was perceived to be, and the more frequent conflicts were between the roommates, the more likely they were to use an avoidance strategy—a strategy that left the conflict unresolved and left the roommates less satisfied with each other.

We would like you to be more successful with your conflict resolution attempts. In particular, we would like you to attempt to use some of the conflict resolution techniques mentioned in this chapter. Conflict management is serious business, and conflicts can have serious consequences for a relationship. For those reasons, we do not want you to go out and initiate conflict just so you can try out your new resolution techniques. However, next time the situation warrants it, and the conflict is appropriate, try to use some of the following suggestions.

Knowing that blaming the other can result from actor-observer differences in attributions, try to empathize with the person with whom you are having the conflict. Listen carefully to his or her explanations of events (this itself is difficult to do in many conflict situations). Rather than avoiding the conflict as a resolution strategy, try to assert your position, while using nonaccusing language. Try to stress that it is your common problem that needs to be resolved, not just the other's personality or behavior that needs to be changed. Encourage the other to listen to your position and empathize with you. Try to use a problem-solving strategy that seeks to maximize each person's goals. If other issues are brought up, try to keep them untangled. Resolve one issue at a time. If necessary, promise to come back to other unresolved issues, even if you have to postpone that until a later date. Be sure you fulfill any such promises. Measure the success of your resolution by its benefits for the relationship rather than by your personal gains.

◾ Summary

Relationships remain a valuable and important part of our lives. Although there are a number of prevailing misconceptions about relationships and their dynamics, social science research attempts to uncover a more accurate picture. Relationships are not a simple matter of matching personality traits. Communication plays a vital role in relational formation and change. This is not to suggest that communication is a magic wand that can cure all relational ills; rather, it is a tool for working on them.

This chapter focused primarily on close relationships. The defining features of such relationships are interdependence—a sharing of common goals and coordinated behavioral sequences, and a history of interaction over time (with some anticipation of future interaction). These relationships can be classified by the type of communication that is typically used. They can differ in how cooperative and friendly or competitive and hostile they are. Some relationships are intense and demanding, whereas others are quite superficial. Relationships can be based on equality of the participants or on dominance by one. We have all experienced relationships that are formal and cautious and others that are informal and open. We can also distinguish between relationships that are task oriented and others that are nontask oriented.

It is clear that relationships do not instantly appear and then remain the same. Relationships change. In this chapter, we described the processes of relationship initiation, maintenance, and termination. Initiation can be viewed as a filtering process, and is characterized by certain communication patterns, such as small talk. Relationship maintenance requires the participants to balance the competing needs of independence and interdependence and to fulfill the relational expectations of each other. Relationship termination is not a mirror image of initiation, as was previously believed. Instead, it involves profound relational changes and can be instigated by a number of communication strategies. The primary differences between these strategies is the degree to which they show concern for the other person's feelings, and their directness—the degree to which they explicitly state that the relationship is over.

Mark Knapp's (1978) theory of relational stages provides a useful explanation for the dynamics of relational change. According to this theory, relationship escalation involves the stages of initiating, experimenting, intensifying, integrating, and bonding. Relationship termination is a process that goes through the stages of differentiating, circumscribing, stagnating, avoiding, and terminating. Movement from stage to stage tends to be sequential, but is not fixed. Relational partners can cycle through stages, and reaching one stage does not necessitate progression to the next stage.

In the final section of the chapter, we discussed the management of conflict. Conflict is an inevitable product of the competing demands of independence and interdependence, which are present in all relationships. If managed effectively, conflict can actually provide beneficial results for the relationship. Unfortunately, there are some common mistakes that people make when attempting to deal with conflict. One mistake is the automatic use of avoidance as a conflict resolution strategy. Though it can be a necessary and useful strategy when employed under the right circumstances, its indiscriminate use can lead to the problem of gunnysacking and a spiraling of escalating conflict. An alternative is to confront conflict situations directly, while being concrete and specific about the troublesome issues.

Blaming the other is a second common mistake in conflict management. Rooted in perceptions and language use, this problem can lead to conflict deadlock, ego-defensiveness, and avoiding strategies. To overcome this problem, the participants need to empathize with each other, use language that accepts ownership of their own feelings, and focus on the shared goals of the relational partners.

The last problem mentioned was the use of an "I win, you lose" strategy. Once applied, this strategy leads to an escalation of the conflict and an inability to find a compromise solution. A more desirable approach is to pursue a strategy that seeks to maximize what each person wants. Conflict management is complex, and we can only begin to discuss its intricacies here. Still, a thoughtful approach to conflict management is probably one of the biggest steps toward improving relationship maintenance.

Exercises

1. Characterize three of your relationships using the five dimensions of Wish and Kaplan (see Figure 8.1). Select three relationships, one with a family member, one with a good friend, and a third of your choice (for example, a coworker, a romantic relationship, a teacher, etc.). If it helps, draw the dimensions on a sheet of paper and scale them from left to right, with the right side of the scale being (1) and the left side represented by a (7), with (4) as the midpoint. For example, on the first dimension, *cooperative and friendly* would be a (1), and *competitive and hostile* would be a (7). Rank each relationship on these five dimensions. Next, consider how these relationships have changed over time. Think about these relationships three years ago. Rank them again, basing the rankings on the relationship at that time. Finally, if you had your choice, what would they ideally be like along these dimensions?

2. Both Duck (1985) and Wilmot (1987) characterized relationship development as a filtering process. Wilmot emphasized the idiosyncratic nature of this filtering process. He noted that the standards or criteria used to elevate a friend to a buddy may differ from person to person. In fact, the categories themselves may not be universal. You might not have a buddy category. For you, friends may just become "close friends." Or, between friends and close friends, you may have a category of "confidantes." For this exercise, evaluate your friendship hierarchy. Distinguish between the different types or classifications of friendship that you use, from acquaintances to best friends (or any other categories that you use). Then, define your filter system. What does a person have to do to graduate from one category to the next? Note that each filter will probably be different. Moving from acquaintance to friend may only require the other person's apparent interest in doing things together and a willingness not to cause great public embarrassment. However, to move beyond the general category of friend to buddy or best friend, you may require quite a bit more. Write a short essay covering these questions.

3. Evaluate the portrayal of conflict resolution on TV. Most situation comedies and many other dramatic TV episodes focus on a conflict between two or more characters. Not surprisingly, they always seem able to resolve the matter within their hour or half-hour time slot (too bad it's not usually so simple in real life). Have two or three of your classmates watch the same show. ("Seinfeld," "Murphy Brown," "Home Improvement," and "Northern Ex-

posure" would all be appropriate.) In a small group, discuss the conflict. Identify the conflict issue. Discuss how it developed and was handled. What mistakes were made in managing the conflict? How did the characters repair their mistakes and eventually resolve the conflict? How realistic was the portrayal of conflict? What techniques did the characters use that you could adopt to improve your conflict management? Be able to discuss these issues with the class after your small-group discussion.

Related Readings

Kelley, H. H., Berscheid, E., Christensen, A., Harvey, J. H., Huston, T. L., Levinger, G., McClintock, E., Peplau, L. A., and Peterson, D. R. (Eds.) (1983). *Close relationships.* New York: W. H. Freeman.

This edited text brings together some of the most prominent social psychologists working in the area of interpersonal relationships. The authors provide thorough literature reviews on a broad range of topics, from emotion to the role of power in relationships. This is a scholarly book of broad scope.

Hocker, J. L., and Wilmot, W. W. (1991). *Interpersonal conflict* (3rd ed.) Dubuque, IA: William C. Brown.

This text sets the standard for other books on communication and interpersonal conflict, with interesting examples, clear writing, and a solid research foundation. Particularly useful is the section explaining the advantages and disadvantages of various conflict tactics.

Roloff, M. E., and Miller, G. R. (Eds.) (1987). *Interpersonal processes: New directions in communication research.* Newbury Park, CA: Sage.

This is a collection of articles from scholars in communication, who address a variety of topics concerning interpersonal relationships and interpersonal communication. Notable are Steve Duck's article ("How to Lose Friends Without Influencing People") on the process of relationship deterioration, and Sillars and Weisberg's article ("Conflict as a Social Skill"), which poses some distressing questions about the usefulness of using skills training to improve people's conflict resolution techniques.

Family Communication

Chapter objectives

After reading this chapter you should be able to:

1. define what a family is, and recognize the potential difficulties of creating the definition

2. list the functions of the family

3. explain the different methods of decision making in families

4. understand the dynamics of power in the family

5. describe how families cope with change

6. understand the critical features of the primary relationships in the family

7. explain the factors that lead to relational satisfaction in the family

Key terms and concepts

family
extended family
nuclear family
consensus decision
   making
accommodation decision
   making
de facto decision making
power
punishment
reward power
expertise
legitimacy
identification
persuasion
independent marital types
separate marital types
traditional marital types
support
control

What is wrong with families these days? The statistics could lead us to despair. Divorce rates are rising. Teen pregnancy seems out of control. The stories on the news are shocking. Some parents sexually abuse their children. Physical abuse of children, spouses, and elderly family members seems to occur with shocking regularity. As though it were not bad enough that these events pervade the news, now the same material has become the fodder for so-called entertainment. It seems that every weekend brings another series of sensationalized TV movies in which family members are physically, sexually, or emotionally abused. Why can't we go back to the "good old days"?

Certainly, there are dysfunctional families today, but, sad as it may seem, they have always been with us. As much as some political and social leaders would have us believe otherwise, there has never been a magical era we can return to in order to resolve the troubles of our families. Much has been said lately about the need to return to "traditional family values." Often accompanying this plea is the belief that during the 1950s the structure of the American family was bedrock solid, and that this provided a foundation for all that was good in our culture. In fact, writers have looked back to the fifties and found that the lives of the Cleavers, the Andersons, and other TV families were not characteristic of what most American families faced. The following are just a few of the common misconceptions uncovered by author Diane Crispell (1992) in her article "Myths of the 1950s."

Myth 1: People were more religious in the fifties, and these religious values held the family together.

Reality: More people attended church services in the fifties, but when asked whether they consider themselves religious, just as many people today respond yes as they did in that earlier era. Crispell concludes, "Americans were not necessarily more religious in the 1950s…they simply showed it in different ways" (p. 42).

Myth 2: The decline of the family is tied to the fact that women today are more concerned with their careers, and therefore spend less time raising and socializing their families.

Reality: World War II had a dramatic effect on the role of women in the work force. Even after the war, in the 1950s, about a fifth of American mothers had paying jobs. Although this rate has increased, the notion that families were universally secure because mothers didn't work outside the home is clearly unfounded. Research indicates that there is little relationship between married women's employment and couples' ratings of marital quality (Bumpass 1990).

Myth 3: Because of the strong family values in the fifties, the problem of unwed mothers was rarely seen. Back then, "good girls" didn't get pregnant.

Current Research 9–1
In his classic study of the phenomenon of childhood from medieval to modern times, historian Philippe Aries describes the concept of family as a fairly modern invention and contends that from medieval times until the nineteenth century, most children did not live with their biological parents but were placed in other families for care and instruction. (Aries, Phillipe, *Centuries of Childhood.* New York: Alfred Knopf, 1962).

Cross-Reference 9–1
The discrepancy between individual and cultural perceptions and reality was explored in Chapter 2.

Reality: Although there were fewer births out of wedlock in the 1950s, this can be explained by the tendency of expectant couples to marry before the child was born. In other words, this doesn't necessarily indicate a change in sexual behavior, but a change in how the consequences were dealt with. Parents were not necessarily giving their children different sets of moral values; however, children who did get pregnant were encouraged by their parents to marry.

We mention these discrepancies not to soil the view of the family of the 1950s or to bring it down to its present status. Rather, we want to point out that it is futile to seek solutions to our present social problems in an illusory past. Perhaps more importantly for this chapter, it is not useful to look for some model of an "ideal" or "normal" family. Family success is more likely to result from understanding the dynamic forces in effect in a family, and from seeing how communication skills can improve family functioning. Turning back the clock is impossible, and efforts to do so will be fruitless.

Many authors (Trenholm and Jensen 1988; Bochner and Eisenberg 1987; Fitzpatrick and Badzinski 1985) note that the ideal family is a myth that we should not hope to duplicate. Even if your family doesn't face the tragedies and horrors mentioned above, you inevitably argue, disagree, or get mad at each other. To expect otherwise is unreasonable. In this chapter, we cannot provide you with a magic formula to turn your family into something out of "The Cosby Show." Not every problem can be solved in thirty minutes nor every difficulty soothed by sage advice from an all-knowing parent. Instead, this chapter offers a better understanding of the dynamic features of families—how they work and why they don't always work as well as we'd like them to. To this end, we explore what a family is, the critical functions served by families, and how families adapt to change. Additionally, we investigate the basic family relationships, and we identify some of the features that distinguish families that are satisfied from those that are dissatisfied with their family relationships.

Teaching Objective 9–1
Introduce the concept of family as broader, more fluid, and more inclusive than traditional conceptions and myths.

DEFINING THE TERM "FAMILY"

What is a family? To many readers this may seem an absurd question. After all, we all know what a family is. Or do we? Every time you start to define the boundaries of the family, exceptions and additions can be quickly generated. To get some sense of how complex and convoluted the notion of family can be, consider this: Hallmark, the greeting card company, makes cards for 105 different types of family relationships (Conn and Silverman 1991). If that still leaves you unimpressed, let's consider an example of the complexity of modern family life.

Assume we begin with a couple and their two children. If the parents divorced when the children were infants and the father hasn't seen them for fifteen years, would you still consider the father part of the family? If the wife remarried, at what point would the stepfather then be part of the family? What about the stepfather's parents? Are the new grandparents part of the family? Imagine that the stepfather has a son from his previous marriage. This boy still lives with the stepfather's ex-wife but visits regularly and spends some holidays

Current Research 9–2
"For a society almost entirely accustomed to nuclear families, the rapid growth of stepfamilies in the 1970s produced a cultural shock to our kinship system . . . . The first problem that comes up in describing stepfamilies is who gets counted as a stepfamily . . . . This is the demographic reality of stepfamilies. But there is a psychological reality as well. Not everyone living in stepfamily households has a common definition of who's included in *their* family." (Furstenberg, Frank and Cherlin, Andrew, *Divided Families: What Happens to Children When Parents Part.* Cambridge, Mass: Harvard University Press, 1991, pp. 78–79)

Discussion Question 9–1
What are the characteristics of the most atypical family you know?

Discussion Question 9–2
Where would you draw the line concerning family boundaries—a homosexual couple with an adopted child? a homosexual couple without children? the residents of a group home for mentally handicapped adults? a heterosexual couple co-habitating?

Teaching Objective 9–2
Explore the various definitions of family and seek commonalities between them.

with this group—is this stepbrother part of the family? How about the mother's niece whose own mother couldn't control her, but who has settled down since moving in with this group about a year ago. Is this niece now part of the family? At what point did she become family? If the son of the original couple moves out of the house to live on his own, is he still part of the family? If he moves in with his girlfriend, and though not married to each other, they display a deep relational commitment over several years, does she become part of the family? What if he were to move in with a same-sexed lover and they maintained a committed relationship over several years. Would the son's lover then be part of the family? And so on. . . .

It is likely that different people would draw the family boundaries at different points. In all, this suggests that the definition of family is not simple by any means. It is certainly clear that biological ties alone cannot be relied on to determine the boundaries of the family. How, then, are we to define what a family is? Three common approaches to defining the **family** are the family structure approach, the task approach, and the transactional process approach (Fitzpatrick and Wamboldt 1990).

The *family structure approach* uses both biological and legal connections to define the family. Marriage, genetic ties, or adoption can all be used to connect family members. The presence of any genetic, marital, or adoptive ties defines the **extended family**. Narrowing further, extended family members who live in the same household are considered a **nuclear family**. As demonstrated by the preceding example, not every person connected through marriage, blood, or adoptive ties feels like family. Hence, this definition isn't completely satisfying.

An alternative definition is based on what people do for each other, not their genetic and legal ties. The *task approach* looks at who fulfills certain family obligations. For example, parents instruct and nurture their children. If a man were to move in with a woman and her daughter, and if he were to read to the daughter, get her a glass of water in the middle of the night, and engage in other such parental behavior, according to the task approach he would be considered part of that family.

The third view is the *transactional process approach,* which focuses on how people interact with each other. Family members relate to one another in special ways. Fitzpatrick and Wamboldt (1990) suggest that according to the transactional process approach, the family is "a group of intimates who generate a sense of home and group identity, complete with strong ties of loyalty and emotion, and an experience of history and a future" (p. 425). Thus, family members see themselves as family and treat each other as such.

These definitions need not be mutually exclusive. In fact, one text on communication in the family characterizes the family in a way that seems to incorporate aspects of all three definitions. According to Galvin and Brommel (1986), families are "networks of people who live together over long periods of time bound by ties of marriage, blood, or commitment, legal or otherwise, who share a future expectation of connected relationship" (p. 4). Perhaps the most important point to remember is that the term *family* needs to be broad and inclusive. When we consider what is and what is not a family, we should not immediately flash to some ideal of a husband, wife, and their 2.3 biological children. Instead, we need to consider other combinations that also function as a family.

From a communication point of view, the biological ties are less important than the social connections—the interactive roles played by the participants—and an understanding of how these roles get played out (more or less successfully) using communication strategies. The face of the American family is changing. Because the family is a changing institution, communication is important. Roles, power, and expectations were clearer in the "traditional" nuclear family. Now that there are more two-income families, more divorces with resulting step-relations, and other changes, communication has become more vital as a tool for understanding and negotiating family relationships. To come to grips with the role of communication in the family, we first need to look at some of the universal functions served by families.

FUNCTIONS OF THE FAMILY

The family serves a variety of critical functions that enable our species to continue to survive. By exploring the functions of the family, we realize that family members are interdependent. By this we mean that family members rely on one another for rewards, and that a change in any member of the family can impact on the whole family. For example, the death of a family member can have devastating effects on all members. When a family member achieves a great success, the repercussions can also be felt throughout the family. If Kurt were to get a new prestigious job with a big salary, his sister Ashley may be proud and supportive, whereas his other sister, Sue, may get jealous and more distant.

Following are some of the functions that we expect families to fulfill. Some families fulfill them better than others. Unfortunately, some families do not accomplish them very well at all. As a result, some people are less satisfied with their family life. Though we cannot expect to solve every family difficulty in one chapter, we may note that successfully fulfilling these functions is largely dependent on effective communication in the family.

Providing Affection and Support

Among the basic needs we have as humans are those of affection and interpersonal support (or inclusion) (Schutz 1966). That is, we have a need to give and receive love, and a need to feel a part of a group. Families give their members a sense of belonging and a feeling of acceptance. For most of us, the family is the primary means through which we initially have these needs fulfilled. Even as we grow older and find these needs being fulfilled through friends, lovers, and perhaps spouses and our own children, most of us still receive some level of affection and support from our family of origin.

In times of doubt, uncertainty, or trouble, we may turn to family members for support and guidance. They may help us maintain a sense of identity and self-worth through difficult times. Consider how your family members, through

Discussion Question 9–3
Which of these approaches seems to be the most accurate? Which seems to be most adaptable to the changing nature of families?

Current Research 9–3
Psychoanalyst and author Alice Miller writes: "Each child needs among other things: care, protection, security, warmth, skin contact, touching, caressing, and tenderness. These needs are seldom sufficiently fulfilled; in fact, they are often exploited by adults for their own ends (trauma of child abuse). Child abuse has lifelong effects." (Miller, Alice, *Thou Shalt Not Be Aware: Society's Betrayal of the Child*. New York: Farrar, Straus, Giroux, 1985, p. 316)

their communicative behaviors, provide you with identity and self-worth. One way is through confirming messages. The concept of confirming versus disconfirming messages was introduced in Chapter 7. In part, family members are given support through the use of confirming messages—messages that acknowledge your value as a person and support the identity you seek to portray.

Nurturing and Socializing Children

Compared to other species in the animal kingdom, human offspring must be provided with care and sustenance for a very long period of time. It is the role of the family to provide nurturance of children's physical and social development. Consider the many ways this is accomplished.

Important social values are conveyed from parents to children. Parents help children to develop a set of moral standards and criteria for distinguishing right from wrong. If, as a child, you grabbed candy off the grocery store shelf without offering any money, it was probably your mother or father who explained to you that this was stealing. Children also learn what behavior is appropriate in their subculture or ethnic group. In short, parents are the first ones to teach children how to be competent social actors.

To become competent social actors, children must also learn the rules of communication. Children learn basic communication skills, such as conversation guidelines, from their parents. When parents treat a baby's coos, grunts, and babbling as conversational turns, the child learns that turn-taking (waiting while the other speaks) is a normal part of competent interaction.

In addition to social values and interaction skills, parents provide their children with important information about the world. They become the child's first educators. Children typically learn their numbers and the letters of the alpha-

Not all families fit into a traditional mold. The definition of family has to take into account many non-traditional arrangements.

bet from their parents or older siblings. Of course, some parents are better at providing critical information than others. According to one poll, 17 percent of respondents said that they learned the "facts of life" from their mothers, while 2 percent were told by their fathers (Conn and Silverman 1991). In other words, over 80 percent of the people asked were not informed about sexuality by either parent. As you can see, families may be better at conveying some types of information to their children than other types.

Providing Economic Support

In order to provide many of its other functions, a family must provide for its members' physical needs. Basic physical needs, such as food, clothing, and shelter, are attainable because family members contribute to the family's financial support. In lieu of financial support, other family members may provide domestic support so that another can dedicate more time to an income-earning profession. In the "traditional" American family, the wife attended to domestic concerns. Although she did not earn an income for doing the wash, cooking, and child rearing, her efforts allowed the husband to devote more time to an income-earning job.

Times have changed, yet many aspects of family life remain the same. More married women are in the workplace, earning a second income to provide financial support for the family. According to Fitzpatrick and Badzinski (1985) over half of all married women in the United States now work outside the home. This may be due in part to the financial necessity of maintaining a desired standard of living and in part to increased awareness of women's rights and equality. Together with the move of women into the workplace there is an ongoing shift in the responsibilities of husband and wife. Both spouses are expected to broaden their family responsibilities. As women accept increased responsibility for the financial well-being of the family, men are expected to take up more of the housekeeping and child-rearing responsibilities. Between 1965 and 1985, men more than doubled the amount of time they spent doing housework (Robinson 1988). Unfortunately, there is still considerable disparity in who does most domestic chores. Even with the substantial increase in their participation, husbands still devote about half as much time as their wives to domestic chores (Bumpass 1990; Kamo 1988; Robinson 1988). Some critics argue that women's role in the work force has not liberated them from the drudgery of housework. Instead, it is argued, married women often take on a full-time job in addition to their domestic work (Hochschild 1989). Others view the transition more positively. They argue that husbands are doing more household chores, and that the time devoted to housework and paid work is roughly equal to about 60 hours per week for both husbands and wives (Ferree 1991). However, this figure excludes child-care responsibilities, which still predominately belong to women.

In addition to providing emotional support, economic support, and child-rearing functions, families serve other needs. For instance, families vacation together, play games, and generally entertain one another. Hence, Trenholm and Jensen (1988) refer to a *recreation* function. When the kids move away from

Teaching Objective 9–3
Describe the basic functions of family life.

Current Research 9–4
Furstenberg and Cherlin cite these harsh economic realities for many American families: sixteen per cent of all U.S. families with children under 18 were poor in 1988; in female-headed families with kids under 18, forty-five per cent were poor; in one study, ten per cent of white children and fourteen percent of black children became poor the year following their parents' separation; white children in single-parent families spend on average 3.2 years in poverty while growing up. (Furstenberg, Frank and Cherlin, Andrew, *Divided Families: What Happens to Children When Parents Part.* Cambridge, Mass.: Harvard University Press, 1991, p. 45)

Discussion Question 9–4
Are there other functions that you believe are a part of family life? Must there be children to be nurtured and socialized for a family to exist?

Cross-Reference 9–2
Compare the functions of the family to the functions of interpersonal communication described in Chapter 7. Would it make sense to consider establishing and negotiating identity as a fundamental function of family life?

home, they may call Mom and Dad to see how everyone in the family is doing. Hence, by serving as an information clearing house, the parents engage in an *information-processing* function. These and other functions suggest that the family plays a crucial role in developing and sustaining the way we live.

It is important to note that the family does not remain the same over time. It must constantly change to deal with the many changing features of the world around it and to accommodate the changes that take place to each of its members. The dynamic, adaptive features of the family are what we turn to next.

■ FAMILY PROCESSES

Families must adapt and change. Various communication skills provide the primary tools with which families deal with change. In this section, we look at how families make decisions, exercise power, and adapt to changing family roles, including divorce.

Family Decision Making

"When should we get a new car?" "What sort of religious training should the kids get?" "What health insurance options can we afford?" "Where will the kids be able to go to college when they're old enough?" Families have quite a few decisions to make, addressing both long-term and short-term needs. How they make these decisions can vary considerably from one family to another. According to Turner (1970), each family adopts its own decision-making style. Depending on the family, that style may remain constant or may vary with time and different decision issues. Turner characterized three basic styles of family decision making: consensus, accommodation, and *de facto*.

Consensus decision making requires that an agreement be reached among all family members in order to make the decision. Without a unanimous agreement the decision would not be finalized. A majority rule or voting would not be sufficient for this decision style. Obviously, the style would require a large investment of time and effort. Good negotiation skills and a willingness to search for common goals would be a great advantage to a family adopting this style. Flexibility and patience would be a must. The benefit would be a strong sense of commitment to the decision once it is made. Given its obvious benefits, it is unfortunate that this is the least used decision-making style among families.

A more frequently used style, **accommodation decision making**, occurs when some members concede to others, assuming that further discussion would be fruitless. Using a "majority rules" decision would be characteristic of this style. It can benefit a majority of the family, but those in the minority can be left unsatisfied. Imagine a family with a husband, wife, and three children. Two of the older children and the father enjoy golfing. Every year when it comes time to decide on a vacation spot, they want to go to a golf resort. The mother and other child have no interest in golf, but every year they get "outvoted." After just a few years, a considerable amount of resentment is likely to develop. In addition to building resentment, this style teaches family members that it is

Current Research 9–5
Psychologist Dorothy Corkille Briggs tied family decision-making, power, and discipline together in her classic parenting guide: "There are only three basic approaches to limit-setting: *power kept, power given away,* and *power shared.* And the method you use influences who makes the rules in your family and how they are enforced." Briggs associates "power kept" with authoritarian decision-making, "power given" with overpermissiveness, and "power shared" with democratic decision-making, characterized by Briggs as "cooperation through unanimous consent." (Briggs, Dorothy Corkille, *Your Child's Self-Esteem.* Garden City, New York: Doubleday & Company, 1975, pp. 231–260)

more important to build winning majority coalitions than it is to accommodate the desires of all members. It also rewards communication behavior designed to dominate others, such as being verbally aggressive, belittling the positions of others, or taking extreme initial positions.

The third style, **de facto** decision making, occurs when a stalemate prevents the family members from reaching a commonly agreed-upon decision. In the face of such a stalemate, one family member may make the decision unilaterally. For example, if a family were unable to decide which movie to go see, the father might get fed up and eventually declare that he's going to see one particular film and that anyone who doesn't want to see that movie can just sit home. Another version of the *de facto* style occurs when the failure to reach a decision lasts until the opportunity to choose from alternatives expires. For instance, the family may argue over what movie to see until only one is left showing that evening (or worse yet, until the theater closes for the night). *De facto* decisions are unlikely to satisfy everyone, and in the case of the unilateral decision, there will likely be criticism of the decision reached.

Some families may be able to adapt their decision-making style depending on the importance of the decision and who it affects. Some families are flexible

Discussion Question 9–5
How would you characterize family decision-making in most of the families you have known, including your own? Do these categories include a place for the decision-making patterns you have observed?

SELF-ASSESSMENT   **Assessing the Decision-Making Style of Your Family**

Analyze the dominant decision-making style in your family of origin (that is, the family you were raised in). What decision style was used most frequently? Did the style differ depending on the type of decision being made? Use the following matrix to help you.

	Decision-Making Style		
	Consensus	Accommodation	*De facto*
Major change (for example, moving)			
Major purchase (new car)			
Major event (annual vacation)			
Minor event (movie choice)			
Your territory (paint color in room)			
Other decisions			

in this respect, whereas others are rigid. As you can imagine, one of the most difficult adjustments anyone can make is adapting to a new family decision-making style as a result of family structure changes (marriage, remarriage, loss of a family member from moving out or death). If the initial decision-making style had been unproductive or dissatisfying, the change could be welcomed. However, in other instances, it is much like changing the rules in the middle of a game. (Complete the Self-Assessment exercise.)

Power in the Family

All family members do not have an equal vote in family discussions. This emphasizes the important role of power in family interactions. Power relationships themselves are dynamic, and they influence how family members deal with change. Let's explore the nature of power, where it comes from, and how it gets used.

Family **power** has been described as "the ability of individuals to change the behavior of other family members" (Galvin and Brommel 1986, p. 128). As such, power should be viewed as a feature of a relationship, not as a possession of an individual. A person doesn't carry power in her back pocket. Rather, the nature of the power depends on the relationship between people. One person may assert power, but the same power move will not necessarily have the same effect on each family member. A girl may exert power over her younger sister by threatening not to share the use of her dolls, and be quite successful. However, the same power move would not have much impact on the girl's older teenage brother. Power is relationship dependent. Obviously, control of the household toys is not the major source of power in most households.

French and Raven (1962) list several sources of power in families. **Punishment**, or coercive power, is probably the first source of family power that comes to mind for many of us. The ability to inflict physical punishment is an extreme example, though punishment also includes the sister who refuses to share the use of her dolls. Withholding any desired commodity (for example, money, affection, sex, food, even a smile) is a widely used form of punishment. Further, if a family member can provide you with a desired reward, he is said to have **reward power** over you. The brother who gets you to wash his car in return for its use is exerting reward power.

Expertise can serve as a source of power, such as when a boy accepts his sister's swimming instructions, knowing that her years in competitive swimming give her knowledge in that area. We accept power moves from people when we perceive they know what they are talking about.

Often families rely on **legitimacy** as a source of power. If a child asks why she should do something and her father replies, "Because I said so," he is relying on his legitimacy as a parent as the source of power. Typically in American homes, parents hold legitimate power over their children, and older children try to use legitimate power over younger siblings. This can be taken to humorous extremes, such as when a boy tries to play the "I'm older than you" card on his twin sister, who was born only minutes later than he. Children often find they can get younger siblings to do their bidding simply because the younger

Current Research 9–6
Miller links childhoods damaged by the use of coercive punishment power to the later lives of Adolph Hitler and other violent individuals. (Miller, Alice, *For Your Own Good: Hidden cruelty in child-rearing and the roots of violence*. New York: Farrar, Straus, Giroux, 1984)

child looks up to or admires the older one. In these cases, **identification** is said to be the source of power.

Finally, power may result from well-reasoned arguments, or **persuasion.** A husband may convince a wife that the best fitness equipment investment for the family is a stationary bike. If she goes along with him based on the weight of his arguments, it could be said that he exerted persuasion (also known as *informational power*).

Though not an exhaustive list, these types of power provide some sense of how different members of the family can exert power over other members. After all, power can come from different sources. It is equally important to note how power gets used. Given the definition of *power* as the ability to change the behavior of other family members, it is not necessary to think of power as a blunt instrument used to coerce others. Certainly, a family member can threaten or bully others into submission. However, power may be used with a more subtle touch. For instance, claimed incompetence can be a powerful move. The sister who implores her brother to help fix her car because he knows about cars, and the husband who imposes on the wife to sew a button because he's "no good at those things," are two examples of exercising power through submissiveness. This suggests that the source of power may provide an indication of how the power will be used. (See the Mastering Communication Skills box.)

Discussion Question 9–6
Which power do you think is employed most often by parents in families? Which power is used most often by children with their parents? Which power is used most often by siblings with one another?

Family Evolution

Families constantly undergo change. Such change may be driven by outside factors (for example, a downturn in the nation's economy necessitates that both spouses earn full-time incomes), by the decisions of family members (for example, the eldest son's decision to go away to college sends the remaining children scrambling to claim a new bedroom), or by the passage of time (for example, a daughter becomes old enough to date, sending her parents into lengthy debates over the appropriate restrictions on her dating behavior).

Change drives people out of old familiar habits and, therefore, can cause stress. By trying to avoid or resist change, families attempt to hold onto security, but such resistance to change often causes additional stress. As Bochner and Eisenberg (1987) note, a family progresses through different stages of develop-

MASTERING COMMUNICATION SKILLS	**Learning from the Past in Family Communication**
	It has been said that we learn parenting skills from the successes and mistakes of our own parents. Think back to your upbringing. Which parenting practices would you like to emulate? Which would you hope to avoid when raising your own family? In particular, focus on a preferred decision-making style, the use of power, and how you would accomplish critical family functions.

ment regardless of whether the members are ready for the changes. With a little foresight, the family members can anticipate and prepare for certain changes. For example, parents will eventually retire and spend more time with each other. Children will reach puberty and deal with the awkwardness of that life stage. Other changes, however, are more sudden and unexpected—a death in the family, the loss of a job. Ultimately, it is these unexpected changes to the family structure that are the most difficult to deal with.

Change is stressful because it often alters the roles of family members. As noted in Chapter 7 on interpersonal communication, the roles we adopt influence the rights and responsibilities that guide our behavior. When family change alters family roles, the rights and responsibilities of family members will likely change as well. Consider the example discussed earlier in the chapter of women's increasing role as co-breadwinner in the family. This role necessitates that women spend more time away from home and devote more energy to non-family activities. However, women's taking on of the responsibilities of an income earner is not consistently matched by their spouses' acceptance of more responsibilities on the domestic front. As you can see, it is often necessary to negotiate rights and responsibilities in the face of family change.

Discussion Question 9–7
What do you think are the biggest changes that affect the structure and evolution of families?

A family's new rights and responsibilities do not "automatically" go into operation. Family members have to sit down to discuss them. Hence, communication skills are crucial to deal with change effectively. The daughter who gets her driver's license may be able to claim the right to use the family car on occasion. If that right is attached to certain responsibilities, such as going to the store for groceries when asked, then her parents must make that bargain clear. The failure to clarify the emerging connection between new rights and responsibilities can easily lead to accusations, recriminations, and conflict.

Divorce is a striking example of how a family must deal with change. Unlike a single event, such as the death of a family member, divorce is a series of progressive steps through which the family must continue to change. Family members change their individual perceptions, their communication strategies, and often their emotional bonds to one another. To fully understand its ongoing, changing nature, think of divorce as the official legal step within the larger process of "uncoupling." The divorce is the legal recognition that the couple has decided to pursue separate lives, but it is not a full picture of the breakup of a marriage. As Table 9.1 shows, the process of uncoupling involves numerous stages (Vaughan 1985).

Teaching Objective 9–4
Emphasize the importance of decision-making patterns, power distribution, and relationship evolution to the structure of family life.

Although some couples are able to move through the uncoupling steps quickly and with little attachment for one another, this is by no means the norm. Living within a family, the husband and wife establish bonds of attachment based on familiar shared routines. Even after love fades in the relationship, a sense of attachment and personal routine may persist. For example, a couple in an otherwise stormy relationship may have enjoyed a temporary calm on weekends when they prepared elaborate Saturday breakfasts or went hiking on nearby nature trails. The sense of attachment gained through these activities may not be enough to sustain the marriage, but its loss does help explain why uncoupling can be painful, even if the marriage is no longer satisfying to either spouse.

Table 9.1
The Steps of Uncoupling

Step in the Sequence	Features
1. *Initiation of uncoupling*	One member of the couple (the "initiator") begins to question their common identity. The initiator begins to get the other to see the marriage as troubled.
2. *Accompanying reconstruction*	Dissatisfied, the initiator redefines the relationship. "I don't like what I have, so I'll view it as something else." Begins viewing the other in a way that makes self feel good about "the new me." For example, "She (or he) is too dowdy and anti-intellectual, and that holds me back."
3. *Self-validation outside the marriage*	The initiator seeks out new ways to find self-fulfillment, ways that emphasize the "me" instead of the "us" in the marriage. If this involves a new circle of friends, the initiator begins to discuss the marital troubles with those in the new circle. Meanwhile, the spouse is left seeking fulfillment in a crumbling marriage.
4. *Trying*	By now both spouses share the view that the marriage is troubled, though the initiator now sees it as unsavable. The initiator has psychologically prepared for the divorce, and is trying to prepare the spouse. The initiator may encourage the spouse to better him-or herself so the spouse will be better off after the divorce.
5. *Restructuring*	At this point the spouses may separate, though remain in an ambiguous state of connectedness. They can't plan separate finances, but don't want to be vulnerable to the other's financial abuses. They may begin to display their separateness, including telling their friends that they are no longer a couple.
6. *Divorce*	The legal switch from mutual identity to separate identities. Uncoupling is complete when the separate new social world of each is complete. If one or both "carry a torch," the final sense of the split may be delayed until a remarriage or similar event.

Source: D. Vaughan, "Uncoupling: The Social Construction of Divorce," in J. Henslin (Ed.), *Marriage and Family in a Changing Society,* 2nd ed. (New York: Free Press, 1985), pp. 429–439.

It has been noted that after the marriage has broken up, the former spouses go through a so-called "grave-dressing" phase (Knapp 1978). During this phase, each ex-spouse attempts to put the relationship to rest, explaining to friends and family the reasons behind the split. Each attempts to characterize the end by developing a story to provide a final word—a sort of official chronicle from his or her own point of view. This is done to help make sense of the uncoupling. It is interesting to note that there is a distinct gender difference in the themes that typically emerge in these stories (Fitzpatrick and Badzinski 1985). The ex-wives typically explain the breakup as being the result of interpersonal problems (for example, "He just stopped talking to me; he no longer shared what was important in his life"). In contrast, the ex-husbands typically attribute the split to structural changes in the family (for example, "With each of us pursuing career goals, we just didn't have time for each other").

When there are children in the family, the consequences of divorce are more widespread. One study of therapeutic interventions (Wallerstein and Kelly 1985) noted some of the reactions of nine-and ten-year-olds to their parents' divorces. Some children developed fears or phobias, especially of being abandoned. They experienced a greater sense of loneliness and isolation. There were attempts to get the parents to reconcile, even when there had been patterns of physical abuse in the family. Finally, in some cases, the children would align themselves with one parent in order to hurt or punish the other. This alignment occurred even in cases where the child previously had a close relationship with the parent who fell out of favor.

In spite of these undesirable effects, divorce can have beneficial consequences. Being raised in a household dominated by conflict between parents places great emotional and psychological stress on children. If a divorce reduces the hostility between the parents, it can improve the overall well-being of the children in a household (Amato 1993). It is easy to see that divorce has profound effects on the entire family.

■ PRIMARY ROLE RELATIONSHIPS

To understand family communication, we must also understand family relationships. These relationships place demands on family members, and the patterns of interaction that emerge help us characterize typical approaches to family life or types of families. Given that husband-wife relationships are different than parent-child relationships and sibling relationships, we deal with each of these in turn.

The Husband-Wife Relationship

Within the husband-wife relationship, the spouses must address many shared concerns—finances, domestic upkeep, housing, and child rearing are just a few. Perhaps the central concern of this relationship is the need to strike the proper balance between individual independence and interdependence (Bochner and Eisenberg 1987). The spouses must each contribute enough to develop a shared identity within the relationship, yet each must also have some sense of personal identity apart from the marriage. Much communication within the husband-wife relationship is devoted to exploring where this balance lies.

Some people have a greater need for independence than others, so it is not surprising that marital relationships can be characterized into different types.

Table 9.2
Fitzpatrick's Marital Types

Marital Type	Characteristic Features
Traditionals	These couples subscribe to traditional male-female role models. The wife is likely to take the husband's last name, and they are both guided by traditional values. They prefer stability to spontaneity, uncertainty, and change. The value of interdependence is emphasized over independence. They maintain a regular daily schedule. There is a lot of sharing, and when issues arise, they confront conflict rather than avoid it.
Independents	These couples are open to uncertainty and change. They reject rigid male-female sex roles and other traditional values. They feel that the relationship should not restrict either individual's freedom (high autonomy). Because they stress independence, they find it difficult to maintain a regular daily time schedule. They tend to deal with conflict, rather than avoid it.
Separates	Separates seem to hold a surprising mix of attitudes. Though they hold conventional views on family issues, they also stress the importance of individual freedom over interdependence. They avoid conflict and share little in common, though they do try to maintain a regular daily schedule with each other. They seem to stay together without a strong commitment to the relationship. There is less companionship and sharing in the marriage.
Separate-traditionals	This is a a "mixed couple" in which the husband and wife disagree about the type of marriage they have. Although about 40 percent of all couples fail to agree on a single marital type, the most common mix involves a wife who sees herself as a traditional and a husband who characterizes himself as a separate. This mix occurs far more frequently than any other combination, where the spouses' views of the marriage differ.

Source: M. A. Fitzpatrick and P. Best, "Dyadic Adjustment in Relational Types: Consensus, Cohesion, Affectional Expression, and Satisfaction in Enduring Relationships," *Communication Monographs* (1979), *46*(3), 167–178.

These category schemes of marital types attempt to capture not only differences in the need for independence, but also variations in other marital attitudes and overt communication behavior. Perhaps the most influential category system presently in the communication field comes out of Fitzpatrick's couple-oriented research. Fitzpatrick and her colleague (Fitzpatrick and Best 1979) looked at the

Table 9.3
Cuber and Harroff's Marital Types

Marital Type	Characteristic Features
Conflict-habituated	These couples are characterized by a high level of conflict interaction. Though there is a lot of bickering and nagging, the conflict is controlled; it does not escalate beyond a set level. A lot of tension is visible to the immediate family, but it is usually hidden from friends. This may be a brief phase that the couple is going through, or it might last the duration of the marriage.
Devitalized	Typically, this stage settles in after the deep love of earlier years fades. The couple moves from interdependence to more independence. Emotional distance begins to separate them as they share fewer common interests. Routine and the lack of better alternatives seem the only bonds that hold them together.
Passive-congenial	Much like the devitalized couple, except that the emotional indifference has always characterized these couples. This mode allows the couple to maintain a high degree of independence since there is little that holds the couple together.
Vital	They are very interdependent, sharing key interests and having these interests heightened by engaging in them together. Most activities are diminished if the spouse is not involved. Conflicts do occur, but unlike the conflict-habituated couple that argues over trivial matters and seeks to place blame, the vital couple deals with conflict honestly to resolve important issues.
Total	Much like the vital couple, except that the move from independence to interdependence is even more complete. The couple shares practically every interest. Conflicts are resolved swiftly with effort taken to reduce the possibility of having a winner and a loser.

Source: J. F. Cuber and P. B. Harroff, "Five Types of Marriage," in J. Henslin (Ed.), *Marriage and Family in a Changing Society,* 2nd ed. (New York: Free Press, 1985), pp. 289–297.

Current Research 9–7
Recent research by Segrin and Fitzpatrick found that pure couple types (both partners of the same type) displayed less distress than mixed couples, and that couples in the Traditionals type were distressed the least. This study also found the lowest level of depression in the Traditionals type couples and the highest levels of both depression and verbal aggressiveness among members of Separates type couples, as well as a strong link between depression and verbal aggressiveness across couple types. (Segrin, Chris and Fitzpatrick, Mary Anne, Depression and verbal aggressiveness in different marital types, *Communication Studies* 43, 2, 1992, 79–91)

attitudes and behaviors of couples in a variety of areas: their views on sharing and interdependence and on autonomy and independence; how closely they adopted "traditional" male-female family roles; their tolerance for uncertainty and change; and their willingness to deal with conflict, to name a few. From the couples' responses, Fitzpatrick was able to characterize four basic relational types: **independents**, **separates**, **traditionals**, and **separate/traditionals** (see Table 9.2). She did not label one marital type as better than another. However, it

Table 9.4
Changes in the Marital Life Cycle

Marital Stages	Features of the Stage
Courtship and early marriage	Both husband and wife begin distancing themselves from their families of origin and develop a commitment to each other. Friendship and extended family circles are realigned to include the new spouse. Couples who looked beyond conflict in the courtship phase find that these issues must now be resolved or they will bring the marriage to an abrupt end.
Family with young children	The couple must make room in the marriage for children, who will require enormous investments of time, energy, and social attention. Arrival of children may strengthen the bonds of the husband and wife to their extended families. The couple must adopt parenting roles and address issues of long-term importance (education, financial stability, change in career roles).
Family with adolescents	The parental roles must shift to deal with increasing independence in the children. Parents cannot expect to maintain complete authority in the household as adolescent children begin to assert their independence. Parents' concerns of career goals and directions, put on hold during the children's early years, are readdressed.
Family as launching center for children	Children leave for college, pursue careers, and get married. With no more dependents in the house, the husband and wife may feel a void. They may fill this void by turning to each other. However, many husbands and wives suddenly find that, in the absence of the children, the spouse has become something of a stranger. The couple may try to hold onto the last child in order to stall the inevitable change. The husband and wife may be losing their own parents to death, placing additional stress on their relationship.
Family in later life	Retirement leaves the couple with considerably more time together, which they may not be prepared for. They may renew shared interests or experience friction from being with each other close to twenty-four hours per day. The presence of grandchildren may soften adjustment difficulties. The greatest adjustment—the loss of a spouse—usually occurs in this stage, and may require the survivor to reorganize his or her entire life.

Source: M. McGoldrick and E. A. Carter, "The Stages of the Family Life Cycle," in J. Henslin (Ed.), *Marriage and Family in a Changing Society*, 2nd ed. (New York: Free Press, 1985), pp. 43–54.

is clear that the type of communication and family atmosphere would vary considerably from one family type to another.

Another marital category system, introduced by Cuber and Harroff (1985), also characterizes couples based on their marital attitudes and behavior (see

Families serve many functions, which include providing their members with affection, support and nurturing.

Table 9.3). Unlike Fitzpatrick's types, Cuber and Harroff place a heavier value judgment on their marital types. According to this category system, the "vital" and "total" couples are seen as better or more desirable than the other three types. Still, these categories give us some insight into how couples differ from one another.

Discussion Question 9–8
Which husband-wife role relationship do you think would provide the best parent-to-child relationships as well?

As you can imagine, husband-wife relationships can change over time. Age, responsibilities, other family interactions can all influence how husband and wife deal with one another. Numerous researchers have described family life cycles, which typically describe how the husband-wife relationship changes over time. Though the descriptions vary somewhat, most life cycles include the following five stages: courtship and early marriage; the family with young children; the family with adolescents; the family as a launching center for children; and the family in later life. Table 9.4 (based on McGoldrick and Carter 1985) lists some of the changes that are likely to occur over the duration of these life stages. Couples may reach these stages at different paces. Furthermore, if there are no children, the pattern can change considerably. Still, the life stage model helps us anticipate some of the more predictable changes in the marital relationship.

The Parent-Child Relationship

Traditionally, researchers interested in the parent-child relationship looked at how the communication efforts of parents affect their children. In this area, it was found that parents' messages either communicate a sense of **support** (which makes the child feel more comfortable with the parent) or **control** (which is designed to gain the child's compliance). Support messages include praising, approving, encouraging, displaying affection, and giving help. Control messages include threats of punishment, revoking privileges, lecturing on consequences of action, threatening the withdrawal of love, and generally showing disapproval of the child's behavior.

The use of these strategies has clear consequences. Supportive messages lead to increased self-esteem in the child, a higher level of conformity to parents' wishes, low levels of aggression, and low levels of antisocial behavior by the child. In contrast, the use of extreme controlling behavior (such as telling children when they can speak, or severely limiting their friendship networks) leads children to be more dependent on parents, so that they require parental approval to distinguish right from wrong. In addition, children don't learn to internalize moral standards, but distinguish right from wrong depending on whether a punishment is administered. Children also learn to use aggressive behavior themselves after receiving physical punishment (Fitzpatrick and Badzinski 1985).

Although most research stresses the effects of parents' messages on children, it is obvious that what children say has an impact on their parents. Unfortunately, most of the research in this area has focused on the infant and caretaker. Still, you can imagine how an infant "trains" its parents through crying, cooing, fussing, and other early communicative behavior.

The Sibling Relationship

Looking back on what determined their early development, most people agree that their siblings (brothers and sisters) had a significant impact. Siblings play many roles in the family. They allow us to practice new social skills on peers for the first time. The parent-child relationship is not a peer relationship; rather, it is based on an exquisite inequality whereby each participant gives the other something different. Among other things, the child gives the parent a sense of being needed. The parent nurtures the child and gives support. The parent is clearly dominant, which makes the relationship work.

In contrast to the parent-child relationship, the sibling relationship is more strongly rooted in equality. As a result, children can practice using social skills designed for peers, which would be less appropriate to use on parents. Siblings learn how to build friendships. They learn to address conflict with siblings, using strategies that are not designed to work with adults. After all, when confronted with a child's demand, parents can counter with a simple, "No, because I said so." This use of legitimacy as a source of power is less likely to occur when children deal with peers. Siblings may find that bargaining and trading are more successful strategies with each other than with a parent. Unfortun-

Discussion Question 9–9
Which kinds of parental messages are more common in your experience—support or control messages?

Current Research 9–8
Two recent pieces of research support the importance of supportive parental messages. Beatty and Dobos found a relationship between adult sons' perceptions of criticism and sarcastic messages from their father and their female partners' perceptions of disconfirming behavior. (Beatty, Michael J. and Dobos, Jean A., Direct and mediated effects of perceived father criticism and sarcasm on females' perceptions of relational partners' disconfirming behavior, *Communication Quarterly* 41, 2, 1993, pp. 187–197). In another study, the same authors report: " . . . these findings appear to suggest that fathers who are concerned about their sons' satisfaction with the relationship should probably focus on messages that illustrate supportive-interest; criticism and sarcasm should be avoided or reduced." (Beatty and Dobos, Relationship between sons' perceptions of fathers' messages and satisfaction in adult son-father relationships, *The Southern Communication Journal* 57, 4, 1992, p. 282)

ately, siblings may also find that aggression and violence help achieve short-term goals with younger or smaller siblings, although these strategies would fail outright with parents. A variety of social skills are tried and tested with siblings.

Siblings can also serve as role models and teachers to each other. If you have brothers or sisters, you may remember some examples of this. Perhaps your sister taught you how to play the drums. Or, you might have spent hours teaching your younger brother the finer points of sinking a free-throw. To a large degree, younger siblings learn by imitating their older brothers and sisters. The potential negative side of this pattern is that younger siblings pick up both correct and antisocial behaviors from older siblings. More than one child has picked up smoking or cussin' as a result of trying to be like an older brother or sister.

In addition to experimenting with various social skills and teaching each other assorted "life skills," siblings provide each other with a support system. Siblings find companionship, security, and a shared sense of family identity with each other, even at an early age. As Dunn (1992) points out, by the time the younger sibling turns four years old, he or she becomes both a more effective companion and antagonist.

Another point is that we use our siblings as a benchmark or point of comparison. We measure our own skills or accomplishments through comparison to siblings. It is not surprising that other people often use a sibling to predict the attitudes, behavior, or skills of a brother or sister. Thus, the social comparison value of siblings is widely used (and sometimes abused).

Teaching Objective 9–5
Characterize the boundaries and structure of husband-wife, parent-child, and sibling relationships within the family.

Rivalry and competition are a frequent part of the sibling relationship. Age and sex differences seem to have an effect on the likelihood of conflict. The older brother-younger sister combination has the greatest risk of conflict, whereas the older sister-younger brother relationship is likely to have the least amount of conflict (Fitzpatrick and Badzinski 1985). Though this type of behav-

Older brothers and sisters help to educate and socialize their younger siblings. As a result, children can practice their own parenting skills.

ior is characteristic of siblings in their early years, little attention has been paid to how sibling relationships evolve over time. It is difficult, them, to generalize about these relationships as siblings move through adulthood and later years.

Although it is not possible to discuss every type of family role relationship in a single chapter, we have overviewed the most common relationships in the traditional American nuclear family. However, we should at least mention other important family relationships. Step-relationships, for example, are increasingly prevalent as a result of the high divorce and remarriage rates. Step-relationships affect the overall dynamics of the family. The extended family is also an important feature of many households. Particularly among certain ethnic subcultures, grandparents, in-laws, uncles, and aunts may live with a couple and their children. In such cases, where there is often close and extended contact, these relationships can have a substantial impact on family functioning.

Sibling relationships, parent-child relationships, husband-wife relationships, and others differ somewhat in their demands, their functions, and in how power is exercised. Still, they remain the primary relationships in the family. The success of these relationships is often determined by how the participants use communication skills.

RELATIONAL SATISFACTION IN THE FAMILY

What exactly is a successful family and how can its success be measured? Should we count how many neighborhood children come to play in the yard? Perhaps we could add the number of children raised in the family who pursue profitable careers and subtract the number who end up in prison? Could we determine success by seeing how many of the family members talk to one another? Coming up with a measure of family success is about as difficult as defining what a family is in the first place. Typically, researchers have asked people how satisfied they are with their family relationships. Hence, individual perceptions of satisfaction are used as the primary measure of success.

Satisfaction in Marital Relationships

Most research in the area of family success has focused on satisfaction in the marital relationship. Even so, it is not easy to develop recommendations for what will lead to marital satisfaction. The problem is that it is hard to tell whether specific behavior, such as arguing, causes marital dissatisfaction or if dissatisfaction in the marriage causes people to argue. Still, there are some general trends that emerge.

Generally, happily married couples report that they communicate effectively with one another. This includes high levels of self-disclosure about thoughts and feelings, high levels of openness, frequent enjoyable communication exchanges, and a high level of accuracy in interpreting the nonverbal signals of the spouse. Apparently, the simple quantity of communication exchanges between spouses is not a good indicator of marital satisfaction. Exchanges that are supportive of the other do promote satisfaction, but if the

Current Research 9–9
Research by Canary, *et al.* found support for the hypothesis that, in arguments, "satisfied couples probably develop their ideas more and reciprocate refutations less than dissatisfied couples do." (Canary, Daniel, Weger, Harry, and Stafford, Laura, Couples' argument sequences and their associations' with relational characteristics, *Western Journal of Speech Communication* 55, 2, 1991, pp. 159–179)

couple's idea of more communication is simply more bickering and complaining, the satisfaction will not be enhanced.

All married couples have to deal with stress and occasional conflict. Couples who are satisfied report that they do not let conflicts escalate, and they do not let stress lead to personal attacks on each other. When they do engage in conflict, satisfied couples attempt to find mutually satisfactory resolutions. They do not each try to win personal goals at the expense of the other.

By contrast, dissatisfied couples typically engage in cross-complaining when conflict occurs. Cross-complaining involves an initial complaint by one person, and a countercomplaint by the other. Rather than deal with the issue behind the initial complaint, the second person broadens the conflict with a new complaint, in effect saying "Oh yeah, well, what about you?" This pattern can spiral, with the spouses continuing to contribute additional complaints. Instead of resolving the conflict issue, each tries to lay the blame on the other.

Perception is also an important part of marital satisfaction. All couples occasionally engage in negative or hurtful communication patterns. Typically, these patterns get mixed in with good or supportive patterns as well. Dissatisfied couples have a tendency to focus on and remember the negative patterns much more than satisfied couples do. They also tend to overanalyze the problems in the marriage. Generally, it is a good idea to monitor communication behavior to understand what is going well and what is not. Unfortunately, dissatisfied couples are more frequently looking for a problem. Not surprisingly, they are more likely to find problems as a result. Hence, the focus of attention or perception of the husband and wife is related to marital satisfaction.

Satisfaction in Family Relationships

Though there is less research in the area of family satisfaction than marital satisfaction, some broad trends appear. Members who report satisfaction with their family relationships come from families that are more spontaneous, less rigid in their rules, and more able to adapt to unexpected stressful events. Families with satisfied members work hard to enjoy each other's company.

Discussion Question 9–10
What qualities or characteristics would you say describe the best relationships in which you are involved?

Family structure can influence satisfaction. Members are more satisfied if there are conventional boundaries with a clear power structure. For example, allowing children to call parents by their first names or to make major decisions for the whole family may leave too much uncertainty about who wields power. Nobody would know who to turn to for a decision. Though some people can live with such uncertainty, most would find it difficult and unsatisfying. In addition, it is important to have a strong parental coalition. If Mom says one thing while Dad says another, it leaves the family in chaos. It wouldn't take much time for the children in such a household to learn to play one parent off the other. This would leave parents angry and children with no clear guidance.

As far as communication skills are concerned, Curran (1983) lists eight features of families who communicate well:

1. Parents are willing to demonstrate a close relationship.
2. Control of the TV is held by the parents.

3. Family members are willing to listen and respond to one another.
4. Members recognize the importance of nonverbal messages.
5. Individual feelings and independent thinking are valued in the family.
6. Family members don't try to attack each other at a personal level.
7. Interruptions occur in conversation, but not unequally.
8. Family disputes are reconciled, not left to escalate.

Though not an exhaustive list, it does give some useful suggestions for improving certain areas of family life.

Families are complex systems that can contain a wide variety of personality mixes. It is unlikely that any single list of communication suggestions could turn a dysfunctional family into one that is suddenly happy and trouble-free. However, the preceding discussion of relational satisfaction in the family gives you some initial areas to analyze. (See the Focus on Leadership box.)

Teaching Objective 9–6
Explore the qualities that typify marital and familial satisfaction in relationships.

FOCUS ON LEADERSHIP

Leadership in the Family—What Does It Mean?

When you think of leadership in the family, perhaps you conjure up some mythical vision of a strong father figure who "brings home the bacon," makes all the key decisions, and serves as the rock everyone else leans against in times of trouble. Maybe you think of a strong partnership between wife and husband that serves as the foundation for all family functioning. Let us propose a third alternative. In actuality, anyone can play a leadership role in the family. One or two persons need not accomplish all leadership roles. After all, leadership is any activity that helps the group (in this case, a family) achieve desired goals. In a family, such goals might include economic stability, family harmony, and mutual emotional support. You can play a leadership role as a spouse, parent, sibling, or child. In fact, rather than viewing the family leader as a person who dictates family actions, today's leader probably has to act more as a facilitator—a person who helps family members balance individual and shared family goals. With this view of a family leader, it should be easy to see that leadership is not the sole responsibility of a single family member.

Not only is the central father figure as sole family leader a myth from the past, but it may also be necessary to develop a contemporary characterization, or "prototype," of the family itself. Prototypes are typical examples of a class of items. For example, you may hold a prototype of a dog. Prototypes are useful because they set a standard against which you can compare all other items in that class. If your prototype of a dog is the German shepherd you had as a child, then your evaluation of a toy poodle would likely be different than someone's whose prototypical dog is a chihuahua.

Recently, Vangelisti (1993) suggested that we may be holding onto an unrealistic prototype of the family. The "traditional" American nuclear family may be viewed as a father, who works outside the home; a mother, who serves as the caretaker at home; and two children. However, this characterization accurately represents fewer than 5 percent of American families (Gilbert 1988). As Vangelisti (1993) points out, it is possible that "prototypes of family relationships have not 'caught up' with the changing structure of today's family. Since family associations are involuntary and difficult to dissolve or replace, members may be particularly disappointed when expected features are absent" (p. 46).

As a family leader, you need to maintain realistic expectations for such things as family interaction. Contemporary families, with step-relations and long-distance parents, may not live up to expectations based on "Father Knows Best" or "The Cosby Show" family prototypes (if, in fact, these prototypes were ever realistic). Perhaps you have a half-brother with whom you share no closeness. Or you may have a step-parent you have known for three years, with whom you are still negotiating relationship expectations. It may be difficult, if not impossible, to achieve the expectations of your prototype if it is rigidly based on the model of the traditional family. It may be necessary to maintain some flexibility in your prototype. To play a leadership role in the family, you have to maintain realistic expectations of what is possible given the changing structure of the American family.

▣ Summary

Contemporary families face many difficulties, but in many ways this has always been the case. The family is a complex system that must be able to adapt to change. It cannot simply go back to some magical formula for success. The difficulty in defining what a family is provides some evidence for the complexity of families today. We suggest maintaining a broad definition, stressing social and commitment bonds, in addition to biological and legal ties.

The family is important because of the functions it serves. Families provide affection and support, nurture and socialize children, and maintain economic stability. While trying to serve these functions, the family must adapt to dynamic changes occurring within and outside of the family unit. Families have to make key decisions, deal with power distribution and use, and adapt to the maturation of its members.

The primary relationships in the family include husband-wife, parent-child, and sibling bonds. These relationships differ in how power is distributed, and in the use of communication to achieve relational goals.

In the end, there is no magic formula for success in family interaction. However, we mentioned some of the behaviors that are commonly linked to satisfaction in family relationships.

1. As you can tell from this chapter, defining family boundaries is not easy. In fact, it may be a task similar to defining different levels of friendship. How would you define the boundaries of your family? Are there different senses of family? For instance, is there an immediate family, an extended family, and an "any blood relative" family? What do you use to distinguish your different levels of family? Compare your answers to those of other members of the class.

2. In this chapter, we mentioned several functions of families. What additional functions do you think should be served by the family unit? What happens when a family cannot serve the functions listed in the chapter or the functions you generated? For instance, what if the family is suddenly homeless, or if a trauma to one member prevents the family from adequately providing affection and support to the other members?

3. Families go through life cycles. Key events often signal, or push, a family to move from one phase to another. The result may be a shift in how power is exercised, or in the nature of the rights and responsibilities of the family members. What were some of the key events in the life cycle of your family? These may be events that signal the movement of a child into adult status (for example, the parents don't say anything when Junior wants a glass of wine with dinner), or a change in family roles (for example, Mom takes a job, so the kids must pick up more household responsibilities). Write a short essay identifying the events and discussing how they changed your family.

4. We can often gain insight into the workings of our own family by comparing and contrasting it to others' families. One way to do this is to compare the workings of your family with those of a TV family. Choose two TV families—one that is similar to your own family and another that is different. List the similarities and differences, paying particular attention to the concepts raised in this chapter.

Exercises

Related Readings

Beer, W. R. (1989). *Strangers in the house: The world of stepsiblings and half-siblings.* New Brunswick, NJ: Transaction.

As a result of divorce and remarriage, many people have lived with stepsiblings and half-siblings. There are numerous social consequences to this situation. People are expected to develop instant family ties, share a house, share possessions, and share parental affection with little or no family history. Beer's book details the complexities of step-relationships through a comfortable blend of interviews and family research.

Dunn, J., and Kendrick, C. (1982). *Siblings: Love, envy, and understanding.* Cambridge, MA: Harvard University Press.

This book looks at the developmental changes that occur in children when a new child is brought into the family. It traces initial interactions between children and infant siblings as well as later interaction patterns. Included is a chapter on communication between siblings.

Fitzpatrick, M. A. (1988). *Between husbands and wives.* Newbury Park, CA: Sage.

In this book, Fitzpatrick expands her discussion of marital types overviewed in this chapter. She describes the types in greater depth and discusses their effects on marital interaction and marital satisfaction. One of her most interesting findings is that about 40 percent of couples fail to agree on the type of marital relationship they have.

Noller, P. (1984). *Nonverbal communication and marital interaction.* Oxford: Pergamon.

This is an interesting book that pulls together much of the search on nonverbal communication in the marital context. It is based on research, as opposed to anecdotes or case studies. As a result, it is complex and technical at points. However, it addresses some critical questions: (1) How do men and women use nonverbal communication differently in the marital context? (2) How do married couples use gaze behavior? and (3) How accurate are married couples in interpreting each other's nonverbal messages?

Interviewing

Chapter objectives

After reading this chapter you should be able to:

1. distinguish between the directive and the nondirective interview and understand the roles of both interviewer and interviewee in each

2. identify the various types of interviews and their purposes

3. identify the different kinds of questions used in interviews and describe their functions

4. understand the process of conducting an information-gathering interview

5. describe the steps involved in preparing for and performing in an employment interview

Key terms and concepts

interview
directive interview
nondirective interview
employment (job-entry)
    interview
promotion interview
exit interview
performance appraisal
    interview
grievance interview
information-gathering
    interview
primary question
secondary question
probe question
mirror question
closed question
open question
bipolar question
leading question
neutral question
loaded question

How can my hands be so wet and my mouth so dry? This is just great. When the employment director greets me, I'll grab her hand with my slimy paw and try to force a hello through these parched lips. Wonderful. Why is my leg shaking like that? I didn't have that much coffee this morning. Oh, no, I couldn't be that nervous. There has to be a better way to get a job. This is awful, and the interview hasn't even started yet. What if she asks a question I don't know the answer to? Worse yet, what if she asks a question, and I have no idea what she's getting at? Oh, there goes my leg again. This is just awful.

Hopefully, any interviews you've had or will engage in will begin more smoothly than this. Anxiety and poor performance in the interview context can be traced to a lack of knowledge or misunderstanding regarding the roles of the participants and how to communicate effectively in this situation. In this chapter, we provide you with the information necessary to feel confident and in control in an interview. We describe the distinctive features of the interviewing context, define the roles of the participants, explain the various types of interviews, and cover the use of questions in interviews. In addition, we provide some tips on how to conduct an information-gathering interview, and how to present yourself effectively in an employment interview situation.

THE NATURE OF THE INTERVIEW PROCESS

Defining the Interview

The interview is a unique communication context. Although it is similar to several other contexts, it has its own distinctive features. Stewart and Cash (1978, p. 5) define the **interview** as "a process of dyadic communication with a predetermined and serious purpose designed to interchange behavior and involving the asking and answering of questions."

The interview is "dyadic" in that it involves two parties. Although this could mean more than two people (for example, a panel of three employment officers interviewing a single job candidate), the roles typically break down into two parties or roles (for example, prospective employer and prospective employee). It is common to refer to the person (or persons) conducting the interview and asking most of the questions as the *interviewer*. The person responding to the questions is called the *interviewee*.

One of the unique features of the interview is that it involves a predetermined and serious purpose. At times an interview may resemble an interpersonal conversation. One difference between them is the relative openness of the topic choice. When conversations are joined between friends, practically any topic is open for discussion, and the topic may change quickly, with little connection to what has gone before. In an interview, a specified topic usually brings the participants together. In a journalistic interview, that topic may be a

Leadership Note 10–1
Apprehension in a communication situation such as the interview can do more than just make us uncomfortable. Joe Ayres found that men with a high degree of communication apprehension "perceived their interaction partners to be less trustworthy, less physically attractive, and less satisfying to interact with than did" men with lower levels of communication apprehension. (Ayres, Joe. The impact of communication apprehension and interaction structure on initial interactions. *Communication Monographs*, 56, 1, 1989, p. 85.) This finding, generalized to the interview situation, is a strong argument for the importance of interviewer comfort with the interview process in order to make accurate judgments about interviewees.

Discussion Question 10–1
What kinds of interviews have you been involved in thus far? What was hard about them? What was surprising or unexpected?

Teaching Objective 10–1
Define the unique nature of interviews as involving two parties, with a predetermined and serious purpose and involving the asking and answering of questions.

pressing issue of the day. The participants in a counseling interview are brought together by an emotional, relational, or social need of the interviewee. In an employment interview, the fit of a candidate to a job opening (and vice versa) brings them together. The participants in an interview are not brought together in order to socialize and bond (regardless of whether that occurs as a consequence of their interaction). They have a purpose in mind, and questions that digress from that predetermined purpose are often seen as inappropriate.

Also characteristic of the interview is the dominant use of a question and answer format. If you listen to communication in other contexts, such as interpersonal communication, small-group decision making, and even public speaking, you will notice that questions and answers occur with some frequency. However, their use in these other contexts is overshadowed by their prevalence in the interview context. Questions and answers are the basic components of interviews. As you will see, understanding the structure and consequences of questions is very important for conducting an effective interview—a topic we discuss shortly.

Roles of Interviewer and Interviewee

The roles or expected behavior of the interviewer and interviewee will vary depending on how the interview is conducted. The interviewer is allowed to determine how much control he or she wants to exert over the pace of the interview, the topics covered, and what constitutes an acceptable answer from the interviewee. In a **directive interview**, the interviewer exerts strong control. At the other end of the continuum is the **nondirective interview**, in which the interviewer surrenders control to the interviewee—in essence, the interviewee is allowed to "run with the ball."

Ted Koppel, the moderator of the TV program "Nightline," and Mike Wallace, of TV's "60 Minutes," provide good examples of the directive style. Their questions are carefully framed. They interrupt an interviewee who digresses too far, and point it out when an interviewee fails to answer a question adequately. Talk-show hosts, such as David Letterman and Arsenio Hall, use a more nondirective interviewing style. Their questions introduce a broad topic area and encourage the "guest" to take the topic in any direction he or she may desire. The host may ask, "So, did you have a good flight in?"—knowing that the guest will launch into a story of airport horror. Figure 10.1 represents the continuum of interviewer control.

Teaching Objective 10–2
Describe the roles and purposes of the interviewer and interviewee.

Current Research 10–1
Skopec delineates the roles of interviewer and interviewee in this way: The interviewer is seen as primarily "proactive," or initiating, while the interviewee's role is characterized as "reactive," or responding to the interviewer's initiatives. (Skopec, Eric William. *Situational Interviewing* Prospect Heights, Ill.: Waveland Press, 1986, pp. 20–22.)

Discussion Question 10–2
Who do you think is the best of the TV news or talk show interviewers? Why? How does he or she relate to the interviewees? What kinds of questions does she or he ask?

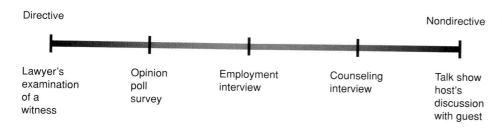

Figure 10.1
A Continuum of Interviewer Control.

In a directive interview, the interviewer's role is to maintain control, primarily by redirecting the interviewee if his or her answer is off track, and by encouraging the interviewee to provide more detail if the answer is insufficient. In order to keep the interviewee on track, the interviewer may have to interrupt, rephrase the question, or put the question in a different context. In order to stimulate the interviewee to provide more detail, the interviewer may try to paraphrase the answer, use probing encouragers (for example, "uh huh," "I see," "go on"), or utilize subtle nonverbal cues (for example, head nodding, leaning forward). Although the interviewer may need to control other features of the interview, acquiring sufficient detail and avoiding excessive digression are the main skills that need to be mastered.

The role of the interviewee in the directive interview can vary considerably, depending on whether the interviewer and the interviewee have similar goals in mind. In a job interview, both the prospective employer and employee are trying to match a person to a job. If not identical, their goals certainly overlap. In such a case, the role of the interviewee is to cooperatively answer the questions in a complete and honest (if somewhat polished) manner. On the other hand, when a reporter is grilling a politician about his or her recent vote on legislation, the goals of the two may be quite divergent. The reporter may be trying to uncover inconsistencies between the politician's campaign promises and voting record. The politician, however, may be trying to minimize or hide any such inconsistencies. In such a case, it would be difficult to argue that it is in the interviewee's best interest to provide complete and open answers to all the reporter's questions, particularly since the reporter can edit the answers to suit his or her own interests. Maddening though it might be, it is not surprising that politicians do not provide direct, unambiguous answers to reporters' questions.

In a nondirective interview, the interviewer's role is to introduce broad topics for discussion, and then follow up by prompting the answers in promising or interesting directions. For the most part, the control is surrendered to the interviewee. The role of the interviewee in the nondirective interview is to provide sufficient information and detail to carry the interview.

Regardless of whether it is a directive or nondirective interview, the interviewee is expected to talk more than the interviewer. The amount will vary depending on the type of interview, but it has been suggested that the interviewer should talk 30 percent of the time, while the interviewee talks for the remaining 70 percent (Stewart and Cash 1978). It is interesting to note that this holds true even in the directive interview, where the interviewer is expected to maintain control. This clearly indicates that control can be exerted through what is said rather than by how much is said.

Types of Interviews

Teaching Objective 10–3
Explain the varieties and diverse purposes of interviews.

When someone mentions the term *interview*, it is likely that the first notion that comes to mind is the typical job interview. That certainly is an important variety, though there are many other types as well. The following is a classification of some of the most common types of interviews.

Leadership Note 10–2
The 1988 pre-election interview of George Bush by Dan Rather, conducted live at Bush's request, offers a rich example of how two strong personalities can have conflicting goals in an interview situation. Rather was seeking to connect Bush to the Iran-Contra scandal; Bush sought to demonstrate that he was not the "wimp" candidate he was perceived to be. Both men used the interview to force their own agendas without accommodation or surrender to the goals of the other.

Job-Related Interviews. There are a number of different interviews used in the workplace. No doubt, the **employment (job-entry) interview** is most widely recognized. These are used to screen prospective employees for job openings, as well as to present the company in a good light to the job applicant. The **promotion interview** is quite similar. It is used to screen applicants within an organization for promotion. A number of organizations also conduct **exit interviews**. When taken seriously, the exit interview can provide the organization with useful feedback, particularly concerning the concerns or difficulties that prompted the employee to leave. When not taken seriously, the exit interview is merely a public relations tool used to keep the departing employee from leaving with a negative impression of the organization.

The **performance appraisal interview** is another type that is commonly used in the workplace. This is used to provide the employee with feedback regarding his or her work in the organization. It helps both the employer and employee to measure success and develop some expectations regarding career paths and promotions. When the action of the employer or organization is evaluated or called into question by the employee, the result is a **grievance interview**. Here the employee levels complaints to the proper authorities in the organization in hopes of having the grievance settled. As you can see, interviews serve a number of important functions in the workplace.

Information-Gathering Interviews. Some interviews can be characterized by the purpose they serve rather than by the setting in which they occur. This is the case with **information-gathering interviews**. Their purpose is to collect information that will later be compiled and distributed to others in the form of reports, stories, research papers, or even speeches.

Current Research 10–2
The employment or selection interview is one of many means of choosing candidates for jobs and is frequently one of several stages in a business's selection process. Nonetheless, it is estimated that 99 percent of all companies use the interview for selection of employees for an estimated 250 million employment interviews nationwide, annually, in the United States. (Stano, M. E., and Reinsch, N.F. [1982]. *Communication in Interviews* [pp. 120–121]. Englewood Cliffs, N.J.: Prentice-Hall.)

Discussion Question 10–3
Which of the various job-related interviews are or have been used at your places of work? How effective are they? What do interviewers and interviewees stand to gain from each of these forms of interview?

The job interview is used to screen prospective employees and present the company in a positive light to the applicant.

A characteristic example of this is the *journalistic,* or *investigative, interview.* Both print and electronic journalism rely on interviews to build news stories. These may include interviews from recognized experts, or "people-in-the-street" interviews that gauge public sentiment. A police detective may also use this type of interview to gain an accurate picture of events.

Surveys and *opinion polls* are also forms of the information-gathering interview. These interviews are typically highly structured and provide a limited range of answers for the interviewee to choose from. The advantage of these types of interviews is that they allow the people collecting the information to make broad generalizations and predictions regarding people's preferences. They are also relatively easy to conduct, since the interviewers require only limited training. Their drawbacks include a limited response range, which might not include the respondent's actual feeling, and a lack of flexibility to explore interesting details in depth.

Social scientists, such as psychologists, sociologists, anthropologists, and communication scholars, may also use interviews to answer the research questions they pose. Such *research interviews* help researchers to explore the motives and behavior of people.

Students may also use information-gathering interviews to gather information for papers, reports, and speeches. Interviews have many advantages over other information-gathering techniques, such as library research. For instance, interview information is relatively accessible and quickly obtained—particularly on a college campus, where there are experts on a wide number of subjects. Interviews can also provide more up-to-date information than that obtained by other methods. Finally, the person interviewed can often direct you to other sources of information, substantially reducing your library search. Chapter 14

Cross-reference 10–1
A discussion of and guide to information-gathering interviews is provided in Chapter 14. Surveys are also briefly discussed in Chapter 13.

People conduct information-gathering interviews for a variety of purposes, including to write reports or journalistic accounts, to conduct surveys and opinion polls, and to gather information for speeches.

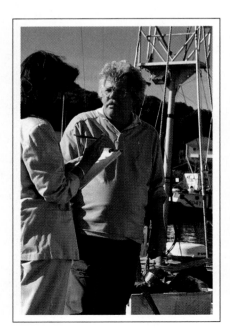

("Discovering Speech Material and Speech Confidence") describes the process of library research and provides hints on conducting interviews for speech material.

Helping Interviews.   Interviews are also used in clinical, therapeutic, and social service settings. The process of interviewing can be used as a form of therapy, as is the case with *counseling interviews*. A psychologist or therapist may use questions to get a client to deal with personal problems more effectively. Interviews may also be used to screen applicants for help in social service agencies, or to direct them to the proper authority. Hence, *social work interviews* are yet another use of the interview format.

Interviews serve a wide variety of functions and are utilized in diverse settings. Clearly, they are important, but how difficult are they to conduct and respond to? One of the keys to success is a good working knowledge of the types of questions that can be used and the effects that they have.

Questions in the Interview

Questions are the primary means of directing the interview. The form and wording of the question can have a significant impact on the response from the interviewee. As a result, it is important to understand questions and their impact. Among other things, questions differ in the degree to which they introduce a new topic area, in the constraints or limits they place on possible answers, and the degree to which they tell the interviewee that a particular response is expected (Stewart and Cash 1978). Table 10.1 summarizes the basic types of questions.

Primary Versus Secondary Questions.   A question that introduces a new topic area is known as a **primary question**. By contrast, a **secondary question** follows up on a primary question to get more elaboration or further detail from the interviewee. This probably makes intuitive sense, but let's see what happens if we put it to the test. Of the following, which are primary and which are secondary questions?

1. Could you tell me about your last job?
2. Why would you say that?
3. Can you think of any other reasons?
4. Can you perform in a job where you are required to work nights?
5. Are you saying that you would enjoy starting in sales?
6. In your last job were you able to utilize your best talents?

If you had any trouble distinguishing the primary from the secondary questions, use this guide: The primary questions would make sense if a stranger stopped you on the street and asked them. It might seem odd that a stranger would ask them, but they would still make sense. Secondary questions would seem odd and out of place if posed without prior interaction, as though you had stepped in on an ongoing conversation. Looking back, you can now see that questions 1, 4, and 6 are primary questions, whereas questions 2, 3, and 5 are secondary questions.

Current Research 10–3
Whereas job-related and information-gathering interviews are of necessity usually directive in order for the interviewer to obtain the information needed, counseling interviews are by their nature usually client-centered and nondirective, initiated by the interviewee and exploring issues and questions introduced by the interviewee. (Donaghy, William C. *The Interview: Skills and Applications.* Salem, Wisc.: Sheffield Publishing, 1990, pp. 286–287.)

Discussion Question 10–4
What would you say are the major differences between job-related, information-gathering, and helping interviews? Would different interviewer skills be required? Would there be differences in interviewer-interviewee relationships? Which type of interviewing do you think would be the most difficult? Why?

Teaching Objective 10–4
Illustrate the differences between primary vs. secondary, open vs. closed, and leading vs. neutral questions.

Table 10.1
Types of Interview Questions

Question Types	Definitions
PRIMARY	A question that introduces a new topic area
SECONDARY	A question that follows up on a previous primary or secondary question
Subtypes:	
Probe	A secondary question that uses a word or brief phrase to encourage the respondent to continue discussing the same issue
Mirror	A secondary question that rephrases the interviewee's response to check for the accuracy of interpretation and to encourage the interviewee to continue
OPEN	A question that leaves the interviewee a wide latitude in deciding how to respond
CLOSED	A question that limits or restricts the range of possible appropriate answers
Subtype:	
Bipolar	A closed question that calls for a "yes-no," "true-false," or "agree-disagree" type of response; acceptable answers are limited to one of two opposites
NEUTRAL	A question that gives the respondent no indication that there is a preferred answer
LEADING	A question that suggests that there is a preferred or more acceptable response
Subtype:	
Loaded	A strongly leading question that uses entrapment, inflammatory language, or polar extremes to indicate the preferred response

The effective interviewer should have a well-prepared set of primary questions as he or she enters the interview. In addition, the interviewer should have a repertoire of secondary questions that can be used when the response to any primary question is incomplete or inappropriate. The interviewee's response may not provide sufficient information, it may not be clear, or it may not address the question that is asked. Another possibility is that the answer may raise an interesting side issue that is worth pursuing. As a result, the interviewer needs to have secondary questions to follow up. Consider the following example:

MASTERING COMMUNICATION SKILLS

Building Your Secondary Question Repertoire

Inexperienced interviewers often fail to follow up on primary questions to gain a more complete and focused answer. Part of this is due to nervousness—trying to think ahead to the next primary question. This problem also occurs because the inexperienced interviewer does not have a wide repertoire of secondary questions to fall back on. Try to build your own repertoire by coming up with an appropriate follow-up question to the following question-response sequences.

Q: How often were you absent at your last place of employment?

R: Not too often.

Q: _____.

Q: Do you enjoy sports?

R: Yes.

Q: _____.

Q: Tell me what you think about the education you received here at the university.

R: It's been okay.

Q: _____.

Q: Who would you rate as the three most important vice presidents this country has had in the past century?

R: Oh, I don't know.

Q: _____.

Q: What kind of car do you own?

R: A Schwinn.

Q: _____.

Q: Do you have any experience with computers?

R: I think we are definitely in the computer age today. Computers are important in the everyday operation of a business, and they will continue to be crucial for some time to come.

Q: _____.

Q: What is your current occupation?

R: I'm a G-7 at the steamer floor, pulling weights and driving a trolly digger.

Q: _____.

Q: Tell me about your last job.

R: I didn't like it very much.

If the interviewer jumped to the next primary question after every brief response like the one above, he or she wouldn't find out much about the interviewee. It would also be a very short interview. Obviously, the interviewer should follow up with a secondary question about why the interviewee didn't like his or her last job. (For some practice developing secondary questions, read the Mastering Communication Skills box and try the exercise.)

Two special types of secondary questions are worth noting—the *probe* and the *mirror* question. The **probe question** is a brief word or phrase that encourages the interviewee to continue the response in the same general direction. A simple "go on," "what else?" "I see," or "uh huh" can prompt the interviewee to continue talking. The interviewer uses a **mirror question** by restating the interviewee's answer or response to the preceding question. "So you're saying that you couldn't work on weekends, is that right?" is an example of a mirror question. It allows the interviewer to check the correctness of his or her interpretation, and it encourages the interviewee to clarify or elaborate on the answer.

Open Versus Closed Questions.   Questions can vary in the degree to which they limit the response options. "Do you support the president's performance in office so far, yes or no?" is quite different from "Tell me what you think of the president's performance in office so far." The first example limits your response options, and is therefore a **closed question.** The second is a relatively **open question** because it allows you to answer the question any way you prefer.

It is useful to think of questions as varying in their degree of openness. Questions are not simply open or closed, but can span a continuum of openness. Figure 10.2 demonstrates this point.

At the far end of continuum are highly closed questions. **Bipolar questions** are a special type of closed question that restrict the respondent to selecting one of two choices. "Either-or," "yes-no," and "agree-disagree" questions are typical examples of bipolar questions.

Both open and closed questions are quite useful, but they allow the interviewer to acquire different types of information. Closed questions are typically easier to respond to and take less time than open questions. It is easier to com-

Current Research 10–4
Hanna and Wilson provide these guidelines for when to use open and closed questions: Use open questions at the start of an interview to relax the interviewee, to learn the interviewee's priorities, to evaluate communication skills and knowledge, to determine values and feelings and to open new areas of questioning. Use closed questions to control both questions and answers, to obtain specific answers, and when time is short, for ease of coding and analysis of answers, when the interviewee's values and feelings are not important and/or when the interviewer is unskilled. (Hanna, Michael S., and Wilson, Gerald L. (*Communicating in Business and Professional Settings.* New York: McGraw-Hill, 1991, pp. 230–233.)

Figure 10.2
A Continuum of Question Openness.

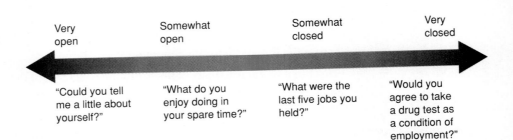

Very open

Somewhat open

Somewhat closed

Very closed

"Could you tell me a little about yourself?"

"What do you enjoy doing in your spare time?"

"What were the last five jobs you held?"

"Would you agree to take a drug test as a condition of employment?"

pare different people's responses to closed questions. This is one reason why opinion polls and questionnaire surveys use closed questions that provide respondents with a range of answers to choose from.

Open questions have several advantages. For instance, they allow an interviewee to elaborate on and explain an answer. The interviewee can also show how strongly she feels about a question or issue, whereas a closed question does not necessarily allow this. Although open questions may take substantially more time than closed questions, they can help uncover interesting insights that the interviewee might have. A closed question can never uncover more than is asked because it restricts the response possibilities. An open question allows the interviewee to display creativity and unique point of view. Consider the example of an employment interviewer who asks a job candidate, "Do you see yourself as more like Lee Iacocca or Leonardo da Vinci?" This closed question may help the interviewer determine whether the candidate is a hard-working pragmatist or a freethinking conceptualist. This might be useful to know, but the answer may tell you less about how the candidate sees herself and what is important to her. An alternative, open-ended phrasing—such as "What person do you emulate most and why?"—would allow the interviewee to answer in a way that is important to her. The closed version may be faster and get at specific information that the interviewer wants. The open version allows the interviewee to respond in a way that reflects what is important to her.

In order to conduct an effective interview, it is necessary to consider the type of questions you are using. As Lahiff (1977, p. 397) explains, "Lack of adequate planning of questions by the interviewer is one of the most frequent causes of inferior interviews." The biggest problem that unskilled interviewers have is using one type of question when they are after the opposite type of information. For example, an interviewer may not understand why he can't get anyone to provide complete detailed answers to his questions. All the respondents are saying is yes and no, with little elaboration. He may fail to realize that he has been asking closed questions, to which these short responses are quite appropriate. Another interviewer may not understand why it takes her so long to conduct an interview. It could be that she is using a series of open questions that require detailed answers, and therefore take more time. An interviewer has to learn how to select the correct tool for the job.

Neutral Versus Leading Questions.   "You'd rather go to the movie tonight than that dumb old party, wouldn't you?" It's clear how the person asking wants you to answer this question. When a question hints at how you are expected to answer, it is known as a **leading question**. Questions that give no such indication of the desired response are called **neutral questions**. The question above could be made neutral by rephrasing it: "Would you prefer to go to the movie or to the party tonight?" Just as questions vary in their "open-closed" nature, they can also vary in the degree to which they are neutral or leading (see Figure 10.3).

When a question is strongly leading it is known as a **loaded question**. A question can be loaded because it (1) includes presumptions that have not been proven, (2) uses inflammatory language, or (3) forces the respondent to choose

Discussion Question 10–5
As an interviewee, would you have different emotional responses to open versus closed questions? Would you be likely to have different responses to the interview and interviewer if questions were more often open or more often closed? How would you tend to feel about leading or loaded questions?

Figure 10.3
Relative Neutrality in
Question Wording.

Neutral

Leading

"Political campaign
rhetoric can vary from
issue-oriented debating
to mudslinging and
character bashing. How
would you rate the campaign
rhetoric of the last presidential
campaign?"

"Do you feel that
there was a lot of
mudslinging and
name-calling in the
last presidential
campaign?"

"Wouldn't you agree
that the last presidential
campaign was the
dirtiest exhibition of
mudslinging and
character bashing ever
to be forced upon the
voting public?"

between opposite extremes. For example, if your instructor were to confront you, saying, "Are you still getting your boyfriend (or girlfriend) to write your speeches for you?" the form of the question presumes that he or she had been writing your speeches in the past. Unless this had been proven at some earlier time, it would be an unfounded presumption. "What do you think about these so-called authors who glorify the worst depravities known to humankind in their twisted attempts to create literature?" would be an example of using inflammatory language ("so-called authors," "worst depravities known to humankind") to strongly bias the question. A question can also be leading because it forces the respondent to select between opposite extremes (neither of which would be the preferred choice): "Are you a true Christian or a godless, heathen Communist?" Such questions ignore anything in between, as well as the possibility that any alternatives fall outside these extremes.

Since leading questions are likely to be answered with biased responses (Kahn and Cannell 1983), it is generally recommended that they be used only by experienced interviewers. Others should try to phrase their questions to be more neutral. A seasoned reporter may ask a politician, "Since the polls indicate that a majority of voters support some form of restriction on handgun sales, how do you intend to vote on the upcoming handgun legislation?" in order to find out whether the politician is willing to express a conviction that goes against the form of the question. It is not surprising, however, that such questions can annoy the person being asked. Since that is part of a reporter's job, it is expected, but such questions should not be used by inexperienced interviewers trying to gain information from cooperating interviewees. As an interviewer, you should word your questions to be neutral in tone. As a potential interviewee, you should be aware of how a question can lead you to a specific answer. Be vigilant in an interview situation. If the interviewer asks you a leading or loaded question, don't be afraid to resist the pull of the question. If necessary, you can always rephrase the question to suit an answer you would prefer to give.

Remember that questions are the basic tools of interviewing. Recognize how these tools work and the effect they have on the interview as a whole.

CONDUCTING AN INFORMATION-GATHERING INTERVIEW

You should understand the interview process from the perspective of both the interviewer and interviewee. You should know how to ask questions and conduct an interview, and should also be able to respond to the questions of an interviewer competently. Understanding both roles will make you more effective when you are in either of them. We begin by explaining how to conduct an information-gathering interview. Some of this material will be expanded on in Chapter 14 ("Discovering Speech Material and Speech Confidence"). Here, we discuss how to prepare your questions and the process of conducting an interview. The Focus on Leadership box provides some specific examples.

FOCUS ON LEADERSHIP

Structuring Questions to Gain Accurate Information

We've noted in previous chapters that leaders need accurate information to make decisions. One way to gain key information is to talk to people—in essence, to conduct information-gathering interviews. In conducting these interviews, it's important to remember that your decision-making ability as a leader will be severely hindered if the people you question only give you information that they think you want to hear. Therefore, you must have access to both favorable and unfavorable information. You can ensure a proper flow of accurate information, in part, by establishing trusting relationships with your subordinates. They have to feel safe to be the bearers of unfavorable news. In addition, you also must be cautious about how you phrase the request for information. The wording of the question can have a significant impact on the answer you receive.

This caution is necessary because of a consistent bias that occurs in the asking of questions. We have a tendency to ask questions in a way that is biased toward confirming our expectations (Snyder and Swan 1978; Snyder 1981). We unwittingly use leading questions that predispose the interviewer to support our existing beliefs. For example, if you wanted to find out whether a person is an extrovert, you might ask, "Do you ever find yourself to be the center of attention in a social gathering?" You may expect that an extrovert will answer yes. Unfortunately, this question does not distinguish introverts from extroverts very well since most people find themselves to be the center of attention occasionally. Your question is worded in a way to confirm your initial suspicions, not to gain accurate information.

This problem is confounded by an unspoken conversational norm, which is the general tendency toward agreement in conversation. We all feel a subtle pressure to confirm what was previously said or asked, unless we disagree fairly strongly. Hence, if you ask, "Are you ever the center of attention?" the respondent will probably say yes, unless he or she is *never* the center of attention. The problem is that you get the answer you expect, regardless of whether the answer is accurate or not. This tendency is even more pronounced in a superior-subordinate relationship (such as leader and follower) in which there are political and social pressures for the subordinate to agree with and support the superior.

You can avoid this problem by being more conscious of how you word your questions. Consider this rewording of the simple question used above: "When compared to other people you know, would you say that you are frequently or infrequently the center of attention at social situations?" This wording does not allow the respondent a simple agreement response. Thus there can be no pressure toward agreement. Obviously, this wording is a bit more complex, and it requires more time to ask and answer this question. However, in cases where accuracy of information is critical and you need to question people to gain that information, it is worth the effort to phrase your questions in a manner that does not automatically confirm your existing beliefs.

Steps Prior to the Interview

Teaching Objective 10–5
Emphasize the importance of interviewer preparation to the successful conduct of an interview.

Though experienced interviewers can make the process look easy, conducting an information-gathering interview involves more than simply carrying on a conversation with another person. One difference is the need to prepare for the interview. In particular, you need to set goals for the interview, and develop a set of primary questions that will help you accomplish those goals.

Developing Goals for the Interview.   Develop goals for the interview by considering the advantages that interviews have over other forms of research, and by considering what information the particular person you are interviewing may possess. Recall that interviews can provide you with up-to-date information. An interview is also a good way to get information with a local focus (as opposed to a national or global scope), and it can provide you with an insider's point of view on a topic. Ask yourself whether the person you select to interview can provide you with the type of information you are interested in. If not, the interview may be a waste of time.

Discussion Question 10–6
Who is the one person you would most like to interview? Why? What would you want to ask? What would you want to know?

Imagine that you are interested in writing a paper or presenting a speech on the nature of crime on college campuses. You would certainly want to get information on national trends from library research. You might gain additional insight into the problem by talking to a local expert on campus crime. Consider the possible candidates. You could talk to members of the sociology department or criminal justice department in hopes that someone would be an expert on campus crime. However, they would likely be more aware of national trends than the local problem. If you have a campus police department, you could interview someone from there. You would probably want information on the general trends of crime on campus (for example, has it increased or decreased?), which types of crimes have changed in frequency, why those changes have occurred, and what the campus police have attempted to do about the changes. Clearly, you would be interested in someone who has access to the figures and could answer policy questions. For that reason, you might want to talk to the head of the department or an assistant. A patrol officer may not be able to answer your questions.

Once you have selected an individual and arranged to conduct a short interview, consider again what information that person would have access to. He or she is more likely to have information on local trends and policy than on the national trends (which you could find out from library research). This person may also be able to tell you some stories of local criminal events, but don't be surprised if there is a limit to the detail that can be provided. Privacy laws might prevent him or her from revealing names or specific addresses of criminal activity. The main idea is to consider ahead of time the type of information that this person can provide, and to have some questions to get at that information.

Developing a List of Primary Questions. Having established some general goals for the interview, break the topics into some logical order—for example, (1) changing trends in crime in this campus; (2) causes of these changes; (3) policy changes undertaken to deal with these changes. Then begin to develop a series of primary questions to uncover what you consider to be the important topics. When developing your list of primary questions, remember that the type of question you ask will help determine the response you receive. If you want specific information in a brief form, ask for it using a closed question—"How many total crimes were reported on campus in the last twelve-month period?" If you want an elaborate answer full of conjecture and opinion, pose an open question—for example, "What are the factors that account for the rise in crime on this campus?"

Avoid making your questions too complex. Develop a well-focused primary question, and consider how you will follow up with appropriate secondary questions. Avoid questions that are really several questions in one—for example, don't ask, "What is this department doing to deal with the changing face of crime on campus, what are the prospects of success for these changes, and how do you think the students will react to any changes you might propose?" Instead, employ the first part of the question, and keep the other two in mind as possible secondary questions.

Be certain that you use neutral questions. Leading or loaded questions are likely to lead to a negative relationship between you and the interviewee, and undermine the interviewee's motivation to give you full, candid answers.

Communicating Your Way Through the Interview

Like many communication events, an interview has a beginning, a middle, and an end. These parts do not just magically occur. You need to steer your way through them by using specific communication techniques.

Begin the interview by arriving on time and greeting your interviewee. Explain the purpose of the interview and tell the interviewee what you intend to use the information for. These steps will give the interviewee a frame of reference, and motivate him or her to be a helpful respondent. It may be useful to explain the major areas that you intend to cover in the interview as a preview of what is to come.

As you conduct the interview, let the respondent know when you move from one major topic area to another. Simple transition statements may help, for example, "You've given me some very useful information on the changing nature of crime on our campus. Now I'd like to turn to the future policies of the university police department. To begin, I'd like to know. . . . " This provides the interviewee with a sense of continuity to the questions you pose.

As you close the interview, it might be helpful to paraphrase some of your major findings. By all means, thank the interviewee for the time and effort put into the interview.

Maintaining Control in the Interview

As the interviewer, you are responsible for maintaining control of the interview process. Primarily, this means that you have to keep the interviewee from digressing too far, and you have to be certain to obtain the necessary information from him or her. The key to both of these is to listen carefully to responses. Too often, the inexperienced interviewer is so concerned about asking the next question that he or she fails to listen to the response to the previous one. Don't be afraid to take along your list of primary questions and refer to it as necessary. Listen closely to the interviewee, determine whether you have to follow up with a secondary question to get the necessary information, and if not, move on to the next primary question. There is nothing wrong with having a short pause between questions as you check your list of primary questions.

Careful listening will also help you determine when an interviewee has digressed too far and gotten off track. Sometimes it is necessary to interrupt the interviewee and get him or her back on track. Be polite, but indicate the need to interrupt by raising a finger, or inserting a verbal break (for example, "Now, . . . "). Gently redirect the interviewee to the question you want answered, or reframe the question to highlight the need for certain information. Remember that you need to maintain control. The interviewee does not necessarily know what information you need. He or she relies on your lead to know where to go.

In order to be an effective interviewer, you must prepare in advance, listen closely during the interview, and maintain control throughout.

PARTICIPATING IN AN EMPLOYMENT INTERVIEW

The process of getting a job, particularly a job on a desired career path, involves more than the employment interview. There are larger issues to be considered, such as what you find rewarding in a potential career, what career path you would like to follow, and how the demands of a career fit in with your overall view of a worthwhile life. Such questions are clearly beyond the scope of this chapter. You can work on these larger questions by talking to a career counselor or by reading one of the many books on the subject, such as Richard Bolles's (1990) ever-popular *What Color Is Your Parachute?* In this section we address issues that will help make you more effective as a job candidate in the interview. In order to be effective, you need to know how to prepare yourself before the interview, and how to conduct yourself during the interview process itself.

Preparing Yourself for the Interview

To be effective in the interview you have to do your homework. Before you talk to the interviewer it is important that you have sufficient information about the company, yourself, and the interview process.

The employment interviewer is trying to match the appropriate person to the available position. The interviewer needs to know that the fit will be proper both ways—the organization must be satisfied with the candidate, and the candidate must be satisfied as well. In order to feel assured that the candidate will be satisfied with the organization, the interviewer must presume that the candidate is familiar with the company. As you enter the interview you are expected to have some information about the organization, and the more you have the better. This helps ensure that you are sincerely interested in this company and that you will be able to ask intelligent questions about it (for example, its style of management, its short- and long-term goals, how you fit into the firm's overall plans, etc.). The importance of these questions cannot be overemphasized. The interview gives the job candidate a chance to find out about the company. Furthermore, the lack of questions by the interviewee may be interpreted as a lack of interest, or an inability to prepare for the interview. Interviewers are not annoyed when you ask questions. They expect it and take it as a sign of mature concern.

You can find out a significant amount of information about a company by doing prior library research. Business publications, annual corporate reports, Better Business Bureau reports, Moody's Manuals, and Peterson's Guides to Employment are all potential sources of information about employers. You may want to ask the reference librarian to help you locate additional information.

The interviewer is going to try to find out about you. Not surprisingly, it is important that you know yourself. In other words, it's time to sit down and ask yourself those long-term and life goal questions that get buried in the rush of

Teaching Objective 10–7
Stress the importance of interviewee preparation and careful impression management to the successful completion of an employment interview.

Current Research 10–6
Hanna and Wilson discuss the importance of understanding the corporate culture of an organization as part of effective preparation for interviewing. (Hanna, Michael S., and Wilson, Gerald L. *Communicating in Business and Professional Settings.* New York: McGraw-Hill, 1991, pp. 273–274.) The importance of assessing corporate culture is clear in light of a finding by Vangelisti and Daly which suggests that there " . . . is the strong probability that different cultural, ethnic, SES, and age groups may achieve success, as well as define success, in different ways." (Vangelisti, Anita L., and Daly, John A. Correlates of speaking skills in the United States: a national assessment. *Communication Education,* 38, 2, 1989, p. 142.)

everyday life. A number of publications can help you through this difficult process. Miller and Mattson's (1977) *The Truth About You: Discover What You Should Be Doing with Your Life* and Haldane's (1988) *Career Satisfaction and Success: How to Know and Manage Your Strengths* are just two examples.

There is also a need to be informed about the interview process itself. This chapter should help you in that area. There are a number of excellent books that can help provide you with a more complete picture of employment interviews, such as Medley's (1978) *Sweaty Palms: The Neglected Art of Being Interviewed* and Helleman's (1986) *Ready, Aim, You're Hired: How to Job-Interview Successfully Anytime, Anywhere with Anyone.*

As part of your preparation for the interview you should think about how you would answer some of the commonly asked questions. It is likely that the interviewer will ask you several or all of the following questions:

What have you accomplished? Be able to give specific examples that demonstrate motivation, technical skills, the ability to work with others, communication skills, and leadership potential.

Why did you select this company? Display your knowledge of the company based on your outside research.

What are your career plans? Show that you have long-term plans that would be compatible with the goals of the company.

What prepares you for this job? Explain how your education, experience, prior employment, or other skills have made you capable of performing in the position.

What are your strengths and weaknesses? Highlight your skills and accomplishments that show your personal strengths. When describing your weaknesses try to explain them as trade-offs with positive sides. For example, describe yourself as deliberate and a perfectionist, noting that this can be a problem when things need to be done immediately. That sounds much better than saying that you are slow.

It is not necessary to memorize your answers to these questions word for word. Instead, be able to talk through the answers, showing that you have given them some consideration.

Performing During the Interview

Even with thorough preparation, there is still pressure to perform during the interview itself. You need to manage the interviewer's impressions of you, answer questions in appropriate ways, and be able to deal with unanticipated questions.

Appearance is a crucial part of your interview performance. Improper dress can quickly place you in the "inappropriate" category regardless of what you say during the interview. There is no single standard or universal interview uniform for all companies. Some organizations are more conservative than others, and the attire of employees will reflect this. It may be worthwhile to visit the company before your interview to find out how employees dress. As a general

---

Discussion Question 10–7
How would you rank-order the factors involved in determining who gets chosen for a job? For example, is appearance more important than accomplishments? Is a personal connection (who you know) more important than the knowledge you possess?

Current Research 10–7
Hickson and Stacks report these findings about nonverbal communication factors in the job interview: Interviewers tend to have stereotyped images of the right candidate for a job. Initial impressions are crucial. Sustained mutual eye contact, appropriate dress, positive facial expression, including smiling and nodding, gestures, and confident vocal quality and body posture are all important to being positively perceived. (Hickson, Mark L., and Stacks, Don W. *Nonverbal Communication.* Dubuque: William C. Brown, 1989, pp. 284–294.)

SELF-ASSESSMENT   Nonverbal behavior in the interview

It is hardly surprising that nonverbal behavior should be important in the employment interview. Obviously, a job candidate should be dressed appropriately and should greet the interviewer with a firm handshake. Gifford, Ng, and Wilkinson (1985) found that some additional nonverbal behaviors are worth monitoring. In particular, they found that interviewers rely on the amount of time the interviewee talks, the use of gestures, and the use of smiling behavior as indicators of the interviewee's motivation. According to their study, an interviewee should spend an average of about six minutes answering a question, should gesture briefly while talking, and should smile occasionally.

It may be helpful to monitor your own nonverbal behavior in interview situations. Engage in a mock job interview (see exercise 3 at the end of this chapter). In addition to the interviewee (you) and the interviewer (a classmate), have a third person—an observer—present. The observer should monitor the interviewee's nonverbal behavior, focusing specifically on the time used to respond to a question, gesture use, smiling behavior, and eye contact. After the mock interview is complete, have the observer give feedback to the interviewee concerning the use of nonverbal behavior.

rule, you should try to match, or dress slightly more formally than, the employees' attire.

The first few minutes of an interview are crucial. This is when the interviewer is particularly vigilant, and early impressions in the interview can color subsequent perceptions of your performance. Early in the interview you want to show yourself to be friendly, curious, honest, and responsive. Greet the interviewer with a firm handshake, and smile occasionally; some limited use of hand gestures is also beneficial. Try the Self-Assessment exercise.

It is particularly important to emphasize positive things early in the interview. Interviewers are engaged in a weeding-out process. The interviewer's job is easier if he or she can reduce the number of job applicants to a manageable few. As a result, he or she may look for information that discounts you as an appropriate job candidate. Negative information is sought out and weighed more heavily in hiring decisions than positive information about the job candidate (Rowe 1989). You do not want to be dishonest, but bringing out negative features early in the interview places you in the "inappropriate" pile before you can display your best characteristics.

Don't speak negatively of others in the interview. Complaining about what a jerk your last boss was will just make you look like a malcontent to the interviewer. The interviewer may also wonder what nasty things you may say about his/her company in the future if you are so willing to be critical now. Even if

Leadership Note 10–3
A study by Johnson and Vinson indicates that negative perceptions of individuals who use powerless language early in an encounter cannot be overcome by the later use of powerful language. The use of powerless language was found to exert a crucial influence on impression formation. (Johnson, Craig, and Vinson, Larry. Placement and frequency of powerless talk and impression formation. *Communication Quarterly*, 38, 4, 1990, pp. 325–333.) Careful management of language is vital to those who aspire to be leaders.

Leadership Note 10–4
Communication Consultant
Roger Ailes describes four
essential qualities of a great
communicator: be pre-
pared, make others com-
fortable, be committed and
be interesting. These four,
and a fifth quality, being
likable, which Ailes calls
"the magic bullet," are
equally appropriate as
essential qualities of a successful interviewee. (Ailes,
Roger, *You Are the
Message.* New York:
Doubleday, 1988, pp.
63–90.)

your last boss was a manic-depressive sociopath who drove you to screaming fits, just tell the present interviewer that your former boss and you decided that you would be better suited for a different career position.

When answering the interviewer's questions it is important to have some idea of what he or she is looking for—the question behind the question. Bolles (1990) suggests that all other questions can be subsumed under four more general questions to which the interviewer wants the answers:

1. Why are you here? Why did you select this organization to apply to?
2. What can you do for us? What useful skills and knowledge will you bring to this company?
3. What kind of person are you? Are you responsible, are you reliable, and are your values and personality compatible with other employees in the organization?
4. Are you affordable? Do your minimum salary needs overlap with the company's maximum offer?

If you are not certain what the interviewer is trying to get at with a question, try to see how it pertains to one of these four basic issues.

You may also encounter problems if the interviewer phrases a question in a way that is difficult to understand. "Give me your perspective on an ideal organizational culture, vis-à-vis interdependencies of work structure" is the type of question that may appear impossible to answer at first. When in doubt, you can follow one of two strategies. You can ask the interviewer to rephrase the question. The alternative strategy is to incorporate your interpretation of the question in your answer: "I assume that you want to know whether I prefer to work in a cooperative work atmosphere, or if I work better when left on my own. Well, I tend to be an independent worker. . . ." This strategy allows the interviewer to check your interpretation of the question, and ask it again if he or she was getting at something else. Either approach is preferable to bumbling ahead, trying to answer a question that was never understood.

It is likely that you can gain further information on employment interviews by contacting a placement center on your campus. These centers often conduct workshops concerning interviewing skills, resumé preparation, job-search strategies, and other employment-related skills.

■ Summary

The interview is a unique communication context. In order to perform well in the role of either the interviewer or interviewee, it is necessary to understand the interviewing process. It is a unique context because the interview involves the two parties meeting for a predetermined and serious purpose, and is conducted primarily through the use of a question and answer format.

Though it may resemble an ordinary conversation, in an interview the roles of the interacting parties (the interviewer and interviewee) are distinct. The interviewer is responsible for maintaining control of the interaction. For the most part, this requires that he or she keep the interviewee on track, and encourage the interviewee to provide complete and thorough answers. Although there are many different types of interviews, the means by which the interviewer maintains control is consistent—it is done by using questions effectively.

Questions are the primary tools of the interviewer. There are different types of questions, and each type can have a different impact on the response an interviewee is likely to give. Questions vary in whether they open a new topic area or follow up on a previous question. Hence, some are primary and some are secondary questions. Questions also differ in the degree to which they restrict a respondent's choices. Closed questions limit the interviewee's response range, whereas open questions provide the interviewee with more latitude. Questions can also vary in how much they indicate the existence of a preferred response. Neutral questions give no indication that one response is preferred over another. Leading questions tell the interviewee that some answers are better than others.

Conducting an information-gathering interview involves prior preparation and careful execution of the interview. To prepare, the interviewer must set clear goals, and determine who can provide the necessary information. Preparation also involves development of a list of primary questions and work on a repertoire of secondary questions that may be brought into play.

To conduct a smooth interview, you should develop a proper opening, body, and closing. The opening should orient the interviewee to the type of information you are after, and motivate him or her to help. The closing of the interview should summarize what you learned and thank the interviewee for his or her help. During the body of the interview, you should primarily be concerned with maintaining control. This may necessitate interrupting the interviewee and getting him or her back on track. It may also require that you use your follow-up questions to obtain the necessary information. Remember that as the interviewer, you are responsible for maintaining control of the interview.

The employment interview should be seen as a part of the overall job-hunt process. In order to perform well in the job interview, you need to do prior work. This includes gathering information about the company, information about yourself, and information about the interviewing process. While engaged in the actual interview, you must establish a strong first impression and avoid negative information. As the interview progresses be certain that you understand the questions asked and the interviewer's rationale for asking the question.

---

1. Unless you are a highly skilled interviewer, it is better to use neutral rather than leading questions. Consequently, it is often necessary to alter the wording of the question from a leading to a neutral form. For the following questions, reword the leading version into a more neutral question.

 Exercises

You prefer the more expensive pair of shoes, don't you?

Do you intend to vote for our candidate or her despicable opponent?

Do you feel that the law-abiding citizens of this country need to take back the streets, or should we turn them over to drug pushers and pimps?

Have you stopped cheating on your taxes?

We can count on your financial support for this fund drive, can't we?

Do you want a strong national defense or bloated social programs?

2. Conduct an information-gathering interview on a friend or classmate. Work on your ability to control the interview by developing strong primary questions and utilizing secondary questions to gain additional detail. You can use any topic. If you can't think of one, interview the person about his or her adjustments to college life. Instruct your interviewee to give you brief answers when you ask closed questions and more developed answers when you ask open questions. You will probably be surprised at how often you end up asking closed questions when you want more developed answers. This exercise will help you be more aware of the needs to develop questions carefully and to use follow-up questions to gain additional information.

3. Take turns conducting an employment interview with a classmate. The interviewer should develop a series of primary questions and be able to ask follow-up questions. Try to cover four key areas discussed in the chapter (Why are you here? What can you do for us? What kind of person are you? Are you affordable?) without using those exact questions. As an interviewee, think through your answers, display poise, and provide sufficient eye contact. Then reverse roles and let the interviewer become the interviewee.

Bolles, R. N. (1990). *What color is your parachute? A practical manual for job-hunters and career changers.* Berkeley, CA: Ten Speed Press.

Though not an interviewing book, this manual is extremely helpful for guiding you through the preinterview questions that you should ask yourself. What are you good at? What are your future goals? What type of people do you like to work with? This book helps you complete a self-assessment so that you will be prepared for the employment interview. Bolles's style is engaging, and the book is updated annually.

Medley, H. A. (1978). *Sweaty palms: The neglected art of being interviewed.* Berkeley, CA: Ten Speed Press.

This book is highly regarded by users and professional placement counselors. It focuses on preparing you for the employment interview.

Stewart, C. J., and Cash, W. B. (1983). *Interviewing principles and practices* (4th ed.). Dubuque, IA: Kendall/Hunt.

This text is a classic approach to interviewing from a communication perspective. The authors cover the various interviewing contexts and specify what is necessary to be competent as either an interviewer or an interviewee. Examples and sample dialogue are used well to explain interviewing concepts.

MASTERING GROUP COMMUNICATION

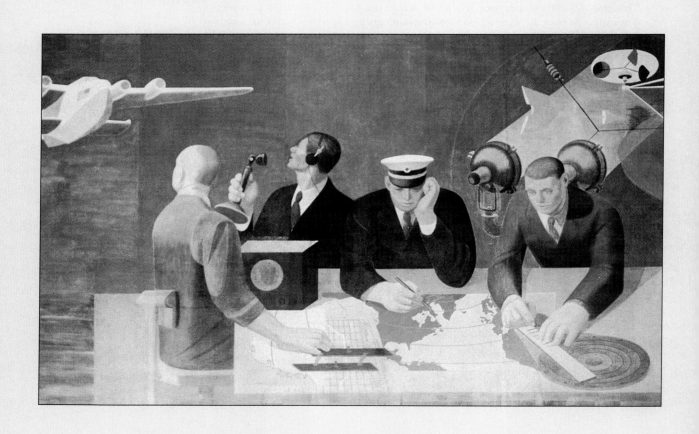

Group Problem Solving and Decision Making

Chapter objectives

After reading this chapter you should be able to:

1. define what a group is

2. identify the major characteristics of groups that distinguish them from one another

3. understand the value of having groups solve problems and make decisions

4. recognize differences in the requirements of problem solving and decision making

5. participate in both types of groups with increased effectiveness

6. appreciate the need for careful advanced preparation

Key terms and concepts

group
goal
task
norm
position
role
role conflict
structure
status
problem solving
decision making
quality circle
conventional problem
  solving
creative problem solving
criterion
brainstorming
Nominal Group
  Technique
question of fact
question of conjecture
question of value
question of policy

Much of our interaction with others occurs in groups. This is especially true in the case of individuals who are in positions of leadership and responsibility. Such people frequently participate in conferences, serve on important committees in organizations they represent, preside over staff meetings, are members of various civic groups, and the like. Usually, these types of groups meet to solve problems and make decisions about matters of importance to their members, the organizations in which they are involved, and the larger communities of which they are a part. These are the kinds of groups with which we are concerned in this chapter.

Because problem-solving and decision-making groups are so prevalent in our society, and because you are likely to be involved in many of them throughout your lifetime, the more you know about such groups and what contributes to their effectiveness, the better a participant you will become. The purpose of this chapter is to provide you with information about problem-solving and decision-making groups that will enable you to be a more skillful contributor to them. We begin with a discussion of the nature of groups, then discuss their value in performing problem-solving and decision-making tasks, review important aspects of participation in groups having such tasks, and finally, identify special considerations in preparing to participate.

Teaching Objective 11–1
Emphasize the presence and importance of groups in every aspect of modern life, beginning with the family and moving into the workplace and beyond.

Current Research 11–1
Hamilton and Parker (*Communicating for Results*, Belmont, Calif.: Wadsworth, 1990, p. 259) reported on a survey conducted by a management consulting firm which found that business executives spend approximately two full days of each five-day week in meetings.

THE NATURE OF GROUPS

What Groups Are

Teaching Objective 11–2
Define groups and describe their primary characteristics; depict the nature and likelihood of conflict.

Although there are many definitions of a **group** (see Palazzolo, 1988), one we find useful for our purposes is the following: a collection of two or more individuals who share information and exchange ideas to achieve a common goal. Our definition places no upper limits on size, but you can think of the kinds of groups we discuss in this chapter as generally ranging in size from five to seven members. We are primarily concerned with what many writers refer to as *the small group*.

Characteristics of Groups

Discussion Question 11–1
Are group and interpersonal communication contexts one and the same? See Chapter 7.

As is true of individuals, groups have many different characteristics. Among the most important of these are (1) goals, (2) norms, (3) positions, (4) roles, and (5) structure. These aspects of groups have a significant effect on how their members communicate and perform tasks. They are the factors that distinguish groups from one another and contribute to the development of their unique cultures (Bormann, 1990). Let's briefly examine each of these characteristics.

Goals.   A **goal** is the end state a group seeks to achieve (Zander, 1971); in other words, what the members hope to accomplish by the performance of a task. Raising a certain amount of money for charity, ensuring fairness in a company's hiring practices, and identifying steps that can be taken to control the costs of medical care are all examples of goals that various groups might hope to attain.

Occasionally, people confuse the notion of a goal with that of a task. Have you ever heard someone say, "I achieved my task," when the person probably meant, "I completed (or performed) the task"? A good way to avoid this confusion is to remember that a goal is an end and a task is a means to that end. Specifically, a **task** is the set of activities a group performs to achieve a goal.

Goals vary in a number of respects, including their origin, importance to the group members, clarity, and reasonableness. Each of these aspects of a goal can affect how the members of a group interact and perform tasks. A group given a goal its members consider unrealistic, for instance, is not likely to take its task very seriously. On the other hand, a group setting for itself what the members believe to be an achievable goal would undoubtedly be more enthusiastic in the performance of a task and exert more effort to accomplish it.

Norms.   A **norm** is a standard that defines acceptable behavior in a group. Sometimes we refer to norms as "rules" (Shimanoff, 1980). Norms apply both to the performance of a task and to relationships among group members. An example of a task-related norm in some groups might be that members are expected to keep their comments brief. In contrast, a relational norm could be that group members are to refrain from abusive language in reacting to one another's comments.

Norms are usually not expressed. Group members often do not become aware of a norm until they have violated it. If the violation is serious, the norm may become evident in a comment such as "May I remind the members of this group that we have had a history of showing respect for others' opinions." The violation of a norm often leads to pressure on the violator to conform (Aronson, 1988). Repeated violations of norms, especially those a group considers important, can even lead to rejection or expulsion of a member (Schacter, 1951).

Not all norms, of course, are equally important to the members of a group. When a norm is not especially important, members will frequently not even respond to a violation of it. In such cases, there is little noticeable impact on communication. When the norm is important, however, violations may divert a group's attention from its task and center it on dealing with the violator. Norms, then, have much to do with how groups conduct themselves in the performance of a task.

Positions.   In addition to goals and norms, groups have positions. A **position** is the part a member has in a group (Shaw, 1981). The positions in a group may be formal and specialized; for example, chair, vice-chair, secretary, and treasurer. Positions may also be informal, limited in number, and not strongly differentiated; for example, facilitator and member. Whatever the classification of a member's position in a group, the part he or she plays has much to do with

Cross-reference 11–1
Note that the effective attainment of goals was presented as a measure of interpersonal communication competence in Chapter 7.

Discussion Question 11–2
What are the norms that govern classroom behaviors? How do the norms of this class differ from those of other classes in which you've been a student (or teacher)?

Cross-reference 11–2
Tie norms to earlier discussions of context in relation to perception (Chapter 2) and verbal and nonverbal communication (Chapters 4 and 5).

Cross-reference 11–3
The particular role of leader will be discussed in greater detail in Chapter 12.

what the person contributes. Leaders function differently from followers, chairs engage in different activities from secretaries, and so on. Remember, then, that your position in a group partly defines what you do and legitimately can do.

Roles.   Roles are closely related to positions (Biddle and Thomas, 1966). Whereas a position is the part a member has in groups, **role** refers to the behavior associated with the position. You can think of a participant's position as a title and a role as what the title holder does or is expected to do. Roles may be designated, in which case a group member is told what others expect. Roles may also emerge. If a member behaves in particular ways in a group, others may come to expect such behavior from that individual on future occasions. Whether designated or emergent, roles evolve. No group member occupying a position behaves in consistently the same way. Instead, occupants continually bring new elements to their roles and modify their behavior accordingly. The common observation that a person "is growing" in his or her role acknowledges this evolutionary process.

In some groups, roles are loosely defined and allow members considerable freedom. The members of a jury, for example, are all generally free to explore any aspect of the issues before them. The foreperson has some specifically designated responsibilities, but the roles of the remaining jurors impose few specific limits on what they may say and do. The executive board of a major corporation, however, would likely be much different in the freedom members have to enact their individual roles. In such groups, the chair often designates who can speak and when, controls the agenda, and calls on specific individuals only when their particular input appears to be relevant. Other members also

Discussion Question 11–3
How many groups are you a member of at this moment in time? Are these groups formal or informal? What is your position and/or roles in each? In how many of these groups do you play multiple roles?

Current Research 11–2
Cragan and Wright suggest that conflict flows from a variety of sources, including roles, personality differences, and the problem-solving process itself. (Cragan, John F., and Wright, David W. *Communication in Small Group Discussion*. St. Paul: West Publishing, 1991, p. 6).

As a group, jurors experience relatively few constraints during the deliberation process. Within the confines of the law, each member is afforded the opportunity to fully express his or her own opinion about how to reach a verdict

tend to "know their place" in the group. A representative from sales would not be likely to make many comments about production, nor would a representative from the engineering division be inclined to contribute actively to a discussion of marketing strategies, unless, of course, he or she was invited to do so.

Roles can be in conflict. In this context, **role conflict** refers to some incompatibility in views about the proper enactment of a role. There are two ways in which such conflict frequently comes about: (1) from differences between how a group member enacts a role and how other members think it should be enacted, and (2) from a group member's performing acts that another member believes he or she has the responsibility to perform. An example of the first type of conflict would be a chair's failure to follow parliamentary procedure when the group has previously agreed to do so. The second type of conflict involves the crossing of role boundaries. A group member who says something like "Let's get this show on the road," when it is the responsibility of the chair to call the meeting to order takes the risk of being perceived as assuming another's role.

Role conflict can be harmful to the performance of a group. Among other things, it often contributes to poor interpersonal relationships among group members. If role conflict is left unresolved, a group may be unable to complete its task. At the very least, role conflict diverts attention from the task and consumes members' emotional energy. The angry department head who says, "Why does everyone around here seem to know how I should do my job?" shows signs of the tension that can follow from a perceived role conflict. It is therefore important that you be aware of what roles are and how their enactment may affect group members' performance of tasks and the kinds of relationships that develop among them. (Read the Focus on Leadership box.)

Structure. Positions and roles in groups do not exist in isolation. One cannot be a leader if there are no followers. A member cannot preside if there is no one to preside over. A participant cannot play the role of devil's advocate if there is no one contributing ideas with which to disagree. The patterns of relationship among the positions and roles represented in a group are what we have in mind when we refer to **structure**. Some groups are highly structured. In them, positions and roles are clearly defined, especially in respect to which members have authority and power. Other groups have positions and roles that are somewhat loosely defined. Members may share authority and power. The first type of group is often called *centralized*, and the second type *decentralized*. In centralized groups, members tend to vary in **status**; that is, the importance assigned to their positions and roles. In decentralized groups, members tend to be roughly equivalent in status.

The structure of a group and the related distribution of authority and status affects who speaks to whom and in what manner. Structure determines who exercises the greatest amount of influence (Gouran and Geonetta, 1977). In centralized groups, members with the least authority and status may withhold comments they would like to make. This apparently occurred in the case of the *Challenger* disaster in 1986, when engineers opposed to the launch failed to

Discussion Question 11–4
Are there other sources of conflict in groups than conflicts over roles?

Current Research 11–3
Poole sees group structure as "both the medium and outcome of group interaction . . . The factors that influence this structuring process . . . influence how decisions develop and emerge and also how relationships among members (e.g., cohesions, power structures, status) evolve over time." (Poole, Marshall Scott. Do we have any theories of group communication? *Communication Studies*, 41, 3, 1990, p. 240).

FOCUS ON LEADERSHIP

The Leadership Role

Of all the roles that exist in a group, the one that has been of greatest fascination is that of leadership. The concern is understandable because leadership may be the single most important influence on how a group performs. Leadership alone, of course, does not determine whether a group will function effectively or ineffectively. When a group has the necessary ingredients for successfully executing a task, however, the quality of leadership present has a significant bearing on the likelihood that it will do so.

Groups do not accomplish tasks simply because the members are equipped to do so. The activities necessary must somehow be coordinated. If such coordination does not occur, the members of a group will have no clear direction in which to move or means by which to progress. Leadership activates the process of interaction in groups, sustains it, and brings it to completion at the appropriate time. Leadership also addresses the difficulties the members of the group encounter or even create in the course of solving a problem or making a decision. Finally, leadership affects the atmosphere in which groups perform. The extent to which members cooperate, remain focused on the task, feel involved, and experience a sense of accomplishment is a direct consequence of leadership.

As a member of a problem-solving or decision-making group, you need to recognize the value of good leadership. Not only is leadership an indispensable aspect of group process—often it is also the margin of difference between groups that succeed and those that fail.

Discussion Question 11–5 In a sense, family life is our first and central experience of group membership; it was where we first learned how to be group members and what to expect from group involvement. How would you describe the status and authority structure of that first group experience of yours? What did you learn from that experience about being a group member?

press their case in discussions with management (Gouran, Hirokawa, and Martz, 1986). Members of decentralized groups are more likely to reflect a diversity of input (Janis, 1982).

It would be easy to conclude from the preceding discussion of structure that centralized groups always perform poorly in comparison to decentralized groups. To conclude such, however, would be a mistake. Sometimes centralized groups perform very effectively, and decentralized groups not so well. Much depends on the circumstances. A football team, for instance, cannot afford to distribute authority among team members during a huddle. To perform well, the team has to rely on the judgment of its quarterback or coach. The point we are making is simply that the ways in which positions and roles in groups are related to one another affects communication and the performance to tasks. To be unaware of this influence is to limit your potential effectiveness.

Thus far we have examined the nature of groups and discovered how their characteristics can influence what members say and do. We now turn to a discussion of the value of having groups perform particular kinds of tasks—specifically, those labeled *problem solving* and *decision making*.

THE VALUE OF GROUP PROBLEM SOLVING AND DECISION MAKING

Because participation in groups can be a frustrating experience, people are sometimes inclined to question their value. Bad experiences in groups inspire jokes, such as "A camel is a committee's idea of a horse." Characterizations are not always intended to be amusing, however. The nineteenth-century philosopher Friedrich Nietzsche reportedly observed that among individuals, madness is the exception, but in groups, the rule. Whatever unfortunate incidents prompt such reactions, there are good reasons for having groups perform problem-solving and decision-making tasks. Before we discuss these reasons, we need to distinguish between the two categories of activity.

Problem Solving Versus Decision Making

Problem solving is any set of activities an individual or group performs to reduce or eliminate some perceived difficulty. If the officers of a fraternity were concerned with its image on campus and attempted to identify ways of improving that image, they would be engaged in problem solving. Similarly, if a city council were expecting a shortage of tax revenues, and therefore explored ways of maintaining current services with reduced income, it too would be engaged in problem solving. Problem solving typically involves devising means or developing a plan for managing whatever difficulty an individual or group is confronting.

Problem solving is a term that some people use interchangeably with *decision making*. The two concepts are not equivalent, however. **Decision making** refers to the act of choosing among alternatives. Usually, the choice involves competing answers to a question—for instance, "Did the accused commit the crime for which he is being tried?", "Should the university change from the semester to the quarter system?", or "Will an increase in rates improve the efficiency of the Postal Service?"

Although problem solving and decision making are different concepts, they frequently go hand in hand. If a group of executives is seeking ways to enhance employee morale in an organization (a problem-solving task), for instance, it will have to make decisions about which of several possible courses of action is likely to have the desired effect. We will have more to say about the activities appropriate to problem-solving and decision-making discussions later in this chapter. To ensure that you understand how they differ in general, however, try the Self-Assessment exercise.

Teaching Objective 11–3
Describe the difference between problem-solving and decision-making, but acknowledge that they are often both utilized in group processes.

Current Research 11–4
According to Poole, McGrath's research on groups indicates the influence of the task assigned to the group on both interaction and outcomes, task is seen as a central determinant. (Poole, Marshall Scott. Do we have any theories of group communication? *Communication Studies*, 41, 3, 1990, p. 240).

Distinguishing problem-solving from decision-making tasks

For each of the descriptions below, identify whether the group involved would be performing a problem-solving or decision-making task. Place PS for problem-solving or DM for decision-making in the blank by each item.

_____1. judging the desirability of intervening in other countries' affairs.

_____2. recommending measures for improving the graduation rate of college athletes

_____3. determining whether trade restrictions on imported goods should be reduced

_____4. identifying ways to eliminate sexual harassment in the workplace

_____5. assessing the likelihood that implementation of a cultural diversity requirement will improve interpersonal relations among college students

_____6. generating ideas for increasing the supply of American scientists and engineers

Answers: 1. DM; 2. PS; 3. DM; 4. PS; 5. DM; 6. PS

Teaching Objective 11–4
Accentuate the benefits of group approaches to problem-solving and decision-making.

Current Research 11–5
Gorden and Infante found that employees desire freedom of speech in the workplace and that perceptions of possessing freedom of speech were positively tied to organizational commitment, commitment to product quality, and commitment to work-life quality. Group problem-solving and decision-making encourages freedom of speech. (Gorden, William and Infante, Dominic, Test of a communication model of organizational commitment. *Communication Quarterly* 39, 2, 1991, pp. 144–155.)

Reasons for Group Problem Solving and Decision Making

The involvement of groups in problem solving and decision making reaches well into history and is one of the hallmarks of democratic societies. An important assumption of this tradition is that if people are to be affected by the consequences of attempted solutions to problems and decisions, where possible, they should have the opportunity to share in their production. Such sharing of responsibility for actions that may affect the collective good is consistent with the themes of leadership and social responsibility discussed throughout this book. Upholding an historical tradition, of course, is not the only reason that groups rather than individuals are so frequently asked to perform problem-solving and decision-making tasks.

Often, the requirements of a problem-solving or decision-making task are so demanding that an individual acting alone could not easily satisfy them. If a company is attempting to develop a plan for marketing a new line of computer hardware, for instance, it would be helpful to have a combination of individuals with different types of expertise involved. Representatives from the production, sales, and advertising divisions collectively could probably do a better job of identifying the features of the hardware most likely to have consumer appeal than any single one of them could.

Another reason for having groups solve problems and make decisions is the increased likelihood that misinformation will be spotted and corrected. The total knowledge of a group is at least as great as that of the most knowledgeable member and usually much greater. As a result, a member of a group who individually might act on misinformation is subject to the corrective influence of other members (Shaw and Gouran, 1990). A high accident rate at a particular intersection in a community, for example, could suggest the need to replace a stop sign with a traffic signal. A person familiar with the intersection, however, might have noticed that the current placement of the stop sign obscures its visibility. The sharing of that piece of information would serve to prevent implementation of a more expensive and unnecessary solution to the problem.

In addition to improving the prospects for discovering better solutions to problems and making defensible decisions, the use of groups often has other benefits. For instance, organizations that have expanded employee participation by the introduction of quality circles have noted gains in morale, productivity, and satisfaction (Ouchi, 1981; Peters and Waterman, 1982). A **quality circle** is a small group of employees who meet regularly to discuss ways in which to improve various aspects of their working conditions and thereby to increase the productivity of the units they represent.

Groups often give us the opportunity to affect our own futures. But even when we have no involvement in a problem-solving or decision-making process, we may be more accepting of actions taken and conclusions reached when they are the product of group effort. We tend to place less confidence in the judgment of individuals acting alone on matters that have consequences for others.

Discussion Question 11–6
What particular skills, talents and abilities do you bring to the groups of which you are a member?

Leadership Note 11–1
DePree provides this answer to what it is we humans want from our work: ". . . a work process and relationships that meet our personal needs for belonging, for contributing, for meaningful work, for the opportunity to make a commitment, for the opportunity to grow and be at least reasonably in control of our own destinies." Perhaps this is what makes group work generally satisfying to those who engage in it. (DePree, Max, *Leadership Is an Art.* New York: Doubleday, 1989, p. 21.)

Many businesses use the quality circle to solve problems. Here, workers meet regularly to discuss ways to improve product quality and productivity.

◼ PROBLEM-SOLVING AND DECISION-MAKING DISCUSSIONS

Earlier, we distinguished between the activities of problem solving and decision making. We now turn to the mechanics of participating in discussions of groups that perform these activities. Not all groups solve problems or make decisions in the ways we shall be describing. Our purpose, however, is to acquaint you with those means of solving problems and making decisions in groups that make it more likely that the process will be effective.

Group Problem Solving

Those who write about problem solving in groups have identified two general approaches to the task. The older of these is often called *conventional*, and the other *creative*. **Conventional problem solving** involves a systematic set of steps in which a group (1) identifies the problem to be solved, (2) establishes criteria for evaluating solutions, (3) generates possible solutions, (4) examines each solution in relation to the criteria, and (5) selects the solution that best satisfies the criteria. **Creative problem solving** is a process in which group members attempt to identify as many different and imaginative solutions as they can for an acknowledged or established problem while refraining from evaluating their merits. Conventional and creative problem solving are not competing processes. Each is useful under different circumstances. A group may even have occasion to take both approaches in dealing with the same issue.

Conventional Problem Solving.   We have already sketched the steps involved in conventional problem solving. They are sometimes called *the method of reflective thinking* and are attributed to the American philosopher John Dewey, who was concerned with the habits of mind that people bring to problems they confront for which solutions are not obvious. The process Dewey (1910) described is captured in the sequence of steps listed above.

Suppose you were asked to participate in a discussion of how to ensure that students at your college or university receive a high-quality education. The first step would be to determine what, if anything, is preventing students from receiving a high-quality education or at least is threatening to have that effect. On the basis of the information available to the members, your group might identify large classes, inadequate facilities, a shortage of full-time instructors, or some combination of these as problematic or potentially problematic. You would now be ready to proceed to the next step.

Assume your group has singled out large classes as the matter that needs to be addressed. Before considering possible solutions to the problem, however, you would need to establish the criteria that any solution, to be acceptable to the group, should satisfy. A **criterion** is a factor to be considered in making assessments. When an athletic coach is considering the positions for which a team member may be best suited, he or she uses such criteria as speed, height, experience, and agility. In the case of how to deal with the problem created by large classes, relevant factors to consider might be cost, length of time required for implementation, and attractiveness to students. A solution that is costly, requires a great deal of time to implement, and is likely to be unattractive to students would be a poor one. A solution that is relatively inexpensive, easily implementable, and attractive to students would obviously be preferable.

Having reached agreement on the criteria, your group would now be ready to introduce possible solutions. Among these might be (1) reducing the number of students admitted, (2) increasing the number of classes that professors teach, (3) raising tuition to hire more instructors, and (4) reducing the number of administrators and staff to allow for an increase in academic appointments. Simply on its face, each solution would appear to lead to the desired result, but careful consideration of them could reveal substantial differences in how effective each is likely to be. It might even reveal that none of the alternatives provides a satisfactory solution. The criteria your group previously selected now become very important.

In the fourth step, your group would examine each solution in relation to each criterion. In the process, you might conclude that the solution of reducing the number of students fails to satisfy the criteria of cost and length of the time required for implementation very well. Fewer students would mean reduced income, and with fewer financial resources, faculty size might have to be cut. In this case, average class size could even increase. Similarly, if to avoid problems created by a sharp reduction in income, the solution had to be phased in over a period of several years, whatever difficulties large classes had been causing would remain.

Discussion most likely would produce different assessments of how well each solution satisfies each criterion. In this phase, you might even discover that none of the solutions completely satisfied the criteria. At that point, your group would have two choices. It could either endorse the solution that comes closest to satisfying the criteria, or it could move back to the previous step and begin to identify more possible solutions.

Another thing that can happen in the assessment of alternatives is that a group comes to the conclusion that while one or more solutions satisfy the criteria, there are possible consequences that would make implementation undesirable. For instance, increasing the number of classes that professors teach would appear to satisfy the three criteria being used. It is possible, however, that professors would not like this arrangement and might begin looking for other jobs, spend less time preparing for class, and the like. Because of this possibility, the group might have to return to the second step and reconsider its criteria. Are there factors that should be considered that were not included in the original list? In either of the situations we have described, the group would not move forward. Instead, it would have to recycle its way through some or all of the steps of the process. This can and often does happen in problem-solving groups (Poole, 1992). You should be prepared for such possibilities.

If your group agrees that one of the solutions satisfies the criteria reasonably well and better than other solutions and sees no additional difficulties, the final step is an easy one to take. The group offers as its solution the one that best meets its criteria. Usually, the final step takes very little of a group's time. The exception would be a situation in which two or more of the possible solutions appear to satisfy a group's criteria equally well. If the group cannot find some basis for selecting one through further discussion, it might simply make an arbitrary choice or decide on the basis of the personal preferences of the members.

Conventional problem solving, then, involves an ordered sequence of steps, in which a group may have to repeat some steps until such time as the members identify a solution that best meets criteria they have established. The steps are summarized for your convenience in Figure 11.1.

Creative Problem Solving.   Many times a group faces a situation in which it is unnecessary to identify a problem. The problem is clear; for example, falling profits, a losing season, group insurance that does not provide adequate coverage in light of rising costs of medical care, and so on. When groups are asked to problem-solve under these sorts of circumstances, the accent is on solutions rather than problems or the criteria for evaluating solutions.

In the 1950s, an advertising executive by the name of Alex Osborn (1957) published an influential book entitled *Applied Imagination*. In it, he introduced the concept of brainstorming, which he described as a creative technique. **Brainstorming** is a process of generating ideas as rapidly as possible and without consideration of their strengths and weaknesses. The principle behind this approach to problem solving, especially when taken by a group, is that the best solution to a problem is more likely to surface in a large number of possible solutions than in a small number. In addition, Osborn believed that evaluation can hamper creativity. If a group stops to evaluate every idea for solving a problem, not only will the number of ideas produced be relatively small, but participants can become easily discouraged as well. How many times, for instance, have you stopped contributing to a discussion because you felt that your ideas were being "shot down"?

Participation in brainstorming groups is not nearly as structured as it is in conventional problem solving. The procedure is quite simple. For any specified problem, members are asked to think of as many different ideas as they can for solving it and to contribute them as they occur to them. They are discouraged

Cross-reference 11–4
Brainstorming is a tool which can also be useful as a method of generating public speaking topics for presentation in classroom settings. Chapters 13 and 14 talk about subject selection.

Figure 11.1
Steps in Conventional Problem Solving.

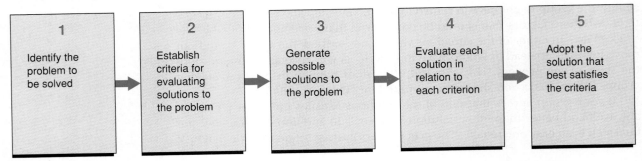

1	2	3	4	5
Identify the problem to be solved	Establish criteria for evaluating solutions to the problem	Generate possible solutions to the problem	Evaluate each solution in relation to each criterion	Adopt the solution that best satisfies the criteria

Participants in Outward Bound programs, in which members attempt to overcome physical and psychological barriers, often rely on creative problem-solving techniques.

from withholding any idea, no matter how extreme or irrelevant it might appear. In fact, an instruction often given to brainstorming groups is along the following lines: "Think of as many different imaginative ways for solving this problem as you can. The wilder, the better."

In a brainstorming session, one member has the role of recorder. That individual keeps track of all of the ideas introduced and determines, if possible, which ones are unique and which are overlapping. The other members spend their time and energy providing input. When contributions cease or the number of new ideas decreases sharply, for all practical purposes, the brainstorming session is over.

Brainstorming groups frequently serve merely to provide novel ideas for someone else to consider in determining how best to solve a problem. Such was the case in the economic conference then President-elect Clinton held in Little Rock, Arkansas, in the weeks prior to his inauguration. In other cases, however, those involved may have the added responsibility of recommending a particular solution. At this point, the members would have to shift out of their "creative" mode of thinking and draw on the sorts of analytical and evaluative skills that conventional problem solving requires. There is nothing in the brainstorming process that makes the best solution to a problem jump out. The quality of ideas and their suitability has to be determined by other means.

An adaptation of brainstorming, called Nominal Group Technique, was introduced several years after Osborn published his book (Delbecq, Van de Ven, and Gustafsen, 1975). The term *nominal* is used because the groups involved in this category of creative problem solving are groups in name only—at least, throughout the idea-generation phase of their work. Members of groups using

Nominal Group Technique are instructed in exactly the same way as brainstorming groups to think of as many different and imaginative solutions to the problem as they can. The only difference is that they are asked to list their ideas on paper. They are not aware of what anyone else has thought until after all members have completed their individual tasks and a facilitator either asks the other members to present their individual lists or gathers and reproduces them on a flowchart. See how creative you can be by trying the exercise in the Mastering Communication Skills box.

Delbecq and his associates developed this alternative approach to brainstorming because previous experience had shown that participants in interacting brainstorming groups (1) do not refrain from making evaluative comments, (2) find it easy to claim to have the same ideas as other group members, and (3) are sometimes inhibited by the presence of members having high status. Whether brainstorming as originally developed or Nominal Group Technique will prove to be consistently superior remains a question among scholars who study such processes. For our purposes, however, the more important consideration is that you be aware of creative problem-solving methods and the circumstances under which they can most profitably be employed.

We also should emphasize that creative problem solving can be combined with conventional problem solving, particularly in the steps of identifying criteria and possible solutions to a problem. As we indicated earlier, conventional problem-solving groups do not always have a sufficient number of criteria or possible solutions to consider. In many instances, it would be better to start with a larger number of each and then limit them than to begin with a small number. This can reduce the amount of recycling through the steps in conventional problem solving that we suggested sometimes becomes necessary.

MASTERING COMMUNICATION SKILLS

Increasing Your Creative Problem-Solving Skill

Identify and write down as many different ways as you can think of for controlling the costs of higher education. Do not stop to think about any idea once it has occurred to you. Simply record it, and continue thinking of other ideas. Allow yourself five minutes to complete the task. Then ask an acquaintance to do the same thing under the same time limit. Compare your list with the one produced by your acquaintance.

1. How many ideas did you both generate?

2. How many of these ideas were common to both lists?

3. What percentage of the items appears to be reasonably realistic? (Count an item appearing on both lists as one.)

4. How many of the ideas that appear to be realistic would be worth exploring further?

Group Decision Making

A problem-solving group cannot successfully complete its task without making decisions. It has to decide which criteria it will use, how many solutions to consider, whether to repeat a step or to move forward, and the like. In some respects, then, we have already introduced you to various aspects of decision making in groups. In this section, however, we are concerned with the activities of groups that involve choices but are not necessarily directed at the reduction or elimination of some perceived difficulty. The kinds of discussions for which the label *decision making* is appropriate, in general, deal with matters involving (1) what is true, (2) what is probable, (3) what is acceptable, and (4) what should be done.

Discussion Question 11–7
How do you make decisions when faced with them? Have you ever used a systematic approach? Have you ever made a snap decision? Have you ever thought about how you make decisions?

Types of Questions. The issues addressed by groups that correspond to the matters mentioned above are referred to as questions of (1) fact, (2) conjecture, (3) value, and (4) policy. Although the approach to developing answers to these four types of questions is generally the same, it is important that you understand more fully the differences among them.

Teaching Objective 11–6
Discuss the questions of fact, value, policy and conjecture; distinguish these types of questions from one another.

When a group is called upon to discuss a **question of fact**, its purpose is to resolve an issue pertaining to what is true in a given case. Deciding "what is true" usually takes two forms: (1) determining whether a particular condition exists (for example, "Are we being successful in our efforts to attract students from minority populations?") and, if a particular condition exists, (2) identifying the causes or underlying reasons (for example, "Why has the community's educational program on substance abuse failed to produce a better result?"). The answers to such questions often have implications for actions a group may later take. The wrong answer, therefore, could have unfortunate consequences. An example would be a corporate board that decides an organization's profits have fallen because of general economic conditions when the actual reason is that its advertising program is weak. By singling out the wrong cause, the company could miss a good opportunity to improve its situation.

A group's purpose in discussing a **question of conjecture** is to form a judgment about what is probable or likely under specified conditions. An example of this type of question is "Will an increase in tuition lead to a reduction in the number of students who apply for admission to our college (university)?" The answer to this type of question can vary according to what conditions a group specifies. In the example given, a group's response might be yes if the members were talking about a 10 percent increase, but no if the increase being considered were only 2 or 3 percent. As in the case of questions of fact, the decisions reached can have effects on other decisions a group may have to make. If a group dealing with the probable effects of a tuition increase concluded that 10 percent would not lead to a reduction in applications, it might be more inclined to recommend such an increase. If later events showed that the conjecture was in error, the group responsible might find itself with a financial crisis to manage.

A **question of value** arises when a group is attempting to decide what is acceptable in a given case. Acceptability refers to matters focusing on what is right and wrong, desirable and undesirable, justifiable and unjustifiable, and the like. "Was the United State's intervention in the Persian Gulf justified?" is an example of a question of value. Decision-making groups, however, are usually not called upon to resolve such issues after the fact. Rather, they discuss questions of value in relation to possible courses of action. The censoring of news that occurred during the war in the Persian Gulf, for example, apparently was the result of discussions among military and government officials concerning whether possible threats to the achievement of military objectives and to the well-being of allied forces justified withholding of some types of information from news sources and the public.

A group discussing a **question of policy** attempts to decide what should be done in a given case. "Should the Undergraduate Student Association revise its election procedures?" is an example of the kind of policy question you might find yourself discussing on your campus. The purpose of such a discussion would be to determine whether a certain action should be undertaken. The task of a group discussing this kind of question would be to establish what grounds, if any, exist for considering a change in the way something is presently done.

Table 11.1 summarizes the types of questions appropriate for decision-making discussions and gives an example of each. Test your understanding of the four types of questions that decision-making groups discuss by completing the exercise in the box. Use the examples in Table 11.1 as a guide.

Teaching Objective 11–7
Distinguish among the stages or requirements of group decision-making.

Cross-reference 11–5
The importance of clarity of language use to effective communication is discussed in regard to public speaking in Chapter 16; the need for clarity extends to all communication contexts.

Requirements of Group Decision Making. In our discussion of problem solving, we identified steps and procedures related to both the conventional and creative types. Decision making is somewhat different, in that formal procedures are not usually spelled out. This is not to suggest that decision-making tasks have no requirements, however.

For a group to make a decision, it is often necessary to *define any ambiguous or problematic terms* in the question under review. A group discussing the question "Would a change in the length of the workweek be desirable?" for instance, probably would have difficulty reaching a conclusion unless its members achieved a common understanding of "length of workweek" and "desirable."

Table 11.1
Types and Examples of Questions Addressed by Decision-Making Groups

Type	Example
Fact	What have been the social effects of dual-career marriages?
Conjecture	Is the number of homeless citizens likely to increase?
Value	Under what circumstances, if any, can euthanasia be justified?
Policy	Should the military draft be reinstated?

> ### Recognizing differences in decision-making tasks
>
> For each question below, place the label (*fact, conjecture, value,* or *policy*) that you believe is most appropriate in the blank provided.
>
> _____ 1. Should SAT scores be discontinued as a basis for admitting students to college and universities?
>
> _____ 2. What will be the effects of raising the minimum hourly wage on the number of people below the poverty line?
>
> _____ 3. Has increased reliance on technology contributed to greater levels of stress in society?
>
> _____ 4. Are minority quotas in the labor force fair?
>
> **Answers:** 1. policy; 2. conjecture; 3. fact; 4. value

A second requirement often imposed by decision-making tasks is for group members to *recognize what type of information is necessary for answering the question* and whether or not such information can be acquired. Self-reports on an issue such as "Does our organization have a morale problem?" might be entirely appropriate for reaching a decision, whereas expert opinion would probably be more desirable if the question were "What are the main causes of employee dissatisfaction in American business and industry?" In some cases, only factual and statistical data could be of much value. For a question such as "How great is the incidence of white-collar crime in the United States?" opinions would not have much use.

Once a decision-making group has acquired the kind of information it needs, a third requirement is to *determine what the information in general suggests about the answer to the question.* Rarely, if ever, does available information uniformly point to the same conclusion. Remember, you are discussing the question in the first place because the answer is in doubt.

As with other impressions, the first one decision makers form from the information they consult is not necessarily the best one in determining the answer to a discussion question. A group needs to *consider whether there are grounds for doubting the apparent answer.* Appropriate considerations include the reliability and trustworthiness of the sources of information, evidence of bias, and direct relevance to the issues. Sometimes a limited amount of information supporting one answer to a question is much better than a larger quantity supporting another. Engaging in these kinds of assessments before a group makes its final choice is very important.

The last requirement of decision making is to *make a choice,* even if it is only to reach the conclusion that the group is not able to resolve the issue. In this sense, no decision is a decision. In most instances, however, a group that has satisfied the other requirements mentioned will be able to make a substantive choice about what is the most defensible answer to its question and will not have to be noncommittal.

Current Research 11–7
Bullis reports that participative decision-making in organizations can be a form of member self-indoctrination. "Through participation, members are more likely to behave on and internalize both the premises and the decisions. . . . " In her study, Bullis found that participative team decision-making was in fact an example of managerial control in organizations wherein leadership obtained the desired decisions through unobtrusive control. (Bullis, Connie, Communication practices as unobtrusive control: an observational study. *Communication Studies* 42, 3, 1991, pp. 254–271)

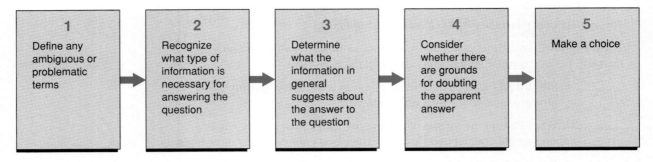

Figure 11.2
General Requirements of
Decision-Making Tasks.

Decision-making groups that satisfy the requirements we have been discussing have a better chance of making the best possible choices. So that you can refer to these requirements more easily, we have summarized them in Figure 11.2.

The Relationship of Decision Making to Problem Solving

We stated earlier in the chapter that problem solving and decision making go hand in hand. Now that you know more about each, you should be able to understand how the two processes may be involved in the work of the same group. A group that has been asked to recommend how recruitment of members for a fraternity or sorority might be improved, for example, would be performing a problem-solving task. Nevertheless, it would need to engage in decision making at several points. It might have to decide why present methods of recruitment are not working (question of fact), why it is desirable to increase the number of recruits (value), and which of several measures for improving recruitment should be adopted (policy). As you develop experience with both types of discussions, you will become more skillful in utilizing decision-making practices for the purpose of solving problems and begin to see these two types of group activity as natural and sometimes inseparable companions.

■ PREPARING FOR PROBLEM-SOLVING AND DECISION-MAKING DISCUSSIONS

Teaching Objective 11–8
Emphasize the need for preparation in order to make effective use of group process, and explore the various facets of preparation and their benefits.

Knowing what is involved in problem-solving and decision-making discussions is important but not sufficient for a group to perform well. There are several other considerations that you need to be aware of, which can help you and other members of the groups in which you participate to do a better job of addressing issues:

   1. *Become as well informed as possible on the subject to be discussed.*   For some issues, you may already be well informed and not need to engage in much gathering of new or additional information. For other subjects, however, the knowledge you already possess will not be sufficient for developing effective solutions to problems or making good decisions. The more you know, the better able you will be to analyze issues, identify strengths and weaknesses of alternatives, and make sound judgments about what your information establishes. Sometimes, the information you need is already available (as in the case of a discussion on the causes of occupational stress). In other instances, you have to generate information (for instance, a discussion involving whether employees would be receptive to implementation of flextime). Whatever the case, you should leave yourself enough time to become familiar with the subject and to acquire any information you may need in order to maximize your contribution to a discussion and improve your group's chances of successfully achieving desired objectives.

2. *Determine whether there is to be an agenda.* An **agenda** is a listing of points or topics in the order in which they are to be taken up in a meeting. For the kinds of group situations on which we have been focusing, the agenda may simply be the steps in the problem-solving sequence chosen or the listing of requirements necessary for making a decision. A quick review of Figures 11.1 and 11.2 will help you see how an agenda can emerge naturally from the type of task to be performed.

3. *Consider the other group members and possible complications they may pose.* In the first part of this chapter, we discussed group characteristics and some of the problems to which they can lead. Anticipating how other members may react to violations of norms, role conflict, status differences, and the like may help you avoid some interpersonal difficulties that would otherwise distract your group from performing its task.

4. *Attend to the physical environment in which the discussion is to occur.* For the types of tasks we have described, it is helpful to have groups seated in arrangements that facilitate the exchange of ideas; for example, a circle or semicircle (Burgoon, 1988). Temperature, ventilation, and room appearance should also be considered. Group members are easily distracted when they are physically uncomfortable. Finally, if you are going to be in need of certain kinds of equipment or materials, you should take steps to arrange for them in advance.

5. *Take steps to minimize the possible influence of preformed judgments.* Most of us enter discussions with some preformed notions about the best solution to a problem or the most defensible answer to a discussion question. To enter with a blank mind is probably neither possible nor desirable. On the other hand, initial preferences can influence judgments, lead to misinterpretations of information, and cause group participants to engage in persuasion rather than exploration (Janis, 1989). When group members make a deliberate effort to suspend previously formed views, it is easier for them to conduct discussions in ways that maximize the chances that desired outcomes will be achieved (Hill, 1976).

Following the preceding recommendations, of course, does not guarantee that the members of a problem-solving or decision-making group will be successful in achieving their objectives. What they can do, however, is remove some potential obstacles to effective problem solving and decision making in advance of a discussion. The more that participants can do along these lines, the easier it will be for them during their interactions to satisfy the requirements of their task.

Leadership Note 11–2
"We must understand that access to pertinent information is essential to getting a job done. . . . Moreover, it is better to err on the side of sharing too much information than risk leaving someone in the dark." (DePree, Max, *Leadership Is an Art*). New York: Doubleday, 1989, p. 92)

Discussion Question 11–8
Take a close look at the room you're in. How well or poorly suited is it for a group process? What is needed? How should the space, seating and other aspects be arranged? Design a "group communication room."

Cross-reference 11–6
The importance of physical space was discussed more fully in Chapter 5.

◾ Summary

Groups are collections of two or more individuals who share information and exchange ideas to achieve a common goal. Among the characteristics of groups that distinguish them from one another are goals, norms, positions, roles, and structure. A goal is an end state a group seeks to achieve. Norms are the standards that define acceptable behavior in a group. Position refers to the part a member of a group has, and a role is the behavior associated with a position. The structure of a group is determined by the ways in which positions and roles are related to one another. All of these characteristics affect the manner in which communication occurs in groups and can pose certain kinds of difficulties for how well the members of groups are able to perform their tasks.

Groups have significant value in problem solving and decision making. Whereas a problem-solving group aims at reducing or eliminating some perceived difficulty, a decision-making group is concerned with choosing among competing answers to questions of particular kinds. There are several reasons for having groups solve problems and make decisions, including consistency with social, political, and cultural traditions, diversity of input, expanded knowledge, and increased acceptability of outcomes.

Problem solving falls into two general categories: conventional and creative. Conventional problem solving reflects efforts to identify a problem, establish criteria for evaluating solutions, generate possible solutions, examine potential solutions in relation to criteria, and select the solution that best satisfies the criteria. Creative problem solving is a process of idea generation in which group participants are encouraged to think of as many different imaginative solutions to an acknowledged problem as they can without evaluating them. This process can be performed by interacting and noninteracting groups. The term *brainstorming* is used to refer to the activities of the first type of group, and *Nominal Group Technique* to those of the second type.

Decision-making groups attempt to resolve questions involving fact (what is true), conjecture (what is probable or likely), value (what is acceptable), and policy (what should be done). Although decision-making groups typically do not have formal procedures to follow, their tasks do have certain requirements that pose needs to (1) define ambiguous or problematic terms, (2) recognize what type of information is necessary for answering the question, (3) determine what the information in general suggests about the answer to the question, (4) consider whether there are grounds for doubting the apparent answer, and (5) make a choice.

A knowledge of the nature of group problem solving and decision making, while important, is not sufficient preparation for effectively performing such tasks. Individuals involved in such groups should become as well informed as possible, determine whether there is to be an agenda, consider the other group members and possible complications they may pose, attend to the physical environment in which a discussion is to occur, and take steps to minimize the possible influence of preformed judgments. Although these aspects of preparation do not ensure success, they can minimize some of the difficulties that a problem-solving or decision-making group may otherwise experience.

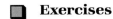

Exercises

1. Try to recall a discussion in which you participated and in which a characteristic such as the group's status structure had a negative influence on the performance of your task. How did the members attempt to manage the problem? Were they successful or unsuccessful? Could they have managed the problem more successfully? How?

2. Devise two creative problem-solving exercises. Then ask several of your friends to use brainstorming in one and Nominal Group Technique in the other. Compare the results in terms of both the total number of ideas produced and the number of noncommon (unrepeated) ideas. Determine which procedure produced the better result.

3. Select a topic in which you are interested and prepare a question of fact, a question of conjecture, a question of value, and a question of policy related to it.

4. For any of the questions you have identified in exercise 3, develop an agenda based on the general requirements for decision-making discussions outlined in this chapter.

5. Identify three people who have written about the subject you have selected who you believe are well qualified. Then write a short paragraph about each one in which you give your reasons for believing that he or she is a good source of information.

Related Readings

Bormann, E. G. (1990). *Small group communication: Theory and practice* (3rd ed.). New York: Harper & Row.

This book is especially good to read because of its emphasis on the culture of groups and how communication contributes to their uniqueness.

Brilhart, J. K., and Galanes, G. J. (1991). *Effective group discussion* (7th ed.). Dubuque, IA: William C. Brown.

Brilhart and Galanes offer a thorough review of principles and practices of problem solving and decision making in groups. The volume also contains useful material on the evaluation of groups.

Cragan, J. F., and Wright, D. W. (1986). *Communication in small group discussions* (2nd ed.). St. Paul, MN: West.

The authors illustrate principles of communication in groups through the examination of cases.

Fisher, B. A., and Ellis, D. G. (1990). *Small group decision making: Communication and the group process* (3rd ed.). New York: McGraw-Hill.

Fisher and Ellis bring a strong theoretical focus to the study of communication in groups. The book is more useful to read after one has had some experience participating in groups.

Folger, J. P., Poole, M. S., and Stutman, R. K. (1993). *Working through conflict* (2nd ed.). Glenview, IL: Scott, Foresman.

The authors present a thorough discussion of conflict, how to minimize its negative aspects, and how to use it constructively in solving problems and making decisions in groups.

Galanes, G. J., and Brilhart, J. K. (1991). *Communicating in groups: Applications and skills.* Dubuque, IA: William C. Brown.

Galanes and Brilhart explore the dynamics of group process and the social influences that affect it.

Gouran, D. S. (1982). *Making decisions in groups: Choices and consequences.* Glenview, IL: Scott, Foresman.

Gouran focuses on decision making in groups and deals with the preparation necessary for participation, as well as how to function once a decision-making discussion is under way.

Scheidel, T. M., and Crowell, L. (1979). *Discussing and deciding: A desk book.* New York: Macmillan.

The authors present a catalogue of activities, resources, and necessary skills that participants in decision-making groups should have to ensure effective performance. The book is especially useful for individuals who are untrained in group process.

Wood, J. T., Phillips, G. M., and Pedersen, D. J. (1986). *Group discussion: A practical guide to participation and leadership* (2nd ed.). New York: Harper & Row.

Wood, Phillips, and Pedersen take the reader through a step-by-step process they call the "standard agenda" and provide information about what participants need to know and be able to do at each stage.

Leadership in Problem-Solving and Decision-Making Groups

Chapter objectives

After reading this chapter you should be able to:

1. understand what leadership is

2. distinguish among the four perspectives from which leadership is viewed

3. describe the difference between designated and emergent leadership

4. appreciate the role leadership plays in problem-solving and decision-making discussions

5. perform the prediscussion, in-process, and postdiscussion responsibilities of leadership

6. identify personal qualities that promote effective leadership

Key terms and concepts

leadership
leader
trait
acquired traits
leadership style
group-centered style
leader-centered style
contingency theory
function
designated leader
emergent leader
unsung hero
climate
interpersonal sensitivity

In Chapter 11, we discussed problem-solving and decision-making groups, the requirements of the tasks they perform, and factors that contribute to their effectiveness. In this chapter, we deal with what sets such groups in motion, keeps them in motion, and enables them to attain their objectives. These matters are the concern of leadership. Since you could easily find yourself having the role of leader in a small group, the more you know about the subject, the more effectively you will be able to meet the responsibilities of leadership and exert the kind of positive influence it entails.

Of all the conditions that determine how well or poorly problem-solving and decision-making groups perform, the most frequently noted cause is leadership. This is understandable because leadership relates directly to the ability of group members to combine their talents and resources to achieve common goals. If no one in a group is capable of bringing about this type of integration, the potential of the members to solve problems and make good decisions is likely to go unrealized.

To become a successful leader, you need to know as much as you possibly can about four areas:

1. the nature of leadership;
2. the role leadership plays in problem-solving and decision-making groups;
3. the responsibilities of leadership; and
4. the qualities that contribute to effective leadership.

The information that follows, we hope, will give you a good start.

■ THE NATURE OF LEADERSHIP

Because of its importance to the successful performance of problem-solving and decision-making groups, it will be useful for you to be aware of how others have thought about leadership. With this background, you can better understand the mechanics involved in its exercise and why the qualities we later discuss are of value to leaders.

A Definition of Leadership

Teaching Objective 12–1
Define leadership as actions influential toward the accomplishment of goals and leaders as those who exert such actions. Seek real leaders, familiar to the audience, to use as examples.

In a recent review of research and theory dealing with leadership, Bass (1990) reports finding numerous definitions. Table 12.1 contains a sampling of these. Despite differences among them, these and other definitions have in common the notion of influence. Those who exercise leadership, then, in some way influence the manner in which groups perform tasks. The various definitions also convey the sense that such influence is positive. It contributes to the achievement of a group's goals. For the types of situations we are discussing, **leader-**

Table 12.1
Representative Definitions of Leadership

1. "The process of influencing the activities of an organized group in its efforts toward goal setting and goal achievement"	Stogdill 1950
2. "Influencing change in the conduct of people"	Nash 1929
3. "Interpersonal influence, exercised in a situation and directed, through the communication process, toward the attainment of a specified goal or goals"	Tannenbaum, Weschler, and Massarik 1961
4. "An interaction process in which an individual, usually through the medium of speech, influences the behavior of others toward a particular end"	Haiman 1951
5. "The presence of a particular influence relationship between two or more persons"	Hollander and Julian 1969

ship consists of any act that has positive influence in ensuring that the requirements of a problem-solving or decision-making task are satisfied. It follows from this definition that a **leader** is any member of a group who performs such acts.

Imagine yourself in a discussion about what students could do to encourage better teaching at your school (a problem-solving task), in which other members are presenting endless examples of poor teaching. If you were to say something like "I think we know what the problem is," you would be exercising leadership. Similarly, if the other members were continually interrupting one another and you were to observe, "There is plenty of time for all of us to have our say," again you would be exercising leadership. Finally, if you invited another member who had remained quiet throughout the discussion to share his or her thoughts with the group, this effort to achieve greater total input would also be an instance of leadership.

These examples all represent acts of leadership because they contribute to a group's ability to satisfy the requirements of its task. In the first case, you would be trying to move the group forward. In the second case, you would be taking a step to ensure that potentially good ideas would be fully expressed and heard. And in the last case, you would be attempting to maximize use of the group's collective knowledge. These examples show that leadership can occur in many different ways. It is also clear that a group member does not need extraordinary skills to exercise leadership. As Fisher (1988) has noted, leaders differ from others not so much in what they do, but in how frequently they do it.

Perspectives on Leadership

Those who study leadership tend to view it from one of four perspectives, or points of view—(1) the trait perspective, (2) the stylistic perspective, (3) the situational perspective, or (4) the functional perspective (Gouran 1970). Each perspective represents a different set of concerns, yet each has value for understanding the practice of leadership.

Discussion Question 12–2
What traits do you think of when you think of leaders and leadership? How are they similar to or different from the traits you find in the people you most admire?

The Trait Perspective.   A **trait** is any identifiable characteristic an individual possesses or appears to possess. From the trait perspective, leaders presumably differ from others in respect to personal characteristics. This perspective derives from the "Great Man" theory of leadership (Stogdill 1974). This theory essentially endorses the view that "leaders are born, not made." The thinking behind it is that individuals vary naturally in their capacity to exercise influence. Those with the greatest capacity for influence will more often than others be in positions of leadership. By comparing leaders with nonleaders, then, we should be able to determine how they differ in other respects.

Despite many studies of leader profiles involving such attributes as intelligence and physical size, available evidence has not established that leadership is the result of some set of inherited traits (Shaw 1981). What research on leadership has revealed with some consistency are differences between leaders and others in what we might call **acquired traits**, or characteristics an individual takes on and develops. Social participation, dependability, responsibility, self-confidence, independence, objectivity, and communication skill are among the acquired traits that leaders often appear to possess in greater degree than nonleaders (Bass 1990). The possession of such traits, of course, does not ensure that anyone will become a leader of a group or be able to exercise leadership when called upon to do so. Those who acquire them, however, have a better chance of getting into positions of leadership.

Current Research 12–1
Fairhurst and Chandler comparatively tested two approaches to leadership, one which defined and sought an "average leadership style" to characterize a leader's communication with members, and another which observed differences in leader-member exchanges between members described as in-group and those seen as out-group members. Fairhurst and Chandler found support for both views, a general leadership style displayed by the leader studied as well as differences in communication behavior with different group members. (Fairhurst, Gail, and Chandler, Teresa, Social structure in leader-member interaction. *Communication Monographs, 56,* 1989, pp. 215–233.)

The Stylistic Perspective.   Below is a list of ways in which one might behave in a group. Check the ones that you think best describe your own tendencies. Do not read further until you have completed the Self-Assessment Exercise.

If you checked more of the even-numbered items in the exercise, you may be inclined toward a group-centered style of leadership. If you checked more of the odd-numbered items, you may be more leader-centered in your style. What exactly does this mean?

Style refers to the characteristic manner in which individuals behave. The term **leadership style**, refers to the characteristic manner in which a person in a position of leadership or who is exercising leadership behaves in a group. Leadership style has been classified and labeled in a variety of ways, for example, as "democratic," "nondirective," "participatory," "directive," "structuring," and "authoritarian." In the context of problem-solving and decision-making groups, however, it is useful to think of leadership style as falling into two general categories: group centered and leader centered.

Discussion Question 12–3
Imagine and describe a variety of situations in which some kind of leadership would be needed. For each of these situations, would a group-centered or leader-centered style of leadership be more appropriate? Why?

A person exhibiting a **group-centered style** of leadership actively invites participation, guides discussion, asks for reactions to input, abides by the will of the majority, and seeks consensus for decisions and actions to be taken. He or she is likely to possess the attributes suggested by items 2, 4, 6, 8, and 10 in the Self-Assessment Exercise you just completed. In contrast, a person having a **leader-centered style** initiates and controls interactions, gives directions, uni-

SELF-ASSESSMENT   **Evaluating your leadership style**

Read each statement below, and place a check in the blank beside each item that you feel describes you reasonably well.

_____ 1. I like to be in charge.

_____ 2. Having majority approval is important to me.

_____ 3. It bothers me when someone else tries to do what I am supposed to be doing.

_____ 4. I am a firm believer in the saying that "two heads are better than one."

_____ 5. I agree with whoever said that "too many cooks spoil the broth."

_____ 6. I think that people should have a say in things that affect their lives even if they make the wrong judgments.

_____ 7. I do not like being slowed down by other people when I am trying to get something done.

_____ 8. I usually find other people's ideas interesting.

_____ 9. It seems like two people working together do about half as much as one person working alone.

_____ 10. In the long run, doing things democratically works out for the best.

laterally decides when to move discussion forward, and generally takes responsibility for determining what a group's solution to a problem or decision is. This type of leader is likely to have several of the characteristics suggested by items 1, 3, 5, 7, and 9 in the Self-Assessment Exercise. Carried to an extreme, the first style can result in little or no progress toward a group's objective, and the second style can contribute to inadequate attention to the requirements of a task. Few, if any, individuals, however, are completely group-or leader-centered in their style.

Early studies of leadership tended to favor the group-centered style, especially in respect to group member satisfaction (White and Lippitt, 1960). This is not surprising, since most of us find group-centered leaders more pleasant to be around and appreciate their apparent respect for our ideas and contributions. A person who is leader-centered in his or her style often leaves the impression that others' views on issues are merely to be tolerated. It is not always the case, however, that groups perform better under a group-centered style of leadership or that they are dissatisfied with those who take on a leader-centered style. In fact, we often refer admiringly to such individuals as a "take-

Current Research 12–2
Wheeless and Reichel found a relationship between the general communication styles and the conflict management styles of supervisors. In addition, they found a relationship of positive attraction by subordinates to supervisors who were noncontrolling and solution-oriented. (Wheeless, Lawrence, and Reichel, Lisa, A reinforcement model of the relationships of supervisors' general communication styles and conflict management styles to task attraction. *Communication Quarterly, 38,* 4, 1990, pp. 372–387.)

Different types of groups lend themselves to different styles of leadership. These mental health workers, who meet regularly to address the needs of their patients, may prefer a group-centered style of leadership.

Leadership Note 12–2
"Progressive leaders in any field never hide behind elitism and hierarchies. They lead through cooperation." (Dreher, Diane, *The Tao of Peace*. New York: Donald I. Fine, 1990, p. 181.)

Cross-reference 12–1
Recall that in earlier chapters the pervasive influence of the situation on the subsequent communication was emphasized. (Chapter 1, Chapter 4, and Chapter 7.)

charge kind of person." We also sometimes speak disparagingly of group-centered leaders as "wimps" and fault them for their apparent inability to act decisively.

Neither of the two general styles of leadership in itself is either good or bad. Negative reactions to either are usually the result of other factors that accompany a leader's style; for instance, his or her motives, attitudes toward others, and commitment to the group and its work and various aspects of the leader's personality. The important consideration in adopting a style of leadership is whether it is appropriate to the particular set of circumstances in which a group is performing a task and the characteristics of the participants. A group having limited time, no history as a group, and an unclear understanding of what is expected of it would probably function better under a leader-centered style. On the other hand, groups whose members know one another well, have experience in problem solving and decision making, and are used to the give-and-take of interaction likely would perform more effectively under a group-centered style of leadership. The recognition of the role that other factors play in determining the suitability of a particular style of leadership led to the next perspective we discuss.

The Situational Perspective.   Fred Fiedler, a social and industrial psychologist, began studying a wide variety of task-oriented groups to determine what accounted for success and failure. Over a twenty-year period, he came to the conclusion that leadership plays a pivotal role. Interestingly, however, he uncovered no evidence that any one style consistently explains good performance. Instead, he discovered that the effectiveness of a given style of leadership depends on the circumstances in which a group functions. A leader-centered style appears to be best under extremely unfavorable or favorable conditions, whereas a group-centered style appears best under moderately favorable conditions (Fiedler, 1967).

According to Fiedler, conditions for a task-oriented group are favorable when a leader has power, relationships with other group members are good, and the task is structured. Unfavorable conditions are just the opposite. As an illustration, a decision-making group with a new leader (low power and weak relationships) and no agenda (unstructured task) would probably perform better if the leader adopted a leader-centered style. This style would provide greater assurance that the requirements of the task would be satisfied. But why would the same group also perform better under a leader-centered style if conditions were highly favorable (an established leader, strong relationships, and a structured task)? Under such conditions, a group can move forward without a great deal of collaboration or interaction. The task becomes routine, the members value the leader, and they have entrusted him or her with authority. Between the extreme cases, other group members apparently feel a greater need to bring clarity to the task and may resent leader interventions that seem to deny them that opportunity.

Fiedler's pioneer work was important and led to what many people now refer to as contingency theory (Chemers, 1987). **Contingency theory**, a formalization of the situational perspective on leadership, states that the effectiveness of a leader's style depends directly on the characteristics of the situation in which leadership is being exercised.

As a leader of a problem-solving or decision-making group, you could easily find yourself having to change your style as circumstances in the group change. If the other members are spending too much time on an insignificant point, you might have to become directive and move on in the agenda. On other occasions, circumstances might suggest a switch from a leader-centered to a group-centered style. Suppose, for example, that a group you are leading has reached a tentative conclusion, but you sense that the members are uncomfortable with it. Something like this could occur in a meeting of fraternity or sorority officers concerning the expulsion of a member from the organization. Under these conditions, an invitation such as "Do you want to discuss the issue further?" or "Should we delay making a decision until the next meeting?" would be preferable to deciding on your own to end or prolong the discussion.

The Functional Perspective. The functional perspective on leadership grew out of the work of Raymond B. Cattell (1951). Cattell's contribution was to separate leadership from the formal position of group leader. In his view, acts that have impact on the performance of groups are leadership. What evolved from this notion was a more refined concept that portrays leadership as acts that serve necessary and desirable functions in moving a group toward its goals. Our definition of leadership reflects this perspective.

A **function** is anything an individual or group does that has a consequence. In this sense, every communicative act serves some function. Such acts may relieve or create tension, clarify or confuse issues, lead to or resolve differences of opinion, build or destroy cohesiveness, and the like. Some functions are

---

Current Research 12–3
Putnam and Stohl argue that much existing research on groups has insufficiently understood the importance of the broader situation or climate in which most bona fide or natural groups exist and the ongoing influence of those broader factors on the group's existence and interaction. (Putnam, Linda, and Stohl, Cynthia, Bona fide groups: a reconceptualization of groups in context. *Communication Studies, 41*, 3, 1990, pp. 248–263.)

Leadership Note 12–3
Covey's approach to leadership is functional, focused on what leaders should do rather than what they should be. Leaders should assume responsibility, create and sustain a vision, set priorities on the basis of what matters most, expect the best from people and situations, listen often and well, build a climate of creative cooperation, and continually seek personal renewal. (Covey, Stephen R., *The Seven Habits of Highly Effective People.* New York: Simon and Schuster, 1989.)

more important to a group's performance than others. For example, telling a joke may make others laugh, but in no other way have any significant effect on what a group does. On the other hand, offering clear definitions of ambiguous terms in a question such as, "What can be done to create more school spirit?", could facilitate progress in identifying the possible solutions to a problem a group is addressing.

Functions that facilitate movement toward a group's goal are sometimes specified. This is usually the case when a member of a problem-solving or decision-making group is assigned a leadership role. In this situation, the leader performs such functions as calling a meeting to order, reviewing the agenda, summarizing discussion at various points, stating the apparent consensus, and the like. In other instances, group members not designated as leaders may nevertheless perform leadership functions; for instance, intervening in a conflict, calling for additional information on a particular issue, and suggesting changes in procedure that could increase the efficiency of the group.

An important value of the functional perspective is its recognition that any member of a group can exercise leadership. This sharing of responsibility for the successful completion of problem-solving and decision-making tasks often is what sets effective and ineffective groups apart. There is no good reason for believing that the only person capable of exercising leadership is the one who is selected to lead a group. To understand this point better, complete the exercise in the Mastering Communication Skills box.

Discussion Question 12–4
Which is more important: (1) what a leader needs to do or what a leader needs to be; (2) skill at handling tasks or skill at handling people; (3) the kind of person you are or the power you have been given?

Were you able to identify a way to deal with each of the situations described in the exercise? If so, you show potential for exercising leadership. From the functional perspective, the key to successful leadership is realizing what needs to be done in a given situation and then proceeding to do it.

The four perspectives on leadership are valuable to prospective leaders because they suggest that leadership effectiveness depends on a combination of personal qualities, manner of behavior, ability to adjust to different circumstances, and knowledge of what problems must be overcome if a group is to

---

MASTERING COMMUNICATION SKILLS

Solving Group Problems

For each of the following situations, indicate how you would try to solve the problem mentioned.

1. Your group is off track.

2. One member of the group is dominating.

3. Two members of the group are engaged in name-calling.

4. A member's feelings are hurt by others laughing at something the individual had said.

5. The group has spent too much time on what you consider to be a relatively minor point.

Table 12.2
Major Perspectives for Understanding Leadership

1. Trait	Focuses on the personal attributes that distinguish leader
2. Stylistic	Focuses on the characteristic manner in which leaders behave
3. Situational	Focuses on circumstances that determine the appropriateness of given styles of leadership
4. Functional	Focuses on acts that contribute to the achievement of group goals

achieve desired outcomes. All four aspects of leadership are important. No one of them alone gives us a complete understanding of the concept. So that you can more easily recall what each perspective emphasizes, we have summarized them in Table 12.2.

Designated Versus Emergent Leadership

Most problem-solving and decision-making groups designate a member to serve as leader. That person may be called the chair, chairperson, presiding officer, moderator, or facilitator. The success of a group is rarely the result of what the designated leader alone does. As the preceding discussion of the functional perspective suggests, other group members perform leadership acts. This is particularly likely when the designated leader fails to meet his or her responsibilities or lacks the capability to do everything that is necessary to keep a group moving toward its goals.

A **designated leader** is the person who is specifically named to play the leadership role in a group. When someone other than a designated leader performs leadership acts with some degree of frequency, we refer to the person as an emergent leader. An **emergent leader** is an individual who fulfills the functions of leadership without being asked or expected to do so and later achieves recognition for his or her contributions. Because of their impact, emergent leaders frequently become designated leaders at some future point. This occurs because they have shown their capacity for leadership even though they are not in a position of leadership.

As a group member, you should be aware that providing leadership can improve your position. Many people refrain from active participation in the problem-solving and decision-making groups to which they belong because they are not in positions they consider to be influential. This kind of thinking leads to a *self-fulfilling prophecy*, which as we saw in Chapter 4, refers to a future condition that becomes more likely because one has predicted it (Aronson, 1980). In the situation we are describing, a group member does not attempt leadership because he or she expects never to be in a position of leadership—thereby making it very unlikely that he or she ever will attain a position of leadership.

Discussion Question 12–5
Where in your own life do you find evidence or examples of the impact of a self-fulfilling prophecy on what you did or did not accomplish?

Leadership Note 12–4
Leaders, too, can place limitations on future abilities or possibilities by focusing either on the strengths or weaknesses of their members. "Focusing on weaknesses usually reinforces them. . . . You'll get by by improving upon weaknesses, but you'll get great by improving on strengths." (Kriegel, Robert J., and Patler, Louis, *If It Ain't Broke...Break It!,* Warner, New York, 1991, p. 218.)

Nelson Mandela is an example of an emergent leader who, after his release from more than two decades in prison, became the designated leader of the African National Congress.

Leadership Note 12–5
"What managers expect of their subordinates and the way they treat them largely determine their performance and career progress." (Bennis, Warren, *On Becoming a Leader.* Reading, MA.: Addison-Wesley, 1989, p. 198.)

Acts that enable a group member to become an emergent leader are important for other reasons. Even if you do not improve your chances for becoming an acknowledged, or designated, leader, addressing situations that call for leadership is nonetheless valuable. If the work of your group is significant and you wish to see it succeed, then you should try to perform leadership functions that otherwise may be neglected. When their contributions are not recognized, individuals who take such initiative are called unsung heroes. An **unsung hero** is an individual who makes a difference in how well a group performs without others' notice. Remember, then, that even if your attempts at leadership do not result in your emergence as a leader or increase your chances for becoming a designated leader, in the role of unsung hero you can still have an important influence on how well a group performs.

THE ROLE OF LEADERSHIP IN PROBLEM-SOLVING AND DECISION-MAKING GROUPS

Whether you are a designated leader or simply a member of a problem-solving or decision-making group, there are many situations in which leadership will be called for. This necessarily makes leadership an important aspect of the performance of such groups. We discuss these situations in the section dealing with the responsibilities of leadership. Our purpose here is to describe the role of leadership. That role is twofold: (1) ensuring that the requirements of a group's task are satisfied, and (2) creating and maintaining a climate in which such assurance becomes possible.

In the preceding chapter, we reviewed the requirements for conventional problem solving, creative problem solving, and decision-making tasks. Of these, the requirements for the two types of creative problem-solving tasks are perhaps the easiest to meet and hence involve less leadership. Whether task requirements are simple or complicated, however, is not the most important consideration. What is important is that you be aware that a failure to deal with task requirements adequately sharply reduces a group's prospects of arriving at effective solutions to problems and making good decisions. Leadership is the exercise of positive influence on the achievement of a group's goals, and such influence has its greatest value when it ensures that a group does what it must to accomplish its task successfully.

The accomplishment of a problem-solving or decision-making task is not simply a matter of performing the activities the task suggests. Groups encounter many sources of interference. These may be external (for example, poor physical conditions) or internal (for example, dissension among members). Whether external or internal, sources of interference affect the climate in which a group discussion occurs.

A **climate** is the psychological atmosphere that surrounds a group. Some climates are unfavorable for effective problem solving and decision making. If you were in a group discussing how to provide a greater number of community services at reduced cost to taxpayers, conditions that would contribute to an unfavorable climate might include indifference to the question on the part of some group members, the presence of personal agendas, an overly warm room, late-evening scheduling, inadequate information about the topic, poor cooperation, and the uncritical acceptance of expert testimony.

Some of the conditions described above could be avoided; for instance, late-evening scheduling and overheating of the room in which the discussion is held. Others would not become evident until the discussion was in progress. A good leader attempts to create a favorable climate by doing whatever he or she can in advance of the meeting of a group to prevent discussion from getting off to a bad start and then deals with other situations that threaten to alter the climate as they arise. In either case, a leader undertakes such actions in the interest of minimizing problems that adversely affect a group's ability to satisfy the requirements of its task. The discussion of the responsibilities of leadership that follows will enable you to do this more effectively.

Teaching Objective 12–3
Explore the notions of role and climate as they apply to group interaction. Seek parallels to individual social roles and the notions of situational and relational context.

Discussion Question 12–6
How would you go about creating a positive psychological climate for a meeting or gathering?

Discussion Question 12–7
What is the difference between situational influences, context, and climate? What is the same about them? How much is overlap?

RESPONSIBILITIES OF LEADERSHIP

As we noted above, leadership entails efforts to ensure that the members of problem-solving and decision-making groups successfully accomplish their tasks. These efforts stem from either activities that are assigned to designated leaders or activities that untitled members of groups take on themselves to perform. We refer to these activities as prediscussion, in-process, and postdiscussion responsibilities. Pre- and postdiscussion responsibilities fall almost

FOCUS ON LEADERSHIP

Recognizing the Requirements of Group Leadership

For each activity below, use the letters PrD (prediscussion), IP (in-process), or PoD (postdiscussion) to designate the type of responsibility a leader would be performing.

_____ 1. beginning the meeting

_____ 2. putting a proposed solution to a problem into operation

_____ 3. sending out the agenda to group members

_____ 4. settling a disagreement between two group members

_____ 5. preparing a chart containing statistical information about an aspect of the discussion topic

_____ 6. conferring with a superior about what your group wishes to see done

_____ 7. suggesting that it is time for a group to take up another issue

_____ 8. recording a decision and preparing a written summary

_____ 9. seeing to it that the seating arrangement facilitates discussion

Answers: 1. IP; 2. PoD; 3. PrD; 4. IP; 5. PrD; 6. PoD; 7. IP; 8. PoD; 9. PrD

Teaching Objective 12–4
Emphasize the notion of leadership as extending beyond the specific boundaries of actual group meetings to the preparatory and follow-up work which is inevitable and essential to the successful completion of group tasks.

Cross-reference 12–2
Much of what is discussed here as the prediscussion responsibilities of leaders involves preparing for and seeking to create an environment in which effective listening is possible. See Chapter 3.

exclusively on designated leaders. In-process responsibilities, however, are ones that members of a group, in addition to the designated leader, often assume. It is in this domain that you are most likely to function as an emergent leader or unsung hero.

Before reading about the responsibilities of leadership, see if you can identify the appropriate category for each of the activities listed in the exercise in the Focus on Leadership box.

Prediscussion Responsibilities

When a group is asked to perform a problem-solving or decision-making task, certain arrangements usually have to be made in advance. These arrangements are the responsibility of the person in charge and include such items as setting a meeting time, finding a suitable location, and notifying the other group members about the time and place. In addition, a designated leader must identify the topic or question to be discussed, prepare an agenda if one is necessary, circulate relevant background information, and provide members with some indication of the type of preparation that is necessary. Depending on the situation, the leader may also have to arrange for the appearance of resource persons, prepare newly acquired information to be introduced at the meeting, and verify that any equipment the group may need will be available and in working order. The prime responsibility, of course, is ensuring that other group members understand what they are expected to accomplish and why.

As trivial as some of the prediscussion responsibilities mentioned may at first appear, when a leader fails to attend conscientiously to them, the possibilities for productive discussion can be severely hampered. For instance, if a leader were to send out a notice stating, "Our meeting next week will focus on the company's medical benefits package," it is unlikely that the other group members would know what is at issue and what they need in the way of information to be able to discuss the topic intelligently. Proper attention to prediscussion responsibilities, of course, is no guarantee that a group will perform effectively, but inattention to them increases the chances that it will not.

In-Process Responsibilities

The responsibilities of leadership are far from over when prediscussion activities have been completed. Once the discussion is ready to begin, the designated leader must

1. introduce members, if necessary;
2. call the meeting to order;
3. review the task to be performed;
4. make sure that the members understand what they are expected to do;
5. call attention to any potentially problematic requirements;
6. review the agenda (if there is one and it has not been previously circulated);
7. secure agreement about the procedures to be followed; and
8. introduce any relevant background information participants may not already possess.

If there are resource persons, consultants, or others who have been invited to attend the meeting, the leader should also introduce them and indicate why they are present.

Once the formalities have been observed and the participants are ready to begin discussing the topic, the leader often needs to initiate interaction. (An exception would be a creative problem-solving group using Nominal Group Technique, in which case the leader would instruct members to begin recording their ideas for how to solve a problem in writing.) Discussions do not start by themselves, and most participants are reluctant to be the first to offer a comment. Statements like "I suspect that we all now understand what we are supposed to do, so unless there are any questions, why don't we begin by trying to state the problem" are usually sufficient to start things moving. If not, the leader may have to call on someone to respond to a specifically framed question; for example, "Catherine, what is your sense of the problem?"

Leadership Note 12–6
Larson and LaFasto developed a broader vision of the responsibilities of leadership based on a lengthy study of diverse work and athletic teams. On the basis of their research, the authors propose these leader strategies: (1) Create clear and inspiring goals. (2) Create a structure that encourages results. (3) Bring competent people together. (4) Seek unity of commitment. (5) Create a cooperative climate. (6) Inspire excellence. (7) Offer support and recognition. (8) Employ transformational leadership—creating a vision, encouraging change, and freeing talent. (Larson, C. and LaFasto, F., *Teamwork: What must go right/What can go wrong.* Newbury Park, CA: Sage, 1989.)

Once you've gotten the proverbial ball rolling, an important responsibility is to keep it rolling—preferably in a desired direction. This is not easy to do. Some participants may be poorly prepared, apathetic, argumentative, uncooperative, and impatient or exhibit other problematic qualities. They may inadvertently, or even deliberately, abandon the agenda, pursue a hidden agenda, try to dominate, become emotionally upset by one another's comments, disregard the need for backing up their opinions, make confusing comments, express resentments about the procedures being followed (even after they have agreed to them), or withdraw. In brainstorming groups, one of the most difficult problems for a leader is to keep group members from making evaluative judgments. (Remember that members of such groups are specifically instructed not to engage in assessment, but merely to generate as many imaginative ideas as they possibly can.)

When problems like these impede a discussion, members almost always expect the designated leader to deal with them, especially in the early stages when the need for orientation and direction is high (Fisher, 1970). To execute in-process responsibilities well, a leader may have to become some combination of manager, soother, overseer, and referee. He or she must be able to spot digressions from task requirements and regulate interaction accordingly, be prepared for interpersonal difficulties and try to prevent them from becoming a distraction, know when to intervene in conflicts, and be able to raise appropriate questions about how well the group is conforming to its charge. Finally, an effective leader must be able to clarify issues, interpret ambiguous comments, determine when a point has been discussed enough, and identify the emerging group consensus, or if consensus has not been reached, point to the probable sources of difficulty.

The situations we have noted above are not all likely to exist in the same discussion. By knowing what could happen and being prepared for it, however, you will be better able to contend with problems when they do arise.

Postdiscussion Responsibilities

In some instances, a discussion leader's work is finished when the group has completed its task. The leader's final responsibilities under such circumstances are to review the outcome and determine whether others have the same perception of it. These are usually not the last pieces of business for the leader, however. If the group has been charged by some external agent to recommend a solution to a problem or make a decision, then the leader will need to inform those responsible. He or she will have to be prepared to report what was accomplished. Such an accounting might be oral, in writing, or both.

In the postdiscussion period, a group leader might also have to respond to questions from those who appointed the group or some other audience. As a leader, you might find yourself having to defend a particular solution to a problem or decision. The role of spokesperson for a group is not always the most pleasant one to have, especially if others are unhappy with what the group has done. Even if others are accepting, representing a group can be difficult. Senator John Tower in 1988, for instance, had the not-so-welcome duty of informing then-President Ronald Reagan on national television that the commission the president appointed to investigate the Iran-Contra affair had concluded that the president himself bore major responsibility (see *Report of the President's Special Review Board*, 1988).

Other postdiscussion responsibilities that a leader sometimes performs are relatively routine, such as setting a time for the next meeting and seeing to it that minutes are prepared and distributed. Beyond routine matters, a leader may also be responsible for devising means to implement a solution to a problem or decision. Whatever postdiscussion activities entail, you should be aware that as a group leader you will be the most likely candidate for executing them. In short, postdiscussion responsibilities "go with the territory" of a designated leader. Individuals who do not wish to have such responsibilities should think very carefully before agreeing to accept an appointment as leader of a problem-solving or decision-making group.

QUALITIES THAT PROMOTE EFFECTIVE LEADERSHIP

Since leadership has to do with ensuring that the requirements of problem-solving and decision-making tasks are satisfied, you will be better prepared for the role if you attempt to develop several personal qualities that contribute to its effectiveness. These include:

1. commitment to group goals;
2. sense of responsibility;
3. understanding of task requirements;
4. interpersonal sensitivity;
5. ability to manage conflicts;
6. verbal ability;
7. skill in listening;
8. openness to diverse views and opinions;
9. adaptability; and
10. fairness.

Commitment to Group Goals

To exercise leadership with much chance of success, a group participant must be committed to a group's goals. Since most groups' goals are accompanied by some amount of uncertainty, if a leader fails to show commitment, he or she can undermine the confidence of the members (Nixon, 1979). By revealing through your behavior that you take the work of your group seriously and that the outcomes you are attempting to achieve have importance, others are more likely to listen to what you have to say and follow your lead. A good leader sets the tone of problem-solving and decision-making discussions, but this is difficult to accomplish if others fail to see any evidence that a person attempting to exert influence is concerned about attaining the goals a group has set.

Teaching Objective 12–5
Describe and examine the qualities that promote effective leadership and how these qualities match or fit with the trait, stylistic, situational, and functional approaches to leadership.

Discussion Question 12–8
In groups you have been a part of in the past, which of these qualities did you find sufficiently represented most of the time? Which were least often present or represented? Which of these qualities do you think our culture has most successfully taught? And which have been least successfully transmitted?

Sense of Responsibility

Although important, your commitment to a group's goals is insufficient for exercising leadership. Taking responsibility for achieving them is critical. All too often members, while committed to the group's goals, nevertheless feel that their achievement is someone else's responsibility. The "let Mary do it" attitude has been the cause of more than one failure of problem-solving and decision-making groups. Recognizing what needs to be done and calling it to the attention of other group members is certainly an act of leadership, but if you seldom take initiative for doing more than that, over time, your contributions may begin to fall on deaf ears.

Understanding of Task Requirements

You probably have heard another person at one time or another observe about a successful athletic coach, "If I have players with that kind of talent, I could win a lot of games too." Such comments rest on a badly mistaken view of leadership. To be effective, a leader must understand task requirements. If you are deficient in this respect, you will be unable to recognize when your group is failing to perform well, or at least why. Merely sensing that something is going wrong or needs to be done will not enable you to take corrective action. You must be able to speak directly to the problem. You cannot do this unless you understand specifically what the problem is. For instance, a group having difficulty recommending a solution for a problem it has been discussing might have failed to generate a sufficient number of possible solutions. By knowing that problem-solving groups need to generate as many solutions as they reasonably can, you would be better able to advise the group on how it might come to grips with its difficulty.

Interpersonal Sensitivity

Cross-Reference 12–3
Interpersonal sensitivity requires both intercultural communication competence (Chapter 6) and interpersonal communication competence as defined in Chapter 7.

A group member can understand task requirements very well, recognize when they are not being satisfied, and still be ineffective in exercising leadership. The reason often is that the person lacks interpersonal sensitivity. He or she may be too blunt, intimidate other group members, anger them, make them feel foolish, show a lack of consideration for their opinions, and the like. This is unfortunate because the individual's good intentions may succeed only in creating further problems.

Interpersonal sensitivity, as we use the term in the context of problem-solving and decision-making discussion, has to do with one's perceptiveness and awareness of how to act toward others in given situations. A leader who is interpersonally sensitive attends carefully to the social environment of a group, considers how his or her behavior will affect the other members, and takes steps to avoid arousing negative feelings, if possible. You will be a more effective leader if you possess this quality. Consideration for others seldom does any harm and often is identified as one of the most valuable attributes a leader can possess (Hemphill, 1955).

Ability to Manage Conflicts

Because problem-solving and decision-making discussions frequently deal with controversial subjects, interpersonal conflicts are almost inevitable. Conflicts can result in sudden changes in the climate of a group (Pruitt and Rubin, 1986). And if they go unmanaged, a group may fail in its task. Having skill in the management of conflict, therefore, can be a useful asset for a leader.

Those who manage conflict well do so because they are usually able to change the frame of reference of group members who are experiencing conflict (Sherif and Sherif, 1953). Calling attention to what the group as whole seeks to accomplish (reinstating the group goal), trying to clarify the basis of a conflict, acknowledging the merits of competing points of view, and even asking the parties to a conflict to set aside their differences are among the strategies used by leaders who are skillful in conflict management. Whatever tactic may seem to be most appropriate for a given situation, the more sensitive you are to the need to prevent interpersonal conflicts from escalating, the better able you will be to maintain a climate in which the successful performance of a task can occur.

Verbal Ability

Group members who rise to positions of leadership tend to engage in more communicative activity than others (Riecken, 1958; Fisher, 1986). They are more active in many instances because they have well-developed verbal skills. Such skills enable one to define terms clearly, give good instructions, state issues concisely, provide meaningful summaries, integrate ideas and information, and perform many of the other activities associated with the leadership role in a group. It is not surprising, therefore, to find that leaders often exceed the average of their group in verbal skill (Klimoski and Hayes, 1980).

In groups, we establish our competence by what we say and how we interact with others. If other group members see you as competent, they will be more receptive to your attempts at influence. Competence gives a group member credibility, and credibility may be the most important source of interpersonal influence a person can possess (Bettinghause and Cody, 1987). It behooves you, therefore, to have as much verbal skill as possible if you want to do a better job of leading in problem-solving and decision-making groups to which you belong.

Skill in Listening

As we saw in Chapter 3, in addition to having good verbal skills, effective leaders also are good listeners and critical thinkers (Gibson and Hodgetts, 1986; Hackman and Johnson, 1991). Listening involves more than hearing what others say. A leader who uses listening skills tries to understand what other group members are trying to say, not just what they do say. They also share their perceptions to verify that their interpretations are consistent with the intentions of the person speaking. This level of care can do much to ensure a favorable group climate for problem-solving and decision-making discussions.

Current Research 12–4
Fisher and Ury of the Harvard Negotiation Project use this method for resolving conflicts: 1) Separate the people from the problem, 2) Focus on interests, not positions, 3) Invent options for mutual gain, and 4) Insist on using objective criteria. (Fisher, Roger, and Ury, William, *Getting to Yes: Negotiating Agreement Without Giving In,* New York: Penguin, 1981.)

Listening is important if a leader is to exert corrective influence in a problem-solving or decision-making group. Other members can easily fail to attend to what is being said or quickly forget. A group leaning toward a particular decision, for instance, may not recall that earlier in the discussion the members expressed a good deal of negative reaction to the favored alternative. By paying careful attention to the interaction throughout the discussion, a leader might be able to prevent the group from making a choice that its earlier discussion had indicated was not one for which there was much support.

Some ways in which you can be a better listener are to

Teaching Objective 12–6
Suggest that effective group leadership (exerting positive influence toward the accomplishment of group goals) is the shared responsibility of all group members.

1. try, whenever appropriate, to focus on content rather than manner of speaking;
2. recognize when you are being distracted;
3. ask others to repeat or rephrase unclear comments; and
4. anticipate how others may react to what is being said, and be prepared to respond accordingly if your anticipations are confirmed.

By developing these habits, you will become more sensitive to the dynamics of group interaction and miss much less of what goes on than you otherwise would.

Current Research 12–5
Putnam and Stohl find these additional characteristics of bona fide or natural groups: 1) stable yet permeable boundaries, simultaneously defining the group and allowing the influx of new members and new ideas; 2) interdependence with immediate context, an overarching climate of behaviors and message patterns which link the group to other groups and to the larger framework; 3) links between boundaries and context, wherein boundary disputes or conflicts within one group percolate into other portions of the context. Here, too, the overriding influence or importance of context and climate are emphasized. (Putnam, Linda, and Stohl, Cynthia. Bona fide groups: a reconceptualization of groups in context. *Communication Studies, 41*, 3, 1990, pp. 257–259.)

Openness to Diverse Views and Opinions

As leader, you will not always be in agreement with other members of the groups to which you belong. Disagreement, of course, makes it difficult to be receptive to others' thoughts and feelings about a subject under discussion. Despite this difficulty, it is important that you try to be open to ideas that may conflict with your own (Burns, 1978). Remember that the group is meeting in the first place because of uncertainty about what is the best solution to a problem or the most appropriate decision to make. A leader who is not receptive to diverse thinking increases the chances that a group will fail to achieve desired outcomes.

Adaptability

Adaptability is another quality that facilitates the exercise of leadership in problem-solving and decision-making groups (Fisher, 1985). Earlier, we discussed the situational perspective on leadership and indicated that conditions in groups can change quickly and pose the need for adjustments in leadership style. An individual who lacks the ability to adapt to changes in the climate of a group is ill prepared for leadership. Discussions are dynamic, not static, and leaders who cannot keep pace with the ebb and flow of interaction will be less able to exert the type of positive influence on the achievement of group goals that leadership represents.

Fairness

Of the qualities that people say they would like to see in leaders, a frequently mentioned one is fairness. Leaders who fail to deal with others in an even-handed manner are often viewed with contempt or disrespect. Participation in a group represents sacrifice, of time and autonomy. The fact of having made this sacrifice, in turn, will contribute to certain expectations on the part of the members. Among these expectations is that the person leading the group will provide adequate psychological compensation; that is, will acknowledge the other participants' efforts and contribute to the feeling that their membership counts. Without this sense of fair treatment, group members are unlikely to give their best efforts. The value of fairness in shaping the performance of groups has been put well by political scientist James MacGregor Burns. According to Burns (1978), "In real life, the most practical advice for leaders is not to treat pawns like pawns, nor princes like princes, but all persons like *persons*" (p. 462).

Summary

The most frequently noted cause for the effectiveness of a group's performance is leadership. Leadership consists of any act that has positive influence in ensuring that the requirements of a problem-solving or decision-making task are satisfied. Four perspectives from which leadership has been viewed are the trait perspective (what personal attributes distinguish leaders), the stylistic perspective (how a leader's characteristic manner of behavior affects group outcomes), the situational perspective (the influence of circumstances in determining the appropriateness of a leader's style), and the functional perspective (what acts contribute most substantially to the outcomes groups achieve). Leaders are members of groups who perform acts that have positive influence on group performance. They may be designated, or they may emerge. Sometimes group members exercise leadership without being recognized for it. When this occurs, they function as unsung heroes.

The role of leadership in problem-solving and decision-making groups is to ensure that the requirements of the task are satisfied and to create and maintain a climate in which such assurance is possible. This role is fulfilled by the enactment of activities that occur at several points. These are called prediscussion, in-process, and postdiscussion responsibilities. Qualities that facilitate effective leadership include (1) commitment to group goals, (2) a sense of responsibility, (3) understanding of task requirements, (4) interpersonal sensitivity, (5) ability to manage conflicts, (6) verbal ability, (7) skill in listening, (8) openness to diverse views and opinions, (9) adaptability, and (10) fairness.

Exercises

1. Think of a person you consider an effective leader. Try to recall what he or she has done to give you this impression. Then write a short essay in which you explain the basis for your feeling that the person in question is an effective leader. Remember, leadership consists of acts, so be sure that you refer to the person's behavior.

2. Ask several of your acquaintances if they know what leadership is. For those who say yes, ask for a definition. Do the answers reveal a very clear understanding? Do the respondents appear to have difficulty saying what they mean by the term? How many refer to personal characteristics as opposed to behavior?

3. Describe yourself as a prospective leader of a problem-solving or decision-making group. What do you see as your strengths? Your weaknesses? Do you believe that you could manage the responsibilities of leadership? If so, why? If not, why not?

4. Rate yourself on the ten qualities that promote effective leadership discussed in the chapter. Repeat exercise 3 in light of this assessment. Did any of your answers change?

5. Try to think of other qualities that contribute to leadership that are not mentioned in the chapter. Come to class prepared to discuss the reasons for your choices.

Related Readings

Bormann, E. G. (1990). *Small group communication: Theory and practice* (3rd ed., pp. 194–232). New York: Harper & Row.

Bormann discusses leadership in terms of both the requirements of the role and the ability to influence the performance of members. He has an excellent discussion of emergent leadership.

Chemers, M. M. (1984). The social, organizational, and cultural context of effective leadership. In B. Kellermann (Ed.), *Leadership: multidisciplinary perspectives* (pp. 95–112). Englewood Cliffs, NJ: Prentice-Hall.

Chemers reviews the various perspectives on leadership and traces their historical origins.

Chemers, M. M. (1987). Leadership processes: Intrapersonal, interpersonal, and societal influences. In C. Hendrick (Ed.), *Group processes* (pp. 252–277). Beverly Hills, CA: Sage.

In this essay, Chemers reviews the concept of leadership and argues in favor of the contingency approach as providing the best basis for understanding sources of effectiveness and ineffectiveness.

Fisher, B. A. (1985). Leadership as medium: Treating complexity in group communication research. *Small Group Behavior, 16,* pp.167–196.

Fisher makes the point that leaders are not unique in small groups. Rather, they engage in the same behavior as other group members. They tend to be more active, however, and more sensitive to the demands of given situations for particular sorts of acts.

Fisher, B. A., and Ellis, D. G. (1990). *Small group decision making: Communication and the group process* (3rd ed., pp. 222–255). New York: McGraw-Hill.

Fisher and Ellis discuss leadership as a role that develops and evolves in the course of group interaction and that depends heavily on communication.

Gouran, D. S. (1982). *Making decisions in groups: Choices and consequences* (pp. 147–172). Glenview, IL: Scott, Foresman.

In his chapter dealing with leadership, Gouran introduces the notion that leadership involves counteracting influences that threaten to prevent groups from achieving their goals. The chapter contains suggestions for how to exercise counteractive influence.

Gouran, D. S. (1988). Principles of counteractive influence in decision-making and problem-solving groups. In R. S. Cathcart and L. A. Samovar (Eds.), *Small group communication: A reader* (5th ed., pp. 192–208). Dubuque, IA: William C. Brown.

In this essay, Gouran develops the concept of counteractive influence as the key to successful leadership in problem-solving and decision-making groups.

Wood, J. T., Phillips, G. M., and Pedersen, D. J. (1986). *Group discussion: A practical guide to participation and leadership* (2nd ed.). New York: Harper & Row.

The entire book carries through the theme of leadership and explores the role of the leader in group discussion in all phases of development.

MASTERING
PUBLIC
COMMUNICATION

Analyzing Audiences to Choose Subject, Purpose, and Theme

Chapter objectives

After reading this chapter you should be able to:

1. identify several specific areas of audience analysis
2. explain several methods of analyzing these areas
3. describe the importance of an audience's belief system to audience analysis
4. identify several methods for adjusting speech form and content based on your audience analysis
5. identify helpful methods for finding speech subjects
6. select ("target") an appropriate subject
7. define the general purposes of public speaking
8. identify methods for developing an effective theme

Key terms and concepts

audience analysis
audience size
age factor
gender
level of education
income
occupation
membership
culture
time
intermember
   relationships
beliefs
attitudes
values
motives
appropriate subjects
knowledge bull's-eye
interest bull's-eye
speak to inform
speak to persuade
addressing a special
   occasion
addressing multiple
   purposes
theme
foresight
skill
industry

Jaime Escalante, a teacher in Los Angeles, was able to motivate students to excel in the difficult area of mathematics by presenting the subject to appeal to his audience.

Every type of communication—including interpersonal and group communication—requires analytical skills. Successful public speakers are analysts: They take the time and trouble to find out what their audiences are thinking and talking about—what their audiences accept as true, good, and beautiful (or the reverse). Recall the public speakers you have recently seen and heard in person, and then ask yourself: Which of them were more effective, the ones who were convinced that their ideas deserved attention, or those who, in addition to being convinced about the value of their own ideas, were informed about the audience's needs?

In a busy world, effective leaders develop a plan before sharing their talents with people. This plan is valuable whether it is intended to inform people of what to expect, challenge them to prepare for the tasks ahead, or even inspire them to fulfill their destiny. Political leaders build the "platforms" on which they run for office. For instance, economic leaders propose budgets, and social and religious leaders announce their visions of a better future. Educational leaders make the same preparations. Jaime Escalante prepared his high school mathematics students to score so highly in national competition that a motion picture—*Stand and Deliver*—was made in honor of his efforts.

Effective public speakers also develop a plan when they choose a subject, purpose, and theme for each speech. Speech subjects, purposes, and themes reflect your audience analysis.

In this chapter, we investigate the ways that effective public speakers learn to know their audiences. You will read about several areas of audience analysis. Each area provides specific cues about the form and content of speechmaking. This chapter also explains a method of choosing subjects that reflects the interests and knowledge of both you and your audience. Effective speakers need to tailor their subject matter so that it will fit a certain time period. Then we define four major speech purposes—to inform, to persuade, to address special occasions, and to accomplish multiple purposes. Once you choose an appropriate purpose, you then develop a distinctive theme. Themes for your speeches—the special perspectives you bring to your subject matter—flow naturally from your audience analysis.

ANALYZING AUDIENCES

Speeches should reflect an *adjustment* of ideas to people. Some audiences may know a lot about a certain topic. Other audiences may know very little. Effective public speakers find out what and how much audiences already know, and then present the ideas and arguments needed to establish their case. There is no deep mystery about the procedure; there is no pain involved for the speaker or audience. Not surprisingly, though, analyzing an audience requires a little effort.

Taking the task of analyzing her audience seriously, Lesli R. Johnson reflected on what she had seen and heard in the classroom before her presentation in a public speaking class.

Most of us spend a majority of our school years studying, but most of this studying is done under poor lighting and noisy conditions. As a matter of fact, *after I overheard several of you discussing this very problem last week,* I looked into the problem more closely. I found that poor study conditions can have an adverse effect on our health and, as a result, our work suffers. Today I'd like you to learn how to control the conditions in which you study in order to make the most of your study time—as well as reduce potential health hazards such as fatigue, headaches, and hearing loss. *By promoting better study conditions, you can make your work more efficient, you will feel better, and you may have more time to do the things you want.*

Proper lighting can save you from headaches and stiff necks that result from straining your eyes and sitting awkwardly to read books and papers. This can happen *during those late nights when you don't want the light to disturb anyone else.* Poor lighting can cause you to become fatigued and lose your concentration. This could mean, for example, rereading the same passage several times before understanding it. Under these conditions, your study time will not be as productive as it should be.

According to *Current Health* magazine, proper lighting includes the amount of light as well as the way the light is distributed. The

---

Teaching Objective 13–2
Emphasize the importance of finding a balance between one's own ideas and adjustments or adaptations to the needs and belief systems of the audience in order to effectively communicate one's ideas.

Discussion Question 13–1
What is the difference between adjustment or adaptation to an audience and "selling out," or telling an audience what it wants to hear? Where and how do we draw the line?

Leadership Note 13–2
"Although it's risky and hard, seek first to understand or diagnose before you prescribe is a correct principle manifest in many areas of life. It's the mark of all true professionals." (Covey, Stephen, *The 7 Habits of Highly Effective People.* New York: Simon and Schuster, 1990, p. 243.)

Directly acknowledges relationship between audience's concern and her speech

Tells her audience members the benefits they will receive if they listen to the speech

Addresses the fact that many in her audience study late at night

amount of light needed depends on what you are doing. For example, doing homework or reading requires bright lights. But you need less light *when using a computer*—so that the light won't wash out the screen's image or reflect back in your eyes. How the light is distributed also affects your studying. For example, if you don't use other lighting along with your reading lamp, the dark room and the brightly lit page will cause eyestrain and will slow your reading as well. Your study efforts will be relatively worthless!

> *Appeals to her audience's habits*

The other study condition that can be a health hazard is noise. *I have seen many students study with their Walkmans on or with their stereos blasting.* However, prolonged exposure to these loud noises has been found to pose health problems, such as headaches, nausea, sleep disorders, high blood pressure, loss of appetite, and general irritability. Excessive exposure to loud noises can also cause hearing loss by damaging the inner ear. Not only is this noise a potential health hazard, but it also distracts you from your studies. Research has shown that you will get more done in a shorter period of time if you study away from distractions such as loud music.

> *Addresses her specific audience*

Many of us study at the library. But some of the smaller libraries—such as the business library—have very poor lighting. This creates better sleeping conditions than studying conditions! In order to manage your health and your studying time, you can make your own study hall at home. The ideal setup includes a comfortable chair at a desk that has a non-glare, light-colored surface. Your desk lamp should be fifteen inches from your work and the same distance above it. Your desk should not be placed in front of a window since night-time darkness and daytime glare can both cause eyestrain. Also, the ideal study hall should be located away from distractions such as sources of loud noise.

> *Acknowledges audience's habits*

If you follow these guidelines on lighting and noise, you will be on your way to feeling better, making your study time more productive, and having extra time to do what you want.

(Used with permission of Lesli R. Johnson.)

> *"Audience analysis is an element of public speaking that is relatively difficult and time consuming, but in the long run speeches will be more effective because of it. . . . I found audience analysis to be very useful when preparing speeches. Not only was I able to choose a topic that would interest my particular audience, but also I was able to give a speech that kept them interested"* (Lesli R. Johnson).

As a public speaker, you should learn as much about your audience as you can. Learning about audiences enables you to make helpful adjustments in the form of your speeches (the language and delivery you use) as well as their content (the ideas and materials you use).

Teaching Objective 13–3
Provide meaningful examples of what it means for a speaker to adapt to her audience.

Teaching Objective 13–4
Develop the concept of audience analysis as the need to know what is important to know about whom we are addressing.

ANALYZING A SPECIFIC AUDIENCE

Audience analysis is an investigation of audience characteristics, including demographic variables, such as *age, gender, level of education,* and *income,* and audience *values, attitudes,* and *beliefs.*

When analyzing your audience, some of the questions you will need to consider include the following: How large a group is it? Are the group members mostly males or females? What proportion of them are rich, poor, or struggling? Elderly, young, or middle-aged? Are they highly educated? Undereducated? Are they also members of a particular culture? Why are they gathered together? Several types of information have traditionally been meaningful for public speakers, as illustrated in Figure 13.1. Directly observing listeners before speaking to them—as Lesli Johnson did—provides information about audience size, age, and gender. However, unless you are addressing a special group or club, you will also need to ask specific questions before a speech in order to learn about educational levels, incomes, occupations, and memberships. Both observation and questioning are typically needed to learn about cultural traditions in the audience.

Size

Audience size is important because it often determines how formally a speech should be presented and how much detail will be appropriate in a speech's content. While there is no standard measurement of small versus large audiences, small group-researchers define a small audience as having fewer than twenty people.

Unlike small audiences—where a speaker might be able to address each listener by name and look each of them in the eye—large audiences usually require a speech to be presented in a more impersonal manner. For example, you should not try to chat with a group of one hundred listeners; it is seldom, if ever, appropriate. People do not expect a total stranger to engage them in an intimate conversation, or appreciate it when one does. Even if all members of a

Teaching Objective 13–5
Examine the idea that there are some things we can try to ascertain about others through direct observation.

Current Research 13–1
Ti-Grace Atkinson, a contemporary radical feminist, has been a frequent speaker to women's groups and also on college campuses: "Her college speeches illustrate her audience analysis techniques because she found it more difficult to speak to youthful groups who could not easily identify with oppression and who did not understand feminist issues. She solved the rhetorical problem of making feminism relevant to college women by personalizing much of the information in tone, choice of language, ideas, topics, and examples...drawn from her own experiences and from those of college women, and by providing the necessary background information on the movement. . . . " (Duffy and Ryan, *American Orators of the Twentieth Century,* 1987, p. 9.)

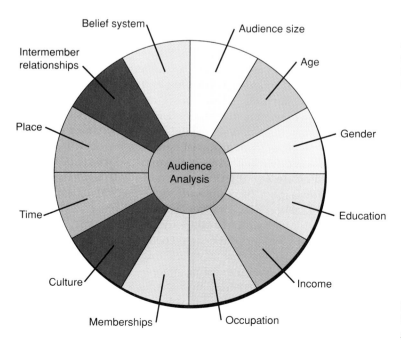

Figure 13.1
Factors in Audience Analysis.

Discussion Question 13–2
What are the tools we normally use to "investigate our audience" when we are meeting a person for the first time at a party or other social gathering?

Cross-reference 13–2
Connect the discussion of audience analysis through direct observation to earlier discussions of how we perceive (Chapter 2) and how we use nonverbal factors to make judgments about others, particularly in the area of first impressions (Chapter 5).

Teaching Objective 13–6
Describe the various standard demographic variables and why they are useful, what kinds of information can be learned and what can be inferred from this type of knowledge, emphasizing again why it is important for a speaker to know these things in order to adapt to the realities of the audience.

Current Research 13–2
Georgie Anne Geyer, author and columnist, delivered the commencement address at St. Mary's College, Notre Dame, Indiana, on May 14, 1988. In "Is Your Generation Doomed to Live in a Second Class America," Geyer made repeated reference to the age and life stage of the generation of young women she was addressing, as well as to their unique role and importance as women. (Geyer, Georgie Anne, Is your generation doomed to live in a second class America? *Vital Speeches,* August 1, 1988, pp. 627–631.)

large audience could hear you, you would find it necessary to exclude some of them from your gaze in order to maintain a chatty approach. Instead, most large audiences expect you to speak more formally or impersonally than if the audience were small.

Large audiences also make it necessary to speak in general rather than specific terms. The reason is simple. It is very hard to predict the specific example or name that will impress a large group because such an audience normally includes people with a wide variety of interests and preferences. When you speak to a large audience, address items of general knowledge and interest, or mentally divide your listeners into smaller groups and then use examples and names of significance to each distinct subgroup. For example, a speech given to a large audience on exciting changes in popular music may require you to talk about the most universal elements of music, such as rhythm, melody, and lyrics. Or, if you address your audience in subgroups, you may be able to talk about specific changes in country and western music, soft rock, and heavy metal music.

Age

Although national organizations such as the Gray Panthers and the American Association of Retired Persons are working to protect their members from discrimination based on age, the fact of age itself is widely accepted as a distinguishing mark among people. In the past, analyzing the age of audiences was not a great concern in the traditional college classroom. However, as more adult learners enroll in college, classroom speeches demand that attention be paid to the **age factor**. Of course, the age of the audience will always be significant beyond the classroom setting.

The form of speeches can be adjusted generally to suit audiences that include mostly older people or mostly younger people. One type of style or delivery may not be appropriate for audiences that contain several age groups. Older audiences may expect a polished type of speechmaking in which the speaker dresses formally, stands erect, and fits the profile of a traditional orator. Younger audiences may not expect traditional forms of speechmaking and may accept a speaker who dresses casually or sits on the edge of a table while speaking. Of course, a youthful group of conservatives may be uncomfortable with an informal style of delivery, while a group of older artists, writers, naturalists, and so forth might be equally uncomfortable with a formal style of delivery. Just knowing one aspect of your audience, therefore, will not provide you with enough information to appeal successfully to it.

Speech content should reflect the different bases of experience of mature audiences and younger audiences. For instance, even a carefully prepared, sincerely delivered speech on "My First Date" may bore both old and young audiences—but for different reasons. People who have dated, married, divorced, and possibly remarried may find the speech cute for a while. However, the speech had better include some very entertaining or poignant stories, or else experienced audiences will not pay attention when the cuteness wears off. On the other hand, people who have recently started dating may have a short attention span because they do not want to hear about social interaction—they want to do it! In addition to different levels of experience, audiences of varying ages draw on different sources of knowledge. A speech on the do's and don'ts of preparing income tax returns may be painfully obvious to an older audience, but completely mysterious to younger listeners. On the other hand, younger audiences will probably understand a speech on the merits of heavy metal music more readily than older audiences.

Gender

Gender is a meaningful factor in audience analysis. Today's public speakers have a difficult task when it comes to accurately perceiving their audiences on the basis of gender. When sexism was the norm, public speakers often assumed that women and men had distinctly different reactions to certain speech topics and modes of presentation. Today, however, women and men share many of the same roles in society—those of worker, spouse, and parent, for instance. Leaders of all types know that the roles we select or find ourselves in exert as great an influence over personal preferences as sexual identity.

Speech content must be adjusted to reflect current trends in *gender roles.* Today, for example, many men are anxious to learn about the essentials of cooking and domestic management. Similarly, many women seek information about paths to business and professional advancement. In choosing topics for informative speeches, you should keep current trends in audience needs in mind.

Education

Education in its full sense occurs in many places and involves a variety of learning activities. While public speakers should not confuse "education" with "intelligence," as a very general rule, the number of years spent in formal schooling are related to a person's ability to understand and appreciate the various forms and contents of speeches.

The audience's **level of education** is significant in formal terms because well-educated people have probably seen and heard several approaches to public speaking at school, on the job, and in society at large. As a result, well-educated audiences are typically receptive to a variety of presentational methods. Less educated audiences may be inattentive to low-key presentations in a public setting, may be distracted by unusual forms of speechmaking, and may actually be suspicious of highly polished speeches.

Well-educated people tend to care more about distant places, long-range planning, and abstract principles than do the less educated. In other words, people who lack education typically focus on the tangible world of "here and now" (Mitchell, 1983). For practical purposes, well-educated audiences may surpass their less educated counterparts in caring about speeches on the Third World, or business needs in the next century. However, a less educated audience may care as much as others about hometown poverty, or how to make a profit tomorrow.

Discussion Question 13–3
How can we discover and use information such as the age and gender of our audience without stereotyping?

Current Research 13–3
While many assumptions are made about gender differences between men and women, there are only two areas in which actual differences have been corroborated by extensive research with children. Girls have greater verbal ability than boys and are more responsive to verbal cues, whereas boys are more responsive to visual cues and have greater skill at developing spatial solutions. (Stewart, Stewart, Friedley, and Cooper, *Communication Between the Sexes,* Scottsdale, AZ: Gorsuch Scarisbrick. 1990, pp. 30–31.)

Discussion Question 13–4
Do you consider yourself well-educated or less-educated? What kinds of presentations and presenters are you most receptive to? What kinds of teachers are able to move you to openness about their subject matter?

As a general rule of thumb, you should not underestimate your listeners' intelligence, nor should you overestimate your audience's ability to infer meaning. *In practice, this means you need to speak clearly, define your terms, and present the needed information to convey your message.*

Income

Income provides special clues about the relevance of certain speech topics. For example, if you are seeking donations to a charitable cause, you definitely should consider the average income of your audience! However, **income** may be the least informative criterion to use as a guide for building speech form and content. In a country like the United States, income is often unrelated to a person's taste; for instance, whether in life-style or speech style. Rather than income, other areas should be analyzed in planning speeches on general topics.

There are times, of course, when income may reasonably be expected to dictate the type of response a public speaker will meet. If your speech is on the tax shelter benefits of buying the paintings of great masters, for instance, common sense indicates that all but the richest audience will be unmoved.

When money is not an issue, however, the average income of the audience may not affect your speech preparation. In fact, income may confound your findings from other types of audience analysis. For example, if you are relatively young, then you may expect an older audience to have a relatively high income. Yet many older Americans live on fixed incomes that are relatively low. In sum, be cautious when interpreting the importance of income in your audience analysis.

Even in a gathering such as a town meeting, in which everyone belongs to the same community, audience factors such as age, gender, income, and occupation may point to the existence of widely divergent interests and needs.

Occupation

Occupation may be important in your analysis because many people define themselves in terms of the jobs or positions they hold. Many students measure the success or failure of their education in relation to the jobs or professions they pursue after graduation. What is the second or third question that an adult is asked by strangers at a party or some other social occasion? Most likely it is "What do you do?" Because work is so central to our culture, retirement, for instance, is considered a major life transition.

Although your analysis of occupation probably will not influence the form of speechmaking you choose, you should consider relevant adjustments in content. If many members of your audience are avid hunters, then you probably shouldn't choose this audience to address the topic of animal rights, at least not if your theme is that killing animals under all circumstances should be banned. Far more important than topic selection is the particular focus, or emphasis, you give the topic. When addressing a group of economists, for example, the focus of a speech on "Getting American Industry Back on Its Feet" should take into account the sophisticated knowledge of the audience. A speech on the same topic to a group of retired steelworkers might stress less technical information, concentrating instead on broad government policies that help or hinder the steel industry. Occupation may also influence your use of illustrations and evidence. For example, an audience made up largely of accountants will probably appreciate "bottom line" information, such as statistics. An audience of artists will probably appreciate visual examples and aids. Whatever occupations seem relevant to your audience, remember that people often equate their work with their survival. Plan your content accordingly! In other words, *structure your message in terms that appeal to the orientations of your listeners. Knowing listeners' occupations is a clue to their orientations.*

Memberships

Memberships can be voluntary (when you choose to join a social club, political party, etc.) or involuntary (when you are born into a family, a citizenship, etc.). Voluntary membership may be renounced if the organization conflicts with personal values. Involuntary membership may be forfeited under a variety of circumstances. Group membership can be rewarding socially and professionally, intangibly and tangibly. As one credit-card-company proclaims, "Membership has its privileges." Because of the various types of rewards offered, memberships influence the way that the individual member thinks and feels. As an effective public speaker and leader, you need to keep track of group loyalties and other affiliations that exert influence on your audience.

Sometimes, the memberships of the audience require adjustments in speech form. For example, addressing criminal justice majors as "Ladies and Gentlemen of the Jury" might break the ice with this audience. Successful public speakers show they care enough about their audiences to make special accommodations to them.

Speech content should also reflect sensitivity to group norms and expecta-

Discussion Question 13–5
What kinds of inferences do we normally draw about people on the basis of their work? How could we test the accuracy of our inferences?

Current Research 13–4
Judith Humphrey, public affairs executive for the Bank of Montreal, adapted her speech to the International Association of Business Communicators on October 27, 1987, by using examples specifically related to corporate communication and executive roles in corporations. (Humphrey, Judith, Writing professional speeches, *Vital Speeches*, March 15, 1988, pp. 343–345.)

Cross-reference 13–3
Remember that in Chapter 4, we observed the ways in which language defines membership. A speaker's adaptations can be used to claim membership or at least kinship with the roles occupied by audience members. Knowledge of occupation allows adaptations to the role, face, and identity management issues discussed in Chapter 7, allowing the speaker to affirm the identities of audience members.

Discussion Question 13–6
In how many groups do you hold voluntary memberships? What do you think those memberships say about you?

tions. For example, in speaking to an audience made up largely of unionized workers, you might state your general appreciation for what organized labor has accomplished. Sometimes speakers are asked to address groups whose values the speaker does not share. In this event, you may decide to forgo the invitation. Adjustment to your audience does not mean that you should give up your personal beliefs or hide them by addressing an audience with insincerity.

Culture

There are many different definitions of culture. For the purposes of public speaking, **culture** should be understood as the shared values, customs, and beliefs of members of your audience. These factors, because of their richness and complexity, provide valuable information about the audience.

Current Research 13–5
"Western and European philosophy is based upon 'I think therefore I am.' Black African philosophy is simply, 'I am.'" (Thomas, William O., as quoted in *Mixed Blessings: New Art in a Multicultural America*. New York: Pantheon, 1990, p. 64.)

On questions of form, for instance, you might mention respect for authority and elders when addressing a group of Japanese listeners. Doubtless, deeply religious members of your audience will not tolerate profanity of any sort. Consider local customs when deciding on humorous anecdotes to include in your speech. Is it effective to poke fun at football in Pennsylvania, hockey in Michigan, or basketball in Indiana? Local culture might even dictate how long you should speak and how many distractions are likely. The British Parliament, for instance, sanctions active heckling of speakers! "Culture influences people so profoundly, constantly, and pervasively that we usually do not realize it is there" (Benderly, Gallagher, and Young, 1977, p. 7).

The audience's culture may also require extensive adjustment of speech content. Race, for example, may influence your choice of topic and purpose. Minorities with a long history of discrimination do not need to have bigotry explained to them; identifying new ways to solve racism might find a more receptive audience. Religion may also influence your choice of evidence. A largely Islamic audience would find quotations from the *Koran* more relevant than *New Testament* gospels.

Public speakers should be curious about people. Your recognition of audience size, age, gender, education, income, occupation, memberships, and culture will indicate relevant adjustments in your language and delivery or in your ideas and evidence. You can also gather important information about audiences by considering their feelings about the time and place of your speech, their intermember relationships, and their belief systems.

Time

Teaching Objective 13–7
Accentuate the value to a speaker of understanding the occasion of a presentation—the size of the audience, the time and place of the gathering, the expectations of the audience as to length of presentation, etc.

The **time** of day, the time of year, and the timing of your speech all influence audience reaction. The *time of day* at which you speak affects audiences' receptivity. Listeners who never rise for breakfast before noon will find it hard to pay attention to your speech in an 8:00 A.M. communication class. On the other hand, people who belong to social or professional groups that always meet for breakfast at 7:00 A.M. will likely be receptive and attentive to an early morning speech. Before agreeing to give a late night speech, you should be confident that your audience will be receptive to such scheduling.

Particular *seasons* of the year may call for speeches of special form and content. For example, some audiences would actually be distracted if you did not wear at least some shamrock green color on March 17. Similarly, a speech given on the first warm and sunny day in many months' time might include acknowledgment of that fact.

Always remember that it is the nature of audiences to grow restless if a speech exceeds its expected length. When a definite time limit has been assigned for your speech, observe it! If you have not been advised of a definite time limit, ask the person in charge of the meeting or a representative listener about the length of speech your audience is expecting.

Place

Before you deliver a speech, become familiar with the *room* or *area* to be used. This may require a quick look at a classroom or conference room, or it might mean surveying a courtyard or mall. What do you "feel" about the place? Do you share enough in common with your listeners to predict that they will feel the same way? An otherwise well-prepared speech may not succeed if the speaker neglects to consider potential reactions to the mood of a place—whether that general feeling is produced by lighting, temperature, furnishings, or other features. Simply expressing your feelings about the place early in your speech might establish a desirable rapport with listeners who feel the same way.

In addition, if the place has special significance for the audience, then referring to that special meaning may provide a comfortable beginning to your speech. For example, you might gather a few bits of information about the person for whom a room has been named or the event to which a courtyard has been dedicated.

Several items you learn through audience analysis may depend on the *geographical region* in which you deliver a speech. A city, county, state, or small group of states is often famous for a particular occupation or culture. For example, this textbook was written under the regional influences of Pennsylvania Dutch folklore and the Indiana limestone industry. Using a few, carefully selected adjectives or phrases ("Nittany Lions," "Hoosier") may demonstrate your attention to regional interests and pride. Using local examples or stories may make your information or arguments especially attractive to a regional audience.

Intermember Relationships

Intermember relationships are the social dynamics among a group of listeners. Although the dynamics of a given group cannot be fully described without sophisticated study, you can look for outward signs of a few important relationships. For example, people who are uncomfortable or unhappy with being part of the audience will typically sit apart from other audience members. They will also avoid speaking to others in the audience or sharing such items as pencils and notebooks. People who hold leadership positions, on the other hand, will frequently be quite talkative. They may even be surrounded closely by admirers.

Cross-reference 13–4
The importance of physical setting was discussed in Chapter 1. Also, the impact of spatial arrangements and furnishings was described in Chapter 5.

Leadership Note 13–3
Sometimes leaders can win over their audiences through a combination of humor and connection to the realities of the place where they are speaking. The comedian Mort Sahl spoke to students and faculty on the campus of Northern Illinois University in DeKalb, Illinois, in the early 1970s; NIU is a sprawling state university dotted with buildings erected at various times and representing various architectural styles. Sahl began by congratulating Northern Illinois University on its "architectural competition," then added, "I'm sorry nobody won."

Teaching Objective 13–8
Explore the notion of intermember relationships and its relevance to a speaker's presentation.

The presence of happy or unhappy leaders or followers may require the public speaker to pay special attention—in word and deed—to these special audience members.

Discussion Question 13–7
Which of the various factors considered in audience analysis exerts the greatest influence on what an audience believes? Why?

Ask yourself related questions about larger aspects of the audience. For example, is the audience split into two or more visibly separated groups? If so, do these subgroups avoid contact with one another? Answers to these questions may indicate how the audience feels about itself. A divided audience may require the public speaker to address each segment differently. Also, subgroups of the audience that appear to dislike other subgroups may require the public speaker to keep the peace in order to get a message across. You need not be an expert in group dynamics to be an effective public speaker; Chapter 11 provides enough information for you to determine the meaning of various dynamics in your audience.

Belief System

Teaching Objective 13–9
Discuss the concept of belief systems and the elements of values, attitudes, and motives which together comprise such a system, clarifying the differences between these elements.

The collection of **beliefs** held by an audience—opinions, feelings, or viewpoints about what is true, good, and desirable, or their opposites—represents a major factor in audience analysis. Consider all the attention paid to public opinion by advertisers, politicians, and others who want to lead people toward a purchase, a vote, or any type of practical decision. Indeed, all of the analytical areas discussed so far influence the formation of beliefs. For example, public speakers try to learn about the effect that ages or occupations will have on the audience's viewpoint on the speech topic. When you reflect on the time and place of your speech, you try to discover the audience's feeling toward the setting. However, a belief system is not simply the sum of age, occupation, time, place, and other factors. To learn audiences' opinion about any subject—including themselves—you should examine relevant values, attitudes, and motives (see Figure 13.2).

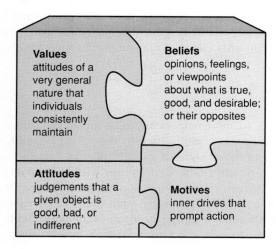

Values
attitudes of a very general nature that individuals consistently maintain

Beliefs
opinions, feelings, or viewpoints about what is true, good, and desirable; or their opposites

Attitudes
judgements that a given object is good, bad, or indifferent

Motives
inner drives that prompt action

Figure 13.2
Audience Belief System.

Values.   **Attitudes** are judgments that a given object is good, bad, or indifferent. **Values** are attitudes of a very general nature that individuals consistently maintain. Anything of value is desirable for its own sake. Many people value their car or house without reference to its so-called market value. Students take a similar measurement of college or professional education: They consider the status of the degree they will earn rather than the amount of money needed for the degree. In a general sense, the value of anything to us may be measured on the same scale. Things that are highly valued are always easy to name but often hard to get. For example, everyone would like to enjoy good health throughout life, but good health is often difficult to maintain. Many people want to be wealthy, but only a few succeed. Also, different individuals may place a different value on the same thing. For example, some people value good health above everything else, including wealth, while other people would rather build their bank balance than invest in a checkup.

While values can be complicated, those that you uncover can reveal a lot about your audience. If you learn your audience's values, then you can choose a highly valued subject for your speech or—without changing your subject—you can discuss relevant values in explaining or advocating your ideas. For an audience that places value on wealth, for instance, you could address investment plans, or you could discuss the economic benefits related to another subject. The same techniques of subject selection or speech development can be used with any audience values you discover. Whatever the relevant values may be, the effective public speaker recognizes and addresses them.

Attitudes.   Most of the public opinion polls you read or see on television measure attitudes. When you analyze attitudes, you learn about people's likes and dislikes as they apply beliefs and values to an object or idea. As we have noted, an attitude is a judgment that a given object is good, bad, or indifferent. An attitude is the result of judging something specific, as opposed to holding a general belief or value. Someone who believes that the human body is a divine gift may have a negative attitude toward another person who eats junk food. Someone who values wealth may think very highly of a successful business merger or skillful corporate takeover. Many attitudes remain fixed throughout a person's life; others fade or change dramatically. True lovers of beauty may never appreciate merely sturdy shoes or a merely reliable car. However, some rugged individualists may lose their distaste for "socialized medicine" and grow to like the idea of national health insurance.

Attitudes are especially informative in audience analysis because they are specifically tied to an object or idea. Discovering values answers the question of *how* an audience sees reality; discovering attitudes answers the question of *why* an audience feels the way it does (See Weisberg and Bowen, 1977, p. 4). If audience analysis is conducted within a reasonable time prior to delivering the speech, attitudes will probably not change.

To discover your audience's values and attitudes, design and use your own opinion polls. These written surveys should be short and to the point, but clearly aimed at producing the kind of specific information you need. (If a survey is not possible, then do the next best thing: talk to those people who are

Figure 13.3
Sample Questionnaire.

1. Each of the following is abused on campus (mark your choices):

   a. Cocaine/Crack Cocaine   _____ Agree   _____ Disagree   _____ Unsure
   b. Heroin   _____ Agree   _____ Disagree   _____ Unsure
   c. Marijuana/Hashish   _____ Agree   _____ Disagree   _____ Unsure
   d. Cigarettes   _____ Agree   _____ Disagree   _____ Unsure
   e. Alcohol   _____ Agree   _____ Disagree   _____ Unsure
   f. Over-the-counter legal drugs   _____ Agree   _____ Disagree   _____ Unsure

2. How widespread a problem is drug abuse on campus? (circle one):

   Extremely Serious   Very Serious   Serious   Mildly Serious   Not serious

3. Some people feel that drug abusers need punishment and not counseling (mark your response):

   _____ I agree
   _____ I disagree
   _____ Unsure

4. Why do you feel the way you do about drug abusers? (write a brief answer)

[Optional] **5.** I abuse (circle one):

   a. Cocaine/Crack Cocaine   Never   Sometimes   Often   All the time
   b. Heroin   Never   Sometimes   Often   All the time
   c. Marijuana/Hashish   Never   Sometimes   Often   All the time
   d. Cigarettes   Never   Sometimes   Often   All the time
   e. Alcohol   Never   Sometimes   Often   All the time
   f. Over-the-counter legal drugs   Never   Sometimes   Often   All the time

members of the group you will be addressing and who are in a position to know the audience's attitudes.) The questionnaire in Figure 13.3, designed for a classroom speech about "Drugs on Campus," illustrates the types of questions you might use in one of your own polls.

You will not need to become an expert in survey research to improve your public speaking. Therefore, the sample questionnaire is not especially sophisticated or subtle. Note, though, that it is relatively brief and devoted exclusively to drug abuse. Although all surveys have flaws, the best surveys make an honest effort to reach their goals with accurate, unbiased questions. In the sample questionnaire, for example, each item requests information about the respondent's current awareness of and attitudes about the problem. Moreover, the questions are of several different types: items 1 and 3 ask for simple agreement or disagreement; item 2 asks for strength of agreement; item 4 is open-ended; that is, it allows the respondent to say any number of things. Using several types of questions is desirable if you wish to gather a wide range of subjective information. If you need only one or two pieces of information, then use only the corresponding type of question. Finally, note that item 5 asks an extremely personal question. The answer is listed as optional, but respondents who choose to answer will identify their stake in the issue.

Motives. No audience analysis is complete without a consideration of motives. While an attitude reflects a value judgment, a **motive** is an inner drive that prompts action. Literally, a motive "moves" us toward some goal in a direction consistent with our values. For example, some athletic coaches are famous for being great motivators: They successfully move their players to perform well by attaching relevant values to that performance. The players then find in themselves gratitude toward sponsors or fans, self-esteem, desire for the tangible rewards of victory, and other values that drive them to their best play. By analogy, the public speaker needs to link up his or her speech with the motives of members of the audience.

You gain valuable insight when you learn what moves your audience toward a certain goal. As a public speaker, you want your audience to be informed or persuaded in some degree after your speech. Though hard to discover, motives can help you accomplish your speech purpose. Perhaps the best way to learn audience motives is to listen carefully. For example, when potential members of an audience remark that price is not that important to them in shopping for goods or services, you could speak about the convenience of buying American-made products. Similarly, if you discover that your listeners value patriotism highly, then you might emphasize a "Buy American" approach to choosing their next purchases. Through organization and evaluation of your audience's comments about a subject, you may discover how the audience justifies its acts on particular occasions. Chapter 18 outlines methods for suggesting relevant motives to your audience when you are supporting a specific belief or action.

Leadership Note 13–4
"This is one of the greatest insights in the field of human motivation: Satisfied needs do not motivate. It's only the unsatisfied need that motivates." (Covey, Stephen, *The 7 Habits of Highly Effective People.* New York: Simon and Schuster, 1990, p. 241.) An effective leader (or speaker) must ask, "What are the unsatisfied needs of this audience and how will my ideas or proposals aid in their satisfaction?"

Discussion Question 13–8
What are the major values, attitudes, and motives in your belief system? Which have changed over time? Which have remained the same?

Understanding your listener's concerns is crucial to the successful public speech. These members of a group of handicapped veterans no doubt share many common concerns that a speaker could address.

■ CHOOSING AN APPROPRIATE SUBJECT

People who make their living as communicators are usually expert analysts, but they are always looking for new subject matter. From nationally televised talk-show hosts to local preachers, the choice of subject is often a crucial first step in speaking effectively. Since these people are frequently opinion leaders as well, their choice of subject matter can exert considerable influence. In many classrooms, and in local meetings of social or service groups, public speakers also search for **appropriate subjects**. Choice of subject matter represents a particularly strategic decision for famous communicators and for beginning public speakers alike.

Sometimes public speakers have no choice when it comes to the subject of their speeches. If, for example, a campus or business organization needs advice on a specific topic, such as finances or publicity, the speaker must fashion subject matter to answer these specific needs. Similarly, if you are called upon to introduce an important visitor, toast a friend, or speak on a topic assigned by a teacher, then you obviously have little choice about subject matter. Those who succeed in speaking on topics dictated by circumstance, however, often find themselves being invited to speak on other occasions. Ironically, these invitations frequently leave the choice of subject up to you—and you are faced with the same strategic decision as are other public speakers!

An appropriate subject for your speech might begin as a broad category of interesting subjects, to be narrowed down at a later time. In order to define these broad subject areas, you can (1) observe the categories that emerge in the world around you; (2) review periodicals; and (3) watch television and listen to the radio with a critical eye and ear (see Figure 13.4).

One place to search for an appropriate subject is your personal knowledge and interests. You may be surprised at how many ideas for speeches you can think of on your own. Your past experiences and current activities may provide the materials for several speeches. People you know and places you have visited may provide worthwhile subjects.

In addition to reflecting on the world around you, review periodicals and other popular sources to find events of international, national, and local significance. For instance, even one issue of a nationally circulated newsmagazine,

Looking for a subject? Consider the following sources:

PERSONAL REFLECTION	to remind yourself that various people and events have been significant in your life
MAGAZINES AND NEWSPAPERS	to review current events
RADIO AND TELEVISION	to identify important topics

Figure 13.4
Choosing an Appropriate Subject.

such as *Newsweek*, contains numerous facts and opinions about the super-powers, the industrialized nations, and other countries. Newspapers also identify national or regional controversies and movements. And when you grow tired of looking at the big picture, consult local and campus publications for profiles of nearby celebrities, politicians, and other interesting people. You may even discover feature articles on the history or development of a noteworthy local institution or custom.

Today radio and television are major sources of ideas. News shows, such as "Nightline," "CNN Special Assignment," and public television's "Frontline," all suggest important subjects. However, you need to be a critical viewer and ask yourself whether the topic of a particular program is worthwhile, whether the program was fair in its coverage, and other similar questions.

Regardless of which source you find most helpful in identifying likely subjects, you still need to decide on the most relevant subject. The first step in making this decision is called *targeting*.

Cross-reference 13–6
Another source of good topic ideas is to ask family and friends what interests them and use effective listening skills (Chapter 3) to find meanings and possible connections in the answers they provide.

Targeting Subject Matter

In choosing subject matter, effective speakers aim for the "bull's-eye" (see Figure 13.5). A perfect shot means that the subject of your speech will reflect your own knowledge and interests as well as those of the audience. By this stage of your speech preparation, you will have already activated your knowledge and interests by consciously reflecting on your experiences, reviewing periodicals, and attending critically to the news media. Moreover, you will not need to guess blindly about your audience's knowledge and interests because you will have already analyzed your audience.

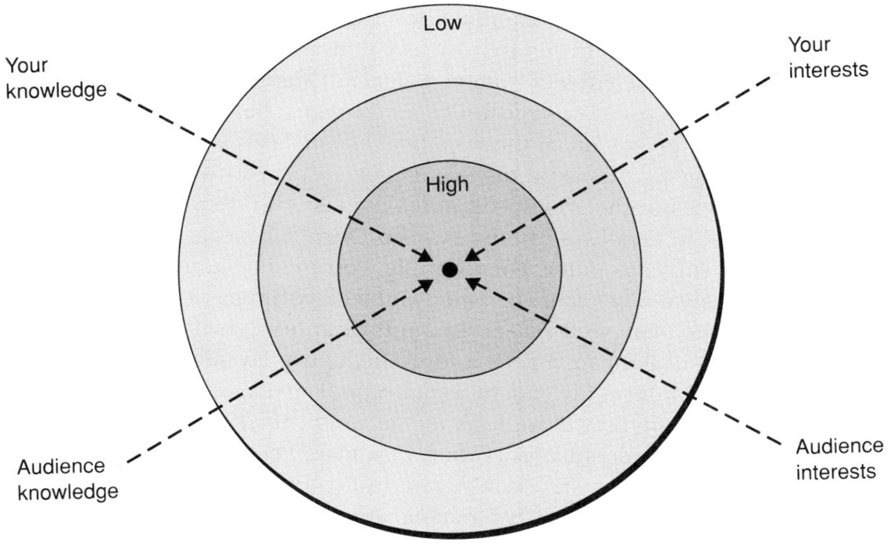

Figure 13.5
The "Target" for Subject Matter.

Current Research 13–6
Sometimes hitting the interest bull's eye may even mean discarding a subject as you stand up to speak: Eugene Lang, a millionaire, was invited to speak to the graduating class of the junior high school he had attended in the South Bronx. He prepared a motivational speech with the theme that if he could succeed, so could these young people. "After looking out at an audience that clearly wasn't interested in him, Lang threw away his prepared speech and said one thing, 'If you graduate from high school'—typically about twenty percent of the youth of the South Bronx would earn a high school diploma—'I will send you to college.' Four years later, the result was phenomenal. All but two of the sixty kids finished high school and many have gone on to the best colleges." (Kriegel, Robert J., and Patler, Louis, *If It Ain't Broke . . . . Break It!* New York: Warner, 1991, p. 37.)

Teaching Objective 13–11
Emphasize the need to limit subject matter to what can effectively and appropriately be covered in the given time period, offering the time, size, place, and utility factors as possible ways of determining limitations.

Hitting the **knowledge bull's-eye** means that you do not need to conduct an unreasonable amount of research on your subject before speaking. If you are totally in the dark about a subject, then the amount of time you spend on research will grossly outweigh the time you spend on organizing, expressing, and rehearsing your speech. Your time should be spent in a more balanced way. For example, if someone chose to speak on the subject of quasars (starlike objects that emit radio waves and radiation) without having had at least an introductory course in a related field, then he or she would have to spend too much time on finding information, learning technical terms, and generally developing an acquaintance with the material. On the other hand, if that same person chose the subject of title searches (tracing the legal ownership of real estate through historical transactions) because he or she had gained some knowledge of that subject while working for an attorney the previous summer, then he or she could devote a reasonably limited time to gathering relevant information and examples. For the public speaker, the bull's-eye represents previous though limited knowledge of subject matter.

In addition, the audience should know something about the subject matter of a speech. If the audience lacks the most basic information about your subject, then your presentation may have to be a lecture rather than a speech. Rather than illustrating only the most intriguing aspects of the subject and speculating on its true worth or meaning, you may find yourself defining too many terms, painfully listing the basic elements of a system, or recounting a lengthy history. For example, even if a person was thoroughly knowledgeable about quasars, choosing this subject for a speech might require spending too much time on explaining basic concepts of mass, energy, and wavelength. However, analysis of the audience might reveal that a speech on title searches could rely on a common understanding of the need to buy real estate only from its legal owner. If you are like the majority of public speaking students, you simply do not have the time in any one speech—or even in a series of speeches—to lecture your classmates on fundamental knowledge.

Hitting the **interest bull's-eye** means that you are genuinely enthusiastic about addressing your subject matter. Later, in Chapter 18, you will read about the importance of speaker credibility, or "image." Part of a public speaker's effectiveness can be traced to the apparent enthusiasm with which a speech is presented. Being enthusiastic does not mean that you have to jump up and down, smile incessantly, and speak at a very fast clip. Rather, the enthusiastic public speaker naturally, sometimes even calmly, reveals his or her sincere interest in the subject matter. For example, you may be genuinely interested in deep space or legal research. For either subject, you may show your interest by presenting substantial, well-researched information—perhaps an expert analysis of the speed of light or a verbal tour through a law library. Audiences will also detect your interest if you relate personal experience with your subject matter—maybe your first close look at the moon through your backyard telescope or your most recent observation of a trial. Personal interest can also be shown by a basic fluency in speaking, an indication that you were enthusiastic enough to practice your delivery—perhaps the correct pronunciation of technical terms.

Audience interest is not usually a mystery when public speakers take time to *listen, analyze,* and *learn.* Rather than a problem of discovery, the only real difficulty here is matching personal interests with the audience's interests. Hitting the interest bull's-eye means that you are willing to discard this or that subject if it definitely will not be interesting to the audience, and to choose another subject that you can still discuss with genuine interest. For example, when an audience is concerned about the number of criminal offenders—drunk drivers, perhaps—who do not receive jail sentences, the effective public speaker will address the ins and outs of plea bargaining even though he or she is more interested in space exploration. As long as personal interest in the subject is sufficiently strong that it will be revealed naturally during the speech, the public speaker hits the bull's-eye by matching personal and audience interests. In fact, the only remaining step at this stage of speech preparation is to accommodate time as well as people. (See the Mastering Communication Skills box.)

Leadership Note 13–5
The famous speaker and writer Charles Osgood suggests that no speaker should seek to hold an audience's attention longer than 12 minutes. Osgood claims this rule of thumb dates back to the days of vaudeville, when only the top act was allowed to go beyond this limit. (Osgood, Charles, *Osgood on Speaking.* New York: William Morrow, 1988)

MASTERING COMMUNICATION SKILLS

Limiting Subject Matter

A good test of subject matter is whether it can be discussed properly in the time allowed. In most instances, however, you can pass this test by limiting or narrowing the material to be covered in your speech, rather than choosing a subject that is perfectly suited to your time limit. Few subjects can be explained clearly, much less exhausted, in a few minutes. Of those rare subjects, fewer still would be located at the bull's-eye of knowledge and interest for most speakers and audiences. Nevertheless, it may be properly narrow on occasion for you to explain a simple process such as making an omelet or addressing letters to public officials so that they actually arrive. On most occasions, though, you will need to limit your coverage of a worthwhile, interesting subject. Your listening and audience analysis provide clues to relevant limitations.

Time Some subjects naturally lend themselves to *narrowing by time,* that is, division into "new" and "old" features. If you are planning to speak about history, a method of inquiry or operation, or people's customs, then discussing only the past or present may be the proper way to satisfy a time limit. For example, many subjects, such as aviation, can be explained briefly in either their historical or their contemporary context. American military aviation might be traced as far back as the use of observation balloons during the Civil War, or the same subject might be limited to the current context of robot aircraft and stealth technology. Further limiting can be done by addressing only a specific decade or quarter-century of aviation history. A speech on weather forecasting could be limited by using the same technique. Ancient methods of divining the right time for planting crops might consume one speech, while another might address contemporary methods of plotting the jet stream and long-range weather systems.

Size   The size of your subject matter may be as significant to you as the size of your audience. Many subjects lend themselves to *narrowing by size* because they involve "big" or "little" dimensions, and these relative sizes may suggest ways to limit the length of your speeches. For example, if a speech on architectural styles would be worthwhile and interesting, you might analyze only the styles of mansions and cathedrals—and save your architectural analysis of cottages and chapels for another occasion. In addition, each of these types of structures could itself be addressed in an even more limited way. Perhaps you and your audience might agree that a speech on personal modes of transportation would be appropriate. In this instance, you could restrict your coverage to mopeds and ultralight aircraft, instead of discussing limousines and private jets. Depending on the time available to you, you might address only the "big" or "little" dimensions of your subject.

Place   You can use *narrowing by place* whenever your subject matter can be divided into elements of place that are "near" or "distant." For example, you could save time by discussing only local examples—whether you are speaking about business organizations, medical treatment, or transportation. Often, however, your audience will already be so knowledgeable about nearby instances of your subject that speaking about foreign or exotic examples will be desirable. For example, you could very briefly mention the nearest McDonald's franchise and then quickly move on to compare or contrast its operation with that of the McDonald's near the Spanish Steps in Rome. A speech on prenatal care and childbirth might be limited to practices in your hometown—although your neighbors might be more captivated by an explanation of related practices in Moscow. You might limit your discussion of urban mass transportation to the trains, buses, and ferries used by people in your own city or state. Then again, you could exhaust your allotted time by explaining the air, land, and water transportation used by city dwellers in exotic places. The smaller the area addressed in your speech, the more limited is your subject. Indeed, "near" and "distant" features may be used to limit speeches on a number of subjects.

Utility   As a final suggestion, *narrowing by utility*—that is, restricting your attention to "practical" as opposed to "impractical" features of your subject—will make your speech fit neatly into a given time period. Many audiences grow impatient with speeches that do not stress the pragmatic aspects of a subject. Did you ever have to sit patiently through a speech on the many good reasons to stop smoking? At the time, even if you were an unconcerned smoker, you no doubt wished that the speaker would have addressed practical ways to kick your habit—rather than reciting evidence of your need to stop smoking. If your time is limited, you may not want to explain the history of a problem or the alternative views on a desirable solution. Getting to the point—the reasons why your solution is the best response to the problem—may be necessary and appropriate. For many audiences, the "bottom line" is a matter of supreme interest. When faced with a decision on what to omit in a brief speech, you might find that the audience will prefer to hear the financial benefits of your proposal rather than the philosophical or aesthetic rewards. If "practical" methods or benefits are generally relevant to your subject matter, then specifically limiting your focus to these features may be the best choice under time pressure.

CHOOSING AN APPROPRIATE PURPOSE

A speaker in a position of leadership uses audience analysis to help establish a desirable speaker-audience relationship. Moreover, once you learn about your audience you are in a much better position to target your subject matter. At this point, you should also consider your choice of speech purpose. There are four major purposes in speaking—informing, persuading, addressing a special occasion, and accomplishing multiple purposes.

Speaking to Inform

When you **speak to inform** an audience, you try to create or improve awareness, understanding, and memory of a subject. For example, your audience analysis may tell you that few if any members of your audience know the specific connection between heart disease and cholesterol—but you and your audience place a high value on health. Your audience may be generally aware of the many health warnings about cholesterol; they may even know that any blood cholesterol level above 200 milligrams per deciliter is generally considered too high. In addition, your audience may include one or two experts who can correctly define cholesterol as one of the fatlike nutrients produced by our bodies and transported through the bloodstream. Nevertheless, you might still choose an informative purpose. For those members of your audience who are generally aware of the warnings about eating foods high in cholesterol, you could create an understanding of specific health problems—for example, clogged arteries leading to the heart. For the expert members of your audience, you could improve an understanding of exactly which foods contribute to high blood cholesterol, or precisely how related health problems are caused. In fact, no one in your audience may know the difference between "bad" and "good" cholesterol, and you could explain the distinction between LDL (low-density lipids, or "bad" cholesterol) and HDL (high-density lipids, or "good" cholesterol).

Speaking to Persuade

The purpose of persuasion is to cause a change in people. When you **speak to persuade**, you should be prepared to identify the type and degree of change you want from your audience.

Teaching Objective 13–12
Explain the importance of clarity of purpose and provide the general purpose categories of informing, persuading, celebrating an occasion, and combining multiple purposes.

Discussion Question 13–11
Do you think a speech always needs to tell an audience what it can do for them or have some direct usefulness?

Current Research 13–7
According to Roger Ailes, media consultant and strategist for both President Reagan and President Bush, "When you know what your mission is in front of an audience, that sense of purpose automatically marshals your best natural resources as a speaker." (Ailes, Roger, with Kraushar, Jon. How to make an audience love you. *Working Woman,* November 1990, p. 119.)

Discussion Question 13–12
Which is easier—to inform or to persuade? Some people say all speeches are persuasive; what do you think?

Cross-reference 13–7
In Chapter 11, leadership was defined as any effort which exerts positive influence toward the accomplishment of a goal. In this sense, then, any successful act of persuasion is an act of leadership.

Cross-reference 13–8
Explore the parallels between these propositions of value and policy and the questions of fact, value, and policy which were discussed in Chapter 10.

Discussion Question 13–13
How many speeches have you heard or do you know of that actually brought about change in an audience or part of an audience?

Leadership Note 13–6
Peters and Waterman advocate continual repetition of the goal or vision of a company by the business leader, whatever the official purpose or occasion of a gathering and whatever other more immediate purposes must also be discussed or implemented. (Peters, Tom, and Waterman, R.H. Jr. *In Search of Excellence.* New York: Harper & Row, 1982.)

Consider the relationship between what you learn from analyzing an audience's belief system and the types of change you might aim for. For example, people who like hot dogs, bacon, and luncheon meats may also understand that these foods are typically high in saturated fat. Regardless of their knowledge, these people might not change their preferences in food. A persuasive speaker may seek a change in values by proposing that these people appreciate the health value of low-fat foods, such as turkey, chicken, and fish. In effect, the speaker is asking the audience to develop a new attitude. Another persuasive speaker may seek a change in policy by proposing that these same people begin substituting foods low in saturated fat for what they normally eat. This speaker, in effect, is asking the audience to develop a new motive—moving toward a healthy diet. In the first instance, the audience responds to an effective speech by thinking differently. In the second instance, the audience responds by behaving differently.

Persuasion also involves degrees of change. For example, a speaker may persuade an audience to change its attitude about seafood from lack of interest to mild interest. In this case, the degree of persuasion would be small. If, however, the same audience had originally hated the idea of eating food perceived as slimy and scaly, then achieving a mild interest in such food would represent a large degree of change. These small and large degrees can be seen in another change. For instance, persuading an audience to eat fatty foods less often would represent a small degree of change in comparison with successfully persuading the same audience to completely replace the beef in its diet with fish. Again, your analysis will reveal which degree of persuasion is desirable for a particular audience.

Speaking on a Special Occasion

Addressing a special occasion, such as a party to celebrate a graduation, retirement, wedding, or the like, may mean that a public speaker retells old stories in new ways or describes vividly a subject that the audience already knows and appreciates. For example, you might address an audience of nutritionists and dieticians gathered together to celebrate the anniversary of their association by recounting their public service in terms that remind them of a proud heritage. Instead of celebrating the past, you could address the same audience by *speaking ritually*—that is, by addressing a required subject in a well-established sequence and in prescribed language. For example, you might carefully observe protocol in reciting a common pledge, introducing honored guests, or even repeating a traditional joke about vegetarians (resulting in good-natured groans from your audience). Finally, when speaking at a graduation, a wedding banquet, or a retirement party, you might anticipate the future. You would not purposefully inform or persuade the audience; instead, you would try to say things about the next phase of life that everyone present would enjoy hearing. In each case, you speak with the purpose of addressing a special occasion.

Special occasion speaking is appropriate whenever the other speech purposes are irrelevant or unrealistic. Your analysis of time and place will no doubt tell you whether addressing a special occasion is the relevant purpose. The settings described above, for instance, typically call for this speech purpose. On other occasions, you might have the same purpose when information or persuasion is relevant but unrealistic.

Speaking with Multiple Purposes

In a sense, there is no such thing as a purely informative, persuasive, or special occasion speech. In fact, you may often find that you need to provide basic information before asking an audience to agree with your point of view. Moreover, you may discover that audiences resist being informed if they are dissatisfied with a subject. Although one purpose will be dominant, public speakers often blend together two or more purposes in a single speech. For instance, consider the teacher who ignores a recent student rally against racism on campus when delivering a lecture on sociology. Some of the students may overcome their preoccupation with the rally and its cause, but many more will miss several important notes because the teacher has not satisfied everyone's need to address racism—if only briefly. Even the proverbial high-pressure salesperson will supply you with at least some information about the merchandise while persuading you to buy it. These and other everyday experiences point out how frequently an audience should be addressed with multiple purposes.

Addressing multiple purposes may be the best way to exhibit leadership through public speaking. If the speaking situation appears to call for both information and persuasion, then address both purposes. If you need to satisfy an audience by addressing a special occasion as well as by being persuasive, then by all means combine your purposes. You should recognize the purposes available to you and plan to achieve as many of them as appear relevant and realistic in your audience analysis. Once you have decided on subject and purpose, you then can develop a theme. (Complete the Self-Assessment checklist.)

CHOOSING AN APPROPRIATE THEME

Throughout history, leaders have brought their plans into focus and made them memorable by using distinctive slogans or rallying cries. Some American presidents of the twentieth century have been particularly successful at defining their plans for the country in a distinctive fashion. Franklin D. Roosevelt, for example, asked Americans to start a "New Deal." John F. Kennedy invited the country to explore a "New Frontier." Public speakers also need to make their subjects and purposes clear and memorable. They accomplish this goal by developing a *distinctive theme.* For example, depending on their choice of subject and purpose, students have frequently used the theme of "Justice for All" ("Let's treat students as fairly as other people!").

A **theme** is a special perspective on the subject matter that the speaker wants to share with the audience. A theme also identifies precisely how the speaker wants his or her audience to respond to the speech. The best themes are distinctive; that is, they keep the subject matter in focus during a speech

Teaching Objective 13–13
Describe the nature and utility of themes as a way of creating a distinctive, focused, and memorable perspective or framework with which to bolster one's presentation.

SELF-ASSESSMENT   **Have I selected an appropriate purpose?**

Speaking to inform

_____ Do I want to create or improve awareness? Understanding? Retention?

Speaking to persuade

_____ Do I want my audience to change its attitudes about a topic?

_____ Do I want my audience to take specific action in response to my speech?

Speaking on special occasions

_____ Am I addressing an audience gathered specifically to celebrate an event, such as retirement, a wedding, graduation, and the like?

_____ Are other speech purposes irrelevant or unrealistic?

Speaking with multiple purposes

_____ Does the match between my subject and my audience suggest that I actually need to address two or more purposes, including speaking to inform, speaking to persuade, and speaking on special occasions?

and make the speaker's purpose memorable after the speech. For this reason, scholars refer to themes as residual messages. Sometimes, you might not recognize your theme until you have worked on your speech for a while. This is normal. In fact, be ready to rework your theme as you near the end of your speech preparations (see Figure 13.6).

Themes Express Special Perspectives

Your audiences lend you their time when you speak, and they expect repayment with interest. One of the ways to repay the loan is to develop an insight into your subject that audiences would not gain unless they attend your speech. This special insight or perspective—the theme of your speech—makes it valuable. By developing an effective theme, you pay dividends on the time that audiences have lent you. Your perspective is special if it reflects superior foresight, skill, or industry.

Foresight. You display the **foresight** of a leader when your speeches anticipate future needs or events. For example, after analyzing an audience interested in applied art, you might display superior foresight in a "Careers Day" speech

Review your speech's theme to be sure it:

Provides a special perspective on your subject matter
Calls for a precise response from the audience
Maintains a clear focus
Conveys enough impact to become memorable

Figure 13.6
Developing an Effective Theme.

about designing furniture. Your distinctive theme might be as follows: "The computer age has just begun and it's time you investigated careers in providing the special furniture needed to accommodate computers at home and at work." If your subject matter has been properly targeted, then your theme would express a timely perspective. For a wide range of other subjects, foresight can be displayed by expressing themes that look beyond the present or expand otherwise narrow perspectives.

Skill.   You show the **skill** of a leader when your speeches reveal a special expertise. Discussing a subject expertly, however, does not necessarily require you to be a genius or a wizard. As long as you have special experience or training in an area, you may have the skill required for a distinctive theme. For example, your summer job as a lifeguard might have prepared you to express a distinctive theme about how to supervise people: "You should understand effective personnel management as a cross between saving a drowning swimmer one day and then kicking him out of the pool for breaking rules the next day." You can display skill in a variety of subjects by describing your theme in terms associated with your special experience or training.

Industry.   You display the **industry** of a leader when your speeches appear well prepared. As the inventor once said, genius is 10 percent inspiration and 90 percent perspiration. For example, you might display industry in a speech on famous journalists by expressing the following theme: "I'd like you to realize that, as I learned from interviewing the three most respected editors in our city, half of the greatest journalists in history are alive right now." Whether you speak about journalism or jujitsu, you can display industry by expressing themes that give clues about your research and speech preparation. The Focus on Leadership box describes a successful speech.

Themes Call for a Precise Response

In addition to revealing special perspectives, effective speakers develop winning themes by telling audiences exactly how they should respond. In most cases, the responses mirror speech purposes. In an informative speech you will want to express a theme that calls for your audience to understand, to appreciate, or

Leadership Note 13–7
Kennedy's theme in his "New Frontier" speech, delivered when accepting the Democratic nomination on July 15, 1960, described the New Frontier in this way: "The New Frontier of which I speak is not a set of promises—it is a set of challenges. It sums up not what I intend to offer the American people, but what I intend to ask of them."

In his inaugural address six months later, Kennedy carried this theme forward in a continued vision of the citizens of the nation working together to accomplish needed changes, a theme memorably summarized in that speech in the now-famous line, "And so, my fellow Americans, ask not what your country can do for you; ask what you can do for your country."

FOCUS ON LEADERSHIP

Lincoln's Masterful Second Inaugural Address

March 4, 1864. The Civil War has torn the nation apart for four years. Despite many military reverses, the president of the United States has been reelected and is about to deliver his second inaugural address. But what will Abraham Lincoln say on this less-than-happy occasion to affirm his national leadership? This is the day he will deliver a speech noted for one of its closing phrases: "with malice toward none, with charity for all."

History tells us that, in his second inaugural address, President Lincoln chose a highly appropriate theme—but many Americans chose to ignore it. With hindsight, we can now judge that Lincoln's speech displayed the *foresight, skill,* and *industry* that expressed a very special perspective. The public outcry over his assassination—which happened not long after his speech—at least suggests that Lincoln's speech affirmed his leadership.

Lincoln expressed remarkable foresight in resisting "malice" toward the South and proposing "charity" instead. The difficult period of American history following the Civil War, known as Reconstruction, caused almost as much stress in the country as the war itself. Hatred between some Northern and Southern leaders plagued the reconstruction of the Union. If Lincoln's theme had been taken up by other leaders, Reconstruction might have been less painful.

President Lincoln also displayed special skill in announcing his theme. He began the speech by recounting his experiences in guiding the country through a terrible war. Not all of his experiences were successful, he admitted, but he hoped that the audience would find his record "reasonably satisfactory and encouraging." As a tool for building his theme, references to his past leadership were highly appropriate.

Even more than the other elements of his special perspective, Lincoln's industry was impressive. In his speech, he referred explicitly to his efforts on behalf of the Union. In fact, he also called upon his listeners to "strive on to finish the work we are in, to bind up the nation's wounds."

Abraham Lincoln was an exceptional leader. Few leaders can hope to rise to his level. All leaders, however, can communicate their speech themes in the same way that Lincoln did—displaying foresight, skill, and industry.

to digest information in some other manner. For example, during a speech on the five most common mistakes in preparing income tax returns, you might express the following theme: "Considering how fearful you probably are of the IRS, you should learn the five most common errors that trigger audits of income tax returns."

Persuasive speeches should be based on themes that call on the audience to agree, to act, or to change in some other way. For example, in a speech that attempts to persuade the audience to buy only biodegradable plastic containers, you might express the following theme: "It's time for you and me to change our ways when it comes to putting out the trash." When you address a special occasion, you should express a theme that invites your audience to enjoy, to celebrate, or to fulfill a ritual. If you were to speak at a local political meeting, for instance, you might express the following theme: "Let us remember the words of Harry S. Truman as we recognize our duty to keep our country on the road to greatness—'the buck stops here.'" In the same way, a speech with multiple purposes should express a theme that asks for a combination of responses from the audience. For example, you might first ask your audience to appreciate the growing popularity of cross-country skiing and then urge them to try it during their next winter holiday.

Whatever purpose or combination of purposes you choose, your theme should define the proper response to be made by your audience. After all, you are taking a leadership role. Let your audience know the way you want them to follow.

Themes Maintain a Clear Focus

An effective theme provides a *focal point* for the speech. Focal points are magnets for people's attention. One way to make your themes effective is to express them early in your speeches; by doing so, you help the audience members to quickly recognize your special perspective and the response they should give. Another way to make your theme serve as a focal point is to refer back to it as your speech unfolds. Early and continuous use of your theme maintains a clear focus on your speech purpose. Trial attorneys often use themes in exactly this way: They introduce the special perspective that a judge and/or jury should adopt, and they renew this proposed focus each time a major piece of evidence is introduced. For example, the prosecutor in a criminal case might refer to the "ladder of evidence" in an opening statement, and then remark that another "rung" has been reached as each witness testifies or as each tangible item is admitted into evidence. By the end of the trial, the ladder of evidence has reached high enough to sustain a verdict of guilty. Your favorite professor might use a similar technique. Introducing his or her lecture with a key phrase—"Eighteenth-century Rome harbored a curious blend of science and sorcery"—the professor then links each main point with either the growth of scientific spirit or the lingering belief in magic.

A well-planned theme maintains clear focus in any speech. Audiences need to know—and deserve to know—the speaker's perspective and the desired response to the speech. By announcing your theme early in your speech, and by indicating how each segment of your speech reflects your theme, you lead your audience to a clear focus on your subject and purpose.

Themes Become Memorable

Leadership Note 13–8
Martin Luther King's now-famous speech on the steps of the Lincoln Memorial in Washington, D.C., on August 28, 1963, had as its purpose to acknowledge racism in our nation and to foster the vision of a future where racism was no longer a national reality. The theme of his presentation, ''I have a dream,'' has become part of our cultural consciousness. His theme, repeated nine times during his address, combined with great effectiveness the elements of foresight, skill, and industry, and offered its audiences, then and now, a clear sense of focus and an obvious memorability.

After a few hours—or even a few minutes—audiences recall only a small portion of the speeches they have heard. Generally, audiences retain only a fraction of the speeches they hear. In this regard, properly expressed themes provide the audience with a guide to what should be remembered. The speaker's distinctive perspective is memorable. And so is the response made immediately by the audience. Most memorable, however, is the theme that is restated in concluding the speech. To ensure a lasting memory of your theme, you should refer back to it at the end of your speech—either through simple repetition or through imaginative rephrasing. For example, you might begin your speech on the presidency of Ulysses S. Grant (1869–1877) by expressing the following theme: "We should all remember that, despite widespread corruption during his administration, Ulysses S. Grant presided over the nation's one hundredth birthday party." Then, in conclusion, you might reemphasize that, although tainted with graft, Grant's presidency was memorable for the country's centennial celebration. By doing so, you would remind your audience of the noteworthy time, place, and circumstances of your subject matter.

The following speech illustrates how Julie A. Goedde developed her theme—"Proper diet may seem like an obvious need but, like so many other so-called obvious things, we don't pay enough attention to it—start now to bring your diet under control before it's too late!"—in a way designed to express a *special perspective*, a *desired response*, a *clear focus*, and a *memorable idea* to other students of public speaking:

Display of "industry" in research

We are obsessed with diets! Fat people are trying to find ways to lose weight, doctors are looking for ways to reduce salt and cholesterol, athletes are looking for foods to provide long-lasting energy, and parents are worrying about junk foods. In his book *The Fit or Fat Target Diet,* Covert Bailey observes that all of us are concerned about the quality of the food we eat. Yet our desire to diet doesn't seem to be working because, as we can see, Americans are getting fatter all the time. A recent Harris poll, for example, found that 64 percent of Americans are overweight—up from 59 percent the previous year. It seems that the more we go on diets, the fatter we get. The steady rise in obesity despite the increasing number of diet books should tell us something—diets don't work!

What I'd like to explain to you is how to achieve a "perfect" diet without actual dieting. As Covert Bailey suggests, you need to obey only four rules in order to achieve a perfect diet: Eat a balanced diet; select foods low in fat; select foods low in sugar; select foods high in fiber.

Some of you might be saying, "Everybody knows that,'' or "That's obvious." Well, maybe it's not so obvious. Just as subjects we've already addressed in class may seem obvious—our responsibility in regard to drinking and driving, for instance—still we don't pay enough attention to them. And just as we may know someone with heart disease or cancer, we probably know twice as many people who are overweight. None of us may even be concerned about this now, but what happens in two or three years, when we're out of college and our activity levels decrease? We'll need to pay attention to our eating habits. Why start then? Start now and get your diet under control before it's too late.

Display of "foresight" in looking to the future2

Getting back to the four rules, rule 1 says to eat a balanced diet. What does that mean? We should eat a variety of foods to make sure we're getting a variety of nutrients. This should be rather obvious since most of us know that different foods contain different elements. Some of you might be thinking, "Yeah, I eat a variety of foods—I have macaroni and cheese for lunch on Monday, Wednesday, and Friday, rice for lunch on Tuesday and Thursday, cereal for breakfast, and popcorn or a hamburger for dinner . . . . That's a variety of foods." Well, it is and it isn't. Eating a variety of foods means that every day you should have two servings from the milk group, two from the meat group, four from the vegetable and fruit group, and four from the bread and cereal group. You may have noticed in the so-called diet I just described that nearly all the items are from one group—bread and cereal. That's not a balanced diet.

Call for a precise response

Clear focus on four rules related to the theme

"When presenting a speech, it's important for me to know that my audience is interested in my subject. This not only motivates me to present significant and useful information, but it also gives me confidence in presenting the speech" (Julie A. Goedde).

Rule 2 says to select foods low in fat. To follow this rule, we don't really need to limit the amount we eat; we just need to make a few changes. For example, instead of drinking whole milk or even 2 percent milk, drink skim milk. Don't eat tuna packed in oil; eat tuna packed in water. You may also want to substitute low-fat cheese, like cottage cheese, for high-fat cheese, like cheddar or cream cheese.

Rule 3 says to select foods low in sugar. One thing you may not realize is that fruit juices are actually high in sugar. Note, however, that the fruit itself is not high in sugar. Other foods, like syrup or some cereals, are very high in sugar and should be eliminated from your diet.

The final rule says to select foods high in fiber. Fiber is a substance that cannot be digested by humans. The most common type of fiber is wheat bran, it can be found in many cereals and in different kinds of bread. Fiber can also be found in lettuce, fruit, and popcorn. Nutritionists recommend that we eat fifteen grams of fiber a day.

Restatement of theme to make it memorable

As I said earlier, some of these diet rules may be obvious. But are we following them? Check your own eating habits. Are you eating a balanced diet? Is it low in fat and sugar? Is it high in fiber?

Control your diet—before it's too late.

(Used with permission of Julie A. Goedde.)

Goedde was concerned—understandably nervous—about speaking in front of an audience of other students. However, she reduced her communication apprehension by choosing a subject, purpose, and theme that suited the time, place, and audience. Afterwards she was pleased to find that the audience could recall her speech and its theme for several weeks.

■ Summary

In public speaking, your relationship with the audience is paramount. Effective speakers are aware of their audiences in much the same way that people who communicate effectively in interpersonal and group relationships are aware of one another's views and feelings. Public speakers may not always agree with audiences, but awareness of the audience is nonetheless essential in creating an honest, strategic rapport.

Audience analysis measures the possible effects of audience size, age, gender, education, income, occupation, memberships, and culture on speech form and content. Features such as size, age, and gender are easily observed if speakers merely take the time to do so. Factors such as education, income, occupation, and memberships may require specific questioning. Culture—whether observed from appearances and habits or identified through specific questioning—often reveals special likes or dislikes.

Audience analysis also measures listeners' feelings toward time and place, their intermember relationships, and their belief system—more specifically, the listeners' values, attitudes, and motives. By reflecting on listeners' answers to specific oral and written questions, the public speaker learns relevant beliefs, values, attitudes, and motives that may significantly influence an audience's receptivity to a particular speech.

Your attention to audience analysis helps you choose an appropriate subject, purpose, and theme. Choosing a subject need not be a helter-skelter hunt. Your personal history and interests are an extremely valuable source of subject matter. Various people and events in your own life may suggest a highly appropriate subject for your next speech. In addition, newsmagazines, local newspapers, radio, and television all identify current events and topics of current interest and importance.

Targeting your subject means comparing potential material to the knowledge and interests of you and your audience. Both you and your audience should already know at least something about your subject before you begin preparing your speech. Otherwise, you may take on an excessively large research project, which will restrict other elements of your preparation, and your audience may need an undesirable number of definitions and explanations during your actual speech. Hitting the bull's-eye of the target also means that you account for your own interests and those of your audience: To some extent, everyone involved in the speech should be basically concerned or enthusiastic about the subject matter.

The same type of analysis should guide your choice of speech purpose. When you speak to inform, you try to enhance awareness, understanding, and memory of a subject. When you speak to persuade, you try to change the audience's attitude or activity in some realistic degree. When you speak to satisfy the needs of a special occasion, you try to celebrate the past, fulfill the present, or anticipate the future. Indeed, on many occasions you combine some or all of these purposes in your speeches.

Your subject and purpose lead naturally to a distinctive theme in your speeches. This theme expresses a special perspective on your subject, and calls for a precise response from the audience. Moreover, an effective theme maintains a clear focus on your subject throughout the speech, and then makes the speech memorable for your audience.

Exercises

1. During your next class meeting, look around the room and take a mental note of the class size and the ages and genders of class members. After class, write down a few speech topics that would probably be relevant or interesting to people of these ages and genders who meet in a group of this size. Compare your list of topics with the topics actually addressed later in the course. Were the speakers well received? Would you have chosen the same topics? Did the form in which speakers presented their ideas satisfy the class expectations as you would have predicted them?

2. As part of a group project, arrange a place to sit that will enable you to view the outward signs of intermember relationships during a speech or lecture. Did you observe groupings within the audience, friendly conversations before or during the presentation, or signs of isolation for some members of the audience? Did you notice any influence of intermember relationships on the type or scope of audience responses to the speech or lecture? Could the speaker or lecturer have adjusted to these influences during the presentation? Discuss your thoughts with the other observers.

3. Before your next speech, compose a brief questionnaire that measures attitudes, values, and motives related to your subject matter. Analyze the results of the survey and outline a plan for adjusting your speech to the subjective setting. If your speech is to be evaluated by an instructor or superior, submit the results of your questionnaire before the evaluation.

4. Spend a few moments skimming a college bulletin or schedule of classes. Then, using your own judgment, list as many interesting, worthwhile speech subjects as you can in three minutes. If possible, compare the number and types of subjects you have listed with those listed by other people who have done the same exercise. How similar are the various lists? How are they different?

5. Talk to people who do a fair amount of public speaking every year. Ask them about the purposes they most often try to accomplish. You may be surprised to find that people you thought were especially persuasive will remark that they see themselves primarily as teachers. Some of these speakers may have a hard time defining just one purpose in most of their speaking. After talking with these public speakers, translate and categorize their stated purposes

into information, persuasion, special occasion, or multiple purposes. Which type of purpose is attempted most often? Which is seen as the most challenging? Are multiple purposes used frequently?

6. Read several speeches in such sources as *Vital Speeches,* the *New York Times,* or anthologies of American public address. Can you identify themes in any of the speeches? Are there phrases or sentences that express special perspectives and desired responses from the audience? How might one or more of the speeches be revised to develop an effective theme? In a group discussion, find out if other people share your observations and suggestions regarding themes.

Fowler, F., Jr. (1993). *Survey research methods* (2nd. ed.). Newbury Park, CA: Sage.

 **Related Readings**

> This handbook briefly outlines the techniques for using polls, questionnaires, and related instruments to gather information.

Tarshis, B. (1979). *The "average American" book.* New York: Atheneum.

> This book outlines common characteristics often found in audiences. You may find this book helpful in devising categories for your analysis of audiences.

Rokeach, M. (1960). *The open and closed mind.* New York: Basic Books.

> This analysis of people's relative willingness to accept new ideas has become a classic. You may find that this book opens your eyes to the task facing public speakers in adapting to their audiences.

Hirsch, E. D., Jr., Kett, J. F., and Trefil, J. (1988). *The dictionary of cultural literacy: What every American needs to know.* Boston: Houghton Mifflin.

> The authors identify items of information—organized in twenty-three categories— that are arguably "the foundation of our public discourse." Whether or not you agree with the choices, these items comprise a handy checklist of potential subjects for speeches.

Wallace, A., Wallechinsky, D., and Wallace, I. (series of publication dates). *The book of lists.* New York: William Morrow and Co.

> In a lighter vein, this series of books, along with a related series by the same authors and publisher, *The People's Almanac,* contains facts and figures about a wide variety of subjects.

Discovering Speech Material and Speech Confidence

Chapter objectives

After reading this chapter you should be able to:

1. explain why speeches should be blends of fact and opinion

2. identify two sources of speech material

3. explain how everyday conversations can produce speech material

4. identify the steps in a successful interview

5. locate library resources in the "reference" section

6. explain methods for finding speech material in card catalogs, vertical files, government documents, and electronic data bases

7. identify the essential items of information on a notecard

8. recognize communication apprehension

9. identify methods of building confidence before, during, and after a speech

Key terms and concepts

fact

opinion

conversation

speaker's diary

card catalog

vertical file

government documents

electronic data bases

Teaching Objective 14–1
Explore the notions of substance and substantiation and meanings and differences in meaning of fact and opinion.

Discussion Question 14–1
What do we mean when we call someone "a person of substance"? How does the notion of substance compare to that of substantiating our ideas?

Cross-reference 14–1
Compare this discussion of fact and opinion with the discussion of fact-inference confusion in Chapter 4, where fact is defined as that which is directly experienced and inference involves conclusions drawn from other sources.

Highly respected leaders are more than merely attractive; they possess depth and substance. Mother Teresa, for example, won the Nobel prize in 1979 for her personal leadership in improving life amidst the slums of Calcutta. She won this recognition because of her deep, long-lived commitment to helping the poor and sick—not because of more superficial qualities or clever publicity. Although people may temporarily follow a shallow or selfish leader, they usually discover their mistake before long. For example, attractive but unskilled actors often lose their fans after one successful play, television program, or motion picture. One-issue mayors and self-centered members of a city council often lose their support among voters after one term in office. To be seen as a speaker of substance, you will need to substantiate your speech with relevant material.

Speeches contain facts and opinions: A **fact** is a deed or event whose truth or accuracy can be confirmed; an **opinion** is a belief or judgment that may be acceptable because of several factors—including the trustworthiness of the speaker. The most effective public speakers usually blend facts with opinions in their materials. A speech built entirely on facts may be truthful, but it may also be dry or impersonal; a speech filled with nothing but opinions may be personal but may lack substance. By gathering both facts and opinions, you develop a substantive speech that is both accurate and interesting.

In this chapter, we identify methods of discovering substance for your speeches. We also discuss how to build confidence in your speaking ability—before, during, and after your speeches.

Mother Theresa's work on behalf of the suffering has gained her credibility worldwide as a speaker of substance.

DISCOVERING MATERIAL THROUGH OTHER PEOPLE

Students of public speaking sometimes think they must spend a lot of time in the library in order to develop their speeches. Making use of library materials is always a good idea, but you should also consider other people as sources of facts and opinions. These people may be experts in a certain field or simply ordinary persons with a wealth of life experiences.

When tourists find themselves in a strange town, common sense tells them to ask natives for useful information—from restaurant recommendations to travel tips. Of course, some tourists are too proud or too shy to ask for help. Ultimately, they, too, find places to eat, and they reach their destinations. But they have to work harder than the tourists who ask for help. No matter how often you prepare speeches, you will probably feel something like a tourist. And no matter how experienced or confident you become at public speaking, you will always benefit from asking other people to share their knowledge and experience with you—if only to make your work a little easier. Discovering these resources can be done informally or formally. The results of informal talk (conversation) are recorded in a diary; the fruits of formal talk (interviews) are recorded in a notebook.

Teaching Objective 14–2
Emphasize the value of other people as sources of ideas, insights, and information.

Conversation

Conversation is informal talk. It normally has no time limits and no "script" in the sense of prepared questions and answers. For these reasons, informal talk is useful when you are in no hurry to gather speech materials. You may not have any advance notice of a conversation. You may not gather much relevant material during some conversations. You may not appreciate a person's special knowledge or experience until after a conversation. In short, you rely on serendipity, or making a valuable discovery by accident.

Write the potentially useful materials you discover through informal talk in a **speaker's diary**—a daily account of what other people tell you about their experiences, ideas, and feelings. A speaker's diary is only distantly related to those we kept as adolescents; it does not feature accounts of your own tragedies and triumphs. Nor is a speaker's diary intended to resemble those journals kept, and later published, by famous writers, politicians, and others. A speaker's diary is a brief record of clever or picturesque materials rather than a monumental collection of brilliant or awesome materials. A speaker's diary preserves the wise sayings, acute observations, genuine humor, and other valuable sentiments you hear in casual conversations. Figure 14.1 shows two typical entries in a speaker's diary. The second of these entries, the story about Fred, might be used when speaking about business risks (or perhaps the true meaning of forgiveness). Entries in a speaker's diary may be used many times or only once—as often as you wish. Whether you keep a speaker's diary for the length of a public speaking course or for the rest of your life, you will create a resource that costs little time and money and is close at hand for easy reference.

Discussion Question 14–2
When was the last time you learned something of real insight or value from a conversation? Sometimes, these serendipitous moments are called "aha" experiences, when we suddenly see or hear something in a new and startling way. When has this happened to you? Did you tell someone else about it? Did you write it down?

Teaching Objective 14–3
Define conversation, and depict a speaker's diary as a mean of preserving the serendipitous knowledge and benefits of conversation.

Figure 14.1
Sample Entries in a
Speaker's Diary.

Sample Entries in a Speaker's Diary:

October 31: Randy, the 4-year-old who lives across the street, excitedly told me he was getting ready to go tweak or treating tonight. I hope he doesn't have to tweak anyone!

February 3: Fred manages a restaurant where I used to work. He told me that, after he had argued for about $75,000 in renovations, business dropped off by 10%. It probably wasn't his fault, or even related to the renovations, but he made an appointment with the owner. Fred went in and said: "You probably want my resignation, don't you?" And the owner answered: "Not after I just paid $75,000 for your education!"

Interviews

Teaching Objective 14–4
Explain the nature and potential benefits of interviews. Describe the stages of the interview process and their importance to the success of the process.

Interviews yield valuable resource material. In fact, it is helpful to think of each interviewee as an "expert." Unlike conversation, an *interview* is best suited to those occasions on which you have limited time and have already targeted your subject.

Some public speakers shy away from using the interview to gather speech materials because they think that people are reluctant to share their expertise. Generally speaking, however, people with special expertise are quite willing to share their experience with others. Most people feel complimented upon being asked for their knowledge and opinions. They also think highly of interviewers who have taken the time to prepare a thoughtful set of interview questions.

Your interview may be in person or by telephone. The most productive interviews follow a few basic guidelines.

Current Research 14–1
Barone and Switzer suggest that information-seeking interviewers begin with these two preparatory questions: What is the information I am seeking? Who is the best person to provide it? In order to answer these initial questions, interviewers must conduct research into the subject area before conducting their interviews. (Barone, Jeanne Tessier and Switzer, Jo Young, *Interviewing Art and Skill*, Boston: Allyn & Bacon, 1994. Chapter 6.)

Obtain Agreements. Most of the time wasted in interviews can be traced to simple misunderstandings. First of all, be sure that the expert has agreed to be interviewed. Make it clear that you are requesting an interview and not simply a conversation. (A brief self-introduction and statement of your purpose would also be appropriate, even though you will be repeating this step at the start of the actual meeting.) In some instances, it will be important to have a complete record of what the expert says: Ask the expert for permission to tape-record the interview. Reach an agreement on the amount of time available to you for the interview. Most experts will accommodate your needs as long as they can be assured of how much time will be involved. Finally, make your appearance and language "agreeable" to the expert. Do not try to radically change your appearance; rather, make the expert comfortable by dressing properly for the setting—whether it is during business hours at the office, a weekend morning at home, or lunchtime in the park. Also use clear and jargon-free language. Experts in

The interview is an excellent way to gather speech materials. People with special expertise and unique histories can offer a wealth of information that would otherwise be unavailable.

Leadership Note 14–1
"One of the attractive features of mastering the indepth information-gathering interview is that its skills transfer nicely to interpersonal conversations with new acquaintances, friends and colleagues. Learning how to ask questions during this type of interview is a skill that you can practice every day in a variety of settings." (Hanna, Michael S., and Wilson, Gerald L. *Communicating in Business and Professional Settings.* New York: McGraw-Hill, 1991, p. 223.)

genetic engineering, for instance, may not be familiar with the vocabulary of marketing. Thus you should ask your questions in words that any reasonably educated person will understand.

Introduce Yourself and Your Purpose.   An interview usually ends no better than it starts. For this reason, the first order of business as you meet the expert is to establish a rapport. After identifying yourself, mention why you need the expert's help. For instance, you may be preparing a series of classroom speeches on current events. Perhaps you are doing a favor for an organization, or fulfilling a professional responsibility. Also mention the specific type and scope of information that you need. This disclosure will cue the expert on what areas to address and how much detail to provide. Initial mention of your specific needs will also justify your courteous reminders to the expert when he or she gets off the track.

Maintain a Quiet or Private Setting.   Although it may not be possible to arrange an ideal time and place for the interview, do whatever you can to screen out distractions and intrusions. Turn off a noisy machine, close a door, or have telephone calls held. These preparations may keep the interview pleasant as well as help the expert to keep a train of thought. If the expert has requested privacy or confidentiality, then your efforts to prevent intrusions will be especially well received. For example, an employee may be more willing to alert you to safety violations on the job if you can minimize the chance that co-workers or a supervisor may overhear the interview.

Cross-reference 14–2
The importance of noise as a barrier to interaction was discussed in Chapter 1.

Use Prepared Questions.   The major advantage of an interview over a conversation is your opportunity to use prepared questions. Prepared questions help you keep a clear focus on your speech subject. They also save time.

Discussion Question 14–3
Have you ever interviewed someone? Have you ever been interviewed? Where and when have you seen interviews conducted and what did you learn from them?

Cross-reference 14–3
Review the discussion of positive listening behaviors and reflective listening skills in Chapter 3.

Leadership Note 14–2
"…if you say to someone, 'That's the silliest thing I ever heard; get on out of here!—then you'll never get anything out of that person again." (Bryan, John, as quoted in Safire, William, and Safire, Leonard, *Leadership*. New York: Simon and Schuster, 1991, p. 132.)

Cross-reference 14–4
The importance of carefully recording and clarifying information obtained in an interview can be easily seen if we refer back to the discussion of the variability of perceptions in Chapter 2.

You may find it helpful to prepare questions that match the likely range and sequence of points in your speech. This technique will reduce your need to reorganize the materials gleaned from the interview. For example, if you are preparing a speech on the history, causes, and effects of inflation, then prepare a series of questions that address your subject in that same sequence.

Should you read your questions from a written list or ask them from memory? When in doubt, read your questions from a written list. You will not run the risk of forgetting to ask a particular question, and you will use exactly the language that you carefully honed when you prepared the material. Memorizing your questions is best reserved for those occasions on which, for some reason, you need to appear especially dramatic or polished as an interviewer.

Use Follow-Up Questions. Keen listening skills are the essence of the interviewer's art. In an interview, you know which items of information are relevant to your speech and you also know that time is short. Therefore, if the interviewee says something that you do not understand clearly, ask for an explanation. If you feel uncomfortable asking for an explanation, simply repeat back the question. This "reflecting" technique usually cues the interviewee to restate his or her remark in a different way.

Avoid Expressing Your Opinions. Remember that the purpose of the interview is to obtain information held by the interviewee. You are certainly entitled to your opinions but they are not useful in an interview. Expressing your opinions will probably cause two unfortunate results: First, you will reduce the amount of time available for questions and answers; second, the interviewee may try to accommodate your opinions by adjusting or withholding answers. Neither result helps you develop speech materials. Imagine what would happen, for example, if census takers always volunteered their own opinions of the ideal family while asking people about their households. Each decade, the U.S. Bureau of the Census would publish a report that showed every family in the country was nearly perfect!

Record Responses. Whether or not you make tape recordings of interviews, you need to create a written record. This notebook should reflect your organization of what the interviewee says into categories that are relevant to your speech. If your prepared questions exactly match the likely range and sequence of points in your speech, then your notebook may simply be a transcript of your tape recording or memory. If your speech preparation is not very advanced at the time of the interview, then your notebook should be organized into generally relevant categories (consider asking the interviewee for suggestions). For example, you may need to divide an interviewee's comments into the historical categories of past, present, and future, or the categories of causes and effects, and so on. After you read Chapter 15, you will have a clearer idea of which points and patterns are available. Finally, make an effort to record the interviewee's remarks accurately in your notebook. As insurance, you may want to doublecheck the accuracy of your notes with the interviewee before presenting your speech.

Although the interview is a more formal activity than the conversation, both are similar methods of discovering speech materials. Both activities require talking to other people and recording potentially useful results in writing. To gather more detailed information, though, you also need to consider library resources.

DISCOVERING MATERIAL THROUGH LIBRARY RESEARCH

Discovering material for your speeches usually requires a visit to the library. Libraries offer the last "best deal" in town. Where else can you go and receive on long-term loan such a treasure trove of goods, including books, magazines, films, tapes and CDs, and even prints and paintings? Libraries are staffed by professionals who take pride in their ability to help you find needed information. Like the source material they help you locate, librarians are an important resource. Aside from talking to the staff—which is an excellent idea whenever you have a question—you should spend most of your time at the library in reading. Unfortunately, many people spend the bulk of their time in finding the materials they want to read. A few minutes invested in attending an orientation tour and in learning the types and locations of library resources will pay you dividends in increased reading time. The following information may be helpful before you actually explore your library.

General Reference Works

The initial stages of your research should probably be done in the reference section. Whether this section is a separate room or a special aisle, you will always find it identified as having "reference" works—books that you read in order to identify other, more detailed resources. For example, at the start of your research, you may need to find a brief identification of the various methods humans have used to keep time (from sundials and water clocks to sophisticated electronic devices). Some of the books you could consult will be as familiar as dictionaries and encyclopedias. To locate the imaginary lines ("meridians") we have drawn to divide the earth into time zones, you could consult maps (books of maps are called atlases). Look closely at the shelves holding these familiar references, though, and you may notice specialized resources that you have never consulted.

In addition to the more common dictionaries, you may see Rosenberg's *Dictionary of Computers, Dataprocessing and Telecommunications* (New York: Wiley and Sons, 1987) or *Black's Law Dictionary* (St. Paul: West, 1990). As their titles indicate, references such as these define the meaning of words used in technical and professional senses. If your library is well financed, you may also find the $2,500, twenty-volume set of the *Oxford English Dictionary* (second edition, 1989), in which 616,500 commonplace and uncommon words are not only defined but also traced back to their earliest known uses. (About the year 1290, for instance, *nice* meant silly. The *OED* also reports that the term *AIDS* may have

Teaching Objective 14–5
Enhance awareness of rich treasures a library provides.

Leadership Note 14–3
"We should never pretend to know what we don't know, we should not feel ashamed to ask and learn...." (Mao Tse-tung as quoted in Safire, William, and Safire, Leonard, *Leadership.* New York: Simon and Schuster, 1991, p. 132.)

Teaching Objective 14–6
Describe the various resources of libraries and how they may be accessed.

Current Research 14–2
A study by Kazoleas compared the effectiveness of statistical versus narrative evidence in affecting the attitude changes of audiences. Kazoleas found that both types of information were equally effective at changing attitudes, but the attitude change caused by narrative evidence was more persistent over time. Also, narrative evidence tended to be remembered longer. (Kazoleas, Dean C., A comparison of the persuasive effectiveness of qualitative versus quantitative evidence: a test of explanatory hypotheses. *Communication Quarterly* 41, 1, 1993, pp. 40–50.)

first appeared in the September 24, 1982, issue of *Morbidity and Mortality Weekly Report.*) Other useful dictionaries include the following:

> Hirsch, E. D., Kett, J. F., and Trefel, J. (1988). *The Dictionary of Cultural Literacy.* Boston: Houghton Mifflin.
> Shafritz, J. M., Koeppe, R. P., and Soper, E. W. (1988). *The Facts on File Dictionary of Education.* New York: Facts on File.
> Williamson, M. T. (1990). *Dictionary of Space Technology.* New York: A Hilger.
> Shafritz, J. M., and Oren, D. (1990). *The American Dictionary of Business and Finance.* New York: Penguin.
> Plano, J. C., and Greenberg, M. (1989). *The American Political Dictionary.* New York: Holt, Rinehart and Winston.

Alongside the encyclopedias you may have already used (for example, *Encyclopaedia Britannica, Encyclopedia Americana,* and *Collier's Encyclopedia*), you may notice the *International Encyclopedia of Communications* (New York: Oxford University Press, 1989), or *The Thames Encyclopedia of Impressionism* (New York: Thames and Hudson, 1990). Rather than being impressed or put off by these specialized references, you should feel encouraged about your chances of finding brief explanations and examples of scholarly and scientific concepts. As with more familiar references, specialized encyclopedias help you find general information about almost any subject. If you need a substantial amount of information on a scholarly or scientific subject, though, you should ask for help from the reference librarian. Public speakers also find the following specialized encyclopedias useful:

> *American Jurisprudence Second* and *Corpus Juris Secundum* (both of these multivolume legal encyclopedias are continuously updated)
> *The New Catholic Encyclopedia*
> *Encyclopedia Judaica*
> *Encyclopedia of Islam*
> *Encyclopedia of Buddhism*
> *Encyclopedia of Advertising*
> *The International Encyclopedia of Education: Research and Studies*
> *World Press Encyclopedia*

As you continue to inspect the reference section, you will notice indexes to serials and periodicals (*serials* are newspapers and magazines that typically are published daily; *periodicals* are published at longer intervals, such as weekly, monthly, or quarterly). You consult these indexes to find out when and where your subject was discussed in the *Washington Post, Time, Gentleman's Quarterly,* or similar publications. These references provide alphabetical lists of authors and subjects; however, unlike the dictionaries and encyclopedias, multivolume works, such as the *Readers' Guide to Periodical Literature* and the *New York Times Index,* are subdivided into annual or slightly longer time periods. You must look through several volumes if you need to discover when stories, articles, or editorials on a particular subject have been published. No matter which volume you choose, be sure to read the directions for interpreting the information in each listing. On nearby shelves you may see indexes to newspapers from various parts of the country (the *Los Angeles Times, Chicago Tribune, Washington Post,* and others). Using these references, you may discover when a subject was reported in a geographical region or city. You might then read particular issues of two or more newspapers to determine whether the subject was treated the same in different areas of the country. Specialized references, such as the *Humanities Index, Social Sciences Index,* and *Education Index,* are organized similarly to the others, but will inform you when a subject was discussed by scholars, scientists, and teachers. The following indexes are often useful:

Applied Science and Technology Index
Business Periodicals Index
Current Law Index
Philosopher's Index
Popular Periodical Index
Subject Index of the Christian Science Monitor
Television Index
Wall Street Journal Index

The reference section also contains very helpful works, called *yearbooks,* that summarize important facts and events on an annual basis. Many of these items of information are not included or identified clearly in the alphabetical lists of encyclopedias and indexes, and so you need to look individually at such references as the *Statistical Abstract of the United States* (a report of everything that the U.S. Bureau of the Census has learned about citizens of the United States since 1879) and the *Facts on File Yearbook* (an annual summary of newsworthy activities and events since 1941). More specialized yearbooks include such references as the *Advertising Age Yearbook* and the *International Motion Picture Almanac.* Worldwide facts and events can be traced through the *World Almanac and Book of Facts.* All these yearbooks address noteworthy subjects that may deserve further attention through your reading of specific books and articles. Other potentially useful yearbooks include the following:

Almanac of American Politics
Information Please Almanac
International Television Almanac
Reader's Digest Almanac and Yearbook

From time to time, you may also need to inspect the biographical resources and directories shelved in the reference section. For example, if you need historical or contemporary information about a particularly noteworthy American, you might find it in the *Dictionary of American Biography, Notable American Women, Who's Who in America,* or *Who's Who of American Women.* For information on our British cousins, you might look at the *Dictionary of National Biography* or *Who's Who.* The *International Who's Who* contains brief biographies on a scale clearly identified in its title. You can also find the business and professional affiliations of some Americans by consulting directories, such as the *Standard and Poor's Register of Corporations, Directors and Executives* and the *Martindale-Hubbell Law Directory.*

Specific or Detailed Resources

Card Catalogs. Later in your research, you will want to read more substantial, detailed treatments of your subject. Very recent issues of newspapers, magazines, and journals may be kept in a special reading room, but books and bound collections of periodicals will be kept on the regular shelves (or "stacks"). To locate these materials, you probably must use the card catalog. Although many libraries have installed computer-assisted services as supplements or replacements, learning to use the card catalog is a traditional step in discovering speech materials. Whether you use manual or electronic means, you might pay special attention to the location of sources, such as the *New York Times* and *Vital Speeches*. These sources contain the full texts of speeches on important, timely issues. You can also find texts of historical speeches in anthologies of speechmaking.

The **card catalog** is a library file system listing the institution's collection of printed materials by title and subject and by author. The card catalog is contained in two series of cabinets—one series under the combined headings "Author/Title" and the other series under the heading "Subject." You can find the location of a printed resource under any of the three headings. For example, if you do not know the author or title of a book, you can still look up the book in the subject area cabinets. Each cabinet has small file drawers. Each drawer contains three-inch by five-inch cards that list several items of information about each book or bound periodical; at this stage in your research, the "call number" is the most important item because it identifies where in the library you can find the resource. Figures 14.2 and 14.3 illustrate the items of information found on catalog cards.

Reference works provide general information and identify sources of detailed information. The card catalog indicates where in the library you can

The card catalog indicates where in the library you can find the sources of detailed information.

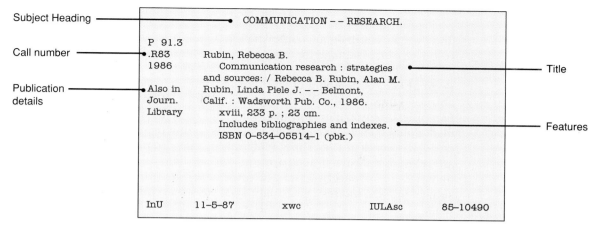

Subject Card

Subject Heading — COMMUNICATION – – RESEARCH.

Call number — P 91.3 .R83 1986

Publication details — Also in Journ. Library

Title — Rubin, Rebecca B.
    Communication research : strategies and sources: / Rebecca B. Rubin, Alan M. Rubin, Linda Piele J. – – Belmont, Calif. : Wadsworth Pub. Co., 1986.
    xviii, 233 p. ; 23 cm.
    Includes bibliographies and indexes.
    ISBN 0–534–05514–1 (pbk.)

Features

InU   11–5–87   xwc   IULAsc   85–10490

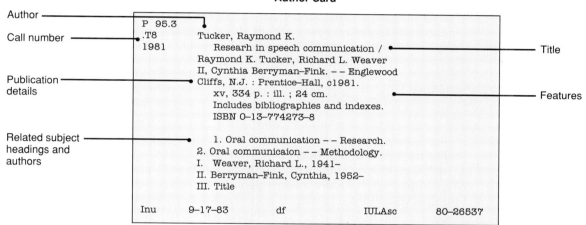

Author Card

Author —

Call number — P 95.3 .T8 1981

Title — Tucker, Raymond K.
    Researh in speech communication / Raymond K. Tucker, Richard L. Weaver II, Cynthia Berryman–Fink. – – Englewood

Publication details — Cliffs, N.J. : Prentice–Hall, c1981.
    xv, 334 p. : ill. ; 24 cm.
    Includes bibliographies and indexes.
    ISBN 0–13–774273–8

Features

Related subject headings and authors —
    1. Oral communication – – Research.
    2. Oral communicaion – – Methodology.
    I. Weaver, Richard L., 1941–
    II. Berryman–Fink, Cynthia, 1952–
    III. Title

Inu   9–17–83   df   IULAsc   80–26537

Figure 14.2
Author/Title and Subject Catalog Cards for Books about "Research in Speech Communication."

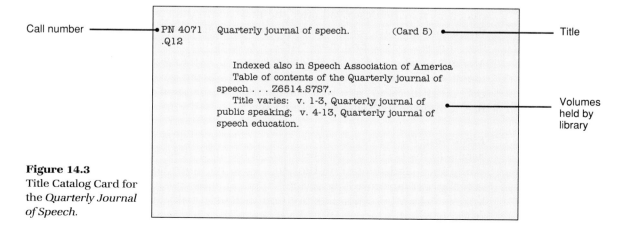

Title Card

Call number — PN 4071 .Q12

Title — Quarterly journal of speech.   (Card 5)

    Indexed also in Speech Association of America
    Table of contents of the Quarterly journal of speech . . . Z6514.S7S7.
    Title varies: v. 1-3, Quarterly journal of public speaking; v. 4-13, Quarterly journal of speech education.

Volumes held by library

Figure 14.3
Title Catalog Card for the *Quarterly Journal of Speech*.

find the sources of detailed information. In addition, you might inspect a special resource organized and maintained by your librarians called the vertical file.

Vertical File.   Members of your library staff are specially trained to recognize and save items of timely or local importance. Whether these resources are pamphlets, newspaper and magazine clippings, or some other item, they are filed alphabetically with similar materials in one or more upright file cabinets, called the **vertical file.** These materials usually are too recent to be indexed or are relevant only to a limited area; in any event, they may provide you with ideas or notes for a speech. In fact, if you are assigned or expected to speak on a subject of local interest, you might start your search for material at the vertical file.

Government Documents.   If you need authoritative information about any level of government, from local to federal, you might need to consult official publications called **government documents.** These documents range from daily accounts of what is said or deliberated in political assemblies, to the legal decisions reached by various courts, to the innumerable publications sponsored by government offices and agencies.

The *Congressional Record* contains actual debates, committee reports, and other materials from the U.S. Senate and House of Representative. To find similar records from your state government, you need to look for books of legislative *Acts,* which are usually kept in the libraries of courthouses and law schools. For the records of political decisions made in your county or city, you need to visit the offices of the county or city clerk (the vertical file may also be useful).

Every type of federal court publishes its decisions. The U.S. trial courts are called district courts; federal courts of appeal are called circuit courts; and, of course, the highest court is the Supreme Court. In addition, other, more specialized courts (for example, the bankruptcy courts) and administrative agencies (for example, the National Labor Relations Board [NRLB]) publish their decisions. At the state level, the decisions of cases that have been appealed beyond a trial court are published. You may temporarily gain access to the documents and decisions in your county or city courts, but you must hurry. These materials may be destroyed after the time allowed for appeals has elapsed. To find legal materials, ask for help from your librarian or county or city clerk.

The best way to find other types of government documents is to consult the *Monthly Catalog of United States Government Publications.* This reference will identify free or modestly priced items, ranging from environmental reports and consumer alerts to informative statements on national and international politics. (Complete the Self-Assessment Exercise.)

Electronic Data Bases.   Many libraries are now able to assist you in gaining access to the electronic resources most useful in speech preparation (as home computers and telephone modems become more common, libraries may actually become more like service centers than like museums). **Electronic data bases** contain information stored on magnetic disks that can be retrieved by using computer terminals. Two types of data bases are especially useful in

SELF-ASSESSMENT   **Discovering Library Resources**

1. To prepare a biographical report on recent Prime Ministers of Great Britain, you might consult _____ .

2. For a speech entitled "Jargon for Computer Junkies," you might consult _____ .

3. To read reports and pamphlets about recent improvements in toxic waste disposal within your city or county, you might consult
_____ .

4. To gather material for a speech on the historical rise and fall of family size in America, you might consult _____ .

5. To criticize speeches made in Washington, D.C., by your state's senators, you might consult _____ .

Answers: 1. *Dictionary of National Biography or Who's Who;* 2. Rosenberg's *Dictionary of Computers, Dataprocessing and Telecommunications;* 3. the vertical file; 4. *Statistical Abstract of the United States;* 5. *Congressional Record*

researching a speech: Reference data bases are electronic equivalents of the printed resources found in reference sections (encyclopedias, directories, etc.); source data bases are electronic twins of the books and other printed materials you locate through a card catalog. You can learn more about these resources in such books as *The Complete Handbook of Personal Computer Communications: Everything You Need to Go Online with the World,* by A. Glossbrenner (New York: St. Martin's Press, 1989), and *Questions and Answers: Strategies for Using the Electronic Reference Collection* (Urbana, IL: Graduate School of Library and Information Science, University of Illinois, Urbana, 1989). In the meantime, Table 14.1 on page 386 shows several electronic resources that are useful in preparing speeches.

Besides the electronic medium, cost is the major difference between traditional and electronic data bases. Library research costs you only time. In order to access an electronic data base, you may have to pay several types of fees. Even if you are literate enough in computers to take advantages of electronic data bases, it is a good idea to talk to your library's specialist before discovering speech materials electronically.

Note Taking

When you properly target your subject, you are already on the path to effective research. You take the next step toward effective research when you talk to other people, and when you examine reference works before exploring the

Discussion Question 14–4
How many times have you used a library for research in your lifetime? How many of the materials described here have you ever used? How many materials are you sure you could find if you walked into your local library?

Teaching Objective 14–7
Introduce the art of note taking as essential to the completion of accurate and effective research.

Table 14.1
Material Available on Electronic Data Bases

Data Base	Resources
ABI/INFORM	Index of business and business-related journals
ERIC	Books and articles on educational subjects
Magazine index	News, stories, and editorials in popular magazines
National newspaper index	News, stories, and editorials in five nationally circulated newspapers
NEXIS	Reports in newspapers, periodicals, newsletters, and encyclopedias

resources on library shelves. In these activities, you first examine sources of general information before seeking more detailed treatments of your subject. The final step is note-taking.

The notes you take will contain one or more types of supporting material. We discuss supporting material more fully in Chapter 17, but for quick reference, Table 14.2 outlines the types and functions of this material.

Your notes should be complete so that you will able to identify your sources. The ethics of speechmaking require that you give credit to the sources from which you borrow facts and opinions. To do otherwise is to plagiarize. (The Focus on Leadership box on p. 388 describes a famous case of plagiarism.)

Your notes should also be accurate so that no individual facts or opinions become divorced from surrounding material. Ethical speakers do not present ideas out of context. Figure 14.4 shows a complete, accurate record of definitions for a speech entitled "Timekeeping."

For most applications, you should record the fruits of your research on three-inch by five-inch or four-inch by six-inch notecards—whether you are quoting selectively from other people's comments or copying the words and numbers from library resources. If you merely use stray bits of paper, then you cannot collect your research notes in a neat stack or box. If you use sheets of looseleaf paper, then you end up with a large, floppy mass of material. Remember, these are the notes you often hold in your hands during your speech.

At the top of each notecard, identify the particular value or significance that the material has for your speech. For example, if you were to research methods of timekeeping, you might collect notes on the distinction between the chronograph and the chronometer, on the earliest timekeeping devices, on the most famous clockmakers, and so on. Record the material's value or significance as you prepare the notecard so that later you can quickly assign your notes to the proper section of your speech.

Most of the space on your notecards will be devoted to the material itself: Doublecheck the accuracy of quotations and numbers—otherwise you might

Teaching Objective 14–8
Offer a reminder of what constitutes plagiarism and why it is both illegal and unethical.

Discussion Question 14–5
What exactly constitutes plagiarism? How is it different from paraphrasing? Why is it important? Martin Luther King's "I Have A Dream" speech contains many lines and phrases borrowed from Bible verses, the sources of which are not cited in his speech. Is this plagiarism?

Table 14.2
Types and Functions of Supporting Material

Type	Function
Definition and explanation	To clarify words and ideas
Quotation and paraphrase	To add authority to ideas
Comparison-contrast and analogy	To point out relationships between ideas
Example and illustration	To provide specific instances, real or hypothetical
Number and statistic	To provide precise measurements

not survive a challenge from the expert who always seems to surface at those times when you cut corners on accuracy! If you find that a particular bit of material requires more than one card, simply add a signal like "Card 1," "Card 2," etc., beside the headings. However, do not attach the successive notecards to one another with staples; if anything, use a paper clip so that you can readily uncover the next card while speaking.

At the bottom, fully record the source of the material. If appropriate, identify the full names of authors or editors. Enclose the titles of articles in quotation marks, but underline the titles of books. Record the place of publication, publisher, and date where appropriate; otherwise, simply make a note of the issue or date. Finally, correctly identify the page number in the resource so that you or others may double check the material's accuracy. A few moments invested in full, accurate note-taking may save you time and trouble during your speech—and afterward. Your notecards, after all, may be useful on more than one occasion.

Figure 14.4
Sample Notecard.

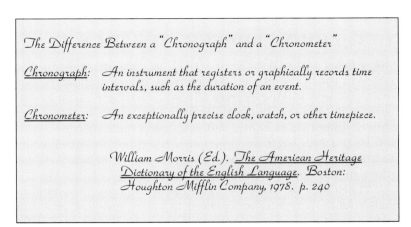

FOCUS ON LEADERSHIP

A Senator and Plagiarism

Senator Joseph R. Biden withdrew from the 1988 presidential campaign in part because he had been accused of plagiarism. He had not properly identified his borrowing of language or his sources in campaign speeches. For example, in his closing statement at an Iowa debate among Democratic candidates, Senator Biden talked about how his ancestors were hard-working people. But despite their working-class status, Biden claimed, they "read poetry and wrote poetry and taught me how to sing verse." Senator Biden made this same statement three days later in a tape recording for the National Education Association. As it turns out, he was quoting from a televised political commercial by Neil Kinnock in Great Britain. However, he did not identify his source either time he used the quotation.

A political reporter for the *New York Times* soon discovered Senator Biden's "borrowing" of the language. Other investigators then discovered similar cases in which Senator Biden had taken language, without saying so, from speeches by Robert F. Kennedy and Hubert H. Humphrey. In fact, investigators found that Senator Biden's problems had begun in school. He had flunked a first-year course at Syracuse University Law School because of plagiarism, writing a term paper that included five pages of text taken from a law review article. But he had not used quotation marks or cited his source.

Plagiarism never helps students or leaders. Considering how easy it is to identify your sources and how favorably teachers view solid research methods, clear note taking, and honest speechmaking in school is excellent preparation for similar communicative duties you will perform later.

◼ DEVELOPING SPEECH CONFIDENCE

Teaching Objective 14–9
Discuss the reality of communication apprehension; emphasize the importance of preparation at every stage and level of the speaking process to building confidence and assuring success.

Discovering material for your speech is a big step toward discovering confidence in your presentation. Nonetheless, even well-prepared speakers react to their task with varying degrees of confidence. Some people are extremely nervous at the thought of speaking in public but deliver their speeches calmly. Others do not seem concerned at all until their speeches actually begin. In a few instances, people are so apprehensive before and during their speeches that they cannot present their ideas effectively. Researchers have labeled this phenomenon *communication apprehension (CA)*.

There may be more than one cause of communication apprehension as well as of the less intense reactions to public speaking. At a fundamental level, public speakers may react negatively to a basic fear of the unknown, or of being stared at, or of being judged. As with other basic fears—fear of the dark, fear of heights, fear of snakes or insects, and so on—communication apprehension may be an innate human trait. If so, communication apprehension may not be caused in the same way as other feelings. People may not learn or develop it at any stage of their lives, and they may not be able to learn to control it. Recently, researchers have found at least some evidence for shyness being an inherited trait.

The best way to develop speech confidence is to approach your speeches methodically. The following sections illustrate several methods to build confidence before, during, and after your speeches. A summary of these techniques is given in the Mastering Communication Skills box on page 390.

Before the Speech

You already know that preparation for your speech must include audience analysis. In addition, you should become familiar with the setting of your speech. Becoming familiar with the time and space in which you will speak offers several benefits. For one, the chances are slim that you will be surprised by the size, lighting, acoustics, furnishings, and other incidentals of your speech setting. You may also find it helpful to visualize how you will physically relate to your audience. You may discover that a bus, train, or plane typically creates outside noise at that time of day. You may learn that the podium is distant and poorly lighted from the audience's point of view. Perhaps the seating arrangement or ventilation in the room is poorly designed. If you learn all of these qualities of the speech setting in advance, you will have time to adapt to them.

Ideally, you should rehearse your speech in the actual setting, as if your audience were already there. A disciplined rehearsal includes full, formal delivery of your subject matter using your theme and your normal speaking voice. Practicing only a part of your speech, or not speaking aloud, reduces the benefits of this preparatory step. For example, practicing only half of your speech does not build confidence in the remainder. It does little good to recognize poor acoustics in a room and then fail to practice the needed adjustments in your delivery.

More than any other factor, thorough preparation of your speech materials and organization will build your confidence. If you know what you want to say, and how you want to say it, your confidence will rise to a level that cannot be reached by any other means.

During the Speech

You can lay part of the foundation for speaking confidently by releasing the tension that people normally feel at the start of their speeches. For example, as you wait for your opportunity, you will probably feel increased energy. You need a certain amount of this extra energy in order to sustain the physical activity of public speaking, but you may find it helpful to slowly release some of this energy just before speaking. Otherwise, your speech might begin on an explosive note rather than a properly energetic one. Slowly point your toes outward, and then bend your feet upward. Stretch and then contract your legs. Open and

Current Research 14–3
Neer reports that communication apprehension or anxiety is reduced when apprehensive persons feel less conspicuous and have acquaintances in the classroom or situation. (Neer, Michael R. Reducing situational anxiety and avoidance behavior associated with classroom apprehension. *Southern Communication Journal, 56,* 1, 1990, pp. 49–71.)

Discussion Question 14–6
How would you rate your own level of communication apprehension on a scale of 1 to 10? Is it different in different situations? Has it gotten better or worse over the years?

Leadership Note 14–4
Kriegel and Patler offer an image of a cycle of fear as it affects a public speaker: first, the speaker imagines looking stupid or being boring; second, the speaker looks out at the audience and perceives hostility or rejection; third, the speaker's physiological fear responses—heart pounding, sweating, etc.—gear up; fourth, the speaker either freezes and forgets main points, stumbles, etc., or talks faster and faster; and, fifth, the speaker thus lives up to her worst expectations and decides she is indeed a terrible speaker. The authors go on to suggest that the best speakers and leaders anticipate all worst-case scenarios before the event and decide in advance how they will handle them. (Kriegel, Robert J., and Patler, Louis, *If It Ain't Broke...Break it!* New York: Warner, 1991, pp. 181–185.)

**MASTERING
COMMUNICATION
SKILLS**

Building Speech Confidence Through Preparation

Before your speech

Content

- Analyze your audience.
- Discover appropriate speech materials and organization.
- Rehearse your speech aloud.

Physical Setting

- Gather appropriate type and amount of furnishings.
- Check on lighting.
- Arrange the room to suit delivery.
- Stage a full, formal rehearsal within the setting.

During your speech

Release Physical Tension

- Exercise hands and feet; while waiting for your turn (and before the audience focuses on you), slowly stretch and rotate hands and feet.
- While approaching the podium, use up excess nervous energy by walking slowly and purposefully.

Introduce Your Speech

- Read a quotation or display a poster (this technique may take the pressure off you by allowing you to rely on someone else's words or directing the audience's attention to the item you are displaying).

Use Gesture and Movement

Conclude Slowly

- In addition to using up some of your energy by restraining the pace of your concluding remarks, a deliberate conclusion helps your audience review the content of your speech.

After your speech

Obtain Feedback

- Actively solicit feedback—by evaluation cards, a formal question period, or informal conversation.
- Seek specific feedback on the quality of your ideas and the overall effectiveness of your speech.

MAKE NEEDED ADJUSTMENTS

close your hands. During your initial observation of the audience, rotate your shoulders and slowly move your head from side to side. These exercises will not appear unusual for someone scanning the audience, and they will begin a process fo methodical rather than random release of energy. When the time for your speech arrives, stand up or approach the speaking position slowly. It takes energy to restrain yourself from rushing into the speaking position. Feel some of your energy being released as you take your position. Again, you will retain plenty of energy for your speech, but you will have begun using it purposefully rather than uncontrollably.

In delivering your first few remarks, be somewhat objective. Repeat words from a written text or display an object, chart, or picture related to your subject. Audiences respect and enjoy relevant quotations or pictures: These items provide early clues to your subject matter and indicate the scope and quality of your speech preparation. For example, you might begin a speech on blacksmiths by displaying a nineteenth-century photograph of a livery stable or by quoting a blacksmith who still plies this trade. Relying on someone else's words at the start of your speech may reduce your fear of making an initial mistake. Displaying an object or picture also uses up more of your energy in a meaningful way.

Throughout your speech, keep physically active. As long as your physical activity is meaningful or emphatic, both you and your audience will benefit. Stepping forward one or two paces to emphasize an important idea is meaningful activity; stepping forward one or two paces simply because your legs are trembling is distracting. Turning from side to side in order to emphasize your attention to the entire audience is altruistic; turning from side to side simply to ease the tension in your shoulders is selfish. In any case, avoid walking from side from side in front of your audience unless you are demonstrating the size or width of an object or area. However, stepping forward or back can emphasize or deemphasize, respectively, the force of your ideas. All these meaningful movements also burn up some of your energy. Gesturing with your hands and arms accomplishes the same goals: Upraised arms can emphasize a high point for the audience, while releasing part of your stress; a chopping motion with your hand can illustrate a division between two ideas for your audience, while burning off a little more of your energy.

You need to maintain your confidence-building efforts until the end of your speech. In general, you should conclude slowly. Although you may be tempted to hurry your remarks as you approach the end of your speech, a hurried conclusion usually confuses or irritates the audience. For example, rushing through a conclusion that summarizes the solutions to an outstanding problem impairs the clarity of the remedies and frustrates a concerned audience. Use your nervous energy to restrain the pace of your conclusion, and you will serve both your self-interest and your audience. Repeating key words for final emphasis or once again reading a relevant quotation may aid you in maintaining a deliberate pace. Whether you rely on a slow-paced rehearsal or other aids, maintain your sequence of confidence building through the conclusion of your speech.

Current Research 14–4
Dorothy Sarnoff, speech consultant and author, offers several suggestions for nervous speakers, including slowly expelling all air from the lungs before getting up to speak (Sarnoff claims this is more relaxing than taking a deep breath), and/or repeating this confidence-boosting message as one faces the audience: "I'm glad I'm here. I'm glad you're here. I care about you. I know what I know." (Sarnoff, Dorothy. *Never Be Nervous Again,* 1990.)

After the Speech

All public speakers feel a certain amount of relief after finishing their presentations. If you plan on speaking publicly again, you will also want to begin building confidence for your next opportunity. The best time to start your next speech preparation is immediately after a prior speech. In most classroom settings, for example, the instructor and students will comment critically on a speaker's performance. Outside the classroom, the use of evaluation cards is commonplace in professionally run programs. After your speech, listen for audience observations. What did your audience notice about your level of confidence? Avoid presuming that the audience observed the quavering in your voice and the shaking in your knees. In most cases, these phenomena are readily evident only to you; your audience will notice few, if any, of these vocal and physical behaviors. After all, during your speech, you are the only one who feels the quavering and shaking. Even if your audience notices a sign or two of communication apprehension on your part, you are primarily interested in the response to your message. Listen for this response.

Discussion Question 14–7
What was the worst public speaking or similar experience of your life? What happened? How did it end?

When your audience analysis reveals that one or more of your methods for building confidence was ineffective, plan to make needed adjustments in your next speech. Whatever the ineffective method may be, you can repair or discard it the next time. However, do not forget to recognize and maintain all of the successful methods you used! Audience analysis—which may include a specially designed opinion poll after your speech—can identify especially helpful steps before and during your speech. Retaining these methods is also a form of adjustment. Learning about your effective techniques should begin the process of building confidence in your next speech. In fact, this process should continue indefinitely as you repeat the sequence of steps and gradually grow more and more confident.

■ Summary

As a public speaker you can exercise leadership when you present well-prepared speeches of substance; that is, speeches that contain sufficient facts and opinions to keep the audience informed, persuaded, or satisfied long after the presentation is over. Facts (materials that the audience can confirm as true) and opinions (materials that the audience may accept as probably true) can be found in a variety of resources, including other people and the library.

You can discover facts and opinions by talking to other people. Informal talk (conversations) is particularly useful in long-range speech preparation when you have a particular subject in mind. By keeping a speaker's diary of other people's stories and viewpoints, you can collect a lasting resource for use throughout a class or throughout a career. Formal talk (interviews) is particularly useful when you have a definite subject in mind and are looking for specific facts and opinions. Unlike conversations, though, interviews require careful preparation and procedures. The most fruitful interviews require that you obtain necessary agreements, introduce yourself and your purpose, maintain a quiet or private setting, use prepared questions, use follow-up questions, avoid expressing personal opinions, and record responses. Whether through conversations or interviews, you will discover speech materials that include personal or, perhaps, expert viewpoints on your subject.

Library research is always a valuable preparation for speechmaking. The reference section is a desirable place to start your library research because this section contains general guides to most subject areas: By consulting dictionaries, encyclopedias, indexes, yearbooks, and biographical references, you can learn generally useful information in a short time. The books and magazines identified in the card catalog, the vertical file, and government documents provide more specific or detailed information. In fact, you may be able to gain access to both general and specific information through electronic data bases (computerized systems of library research).

Talking to other people and library research are useful only if you take complete, accurate notes. The most useful notes—to both speaker and audience—identify the special value of the material, include a complete text or record, and clearly list the source.

A well-prepared speech reduces communication apprehension, a technical term for concern over public speaking, ranging from nervousness to fear. You can reduce the tension that speakers normally feel before a speech by preparing competently and arranging the setting. During your speech, you can build confidence by releasing tension, making an objective introduction, using movement and gesture, and concluding slowly. After your speech, you can extend this process by listening to audience observations on your effectiveness and making adjustments in future speeches.

Exercises

1. If you had to present a biographical speech about any person of your choice—living or dead—who would it be? Why would you select that person? What would be the purpose of your speech? If you had an opportunity to interview the person, how would you arrange the agreements and setting? Which questions would you ask? Where could you find relevant biographical materials in the library? Write a brief report that answers all these questions.

2. Interview two or more people who are experienced public speakers, using the steps offered in this chapter as a guide. Which resources do these people typically consult in discovering materials for their speeches? Which types of notes do they make and how do they use these notes in their speaking? Which types of speech materials do they find most valuable? Discuss the results of your interview in class.

3. Talk to people who do a fair amount of public speaking (such as political office-holders, lawyers, teachers, supervisors, and others who speak publicly on a regular basis). Ask these people about their feelings toward speaking in public. What is their typical level of communication apprehension? Do these speakers have any helpful methods of reducing communication apprehension?

Coordination

A speech has **coordination** when its parts are equal or parallel in importance. Coordinate elements deserve a roughly equal amount of attention—whether that means an equal amount of speaking time or an equal degree of verbal and vocal emphasis. As we point out later in this chapter, coordinate elements can be spotted quickly in a well-prepared outline because they are assigned distinctive symbols and places.

Subordination

A speech reflects **subordination** when it supports or develops major parts with subparts and specific details. Subordinate elements are minor parts of a larger whole. As you might expect, the attention given to all related subordinate elements equals the attention paid to the major element they support. Put another way, no subordinate element should receive as much emphasis as any major element. The principle of subordination, therefore, also indicates how much time you should devote to any given element of a speech. In a well-prepared outline, the subordinate elements can be distinguished by their identifying symbols and placement.

In the following speech by Julie M. Graef, "The Ethical Implications of the Rap Music Controversy" (Oregon State University, 1990), consider the general value of organization and look for reflections of unity, coordination, and subordination.

Leadership Note 15–1
"Leaders have a significant role in creating the state of mind that is in the society. They can serve as symbols of the moral unity of society. They can express the values that hold society together." (Gardner, John W., as quoted in Bennis, Warren, *On Becoming a Leader*. Reading, MA.: Addison-Wesley, 1989, p. 19.)

Discussion Question 15–1
Could these same principles of unity, coordination, and subordination be used to evaluate the organization of any work of art? Can a speech be a work of art?

Remember when they said that rock-and-roll was corrupting the minds of our nation's youth? Now, rap music is under attack. This controversial form of inner-city, urban-based music has raised some serious legal and ethical questions. Are rap groups really influencing our children to be more violent and obscene, or are they simply expressing their right to freedom of speech? What responsibilities do rap groups have in protecting their audiences?

There has been a rise in the last two years in what some call increasingly brash lyrics of rap. Tonight I will talk about three of the most controversial rap groups today: the militant Public Enemy, then the violent NWA, and finally the questionably obscene 2 Live Crew.

Probably the most politically influential rap group is Public Enemy. They are the self-proclaimed prophets of rage. They set role models for black youth. Their songs promote black pride and describe the everyday problems of urban life. On stage, their dancers dress in military uniforms, carrying plastic Uzis. A fringe member was accused of anti-Semitism last spring.

Another rap group that is no stranger to criticism is Los Angeles based NWA—"N——s with Attitude." When asked about the violent lyrics in his album, "Straight Outta Compton," Eazy E., the lead singer, calls himself a street historian. He says his group just tells it like it is when living in the violent culture of the slums of Compton, where being shot by a cop is a very real fear.

The most recent controversy has to do with the question of obscenity with the rap group 2 Live Crew. Their tunes are filled not only with material about women and gays, but also contain dirty nursery rhymes. The June 9, 1990, *New York Times* describes their "explicit depictions of male and female genitalia, as well as anatomical descriptions of copulation in a variety of physical positions. One of the milder songs is titled 'Me So Horny.'"

I've introduced some of the controversial rap groups; now let's look at some of the legal and ethical issues that have arisen.

NWA ran into trouble with the FBI last summer because of their album "Straight Outta Compton." FBI Assistant Director Milt Ahlerich wrote a letter to NWA's distributors, saying that the album "encourages violence against and disrespect for policemen." In particular, the song "F——the Police" was in question.

Newsweek's March 19, 1990, issue asks if "such appalling expressions of attitude are protected by the First Amendment." According to an American Civil Liberties Union official, they are. He said, "The song does not constitute advocacy of violence as that has been interpreted by the courts."

Another legal concern is the question of obscenity in rap lyrics. On June 6 [1990], 2 Live Crew's album, "As Nasty as They Wanna Be" was ruled obscene, punishable by a $1,000 fine and one year in jail. Charles Freeman was arrested on June 9 for selling the album. Freeman was against the attempts to suppress the recording, and to show how strong his feelings were, he ordered a new shipment of the album and began selling it again on the day he was released. Later that night, two members of 2 Live Crew, including lead singer Luther Campbell, were arrested after performing an adults-only concert. Campbell says he had "unfairly been a victim of limitation of freedom of speech and racism." The album's sales recently soared to over 1.7 million.

John Leland, *Newsday*'s music critic, said the ruling was clouded by a lack of understanding of black music. According to the legal definition of obscenity rendered in the 1973 [Supreme] Court decision of *Miller v. California,* to be obscene, "material must be offensive to community standards, and devoid of literary, artistic, political or social value." Leland suggests that whites aren't always aware of black literary devices. *New York Times* critic John Pareles says opponents are failing to see the humor in the lyrics, claiming that it is a black tradition to boast about sexual abilities and encounters. He concludes, "Clearly 2 Live Crew sees itself as part of a comic tradition."

Not only does rap arouse legal questions; ethical questions of social responsibility are also asked.

A father, writing in *Time* magazine, echoed the concerns of many parents when he argued that rap music is sending dangerous messages to our children: Women's only function is for the sexual convenience of man; violence is an acceptable way to solve problems; and bigotry is "hip."

Susan Baker and Tipper Gore founded the Parents' Music Resource Center to place warning labels on certain albums. According to *Time* magazine, Gore says there are "some 14 million children who are at risk and in need of counseling due to the graphic brutality in music lyrics." Still others add that the number of murders and rapes committed by juveniles is continuously rising and teenage pregnancy has reached "epidemic proportions."

But who can say that violent or sexual lyrics influence youthful behavior? A study commissioned by the Carnegie Council on Adolescent Development concluded, however, that few children are harmfully affected by strong lyrics. Donald F. Roberts of Stanford University says, "Kids take it in stride."

Performers themselves are asking if they should take some responsibility for the influence that they might possibly have on their audiences. Young MC believes that they should. As he tells *Newsweek* magazine, "There are a lot of impressionable people listening to the music. If I wasn't to take notice of that, I'd be shirking responsibility."

Luther Campbell of 2 Live Crew feels that they have taken more responsibility than any other musical group. Campbell placed a label reading "PARENTAL ADVISORY: EXPLICIT LYRICS" on his "Nasty" album. In response to criticism, Campbell also made an alternative version of the album called "As Clean as They Wanna Be."

People criticize the militancy of Public Enemy, the violence of NWA, and the obscenity of 2 Live Crew, which raise serious legal and ethical questions. Twenty-five years ago, it was rock-and-roll. Now it's rap. As long as there is freedom of expression, there will be controversy over what is acceptable for society and where the line is drawn.

(Used with permission of Julie M. Graef.)

Discussion Question 15–2 Are the problems discussed by Ms. Graef regarding rap music reflective of racist or of free speech issues?

As an aid to detecting its organization, and its reflection of unity, coordination, and subordination, Graef's speech can be outlined as follows:

Theme: "Rap music is under attack because it has raised serious legal and ethical questions."

Introduction
   A. Like rock-and-roll music in the past, rap music now raises legal and ethical questions: Are rap groups legally responsible for violent and obscene influences? Do rap groups have ethical responsibilities?
   B. On the issue of brash lyrics, three rap groups are controversial.
      1. Public Enemy is the most politically influential group.

"Unity": The three divisions of subpoint B are all rap groups

   a. They are prophets of rage.
   b. They are role models.
   c. They promote black pride.
   d. They describe everyday urban problems.
       (1) Their dancers wear military uniforms and carry plastic Uzis.
       (2) A fringe member was accused of anti-Semitism.
 2. NWA, "N——s with Attitude," based in Los Angeles, uses violent lyrics.
   a. Eazy E., lead singer, calls himself a street historian.
   b. He says his group tells of real life because the slums of Compton have a violent culture—being shot by a cop is a real fear.
 3. 2 Live Crew has recently been accused of obscenity.
   a. Their tunes have questionable lyrics about women and gays, and even contain dirty nursery rhymes.
   b. The *New York Times,* June 9, 1990, describes these lyrics (read quotation).

Transition	I've introduced some of the controversial rap groups; now let's look at some of the legal and ethical issues that have arisen.

"Coordination": Legal and ethical issues are of equal importance

Main point	I. Legal issues include violence and obscenity.

A. NWA lyrics in "Straight Outta Compton" suggest violence against police.

"Subordination": The quotations in 1, 2, 3, and 4 support subpoint A

 1. FBI Assistant Director Milt Ahlerich wrote a letter criticizing the album (read quotation).
 2. The song, "F—— the Police," contains typical lyrics.
 3. *Newsweek,* March 19, 1990, asks a related question (read quotation).
 4. An American Civil Liberties Union official defends the lyrics (read quotation).

"Coordination": All four quotations are of equal importance

B. 2 Live Crew lyrics suggest obscenity.
 1. "As Nasty as They Wanna Be" was ruled obscene on June 6, 1990, with possible penalties of a $1,000 fine and a one-year jail sentence.
   a. Charles Freeman was arrested on June 9 for selling the album, but, because of his strong antisuppression feelings, he ordered more albums and began selling them again following his release.
   b. Two members of the rap group, including lead singer Luther Campbell, were also arrested on June 9 after performing an adults-only concert.
       (1) Campbell complained about his arrest (read quotation).
       (2) Sales of the album soared to over 1.7 million.

2. John Leland, *Newsday*'s music critic, said the ruling lacked understanding of black music.
   a. 1973 ruling in *Miller v. California* defined "obscenity" (read quotation).
   b. Leland suggests whites aren't always aware of black literary devices.
   c. John Pareles, critic for the *New York Times,* agrees (read quotation).

Not only does rap arouse legal questions; ethical questions of social responsibility are also asked.

II. Ethical issues include the danger of rap lyrics and performers' social responsibility.
   A. Many people believe rap lyrics are dangerous to youthful audiences.
      1. A father, writing in *Time,* echoed many parents' concerns (read quotation).
      2. Susan Baker and Tipper Gore founded the Parents' Music Resource Center to place warning labels on certain albums.
         a. Gore addressed these warnings in *Time* (read quotation).
         b. Other people point to the continuing rise in murders and rapes by juveniles, and describe the "epidemic proportions" of teenage pregnancy.
      3. But do violent or sexual lyrics influence youthful behavior?
         a. A study commissioned by the Carnegie Council on Adolescent Development concluded that few children are harmfully affected.
         b. Stanford University's Donald F. Roberts says, "Kids take it in stride."
   B. Many performers ask about their responsibility for influencing youthful audiences.
      1. Young MC tells *Newsweek* that performers should take responsibility (read quotation).
      2. Luther Campbell of 2 Live Crew agrees.
         a. He placed a warning label reading "PARENTAL ADVISORY: EXPLICIT LYRICS" on his "Nasty" album.
         b. He also responded to criticism by making an alternative version called "As Clean as They Wanna Be."

Conclusion
   A. People criticize the militancy of Public Enemy, the violence of NWA, and the obscenity of 2 Live Crew, which raise serious legal and ethical questions.
   B. Twenty-five years ago it was rock-and-roll. Now it's rap. As long as there is freedom of expression, there will be controversy over what is acceptable for society and where the line is drawn.

Leadership Note 15–2
"Public leadership is a product of effective public communication. Although many public campaigns rely on pamphlets, position papers and other written materials, the majority of interaction between public leaders and their followers takes place via public address. Whether you aspire to be President of the United States, a social activist, or the leader of a fraternity or sorority, you must be able to speak effectively in public to influence large numbers of followers....The logic and structure of the ideas presented within a public speech are critical."
(Hackman, Michael Z. and Johnson, Craig E., *Leadership: A Communication Perspective*. Prospect Heights, IL: Waveland Press, 1991, pp. 219–221.)

The form of this speech illustrates that clear organization permits only a limited number of ideas to be addressed in a given speech. Audiences can only learn or be persuaded of so much at one time. For most classroom speeches, it is ineffective to address more than three major ideas in combination with an introduction and conclusion. If you have the relative luxury of being able to speak with liberal time limits, or none at all, you might address as many as five or six important ideas. In her speech, Julie M. Graef addressed two main points.

The organization of Graef's speech also illustrates the principles of unity, coordination, and subordination. The speech illustrates the principle of unity because, first of all, it does not stray from its theme. In addition, its introduction is subdivided into two issues surrounding rap music and three controversial rap groups; each subdivision is unified because it contains only one type of material. The conclusion is arranged in the same unified way. The speech is divided into two main points, each of which is unified because it addresses either legal issues or ethical issues, but not both. Furthermore, the subdivisions of each main point contain unified elements. No single point in the speech contains unrelated ideas; no supporting element contains more than one type of speech material. Otherwise, Graef would not have had clear organization.

The speech also illustrates the principle of coordination. Legal issues and ethical issues are coordinate elements in Graef's speech. Within the first main

MASTERING COMMUNICATION SKILLS

Recognizing the Principles of Organization

Each of the following series of points reflects a violation of the principles of unity, coordination, or subordination. Identify which violation has occurred in each case.

1. I.   Marijuana is a substantial "cash crop" in the United States; other countries grow marijuana for personal consumption.
    II. Marijuana is illegal in most states, but people disagree about its effects on personal health.
    III. Marijuana is a subject of considerable medical testing and legal dispute.

2. I.   Marijuana is a substantial "cash crop" in the United States.
    II. A "cash crop" is something grown for sale and profit.
    III. Americans grow several thousand tons of marijuana each year.

3. I.   Over the years marijuana has been cultivated for various purposes.
    A. The earliest Americans cultivated marijuana for medicinal and ritual uses.
    B. Nineteenth-century Americans began cultivating marijuana for use as a social lubricant.
    C. The cultivation of marijuana has been illegal for many years in most states.

Answers: 1. unity; 2. subordination; 3. coordination

diopulmonary resuscitation (CPR) would not be helpful if it explained the technique backwards. In any event, a speech using the temporal pattern should not skip time periods or steps without an explanation.

Outlining a Temporal Pattern. Commodity trading follows a formal sequence, even though deal making on the trading floor can appear frenzied at times. The following outline illustrates how a speaker might use the temporal pattern to explain trading at a commodity exchange.

I. Telephone agents receive buy and sell orders.
II. Runners deliver the orders to brokers and traders.
III. Brokers and traders shout out their offers.
IV. Exchange employees record deals that are made.

The outline follows the making of a deal from start to finish. A history of commodity trading or a speech on the training of brokers might be arranged in a similar pattern. Because people perceive time as significant, the temporal pattern offers substantial advantages when your subject involves sequences or steps.

The only drawback in using a temporal pattern is related to the art of storytelling. Two people may tell the same story, but their audiences may enjoy one while barely tolerating the other. In other words, the temporal pattern may require a vivid or dramatic recitation of events or steps. If you do not trust your skill at storytelling, then you might want to consider another pattern.

The Problem-Solving Pattern

Audiences are naturally drawn to speeches that solve problems. The benefits of solving a problem readily capture the audience's interest. For example, once an audience perceives a problem, such as unfair tax rates, to be significant, that audience pays attention to suggested remedies, such as the closing of tax loopholes. Once an audience realizes that environmental pollution is a clear and present danger, that audience pays attention to suggested changes in waste disposal methods. In each case, the audience's attention is drawn to a movement or change from need to satisfaction. However, responsible speakers do not address a problem without identifying a reasonable solution. To do less would be to agitate audiences rather than help them.

In the most basic **problem-solving pattern of organization**, the speaker addresses an actual need of the audience, and then explains a desirable way of satisfying that need. Some problems may have two or more equally feasible solutions; for example—depending on the student—the high cost of college may be handled by obtaining grants and scholarships, taking out a student loan, working part time after enrollment, or delaying enrollment and working full time for a while. In a more sophisticated problem-solving pattern, the speaker would address the problem, discuss criteria for judging the best remedy, measure possible solutions against the criteria, and then identify the most qualified solution. The *motivated sequence* is another pattern frequently used in prob-

Current Research 15–3
Ishii compared Western and Japanese Buddhist rhetorical principles and found many similarities. The Buddhist Agui School of rhetorical principles follows a 5-step organization of sermons: (1) Theme glorification (using a sutra verse related to the subject); (2) Tenet explanation (explaining the main idea); (3) Allegory (telling a story that illustrates the idea); (4) Karma (sharing an evidential narrative to prove the idea); (5) Concluding persuasion (summarizing and concluding by offering peace of mind). (Ishii, Satoshi, Buddhist preaching: The persistent main undercurrent of Japanese rhetorical communication. *Communication Quarterly 40*, 4, 1992, pp. 391–397.)

lem-solving speeches. In this five-step pattern, speakers (1) attract the audience's attention; (2) demonstrate the need; (3) identify the satisfaction; (4) help the audience visualize the results; and finally (5) request a response. If the response is to be simple agreement rather than action, then step 5 may be omitted. Similarly, if the speaker's purpose is purely informative, then both steps 4 and 5 may be omitted.

Outlining a Problem-Solving Pattern. In a speech on commodity trading, the problem-solving pattern could be used to explore potential remedies for wild fluctuations in the price of grain. The following outline illustrates a speech in which two solutions are discussed.

I. Wild fluctuations in the price of grain hurt both farmers and consumers.
  A. Farmers cannot survive cycles of boom and bust.
  B. Consumers cannot plan their food budgets.
II. The best solution to this problem would modify price changes while preserving free trade.
  A. Restrained price changes make business and personal finances more manageable.
  B. Free trade is the foundation of our economy.
III. Another solution involves increased federal regulation or self-regulation.
  A. More federal regulation could provide for the closing of trade at times of extreme price swings.
    1. Price changes would be restrained.
    2. Free trade might be delayed but not prohibited.
  B. Self-regulation by commodity exchanges could discourage panic selling and buying.
    1. Price changes would be modified.
    2. Trading would remain as free as farmers and traders would wish.

The outline first identifies the nature of the problem: Both farmers and consumers suffer from unstable grain markets. Next, the outline identifies desirable criteria for solving the problem: Restraints on price swings are good as long as free trade is also maintained. Finally, the outline identifies alternative solutions that meet the criteria: federal regulation or self-regulation. Each of these coordinate points is developed to a roughly equal degree. For an audience attuned to this subject matter, the problem-solving pattern would be predictably easy to follow—just as the human eye is predictably drawn to movement or change in the environment. Of course, the outline does not merely call attention to a problem without also proposing a reasonable solution.

A problem-solving pattern has many advantages and few drawbacks—as long as it is relevant to your subject matter. In fact, failure to gain agreement on the existence of a problem is the only major difficulty associated with speeches of this type. Sometimes, therefore, it is desirable to schedule a problem-solving speech after having presented a speech in which you discuss the causes of a problem.

The Causal Pattern

Cause and effect—stimulus and response—are basic elements of nature. Not surprisingly, people are always interested in discovering the causes of important conditions or events. Causal relationships are among the most difficult to prove, but people are usually receptive to information and evidence about causes and effects. For instance, the whodunit detective novel is a staple in bookstores; the causes of airliner accidents and other tragedies are front-page news; where to place the praise or blame for a political decision remains a popular pastime. Speeches on a number of subjects benefit from the human tendency to perceive causal relationships; as mentioned above, it is often effective to address the causes of a problem before speaking in favor of a solution. If you can clearly identify the relevant stimuli and responses, then you can arrange your points in a **causal pattern of organization**. Whether you speak first of cause and then of effect—or the reverse—is not always significant. It is more important that your speech materials provide accurate, sufficient evidence of causality.

Current Research 15–4
Karlyn Campbell has described what she believes to be a feminine style of rhetoric, which is inductive and employs a narrative or dramatic method of organization. (As discussed in Pearson, Turner, and Todd-Mancillas, *Gender and Communication*. Dubuque: William C. Brown, 1991, p. 227.)

Outlining a Causal Pattern.   The now-familiar subject of commodity trading could be organized into a causal pattern. In the following outline, the speaker is addressing major causes of unstable commodity prices.

    I. A fast-changing commodity market reflects the insecurity felt by both sellers and buyers.
       A. Farmers sometimes feel pressured to sell at prices that do not cover their costs of production.
       B. Distributors sometimes feel pressured to buy at prices that put them at a disadvantage with their competitors.
   II. A fast-changing commodity market responds to natural and artificial forces.
       A. Unusually good or bad weather naturally affects prices by increasing or decreasing the supply of commodities.
       B. Sudden political decisions to subsidize the cultivation of certain crops artificially raise or lower prices.

This outline illustrates an effect-to-cause pattern. The speaker felt that the audience would already be somewhat familiar with unstable food prices (effects) and began the speech with material that needed little explanation. The speech then moved on to more difficult ideas (causes). If both effects and causes were equally unknown, then the speech could have begun with either point. This outline is not fully developed and does not identify the evidence that would prove the causal relationship among weather, politics, and commodity prices. Such evidence, of course, is fundamental to the success of speeches that use the causal pattern.

Discussion Question 15–3
Each of us, when approaching a new problem or experience, perceives it differently, some wanting to know first what it's made up of (conventional pattern), others wanting to know what came first (temporal) or what caused this thing to occur (causal). Of the five patterns your text explains, which best describes your basic or general approach to new experiences or problems? What is it that you first want to know?

    The link between cause and effect is fairly obvious, but similar links or relationships support all five patterns of speech organization. Coordinate points may be related by convention, by time, by space, or by a problem-solution link as well as by the cause-effect link. Relationships are also crucial in designing effective introductions and conclusions. (See the Self-Assessment exercise.)

■ USING INTRODUCTIONS AND CONCLUSIONS

Teaching Objective 15–3
Emphasize the importance of effective introductions and conclusions to the success of a speech; define them in terms of relationships between the speaker and the subject, occasion, and audience.

Discussion Question 15–4
When you need to ask someone you know for assistance, how much thought do you give to how you will begin? For example, how would you introduce the subject of wanting to borrow a large sum of money from your mom or dad?

The importance of introducing and concluding a speech is as widely accepted as the value of organization itself. Effective speakers design their introductions and conclusions to emphasize three "relationships" rather than communicate a great deal of information. At the beginning and end of their speeches, these speakers establish connections between themselves and the *subject, occasion,* and *audience* (see Figure 15.1).

As a practical matter, public speakers need to gain the audience's attention to the speech's main points in the introduction. In the conclusion, a summary or restatement of these same points is necessary. In addition, speakers are often concerned about the proper length of introductions and conclusions. Common sense rules apply. An introduction, after all, is merely a preliminary to the speech; a conclusion is likewise subordinate to the main points of the speech. A traditional measurement dictates that—as long as each part performs its functions as discussed below—only 10 to 15 percent of a speech should be devoted to the introduction, with a similar investment of time and materials in the conclusion. When the desirable relationships are difficult to express, however, you may need to spend additional time on the beginnings and ends of your speeches.

Figure 15.1
Introductions and Conclusions Establish Relationships: Between You and the Subject, Between You and the Occasion, Between You and the Audience.

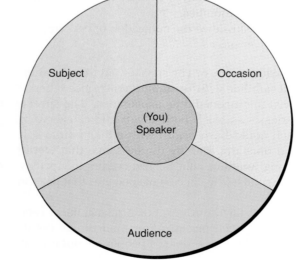

Recognizing patterns of organization

Which of the five patterns of organization would be most suitable for speeches on the following subjects?

1. personal and institutional answers to the question of how to reclaim our polluted environment

2. good spots for bass fishing in the local reservoir

3. duties in the job description of a regional sales manager

4. predictable results of computer illiteracy among college students

5. how to refinish antique furniture

Answers: 1. problem-solving; 2. spatial; 3. conventional; 4. causal; 5. temporal

Introducing Your Speech

Relationship Between Speaker and Subject. Audience attention can first be stimulated by showing a relationship between yourself and your subject. Public speakers are well received when they address a subject related to their personal knowledge or experience. Audiences may also accept a speaker's sincere interest or concern as a substitute for extensive knowledge or experience. For a speech on the need for strict regulation of companies that transport hazardous waste, which of the following speakers would you find more acceptable—the person who tells you that she found this subject to rank highly on a recently published list of public concerns, or the person who tells you that she once worked for such a company but quit her job because she felt torn between her paycheck and her values? Both speakers used appropriate material to introduce their speeches. Although the second speaker's personal example may have improved her acceptability, note that she does not necessarily have special training or experience related to her subject (it is not clear whether her job was closely related to the actual transportation of hazardous wastes). The first speaker may actually have been more knowledgeable—especially if her speech revealed what she had learned from library research and perhaps an interview or two.

Consider how Lesli R. Johnson identified her relationship to her subject—the effects of lighting and noise on study time—in introducing the speech first presented in Chapter 13:

Current Research 15–5
Patricia Weir, President of Encyclopedia Britannica, U.S.A., established her relationship both to the subject and the audience in this second paragraph of her introduction to a speech on corporate success strategies presented to the National Association of College and University Business Officers in Houston, Texas, on July 14, 1987: "Some of what I say may seem obvious, but in the twenty-five or so years in which I have been working, which parallels the history of your organization, many things have changed in the corporate world with regard to women. I think the academic world is changing in similar fashion, and therefore maybe I can offer something that is helpful to you." (*Vital Speeches*, 10/15/87, p. 26.)

Most of us spend a majority of our school years studying, but most of this studying is done under poor lighting and noisy conditions.

As a matter of fact, after I heard several of you discussing this very problem last week, I looked into the problem more closely. I found that poor study conditions can have an adverse effect on our health and, as a result, our work suffers. Today I'd like you to learn how to control the conditions in which you study in order to make the most of your study time—as well as reduce potential health hazards such as fatigue, headaches, and hearing loss. By promoting better study conditions, you can make your work more efficient, you will feel better, and you may have more time to do the things you want. . . .

(Used with permission of Lesli R. Johnson.)

Leadership Note 15–3
Frederick Douglass, writer, orator, and former slave, used the very question, described here as one the audience wants answered in an introduction, to turn the tables on his audience and introduce his very disturbing and uncelebratory speech, "The Meaning of July Fourth for the Negro," delivered in Rochester, New York, on July 4, 1852: "Fellow citizens: Pardon me, and allow me to ask, why am I called upon to speak here today? What have I or those I represent to do with your national independence? Are the great principles of political freedom and of natural justice, embodied in that Declaration of Independence, extended to us?"

By announcing the two major factors of lighting and noise as main points, Johnson previewed her speech for the audience in a way that suggested her command over the material. Also, she clearly identified personal knowledge, experience, and concern related to her subject matter. She identified herself as knowledgeable by remarking on the special research she conducted to prepare her speech; she identified her personal relationship to the subject by talking about her status as a student. This combination of facts and opinion was highly desirable. The speaker's theme—expressed in the next to last sentence of the introduction—called for a precise response from the audience and began the process of making her speech distinctive and memorable.

Relationship Between Speaker and Occasion.   Audiences want to know the relationship between speaker and occasion. In other words, audiences want to answer the question: Why is this speaker addressing this subject here and now? Sometimes the location of a speech is highly relevant and should be addressed. For example, introductory references to the surrounding architecture would be relevant in a speech delivered at the grand opening of a store, office, or some other building. A speech's physical site, however, may be far less significant than its timing. For example, clergy do not typically benefit from reminding the congregation that they are in church. For similar reasons, students of public speaking do not usually benefit from reminding their listeners about the classroom setting. In these instances, references to the time are more important. Why is it opportune for the preacher to address a particular virtue or vice? Why is it timely for the student to address a particular subject?

As we saw earlier in the chapter, the introduction to Graef's speech on rap music clearly establishes a relationship between her choice of subject and the occasion:

Remember when they said that rock-and-roll was corrupting the minds of our nation's youth? Now, rap music is under attack. This controversial form of inner-city, urban-based music has raised some serious legal and ethical questions. Are rap groups really influencing our children to be more violent and obscene, or are they simply expressing their right to freedom of speech? What responsibilities do rap groups have in protecting their audiences?

There has been a rise in the last two years in what some call the increasingly brash lyrics of rap. Tonight I will talk about three of the most controversial rap groups today: the militant Public Enemy, then the violent NWA, and finally the questionably obscene 2 Live Crew.

(Used with permission of Julie M. Graef.)

The speaker expresses her theme in questions about the influence and responsibilities of rap groups. She also emphasizes the timeliness of her speech. Recounting the old attacks on rock-and-roll, Graef compares them with the current attacks on rap music. The speech illustrates that a long, extensively researched introduction is not necessarily needed to establish a relationship

To gain an audience's attention and interest, speakers demonstrate their relationship to their subject, occasion, and audience.

between the speaker and the occasion. Rather, it is more important to express the link between the subject and the place or time.

Discussion Question 15–5
How do you go about attempting to present yourself as believable and trustworthy in your everyday life?

Relationship Between Speaker and Audience. Audiences also want to know their relationship to the speaker. Should they relate to the speaker as a superior, an equal, or a subordinate? What do they share in common with the speaker? How are they different? Rather than allowing or encouraging audiences to guess, you should provide the answer in your introduction. This relationship is particularly important in persuasive speeches and, in Chapter 18, speaker "credibility" will be discussed in considerable detail. For now, you should consider the general effect of establishing an introductory relationship with the audience. In a speech about drug abuse among amateur athletes, for instance, it would be advantageous to mention the sporting events that both speaker and audience enjoy equally. A speech about the social and economic effects of saving the Social Security system might well begin with the speaker's declaration of concern for both the older and the younger members of the audience.

Recall from Chapter 13 how Julie A. Goedde emphasized a relationship with the audience in the introduction to her speech on dieting:

> We are obsessed with diets! Fat people are trying to find ways to lose weight, doctors are looking for ways to reduce salt and cholesterol, athletes are looking for foods to provide long-lasting energy, and parents are worrying about junk foods….And just as we may know someone with heart disease or cancer, we probably know twice as many people who are overweight. None of us may even be concerned about this now, but what happens in two or three years, when we're out of college and our activity levels decrease? We'll need to pay attention to our eating habits. Why start then? Start now and get your diet under control before it's too late.
>
> (Used with permission of Julie A. Goedde.)

The speaker states her concern for members of the immediate audience as well as for who they might become in the years ahead. Using words such as "we" and "us," she establishes common ground with the audience. Indeed, Goedde identifies steps that both she and the audience should take together. She also emphasizes the timeliness of her subject.

Effective speakers establish relationships with the subject, occasion, and audience while introducing their speeches. Few introductions set up all three relationships equally; it is usually sufficient to establish one or two. At the same time, of course, themes should be announced. In ending their speeches, leading speakers complete the process by referring back to subject, occasion, audience, and theme.

Concluding Your Speech

References to subject, occasion, and audience become all the more meaningful and memorable when used at both the beginning and end of a presentation.

Using a technique called *mirroring,* many speakers conclude by referring back to the material they used while introducing the speech. In the same way that effective introductions preview main points, effective conclusions restate these points. You should conclude by amplifying the same relationships emphasized in your introduction.

Relationship Between Speaker and Subject.   When accepting the Democratic nomination to run for president in 1992, Bill Clinton concluded his speech by emphasizing his relationship with the "future":

> I want every person in this hall and every citizen in this land to reach out and join us in a great new adventure to chart a bold new future. As a teenager I heard John Kennedy's summons to citizenship. And then, as a student at Georgetown, I heard that call clarified by a professor I had, named Carroll Quigley, who said America was the greatest country in the history of the world because our people have always believed in two great ideas: first, that tomorrow can be better than today, and second, that each of us has a personal, moral responsibility to make it so. That future entered my life the night our daughter Chelsea was born. As I stood in that delivery room, I was overcome with the thought that God had given me a blessing my own father never knew; the chance to hold my child in my arms.

Early in his speech, Clinton announces that he wants to talk about the future; his conclusion restates this aim as well as his personal connection with his subject.

Relationship Between Speaker and Occasion.   A concluding restatement of the relationship between speaker and occasion is also effective. Particularly during a lengthy speech, an audience may lose sight of the significance of place or time. By referring back to this special significance, a speaker enhances the audience's memory of the entire speech. For example, when concluding a speech to the World Affairs Council in Los Angeles on August 13, 1992, Bill Clinton emphasized how appropriate his remarks were to the time and place:

> Today's leadership is rudderless, reactive and erratic. It is time for leadership that is strategic, vigorous and grounded in America's democratic values. In 1960, John F. Kennedy told America that there was "a new world to be won." Today there is again. My vision is of a world united in peaceful commerce; a world in which nations compete more in economic and less in military terms; a world of dynamic market-generated growth that narrows the gap between rich and poor; a world increasingly engaged in democracy, tolerant of diversity and respectful of human rights.

Current Research 15–6
Jane M. Orient, President, Doctors for Disaster Preparedness, used the technique of mirroring effectively in a speech delivered at a symposium sponsored by the Ethics and Public Policy Center, Washington, D.C., April 23, 1988. Her introduction began: "Nuclear weapons are often thought of as an epidemic or a cancer, so naturally doctors tend to think of themselves as experts on the subject. Various doctors have written prescriptions for the nuclear weapons outbreak. Do we want to take their medicine?" Orient goes on, in the body of her speech, to talk about the lack of a U.S. civil defense plan and defense preparedness in the event of nuclear attack, and concludes in this way: "The policy of not having defenses writes off more than 100 million human beings in the event of an attack. Alternately, it dictates a policy of unconditional surrender as a response to nuclear blackmail, and the consequent destruction of United States of America as a free nation. Ask the doctors who are writing these orders just how sure they are about their prognosis. Then ask yourself whether we need to find another doctor." (*Vital Speeches,* 1/1/89, pp. 186–190.)

This conclusion is short and to the point. The speaker mirrors his introductory reference to "a new world" and emphasizes the relationship between subject and occasion (a meeting of the World Affairs Council).

Relationship Between Speaker and Audience. Concluding with a reference to the relationship between speaker and audience is a powerful reminder to listeners that the speaker is similar to and cares about them. In most instances, this relationship exists alongside the speaker's strong ties to subject and occasion—as it does in the following conclusion to a speech given by Bill Clinton in 1992 at Eastside High School in East St. Louis (the hometown of Olympian Jackie Joyner Kersee):

[W]e ought to realize that the best things we can learn from the Jackie Joyner Kersees of the world is that if you apply that level of effort to other areas of life we can all succeed. Not everybody can be an Olympic gold medalist, but everybody can succeed in life with organized effort in an environment where they can succeed. That's the lesson to learn. I want you to know that after this election's over, I'm not going to hide out in the White House. I'm going to keep coming out here to communities like this, listening to people, answering questions, being accountable, and challenging you to make the most of the opportunities we're going to do our best to create. And if you want that kind of partnership and that kind of challenge, . . . together, you and I, we can change the course of history.

Note the speaker's use of "partnership," "you," and "I" to emphasize his relationship to the audience.

Introductions and conclusions have several important functions. Most important, they amplify the effectiveness of your theme by beginning and ending your speech with clear evidence of how you are related to the subject, occasion, and audience. Just as clear organization improves an audience's grasp of details, a well-constructed introduction and conclusion reveal the personal and timely value of your speech. Of course, you want to ensure that your speech will be delivered as you organized it. Proper outlining technique helps you recall your pattern of ideas and present your materials accurately. (See the Focus on Leadership box.)

■ USING OUTLINES

Teaching Objective 15–4
Review with the students the principles of outlining, including traditional symbol usage and spacing and the phrasing options of substantial quotations, full sentence, and key word outlining.

Proper outlining technique rests on principles and elements that you have already learned. By following the principles of unity, coordination, and subordination, you create main points and subpoints in your speeches. These points are usually arranged in one of five patterns. You already know that an introduction precedes main points and subpoints, and that a conclusion follows. Proper outlining technique applies distinctive symbols, spacing, and phrasing to the basic parts of a speech.

FOCUS ON LEADERSHIP

Women Leaders and Organizational Skills

A sense of organization is valuable to leaders in their profession as well as in their speechmaking. Being organized helps ensure smooth progress and maximum benefits. Strangely enough, although we seldom presume that women are not suited to organizing a speech, some people presume that women are not suited to organizing business or governmental offices. This presumption often restricts career opportunities for women.

The International Women's Forum, founded in 1982, is dedicated to a worldwide exchange of knowledge among women leaders in various professions. A recent survey of members (reported in the *Harvard Business Review*, November–December, 1990, pp. 119–125) includes data on women's leadership styles and related areas of interest. For example, according to the survey, women are more likely than men to motivate others by "transforming their self-interest into the goals of the organization." In addition, women leaders do not covet formal authority. They are more likely to rely on their personal charisma and work record than men—who tend to rely on their official rank and ability to reward or punish.

The results of surveys like the one sponsored by the International Women's Forum suggest that women leaders need to be very well organized in their work. For example, an examination of corporate documents reported in *Fortune* magazine (July 30, 1990, p. 62) prompted the following advice: "Look like a lady; act like a man; work like a dog." Related research by Louis Harris and Associates, Inc., reveals that women managers see barriers to their careers—despite their organizational skills. Of the women surveyed in a Harris poll, 60 percent identified problems in the corporate atmosphere rather than their own training or competency; however, only 25 percent identified problems in the communication between men and women (*Business Week*, August 6, 1990, p. 54).

Communication skills in general—and organizational skills in particular—have proven to be valuable to leaders in business and government. For women leaders especially, these skills can make the difference between a satisfying and an unsatisfying career.

Symbols

Traditional outlines use a combination of numbers and letters to identify the various elements of a speech. Unless you need a special set of symbols, the following roster of numbers and letters is useful—as illustrated by the outline of Julie M. Graef's speech on rap music.

Roman numerals (I, II, etc.) identify main points:

I. Legal issues include violence and obscenity.
II. Ethical issues include the danger of rap lyrics and performers' social responsibility.

Within major elements of a speech, such as point II about ethical issues, speakers use *uppercase letters* (A, B, etc.) to identify subpoints:

A. Many people believe rap lyrics are dangerous to youthful audiences.
B. Many performers ask about their responsibility for influencing youthful audiences.

Supporting material for subpoints is identified with *arabic numerals* (1, 2, etc.):

1. A father, writing in *Time*, echoed many parents' concerns.
2. Susan Baker and Tipper Gore founded the Parents' Music Resource Center to place warning labels on certain albums.

More detailed supporting material, such as that for subpoint II.A.1 in Graef's speech, is identified with *lowercase letters* (a, b, etc.):

a. Gore addressed these warnings in *Time*.
b. Other people point to the continuing rise in murders and rapes by juveniles, and describe the "epidemic proportions" of teenage pregnancy.

Also, note that each symbol is punctuated with a period and that the symbols themselves are needed only when there are two or more subdivisions of an element. Sometimes, a lengthy speech has more subdivisions than can be identified by four symbols. On these occasions, simply add another set of arabic numerals or lowercase letters in parentheses—for example, (1) or (a).

Traditional outlining symbols remind you of each element's relative weight in a speech. Roman numerals and uppercase letters identify major elements that should receive more attention than elements identified by other symbols. Proper spacing is a further visual reminder of weight and function.

Spacing

Traditionally, the more weighty elements of a speech are aligned closer to the left side of an outline than less weighty elements. By this method, the combination of symbols and spacing (often called *indenting*) visually distinguishes main points, subpoints, and items of supporting material. For example, note again the elements of point II in the speech on rap music:

II. Ethical issues include the danger of rap lyrics and performers' social responsibility.
   A. Many people believe rap lyrics are dangerous to youthful audiences.
      1. A father, writing in *Time*, echoed many parents' concerns.
      2. Susan Baker and Tipper Gore founded the Parents' Music Resource Center to place warning labels on certain albums.

a. Gore addressed these warnings in *Time*.

b. Other people point to the continuing rise in murders and rapes by juveniles, and describe the "epidemic proportions" of teenage pregnancy.

3. But do violent or sexual lyrics influence youthful behavior?

a. A study commissioned by the Carnegie Council on Adolescent Development concluded that few children are harmfully affected.

b. Stanford University's Donald F. Roberts says, "Kids take it in stride."

Main point II is located on the left margin of the outline, indicating its relative importance. A less inclusive point, II.A, is indented to the right. Other subordinate points—identified with arabic numerals—are indented even farther. Finally, indented farthest to the right, comes the supporting material that is identified with lowercase letters. This system of spacing, or indentation, adds visual cues to the set of symbols, making it easy to locate the relative weight or the function of any speech element. Furthermore, just as symbols and spacing help you locate elements of your speech, proper phrasing helps your audience recognize these elements.

Phrasing

Several types of phrasing are available; you should learn the preference, if any, of your instructor or your audience. Traditional options in outlining include substantial quotations, full sentences, and key words.

A **substantial quotations outline** subdivides the actual text of a speech into appropriate elements. In effect, the speech is reproduced word for word, but in the several divisions and subdivisions of an outline. For example, in the speech on rap music, points I.A.1–4 would be outlined in substantial quotations if they appeared as follows:

I. Legal issues include violence and obscenity.

A. NWA ran into trouble with the FBI last summer because of its album "Straight Outta Compton."

1. FBI Assistant Director Milt Ahlerich wrote a letter to NWA's distributors, saying that the album "encourages violence against and disrespect for policemen."

2. In particular, the song "F—— the Police" was in question, with lyrics considered to be violent and obscene.

3. *Newsweek*'s March 19, 1990, issue asks if "such appalling expressions of attitude are protected by the First Amendment."

4. According to an American Civil Liberties Union official, they are. He said, "The song does not constitute advocacy of violence as that has been interpreted by the courts."

An outline of substantial quotations clearly shows where all of your words fit into a speech, but this phrasing usually duplicates the material on your notecards. For this reason, either of the other two phrasing techniques is more economical.

A **full sentences outline** clearly reflects the principle of unity. A full sentence expresses a complete thought. Since each point should contain only related ideas, expressing points in full sentences completely reveals whether each point reflects the principle of unity. The outline of the speech on rap music illustrates the use of full sentences to phrase both main points and other elements.

A **key words outline** uses a single word or a brief phrase to express main points, subpoints, and supporting materials. The simplicity of these outlines is their greatest advantage. For example, compare the use of full quotations to outline points I.A.1–4 in the speech on rap music with the following key words phrasing:

    I. Legal issues—violence and obscenity
        A. Violence against police in NWA lyrics
            1. Criticism in FBI Assistant Director's letter
            2. Lyrics in "F—— the Police"
            3. Question in *Newsweek*
            4. Defense by ACLU official

Although simple and easy to follow, key words outlines require you to remember details that may escape you during delivery of your speech. Full sentence phrasing is only slightly more complicated than using key words, yet it includes many of the details found in substantial quotations.

Regardless of which technique you use, consider the benefits of *parallel phrasing* in outlines. When two or more points are expressed in a parallel manner, their coordinate relationship is emphasized. When audiences hear an idea expressed in the same form as a coordinate idea, they are reminded of the speech pattern. For example, to emphasize the equal importance of legal and ethical issues in rap music, these elements can easily be expressed in a parallel way:

    I. Legal issues include violence and obscenity.
   II. Ethical issues include the danger of rap lyrics and performers' social responsibility.

Discussion Question 15–6
How would you outline the pattern of your life?

Parallel phrasing emphasizes the coordinate status of these main points and helps the audience recall that the two ethical issues are just as important as the two legal issues.

Sample Outline

The sample outline that follows is fully developed and illustrates traditional technique in using symbols, spacing, and phrasing for a speech entitled "Little Old Central County Can Become a Big New Industrial Showplace." The speech is designed to inform and persuade members of the Central County Boosters' Club.

Focus of speech

Theme: "We need to remedy flaws in education, transportation, and industrial construction if we want to enlarge Central County's manufacturing base."

Evidence of foresight

Call for a precise response

Introduction

Establishment of speaker's relationship to occasion and audience

A. Our club has recently been discussing the desirability of enlarging our county's manufacturing base.
   1. The countywide 13 percent unemployment rate means that 2,500 of our neighbors need jobs.
   2. At our last meeting, the executive committee placed attracting new industry at the top of our agenda.

Establishment of speaker's relationship to subject

B. As your recently elected president and owner of a small business, I strongly support the club's initiative.

Announcement of desired response

C. Based on my experience and personal concern, I believe that we need to remedy flaws in education, transportation, and industrial construction if we want to enlarge Central County's manufacturing base.

Roman numeral to identify main point

I. New industries won't take a second look at our county unless we make changes in our educational system, transportation network, and industrial park.

Upper-case letter to identify subpoint

A. Our school system suffers from too many dropouts and too few technical programs.

Arabic numeral to identify further subpoint

   1. Modern industries need a well-educated work force.

Lowercase letter to identify supporting material

     a. For example, jobs at Acme Paper Mills require an ability to follow complex instructions and write clear production reports.
     b. Our countywide dropout rate of 27 percent means that less than three out of four of our young people learn complete reading and writing skills.
   2. Modern industries need a technically educated work force.
     a. *Industry Unlimited* magazine recently predicted that eight out of ten industrial workers will soon need a technical understanding of computers and robotics.

Parenthetical numeral to identify very detailed supporting material

       (1) Industrial computing skills are applied to precise measurement and inventory control.
       (2) Industrial robots have replaced many assembly line workers in routine or dangerous jobs.
     b. Our two high schools do not offer sufficient technical coursework.
       (1) The high school catalogs identify merely one course in industrial arts.
       (2) The same catalogs identify no courses in robotics.

Parenthetical numeral to identify very detailed supporting material

B. Our highways and railroad spurs are inadequate.
   1. Any sizable industry needs direct trucking routes to major markets.

> *Supporting material spaced to the right of the point being supported*

         a. Main Street is our only direct link to the interstate highway.

         b. The two lanes of Main Street are only nine feet wide—too narrow to handle heavy truck traffic.

    2. Industries that deal with bulk products need access to rail transportation.

         a. Chris Mack, the county engineer, says that our only existing railroad spur needs repair or replacement.

         b. In view of the rail facilities in prosperous counties, the construction of additional spurs is desirable.

C. Our industrial park lacks enough buildings with suitable size and facilities to house new industries.

> *Full sentence phrasing to reveal unity of the idea*

    1. New industries would require more than the three factory-type buildings in our industrial park.

         a. (Read quotation from *Today's Factory Manager.*)

         b. (Read excerpts from interview with manager of the local plastics company.)

    2. New industries need at least 100,000 square feet of up-to-date manufacturing space.

         a. Recent criticism of our industrial park by representatives of World-Wide Yarn, Inc., emphasizes lack of usable space.

         b. (Read quotation from *Industry Unlimited.*)

> *Parallel phrasing of main points I and II*

II. New industries can't help but take a second look at our county if we apply commonsense solutions to our educational, transportation, and building problems.

> *Main point spaced to the left of subpoints and supporting material*

A. We need to lobby both the school board and our state legislators to support programs that reflect our concerns.

    1. Chris Smith, president of the school board, recently endorsed a method by which students are retained in school by suspending the drivers' licenses of dropouts.

    2. Dana Johnson and Les Clark of the State Assembly have indicated their willingness to sponsor an industrial education bill.

> *Parallel phrasing of subpoints A, B, and C*

B. We need to explore the available state and federal funding programs for new highway and railway construction.

    1. The State of Columbia offers matching grants for county highway construction.

    2. The federal Department of Transportation offers special grants for railroad construction that attracts foreign business ventures.

C. We need to invest local and federal resources in developing the industrial park.

    1. County approval of a bond issue to finance new construction would supply the needed capital quickly and painlessly.

         a. Al Jones, the county auditor, estimates that a bond issue could be approved within six months.

b. Mr. Jones also estimates that the bonds could be paid off by a county tax increase of less than 1 percent.

2. The federal Job Training Partnership Act (JTPA) would make the hiring of local workers attractive to our new industries.

a. The JTPA subsidizes the hiring of displaced workers.

b. Under JTPA, employers are reimbursed 50 percent of the wages paid to formerly displaced workers for a certain period of time.

Conclusion

"Mirroring" of needs stated in the introduction

A. Attracting new industry to Central County is a complex task, but not a mysterious one.

1. Student retention and industrial courses are educational priorities.

2. Highway and railway construction are transportation priorities.

3. Expansion and updating of our industrial park is the other major priority.

Reinforcement of the relationships stated in the introduction

B. I wouldn't have accepted the presidency of our club or planned to keep my business in Central County if I didn't believe that you are as interested in a prosperous future as I am.

You may never speak publicly about your county's need to attract new industry. However, proper outlining technique goes beyond the subject matter of any given speech. This technique helps speakers recall and present their materials in an effective pattern, as well as helping audiences follow and appreciate the speaker's ideas.

Summary

The decisions that public speakers make about their organization flow naturally from prior decisions about the audience, subject, and material. Guiding these decisions are the principles of unity, coordination, and subordination. Unity in speech elements reflects organized thought because unified speeches do not harbor confused or unrelated elements. Coordination also reflects clear organization because elements of equal status are treated accordingly. Moreover, subordination clearly assigns supporting roles to the less weighty elements of a speech. Clear organization alone may not account for success in public speaking, but careful choices of pattern, introduction, conclusion, and outlining technique enhance a speaker's effectiveness.

Human beings are especially good at perceiving certain features of their environment. Effective speakers apply this perceptual ability to their organization of points into patterns. The conventional, or topical, pattern, for instance, reflects the coordinate status of common objects or structures in our perceptual field. These items may be similar or different, comparable or contrasting, but they are commonly perceived as parts or functions of a larger object or structure. The spatial and temporal patterns are related to pragmatic human concerns about place and time. Human attention is readily drawn to movement, and the problem-solving pattern takes advantage of this perceptual tendency by drawing an audience's attention to the movement from problem to solution, from need to satisfaction. Finally, the causal pattern is related to human perception of stimuli and responses: We appreciate knowing how one item causes effects, such as the creation or change of another item.

Just as patterns of organization highlight the links among speech elements, introductions and conclusions should highlight the speaker's relationship to subject, occasion, and audience. The most effective introductions and conclusions make explicit why a speaker chose a particular subject. In the same way, audiences appreciate knowing why a speaker's choice of subject is related to the place and time of the speech. Of course, audiences also like to know how they should relate to the speaker personally, professionally, and so on. These relationships are addressed by using the same types of speech material that support main points. Effective introductions reveal a speaker's theme; effective conclusions restate the theme to make it memorable.

Proper outlining technique arranges all the elements of a speech in a visual display that ensures accurate recall and presentation of your material. Traditional symbols and spacing are vivid reminders of how to address each part of the speech; phrasing options—substantial quotations, full sentences, and key words—enable you to express the character and function of each part of the speech to your audience.

▪ Exercises

1. After rereading the outlines of points for speeches on commodity trading in this chapter, write an introduction for one or more of the speeches that you personally could use. Discuss your composition with other students who have also written introductions to the same speech. Can you detect different "relationships" or different methods of establishing the same "relationships"? Try this same exercise for conclusions.

2. Fill in the blanks with the correct outlining symbols for each point and subpoint.

   _____ Mom and Dad were married in 1968.

   _____ Mom finished her schooling in St. Louis.

   _____ Mom and Dad both grew up in St. Louis.

   _____ Dad had three groomsmen in addition to his best man.

   _____ Dad left St. Louis after high school to attend Texas A & M.

   _____ Mom had three bridesmaids in addition to her maid of honor.

   _____ Dad wants to do a lot of fishing after retirement.

_____ Mom wants to live in a warm climate when she's older.

_____ Mom and Dad plan on moving to the Gulf Coast of Mississippi for their senior years.

3. Correct the phrasing in the following full sentences outline.

    I. Cats and dogs can live together.

        A. Cats' psychology.

        B. Dogs' psychology.

    II. Benefits to owners.

        A. Happy pets cause far less property damage than unhappy pets.

        B. Owners get more love from happy pets.

Answers: 2.   III 'ɐIII 'VIII 'ɐII 'VI 'VII 'I 'ɐI 'II

Amato, P., and Eckroyd, D. (1975). *Organizational patterns and strategies in speech communication*. Skokie, IL: National Textbook Company.

This text is valuable for its special adaptation of general organizing methods to the needs of public speakers. It also contains a clear discussion of the principles underlying effective speech organization.

Katula, R. A., Martin, C. A., and Schwegler, R. A. (1983). *Communication—Writing and speaking*. Boston: Little, Brown.

Especially if you are studying composition as well as public speaking, you may want to read this text for its treatment of organizational patterns and outlining from both perspectives.

Petrie, C. R., Jr. (1963). Informative speaking: A summary and bibliography of related research. *Speech Monographs, 30,* pp. 79–91.

A summary of experimental studies dealing with the effect of organization and skill of speaker on comprehension. You can consult Petrie's article for predictable effects of organized versus disorganized speeches. See also the earlier study by K. C. Beighley, (1952), A summary of experimental studies dealing with the effect of organization and of skill of speaker on comprehension, *Journal of Communication, 2,* (Nov.) pp. 58–65.

Related Readings

Using Oral Language and Skillful Delivery

Chapter objectives

After reading this chapter you should be able to:

1. explain the features of clear, emphatic, vivid, and appropriate language

2. identify four types of transitional language

3. develop an awareness of jargon, dialect, profanity, malapropism, and sexism

4. evaluate the advantages and disadvantages of the four main types of delivery

5. explain the features of volume, rate, pitch, quality, and pronunciation

6. explain the effects of facial and eye control, gesture, and movement

Key terms and concepts

clear language
emphatic language
vivid language
appropriate language
transitional language
repetition
scheme
parallelism
anaphora
epistrophe
antithesis
trope
metaphor
mixed metaphor
simile
alliteration
euphuism
onomatopoeia
jargon
dialect

profanity
malapropism
sexist language
impromptu delivery
extemporaneous delivery
manuscript delivery
memorized delivery
mnemonic device
volume
rate
pitch
quality
pronunciation
facial expressions
gesture
movement

To some extent, public speakers earn respect by choosing their words carefully. Well-spoken people are seen as exceptional, impressive, or trustworthy. Their language reflects an ability or training that is proper to their status. For many people, the skillful use of language also indicates that a leader is thoughtful. For example, the Reverend Jesse Jackson, a leader in the civil rights movement, has drawn many people to the movement by his eloquent use of language in his speeches. While few of us will approach the fame of Jesse Jackson, we can all increase our effectiveness as public speakers by using language skillfully.

Developing a skillful delivery is just as important. In fact an ancient proverb states that the three most important elements of eloquence are first, delivery; second, delivery; and third—as you probably have guessed—delivery! For example, during the Persian Gulf War people of all ages and backgrounds voiced their support or opposition for the war. Exercising leadership by expressing their opinions publicly, these people often drew attention to their messages by skillful delivery.

In this chapter, you will read about four desirable features of oral language as well as the basic skills of delivery. Using oral language effectively means paying attention to the clarity, emphasis, and vividness of your speeches. You can also ensure the appropriateness of your language by avoiding specific errors. There are four main types of delivery—impromptu, extemporaneous, manuscript, and memorized—each having its own special value. Regardless of which delivery type you use, it should reflect appropriate volume, rate, pitch, quality,

Jesse Jackson is renowned worldwide for his eloquent use of language.

and pronunciation. Skillful physical delivery reflects appropriate facial and eye control, gesture and movement.

After reading this chapter, you may be conscious of natural features in your delivery that you did not recognize before. But you should not try to develop new features. Trying to deliver speeches in ways that are unnatural increases tension and misleads your audience. By applying your normal abilities to your speaking, you can establish a sincere rapport with listeners. Your delivery may not be utterly spontaneous—that is, you will have prepared your words and rehearsed your speech beforehand—but it will nonetheless be natural.

USING ORAL LANGUAGE

Oral language has four features that public speakers use to enhance their messages. Each of these features must be understood in relation to a specific audience (see Figure 16.1). **Clear language** aids the audience in capturing the speaker's meaning. Effective speakers gain clarity by using words that are specific and transitional. **Emphatic language** identifies the ideas to which the audience should pay special attention. Emphasis can be achieved by using repetition and stylistic schemes. **Vivid language** makes ideas memorable. Public speakers achieve vividness by using description and stylistic tropes. **Appropriate language** protects the speaker from surprising or offending the audience. Appropriateness can be achieved by avoiding jargon, dialect, and profanity, as well as malapropism and sexism. Again, each of these features must be understood in relation to a specific audience. (See the Mastering Communication Skills box.)

Discussion Question 16–1
How must oral language differ from conversation?

Clarity

Specific Words. Audiences do not readily understand the meaning of general words that refer to abstract ideas. There is nothing intrinsically wrong with words like *truth*, *goodness*, and *beauty*. But you should not expect an audience

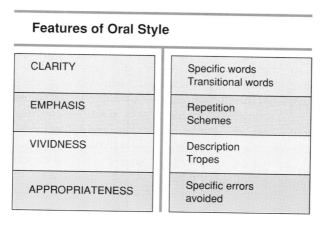

Features of Oral Style

CLARITY	Specific words Transitional words
EMPHASIS	Repetition Schemes
VIVIDNESS	Description Tropes
APPROPRIATENESS	Specific errors avoided

Figure 16.1
Features of Oral Style.

Adapting Language for Oral Delivery

Public speakers use skillful language when they adapt to their oral medium. Several years ago, a popular philosopher of communication argued that "the medium is the message." In this sense, then, your choice of language is a very important part of your speech preparation. You can adapt to the medium of your public speaking by paying attention to the following concerns.

Simple Diction

Teaching Objective 16–1
Emphasize the differences between written and oral language and the need for oral language to be appropriate to the needs of listeners rather than readers.

Diction is a word choice, especially with regard to correctness, clarity, or effectiveness. In writing, the choice of words is limited only by the subject matter. An essay on "The Joys of Soul Food," for example, might contain readily understood words that express the sight, texture, aroma, and taste associated with the subject. However, an essay on "The Differences Between Afro-Centrism and Euro-Centrism" might rely on complex words that express intricate contrasts among the social, cultural, and political roots of blacks and whites. Depending on subject, written language may contain words of many syllables that have complex or unfamiliar meanings.

Current Research 16–1
The prolific writer and teacher Ursula K. Le Guin has more recently in her career been working on developing pieces for speech rather than the written word. Here, she explains why: "It's playing with word as sound, as well as word as meaning. I get tired of word as meaning. People are always saying, 'What does that story mean?' and sometimes I think, does it matter? Listen to me! It's like music. Listen to the story. Hear it! And does it matter what it means if it satisfies you?"
(Le Guin, Ursula K., as quoted in Foss, Karen A., and Foss, Sonja K., *Women Speak, The Eloquence of Women's Lives.* Prospect Heights, IL: Waveland Press, 1991, p. 269.)

Unlike readers, listeners have only one chance to catch the meaning of words. Effective speakers favor words that can be pronounced easily and are familiar to the audience. In most instances, you may assume that your audience is unfamiliar with the meaning of any word that you find hard to pronounce. For example, a writer may properly advocate "enhanced sentences for those guilty of soliciting children for pornographic photographs." Similarly, another writer may advise "a balance between caloric intake and energy expenditure." However, speeches on these two subjects should use easily pronounced, familiar language. Unlike writers, speakers might advocate "more jail time for those guilty of asking children to pose for dirty pictures" and might advise listeners to "eat less and exercise more."

Personal References

Formal writing is often impersonal. In fact, many teachers of composition encourage students to use the third person ("the author") when referring to themselves. Sometimes, an individual is taught to use the editorial plural ("we"). When you read the works of past and present authors who have used this style, notice the overall effect of their language. It is hard to form a mental picture of the person who is "the author," or the individual behind the "we." Warm-hearted or fascinating authors may not appear that way to a reader unless they are masters of their craft.

Even those speeches prepared for formal occasions should have *personal references*—the use of pronouns such as "I" and "you"—in order to establish a relationship with the audience. For example, there is a small

Teaching Objective 16–2
Explain the primary adaptations of oral language through use of simple diction, personal references, flexible grammar, active voice, and short, simple statements.

but significant difference between announcing impersonally, "This speech is about good health," and saying, "I want to talk to you about good health." In the second statement, the words express a personal relationship. Audiences may be temporarily confused by the editorial plural—for example, an individual speaker who announces "our findings" rather than "my conclusion." On the other hand, it is effective to say "we" if you are referring to a belief or action you want to share with listeners.

Personal references are especially appropriate in speeches that have a carefully developed theme. You can emphasize your foresight, skill, and industry by referring personally to yourself. You can also highlight the precise response your listeners should make by addressing them personally.

Flexible Grammar

Correct writing follows the rules of grammar. For instance, a grammatical sentence must have both a subject and verb, the subject and verb must agree in number, and so on. Public speaking is not the same as formal writing; a speech can have *flexible grammar*. For example, sentence fragments—written expressions that lack a subject or verb—are acceptable and often effective in expressing a point. In contrast to formal writing, in which a patriot must say, "I love my country!", a patriotic speaker may state, "My country! I love it!" Formal rules about the use of contractions are also flexible in public speaking. For example, formal grammar requires expressions such as "I will not do it" or "You should not do it." However, a speaker may properly assert, "I won't do it," or "You shouldn't do it."

The grammar required in speeches will vary according to time and place. In analyzing your audience, look for grammatical norms among the other facts and opinions that you need to know for confident speech-making.

Active Voice

Leadership Note 16–3
This famous line from John F. Kennedy's Inaugural Address is a rich example of the power of the active voice in oral address: "Let every nation know, whether it wishes us well or ill, that we shall pay any price, bear any burden, meet any hardship, support any friend, oppose any foe to assure the survival and the success of liberty."

In formal writing, the links between people, objects, or ideas are properly expressed by using the verb *to be* ("He is her spouse." "Their careers are as successful as their marriage."). In writing, a sequence or causal relationship can be expressed in the passive voice ("The evidence was discovered by accident." "He was approached by a stranger.").

In contrast, public speaking has been compared with lively conversation—though adapted to a larger setting and audience. Effective speakers use the active voice that is typical of lively conversation. The *active voice* is the use of verbs other than forms of the verb *to be* to make spoken language lively and dynamic. In speaking, you should express the links between people, objects, or ideas through active verbs ("She married him." "They work at their careers as hard as they work at their marriage."). You should also express a sequence or cause through active verbs

("They discovered the evidence by accident." "A stranger approached him."). In this way, you use the liveliness of conversational style to satisfy the need for dynamism in public speaking.

Of course, it is not always convenient or accurate to speak in the active voice. Observing that "their marriage is successful" may be the most natural way to express a fact or opinion, despite its lack of dynamism. Just as you use full sentences primarily to express main points in your outlines, you should use the active voice to express the most important ideas in your speech (see DeVito 1969).

Relatively Short, Simple Statements

A well-written essay or book contains sentences of varied lengths and types. Length or type of sentence is not troublesome for writers in the sense that they do not run out of breath; in addition, their audiences can always reread a long, complex sentence to find the main idea. Very long sentences, however, are difficult for the average reader; for example, a sentence containing more than twenty-nine words may be "very difficult" to read (Flesch 1949; Gunning 1968).

In contrast, public speaking is measured in terms of "statements"—not sentences. A *statement* is the total number of words spoken in one breath. With flexible grammar, not every statement will be a full sentence. By using relatively short, simple statements, effective speakers ease the burden on listeners to keep track of points. Vague introductory clauses are reduced; the focus of attention remains clear; and verbs quickly follow their subjects. As an illustration, compare the length and type of the following examples of written and oral language:

> *Written Style:*
> Based on careful calculations of the number of executions since the Supreme Court reinstated the death penalty, it is clear that blacks are much more likely than whites to receive death sentences and actually surrender their lives for their crimes.

> *Oral Style:*
> Numbers don't lie. The Supreme Court reinstated the death penalty in 1976. Since then, blacks have died for their crimes much more often than whites.

Discussion Question 16–2
Who are the best story tellers you know among your friends and family? What is it about the way they tell their stories which makes them interesting?

The oral statements can be delivered comfortably in one breath. They do not contain long introductory clauses and they focus attention on the idea that the death penalty has been imposed on black criminals more frequently than on white criminals. Express your speeches in oral statements the same way you maintain simple diction. Translate information from your sources of research into the language of everyday conversation. Speeches do not automatically fail when a long, complex sentence creeps in, but oral language favors relatively short, simple statements.

to understand the ideas behind these words in exactly the same way you do. To achieve clarity, use specific words that clearly identify people or objects or the ideas being addressed. Then both speaker and listeners will have a shared point of reference. For example, consider which of the following statements would be the clearest to an audience:

1. "Racist or sexist policies are bad."
2. "Hiring decisions are unfair when they favor whites over blacks, or males over females."
3. "The boss was unfair when he hired John instead of Mary. She had a higher score on the test."

Statement 1 reflects oral language, but audience members could attach various meanings to the general terms *racism, sexism,* and *policy*. Statement 2 is clearer. It specifically links racism and sexism with favoritism in hiring decisions and defines *bad* as meaning unfair. Using the specific example of John and Mary, statement 3 is the clearest of all because an audience would be reminded of distinctive people and events. Moreover, unfairness would be defined further as the boss's rejection of test results.

Transitional Words.   Speakers also achieve clarity by using **transitional language**—words that identify a shift from one point in a speech to another point. Sometimes called *internal previews, internal summaries,* or *signposts,* transitional words are essential. Even brief speeches often contain more than one idea, and all effective speeches contain a blend of factual and opinion-based supporting materials. Transitional language helps an audience turn its attention at the proper time to your various points or supporting materials. Depending on the type of shift needed, four types of transitional language are useful—words indicating sequence, words indicating coordination, words indicating contrast, and words indicating the beginning of a conclusion (see Figure 16.2).

Transitional language helps you achieve clarity in several ways:

SEQUENCE	First ... Second ... Last Nearby ... Further on ... Most distant Earlier ... Later Now ... Then Before ... After
COORDINATION	And ... In addition ... Also ... Furthermore
CONTRAST	But ... However ... Nevertheless ... On the other hand
CONCLUSION	So ... Therefore ... In conclusion

Figure 16.2
Transitional Language.

Teaching Objective 16–3
Introduce the notion of clarity in language, and develop an appreciation for the use of specific and transitional language to achieve oral clarity.

Current Research 16–2
Joan Davis Ratteray, President, Institute for Independent Education, used transitional language effectively as an organizing tool for her speech on the corporate role in education to The Wisconsin Forum on December 8, 1987: "When we look at what history has taught us, we see three causes of our present dilemma. One is that business has been one of the greatest promoters of government monopoly in education, and this is especially true for African-Americans. The second is that educators were allowed to pick and choose which business management principles they would adopt, yet business did nothing when educators failed to pick the most important one of all. The third is that the corporate sector has been unable to see beyond the cultural myopia of mainstream America. First, let us consider the question of monopoly...." (*Vital Speeches,* 2/1/88, p. 246).

Speeches with a *conventional structure* of points benefit from such transitional words as *first, second,* and so on until the speaker addresses the *last* point. In the absence of these transitions, an audience may not recognize the actual number of main points. Speeches arranged in a *spatial order* benefit from such transitional language as *nearby, further on,* and *most distant.* By using such words as *earlier, now,* and *later,* a speaker clearly identifies the *temporal sequence* of points or illustrations. These transitional words remind listeners that they are hearing a chain of events. The transitional words *before* and *after* clearly identify the sequences of *problem-solution* or *cause-effect.* For example, consider how often you have seen these two words appear in advertisements for weight-loss products or home-improvement companies!

Equally significant points or supporting materials can be clearly identified by using the coordinate transitions *and, in addition, also,* and *furthermore.* These words express a progression among equally weighty ideas. For example, after you quote one expert, you can identify the equally qualified opinion of a second expert by stating, "In addition, (expert 2) has observed. . . ."

When you need to express a contrast between points or supporting materials, you can use such language as *but, however, nevertheless,* or *on the other hand.* These words express a break or clash of opposing points. For example, alternative solutions to a problem may be equally effective, "but" they may differ substantially in time or money. The first solution may be quick; "on the other hand," the second solution may be inexpensive.

Audiences clearly recognize the conclusion of an argument when speakers use such transitional words as *so* and *therefore.* The same language can be used to conclude an entire speech, although the most obvious and popular phrase is *in conclusion.* Any of these transitions express the same thought to listeners: Now is the time to judge the quantity and quality of the speaker's ideas.

Emphasis

Teaching Objective 16–4
Describe the value of emphasis to oral expression, providing definitions and examples of repetition, parallelism (anaphora and epistrophe) and antithesis.

Repetition.   Experienced public speakers have discovered that, if something is worth saying, it is worth saying again. **Repetition** is a simple but powerful method of emphasizing a point or piece of evidence. For example, if the low cost of something should be noted, then this cost factor should be repeated for emphasis: "It will cost merely $150. $150!" If a fact or opinion is especially noteworthy, then you might emphasize that idea by repeating it: "He went to jail again and again rather than compromise his beliefs. Again and again he chose jail over compromise." Simple repetition expresses the importance of an idea and alerts the audience to pay special attention. For example, consider how repetition is used to emphasize the idea of frequency in the following statements:

1. "She never told a lie. Not once did she bend the truth."
2. "I've been injured so many times that I've lost count. It happens so often that I can't remember the first time."

These statements illustrate restatement, or repeating an idea in slightly different language. Whether you use repetition or restatement, consider that public speaking is one medium in which you should ignore the commonplace advice not to repeat yourself.

Schemes. A **scheme** is a figure of speech. Schemes emphasize an idea by expressing it in language that has an unusual structure or pattern. Many schemes are available. Parallelism and antithesis are two of these structural schemes that can be readily adapted to oral language.

For the same reason that outlines should contain parallel phrasing of main points, beginning or ending successive statements with parallel words draws attention to the significance of the statements. **Parallelism** is a stylish version of repetition. When successive statements or sentences begin with the same language, the scheme is called **anaphora**. Ending successive statements or sentences with the same language is called **epistrophe**. For example, the two statements used above to illustrate repetition can also be phrased in parallel schemes:

1. "She never told a lie. She never bent the truth." (anaphora)
2. "I've been injured so many times that I've lost count. I've bumped my head, sprained my wrist, and twisted my ankle so often that I've lost count." (epistrophe)

The scheme of **antithesis** is also a version of parallelism, but it contrasts the importance of successive statements. When you use contrasting transitional language, you often create an antithesis. For example, you might emphasize the difference between alternative solutions to a problem by expressing their respective time and cost in antithetical style: "The first solution is relatively quick but expensive; the second solution takes longer but is cheaper." This antithesis combines parallelism and contrasting transitional words.

Vividness

Description. A speech may be lifeless unless the speaker helps the audience vicariously hear, see, touch, taste, and smell the subject matter. In order to make ideas vivid or lively, effective speakers describe in detail the people, objects, and places mentioned in their speeches. The ancient Greek word for this stylistic device—*ecphrasis*—means that skillful speakers make their ideas "stand out" in the minds of listeners. For example, there is a sizable difference between stating lifelessly, "All adult citizens have the right to vote," and stating vividly, "All adult citizens—the professionals in their tailored suits, the working folks in their well-worn uniforms, and the poor in their hand-me-down jeans—have the right to pull levers or deposit ballots at the polls."

When choosing descriptive language, remember that human beings learn about reality through their five senses. Consider, for example, the vivid alternatives to stating lifelessly, "Max spent the night in jail":

Leadership Note 16–4
Note Martin Luther King's dramatic use of anaphora in this segment of the "I Have A Dream" speech: "We can never be satisfied as long as the Negro is the victim of the unspeakable horrors of police brutality. We can never be satisfied as long as our bodies, heavy with the fatigue of travel, cannot gain lodging in the motels of the highways and the hotels of the cities. We cannot be satisfied as long as the Negro's basic mobility is from a smaller ghetto to a larger one. We can never be satisfied as long as a Negro in Mississippi cannot vote and a Negro in New York believes he has nothing for which to vote. No, no, we are not satisfied...."

"Max spent a night listening to the assorted wails, moans, and screams of fellow inmates." (sense of hearing)

"The drab, gray shades of life in jail made the night feel like an eternity for Max." (sense of sight)

"For Max, a night in jail meant the cold steel and scratchy blanket of his bunk." (sense of touch)

"The spicy beets and bland hamburger scarcely made Max's night in jail a pleasant experience." (sense of taste)

"For Max, jail was a noseful of stale odors." (sense of smell)

As mentioned in Chapter 4, words are merely verbal symbols. By using descriptive words, public speakers express the full context and meaning of their ideas. A master orator is described in the Focus on Leadership box.

FOCUS ON LEADERSHIP

Jesse Jackson—A Master Orator

Speech critics react strongly to the Reverend Jesse Jackson's use of language in speechmaking, either loving it or hating it. The strength of criticisms—pro and con—illustrates that speechmaking is central in the exercise of social and political leadership. Regardless of other issues, however, critics agree that Jesse Jackson is sensitive to the qualities of oral language.

Critics pay attention to Jesse Jackson's use of poetic devices, such as rhyme. For example, in a speech he gave with minor variations many times during his 1988 presidential campaign, Jackson criticized Congress for not stopping the loss of American jobs to foreign competitors. He repeatedly stated: "Right now Congress can merge and then purge workers and then submerge the economy. A process called merging, purging, and submerging." In addition to noting the obvious rhyming words, notice that Jesse Jackson properly used a sentence fragment following the initial full sentence.

Critics also point out Jesse Jackson's use of figures of speech— including alliteration. In his speech to the Democratic National Convention on July 19, 1988, Jackson stated: "This campaign has shown that politics need not be the marketing of politicians packaged by pollsters and pundits." The alliteration of "p" shows an effective technique of oral language that enhances the vividness of a speech.

As mentioned previously, no critics take issue with Jesse Jackson's sensitivity to the qualities of oral language. You should also pay attention to oral language because of the leadership duties you are likely to assume in the near future.

In 1946 Winston Churchill, addressing an audience at Westminster College in Fulton, Missouri, claimed metaphorically that "an iron curtain has descended across the Continent." By this he meant that the then Soviet Union had begun to dominate Eastern Europe under communism.

Teaching Objective 16–5
Introduce the figures of speech known as tropes and, through definitions and examples, seek to enhance appreciation of the power of metaphor, simile, alliteration, euphuism, and onomatopoeia.

Current Research 16–3
Novelist Toni Morrison talks about the oral language of Afro-Americans: "The American English Black people speak has been ridiculed as a sign of stupidity, you know, like lower class, but to me it seems very powerful. It struck my mind even as a child....I was always amazed at the language that people spoke, regardless of their education. The metaphors were fabulous: They used pictures that would make your mind jump...." (Morrison, Toni, as quoted in Lippard, Lucy R., *Mixed Blessings.* New York: Pantheon, 1990, p. 93.)

Tropes. A **trope** is a figure of speech that adds vividness to language by assigning unusual meanings to words. Tropes differ from schemes because tropes give unusual meanings to language rather than changing its structure or pattern. Metaphor, simile, alliteration, and onomatopeia are especially useful tropes.

A **metaphor** is a figure of speech that directly compares two ideas that are not commonly linked together. For example, a speaker may argue that "financial assistance to college students is an investment in our nation's future." This statement is metaphorical because it implicitly compares financial assistance with an investment and college students with our nation's future. The metaphor is effective because it realistically maintains a focus on economic ideas. However, metaphors do not stretch the truth; they do not compare ideas that are not really comparable. Effective public speakers avoid mixed metaphors that contain unrealistic comparisons. A **mixed metaphor** is a flawed figure of speech in which analogy is expressed unrealistically through comparing two ideas that should not be linked together. For example, the statement "We should provide students with an economic lifeboat to save them from the quicksand of debt" undesirably mixes the ideas of rescue on sea and rescue on land.

Metaphors rely on imagery for their effectiveness—that is, they link a commonly held view of an idea with a less commonly held vision. You may develop your skill at using metaphor by considering a few traditional sources of imagery:

Agricultural: "Institutions of higher education yield a rich harvest of future leaders."

Military: "Students fight the battle for grades in their dormitory barracks as well as in the classroom trenches."

Nautical: "No one appreciates more than students how hard it is to steer a straight course through the tempest of moral and ethical questions in our society."

Athletic: "It takes training and stamina to win the race for academic honors."

Economic: "Students pay both a physical and mental price to succeed in college."

A **simile** performs the same stylistic tasks as a metaphor, but makes explicit comparisons of two ideas by using the word *like* or *as*. Traditionally, similes have been evaluated as less "artistic" than metaphors because of their more obvious nature. Then again, similes are more useful than metaphors when your audience analysis shows that listeners may not understand or appreciate the implicit comparison of two ideas. For example, traditional sources of imagery can be used for similes as well as metaphors:

"Colleges are like fertile fields that produce crop after crop of our nation's leaders."

"Students fight for grades as soldiers fight for territory."

"Maintaining good grades is as hard as keeping your head above water in a rising tide."

"To a student, money from home is like a ray of sunshine."

"Like a long-distance runner, a student relies on training and stamina."

"Students endure physical and mental stress as if they were paying for their education with their health."

A simile should pass the same tests as a metaphor to be effective. Consistent, realistic comparisons are necessary—regardless of the source of imagery—for both similes and metaphors to be vivid.

Alliteration is a trope in which the speaker uses a series of words that begin with the same consonant sound. A related trope, **euphuism**, uses a series of words that have the same vowel sound. The effect is highly unusual—almost poetic—and makes that part of a speech come alive for listeners. For example, a speaker might state that "the rich run roughshod over the poor" (alliteration of the consonant *r*) or that "open minds oppose overt racism" (euphuism of the vowel *o*). Alliteration is so obvious, though, that speakers should use it sparingly unless they want to appear extremely conscious of their language.

Another trope that uses sound effects is less obvious and potentially more effective: **Onomatopoeia** is a trope in which the speaker's words make the sounds to which they refer. In a sense, this trope goes beyond description and actually allows the audience to hear an idea! Edgar Allen Poe, a famous nineteenth- century American poet and short story writer, used onomatopoeia in expressing the sound effect of bells as "tintinnabulation." Public speakers, however, do not need to invent fabulous words like *tintinnabulation* in order to express themselves vividly. For example, a student's alarm clock may "clang" or "buzz" early each morning. The campus buses may "roar" and "rumble" as they make their rounds. More delicately, the student sitting behind you may "wheeze" or "gasp" when he or she first looks at the test questions.

Your skill in using onomatopoeia will be limited only by the range of sound effects you can imagine. To increase your range, you might consider the sections of an orchestra as likely sources for a variety of onomatopoeic words.

Woodwinds: "I dreaded the screech of the chalk scraping across the board; it always made the class twitter."

Brass: "The blaring of his lectures was matched only by the whoosh of students leaving class early."

Strings: "As our brains began humming, ideas zinged around the classroom."

Percussion: "The rat-a-tat-tat of the professor's questions continued until the period ended with a ding-dong signal."

The sound effects produced by onomatopoeia are unusual enough that you will not want to use this trope more than once or twice in a single speech.

Appropriateness

Jargon. The technical or professional language of a special field of activity that is often not understood by people outside that specialty is termed **jargon**. Although jargon may add emphasis to some speeches, effective speakers usually avoid it so that they do not confuse or alienate their audiences. For example, you would not want to describe appropriate speaking style as "the rhetorical manifestation of erudition." Instead, you might refer to the "skillful use of words." Otherwise, students might not understand your true meaning—or worse, they might be offended by your use of heavily academic jargon. In the courtroom, lawyers object to testimony that is "irrelevant, immaterial, and prejudicial"; but in speeches to nonlawyers, it would be more skillful to explain the bad effects of testimony that "has nothing to do with the case at hand."

Dialect. Language used in a restricted area of the country is termed **dialect**. Except when illustrating how the same idea is expressed differently in various parts of the country, speakers should use language that is proper to the audience in attendance. Most audiences will eventually decode your meaning if you use dialect. However, you will have at least temporarily confused some listeners—if not irritated them. For example, when explaining the differences between natural and artificial sweeteners, a speaker should decide whether the audience refers to carbonated beverages as "soda" or "pop." When illustrating

Teaching Objective 16–6
Raise the issue of appropriateness in language use for various settings and audiences and offer examples of the use and potential impact of jargon, dialect, profanity, vulgarity, malapropism, and sexist language.

Cross-reference 16–1
See the discussion in Chapter 4 on the use of language to define membership.

Discussion Question 16–3
What are some of the elements of the regional dialect which is native to you? Could we say that college or university campuses have their own dialects as well?

the ease of using recyclable products, a speaker should decide whether the audience carries groceries home in a "bag" or a "sack."

Profanity.   Irreverent, coarse language is termed **profanity**. Profanity cannot be defined without reference to those ideas and objects that a specific audience respects or worships. Although profane language can be very emphatic and vivid, the speaker always runs the risk of being thought irreverent or coarse by members of the audience. A speaker who uses "vulgar" language runs the same risks: Vulgar language is the explicit reference to ideas and objects that an audience considers unsightly or foul. You have heard more (and possibly better) examples of profanity and vulgarity than could be listed here. But consider the proper use of this language. For example, did Malcolm X confuse or insult his audience when he used the phrase "catch hell"? Would you obscure your meaning or offend a local audience by using the word "crap"? In each instance, appropriate style must be defined in reference to audience expectations and feelings.

Malapropism.   In his eighteenth-century comedy *The Rivals*, the Irish playwright Richard Sheridan introduced a character named Mrs. Malaprop. Her humorous misuse of words—especially her substitution of an inappropriate word for one that sounds alike—has been called **malapropism** ever since. Mrs. Malaprop was an object of ridicule, and public speakers avoid her linguistic fault if they do not want to suffer the same fate. For example, a sportscaster might unwittingly amuse listeners instead of informing them by stating that great athletes have a "pension" for making the right moves. *Penchant* is the appropriate word. An otherwise respectable lawyer might inadvertently amuse the jury by denying that a defendant was guilty of income tax "invasion." *Evasion* is the appropriate word.

Inappropriate use of jargon, dialect, or profanity causes audiences to question speakers' thoughtfulness but not their seriousness. Falling into a malapropism makes a speaker look foolish. The best safeguard against malapropism is thorough preparation. Successful public speakers approach their tasks with confidence, including the confidence that speech rehearsals did not reveal any words humorously inappropriate to the subject matter.

Cross-reference 16–2
The communication problems posed by sexist and racist language are discussed more fully in Chapter 4.

Sexism.   Depending on the subject matter, the exclusive use of either masculine or feminine pronouns or titles may indicate that the speaker is excluding either female or male listeners. For example, a speech on careers in law enforcement will not sound encouraging to female listeners if the speaker exclusively refers to the police officer as "he." Similarly, a career in day care will not sound promising to male listeners if the speaker exclusively refers to the day care provider as "she." A related problem occurs when law officers are exclusively called "policemen" and day-care personnel are called "nannies." In addition, references to "female police" and "male nannies" implicitly express the view that it is unusual or even improper for a woman to enforce the law or for a man to care for a child.

Sexist language expresses a lower status for one gender. Constant use of words that have diminutive suffixes when referring to females may indicate that the speaker accepts the inferior status expressed in the language. For example, an informative speech on great authors might inaccurately express higher status for a "poet" than for a "poetess" by adding the diminutive suffix *ess* to poet. A leading critic of our society may be a "prophet" of a better future or a "prophetess." But does the choice of words imply a lower status for one of the critics? Unless you actually intend to express different statuses for males and females, choose language that is appropriate to equal status.

Complete the Self-Assessment Exercise.

SELF-ASSESSMENT   **Evaluating Appropriate Language**

One way to evaluate the use of appropriate language is to compare historical speechmaking with the way you might express the same theme today. Frederick Douglass (c. 1817–1895) delivered a speech that provides material for this type of comparison. Douglass spoke at Rochester, New York, on July 5, 1852. In the following excerpts from his speech, consider the match between audience and language:

> What, to the American slave, is your Fourth of July? I answer; a day that reveals to him, more than all other days in the year, the gross injustice and cruelty to which he is the constant victim. To him, your celebration is a sham; your boasted liberty, an unholy license; your national greatness, swelling vanity; your sounds of rejoicing are empty and heartless; your denunciation of tyrants, brass fronted impudence; your shouts of liberty and equality, hollow mockery; your prayers and hymns, your sermons and thanksgivings, with all your religious parade and solemnity, are, to Him, mere bombast, fraud, deception, impiety, and hypocrisy—a thin veil to cover up crimes which would disgrace a nation of savages. There is not a nation on the earth guilty of practices more shocking and bloody than are the people of the United States, at this very hour.
>
> Go where you may, search where you will, roam through all the monarchies and despotisms of the Old World, travel through South America, search out every abuse, and when you have found the last, lay your facts by the side of the everyday practices of this nation, and you will say with me, that, for revolting barbarity and shameless hypocrisy, America reigns without a rival.
>
> (From *Negro Orators and their Orations* by Carter G. Woodson [Russell & Russell, an imprint of Macmillan Publishing Company, New York, 1969]. Used with permission.)

This speech illustrates the features of clarity, emphasis, and vividness. But would the speaker's language still be appropriate today? With specific diction and transitional language, Frederick Douglass mentioned particular behaviors during the Fourth of July celebration. The speech reflects emphasis in its use of repetition and schemes; Douglass used antithesis frequently in his initial criticisms, and then restated his commands to search widely for examples of abuse. The speech also illustrate, vivid style:

Douglass used detailed descriptions and various metaphors, including an image of America's reigning without a rival.

But does Douglass's language remain appropriate? He avoided jargon and dialect, although he used language, such as "brass fronted impudence" and "bombast," that would not have clear meanings for audiences in the 1990s. He avoided profane or vulgar language when he strongly criticized his audience's religious and political practices—a skillful technique now, as well as in 1852. Finally, Douglass's obvious command of language protected his speech against malapropism, but many current audiences would not appreciate his exclusive use of masculine pronouns for slaves.

▣ USING SKILLFUL DELIVERY

Leadership Note 16–6
"Be a craftsman in speech that thou mayest be strong, for the strength of one is the tongue, and speech is mightier than all fighting." (Maxim of Ptahhotep, c. 3400 B.C., in *Bartlett's Familiar Quotations*, Boston: Little, Brown, 1968, p. 3.)

There four main types of oral delivery (see Table 16.1). Choosing the most appropriate type depends on the audience and speech purpose. Impromptu speeches are best used when the speaker must sound and look spontaneous—almost to the exclusion of other features. Extemporaneous speeches are adaptable to a wide variety of audiences and purposes. Manuscript speeches allow exact wording and careful recitation of a message. Memorized speeches reflect careful preparation but otherwise lack adaptability.

Impromptu Delivery

Discussion Question 16–4
Who is the most effective speaker you have ever seen, in person or on film? What was it about her or his presentation that made her or him so effective?

When the purpose or organization of a speech cannot be determined in advance, or when unanticipated events occur, public speakers use **impromptu delivery**. Many campaign speeches take this form, because the candidate must wait to determine how much time is available or who has assembled to hear the speech. These candidates have preselected subject matter and purpose (gaining votes in the upcoming election!) but must adapt their speech length and structure to variable conditions. Public speaking contests often include a category for impromptu speaking because it tests a person's general knowledge. The contestants know beforehand the length and purpose of their speeches, but not the subject matter.

Teaching Objective 16–7
Describe the four basic types of delivery and the advantages and disadvantages of each, stressing the importance of preparation to each type.

Table 16.1
Four Types of Delivery

Type	Advantage	Disadvantage
Impromptu	Spontaneity	Restricted preparation
Extemporaneous	High adaptability	Variable wording
Manuscript	Precise wording	Restricted physical delivery
Memorized	Extensive preparation	Low adaptability

Impromptu delivery should not be confused with lack of preparation. Speakers must command a wife range of speech materials and must develop an ability to organize their ideas quickly. In full view of the audience, an impromptu speaker spontaneously decides which speech material is relevant and then arranges this material in a clear pattern. Thus, impromptu delivery is not suitable for beginning speakers or for persons who suffer from communication apprehension. It adds spontaneity to public speaking, but it taxes the speaker's adaptability.

Extemporaneous Delivery

Extemporaneous delivery combines extensive planning with adaptability to the audience and occasion. This type of delivery depends on a carefully prepared outline that does not necessarily bind the speaker to particular wording. Moreover, extemporaneous delivery is valuable whether or not the audience

Politicians are often in situations that call for impromptu delivery.

Current Research 16–4
Craig R. Smith, former speechwriter for President Ford, Vice President Bush and Chrysler CEO Lee Iacocca, described Iacocca's use of manuscript delivery in this way: "His secret for success is that he rehearses in front of a mirror. He used to rehearse them in front of me before he gave them. The real advantage in Lee's case was that I have seen him deliver a manuscript—he always spoke from manuscripts—51 pages long, big type…flipping through the thing, delivering the whole speech, getting a standing ovation, people coming up to him afterward and saying, 'I don't know how you memorized that.' He had just stood in front of them the whole time flipping pages. He was that good at delivering a speech from a manuscript." (As quoted in Duffy, Bernard K., and Winchell, Mark Royden. 'Speak the speech, I pray you.' The practice and perils of literary and oratorical ghostwriting. *Southern Communication Journal*, *55*, 1, 1989, p. 107.)

responds as expected to a speech. For example, if all listeners nod in agreement and no one raises an objection, then a speaker may continue delivering proposals for changes in policy or procedure as outlined. If some listeners frown or look puzzled, and if one or two people interrupt with troubling questions, then the speaker may backtrack on the outline of proposals or restate a troublesome idea in different terms.

In contrast to impromptu delivery, the purpose and structure of extemporaneous speeches do not change. Rather than trusting memory, the extemporaneous speaker assembles notecards filled with relevant facts and figures. However, the speaker must remain flexible in wording his or her ideas. In short, the speaker relies more on prior analysis of the audience and occasion than on spontaneity, but still remains adaptable. Problems occur only when adaptability is confused with lack of preparation!

The suggestions in the preceding three chapters are most relevant to developing skills in extemporaneous delivery. Analysis of the audience and setting is crucial. Based on this prior analysis, you select a relevant purpose and theme; you discover useful speech material; you arrange ideas in an appropriate pattern; and you practice expressing these ideas in oral language.

Manuscript Delivery

Manuscript delivery permits speakers to express their ideas in exactly the words they had planned. A manuscript speaker reads aloud from the full text of a speech. This type of delivery is appropriate when minor mistakes in wording may be disastrous. For example, because their audiences will pay close attention to every word and nuance, highly renowned or professional lecturers often

To be effective, speeches prepared for manuscript delivery should be written in oral style.

choose manuscript delivery. World leaders often deliver their remarks from manuscripts on formal occasions or in times of crisis. Some teachers routinely deliver classroom lectures from manuscripts, but students' bored responses to at least some of these lectures illustrate that manuscript delivery should be reserved for special occasions.

Manuscript delivery is surprisingly difficult. Although many speakers think that relying on a speech text solves problems with organization or wording, manuscript delivery often becomes inflexible and uninteresting for audiences. Consider, for example, the plight of clergy or even sales representatives who deliver a prepared text without adapting to last-minute changes in the setting or unpredictable responses from the audience. Congregations who are being drenched by a new leak in the church roof, or customers who have just filed bankruptcy petitions, do not favor prepared texts! In addition, manuscript speeches often fail when speakers do not appreciate the difference between written and oral style. Speakers should also recognize the restraints imposed on physical activity while delivering a manuscript speech: It is awkward to emphasize a point by raising a clenched fist when the manuscript must be held in both hands!

Skillful manuscript delivery requires careful preparation of the text. The lettering is large for easy reading. Margins are wide. Double or triple spacing is used. After all, reliance on exact wording makes it crucial for speakers not to lose their places. In addition, manuscripts contain written cues in the margins or between the lines indicating particularly important language. Otherwise, the text might be read in a manner that invites daydreaming by the audience. Careful preparation of the text also requires repeated practice sessions in order to ensure familiarity with the words. This familiarity makes it possible to look up from the text during delivery and gauge the audience's response. Figure 16.3 illustrates simple but effective methods for adding cues to a manuscript.

Preparation of the physical setting is also important. Arrange for the manuscript to rest securely on a lectern (if one is to be used). Interrupting your speech to pick up the scattered pages of a fallen manuscript is the last thing you want to happen. Moreover, the height of the lectern, or the height at which you hold the manuscript, should prevent the text from becoming a physical barrier between you and your audience. Notice, for example, how many formal speeches now enlist the aid of teleprompters so that manuscripts are projected onto a clear plastic screen in front of the speaker.

Cross-reference 16–3
Noise as a barrier to listening was examined in Chapter 3. Also, the importance of setting and space to communication was discussed in Chapter 5.

Memorized Delivery

Memorized delivery is rare in speeches of more than a few minutes in length; public speakers do not usually entrust their messages to memory. A memorized speech requires composition of a manuscript, but not using that text in delivery. Manuscript delivery, of course, runs the risk of being vocally dull and physically restrained. Memorized delivery avoids these problems if sufficient time is spent in preparation. In fact, this extensive amount of preparation is the greatest virtue of memorized speeches. The speaker is intimately familiar with every word of the speech and the organization of every point.

What can we do? $_{(Pause)}^{\uparrow}$ Well, we could tell ourselves that substance abuse doesn't happen to nice people like us, our families and friends. But that would be a lie. $\underset{(slowly)}{}$ Instead, it's time we faced up to the scope of this national epidemic and the causes that are found in our own neighborhoods. In addition, we should support neighborhood agencies that provide evaluation and counseling—agencies that tell substance abusers among our families and friends where they can get immediate therapy. No, you don't have to build a treatment center in your own backyard. But you need to vote for local and national candidates who will back public subsidies for centrally located, properly staffed centers that serve everyone who needs treatment.
(Emphasize)

Figure 16.3
Page of Manuscript
Speech with Added Cues.

Attention to exact wording is the greatest failing of memorized delivery. Lacking the flexibility to restate points or adjust language to audience responses, the speaker must ignore any changes in setting or audience that occur after preparation has been completed. In addition to poor adaptability, memorized speeches often end prematurely when speakers forget the exact sequence of words. This often embarrassing lapse of memory is particularly unfortunate because worthwhile speeches are valuable more for their ideas than for their words.

Memorization demands repeated silent reading or oral recitation of a speech's complete text. Oral recitation is preferable because it allows you to gauge whether your organization and language will sound right as well as look appropriate. In addition, lengthy texts are usually memorized in properly ordered segments rather than as a whole; ultimately, each segment is delivered as a minispeech.

Traditional methods called mnemonic devices (*mnemonic* is derived from the ancient Greek word for memory) are available to aid your recall of entire or segmented texts. A **mnemonic device** is a striking formula or code that triggers the memory by helping you recall whatever the formula or code is meant to signify. One mnemonic device is the *acronym,* a word formed from the initial letters of a phrase or title. For instance, KISS is an acronym for "Keep it simple, Stupid" (a phrase meant to remind writers and speakers that simplicity of expression is desirable).

Using Vocal Delivery

The human voice was undoubtedly the first musical instrument. Speech delivery is comparable to musical performance in its instrumental aspects, with the human voice supplying the most basic and natural instruments of speechmaking. Using skillful delivery, therefore, involves appropriate use of the voice. Volume, rate, pitch, quality, and pronunciation should be adjusted to suit your speech purpose (see Figure 16.4). These vocal adjustments can be made naturally and enhance your expression of ideas.

Volume.   No message can inform or persuade anyone if it cannot be heard. The size of the room and of the audience dictate the basic level of **volume,** or loudness, in delivery. Thoughtful speech preparation includes measuring the appropriate volume with a willing listener in advance of the speech—but remember that empty rooms carry sound more readily than crowded rooms. When advance preparation is not possible, look for signs of inadequate volume during the speech—signs such as listeners leaning forward, looking puzzled, or simply ignoring the speech. Ironically, these listeners may begin squinting their eyes if they are not able to hear you—as if they could compensate for impaired hearing with sharper eyesight.

To remedy a lack of sufficient natural volume, either arrange the setting to bring listeners within hearing range or use electronic amplifiers. When possible, arrange audience seating across the width of a room rather than down its length. A fan-shaped seating arrangement is often desirable. If necessary, ask members of the audience to seat themselves front and center when they do not fill the room. You may achieve the same effect without relying on the audience's cooperation by securing a personal microphone and amplifier, or by using a public address system.

The location of a speech also dictates appropriate volume. Speakers often compete for the audience's attention with background sounds and noisy dis-

Cross-reference 16–4
All of the elements of vocal and physical delivery are discussed in detail in Chapter 5 as forms of nonverbal communication, specifically paralanguage (vocal nonverbals) and kinesics (body movement).

Teaching Objective 16–8
Stress the importance of vocal delivery to effective speaking, making sure students understand the elements and impact of volume, rate, pitch, quality, and pronunciation.

Current Research 16–5
Hickson and Stacks report that, in two related pieces of research, Cheris Kramerae determined perceived differences between male and female voices, and perceptions by both men and women of how they compare to idealized vocal qualities. Traits characteristic of male speakers included deep, demanding voices, loud and dominating speech, and forceful and aggressive speech. Female characteristics included clear enunciation, high pitch, gentle and fast speech, and wide range in rate and pitch. In a related study, Kramerae is reported to have found that men perceived themselves as differing from an ideal voice type much less significantly than women perceived themselves in relation to the ideal. (Hickson, Mark L., and Stacks, Don W., *Nonverbal Communication.* Dubuque: William C. Brown, 1989, pp. 156–157.)

Vocal Features of Delivery

VOLUME	Adequacy / Emphasis
RATE	Tempo / Pause
PITCH	Meaning / Expressiveness
QUALITY	Distinctiveness / Attractiveness
PRONUNCIATION	Correctness

Figure 16.4
Vocal Features of Delivery.

tractions. Ventilation machinery, lights, and other equipment may produce humming or whining sounds. Your speech may also be invaded by noise from outside the room—street traffic, lawn mowers, and so on. When background or outside noises cannot be removed, you face a problem with your volume. To solve this problem, do not speak with unnatural loudness: You will not deliver your ideas effectively, and your audience may feel assaulted by the combination of sounds.

Effective speakers develop emphatic volume by eliminating fade-out at the ends of oral statements and by planning variations in loudness. Listeners may get the impression that an idea lacks merit if you do not maintain adequate volume through a full statement of the idea. In other words, fading volume signals a drop in significance. The use of relatively short sentences eliminates much of this problem. To add significance, use various levels of volume. Whether you increase or decrease loudness, you alert listeners to a significant change in your speech. For example, recite the phrase "It's over" three times while using the same volume, then higher volume, and finally lower volume for "over." For most audiences, the lower or higher volume of "over" will mean that a particularly important end has been reached. Higher or lower volume in expressing a repetition or restatement will enhance the emphatic qualities of these stylistic devices. Try saying "It's over—it's over" with higher or lower volume on the second phrase to observe the emphatic quality of changes in volume.

Everyone has a natural or comfortable range of volume that can be used consciously to improve delivery. In most instances, adjustments in seating arrangement or electronic amplification will eliminate the need for unnatural loudness. Avoiding fade-outs and planning changes in volume will add emphasis.

Rate.   Similar to musical rhythm, the pace at which a speech is delivered carries the underlying mood of a message. Your natural **rate** of conversation is the basic tempo at which you should deliver speeches. Unfortunately, people often react to the stress of public speaking by delivering their speech at an unnaturally fast rate.

Depending on your audience or speech purpose, you should plan to change the basic rate of delivery. For example, complex ideas need a relatively slow rate of delivery so that listeners have enough time to mull over the material. A computer technician may quickly recite the sixteen steps for repairing a disk drive to another technician; but if you were to plan a "how to" speech on this same subject, you should assume that your listeners will need a slower-paced explanation. A fast-paced delivery enhances your expression of angry or excited feelings. A slower pace expresses sadness or solemnity. Recall, for example, the rates at which speeches or sermons were delivered when you have attended weddings and funerals. Any change in your natural rate—faster or slower—draws attention to the point being discussed. A rate of 125 to 150 words per minute is usually a desirable tempo (see Petrie 1963). Without changing your basic tempo, you can emphasize a main point or a particularly important example by temporarily speaking faster or slower. The most practical ways of achieving an effective rate are to remind yourself clearly in your notes, outline, or text, and to rehearse a varied pace.

Discussion Question 16–5
What are your emotional and physiological responses when someone shouts at you, or speaks so loudly given the space and situation you're in that it feels like shouting? How about, at the other end of the spectrum, when you have to strain to hear?

Cross-reference 16–5
When arranging space for an oral presentation, keep in mind the nonverbal impact of the proxemic arrangements as discussed in Chapter 5. Also, as discussed in Chapter 3, take steps to eliminate as much of the noise as possible to enhance the listening environment.

Current Research 16–6
Hickson and Stacks also report research findings which suggest that both men and women are perceived as being more competent when they speak at faster rates, men also being perceived as more socially attractive. This perception of competence was higher in normal communication settings than in interviews. (Hickson, Mark L., and Stacks, Don W., *Nonverbal Communication.* Dubuque: William C. Brown, 1989, p. 164.)

Developing a rate appropriate to your subject matter also requires attention to pauses. These breaks in delivery are especially useful for defining sections of a speech and for cuing the audience to consider a particular idea. Just as certain transitional words alert listeners to the beginning of a point, pausing briefly after a point confirms the end of that particular idea. Audiences cannot see the spaces between points on a speaker's outline, but audiences can hear these divisions in the form of a one-second pause. In addition, these pauses allow you to consult your outline before launching into the next point.

Longer pauses are appropriate after you ask a rhetorical question or request your listeners to consider seriously a proposal; stopping your delivery is only natural at such times if you are sincere about your question or request. For example, when you pose a question like "How many times have you personally encountered the problem I'm talking about, but simply wished for it to go away?" a two-second pause before you continue will allow your audience to search their memory and recall the experience. Two seconds seem very brief except when you are delivering a speech, so you will need to practice pausing before it becomes a comfortable part of your delivery.

Despite the simple nature of pauses, some public speakers are uncomfortable with even the briefest moments of silence. During these uncomfortable times, speakers insert "filler"—meaningless sounds, such as "um" or "uh," or quasi-words, such as "you know" or "yeah"—all of which distract audiences. Although silence is preferable, a firm intention to avoid "filler" usually does no good unless you pay close attention to pauses in speech rehearsals. If you habitually use "filler" in your normal conversation, then you might need to tolerate an unnatural speech delivery until you consciously develop a new habit of silent pauses.

Along with volume, rate is a simple vocal feature to adjust. Practice with varying rates to determine your natural range, or comfort zone, and then plan clear or emphatic changes and pauses to match the ideas in your speeches. Other vocal features are examined below, but skillful adjustments in rate and volume are often sufficient to enhance your oral style.

Pitch.   Strong but flexible chords or folds in the larynx vibrate at different rates to produce high or low **pitch** in the human voice. Each individual has a range of pitch that is natural to his or her vocal chords (males often have a lower range than females). Moreover, each person has an optimum pitch (the level at which he or she can speak clearly and forcefully for long periods of time). You should recognize your optimum pitch and deliver the appropriate portions of your speech at slightly varying ranges. This type of *vocal variety* protects you against a monotone delivery, creates interest, and provides emphasis. At the same time you stay within your natural range.

Because the natural range of pitch varies widely from speaker to speaker—and because adjusting pitch or range is a difficult task—you may wish to develop a relatively simple set of related skills. For example, read aloud the following statements with high and low adjustments of pitch on the italicized words:

Is *this* the bozo who wants me to move my car?

Is this the bozo who wants *me* to move my car?

Is this the bozo who wants me to move my *car?*

Current Research 16–7
Some research has found that women tend to use more vocal fillers than men; there is also research indicating that men tend to use fillers as a way of holding onto available air space between expressions. (Pearson, Turner, and Todd-Mancillas. *Gender and Communication.* Dubuque: William C. Brown, 1991, p. 113.)

By adjusting pitch in either direction on the italicized words, you cause the three statements to have different meanings. A high-pitched recitation of *"this"* would typically indicate that this person is foolish and generally not deserving of respect; a low-pitched recitation of *"me"* would indicate comparatively greater seriousness and importance. As to the *"car,"* any change from optimum pitch emphasizes the object of attention. This illustration draws attention to people and objects, but the same effect can be achieved with actions.

Discussion Question 16–6
All of us can describe certain kinds of voices which we find it difficult to listen to—what are the ones that get to you? Why? What is it about them that bothers you?

Some adjustments in pitch are necessary in order to convey special forms of expression. For example, audiences may not recognize that a question is being posed unless it ends on a higher pitch than simple declarations. Very solemn declarations are expected to be delivered at a lower pitch than other statements. You make these types of adjustment naturally in everyday conversation, but the strain of public speaking sometimes restricts your natural range—causing a monotone, or single-pitch delivery. As with "filler," only repeated practice can rid you of monotonous delivery. However, it may be helpful to remember that audiences expect a high-pitched delivery at times when you naturally speak at a rapid rate, and low-pitched delivery when you naturally speak at a slow rate. For example, try reciting aloud the statement "We won!" at an unnaturally slow rate. The pitch will also be unnaturally low. As another exercise, try reciting aloud the statement "She died" at a solemnly slow rate. Note that your pitch also becomes properly low. Adjusting your rate—an easier task than changing pitch—may satisfy audience expectations about your delivery.

Pitch is usually more difficult to adjust than other vocal features, but relatively simple changes in anyone's natural range can enhance meaning and create emphasis. Again, the key word is *natural*. This same basic value is crucial to vocal quality.

Quality.   Audiences judge the **quality** of a speaker's voice on the basis of frequently intangible, always subjective standards. As the old maxim states, there is no accounting for taste. Some listeners place a premium on crisply articulated words: Each word is constructed of letters, and each letter must be sounded distinctly if the language is to be treated with respect. Other listeners focus on more generally attractive qualities and judge nasality, breathiness, and hoarseness. Because concerns about distinctiveness and attractiveness vary from audience to audience, successful public speakers avoid features that generally distract any audience.

Distinctive delivery avoids the slurred or incomplete expression of words. These types of poor articulation often confuse listeners as well as distract them. For example, an audience of concerned consumers might react with dismay to a speaker who states, "Yawonwanna buyese lessya doncare boutsafety," instead of "You won't want to buy these unless you don't care about safety."

Distinctive articulation also expresses differing moods and degrees of formality. For instance, saying "Luv ya" instead of "I love you" may express the same message in two significantly different ways: The first is casual and cute; the second is formal and impressive. Your audience analysis is never complete, therefore, until you have become sensitive to the level of articulation preferred or expected by your listeners. In most cases, you will find that audiences expect only a reasonably clear articulation—certainly not the extreme precision of sounding the *t* in "often" or the *b* in "plumber."

Attractive delivery avoids extremes of nasality and breathiness. An extremely nasal tone draws attention to your voice and away from your ideas. To appreciate the vocal effect of extreme nasality, record your voice while pinching your nostrils.

Breathy voices have commonly been used by actors and singers (recall Marilyn Monroe and her 1990s counterpart, Madonna) to enhance audience perceptions of their sensuality. This type of delivery will predictably draw the audience's attention to your voice and not your message. Public speakers avoid breathiness by not running up to the place where they are delivering their address. Catch your breath before beginning your speech.

Try as you might, you may never develop a vocal quality that will win prizes. No matter. Effective speakers realize that other features of vocal delivery enhance their expression of ideas. Pronunciation is certainly one of these features.

Pronunciation. Some listeners are offended when a speaker mispronounces words because incorrect **pronunciation** suggests inadequate preparation. Correct delivery avoids the mispronunciation of names and uncommon words, which could evoke negative feelings about the speaker (see Kibler and Barker 1968, 1972). The simple diction that is characteristic of oral style reduces the chances of incorrect pronunciation, but the problem never goes away completely. For example, when strangers try to pronounce the names of people to whom they have just been introduced, the results are sometimes comical. Distractions also occur during religious services, when both clergy and laypeople mispronounce the unusual names and places mentioned in sacred texts.

In addition to standards of skillful delivery, common courtesy demands that speakers correctly pronounce the names of unfamiliar people, places, and objects. Should "Ehninger" be pronounced with a soft or hard *g*? What is the correct way to pronounce "Zimbabwe"? What about "cyclotron"? In essence, you should prepare each speech as if you were addressing exactly those people who will be distracted by incorrect pronunciation.

Sometimes correct pronunciation may simply be a matter of accent—the stress placed on a particular syllable within a name or word. For example, is the city properly called "*De*troit" or "De*troit*"? When in doubt, consult a pronouncing dictionary of the English language, a foreign-language dictionary, an encyclopedia, or related works in the reference section of your library.

Vocal quality is difficult to adjust. For the long run, though, it may be worthwhile to begin developing a distinctive and attractive voice. In the short run, you may find that adjustments in volume, rate, and pitch are more practical. Your pronunciation also has practical consequences. Equally valuable are aspects of your physical delivery.

Discussion Question 16–7
Have you ever had someone mispronounce your name? How did you feel? How did you respond?

Using Physical Delivery

Teaching Objective 16–9
Examine the necessity and
impact of physical delivery
in effective speaking, particularly in the areas of
facial expressions and eye
contact, gestures, and
movement.

In Chapter 5 you learned about the central role of nonverbal behaviors in human communication. The elements of physical delivery—facial and eye control, gesture, and movement—are all nonverbal behaviors (see Figure 16.5). The use or misuse of these nonverbal cues can win over or alienate an audience.

Facial and Eye Control.   Audiences traditionally rely on facial expressions and eye contact to judge a speaker's sincerity. The frozen, insincere smile on a salesclerk's face—an expression that quickly disappears if you mention how expensive the merchandise seems—does not encourage you to shop. In myth and folklore, the eyes have often been called "windows to the soul." Lacking other evidence, people often rely on what they see to draw conclusions about a speaker's message.

Three **facial expressions** are fundamental to enhancing a message. First, you should plan to smile—but not force an exaggerated grin—when your subject matter is pleasant, cheerful, or positive in some other way. Some speakers are caught up in their tasks and simply forget to smile when they celebrate personal or public achievements, when they discuss the benefits of a proposed course of action, or when they recall the happy times of a bygone era. As always, use only your natural facial resources. This portion of your physical delivery should reflect your customary smile, whether it is toothy, closed-mouth, or somewhere in between. Second, you should frown naturally—but not force an awful glare—when your subject matter is sad, threatening, or negative in some way. This type of physical delivery is consistent with speeches about the problems caused by war, poverty, crime, and related subjects. Third, remember to raise your eyebrows and naturally adjust your other features to look puzzled when you ask a question. Combined with appropriate adjustments in vocal delivery, this type of facial expression amplifies your search for answers.

Public speakers have been cautioned for centuries to maintain eye contact with listeners—otherwise the audience might become suspicious of the speaker's sincerity. Skillful eye contact, though, does not require fully memorized

Physical Features of Delivery

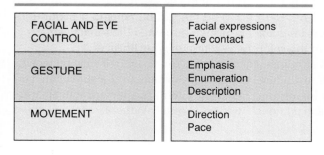

Figure 16.5
Physical Features of
Delivery.

speeches. Extemporaneous speaking—as well as impromptu and manuscript speaking—allows you to look directly at listeners except when you are (1) reciting especially precise or complicated material, (2) pausing between points, or (3) directing the audience's attention to an audio-visual aid (see Chapter 17). None of these behaviors suggest that you are hiding true feelings or avoiding your audience. Indeed, listeners do not expect you to memorize the words or numbers taken directly from other sources. Neither will your audience expect you to maintain eye contact during those times when you must consult your outline and notecards, or during those moments when you reach for a picture or begin using a projector. However, audiences do appreciate eye contact when speakers retell personal experiences, promote their own opinions, or explain a complex subject. Eye contact at these times also benefits speakers by providing a clear view of audience reactions. As a general rule, eye contact should be maintained during 80 to 90 percent of an extemporaneous speech.

If your distance from listeners allows you to look at all of them simply by raising your head, remove obstacles—such as podiums, books, and visual aids—between your face and the audience. If you are located near your listeners—or if they are spread out widely around you—then scan the audience. Scanning involves looking at portions of the audience in sequence as you deliver a speech, or perhaps continuously shifting your gaze around the room. Your own experience is the best guide concerning which method of scanning is right for you. Especially anxious speakers sometimes look slightly above the heads of the audience or look only at friendly faces. However, both of these methods restrict adaptation to the audience: You need to observe reactions from the

Leadership Note 16–7
Sustained eye contact in public speaking situations enhances listener perceptions of speaker credibility. (Beebe, S. A. Eye contact: a nonverbal determinant of speaker credibility. *Speech Teacher, 23,* 1974, pp. 21–25.)

In public speaking, gestures should be timed naturally to physically describe and emphasize relevant parts of a speech.

entire audience in order to determine whether adjustments are needed in your content or delivery.

Gesture.   The study of how to move the head, hands, and arms in concert with a message, the use of **gesture,** has traditionally provided a bridge between theater and public speaking. Of course, leading speakers draw the line between theatrics and expressive gesturing. Gestures are effective only when you use them naturally—that is, as you would in a conversation. Unnatural use of a gesture makes your delivery theatrical rather than skillful.

Discussion Question 16–18
Different cultures can have different gestural repertoires or habits. How would you describe the gestural habits of your family or ethnic background?

When emphasis is desirable, effective speakers tend to point at a person or object, make a fist or wave, and nod or shake their heads. All of these gestures emphasize the point being discussed or indicate agreement or disagreement. For example, some speakers point at themselves to emphasize their genuine concern or personal stake in the subject at hand. Others use a slashing arm or raised fist to indicate the strength of their feelings. In any event, avoid becoming predictable or dependent on a particular gesture. Variety is necessary in order to avoid staleness.

When enumeration is desirable, speakers hold up however many fingers are appropriate to identify a main point, a quantity of objects, or a place in a hierarchy. For example, sports fans now enthusiastically point with their index finger to identify the ranking of their favorite team ("We're Number 1!"). Some speakers effectively gain their listeners' attention by enumerating the few points to be addressed. However, these gestures are so common that you may wish to consciously limit your use of them.

When description is desirable, speakers gesture in various ways. They may physically imitate the act of climbing hand over hand, waving hello and good-bye, or some other act. They may identify the shape or size of an object by drawing it or enclosing it with their hands (for example, the legendary "fish that got away"). They may illustrate the position or movement of an object by pointing at a place or moving hands and arms quickly or slowly. For example, you could easily describe the relative positions and speeds of two airliners immediately before a midair collision by using each of your hands as illustrations. Speakers vary widely in their natural use of descriptive gestures, and some people must develop self-control rather than increased activity. Otherwise their gestures may become distracting to the audience.

Developing an appreciation for the size and timing of effective gestures is more important than recognizing their types. For practical as well as aesthetic reasons, gesturing should be kept within the limited area outlined by your waist, sides, and head. Keeping gestures within this area maintains the audience's attention on you the speaker as principal source of the message, while allowing you at the same time to use other physical features, such as facial expressions and eye contact. Furthermore, gestures should be timed naturally to emphasize, enumerate, or describe while these functions are relevant to your speech. You can appreciate the effects of poorly timed gestures by standing in front of a mirror and holding up your index finger a mere one second after stating "My first point is...."

Gestures provide more physically obvious clues to a speaker's meaning than most other features of physical delivery. And the larger the feature, the greater the benefit or harm to public speaking. In this sense, the final type of physical feature—movement—deserves careful study.

Movement. Skillful use of the face and eyes calls for relatively small adjustments. Gestures with the head, hands, and arms are most effective when restrained. However, speakers add major physical features, or **movement,** to speech delivery when they move from place to place in front of an audience. Effective speakers develop a sensitivity to the natural direction and pace of these movements. You can adopt the same techniques if these movements are natural to your everyday expression of ideas.

Stepping forward or backward are especially meaningful movements in public speaking. These two directions either reduce or increase the distance between speaker and audience, thus changing the speech setting while addressing a particular idea. Movement to the side carries little or no meaning, and occasionally distracts the audience. When speakers take a step or two forward, they physically indicate the urgency of a point or their willingness to be identified with a proposal. Taking a step or two backwards indicates that the speaker has reservations or fears about a point. For example, by stepping forward with a petition in hand, a speaker can impress listeners with the immediate need to show their commitment to a plan or reform. By stepping backward while grasping the same petition, another speaker can indicate reluctance to hurry the plan or reform along.

In most instances, slow to moderately slow movement is appropriate. Smaller physical features may be adjusted quickly, but quick movements of the entire body disrupt the setting. A slow pace reflects care and deliberation on the speaker's part and allows listeners to "catch up" mentally with the speech. If a speaker were to leap forward quickly with a petition in hand, an audience might well recoil from the advance instead of embracing the speaker's plan. A hasty retreat might well express dislike for an audience rather than the speaker's disdain for an idea. Slower movements have a more predictable effect on listeners and can be blended naturally into the physical delivery of a speech.

Summary

The first step in using oral language is to appreciate its traits. Effective speakers use simple diction—easily pronounced, familiar words, such as "food" rather than "nourishment." They make personal references to themselves and their audiences, as well as allowing themselves more flexibility in grammar. For example, they make effective use of sentence fragments and word contractions. The active voice is particularly useful in speechmaking because audiences expect the language of speeches to be dynamic. Relatively short, simple statements—not always sentences—are appropriate because speakers can deliver them comfortably and because audiences can follow the meaning of such statements readily.

Four features guide the skillful use of oral language. These features are clarity, emphasis, vividness, and appropriateness.

Clear language contains words with specific rather than general meanings, as well as verbal transitions from idea to idea. "Food," for instance, could be stated more specifically as "cereal," or perhaps more specifically yet as "Wheaties." Depending on your speech organization and supporting materials, you might use sequential, coordinate, contrasting, or conclusory transitions between ideas.

Emphatic language reflects repetition and the use of schemes, such as parallelism (with its subdivisions of anaphora and epistrophe) and antithesis. Simple repetition of ideas confirms their importance for listeners. A more stylish repetition in the form of parallelism accomplishes the same goal, while antithesis emphatically contrasts one idea with another.

Vivid language rests on detailed description and the use of tropes, such as metaphors, similes, alliteration, and onomatopoeia. When speakers describe a person, event, or object with sensory details, they help the audience form a lively impression of the subject matter. Metaphors and similes help the audience draw vivid relationships between comparable ideas or things. With special sound effects, alliteration and onomatopoeia make a subject come alive for listeners.

Appropriate language does not surprise or offend listeners. By avoiding jargon, dialect, and profanity, speakers reduce their risk of using words that may be confusing or insulting to audiences. Malapropism—the often comical misuse of language—should be avoided for obvious reasons. By avoiding sexist language, speakers completely and evenly address both male and female listeners.

Skillful delivery is natural. Effective speakers stay within the natural bounds of their abilities and inclination while revealing their special perspective, and their relationship to subject matter, occasion, and audience. A natural delivery thus serves the same goals as those achieved by choosing an appropriate theme, and highlighting it in introductions and conclusions.

Skillful delivery is also adaptable. Public speakers may choose from among four main types of delivery in order to relate to specific audiences and speech purposes. An impromptu delivery is suited to those occasions when a speaker cannot preselect purpose and organization; instead, based on substantial prior reading and reflection, the speaker addresses an audience spontaneously on a subject of interest. An extemporaneous delivery is suitable for most occasions. Using an outline or notecards, the extemporaneous speaker addresses a subject with well-prepared organization and supporting materials but with flexible wording. A manuscript delivery is based on thorough preparation and allows precise wording, but often taxes the speaker's physical delivery. Finally, a memorized delivery also requires thorough preparation but may lack adaptability to changes in the setting and audience. Moreover, memorization is tedious and may restrict the speaker's vocal delivery.

Regardless of their type of delivery, successful speakers apply the full range of their natural voices to speechmaking. They take an inventory of their customary volume, rate, pitch, vocal quality, and pronunciation, and then use those features that will enhance their expression of ideas. Volume must be adequate for the setting, and occasional variations in volume should be used to emphasize specific points. Adjustments in rate can be used to compensate for marginal volume, but changes in tempo are even more valuable for clarifying ideas, expressing feelings, and emphasizing points of significance. Combined with thoughtful pauses and an avoidance of "filler" sounds, a speaker's rate provides meaningful rhythm in delivery. Pitch is more difficult to adjust, but fairly minor changes in this vocal feature enliven delivery. Some adjustments are mandatory: Speakers must end questions on a higher pitch and conclude solemn statements on a lower pitch. Vocal quality may be the most difficult of all features to adjust. Nonetheless, long-range benefits make the development of distinct articulation and an attractive voice worthwhile. Correct pronunciation is often a courtesy to listeners and merely requires preliminary attention to unfamiliar names and other words.

Skillful physical adjustments visually enhance vocal delivery. Facial expressions and eye contact have traditionally provided audiences with evidence of a speaker's sincerity. These physical features should be visibly consistent with the speaker's true feelings about the subject matter being addressed. Head, arm, and hand gestures should also be consistent with the speaker's feelings—that is, they should not be prepared artificially as conscious features of delivery but rather should reflect a natural tendency to emphasize, enumerate, or describe ideas. Public speakers also use movement—their natural inclinations to step forward or backward—when underscoring their enthusiasm or reluctance about a plan or proposal. However, physical movement is a highly visible feature of delivery and should be enacted at a relatively slow pace so as not to distract the audience.

Exercises

1. Reread the following passage from the introduction to Lesli R. Johnson's speech (printed in Chapter 13):

> Most of us spend a majority of our school years studying, but most of this studying is done under poor lighting and noisy conditions. As a matter of fact, after I heard several of you discussing this very problem last week, I looked into the problem more closely. I found that poor study conditions can have an adverse effect on our health and, as a result, our work suffers. Today I'd like you to learn how to control the conditions in which you study in order to make the most of your study time—as well as reduce potential health hazards such as fatigue, headaches, and hearing loss. By promoting better study conditions, you can make your work more efficient, you will feel better, and you may have more time to do the things you want.
>
> (Reprinted by permission of Lesli R. Johnson.)

Write a brief report or prepare to discuss orally whether Johnson expressed her ideas in oral style or written style. Consider whether the diction is simple and the grammar flexible. Did she use personal references to establish a relationship with the audience? Did she use the active voice? Which words or statements could be improved?

2. After attending a family picnic or gathering of some type, jot down two or three obvious behaviors that seem natural to one adult member of the family. The list might include a person's typical volume, rate, and vocal quality, as well as that person's habits of walking, smiling or frowning, gesturing, and so on. (If you can obtain a videotaped recording of the scene, then you could compare your list with similar notes made by other viewers.) Prepare a written report or discussion of the following: Which of the behaviors could be adapted to effective speech delivery? Which could not? Which of the persons in the videotape seem more naturally suited to speechmaking? Why?

3. Neil Armstrong uttered a now-famous statement in 1969 when he first stepped onto the moon: "That's one small step for a man, one giant leap for mankind." To appreciate the possible changes in meaning and emphasis, recite and tape-record Neil Armstrong's words—using higher volume for "small" and "giant" in your first recital and for "man" and "mankind" in a second recital. (If a recording of this statement is available in your library's media center, compare your two recitations with the vocal delivery actually used by Armstrong.)

4. Consider a famous statement from John F. Kennedy's inaugural address: "Ask not what your country can do for you, ask what you can do for your country." Where should pitch be raised or lowered to express this statement most emphatically? Why? (If a recording of this speech is available in your library's media center, check your answer against the vocal emphasis actually used by President Kennedy.)

5. Find magazine advertisements for competing brands of the same product that use spokespersons or models. Are there differences in faces and eyes? Which of these features are the same in the advertisements? Why would the advertiser use these physical features to sell the product?

Related Readings

Blankenship, J. (1968). *A sense of style: An introduction to style for the public speaker.* Belmont, CA: Dickenson Publishing.

Professor Blankenship provides a thorough and still timely analysis of how public speakers should adjust their language to their purpose.

Havelock, E. A. (1988). *The muse learns to write—Reflections on orality and literacy from antiquity to the present.* New Haven: Yale University Press.

This scholarly book is difficult reading, but it may increase your appreciation of how spoken and written styles became distinct through the ages.

King, R., and DiMichael, E. (1978). *Articulation and voice: Improving oral communication.* New York: Macmillan.

Many texts are available for further study of vocal development. This particular text is complete and offers practical guidelines for students of public speaking.

Knapp, M. (1978). *Nonverbal communication in human interaction* (2nd ed.). New York: Holt, Rinehart and Winston.

Of the several well-researched, clearly written texts on physical features of delivery, this book has become a standard reference for students of public speaking.

Strunk, W., Jr., and White, E. B. (1979). *The elements of style.* New York: Macmillan.

This book is a standard reference for writers. Even though you are primarily concerned about using language skillfully in public speaking, the book offers many relevant explanations and examples of clear, emphatic, vivid, and appropriate style.

Webster's new world guide to pronunciation (1984). New York: Simon and Schuster.

This text provides an up-to-date and inexpensive guide for your development of correct pronunciation.

Speaking to Inform

Chapter objectives

After you read this chapter you should be able to:

1. explain the process of information
2. recognize the organization suitable for each stage of the informative process
3. identify the three goals of informative speaking
4. define five types of supporting material
5. identify the functions of each type of supporting material
6. identify four types of audio-visual aids
7. evaluate the uses of each type of audio-visual aid

Key terms and concepts

information
recognition
understanding
false impressions
retention
interpretation
description
demonstration
definition
explanation
quotation
paraphrase
comparison
contrast
analogy
example
illustration
anecdote
number
statistic
audio-visual aid

In Chapter 13, we briefly discussed the four major purposes in public speaking: speaking to inform, speaking to persuade, speaking on a special occasion, and speaking with multiple purposes. Informative speeches are important in today's world because people realize that in our "information society," in which events change at lightening pace, success at school, at work, or at home frequently hinges on up-to-date information. As author Harlan Cleveland has noted in his text *The Knowledge Executive*, those who know how to effectively use the resource of information will be able to lead (Cleveland, 1985). When speaking to inform, your goal is to create or improve your listener's grasp of a subject by interpreting, describing, or demonstrating it.

Leadership Note 17–1
Consider the value of the notion that "Knowledge is power." (Francis Bacon)

Not surprisingly, today's leaders often assume the role of information giver. For example, while speaking as the nation's Surgeon General in 1988, Dr. C. Everett Koop described various health problems—from cigarette smoking to AIDS—and he explained what could be done to prevent or solve these problems. The Focus on Leadership box provides more details about Dr. Koop's speech.

In this chapter, we address information as a process—a give-and-take between speakers and their audiences. Developed consciously as part of a larger process, informative speeches help audiences to recognize, understand, and retain worthwhile knowledge. Informative speeches can be broadly classified as speeches of interpretation, description, or demonstration, or some combination of these, according to the speaker's goal.

During his tenure as Surgeon General of the United States (1981–1989), Dr. C. Everett Koop used informative speaking to educate the nation about health problems ranging from teenage pregnancy to AIDS.

FOCUS ON LEADERSHIP

Teaching the American People About AIDS

The threat of AIDS did not become a part of the national consciousness until 1988. In that year, Surgeon General C. Everett Koop addressed the American people in a pamphlet, "Understanding AIDS" (the pamphlet was available free of charge by calling an 800 toll-free number). The pamphlet illustrates Dr. Koop's grasp of the informative process as well as his conscious attention to health care leadership. With minor changes in the pamphlet's wording to promote the qualities of oral language, "Understanding AIDS" would be an effective speech.

Dr. Koop's brief, personal introduction stressed his leadership in health care by expressing his concern about the American people. He wanted people to recognize and understand AIDS so that they would know how to fight the disease. More specifically, he stressed the importance of having "the best information" about the disease and clearly announced his theme: "We all must know about AIDS." Using repetition, he drove home the need to "stop" the disease.

Within the pamphlet, Dr. Koop promoted understanding and retention of AIDS information by using a variety of supporting material. He defined *acquired immunodeficiency syndrome*. He contrasted giving blood to receiving a transfusion. He used numerous examples of how people can be infected with AIDS and, just as important, how the disease is *not* spread. He quoted several doctors, counselors, and other experts about each fact outlined in the pamphlet. However, he avoided using numbers or statistics—apparently in the belief that people needed more concrete, down-to-earth material.

Dr. Koop also included photographs of several of the people he quoted. There was even a quiz at the end of the pamphlet. These visual aids, of course, did not provide additional information—but they did enhance the facts already announced in the pamphlet. They also made the material memorable.

Any leader could profit from studying Dr. Koop's example. Any informative speaker could profit from studying the techniques in Dr. Koop's address to the American people.

All informative speeches are built by using the five main types of supporting material we briefly introduced in Chapter 14. In addition, using four types of audio-visual aids enhances your supporting material—especially if you follow a few simple guidelines.

Informative speeches help audiences to recognize, understand, and retain important information.

Teaching Objective 17–1
Introduce the concept of information not as facts but as the process by which facts, figures, and ideas are shared, a process involving both speaker and listener and one which requires recognition, understanding, and retention of what is conveyed.

Cross-reference 17–1
Refer back to the stages in the communication sequence as described in Chapter 1. Consider the overlap or correspondence between the stages of recognition, understanding, and retention described here and the stages of reception, interpretation, and reaction discussed there.

UNDERSTANDING THE PROCESS OF INFORMATION

Information is not the product of a speech. **Information** is a process of *recognition*, *understanding*, and *retention* in which both speakers and audiences play active roles. Skilled teachers and reporters, for instance, have learned that they cannot simply insert facts and figures into people's heads. Rather, people must recognize and understand information before they can retain it (Frandsen and Clement, 1984). In this sense, both speaker and audience are involved in the process of information.

Recognition

Recognition occurs when a speaker introduces listeners to facts and figures that were previously unknown. In a few instances, recognition might be achieved simply by revealing new or previously obscure facts and figures that are relevant to listeners. Most of the time, though, the audience needs to hear a link between the novel and the familiar—between the unknown and what they already know (Deutsch and Deutsch, 1970). To build this link, public speakers choose themes that identify not only the scope of research but also the information's value to listeners. Then, throughout the speech, the benefits of listening to the informative report are reaffirmed. For example, in reporting to the officers of an oil company, a geologist might use the following theme: "Extensive analysis has produced new evidence of untapped but valuable reserves in field 36." In this report, a temporal pattern of organization might be used to clarify the steps taken in finding the valuable oil:

I. An assessment of the already productive regional strata was favorable.
II. A later assessment of profitable, contiguous fields was favorable.
III. A final assessment of field 36 was favorable.

Or a conventional pattern might be used to reveal the various methods used to assess field 36:

I. Mineral analysis of regional strata identified favorable conditions.
II. Seismic analysis of the field indicated sizable reserves.
III. Exploratory drilling produced high-quality core samples.

Using relatively short, simple statements ("We used three methods of analysis. All three had favorable results."), the geologist could draw attention to the new oil. Linking these untapped reserves with the profits made from nearby drilling projects would help listeners recognize the information's value. In fact, this informative technique might even compensate for a less than exciting style and delivery. Predictably in such reports, technical jargon would be needed. Chances are that the geologist would read from a manuscript with unvarying rate, and that little physical delivery would be used. Despite the geologist's style and delivery, the listeners' interest as oil company executives would favor their recognition of the information.

More frequently, simple recognition is not enough. Imagine, for example, your response to a chemist's report that your drinking water contains toxic substances. Even if you were familiar with the general problem of water pollution, you would still want to know how these substances were introduced into the water and their particular dangers. In other words, recognition is the first stage of the informative process. Being aware of new information is the foundation on which listeners build understanding.

Understanding

People sometimes recognize a fact or figure without comprehending its significance. To enhance an audience's **understanding**, effective speakers answer predictable questions about a subject.

For example, some audiences are already aware of "continental drift" but do not understand how or why land masses have moved across the earth's surface through eons of time. In a hypothetical case, listeners may recognize the existence of an island named Xanthia but not know its location, the history of its political development, or the characteristics of its people. For this speech, it would be appropriate to use the following theme: "After interviewing teachers and counselors at our school, I became convinced that we need to learn more about global neighbors like the people of Xanthia." In addressing the question "Where is Xanthia?" as main point I, spatial organization could be used:

Discussion Question 17–1
How does information as a process differ from our normal understanding of this term? Who bears the greater responsibility for the successful completion of this process?

Cross-reference 17–2
See Chapter 2 to review perceptual barriers to recognition and understanding information and Chapter 3 to review the listener's responsibility in this process.

A. Xanthia is in the Western Hemisphere.

B. Xanthia is an equatorial island.

C. Xanthia is southwest of Bermuda.

Temporal organization would clearly be appropriate for addressing main point II, "How did Xanthia develop politically?":

A. Xanthia was settled by pirates in the 1500s.

B. Xanthia was later colonized by several European nations.

C. Xanthia gained its independence in 1906.

Conventional organization would be useful in addressing main point III, "Who are the people of Xanthia?":

A. The people of Xanthia distrust outsiders.

B. The people of Xanthia worship the sun.

C. The people of Xanthia prefer small families.

Since this hypothetical island would be literally foreign to the audience, the speaker would want to use statements that contain specific details and are linked by transitional language ("The people of Xanthia are an almost equal blend of European and Caribbean cultures. However, their religious and social practices reflect unique traditions."). Vivid descriptions of the country's geography would also be appropriate ("Soaring volcanic peaks divide the country in half, but sky-blue ponds dot both sides of the central mountain range."). For similar reasons, the speaker's rate of delivery should be relatively slow to give listeners an opportunity to mull over the information. If the audience seemed unconcerned about the subject or even resistant to the information, then the speaker would at least try to maintain an attractive vocal delivery and, at best, display facial expression and gestures to emphasize a personal enthusiasm for the subject.

Cross-reference 17–3
False impressions or understanding could also result from differences in connotative meaning on the part of speaker and audience. See Chapter 3.

Eliminating False Impressions.   Understanding may also require the correction of **false impressions**. After having recognized a bit of information on their own, some listeners jump to conclusions about its relevance or significance. In these cases, effective speakers clear up any misunderstanding. During emergencies, for example, people often believe the first rumor they hear: "Everyone will take a pay cut under the new boss"; "No one survived the plane crash." Addressing concerns such as these, a speaker might use causal organization to clarify the actual events that are unfolding. In addition, the speech would contain emphatic as well as clear language to dispel listeners' fears and correct their misunderstanding. In delivering a corrective speech, the speaker's volume and rate would most likely be steady—expressing personal confidence. By appearing unruffled and maintaining eye contact, skilled speakers reinforce their corrective message.

Clear organization, appropriate language, and skillful delivery help a speaker promote recognition and understanding. These same factors aid an audience's retention of information.

Retention

Just as simple recognition does not automatically mean that an audience will understand information, understanding should not be confused with the retention of facts and figures. **Retention** means to keep, or remember. People forget information for many reasons, but it is most frequently lost for the same reason that fluency in a foreign language is lost. It is not used. Successful speakers illustrate the usefulness of their subject to their audiences in their themes. For example, a speech on defensive driving might be made memorable by emphasizing that members of the audience can protect their own lives as well as make a more valuable contribution to a city or county committee on driving safety. Such a speech might be organized in a causal pattern that emphasizes the links between specific driving skills and highway safety. Personal references by the speaker and use of the active voice could emphasize genuine belief in the speech's utility; vivid descriptions of the unsafe alternatives might reinforce the speech's purpose. The speaker might also emphasize the usefulness of defensive driving by varying volume, rate, and pitch when addressing the ease with which specific skills can be learned. The information could be made more memorable by gesturing with hands and arms to illustrate driving techniques.

Successful speakers also help audiences retain information by *limiting their subjects*. The speech on defensive driving, for instance, might be limited to the desirable effects of defensive techniques in three common situations:

I. Defensive driving ensures your arrival at work.
II. Defensive driving protects you on shopping trips.
III. Defensive driving safeguards your vacation.

Or the speech might be limited to the desirable effects of using three controls defensively:

I. Daytime use of headlights increases your visibility to other drivers.
II. Consistent use of turn signals advertises your lane changes.
III. Restricted use of brakes reduces your chances of skidding.

The speaker could develop a memorable speech by revealing personal training in the introduction, and by calling for the audience to seriously consider the same course of training in the conclusion.

REACHING INFORMATIVE GOALS

In the process of informing audiences, public speakers try to reach at least one of three goals: interpretation, description, or demonstration. We will discuss them briefly as separate goals, although public speakers occasionally need to combine them—similar to the way people sometimes speak with multiple purposes.

Cross-reference 17–4
Chapter 3 (on listening) discusses the value of repeating the message to aid retention. Chapter 16 discusses the use of mnemonic devices to aid memorization; such devices could also be used as aids to listener retention.

Teaching Objective 17–2
Describe the speech goals of interpretation, description, and demonstration.

Leadership Note 17–2
Listen to these words of description from Rachel Carson, an environmental leader whose *Silent Spring* (1962) early alerted a wide segment of the nation to the damage being inflicted on the earth: "Since the mid-1940's over 200 basic chemicals have been created for use in killing insects, weeds, rodents, and other organisms....These sprays, dusts, and aerosols are now applied almost universally to farms, gardens, forests, and homes—non-selective chemicals that have the power to kill every insect, the 'good' and the 'bad,' to still the song of birds and the leaping of fish in the streams, to coat the leaves with a deadly film, and to linger on in the soil—all this though the intended target may be only a few weeds or insects. Can anyone believe it is possible to lay down such a barrage of poisons on the surface of the earth without making it unfit for all life? They should not be called 'insecticides' but 'biocides.'" (As quoted in Ravitch, Diane, *The American Reader: Words that Moved a Nation*. New York: HarperCollins, 1990, p. 324.)

Discussion Question 17–2
Which of these three informative speech goals best corresponds to the way you are most likely to recognize, understand, and retain information? Which do you think is the easiest goal for a speaker to attain—explaining, describing, or showing?

Interpretation

Effective speakers provide an **interpretation** when they make their subject matter simple and familiar to audiences. Speakers select the goal of interpretation (also called explanation) when they must inform audiences about complicated or difficult ideas. For example, when C. Everett Koop spoke to Americans about AIDS, he explained the several different groups at risk and the many ways in which a person might get AIDS. A student speaker might need to explain the structure and purposes of his or her campus organization.

Description

Speeches of **description** are designed to provide listeners with a mental image or picture of the subject matter. More detailed and vivid than a simple explanation, a descriptive speech helps the audience to vicariously see, smell, and otherwise sense physical details. Doctors, such as C. Everett Koop, often need to make people aware of the symptoms of a disease or the physical harm caused by certain injuries. To reach this descriptive goal, a speaker might announce the specific aches and pains associated with a disease, or describe the specific scars and loss of mobility associated with an injury. A student speaker might need to describe the details of meeting with parents and teachers after an especially bad grading period. On the brighter side, descriptive speakers also need to announce the specific physical benefits of healthy nutrition and exercise, or the enjoyable feelings associated with academic success.

Demonstration

Public speakers select the speech goal of **demonstration** when their task is to help audiences learn how to do something. Unlike speakers who pursue the goals of interpretation or description, demonstrative speakers are not satisfied with telling an audience about the subject matter. They want to show listeners the subject matter. Patients usually need a doctor or nurse to show them how to use an item of medical technology—whether it is a syringe or a knee brace. Likewise, student speakers are often called upon to demonstrate how to use educational technology—from a new computer to a well-used slide projector.

Informative speaking benefits from all of the analytical, organizational, and presentational methods discussed in preceding chapters. However, these methods are intended to set the stage for your effective use of supporting material. This material is the heart of informative speaking. With this thought in mind, consider how the following types of supporting material can be used to interpret, describe, and demonstrate information.

BUILDING THE SPEECH WITH SUPPORTING MATERIALS

To select the appropriate information to include in your speech, you should draw upon the notes you made during the research process (discussed in

Chapter 14). Informative speeches ideally contain several types of research, or support. Each of the five main types of supporting material has a specific function (see Table 17.1).

Definition and Explanation

Audiences need definitions of words and explanations of ideas that are unusual, technical, or ambiguous. **Definitions** and **explanations** reveal the meaning of a subject or the category in which it belongs. Speeches of interpretation often rely heavily on definition and explanation.

Unusual Information.   A word is unusual if most members of the audience do not regularly use it themselves. For example, most audiences would need definitions of the words *chronograph* (a stopwatch or similar timepiece) and *chronometer* (an extremely accurate timepiece). Generally speaking, most people would say "watch"; a small portion might say "timepiece." But how many people recognize or understand chronographs and chronometers? In the same way, political analysts needed to explain their use of the word *synergy* in describing the appeal of a Clinton-Gore presidential ticket: When the images of the two candidates were fused in the public mind, the sum appeared greater than the parts.

As illustrated here, a speaker does not necessarily have to use a dictionary in order to inform the audience. Rather, clarity simply demands that you speak the language of the audience. When you must use an unusual word or idea you should offer a definition or explanation.

Technical Information.   Technical words reflect the special vocabulary of a particular art, science, or profession. One artist, for instance, may talk to another artist about a "fret" without defining this word. However, most audiences will interpret "fret" as an act of worrying rather than as a symmetrical design within a border or hem. In fact, an audience of musicians would probably assume that a "fret" is one of the ridges on the fingerboard of a stringed

Teaching Objective 17–3
Explain, with relevant examples, the various types of supporting material.

Leadership Note 17–3
Founding member of the modern feminist movement Betty Friedan defines "the feminine mystique": "The feminine mystique says that the highest value and the only commitment for women is the fulfillment of their own femininity….It says this femininity is so mysterious and intuitive and close to the creation and origin of life that man-made science may never be able to understand it….The mistake, says the mystique, the root of women's troubles in the past is that women envied men, women tried to be like men, instead of accepting their own nature, which can find fulfillment only in sexual passivity, male domination, and nurturing maternal love. . . ." (As quoted in Ravitch, Diane, ed., *The American Reader: Words that Moved a Nation* New York: HarperCollins, 1990, pp. 337–338.)

Table 17.1
Types and Functions of Supporting Material

Type	Function
Definition and explanation	To clarify words and ideas
Quotation and paraphrase	To add authority to ideas
Comparison and analogy	To point out relationships between ideas
Example and illustration	To provide specific instances, real or hypothetical
Number and statistic	To provide precise measurements

Discussion Question 17–3
How would you define yourself? How would you explain yourself? What is the difference?

instrument. Without a definition, the technical meaning of "fret" would be lost. Similarly, if we lacked books like *Roget's International Thesaurus*, it would be difficult to understand the technical differences among the two hundred "phobias," such as *kakorraphiaphobia* (fear of failure) and *aulophobia* (fear of the flute).

When you fail to define technical terms—whether you are talking about a fret or a phobia—you exclude at least some listeners from your speech. No one enjoys being left out of a conversation. As a leader, you need to maintain lines of communication with your audience even if your subject is highly technical.

Discussion Question 17–4
Suppose you wanted to give a speech on the subject that human beings need love to survive. How would you go about clarifying what you mean by the ambiguous word "love" in this instance?

Ambiguous Information. Words are ambiguous when they can mean different things to different members of the audience. For example, after someone describes a friend as "funny," you may hear another person ask whether the friend is funny as in "ha ha" or funny as in "peculiar." Sometimes a critic will avoid being insulting by ambiguously describing an idea or performance as "interesting"—although the critic means "odd" and not "attractive." Words such as *funny* or *interesting* are ambiguous and usually need to be defined.

Ideas can be just as ambiguous. For example, what does it mean to be a "refugee"? Depending on the speaker's choice of subject, the millions of Africans who fled from drought and famine are refugees, but so are the thousands of Muslims who fled warfare in the Middle East or the Balkans.

Definitions and explanations help the audience recognize and understand the nature of information. Beware of two warning signs, however. First, if you find that more than a few definitions or explanations are needed, you should consider whether you have properly targeted your subject matter. You may need to further limit your subject. Second, be alert to introducing words and ideas that require further definition and explanation. You should check your own command of unusual, technical, or ambiguous information if you cannot explain it to others in commonly understood language.

Discussion Question 17–5
What is your favorite quotation? What is it about the quotation that speaks to you just the way it is? What is the source of its power to move you? Would it lose some of its power if it were paraphrased?

Quotation and Paraphrase

One of the most effective ways to borrow experience or expertise is to use other people's words. A **quotation** is an exact ("verbatim") borrowing of someone else's words; paraphrases are looser but still accurate restatements. In addition to the use of definitions and explanations, speeches of interpretation rely heavily on quotation and paraphrase.

Direct quotation adds precision and authority to a speech. For example, if you want your audience to feel the same way as victims of a recent accident, you might quote verbatim the firsthand reactions of a victim.

Leadership Note 17–4
Consider the value of this comparison by former Chief Justice of the Supreme Court Warren Burger: "Our Constitution has had as great an impact on humanity as the splitting of the atom." (In Bowen, C.D., *Miracle at Philadelphia.* Boston: Little Brown, 1966, p. x.)

Quoting experts provides an audience with authoritative facts. However, a quotation from an expert—especially a lengthy quotation—may be hard to understand and require further definition or explanation. A **paraphrase**, then, is a brief but accurate way of providing the same information contained in a quotation.

Effective speakers decide whether they need the precision of a quotation, or whether their message will be just as effective if a paraphrase is used. In either case, first identify the source of the information and then briefly explain the person's credentials—whether these are based on simple experience or expertise. This explanation allows the audience to judge whether the quoted or paraphrased language is authoritative.

Comparison and Analogy

Comparison is useful in pointing out similarities among objects, qualities, or actions of the same general type or classification. At an auto show, for instance, a speaker might compare different makes and models that, though dissimilar in some ways, belong to the classification "new cars." **Contrast**—a close relative of comparison—is used to point out differences among objects, qualities, or actions of the same general type or classification. For example, new cars can be contrasted as to their color, equipment, etc. **Analogy** is a comparison of basically different objects, qualities, or actions. Analogy is especially useful when relating familiar ideas to unfamiliar ones. A speaker who was magically transported to the past or future might use analogies—respectively, analogies to horse-drawn carts or solar-powered air scooters—when describing cars of the 1990s. Most speeches of description include a substantial amount of comparison-contrast and analogy.

Comparison links subjects of the same type. Restricting comparisons within one class or type of subjects is important because otherwise audiences could become confused about the basic qualities of your subject. For example, you can compare or contrast hospitals and clinics because they are both health care facilities. But you cannot properly compare or contrast hospitals and roller-skating rinks: They are different types of institutions having different purposes. J. Jeffery Auer (1989) used comparison and contrast properly when he commented on former Prime Minister Margaret Thatcher's political speaking: "The young in England, like the young in America, are much less concerned about niceties of voice and diction than middle-aged and older citizens." People are people, so their nationalities can be compared and their ages can be contrasted. You should use comparison or contrast whenever your audience needs to know the similarities or differences between related subjects.

Analogy is used to link two subjects of different types. To make information meaningful, a teacher or reporter draws an analogy between the unfamiliar idea and an unrelated but familiar one. For example, most of today's audiences are familiar with recycling but need further information about job retraining programs. Community leaders may draw an analogy between retraining unemployed or underemployed workers and recycling valuable resources that might otherwise be wasted. In another case, a speaker might refer to newly hired workers as "diamonds in the rough." Analogies help the audience see the relationship between ideas—even though workers cannot be compared directly with recyclables or diamonds.

Especially clever or vivid relationships become memorable. However, you should always be alert to the requirements of comparisons and contrasts. The two ideas being related must be of the same type or class. They must share

Leadership Note 17–5
Frances Moore Lappe, best known for her authorship of *Diet for a Small Planet*, used contrast in this article entitled "For The Future": "We ourselves must believe that those of us working actively for peace and justice are not cursed with the burden of saving the world, but blessed with what many many…yearn for….Our lives must not say: 'You must come help us shoulder the mighty burden of making the world better.' Instead…we must demonstrate how government can be reclaimed as a vehicle through which we can act on our deepest values, rather than remain an instrument of authoritative (or corrupt) control." (As quoted in Gioseffi, Daniela, ed., *Women on War*. New York: Touchstone, 1988, p. 321.)

Current Research 17–1
In a speech at California State University in San Bernadino, California, Distinguished Visiting Professor Anita Taylor suggested that "exchange" is the most common analogy used within U.S. culture to explain the education process, with students and professors assuming that a student exchanges time, energy, and money for skills or future monetary potential. Later in the speech, Taylor questions whether this analogy is accurate or useful. (What are we doing here? *Vital Speeches*, 9/15/88, pp. 718–722.)

Discussion Question 17–6
What would you say is a good analogy to help someone who has never been to college understand what college is like?

Leadership Note 17–6
Shirley Chisholm, U.S. Congresswoman, educator, and former presidential candidate, made power-ful use of statistics in a speech entitled "Economic Injustice in America Today" which was delivered in various forms during her presidential campaign: "Ask the Chicanos in East Los Angeles in which 35% of the housing is substan-dard whether President Nixon's announcement of 2 million housing starts in 1971 had anything to do with improvement of hous-ing in East Los Angeles. Or talk to the Spanish-speaking migrant worker (who) knows that infant and maternal mortality among his or her people is 125% higher than the national rate: that influenza and pneumonia death rates are 200% higher…that death from tuberculosis and infectious disease is 260% higher; and life expectancy itself for migrant workers is 49 years—compared with the 67.5 years for the members of the silent majority." (As quoted in Duffy, Bernard, and Ryan, Halford, *American Orators of the Twentieth Century.* New York: Greenwood Press, 1977, p. 65.)

basic characteristics. Although analogies are less rigorous, you should avoid far-fetched ones that will not immediately appear relevant or significant to your audience.

Example and Illustration

An **example** is a brief reference to an actual or hypothetical case that makes a subject realistic and present to the audience. An **illustration** is a highly detailed example. Lengthy, occasionally humorous or poignant illustrations are called **anecdotes**. Speeches of description usually contain a substantial amount of example and illustration.

Audiences may comprehend a word or idea, and they may understand the nature of your subject matter, but they will better realize its existence if you pro-vide an example. For instance, in developing a speech on the complex problems of refugees, you might refer to the real experiences of people in Sudan who have suffered hunger and homelessness during their country's long civil war between northern Muslims and southern Christians. Your audience may not need an explanation of what it means to be a refugee. Instead, they might need to hear an actual example.

Illustrations offer the same benefits as examples but, because they are developed in more detail, illustrations provide special depth. To provide an in-depth understanding of recycling, you might illustrate your subject with related methods in Germany. German manufacturers and stores are required at their own expense to take back the packaging used in shipping and selling goods: packaging used in transportation of goods (including cardboard boxes and Styrofoam) and in selling goods (including plastic cups and wrapping paper) can be returned. Though lengthier than an example, this illustration of German recycling is relevant and adds worthwhile details.

Examples and illustrations help the audience sense a subject as if it were actually present. Overuse of examples and illustrations leads to confusion over the point being supported. For any given idea, effective speakers use just enough of these types of support to provide listeners with a sense of reality. To ensure realism, an example or illustration must be typical, or representative. If listeners do not quickly recognize the reality of instances or cases, then the speaker has not improved their understanding.

Number and Statistic

Measurements of quantity provide listeners with very useful information. A **number** is a simple measurement that answers such questions as "How many?" "How long?" "How deep?" and so on. A **statistic** is a more complex mea-surement of the relationship between two or more numbers. Typical statistical measures include the mean (an average of other numbers), the median (the midpoint in a series of numbers), and the mode (the most frequent number in a group). Speeches of description frequently rely on numbers and statistics.

Numbers add precision to speeches. But numbers are abstract and fre-quently need explanation. For instance, a critic of burn-out in the legal profes-

SELF-ASSESSMENT   Identify the Supporting Materials

1. The coach explains: "Okay. So we've lost a few games. We lost the first two games by scores of 152–0 and 145–0; then we lost 144–0. But we're getting better. Last week it was only 3–0. We used to lose by an average of 147 points!"

2. The complainer moans: "All of my friends are complicated people. Even their names are complicated: Pillersdorf, Drakulich, Ruthizerson, and Klaskovich."

3. The skeptic wonders aloud who can be trusted: "Even the former president said, 'Read my lips,' but then broke his promise."

4. The speeder responds: "But officer, to drive at 55 miles per hour on this road you'd have to be like the people who don't cross the street unless the walk sign is flashing."

5. The parent scolds: "Respect means obedience, and obedience means doing what I say."

Answers: 1. numbers/statistic; 2. examples; 3. quotation; 4. comparison; 5. definition and explanation.

sion might state: "Most lawyers put in 1,800 to 2,200 hours a year on the job—an average of 2,000 working hours annually." But note how the numbers and statistics become clearer when the critic adds: "Put into simple terms, that means 7 hours a day, 6 days a week, 52 weeks a year." If the critic does not explain the mean, or average, of lawyers' workload, then the audience might not appreciate how stressful the workload is.

Public speakers use numbers and statistics whenever their audience needs precise information about quantity, extent, and related measurements. However, rounding off a number usually makes it memorable without seriously harming its precision. The critic of burn-out in the legal profession may count precisely 2,000 hours as an average workload, but we may assume the actual number is slightly more or less. Furthermore, the abstract quality of numbers makes it desirable for speakers to use accompanying explanations or examples (Taylor and Thompson, 1982). (Complete the Self-Assessment exercise.)

To appreciate the vital role of supporting material in informative speaking, consider the following response to our country's shortage of health care professionals. Carol J. Brookshire, a registered nurse, delivered this speech in 1989 to satisfy course requirements in public speaking. Although Brookshire injected her personal opinion here and there, her primary purpose was to interpret and describe information about the recruitment and retention of health care workers.

Current Research 17–2
Kathleen C. Bailey, Assistant Director, U.S. Arms Control and Disarmament Agency, made this use of numbers in a speech on chemical weapons proliferation to the Dallas Market Rotary Club on July 16, 1988: "Twenty-five years ago, only five countries were estimated to possess chemical weapons. Today, this figure has risen to about 15 and there are others which are trying to acquire them." (Bailey, Kathleen C., Chemical weapons proliferation. *Vital Speeches*, 10/1/88, p. 749.)

<table>
<tr><td>

A "scenario" for comparison

</td><td>

1. It's 7:00 A.M. You've just arrived at work, and you find a pink resignation slip on your desk. Another employee is leaving your hospital. You're already understaffed because two employees resigned last spring. And you don't have any prospects for filling these positions because of a shortage of health care workers. Sound grim? Sound familiar? I think this scenario is something we are all experiencing now with increasing frequency.

</td></tr>
<tr><td>

Paraphrase of research findings

</td><td>

2. The dwindling supply of health care professionals and high turnover rates are prompting those of us in hospital management to learn the means of finding and keeping top-notch workers. According to experts at Hershey Medical Center in Pennsylvania, recruitment and retention strategies are the answer to the present crisis. Recruitment strategies must be both short term and long term, or we are just putting a Band-Aid on the problem.

</td></tr>
<tr><td>

Definition of "long-term recruitment"

</td><td>

3. Long-term recruitment strategies are meant to replenish the supply of health care professionals in four to eight years, and they involve two steps: to inform and to encourage.

</td></tr>
<tr><td>

Examples

</td><td>

4. High school students are not attracted to a career in health care unless we let them know this career exists—for example, during high school career days. Most high school students have heard of nurses and pharmacists, but are they aware of medical technologists, respiratory therapists, or cytotechnologists? I doubt it. They need to be informed about all of these professions.

</td></tr>
<tr><td>

Examples

</td><td>

5. The second means of informing is by educating high school counselors about the specifics of health care careers, such as academic requirements, job benefits, and salary ranges. At our hospital, we have received several letters from grateful counselors after we sent them photocopies of salary surveys published by nursing journals.

</td></tr>
<tr><td>

Personal example

</td><td>

6. The next step is to encourage students to choose a health care profession by giving them a positive, hands-on hospital experience. This can be accomplished by hiring summer interns, conducting hospital tours, or sponsoring an in-hospital health fair. Our hospital held a fair last spring, with every department represented by an individual booth. We used videos, slides, pamphlets, posters, and demonstrations. Attendance was beyond our expectations, and we plan to hold another fair this spring.

7. Long-term recruitment is vital, but we must understand short-term strategies as well.

</td></tr>
<tr><td>

Explanation and examples

</td><td>

8. Specific advertising information in both newspapers and professional journals is a first step. Truly informative advertising is explicit about qualifications and shift requirements, as well as being clear about opportunities for educational aid, sign-on bonuses, even highlights of your community.

</td></tr>
<tr><td>

Extensive explanation

</td><td>

9. During interviews, prospective employees deserve the whole truth—desirable features of the job along with its disadvantages. Prospective employees also appreciate a tour of your department.

</td></tr>
</table>

They like to be introduced to one or two key people, and have a chance to talk to an enthusiastic employee—alone. If the candidate is from out of town, housing, schools, and community benefits are relevant points of interest. For example, if a spouse needs help in finding a job, the prospective employee appreciates learning the phone number of the human resources department.

10. Now, even if you master recruitment strategies, you still have to worry about someone leaving to go to another hospital, or into research, or even industry. With low supply and high demand, turnover rates in health care are frightening. According to the *Medical Laboratory Observer Journal*, a typical annual turnover rate is 30 percent. Since it's less expensive and less disruptive to retain than to replace, we must learn about retention strategies.

Number

11. How can we keep the employees we have? According to a recent study using exit interviews, the most important retention strategy is effective coaching and team building by supervisory staff in an atmosphere of respect and appreciation. According to this same study, employees will tolerate tremendous adversity if they feel respected and have a sense of input and belonging.

Paraphrase of research findings

12. A second important strategy is career development, which relies on subsidized attendance at educational and professional meetings, and tuition reimbursement. We should also consider scheduling options, such as flextime.

Examples

13. Work environment is important. It may sound trivial, but temperature and aesthetics are just as important to retention as state-of-the-art equipment.

14. And last but not least, money. Financial incentives play a very important role in retention strategies. Renewal bonuses, shift differentials, overtime pay, personal or merit raises, and cash awards for suggestions and perfect attendance are all effective incentives. Of course, a competitive salary range always helps.

Examples

15. You know, we like to believe that other companies or hospitals are enticing our staff away. But the truth may well be that our employees find their jobs undesirable. By learning about retention strategies, we may begin the process of limiting our turnover rate; and in conjunction with recruitment strategies, we may survive this shortage crisis in the health care professions.

(Used with permission of Carol J. Brookshire.)

As Brookshire's speech illustrates, each type of supporting material has a distinct function. Audio-visual aids enhance or amplify these functions.

▪ USING AUDIO-VISUAL AIDS

Teaching Objective 17–4
Describe the various types of audio-visual aids.

Have you ever heard a fascinating bit of information and then quickly forgotten it? Because each of the five senses is limited, combinations of visual and audible cues often make information particularly impressive and memorable. Effective speakers use at least four types of **audio-visual aids** to enhance or amplify the functions of supporting material (see Table 17.2). In particular, speeches of demonstration rely on audio-visual aids.

Types of Audio-Visual Aids

Objects and Models. Objects and models enhance the functions of definition and example by appealing to the audience's senses of sight and touch. Also, these visual aids typically save time. Because it might otherwise take many words of explanation or description, displaying an object enables you to address other details. For example, a speaker might display a new type of golf club or tennis racket in order to quickly illustrate recent changes in design. Then, the time saved could be spent on explaining how the new design improves performance.

Obviously, you will not want to use an object unless it can be seen clearly by listeners at the rear of your audience. Conversely, if an object is too large—or too dangerous—for display during a speech, you will want to use a smaller or safer model to obtain the same benefits. For example, new approaches to urban planning or recent dangers posed by automatic weapons could be illustrated by displaying a plaster model of "the city of the future" or by displaying realistic toy versions of the weapons. Use of a model rather than an object may require you to explain actual size and other features, but the convenience and safety of models are often worth the extra time needed for explanations.

Discussion Question 17–7
Is a picture really worth a thousand words? When has this been true in your own experience?

Pictures and Drawings. Pictures and drawings enhance an audience's ability to recognize specific effects or the scope of a problem. Comparisons can also be enhanced by presenting them pictorially. Indeed, these visual aids allow audiences to judge examples as closely as the speaker. For instance, a picture of a

Table 17.2
Types and Functions of Audio-Visual Aids

Type	Function
Objects and models	To enhance definitions and examples
Pictures and drawings	To enhance examples, comparisons, and quotations
Graphs and charts	To enhance comparisons and numbers
Film, video, and sound recordings	To enhance examples and quotations

barren landscape might be the clearest example of the effects of "slash and burn" land management in rain forests. Careful scale drawings of Venus, Earth, and Mars might best explain the similarities and differences between the orbits and sizes of these neighboring planets. Speeches about art and artists, of course, benefit from visual displays of the relevant styles and techniques being addressed.

You do not always have to rely on your own artistry in preparing pictures and drawings. Library research can introduce you to articles and books in which the authors have illustrated their subject matter—and you can trace or make photocopies of these illustrations for enlargement and display. In fact, many libraries lend selected pictures and drawings as well as books.

Charts and Graphs. Charts and graphs help audiences understand and recall numbers and statistics. Because numerical information is abstract, audiences appreciate its translation into visual displays. The pie chart, for example, is a traditionally effective method of displaying the distribution of resources: Typical pie charts show the several proportionate "slices" of a budget or "pieces" of a whole. Bar graphs (also called bar charts) also show comparisons between quantities and thus can be used to show the increase or decrease of a quantity over time. Line graphs typically show the increase or decrease of a quantity over time or in relation to some other variable. See Figure 17.1 for a typical pie chart, bar chart, and line graph.

Beware of trying to express too much information in one chart or graph. The most effective displays reveal one type of measurement or numerical relationship.

Figure 17.1
Drawings of a Line Graph,
Bar Chart, and Pie Chart.

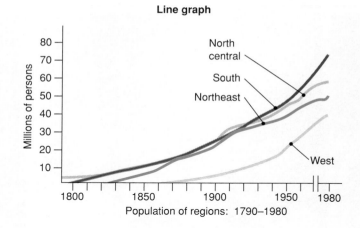

Line graph

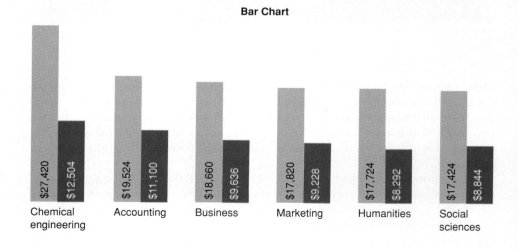

Bar Chart

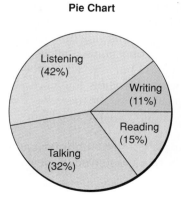

Pie Chart

Film, Video, and Sound Recordings.   Film, video, and sound recordings are dramatic—helping the audience to recognize actions and events. Like amplified quotations, recordings of speeches, press conferences, and other forms of public address are especially helpful in recognizing the original delivery of words and ideas. For example, General Douglas MacArthur's 1962 farewell speech at West Point—despite its powerful language—was originally delivered in a tired, halting manner. Examples or illustrations of the performing arts come alive when played for audiences. In addition, recordings of the sights and sounds of faraway peoples and cultures often enliven related speeches.

As with the other types of audio-visual aids, recordings can often be obtained inexpensively. Contact your campus services agency or local library to obtain catalogs of available materials and to receive training in the use of equipment.

Considering their costs and benefits, objects or models, pictures or drawings, charts or graphs, and film, video, or sound recordings offer considerable value. They are most valuable, though, when the speaker maintains a proper perspective on their function. They should not become the focal point of a speech. Instead, they should be used to amplify supporting material that itself is subordinate to a main point. Other, more specific guidelines should also be considered.

Guidelines on the Use of Audio-Visual Aids

Invest Time in Preparation and Practice.   Public speakers occasionally take a few shortcuts, but they seldom discount the preparation and practice of audio-visual aids. In fact, Murphy's law is clear on these matters—if something can go wrong, it will! By preparing your aid well in advance of a speech, you reduce the chances of overlooking a flaw. The rushed speaker who draws accurate pictures of Union and Confederate flags for a speech on the Civil War but then incorrectly labels the flags suffers a worse fate than if no visual aid had been prepared. For this same reason, use chalkboards only when you can write or draw on them well in advance of your speech. Audio-visual equipment has a nasty habit of displaying information out of sequence or breaking down at just the wrong time. Check electrical equipment thoroughly before your speeches.

Advance preparation also makes it possible to practice using your aid realistically. Pretending to play a cassette tape without securing batteries or an extension cord makes your rehearsal unrealistic. Pretending to display a large, floppy poster while practicing a speech does not simulate the actual conditions of struggling with an awkward, distracting picture or chart. Practice will make you familiar and comfortable with using audio-visual aids.

Ensure Audience Hearing and Sight.   Advance preparation and practice should include special attention to the volume of audio aids and the size of visual aids. Spend a few moments checking desirable sound levels at the actual site of your speech; decide which level will be loud enough for listeners at the rear of your audience but not too loud for those at the front. If possible, avoid

Teaching Objective 17–5
Emphasize the importance of using audio-visual materials well and reinforce the guidelines for use suggested by the authors.

this decision by arranging for speakers to be distributed throughout the area. Many stereo cassette players, for example, are equipped with detachable speakers. For your visual aids, check overall size, and the size of details, such as letters or numbers. Ask another person to do this because you already know the content of your material! Your audience is entitled to see your supporting materials, regardless of which types you use. Remember that your aid should speak for itself in most respects—that is, you should not have to repeat aloud the words and figures in the aid.

Planning a central location for your aid often eases the job of determining proper sound level and size. When appropriate, locate audio-visual aids in the same area where you will be speaking: If you are satisfied with the audience's ability to hear and see you clearly, then you can also be confident about the location of your audio-visual aid. However, on those occasions when you yourself will be distant or obscured, your visual aids do not have to share the same fate. For example, a speaker of average height may locate illustrative drawings in front of a tall podium, or at the side.

Establish Proper Timing.   Since audio-visual aids should enhance your supporting material—rather than replace it—plan to use each aid only when it is directly relevant to an idea in your speech. Playing rock music when you are discussing Appalachian folk music is highly distracting. Displaying a graph before or after the proper moment is just as distracting as playing music out of sequence. Chapter 16 outlines related rules for timing physical gestures and movements; think of audio-visual aids as extensions of yourself and plan accordingly!

Passing a visual aid among members of the audience usually harms a speech, even if the timing is perfect. After all, audiences already have the option to ignore a speaker and pay attention to themselves, the time, or the place. When you pass an object or picture among listeners, you simply add another option to the list. Distributing handouts during a speech runs the same risk. Instead, display your material in an amplified form at the proper moment and then provide small, individual handouts after the speech. This method requires extra preparation and expense but it saves you from the indignity of finishing second to a piece of paper in the competition for your audience's attention.

Explain Briefly the Meaning or Significance.   As mentioned above, audio-visual aids should speak for themselves in most respects. However, speakers fail to exploit all the power of an aid if they do not discuss its meaning or its significance. These features do not typically emerge by themselves. For example, most audiences do not know the meaning or significance of the battle flags used during the Civil War regardless of how clearly these emblems are depicted. Even high-fidelity recordings do not automatically express the meaning and significance of various musical styles. Numerical charts and graphs are often obscure to audiences. Therefore, offer explanations just as you do elsewhere in your speech—by directly addressing the audience. Speaking to the aid instead of to your listeners suggests confusion on your part about the real audience and speech purpose.

MASTERING COMMUNICATION SKILLS

Using Audio-Visual Aids

1. Did I invest plenty of time in preparation and practice?
    a. Did I allow enough time to prepare my audio-visual aid as an important element in my speech, or did I hurriedly "throw it together" just for the sake of using an aid?
    b. Did I practice using my audio-visual aid while I rehearsed my speech, or did I omit that part of my practice—assuming the aid would fit in neatly?

2. Did I ensure that my audience could hear and see?
    a. Did I ask a friend to help me during a rehearsal by listening from the rear of the room? Did I walk to the rear and sides of the room to see whether my aid was large enough?
    b. Did I use my audio-visual aid in a central location, especially if it seemed that volume and/or size would be a problem?

3. Did I use proper timing?
    a. Did I use the aid only when it was relevant to what I was saying? Did I avoid displaying my visual aid too early or too long? Did I avoid playing more of my audio aid than was necessary to enhance my idea?
    b. Did I limit the sharing or distribution of my visual aids?

4. Did I explain briefly the meaning or significance of my audio-visual aid?
    a. Did I avoid turning away from the audience while using my audio-visual aid?
    b. Did I focus on my speech, speaking only briefly about my audio-visual aid?

Although you may spend considerable time and money in preparing an audio-visual aid, your explanations should be brief because the aid merely enhances one item of supporting material. Common sense dictates that a five-minute informative speech does not allow a speaker to play a three-minute audio or video recording—even to support a main idea. In the same speech, a three-minute explanation of an audio-visual aid would be equally improper. If your rehearsal indicates that an aid requires lengthy explanation, then seriously consider not using the aid.

As amplifiers of supporting material, audio-visual aids increase the accessibility of your information. By appealing to as many senses as feasible, you help the audience's recognition, understanding, and retention of facts and figures. You also help yourself reach your informative goals. (See the Mastering Communication Skills box.)

◾ Summary

The process of information challenges speakers and audiences to join forces in order to improve their recognition, understanding, and retention. Recognition is improved when audiences become aware of new or obscure facts and figures. In most cases, however, recognition is merely the first phase in the process. Understanding is improved when audiences appreciate the meaning or significance of information, or when misunderstanding is corrected. Retention is evident when audiences use information privately or publicly.

Recognizing the process of information helps you reach the informative goals of interpretation, description, and demonstration. Public speakers make their information simple and familiar when they interpret it for audiences. Descriptive speakers help their audiences form a mental picture of information. Speeches of demonstration show listeners how to do something.

Effective speakers use a variety of supporting material to reach informative goals. Each of the five main types of support has a specific function: A definition or explanation reveals the precise meaning of a word or idea; a quotation or paraphrase expresses ideas from an authoritative perspective; a comparison or analogy identifies the relationships between ideas; an example or illustration provides specific, realistic instances of an idea; a number or statistic provides precise measurements of quantities. Developing several types of support for each speech increases the chances that an audience will recognize, understand, and retain information.

Each type of supporting material can be enhanced or amplified with audio-visual aids: An object or model saves time when a speaker needs to define or illustrate a subject; a picture or drawing clearly displays comparisons and examples; a chart or graph makes numbers more tangible; a film, video, or sound recording dramatizes examples and quotations. The most effective use of audio-visual aids reflects extensive preparation and practice, ensuring the audience's hearing and sight, as well as proper timing and brief explanations of each aid.

◾ Exercises

1. For a class report or discussion, obtain copies of two or three of your favorite magazine advertisements. Take a few moments to examine how these ads enhance the process of information. Are the facts and figures novel? How many questions about the product or service are answered? What uses are identified to make the product or service memorable?

2. Arrange a brief meeting with two or three students after one of their lecture classes and interview the students about the content of that day's lecture. Based on the results of your interview, can you identify specific techniques used by the lecturer to help students recognize, understand, and retain information? Based on the students' responses, what might the lecturer do to improve his or her classroom presentations?

3. Reread the speech on pages 476–477 by Carol J. Brookshire. What type(s) of

audio-visual aids would have been appropriate for use during the speech? How might a picture or drawing be used to enhance the discussion of "health fairs" in paragraph 6? How might the speaker have used a chart to enhance the memorability of the five aspects of advertising in paragraph 8? Would a sound recording have been useful? Where in the speech might it be used?

Campbell, J. (1982). *Grammatical man: Information, entropy, language, and life.* New York: Simon and Schuster.

Related Readings

> This book offers a readable introduction to information theory, a field presently characterized by investigations of cybernetics and artificial intelligence.

Cleveland, H. (1989). *The knowledge executive.* New York: E. P. Dutton.

> You will enjoy reading this author's reflections on the dawning of the "information age" and on how each of us can play a leadership role every day by using information wisely and efficiently.

Speaking to Persuade

Chapter objectives

After reading this chapter you should be able to:

1. explain persuasion as a process of changing attitude and behavior

2. define the four persuasive themes of fact, conjecture, value, and policy

3. identify three types of persuasive appeals

4. explain how knowledge, character, good will, and dynamism support a speaker's credibility

5. evaluate the appropriateness of emotional appeals in speeches addressing the four persuasive themes

6. outline the types of reasoning and evidence

Key terms and concepts

persuasive change
attitude
behavior
motives
credibility appeal
dynamism
knowledge
character
good will
emotional appeal
physiological needs
safety needs
belongingness needs
self-esteem needs
self-actualization needs
rational appeal
deductive reasoning
inductive reasoning
evidence

Teaching Objective 18–1
Explore the relationship
between leadership skills
and persuasive skills.

Leadership Note 18–1
"And listen: for me the
most beautiful monument
to human dignity is still the
one I saw on a hill in the
Peloponnesus. It was not a
statue, it was not a flag,
but three letters that in
Greek signify No: oxi. Men
thirsting for freedom had
written them among the
trees during the Nazi-Fascist
occupation, and for thirty
years that No had remained
there, unfaded by the sun
or rain." (Fallaci, Oriana,
Interview with history, as
quoted in *Women on War*.
New York: Touchstone,
1988, p. 302.)

Leaders who improve people's lives by changing public thought and action usually gain recognition of their efforts. Because there is often great risk or pain in speaking out publicly for beneficial changes, these leaders also gain respect. Rigoberta Menchu, for example, won the Nobel Peace Prize in 1992 for promoting social justice and reconciliation among ethnic and cultural groups in Latin America.

On a smaller scale, in your own city or county, you have probably admired at least one political, social, or religious leader who put aside personal comfort or special interests and successfully called for changes that helped the entire community. This leader was persuasive because he or she was an agent of change. You can become an agent of change in your community by applying well-established principles of persuasion to your own speaking.

In this chapter we explain the goal of persuasive speaking as seeking a change in the audience's attitudes and/or behavior. Persuasive speeches address themes of fact, conjecture, value, or policy—the same questions addressed in decision-making groups. As in informative speaking, audience analysis, organization, language, and delivery are important in persuasive speaking. In fact, persuasion requires the same types of supporting material as informative speaking. Using this material, persuaders build credibility appeals, emotional appeals, and rational appeals as instruments of change. The Focus on Leadership box describes the National Speaker's Association.

UNDERSTANDING THE PROCESS OF PERSUASION

Speaking to persuade means that you want your audience to change. The key term is **persuasive change**—a measurable difference in thought or action.

Change

We can define the process of persuasion in terms of the desired change the speaker seeks to bring about in his or her audience. At one extreme, change can result from coercion—or denial of choices to people. An armed terrorist coerces victims to obey by removing all options other than life or death. At the opposite extreme from coercion is compliance. After minimal effort by friends or loved ones—often mere looks or shrugs—a person may comply with their whims or wishes. In general, public speakers who use persuasion steer clear of both coercion and unthinking compliance. Instead, you should provide solid evidence so that listeners freely and consciously will make a decision about your message.

Discussion Question 18–1
Must one be a skilled persuader to be a leader? Are
leadership and persuasive
power synonymous?

To appreciate the process of persuasive change, recall the process of information we discussed in the previous chapter. We saw there that an audience

FOCUS ON LEADERSHIP

The National Speaker's Association

The National Speaker's Association (NSA) is a seventeen-year-old society of professional speakers and others who want to be professional speakers. With headquarters in Phoenix, Arizona, the NSA counts 3,700 members from every state and twelve foreign countries.

The association's stated purpose is to ensure a high standard of excellence in the profession of speaking and to promote professional speaking through

a belief in and adherence to the highest standard of ethics;

demonstrated professional competence;

a commitment to continued development of expertise and knowledge; and

a responsibility to clients and the profession.

Recently the NSA has awarded $2,000 scholarships to junior, senior, or graduate students majoring or minoring in speech or a directly related field. Among the criteria for the award is that the student be capable of leadership, with the potential to make a future impact using skills of oral communication.

will most likely retain information if the speaker has accurately gauged its relevance and usefulness to the audience. We also noted that the process of information involves a joint effort by speaker and audience. Similarly, the process of persuasion requires this joint effort. The persuasive speaker proposes a change that is beneficial to listeners, and then provides material to support the proposed change. For instance, as opposed to simply informing customers about the high quality of a car's construction, a salesperson might ask for a change in buying behavior by insisting on a quick decision about purchasing the car. In turn, the audience (in this case, the customer) ponders this persuasion when deciding whether to accept the change as beneficial, or actually make the proposed change. However, since persuasive speakers seek a change and not just recognition, understanding, or retention (stages in the process of information), the joint effort between speaker and audience becomes all the more crucial. In the case of the customers, for example, changing their position may ensure reliable transportation—or it may drive them into debt!

Current Research 18–1
Roger Ailes, communication advisor to U.S. presidents and corporate executives, summarizes the relationship between leadership and change in this way: "A successful communicator is prepared to go into any kind of communication process and change the flow of thought. This is control of the atmosphere through assertion of skill, personality, knowledge and belief, and through the energy of enthusiasm." (Ailes, Roger, *You Are the Message*. New York: Doubleday, 1989, p. 211.)

The Relationship Between Attitude and Behavior

Teaching Objective 18–2
Examine the relationships between attitudes, motives and behavior.

Recall that in Chapter 13 we described an **attitude** as a judgment based upon a person's belief about a given object or idea. **Behavior** involves *action* and *response* in addition to judgment or state of mind. This distinction is important in developing a persuasive speech. Remember that the investigation of attitudes is an important part of audience analysis. Attitudes are related to **motives**—which are the driving forces behind people's behavior. Changes in attitudes lead to changes in behavior. For example, a public health nurse can rely on patients to take their medicine after the nurse leaves if they believe that the medicine is vital to their health. A supervisor can depend on employees to use a new assembly method that they accepted as efficient and safe during a training session. If no relationship existed between attitudes and behaviors, then persuasion would become a much more complicated process than information. In fact, the public health nurse, the supervisor, and all other speakers would need to learn different methods for proposing changes in thought as opposed to action.

Cross-reference 18–1
Refer to the discussion of attitudes, motives, and beliefs in Chapter 2, "Perception and Communication."

Discussion Question 18–2
Which is easier to change—attitudes or behavior? Are both basically habits, one of thought and the other of action? Can they be changed all at once or must they be gradually unlearned?

In the following pages, you will read about techniques that assume informative and persuasive speaking are closely related. Persuasive speaking is not necessarily more complicated than informative speaking. The key difference is that while informative speakers seek to build audience comprehension or knowledge, persuasive speakers ask audiences to change. (See the Self-Assessment box.)

SELF-ASSESSMENT Planning Your Persuasive Goals

Visualizing the desired results of any persuasive speech as movement—sometimes a very slight movement—can help you determine your goal. Figure 18.1 illustrates the type of scale that you might use after analyzing an audience. This visualization shows that a persuasive speaker may ask listeners to change in two ways. They may change the *direction* of their attitudes, beliefs, or behaviors, or they may change the *degree* to which they feel committed to them. To visualize your persuasive goal, or movement toward your proposed change, you would initially mark the audience's favorable (+), neutral (0), or unfavorable (—) position regarding your subject on the scale. This mark would show the change that is needed. Using questionnaires and observation to measure audience response, you would then mark the audience position after your speech—drawing an arrow from the first mark to the second mark.

Persuasive direction refers to audience movement away from previously held attitudes or behavior. But avoid the trap of thinking that a significant change in direction occurs only when an audience has shifted its position dramatically on the scale. Adopting a neutral stance—moving from either "+" or "–" toward "0"—is meaningful if it reflects a decision by listeners to take a different position after they listen to you (see Figure 18.2). Consider, for example, the situation in which striking workers picket

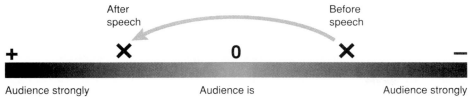

Figure 18.1
A Scale for Visualizing Persuasive Change.

a store and stop customers from entering it. If the store manager persuades workers to step aside and allow customers to enter the store, then a meaningful change in direction has occurred. The workers have been directed toward a neutral position toward customers—allowing them to support the strike or not, boycott the store or enter it.

Moving previously neutral or apathetic listeners toward a positive or negative position is also a meaningful change in direction. You make a measurable change in your friends by persuading them to support or to reject a candidate for political office when they previously cared very little about the election—one way or the other. These voters have been moved in a measurable, meaningful direction on the scale.

One persuasive speech is usually not enough to cause dramatic changes in an audience. In many instances, such as classroom speeches, you should interpret any measurable change in direction as meaningful. You may want to interpret changes in degree the same way.

Persuasive degree refers to the intensity of change in audience attitudes or behavior (see Figure 18.3). This change can be as significant as a change in direction. For example, you might move your friends to strongly favor a political candidate whom they had only supported weakly before your speech (their support has intensified). When workers stop picketing a store entirely at their employer's urging—instead of picketing only on sunny days—a meaningful change in persuasive degree has happened. Note that you have not affected the direction of the workers' attitudes— they still support the candidate—but you have changed the degree to which they support that candidate.

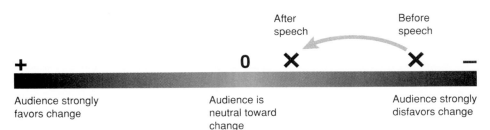

Figure 18.2
A Meaningful Change in Direction.

Although changes in attitude and behavior are related, they often reflect different persuasive degrees. It is sometimes easier to measure progress toward persuasive goals when an audience is asked to change its attitudes but not its behavior. For example, a minister may notice that members of the congregation enthusiastically nod their agreement with a sermon on the plight of abused women and children. But collection baskets may not show an increase in donations to a local shelter. Then again, people sometimes act in a way that suggests a greater degree of change in their attitude than has really happened. Without really changing a deeply negative attitude toward co-workers who have recently arrived from Asia, a person might refrain from using derogatory nicknames for these co-workers simply to avoid getting into trouble with the employer.

Classroom speeches and other brief speeches usually do not evoke more than a modest change in persuasive degree. Beyond the classroom, you may seek change in longer speeches or a campaign of speeches. In either setting, though, a visual scale is helpful in planning your persuasive goal. Rely on careful audience analysis to determine which persuasive degree is realistic.

Leadership Note 18–2
"There is only one way under High Heaven to get anybody to do anything. Did you ever stop to think of that? Yes, just one way. And that is by making the other person want to do it. Remember, there is no other way." (Carnegie, Dale, as quoted in Safire, William, and Safir, Leonard, *Leadership.* New York: Simon and Schuster, 1990, p. 149.)

Discussion Question 18–3
How much direction and degree of change is it realistic for a persuasive speaker to expect from one persuasive effort?

THEMES OF PERSUASION

In Chapter 11, we discussed the questions of fact, conjecture, value, and policy that are relevant to group decision making. When speaking persuasively, you ask listeners to reach decisions about one or more of these same questions (see Figure 18.4). These decisions are the responses that public speakers stress in their persuasive themes.

Fact

Resolving questions of fact in group communication requires decisions about what has happened or what is true in a given situation. A public speaker may also ask audiences to believe that something exists or does not exist or that

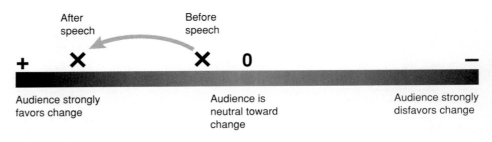

Figure 18.3
A Meaningful Change in Degree.

something is true or false. For example, one speaker might address the following theme: "Recent studies of the earth should alert us to the greenhouse effect—an alarming rise in global temperature." Another speaker might pose the following question: "Do factory closings, stock market declines, and trade imbalances mean that our economy is sinking?"

In addressing a factual theme, you should locate or visualize the audience's position on your subject as contrary to your own, or at least neutral. Otherwise you would not be seeking a change. For example, a speaker might try to persuade a skeptical, or at least uncaring, audience that alcohol abuse is involved in the majority of automobile accidents.

Several patterns of organization are useful, but the conventional, spatial, and temporal patterns of main points are most valuable in addressing a factual theme. In a speech about drinking and driving, the speaker could identify evidence of alcohol abuse in various types of accidents (conventional pattern), the alcohol-related accidents reported in each region of the country (spatial pattern), or the steady growth in alcohol-related accidents over the past twenty years (temporal pattern).

Effective speakers also address factual themes with concrete, specific words. For instance, instead of referring generally to "alcohol abuse," the speaker could specifically mention "drinking a six-pack of beer."

Persuasive themes of fact are different from informative themes because the speaker seeks *belief* in addition to understanding. Seeking a change of belief, though, does not mean that audience recognition and retention lose their value. Accordingly, the factual type of persuasive purpose demands attention to many of the features involved in achieving an informative purpose.

Conjecture

Just as in group decision making, conjecture might be thought of as "future fact." When speakers address a conjectural theme, they ask audiences to believe that something could exist, will exist, or might have existed. Sample themes

Teaching Objective 18–3
Reexamine the questions of fact, conjecture, value, and policy as themes in persuasion and consider the differences between them in terms of patterns of organization and what is expected of the audience.

Cross-reference 18–2
Previous discussion of questions of fact, conjecture, value, and policy can be found in Chapter 11, "Group Problem-Solving and Decision-Making."

Persuasive Themes

FACT	Audience might be asked to believe in the existence of police brutality, or the nature of local pollution problems.
CONJECTURE	Audience might be asked to believe in the possibility of alternative energy sources, or in future contact with extraterrestial life.
VALUE	Audience might be asked to judge the rightness of sending troops to a world trouble spot, or the acceptability of lying to protect a friend.
POLICY	Audience might be asked to commute with bicycles instead of cars, or eat less red meat.

Figure 18.4
Persuasive Themes.

Leadership Note 18–3
Harvey Milk, San Francisco city leader and city advocate, made this use of conjecture in a fund-raising speech not long before he was assassinated in 1978: "For all practical purposes, the eastern corridor from Boston to Newark will be one vast strip city. So will the area from Milwaukee to Gary, Indiana. In California, it will be that fertile crescent of asphalt and neon that stretches from Santa Barbara to San Diego. Will urban blight travel the arteries of the freeways? Of course it will—unless we stop it." (Milk, Harvey. A city of neighborhoods, in Ravitch, Diane, ed., *The American Reader: Words that Moved a Nation.* New York: HarperCollins, 1990, p. 356.)

include the following: "Could our governor be neglecting the state while preparing to run for the presidency?" "Oil spills will not be a danger in the future because tankers will be designed differently." "Might Cuba have remained an ally if Fidel Castro had not risen to power?"

Questions of future fact can only be answered tentatively. For example, listeners who are proud of their American heritage could be asked to believe that the United States will someday surrender its leadership in business and industry to foreign competitors.

Conventional, spatial, and temporal patterns of organization remain useful when addressing a conjectural theme, but the causal pattern of main points is also valuable. For instance, in a speech about business trends, you might address the types of business/industrial competition (conventional pattern), the leading sources of international competition (spatial pattern), or the historical decline of American business and industry (temporal pattern). You could also address the future effects of international competition (causal pattern).

Conjectural themes should be addressed in vivid language to help listeners look ahead in time. For example, future changes in business/industrial power could be described in detail so that listeners will appreciate the change from present levels of competition: "In the years ahead, when American business executives go abroad to beg for loans from foreign banks, they will see bustling factories, thriving shopping centers, and prosperous neighborhoods that used to be common at home."

Persuasive speeches on fact and conjecture share several features, although two different types of belief are sought. The other two persuasive themes, value and policy, require substantially different preparations.

Value

In Chapter 13 we defined *values* as general, enduring interpretations that people place on reality. As such, values are difficult to change. However, when values are applied to specific objects, people, or events, the resulting attitudes are particular and changeable. In addressing a persuasive theme of value, the speaker asks listeners to change their judgment of a particular subject. Most frequently, audiences are asked to judge the rightness or wrongness of a specific action or event. For example, a speaker might address the theme "Should employees report an employer's illegal business activities, even if it will cost them their jobs?" or the theme "Is it all right to lie about a relatively insignificant matter when the truth will embarrass you or your family?"

Change remains a crucial element in addressing themes of value. These themes should be used when the audience is undecided about the speaker's position—or opposed to it. For example, a speaker could ask homeowners to agree on the desirability of using property taxes to support both private and public schools.

All major patterns of organization are useful in addressing the persuasive theme of value. In the speech on public assistance to private schools, the problem-solving and causal patterns would be especially useful if listeners already knew the conventional uses of tax money, the places where private schools already receive tax support, and the history of dual school systems. Relying on the audience's interpretation of education as general, enduring value, the speaker could explain how tax support for private schools would solve the problem of overcrowded classrooms in public schools. Or the speaker could explain the limited curriculum and sports programs in many private schools as the effects of prohibiting tax support.

Effective speakers address themes of value with language that clearly expresses judgments—rather than simply describing facts. For instance, public assistance to private schools could be described as "fair and just" rather than as simply a matter of economics.

The persuasive theme of value calls for a judgment on rightness or acceptability, not a belief in fact or conjecture. All three responses, though, involve attitudes rather than behaviors. The final theme—policy—is distinctive because it calls for a definite *behavioral response*.

Policy

Whether in interpersonal, group, or public settings, people are constantly asking the question "What must we do?" In addressing a theme of policy, you should ask people to commit themselves to a specific action or refrain from a particular behavior. For example, a speaker might say, "Send a message to the local police that we must reduce crime on campus without violating civil rights," or might urge, "Volunteer now at the library to help eliminate illiteracy in our community."

The audience may already share your belief in a fact or conjecture, and no one may disagree about how values should be applied to a specific situation. Nonetheless, themes of policy should be addressed if audience analysis shows that listeners are doing little or nothing *to act on* their beliefs and judgments. For example, observing that students frequently tear out pages from library books because they either cannot afford the cost or won't take the time to photocopy, an officer in student government could ask for a reasonable amount of free photocopying from school authorities. The student government officer knows that many officials are aware of this problem; his or her task is to persuade them to act on their beliefs.

In most cases, the problem-solving pattern of organization is best suited to themes of policy. Other patterns can be used to develop subordinate points within the main problem-solving sequence. To advocate free photocopying, the speaker could discuss the history of mutilated library books and the financial causes of the problem (temporal and causal subpoints), and then outline a schedule for adopting the solution as well as ideal places for the needed machines (temporal and spatial subpoints).

Emphatic language is especially valuable in addressing policy. Since many audiences are agreeable but inactive, effective speakers use repetition and unusual schemes of language to audibly jar the audience and move it from thought to action. For instance, a speaker might advocate "Free copies for good students. Free copies for bad students. Free copies for all students."

Selecting one of the four themes discussed above is just as important as

Discussion Question 18–4
Which is easier—to convince someone of facts, probabilities, judgments, or needed actions?

planning your persuasive goal. Once you have properly set a goal, you can assess your need for persuasive appeals—the instruments of change.

■ USING PERSUASIVE APPEALS

Discussion Question 18–5
How could we measure the impact of a persuasive effort? When should we measure it? Would when we measured make a difference?

Whether they seek a change in direction or in degree, public speakers must prove the necessity or desirability of the change. At least from the time of Aristotle (384–322 B.C.), students of persuasion have analyzed proof from three perspectives: *credibility appeals*, or the impression created by the speaker; *emotional appeals*, or the feelings aroused in the audience; and *rational appeals*, or the argument within a speech (see Figure 18.5). Moreover, all three of these appeals are used in combination for the most effective persuasion.

Credibility Appeal

Teaching Objective 18–4
Emphasize the importance of credibility and describe the factors contributing to an audience's perception of speaker credibility.

Speakers use a **credibility appeal** when they present themselves to an audience as believable, ethical, and trustworthy. If we see a person as generally believable and ethical, then we tend to trust what that person says about a particular subject. If we have not already formed an impression of a speaker's credibility, then we must rely on our perceptions of him or her during the speech. Effective speakers establish their credibility early in their speeches.

Traditional theories of credibility address only the impression created during a speech. Today it makes just as much sense to account for the total impression created by a speaker—before and during a speech. But how do we form our impression of a speaker? Traditional theories hold that we judge whether a speaker seems knowledgeable, upright in character, and concerned about our welfare. These three elements—knowledge, character, and good will—have been analyzed extensively through the years and are primary factors in establishing credibility. Another element, "dynamism," has emerged from studies of image making in the mass media (see Boulding, 1961; and Boorstin, 1978). **Dynamism** refers to the energy, attractiveness, and amount of enthusiasm with which people present themselves. Dynamism is thus a means of enhancing the audience's response to the three other elements of credibility.

A speaker can use:

CREDIBILITY APPEALS	The knowledge, character, good will, and dynamism displayed by the speaker through words and deeds
EMOTIONAL APPEALS	The feelings aroused in the audience at appropriate times by careful choices of theme and language
RATIONAL APPEALS	The acceptability of a change as measured by a speaker's reasoning and evidence

Figure 18.5
Types of Persuasive Appeals.

conjecture, value, and policy suggests general guidelines on when to use an emotional appeal.

First, it is seldom appropriate to arouse the audience's feelings when addressing themes of fact or conjecture. Rather, factual examples and unvarnished statistics are useful. Imagine the confusion that could result if scientists or historians routinely asked colleagues to believe findings based on their feelings instead of their research. Past and present facts could be distorted instead of clarified. Future facts could be arbitrary guesses instead of careful estimates.

Second, emotional appeals should be used cautiously when addressing the theme of value. Efforts to change people's feelings toward social, political, and moral issues fall into this category of themes. However, using quotations from a person who is deeply committed to one side of a social movement, political protest, or moral cause can be troublesome unless you quote representatives from the other side. People invest their entire being—including their emotions—in personal values; speeches aimed at changing social, political, and moral attitudes derived from these personal values automatically arouse the audience's feelings. In many cases, the persuader will not be able to predict and manage these feelings.

Third, it is frequently appropriate—and even necessary—to address the audience's emotions when speaking on policy. You can confirm this guideline by recalling the times you have been asked to donate time or money to a worthwhile cause. Anecdotes about personal experiences under a new policy are often emotionally compelling. If you want your listeners to change their actions, then you should assist them in generating the emotional energy needed to pursue the new direction or degree of behavior. The proper timing of emotional appeals, regardless of persuasive theme, often depends on the human need being addressed.

Matching Emotional Appeals to Human Needs.   According to a theory proposed by Maslow (1970), human behavior is driven by five categories of needs that can be arranged in a hierarchy (see Figure 18.7). These categories, in ascending order, include physiological, safety, belongingness, self-esteem, and self-actualization need.

People fulfill **physiological needs** when they breathe, eat, drink, and attend to other basic requirements and urges. Unlike lower animals, however, we do not live by instinct. Anyone is capable of conscious self-denial—whether it is a hunger strike for political protest or holding one's breath in a tantrum. Because audiences have a choice, appeals to physiological needs can be used to either change audiences or help them resist change—to fulfill a need ("Buy bottled water…because you can never be sure what's coming out of your faucet") or postpone fulfillment for a worthy cause ("For the price of a pizza, you can provide a needy child with shoes for school").

Most **safety needs** are fulfilled after physiological needs have been met. We feel safe when we know where our next meal is coming from, where shelter can be found, and so on ("buy a freezer and take the guesswork out of planning your meals"). Survival is a struggle against the unknown. Once we no longer fear the unknown, we feel safe. Suggesting ways to achieve security can be very

Teaching Objective 18–5
Explore the premises and levels of Maslow's hierarchy of needs and examine ways that emotional appeals can be tied to these levels of need.

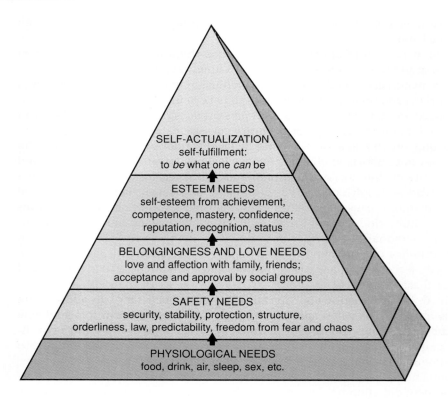

Figure 18.7
Hierarchy of Human
Needs.

Current Research 18–4
In his classic work on
human need, *Touching*,
scholar and writer Ashley
Montagu reported that,
during the 19th century,
half of all infants died from
a disease called "maras-
mus," which means "with-
ering away." Even in U.S.
orphanages as late as up to
around 1920, the death
rate for infants under a year
of age was nearly 100%.
These infants were fed, but
they were not touched;
researchers eventually
decided that the cause of
marasmus was a lack of
love. (Montagu, Ashley,
Touching. New York:
Harper & Row, 1971,
pp. 92–95.)

attractive to listeners who cherish an orderly, predictable existence ("Now is the best time to plan for your retirement").

People fulfill **belongingness needs** through group membership and inter-personal bonding. These urges are often called love needs. Once we feel our basic individual needs are fulfilled, we reach out to others in an effort to form circles of friends and, in most cases, smaller circles of loved ones ("Come to the company picnic to meet old friends and make some new ones"). Appeals to companionship and affection can move audiences to adopt new thoughts and actions that will relieve feelings of loneliness or isolation ("Cosmic Dating Service—meet someone who's out of this world").

Self-esteem needs drive people to develop positive self-images and to acquire social status. We want to feel confident about our place in the world, and we measure at least part of this confidence in terms of how highly other people regard us. Appeals to a sense of achievement and prestige are used com-monly in the type of advertising that teachers and scholars criticize as base or manipulative ("EuroSedan is for the discriminating driver"). As a speaker, you should appeal to self-esteem when it will move audiences to improve the human condition—not flatter personal vanity ("Everyone's a winner when you support the Special Olympics").

Few people succeed in fulfilling their **self-actualization needs**. Several years ago, a well-crafted advertisement challenged young people to "be all that you can be. . . . Join the Army." The same appeal could have been used to recruit future poets or chemical engineers since people want to fulfill their destinies, whatever they may be. This need is far less concrete than hunger or thirst, but it can be just as persuasive ("What do you want to be when you grow up? Let the Campus Placement Service help you decide.").

Maslow recognized that people also want to fulfill their curiosity and aesthetic needs, but these categories did not fit neatly into his hierarchy. Regardless of its incompleteness, though, Maslow's hierarchy is valuable to leading speakers for at least three reasons.

First, according to Maslow's estimates, the average person usually feels fulfilled about his or her needs in the following amounts:

self-actualization needs—10 percent
self-esteem needs—15 percent
belongingness and love needs—55 percent
safety needs—70 percent
physiological needs—85 percent

These estimates remain inexact but they suggest that you may generally expect audiences to feel more concerned about their self-esteem and self-actualization needs than about their physiological and safety needs. For example, you might define, explain, compare, or contrast, the social and personal fulfillment to be gained from a sensible diet and exercise program—rather than a decreased risk of serious illness.

Second, although research has not always supported this part of his theory, Maslow suggested that people may not respond to appeals directed at the top of the hierarchy unless the lower categories of needs have already been addressed. In other words, if people are hungry or fearful for their safety, then they may not pay attention to a speech about building self-esteem. A speaker should analyze audience needs in a particular area when preparing to address that subject persuasively. For example, even the most sincere testimonials from club members who have made new friends (thus satisfying their belongingness needs) may not be appealing to people who cannot afford to join the club.

Third, Maslow observed that each change in thought or action may result from a person's desire to fulfill several categories of needs. A speaker who plans otherwise would be ignoring the complex character of human audiences. In practical terms, the most effective speeches on physical fitness invite listeners to consider both tangible and intangible benefits. You might, for example, use numerical or statistical evidence to persuade listeners that they will "feel better" (physiological need), "look better" (belongingness need), and "achieve better" (self-actualization need) as a result of a sensible diet and exercise program.

Needless to say, emotional appeals are common in the advertisements and other persuasive communications you see and hear every day. Combined with a credible source, these appeals encourage audiences to "buy" ideas as well as products and services. Another persuasive appeal—rational appeal—also benefits from a credible source, but it offers an argument for the audience's judgment.

Discussion Question 18–9
Do you agree with Maslow's percentages? How would you assign them?

Rational Appeal

Teaching Objective 18–6
Describe what is meant by rational appeals and the nature of evidence. Contrast deductive versus inductive reasoning.

Persuaders do not argue with audiences in the popular sense of picking a fight. In fact, successful speakers are usually not seen by listeners as contrary or combative. Instead, these speakers rely on **rational appeal**—giving reasons or arguments for why an attitude or behavior is desirable or not, and supporting these reasons with evidence. In many cases, public speakers use rational appeals to show how they themselves came to believe a fact or conjecture, accept a value, or enact a policy. In this way, a speaker links personal credibility and emotional energy with reasonable attitudes and behaviors.

Types of Reasoning.   Reasoning takes two basic forms: deduction and induction. These two forms are the theoretical bases of all argument.

Deductive reasoning moves from a general point on which the speaker and audience already agree to a specific conclusion. Some scholars refer to variations in reasoning from the general to the specific as *arguments from generalization* and *arguments from cause*. When speakers argue from generalization, they begin by discussing a generally acceptable principle. ("Green space is desirable in choosing a place to live.") Then they ask the audience to accept a specific subject linked to that principle. ("This apartment complex has green space and therefore will be a desirable place to live.") When speakers argue from cause, they begin by identifying an observable influence. ("Polluting the environment causes a decline in the quality of life.") Then they ask the audience to accept a previously unnoticed effect. ("The city's excessive use of chemical fertilizer in public parks is gradually harming our daily lives.")

In deduction, a persuader begins by identifying a generally acceptable value or policy. Listeners might be reminded, for instance, that they have always supported economy in government. Then they are asked to include a more specific fact, conjecture, value, or policy within their general frame of acceptance. ("Closing military bases that are no longer vital to our nation's defense will save tax dollars.") Finally, the persuader recommends an attitude or behavior consistent with both the general and specific acceptance. ("Write your representatives and support the closing of underused military bases.")

Inductive reasoning moves from a specific point on which the speaker and audience already agree to an equally specific conclusion, or a more general one. Some scholars refer to variations in reasoning from a specific agreement to a specific conclusion as *arguments from specific instance, arguments from effect,* and *arguments from sign* (*arguments from analogy,* as the phrase suggests, are based on less directly related points of agreement). Arguments from specific instance are the reverse of arguments from generalization—the speaker reasons from a clearly supported and specific subject to the existence of a general principle (try reversing the argument about green space cited above). Arguments from effect similarly reverse the order in arguments from cause (again, try changing the argument about pollution cited above). Arguments from sign are related to the process of physical diagnosis used by your doctor: The doctor reasons that symptoms, or signs, such as fever and coughing, indicate that you have the flu. By analogy, a speaker might argue that our earth is suffering from the greenhouse effect because average annual temperatures are rising and the atmosphere is choked with dust and fumes.

In induction, a persuader begins by identifying a specific fact or conjecture. ("The seldom used military base near Smithville was closed at a savings of $30 million a year. Other useless bases near Jonesville and Johnson City were closed with annual savings of $20 million and $40 million.") Then the audience is asked to make a related and equally specific decision, or a more general decision, that reflects the desirability of the initial fact or conjecture. ("Urge your representative to vote in favor of closing the underused military base near Brown City" would call for an equally specific conclusion. "Let your representative know that you support economy in government by closing underused military bases" would call for a more general conclusion.)

Deductive and inductive reasoning are patterns or structures in which persuasive speakers develop arguments. However, reasoning is hollow without supporting evidence.

Types of Evidence. **Evidence** is the substance of persuasive reasoning by which you provide listeners with proof. Evidence is fashioned from the same five types of material—definition and explanation, quotation and paraphrase, comparison and analogy, example and illustration, and number and statistic—that we have already discussed in previous chapters. Until now, we have treated these five types of material as the means for supporting your answers to listeners' questions, such as "What do you mean?" or "How can we do it?" In persuasive speaking, though, you use these types of material (now being used as *evidence*) to prove your answer to a more crucial question in your listeners' minds: "*Why* should we change our attitude or behavior?"

Without evidence, there can be no reasoning. As you review the evidence that you prepare for a persuasive speech, consider whether the support for your reasoning is up to date and confirmed in at least one other, unbiased source.

Definition and Explanation. Persuasive speakers aim at a different goal than revealing the meanings of words. When using definitions and explanations, you prove that an agreement exists between yourself and your audience by defining or explaining it. Definition and explanation can also be used to argue that other evidence in your speech is relevant to your reasoning—that is, that it properly belongs in the same category as the decision you want listeners to make. Salespeople use this type of evidence all the time. They persuade customers that the cost of a camera, for example, is reasonable by explaining its quality features. Or they argue that a customer should buy a certain carpet because, by definition, its fiber and density is suited to the customer's needs.

Quotation and Paraphrase. The flavor of authority in quotations and paraphrases allows persuasive speakers to use this material as evidence. However, unlike the persuasive force of other types of evidence, the persuasive force of a quotation or paraphrase depends on other evidence—the credibility of its source. A prosecutor may quote an eyewitness as evidence that the defendant is guilty, but the evidence might fail if the witness were known to be a convicted criminal. As an argument, "Do unto others . . . " may be more persuasive if quoted from a biblical author rather than a popular cartoonist.

Discussion Question 18–10
Which type of reasoning do you find more powerful or convincing—moving from a general to a specific point of agreement, or vice versa?

Discussion Question 18–11
Which of these types of evidence do you believe is the most convincing?

Discussion Question 18–6
How would you rate your own credibility on the basis of your knowledge, character, general goodwill, and dynamism? Do you think we tend to assume most people are credible or that they are not?

Comparison and Analogy. Unlike informative speakers, persuasive speakers use comparison or analogy as evidence that a change is desirable because it is similar to what listeners have thought or done previously. Sometimes, you cannot define or explain precisely—or you do not wish to be precise. A comparison or contrast is the next best means of supporting a change. Social critics occasionally use this type of evidence to express their visions of an ideal society (for example, a "New Frontier" or "new world order")—visions that cannot be defined easily. Religious speakers, of course, frequently address faith and morals by contrasting the earthly and supernatural bases of decisions about these matters.

Example and Illustration. Examples and illustrations can be used as evidence that a proposed change is realistic, even if the audience has never experienced anything like it. Historical or contemporary evidence of beneficial results makes listeners feel confident about the decision they are being asked to make. For instance, a business consultant who is aware that Mr. Smith has never used laser printing before argues that he will like it because all of the consultant's other clients have been pleased with documents that were laser printed.

Number and Statistic. When evidence must be very precise in order to sustain an argument, numerical or statistical material is valuable. But recall from Chapter 17 that numbers and statistics frequently require further explanation. For example, a health care professional may use a blood pressure of 210/120, a pulse rate of 90, and other measurements as evidence of the patient's need for a particular treatment. However, these numbers are often far less persuasive to the patients themselves. They need an explanation of why the numbers "add up" to general health problems. The Mastering Communication Skills box discusses fallacies in evidence.

MASTERING COMMUNICATION SKILLS

Spotting Fallacies in Your Evidence

Fallacies are flaws in the way evidence is used in an argument. Fallacies are not always intentional, but speakers remain responsible for these flaws. To check your own use of evidence, be wary of the following flaws.

Equivocation and *half-truth* are fallacies in the use of definition and explanation. A definition is an equivocation when it fails to clear up ambiguity. A salesperson may argue equivocally when stating that a particular camera should be purchased because it is "imported." "Imported" could mean that the item came from any number of countries other than those that are noted for quality goods. An explanation is a half-truth when it ignores "the rest of the story." It is a half-truth to state that a particular carpet fiber is best suited to a customer's needs when the salesperson knows that it is durable but does not clean well.

The *either/or fallacy* and *faulty analogy* are flaws in the use of comparison and analogy. The either/or fallacy suggests that only two contrasting positions are realistic. When confronted with a contrast such as "Either love this country or leave it," listeners are asked to decide between unrealistically limited options. All analogies are faulty to some degree, so persua sive speakers should be careful in how they use this type of supporting material. For instance, using an analogy between people's marriages and corporate mergers would be especially faulty if the speaker intended to compare depth of feeling in each case.

Flaws in the use of example and illustration lead to *faulty generalization*. Despite the detail or vividness in an example, it might not support a broad conclusion. Other people's success with a product might not be sufficient support for your success if the other people have peculiar needs or standards that are different from your own.

The misuse of quotations often leads to a fallacy called *begging the question*. If a speaker quotes a source who is not trustworthy or not an authority, then the question of whether a proposed change is desirable remains unanswered (or "begged"). "Your Honor, in view of the (twice-convicted) witness's testimony, all charges against the defendant should be dismissed" is an example of begging the question.

In addition to faulty generalization, flaws in the use of number and statistic can lead to a *red herring*. This colorful phrase refers to the old trick of dragging a smelly fish across the trail left by an animal so that pursuing hounds lose the scent. One kind of red herring is an irrelevant issue. Another kind is a confusing mass of unnecessarily technical information; for instance, if numerical data become so complex that only mathematics majors can follow the argument, then other listeners will lose their way in evaluating the supporting material. "Sixty-two percent of the 175 patients who had blood pressures between 195/90 and 265/110 in the thirteen hospitals surveyed benefited from a three-fourths cut in the amount of their carbohydrate intake" is an example of the second kind of red herring.

One dynamic way to appreciate the various types of reasoning and evidence is to analyze both sides of a lively debate. In the following example, Timothy B. Dyk, a media lawyer, and U.S. Bankruptcy Judge Bernice Donald debate the question, "Should Supreme Court Proceedings Be Televised?"

YES: Timothy Dyk

Numbers and examples as evidence

1. Forty-four states have eliminated the blanket ban on cameras in their courts. The president, the House, and now the Senate appear on television. But the Supreme Court is still seen only by that miniscule portion of the public that can fit into the Court's 150 public seats. The long, slow waiting lines attest to the unsatisfied demand. At important arguments even members of the bar have had to wait, as I have done twice this term. The other federal courts also remain closed to cameras.

Credibility appeal

2. On Nov. 21, [1988], the Supreme Court authorized a group of news organizations to use the courtroom for a demonstration of the technology available for coverage of arguments, and three justices attended. Whether the Court's policy will change in the near future is not certain; my view is that it should.

Theme of policy

3. Historically, and since [the case of] *Richmond Newspapers,* as a matter of constitutional law, the press, as surrogate for the public, has enjoyed a right to attend criminal trials, and it is generally accepted that the right should extend to other court proceedings. Press coverage, though often imperfect, is viewed as indispensable to fairness and the education of the public. The same interests support the admission of cameras.

Deductive reasoning

4. The Court's decisions affect all of us, but surveys show that it is one of the least understood features of modern American government. Camera coverage is all the more important since television is, for many, a primary news source.

5. Why, then, ban cameras? Four arguments are usually advanced. Not surprisingly, I find none persuasive.

6. First, it is urged that camera coverage is disruptive. In our demonstrations we attempted to show that cameras are unobtrusive, can operate in normal light, can use the Court's existing sound system, and will not encroach on the seating for members of the bar or the public.

Example as evidence

7. Second, it is suggested that participants in the proceedings would be adversely affected. The Court in *Chandler* found no such adverse effect even in criminal trials, and the effects seem even less likely at the appellate level. I don't believe that the bar or the justices themselves would be inhibited or seek to become television personalities, and the experience with cameras in state appellate arguments supports this view.

Paraphrase as evidence

8. Third, it is urged that public knowledge will not be increased either because broadcasters won't cover the Court, or the public won't watch. No one is claiming that the Court will achieve Super-Bowl ratings or that broadcasters will routinely pre-empt their daytime schedules for Court arguments. But, like the House and Senate debates, Court arguments will be on C-Span or another cable channel for those who want to watch. The mass audience will see those few landmark cases such as *Brown v. Board of Education*, the Pentagon Papers case, and *U.S. v. Nixon*—and it will see excerpts from others.

Comparison as evidence

9. The Court itself appears to recognize that brief exposure to the Court has value, because it maintains a separate "three-minute" line for members of the public. Just as the public learns by seeing the

Comparison as evidence

Court in person for brief periods, the public would surely learn by seeing the actual proceedings rather than a secondhand summary.

Emotional appeal

Credibility appeal

10. Finally, it is said that seeing the Court on television will dissipate its mystique, undermining its authority. I think the opposite is true. I am not arguing that the confidentiality of the Court's inner workings is unimportant; it is critical. I do urge that broader knowledge of the Court's *public* proceedings will lead to greater understanding and support for the process. I find it difficult to believe that the Supreme Court, one of the glories of our American democracy, depends for its authority on a lack of public understanding of what it does.

11. I suggest that the real issue will arise a few years after coverage is allowed: What were we arguing about so heatedly, and how did we do without television for so long?

NO: Bernice Donald

Emotional appeal

1. The Supreme Court is the highest court in the land. As the final forum for appeal, it decides issues that are fundamental to our existence. For over 200 years, the Court has handed down written decisions, and attorneys have argued and responded to questions of the justices, unmolested by the unblinking eye of the camera. Any argument for change must be compelling.

Theme of policy

2. While there has been substantial relaxation of rules against cameras in the courtroom (primarily on policy grounds), some of the initial objections are still valid today:

3. Cameras may have a prejudicial effect on juries. This is supported by reports showing that televised trials put undue psychological pressure on jurors.

Inductive reasoning

4. Cameras may place an increased burden on the trial judge, who must protect the right to a fair trial, while policing the press.

Emotional appeal

5. Cameras may cause a chilling effect by deterring witnesses who are intimidated by cameras or who simply do not want to be filmed.

Example as evidence

6. Furthermore, some witnesses will watch television and later alter their testimony to conform to what's in the record. This tends to moot the effect of witness sequestration.

7. Finally, courts must be mindful of the harmful effect that cameras have on the defendant, and on the defendant's lawyer. Some lawyers have reported that cameras put tremendous pressure on them and hamper their efforts to argue effectively. Lawyers also fear that highly sensitive microphones could greatly inhibit attorney-client communications.

Example as evidence

Quotation as evidence

8. The Supreme Court acknowledged in *Estes v. Texas* (381 U.S. 532 [1965]), "We are all self-conscious and uneasy when being televised. Human nature being what it is . . . a juror's mind will be preoccupied with the telecasting rather than the testimony."

Paraphrase as evidence

9. Proponents also suggest that there is no justification for denying cameras at appellate levels, since there are no juries, and presumably only the most capable advocates participate at this level. They contend that the problems of bias and fair trials do not apply here and that televised arguments will provide an excellent learning tool for the bench, the bar, and law schools.

10. At the Supreme Court level, however, the stakes are much too high to work up demonstration films for law schools or bar groups. An attorney who goes to argue before the Supreme Court does not consent to having his argument panned across the country, to have it dissected and criticized by overzealous law professors. Even though the Supreme Court is public, such contemplated use goes beyond that which a lawyer reasonbly anticipates and consents to when he enters those hallowed halls. Furthermore, a lawyer has a reasonable expectation that his performance in the Court will be private.

Deductive reasoning

Indirect credibility appeal

11. Cameras in the courtroom are not conducive to the type of sobering, deliberate, reflective thinking that is the cornerstone of judicial proceedings. Even though this arguably may be less valid at the Supreme Court level since the parties must submit written briefs and have limited time for oral arguments, cameras may inhibit the free-flowing dialogue between justices and counsel that is essential to the process, even though it does not work its way into the final opinion.

12. The Court has spoken through its written opinions. Its deliberation process—the internal debate, tentative positions taken by justices, preliminary notes, drafts of opinions, negotiations, confrontations and compromises—all have been out of public view.

Emotional appeal

13. It is a system designed to preserve and protect the integrity and independence of the judiciary. A move to allow cameras access to the oral arguments will inevitably lead to a demand for access at every stage of the process. The right of the public to know must never overshadow the need for a strong judiciary, and the integrity of the process must be vigilantly safeguarded.

(Reprinted with permission from the March 1989 issue of the *ABA Journal*, the Lawyer's Magazine, published by the American Bar Association.)

The debaters address an action to be taken (a theme of policy): "Should Supreme Court Proceedings Be Televised?" Attorney Timothy Dyk's statements indicate that he has planned to move the audience from a neutral position toward one favoring his proposed change. He quickly establishes his knowledge in the first paragraph, citing his personal experience. Later, in paragraph 10, he implies his character and good will by endorsing public understanding of the Supreme Court, "one of the glories of American democracy." Dyk's emotional appeal—based on safety needs associated with law and order—is clear. He reasons inductively in paragraphs 1 and 2, where the specific policies of forty-one states and a recent Supreme Court demonstration in support of televised proceedings are cited. For the most part, though, Dyk's reasoning is deductive; he argues that televising the Supreme Court fits within the general, constitutional right of the public to attend court proceedings. In paragraphs 3 and 4, the speaker uses definitions—of legal precedent, of prevailing opinion, of the primacy of television as a source of news—to support cameras in the Court. After reasserting his point of view in paragraph 5, Dyk then cites other evidence (in paragraphs 6–10), including examples from a courtroom demonstration, a paraphrase of findings in the *Chandler* case, and several comparisons between televised court proceedings and other programs.

Judge Bernice Donald's statements indicate that she has planned to strengthen the audience's existing agreement with her position. (Under the rules of debate, Judge Donald is entitled to this position—called *presumption*—because she is not advocating change. In contrast, Dyk holds the "burden of proof" because he supports a change.) Consistent with her professional status, Judge Donald makes no direct references to her credibility. Instead, she skillfully speaks of the "sobering, deliberate, reflective thinking" typical of all judges (paragraph 11). Appealing to safety needs, she addresses issues of "existence" (paragraph 1) and protection (paragraphs 4 and 13). Like her opponent, Judge Donald reasons both inductively and deductively. First, she cites specific instances in which televised trials have harmed or at least worried judges, jurors, and lawyers (paragraphs 3–7). Then she cites the general expectations of lawyers and judges that specifically support a ban on television (paragraphs 10–11). Throughout her statement, Judge Donald uses examples (the generally "valid" objections to having cameras in courtrooms cited in paragraphs 2–7) as well as quotations and paraphrase (the Supreme Court case cited in paragraph 8 and the paraphrase of suggestions by "proponents" in paragraph 9). In later paragraphs, she relies on comparisons and contrasts.

Regardless of how you may personally feel about televising the Supreme Court, you should recognize how the debaters in this example use certain types of appeals to address the theme and reach their persuasive goals.

Summary

Persuasive speaking seeks change. The process of change is best understood in relation to the similar process of information: Both informative and persuasive change rely on thoughtful audience analysis and appropriate supporting material. Whether addressing listeners' attitudes or behaviors, effective speakers visualize a goal of movement in direction and degree. This measurement of movement reminds you of the type and amount of change that you are asking of your audience.

In addition, an accurate analysis of persuasive theme alerts speakers to the most suitable organization and style. When addressing themes of fact ("what is"), speakers should consider the benefits of using conventional, spatial, and temporal organization. Themes of conjecture ("what will be") can be addressed by using causal organization. Themes of fact are best expressed in concrete, specific words, while themes of conjecture require vivid, detailed descriptions. Any of the five major patterns of organization are suitable to a theme of value ("what should be"), but the speaker's language should express judgments. Finally, when addressing a theme of policy ("what must be done"), problem-solving organization and emphatic style are especially suitable.

Public speakers use three persuasive appeals: credibility appeals, emotional appeals, and rational appeals. Credibility is achieved in four ways: (1) providing examples of the speaker's knowledge (or borrowing knowledge by quoting an expert); (2) providing comparative support for the speaker's character; (3) explaining the speaker's good will; and (4) enhancing the presentation with dynamic delivery.

Emotional appeal is achieved by linking the persuasive theme with an appropriate feeling or mood in the audience. Persuaders commonly establish this link by addressing one or more needs that the audience wants to fulfill: physiological, safety, belongingness, esteem, or self-actualization needs.

Rational appeal requires attention to the types of reasoning (or argument) and evidence. Speakers may argue from the general to the specific (deductive reasoning) or argue from the specific to either an equally specific conclusion or a more general one (inductive reasoning). In either case, the speaker draws persuasive evidence from the five major types of supporting material: definition and explanation, quotation and paraphrase, comparison and analogy, example and illustration, and number and statistic.

■ Exercises

1. For each of the following subjects, compose four separate themes that address fact, conjecture, value, and policy. For example, a theme of fact could state that "computer theft did not exist before the 1970s"; a theme of conjecture could state that "computer theft will account for the majority of thefts by the year 2010"; a theme of value could state that "computer theft is a more serious crime than robbery"; and a theme of policy could state that "we must elect representatives who will sponsor tough criminal laws against computer theft."

   Computer Theft
   The Role of Teachers in a Democratic Society
   Photography as Art
   The Rights of Drug Abusers
   Efficiency on the Job

Compare your themes with those composed by three or four other people. Discuss the directions and degrees of change that would be needed if a persuader were to address your group about the themes. You may want to prepare several copies of a "visualization scale" so that your group can show what changes in direction and degree would be meaningful.

2. Take a moment to recall three or four people you consider believable and trustworthy. What is it about these people that has made them credible to you? If you dislike exercises that require memory, then watch a typical "courtroom" scene in a soap opera or motion picture and analyze the credibility of one or more of the witnesses. Which elements were credible—Knowledge? Character? Good will? Dynamism? Which evidence clearly revealed credibility, or lack of it?

3. Compare your feelings with those of others about the following subjects:

> Beauty Pageants
> Big Business
> Salaries of Professional Athletes
> Competency of Teachers
> Medical Ethics

Discuss how many different emotions are attached to the five subjects. Which types of needs, as defined in Maslow's hierarchy, are related to each of the subjects?

4. Patrick Henry is famous for a Revolutionary War speech in which he declared, "Give me liberty, or give me death." In terms of emotional appeal, why would it be inappropriate to declare, "Give me a healthy lawn or give me death"? What about the declaration "Give me open access to government secrets or give me death"? Can you think of other famous quotations that if reworded slightly, would make their emotional appeals inappropriate—or even humorous? Consider the following common but significant statement by one person to another: "You mean more to me than _____." Can you fill in the blank with a word or phrase that would elicit an appropriate emotion? An inappropriate emotion?

5. Collect three different editorials from newspapers or magazines. Outline the types of reasoning and evidence used in each editorial. Does the reasoning reveal the editor's estimate of readers' attitudes toward the subject? For example, does the editor assume that readers generally agree on a value or policy? Does the editor favor one type of evidence? Which type(s) of evidence would you have used?

514   *Mastering Public Communication*

**Related
Readings**

Bailey, F. G. (1983). *The tactical uses of passion*. Ithaca, NY: Cornell University
Press.

The author examines the necessary relationship between emotion and reason in
persuasion. Before concluding his book, Bailey illustrates how rules for emotional
appeal can be extracted from several examples of actual political argument.

Thompson, W. N. (1975). *The process of persuasion: Principles and readings*.
New York: Harper & Row.

This book includes a collection of well-regarded essays that treat persuasion as a
process or movement. Thompson also comments thoughtfully on the principles
addressed within the essays.

Weddle, P. (1978). *Argument—A guide to critical thinking*. New York: McGraw-
Hill.

This brief, paperback book examines important issues in reasoning and argument.
The problem of fallacy receives especially clear, concise treatment.

Glossary

Accommodation decision making   A family decision making technique in which some family members concede to the wishes of others. "Majority rules" is one example.

Acculturation   A method individuals use when crossing cultural boundaries. Acculturation involves trying to fit in, to the extent of becoming a member of the new culture, no longer identifying with one's culture of origin.

Acquired traits   Any characteristics an individual takes on and develops.

Active voice   Use of verbs other than forms of the verb *to be*, to make spoken language lively and dynamic.

Actor-observer difference (in causal attributions)   The tendency to judge another person's actions as a consequence of his or her underlying personality, and a corresponding tendency to attribute one's own behavior to external causal forces.

Adaptors   Individual movements that people adopt because the particular behavior(s) tend to gratify some sense of who they are, of what they are doing, or of how best they relate to one another.

Affect displays   Movements of the face and body that serve to reveal an emotional state.

Agenda   A listing of points or topics in the order in which they are to be taken up in a meeting.

Alliteration   Figure of speech in which the speaker uses a series of words beginning with the same consonant sound.

Altercasting   Attempts to manage another's identity; a communicative strategy used to negotiate identities and the social rights and responsibilities that correspond to them.

Analogy   Type of supporting material that points out the not-so-obvious similarities among objects, qualities, or actions of different classes.

Anaphora   Figure of speech in which successive statements or sentences begin with the same words.

Anecdote   Type of supporting material that makes subject matter realistic and present by referring humorously or poignantly, as well as in detail, to a case.

Antithesis   Figure of speech in which two ideas are contrasted through the use of parallel language.

Anxiety   A type of arousal of uncertain origin.

Articulation   Quality of vocal delivery in which sounds are produced distinctly and crisply.

Artifacts   Objects we wear or manipulate that have an impact on our appearance or others' impressions of us.

Assimilation effect   A type of distortion in which one perceives the position expressed in a message as closer to one's own than it actually is.

Attitudes   Judgments built upon beliefs that a given object is good, bad, or neither, and should be accepted or rejected; the inclination a person has to evaluate objects of perception favorably or unfavorably.

Attribution training   A method of intercultural communication training. This method focuses on helping trainees understand the intentions of people from another culture.

Audience analysis   Investigation of listeners' characteristics, including demographic variables, such as age, gender, education, and income, and audience beliefs, values, attitudes, and motives.

Audio-visual aids   Devices for enhancing or amplifying types of supporting material.

Beliefs   Opinions, feelings, or viewpoints about what is true, good, or desirable, and the opposites of these.

Belongingness needs   Requirements and urges, such as group membership and interpersonal bonding, that are addressed in emotional appeals.

Bipolar question   Special type of closed question that restricts the respondent to selecting one of two choices.

Brainstorming   A process of generating possible solutions to a problem as rapidly as possible without consideration of their strengths and weaknesses.

Bypassing   A language-related problem that occurs when people fail to share the same connection between a word and what it stands for (its referent).

Card catalog   Library filing system that lists printed materials by author, title, and subject.

Cathartic communication   Communication to share information in order to elicit emotional support and understanding.

Causal pattern of organization   System of organizing speeches according to a sequence of stimulus and response.

Character   One component of a speaker's credibility appeal, based on perceived integrity, consistency, and similarity to the audience.

Chauvinistic   A method individuals use when crossing cultural boundaries. This approach involves rejecting the norms of the new culture, and strongly embracing one's culture of origin.

Chronemics   The study of how humans structure and use time.

Clear language   Use of specific words that identify the people, objects, or ideas being addressed.

Climate   The psychological atmosphere that surrounds a group.

Closed question   Question used in interview context that limits the responses an interviewee can give.

Cognitive-behavior modification   A method of intercultural communication training. Trainees are asked to identify things they find rewarding or punishing. Then they are told how to seek these rewards and punishments in the host culture.

Communication   The purposeful production and transmission of a message by a person to one or more other persons.

Communication appropriateness   The extent to which communicative behavior reflects verbal sensitivity and is suited to the relational and situational context of the interaction.

Communication competence   The ability to communicate in a personally effective and socially appropriate manner.

Communication effectiveness   The ability to accomplish interactional goals through communicative behavior.

Comparison   Type of supporting material that points out the obvious similarities among objects, qualities, or actions of the same general class.

Confirming response   Interpersonal response that acknowledges the value of an individual.

Conflict   An expressed struggle between at least two interdependent parties who perceive incompatible goals, scarce resources, and interference from the other party in achieving their goals.

Connotative meaning   The rich personal definition brought to a word that includes all the examples, emotions, and associations that individuals attach to it.

Consensus decision making   A family decision making technique that requires unanimous agreement among all family members.

Consistency   The degree to which a message is free of contradictions.

Contingency theory   A formalization of the situational perspective on leadership, which develops the proposition that the effectiveness of a leader's style depends directly on the characteristics of the situation in which leadership is being exercised.

Contrast   Type of supporting material that points out the obvious differences among objects, qualities, or actions of the same general class.

Contrast effect   A type of distortion in which one perceives the position expressed in a message as further from one's own that it actually is.

Control   Messages used by parents (threats of punishment, lecturing, revoking privileges) which show disapproval of a child's behavior. These messages make the child feel uncomfortable and more dependent on the parent.

Conventional pattern of organization   System of organizing speeches according to basic parts or functions of a subject that are commonly spoken of together.

Conventional problem solving   A systematic set of steps in which a group (1) identifies the problem to be solved, (2) establishes criteria for evaluating solutions, (3) generates possible solutions, (4) examines each solution in relation to the criteria, and (5) selects the solution that best satisfies the criteria.

Conversation Informal, everyday talk; used to discover speech material.

Coordination Quality of speech organization that is achieved when elements of equal importance are emphasized equally.

Creative problem solving Any process in which group members attempt to identify as many different and imaginative solutions as they can for an acknowledged or established problem.

Credibility appeal Perception of speaker as believable, ethical, and trustworthy.

Criterion A factor to be considered in making assessments.

Critical thinking A process by which one makes inferences about the believability of message content.

Cultural awareness training A method of intercultural communication training. Emphasis is placed on helping trainees understand how the features of any culture influence the social interaction of people.

Cultural-level knowledge The shared knowledge that members of a culture possess.

Cultural stereotype A fixed view of a group of people, united by some common characteristics, that disregards differences among the members.

Culture A system of shared knowledge, beliefs, values and symbols that unite and define a group of people.

Culture shock The failure to adjust to a different culture, that results from the loss of expected cultural routines and social anchors (like how and when to give tips).

Decision making The act of choosing among alternatives.

Decoding A mental process by which one assigns meanings to messages and determines what the message producer presumably intends to say.

Deductive reasoning Argument toward a specific conclusion from a general point on which the speaker and audience already agree.

De facto decision making A family decision making technique which results from a stalemate. The failure to reach a shared decision often has consequences (another party buys the used car the family considered buying) and therefore becomes a decision itself.

Definition Type of supporting material that reveals the meaning of words.

Deliberate ambiguity A tendency to be vague when clarity might elicit a negative reaction.

Demonstration Informative goal in which a speaker helps listeners learn how to do something.

Denotative meaning The official meaning of a word; the meaning that appears in a dictionary.

Description Informative goal in which a speaker provides listeners with a mental image of subject matter.

Designated leader The person who is specifically named to play the leadership role in a group.

Dialect Language used in a restricted area of the country.

Diction Choice of words, especially with regard to correctness, clarity, or effectiveness.

Directive interview Interview in which the interviewer exerts strong control.

Disconfirming response Interpersonal response that fails to acknowledge the value of an individual.

Doublespeak The deliberate misuse of language to deceive.

Dynamism One component of a speaker's credibility appeal, based on perceived energy, attractiveness, and amount of enthusiasm in delivery.

Ego-involvement The strength of one's interest in or belief about some matter.

Egocentric listening Listening in which the message receiver concentrates more on him- or herself than on the incoming message.

Electronic data bases Information stored on magnetic disks for use in computers that is similar to the printed resources in libraries.

Emblems Visual movements that can be directly translated into verbal equivalents.

Emergent leader An individual who fulfills the functions of leadership without being asked or expected to do so and later achieves recognition for his or her contributions.

Emotional appeal A speaker's encouragement of the audience to experience particular feelings in relation to selected speech material.

Empathy The ability to understand another person's behavior from that person's perspective.

Employment (job-entry) interview Interview used to screen prospective employees for job openings, as well as to present the company in a good light to job applicants.

Encoding The translation of thoughts into words and other types of symbolic expression that enable others to understand what the source of a message wants them to know, think, feel, believe, or do.

Epistrophe   Figure of speech in which successive statements or sentences end with the same words.

Ethical communication   The display of appropriate sensitivity to the well-being of those to whom messages are directed.

Ethnocentrism   The tendency to judge other cultures, or members of other cultures, using your own cultural values.

Euphemism   An inoffensive word or phrase that is used in place of a term that people may find too explicit or tactless.

Euphuism   Figure of speech in which the speaker uses a series of words having the same vowel sound.

Evaluative listening   Listening while thinking critically.

Evidence   Substance of persuasive reasoning by which a speaker offers proof to the audience.

Example   Type of supporting material that makes subject matter realistic and present by briefly referring to an actual or hypothetical case.

Exit interview   Interview conducted when an employee leaves the firm; feedback on the concerns or difficulties that may have precipitated the exit is sought by the interviewer for later constructive use by the organization.

Experiential learning   A method of intercultural communication training. Role playing and other methods are used to help trainees experience features of life in the host country.

Expertise   A form of family power that can be used if the person attempting to exert the power is viewed as knowledgeable, or an expert on a topic.

Explanation   Type of supporting material that reveals the meaning of ideas.

Extemporaneous delivery   Type of presentation that is used when a speech's purpose and organization are carefully planned but exact wording is adapted to the audience and occasion.

Extended family   A family broadly defined through biological and legal ties. This might include aunts, uncles, in-laws, and grandparents. It extends beyond the basic nuclear family consisting of parents and their immediate offspring.

Face   The positive sense of social worth that a person claims for him- or herself.

Facial expressions   Element of physical delivery in which the speaker uses face and eyes in concert with a message.

Fact   Deed or event whose truth or accuracy may be acceptable to an audience because the fact can be confirmed.

Fact-inference confusion   A language-related problem that occurs because we cannot determine from language alone whether a speaker is describing a direct experience or stating an inference drawn from assorted information.

Fallacies   Flaws in the way evidence is used in an argument.

False impressions   Process in which listeners jump to conclusions about the relevance or significance of information after having recognized it on their own.

Family   A social unit which typically functions to provide affective and economic support for its members. Families are not easily defined through biological and legal boundaries alone. A family may be any group that defines itself as a family and whose members play the necessary roles.

Feedback   A special type of message revealing a person's reactions to what another person has said.

Fidelity   The correspondence between what a message producer has in mind and what a message recipient understands that person to have in mind.

Flexible grammar   Use of language in speaking that is considered inappropriate in formal writing, such as sentence fragments and contractions.

Function   Anything an individual or group does that has a consequence.

Fundamental attribution error   The tendency to misassign intentions to others' behavior.

Generation   The set of mental operations by which a communicator thinks about what he or she is going to say or wishes to say.

Gesture   Element of physical delivery in which the speaker uses head, arms, and hands in concert with a message.

Goal   The end state a group seeks to achieve.

Good will   One component of a speaker's credibility appeal, based on perceived interest in the audience's welfare.

Government documents   Library materials published by federal, state, and other political agencies that identify and explain new policies, laws, and programs.

Grievance interview   Interview used by employees to level complaints to the proper authorities in the firm in hopes of having the grievance settled.

Group   A collection of two or more individuals who share information and exchange ideas to achieve a common goal.

Group-centered style   The manner of behavior of a group leader who invites participation, guides discussion, asks for reactions to input, abides by the will of the majority, and seeks consensus for decisions and actions to be taken.

Gunnysacking The tendency to build up a store of unresolved issues as a result of avoiding confrontation; results in a deferred and inappropriate burst of anger in which the issues are brought up.

Haptics Messages associated with or conveyed by touch.

Hearing The physiological process of picking up outside acoustical energy through the ear and transmitting it to the brain.

Identification A form of power which may be used in the family. This form of power can be exerted if one family member admires another. The admirer is likely to do the bidding of the other.

Illustration Type of supporting material that makes subject matter realistic and present by referring in detail to an actual or hypothetical case.

Illustrators Movements that help describe or clarify what is being said in the verbal (symbolic) message.

Impromptu delivery Unplanned type of presentation that is used when the purpose or organization of a speech cannot be determined in advance or when unanticipated events occur.

Independent marital types One type of marital relationship, in which couples reject rigid male-female sex roles. These couples are more open to uncertainty and change when compared to other married couples.

Individualism-collectivism One dimension along with cultures vary. Individualistic cultures emphasize the importance of personal achievement, whereas collectivist cultures place a high premium on shared, group accomplishment.

Inductive reasoning Argument toward a specific or general conclusion from a specific point on which the speaker and audience already agree.

Information-based intercultural training A method of intercultural communication training. This classroom approach provides trainees with information about host culture (norms, the economy, daily routines, decision-making styles).

Information-gathering interview Interview used to collect information that will later be compiled and distributed to others in the form of reports, stories, research papers, or speeches.

Informative communication Communication to exchange information.

Intensional orientation The tendency to treat labels or words as real.

Interaction training A method of intercultural communication training. In a relaxed, non-threatening setting, trainees are able to interact with people from the host culture and people who have traveled through the host culture.

Intercultural communication Communication between members of different cultures or subcultures. To be intercultural, the communication event must be influenced by the cultural differences between the interactants.

Interpersonal communication (contextual definition) Communication in which (1) few participants are involved; (2) interactants are in close proximity to each other; (3) interactants can see, hear, touch, and smell each other; and (4) immediate feedback is available.

Interpersonal communication (developmental definition) Communication in which people interact over an extended period of time, and in which the interaction is adapted to the other as a unique individual, rather than communication in which actors play out well-defined roles, such as waiter and customer.

Interpersonal sensitivity Perceptiveness and awareness of how to act toward others in given situations.

Interpretation Informative goal in which a speaker makes subject matter simple and familiar to listeners.

Interview A process of two-way communication with a predetermined and serious purpose designed to interchange behavior and involving the asking and answering of questions.

Intimate distance The amount of distance typically maintained in communication—generally ranging from zero to eighteen inches—by those who are emotionally close.

Jargon Technical or professional language of a special field of activity that is often not understood by people outside that specialty.

Kinesics All body movement, other than touch, used to communicate. This would include gestures, eye contact, facial expressions, posture, and movement.

Knowledge One component of a speaker's credibility appeal, based on words and deeds that reflect maturity and intelligence.

Labeling The process by which individuals develop a self-concept from the terms others use to describe them.

Leader Any member of a group who performs acts that have positive influence in ensuring that the requirements of a problem-solving or decision-making task are satisfied.

Leader-centered style The manner of behavior of a group leader who initiates and controls interaction, gives directions, unilaterally decides when to move discussion forward, and generally takes responsibility for determining a group's solution to a problem or decision.

Leadership   Any act that has positive influence in ensuring that the requirements of a problem-solving or decision-making task are satisfied.

Leadership style   The characteristic manner in which a person who is in a position of leadership or is exercising leadership behaves in a group.

Leading question   Question that attempts to elicit a predetermined response from an interviewee.

Legitimacy   A form of power which may be used in the family. It is based on expected power relationships. For example, parents are afforded the right to exert control over their children. The parents are seen as having a legitimate right to exert this control.

Listening   The process of attending to aural symbols and assigning meaning to them.

Loaded question   A strongly leading question.

Malapropism   Incorrect use of a word for one that sounds alike.

Manuscript delivery   Type of presentation that is used when a speech is read word for word from a text.

Marginal   A method individuals use when crossing cultural boundaries. The marginal approach involves trying to accept the norms of a new culture and one's culture of origin, even when those norms are incompatible. Individuals using this approach often fail to fit in, or end up on the margins of both cultures.

Masculinity-femininity   One dimension along with cultures vary. Masculine cultures value individuals who exercise power and are assertive, whereas feminine cultures value personal relationships and role flexibility.

Mediating   A method individuals use when crossing cultural boundaries. This approach is rare. It results when an individual is able to combine the important features of the new culture, and his or her culture of origin.

Medium   A particular means of communication.

Memorized delivery   Type of presentation that is used when a speaker recites the text of a speech from memory.

Message credibility   The apparent degree of truth in a communicator's utterances.

Metacommunication   Communicating explicitly about the "frame" rather than the context of communication.

Metaperception   The process of inferring what another person is experiencing.

Metaphor   Figure of speech that directly compares two ideas that are not commonly linked together.

Mirror question   Used in interview context, question that restates the interviewee's response to a preceding question; used to aid the interviewer in checking the cor-

rectness of his or her interpretation of the interviewee's response. Also encourages the interviewee to clarify or elaborate on his or her answer.

Mixed metaphor   Flawed figure of speech in which an analogy is expressed unrealistically through comparing two ideas that should not be linked together.

Mnemonic device   Striking code or device that helps a speaker remember specific information signified by the code or device.

Motivation   A psychological condition that sets the direction for one's behavior.

Motives   Inner drives that prompt action; the reason behind an action that causes an individual to behave in a particular way.

Movement   Element of physical delivery in which the speaker changes physical location in concert with a message.

Neutral question   Question that gives no indication of the desired response.

Noise   Any source of interference that limits reception of a message.

Nominal Group Technique   An adaptation of brainstorming in which group members record their ideas in writing instead of stating them orally.

Nondirective interview   Interview in which the interviewer surrenders control to the interviewee, allowing the interviewee to supply information as he or she decides.

Nonverbal communication   Communication that is not encoded in a verbal language system, but involves signals other than words.

Norm   A standard that defines acceptable behavior in a group.

Nuclear family   Family members who live in the same household. Typically, the parents (or parent) and their immediate offspring.

Number   Type of supporting material that provides a simple measurement.

Objective   The end toward which communicative activity is directed.

Onomatopoeia   Figure of speech in which the speaker's words make sounds associated with the idea being addressed.

Open question   Question used in interview context that permits the interviewee to respond freely.

Opinion   Belief or judgment that may be acceptable to an audience because it holds the same opinion or is impressed by such factors as the speaker's credibility.

Paralanguage   The study of all cues in oral speech other than the context of the words spoken.

Parallelism   Figure of speech in which the same words are repeated in successive statements or sentences.

Paraphrase   Type of supporting material that provides a loose but accurate restatement of someone else's words.

Paraphrasing   Restatement to convey support and understanding.

Perception   The process of determining and interpreting what we experience.

Perceptual selectivity   The process of selecting out of an environment those sights, sounds, and other stimuli you will attend to, while ignoring others.

Performance appraisal interview   Interview used to provide the employee with feedback regarding his or her work in the organization.

Personal distance   The amount of distance maintained —generally ranging from eighteen inches to approximately four feet—while conducting conversations with friends and acquaintances.

Personal references   Use of pronouns such as *I* and *you* to establish a relationship with a listener.

Personal space   The psychological and physical comfort zone that surrounds a person as he or she moves about.

Persuasion   A form of power which may be used in the family. It is based on the ability to use well reasoned arguments to exert control over another.

Persuasive change   A measurable difference in the audience's thought or action.

Persuasive communication   Communication to influence others.

Persuasive degree   The intensity of change in audience attitudes or behavior.

Persuasive direction   Movement by audience away from previously held attitudes or behaviors.

Phatic communication   "Small talk." Communication in which the primary goal is to socialize and cover non-controversial topics as a means of getting to know the other person.

Physiological needs   Basic requirements and urges, such as breathing, eating, and drinking. These needs are addressed in emotional appeals.

Pitch   Level of human voice, high to low, that is produced by vibrations in vocal chords.

Plausibility   The extent to which a message, on its face, rings true.

Polarization   The tendency of language to force us to think or talk about extremes.

Position   The part a member has in a group.

Power   The ability of an individual to change the behavior of other family members.

Power distance   One dimension along which cultures vary. High power distance cultures accept the distinction between high power and low power positions in society. Low power distance cultures value equality, and have fewer outward signs to distinguish the powerful from the powerless members of society.

Primary question   Question used in interview context that introduces a new topic area.

Probe question   Used in interview context, question posed as a brief word or phrase that encourages the interviewee to continue the response in the same general direction.

Problem solving   Any set of activities an individual or group performs to reduce or eliminate some perceived difficulty.

Problem-solving pattern of organization   System of organizing speeches according to a sequence of need and satisfaction.

Profanity   Irreverent or coarse use of language.

Promotion interview   Interview used to screen applicants within an organization for promotion.

Pronunciation   Expression of words in which the speaker uses correct sounds and accent.

Proxemics   The use of space by humans.

Psychological-level knowledge   The knowledge we possess of others as individuals; includes knowledge of personal preferences, beliefs, and values.

Public distance   The amount of distance typically maintained in public speaking and ceremonial events— ranging from twelve to twenty-five feet.

Punishment   A form of power which may be used in the family. It involves inflicting physical punishment or withholding a desired commodity.

Quality   Subjective evaluation of human voice based on factors such as volume, rate, pitch, articulation, nasality, breathiness, and hoarseness.

Quality circle   A small group of employees who meet regularly to discuss ways in which to improve various aspects of their working conditions.

Question of conjecture   An issue involving decisions about what is probable or likely under specified conditions in a given case.

Question of fact   An issue involving decisions about what is true in a given case.

Question of policy   An issue involving decisions about what should be done in a given case.

Question of value   An issue involving decisions about what is acceptable in a given case.

Quotation   Type of supporting material that provides a word-for-word borrowing of someone else's words.

Racist language   Language usage that has the effect of

demeaning or otherwise offending a specific group or groups.

Rate Basic tempo of vocal delivery.

Rational appeal Reasoning or argument why an attitude or behavior is desirable or not; supported with evidence.

Reaction What an individual understands, believes, feels, or does as a result of his or her interpretation of a message.

Reception The activity of becoming aware of a message and recognizing it as such.

Recognition Process in which a speaker introduces listeners to information that was previously unknown.

Reflective listening Listening to help others deal with personal problems or concerns. It usually involves restating what the other person said to give him/her a sense of support and understanding.

Regulators Nonoral and oral behaviors that serve to maintain and coordinate the sequencing and turn taking that occurs when two or more people interact.

Relational message An utterance that reveals how a communicator feels about the person with whom he or she is interacting.

Relationship initiation The process of building relationships, moving from initial interaction to greater levels of intimacy.

Relationship maintenance The process of sustaining a relationship and fulfilling relationship expectations.

Relationship termination The process of moving from greater to diminishing levels of intimacy.

Repetition Emphasizing important ideas by saying them again using the same words.

Retention Process in which a speaker helps listeners to remember information.

Reward power A form of power which may be used in the family. It involves providing a desired reward in order to change another family member's behavior.

Rhetoric System of public speaking and writing created by ancient Greeks.

Role A social category that designates your social rights and responsibilities; the behavior associated with a position.

Role conflict Incompatibility in views about the proper enactment of a role.

Safety needs Requirements and urges for a sense of security or order. These needs are addressed in emotional appeals.

Sapir-Whorf hypothesis A linguistic theory suggesting that language determines thought.

Scheme Figure of speech that emphasizes an idea by expressing it in language that has an unusual structure or pattern.

Secondary question Question used in interview context that follows up on some aspect of a primary question; used to get more elaboration from the interviewee.

Selective listening The tendency to listen to what you already agree with. As a result, you may rationalize or support your existing beliefs because you ignore any opposition.

Self-actualization needs Requirements and urges to be all that one can be. These needs are addressed in emotional appeals.

Self-disclosure The act of voluntarily communicating information about oneself that the recipient is unlikely to uncover from other sources.

Self-esteem needs Requirements and urges for a positive self-image and social status. These needs are addressed in emotional appeals.

Self-presentation Managing your own identity in a communication encounter; a communicative strategy used to negotiate identities and the social rights and responsibilities that correspond to them.

Semantic difficulty A problem in achieving shared understanding that occurs when two people assign different meanings to the same word(s) because their past experiences with the word(s) are dissimilar.

Separate marital types One type of marital relationship, in which the couple holds conventional views on many family issues. In surprising contrast, however, these couples also value individual freedom over strong relational interdependence.

Sequencing The conventional patterns we follow when we use language.

Sexist language Language usage that has the effect of demeaning or otherwise offending a specific gender.

Sign Anything that represents something else.

Simile Figure of speech that compares two ideas by using the words *like* or *as*.

Social distance The amount of distance typically maintained—generally ranging from four to twelve feet—while engaged in impersonal, role-related interactions.

Sociological-level knowledge Knowledge of the groups to which a person belongs. This knowledge allows us to tailor our messages more closely to a recipient.

Social validation Acceptance by others in response to the revelation of personal information.

Sophists Ancient Greek teachers and orators who claimed that no "truth" existed and therefore public speakers could never be accused of deceiving audiences.

Source reliability   One's reputation for accuracy and truthfulness.

Spatial pattern of organization   System of organizing speeches according to physical place, as determined by geographic location, distance, height, and depth.

Speaker's diary   Daily account of experiences, ideas, feelings, and impressions of other people and events; used to discover speech material.

Statement   Total number of words spoken in one breath.

Static evaluation   The tendency to allow words to capture an object, event, or feeling at a particular point in time, regardless of intervening events.

Statistic   Type of supporting material that provides a complex measurement of the relationship between two or more numbers.

Status   The importance assigned to positions and roles.

Stereotype   A fixed view of the common characteristics of the objects in a class of objects that ignores individual differences.

Stimulation   Any type of sensory or mental experience of which we become aware.

Structure   The pattern of relationships among the positions and roles represented in a group.

Subculture   A distinct group within a larger social culture, for example, many ethnic or racial groups in the U.S. The racial or ethnic group would be considered a subculture if members of the group shared common beliefs, practices, or aesthetic tastes (in cooking, music, family structure, and such) which are distinct from the general culture at large.

Subordination   Quality of speech organization that is achieved when elements of lesser importance support elements of greater importance.

Support   Messages used by parents (encouraging, praising, approving) which show approval for a child's behavior. These messages make the child more comfortable with the parent.

Symbol   Something that is intentionally used to represent something else. Symbols are a special class of signs.

Task   The set of activities a group performs to achieve a goal.

Temporal pattern of organization   System of organizing speeches according to a forward or backward sequence of time or steps.

Territoriality   The impulse to establish and maintain control over a physical area or space.

Theme   Special perspective on the subject matter of a speech; identifies how the speaker wants the audience to respond.

Traditional marital types   One type of marital relationship, in which the couple subscribes to traditional male-female role models and is guided by what have become known as traditional values.

Trait   Any identifiable characteristic an individual possesses or appears to possess.

Transmission   The process by which a message is conveyed from the sender to the person or persons for whom it is intended.

Transitional language   Words that identify a shift from one point in a speech to another point.

Trope   Figure of speech that adds vividness to language by assigning unusual meanings to words.

Uncertainty avoidance   One dimension along which cultures vary. Cultures that rank high in uncertainty avoidance value clarity in social roles and have a low tolerance for ambiguity. Cultures low in uncertainty avoidance tolerate deviance and encourage risk taking.

Understanding   Process in which a speaker answers listeners' predictable questions about a subject.

Unity   Quality of speech organization that is achieved when all elements are directly related to the theme/purpose and each part of a speech contains related ideas and material.

Unsung hero(ine)   An individual who makes a difference in how well a group performs without others' notice.

Values   Attitudes of a very general nature that people consistently maintain.

Verbal communication   Any language system that employs arbitrary symbols shared by a group of language users.

Verbal style   One measure of cultural variation. The flavor or tone of language use within a culture, which can vary in terms of how direct, elaborate, personal, or instrumental (goal directed) it is.

Verifiability   A characteristic of messages relating to the possibility of establishing the authenticity of the factual claims they embody.

Vertical file   Library filing system that contains pamphlets and newspaper and magazine clippings of timely or local importance.

Vocalics   Sounds and related features of oral message presentation that invariably accompany symbolic exchange, but themselves are not linguistic symbols.

Volume   Force of vocal delivery.

References

Chapter 1

Berlo, D. K. (1960). *The process of communication.* New York: Holt, Rinehart and Winston.

Bettinghaus, E. P., and Cody, M. J. (1987). *Persuasive communication* (4th ed.). New York: Holt, Rinehart and Winston.

Burgoon, M., and Miller, M. D. (1990). Communication and influence. In G. L. Dahnke and G. W. Clatterbuck (Eds.). *Human communication: Theory and research* (pp. 229–258). Belmont, CA: Wadsworth.

Gregg, R. B. (1984). *Symbolic inducement and knowing.* Columbia, SC: University of South Carolina Press.

Johannesen, R. L. (1990). *Ethics in human communication* (3rd ed.). Prospect Heights, IL: Waveland.

Keltner, J. W. (1970). *Interpersonal speech-communication: Elements and structure.* Belmont, CA: Wadsworth.

King, S. W. (1988). The nature of communication. In R. S. Cathcart and L. A. Samovar (Eds.). *Small group communication: A reader* (5th ed., pp. 250–259). Dubuque, IA: William C. Brown.

Littlejohn, S. W. (1992). *Theories of human communication* (4th ed.). Belmont, CA: Wadsworth.

Pierce, J. R. (1960). *Symbols, signals, and noise: The nature and process of communication.* New York: Harper Torchbooks.

Poole, M. S., and Doelger, J. A. (1986). Developmental processes in group decision-making. In R. Y. Hirokawa and M. S. Poole (Eds.). *Communication and group decision-making* (pp. 35–61). Beverly Hills, CA: Sage.

Chapter 2

Asch, S. (1948). The doctrine of suggestion, prestige, and imitation in social psychology. *Psychological Review, 55,* 250–276.

Asuncion-Lande, N. C. (1990). Intercultural communication. In G. L. Dahnke and G. W. Clatterbuck (Eds.). *Human communication: Theory and research* (pp. 208–225). Belmont, CA: Wadsworth.

Berger, P., and Luckman, T. (1966). *The social construction of reality.* Garden City, NY: Doubleday.

Brehm, J. W. (1966). *A theory of psychological reactance.* New York: Academic Press.

Bruner, J. S. (1957). On going beyond the information given. In J. S. Bruner (Ed.). *Contemporary approaches to cognition* (pp. 41–69); Cambridge, MA: Harvard University Press.

Burke, K. (1966). *Language as symbolic action.* Berkeley, CA: University of California Press.

Clark, W.V.T. (1940). *The Ox-Bow incident.* New York: Vintage Books.

Eco, U. (1976). *A theory of semiotics.* Bloomington, IN: Indiana University Press.

Eco, U. (1984). *Semiotics and the philosophy of language.* Bloomington, IN: Indiana University Press.

Fishbein, M., and Ajzen, I. (1975). *Belief, attitude, intentions, and behavior: An introduction to theory and research.* Reading, MA: Addison-Wesley.

Fisher, B. A. (1979). Content and relationship dimensions

of communication in decision-making groups. *Communication Quarterly, 27*(3), 3–11.

Gregg, R. B. (1984). *Symbolic inducement and knowing: A study in the foundations of rhetoric.* Columbia, SC: University of South Carolina Press.

Harvey, J. B. (1974). The Abilene paradox: The management of agreement. *Organizational Dynamics, 3,* 63–80.

Heider, F. (1958). *The psychology of interpersonal relations.* New York: Wiley.

Laing, R. D. (1967). *The politics of experience.* New York: Pantheon.

Laing, R. D. (1969). *Self and others.* London: Tavistock.

Loftus, E. F. (1979). Eyewitness testimony. Cambridge, MA: Harvard University Press.

Mayer, J., and McMannus, D. (1988). *Landslide.* Boston: Houghton Mifflin.

Millar, F. E., and Rogers, E. L. (1976). A relational approach to interpersonal communication. In G. R. Miller (Ed.). *Explorations in interpersonal communication* (pp. 87–103). Beverly Hills, CA: Sage.

Miller, G. R., and Steinberg, M. (1992). Empathic skills and the development of communication effectiveness. In R. S. Cathcart and L. A. Samovar (Eds.), *Small group communication: A reader* (6th ed., pp. 375–381). Dubuque, IA: William C. Brown.

Nisbett, R., and Ross, L. (1980). *Human inference: Strategies and shortcomings of social judgment.* Englewood Cliffs, NJ: Prentice-Hall.

Sherif, C. W., Sherif, M., and Nebergall, R. E. (1965). *Attitude and attitude change: The social judgment-involvement approach.* Philadelphia: W. B. Saunders.

Wyer, R. S., Jr., and Carlston, D. E. (1979). *Social cognition, inference, and attribution.* Hillsdale, NJ: Lawrence Erlbaum.

Zillmann, D. (1978). Attribution and misattribution of excitatory reactions. In J. H. Harvey, W. J. Ickes, and R. F. Kidd (Eds.). *New directions in attribution research* (pp. 335–368). Hillsdale, NJ: Lawrence Erlbaum.

Chapter 3

Bostrom, R. N. (1988). *Understanding human communication* (3rd ed.). New York: Holt, Rinehart and Winston.

Cantril, H. (1941). *The psychology of social movements.* New York: John Wiley & Sons.

Corballis, M. C., and Beale, I. L. (1983). *The ambivalent mind.* Chicago: Nelson-Hall.

Floyd, J. (1985). *Listening: A practical approach.* Glenview, IL: Scott.

Hamilton, C., and Parker, C. (1990). *Communicating for results* (3rd ed.). Belmont, CA: Wadsworth.

Heinich, R., Molenda, M., and Russell, J.D. (1989).

Instructional media and the new technologies of instruction (3rd ed.). New York: Macmillan.

Hirsch, R. O. (1979). *Listening: A way to process information aurally.* Dubuque, IA: Scarisbrick.

Janis, I. L. (1982). *Groupthink* (2nd ed.). Boston: Houghton Mifflin.

Karlins, M., and Abelson, H. I. (1970). *Persuasion* (2nd ed.). New York: Springer.

Lorayne, H., and Lucas, J. (1974). *The memory book.* Chelsea, MI: Scarborough House.

Okun, S. K. (1977). How to be a better listener. In R. C. Huseman, C. M. Logue, and D. L. Freshley (Eds.), *Readings in interpersonal and organizational communication* (3rd ed, pp. 582–586). Boston: Allyn & Bacon.

Rogers, C. R., and Farson, R. E. (1977). Active listening. In R. C. Huseman, C. M. Logue, and D. L. Freshley (Eds.), *Readings in interpersonal and organizational communication* (3rd ed, pp. 561–576). Boston: Allyn & Bacon.

Ross, R. S. (1986). *Speech communication* (7th ed.). Englewood Cliffs, NJ: Prentice-Hall.

Timm, P. R. (1980). *Managerial communication.* Englewood Cliffs, NJ: Prentice-Hall.

Wovin, A. D., and Coakley, C. G. (1982). *Listening.* Dubuque, IA: W. C. Brown.

Chapter 4

Allen, I. L. (1983). *The language of ethnic conflict: Social organization and lexical culture.* New York: Columbia University Press.

Bernstein, R. (1988, December 11). On language: Youthspeak. *New York Times Magazine.* pp. 22–24.

Brooks, W. D., Scafe, M., and Siler, I. C. (1980). *Verbal language and communication.* Dubuque, IA: Gorsuch Scarisbrick.

Cross, D. W. (1979). *Word abuse: How the words we use use us.* New York: Coward, McCann and Geoghegan.

Dickson, P. (1990). *Slang!* New York: Pocket Books.

Leiter, K. (1980). *A primer on ethnomethodology.* New York: Oxford University Press.

Lutz, W. (1989). *Doublespeak: From "revenue enhancement" to "terminal living": How government, business, advertisers, and others use language to deceive you.* New York: Harper & Row.

Maggio, R. (1987). *The nonsexist word finder: A dictionary of gender-free usage.* Phoenix, AZ: Oryx Press.

Munro, P. (1991). *Slang U.* New York: Crown Press.

Nolan, M. J. (1975). The relationship between verbal and nonverbal communication. In G. J. Hanneman and W. J. McEwen (Eds.), *Communication and behavior.* Reading, MA: Addison-Wesley.

Sacks, H. (1972). On the analyzability of stories by children. In J. J. Gumperz and D. Hymes (Eds.), *Directions in sociolinguistics* (pp. 325–345). New York: Holt, Rinehart and Winston.

Tannen, D. (1990). *You just don't understand.* New York: Morrow.(1969, December 11). The freaks had a word for It. *Newsweek, p. 18.*

Whorf, B. L. (1956). *Language, thought and reality: selected writings.* Cambridge, MA: MIT Press.

Chapter 5

Altman, I. (1975). *The environment and social behavior.* Monterey, CA: Brooks/Cole.

Birdwhistell, R. (1955). Background to kinesics. *ETC, 13,* 10–18.

Burgoon, J. K. (1985). Nonverbal signals. In M. L. Knapp and G. R. Miller (Eds.), *Handbook of interpersonal communication* (pp. 344–390). Beverly Hills, CA: Sage.

Burgoon, J. K., Buller, D. B., and Woodall, W. G. (1989). *Nonverbal communication: The unspoken dialogue.* New York: Harper & Row.

Eibl-Eibesfeldt, I. (1973). The expressive behavior of the deaf-and-blind-born. In M. von Cranach and I. Vine (Eds.), *Social communication and movement* (pp. 163–194). New York: Academic Press.

Eibl-Eibesfeldt, I. (1975). *Ethology: The biology of behavior* (2nd ed.) New York: Holt, Rinehart and Winston.

Ekman, P. (Ed.) (1982). Emotion in the human face (2nd ed.). New York: Cambridge.

Ekman, P. (1973). *Cross cultural studies of facial expression.* In P. Ekman (ed.), *Darwin and facial expression.* New York: Academic Press.

Ekman, P., and Friesen, W. V. (1969). The repertoire of nonverbal behavior: Categories, origins, usage and coding. *Semiotica, 1,* 49–98.

Hall, E. T. (1966). *The hidden dimension.* Garden City, NY: Anchor Books.

Hall, E. T. (1973). *The silent language.* Garden City, NY: Anchor Press/Doubleday.

Heslin, R., and Alper, T. (1983). Touch: A bonding gesture. In J. M. Wiemann and R. P. Harrison (Eds.), *Nonverbal interaction* (pp. 47–75). Beverly Hills, CA: Sage.

Hess, E. H. (1975). The role of pupil size in communication. *Scientific American, 233,* 110–119.

Infante, D. A., Rancer, A. S., and Womack, D. F. (1990). *Building communication theory.* Prospect Heights, IL: Waveland Press.

Jourard, S. M. (1968). *Disclosing man to himself.* New York: Van Nostrand.

Knapp, M. L. (1978). Nonverbal communication in human interaction (2nd ed.). New York: Holt, Rinehart and Winston.

Knapp, M. L. (1990). Nonverbal communication. In G. L.

Dahnke and G. W. Clatterbuck (Eds.), *Human communication: theory and research* (pp. 50–69). Belmont, CA: Wadsworth.

Knapp, M. L., Hart, R. P., Friedrich, G. W., and Shulman, G. M. (1973). The rhetoric of goodbye: Verbal and nonverbal correlates of human leave-taking. *Speech Monographs, 40,* 182–198.

Lewis, P. V. (1975). *Organizational communication: the essence of effective management.* Columbus, OH: Grid.

Lyman, S. M., and Scott, M. B. (1967). Territoriality: A neglected sociological dimension. *Social Problems, 15,* 236–249.

Malandro, L. A., Barker, L. L., and Barker, D. A. (1989). *Nonverbal communication* (2nd ed.). New York: Random House.

Mehrabian, A., and Ferris, S. R. (1967). Inference of attitudes from nonverbal communication in two channels. *Journal of Consulting Psychology, 31,* 248–252.

Morris, D. (1977). *Manwatching: a field guide to human behavior.* New York: Harry N. Abrams.

Nierenberg, G. I., and Calero, H. H. (1973). *How to read a person like a book.* New York: Pocket Books.

Rutter, D. R. (1984). *Looking and seeing.* New York: Wiley.

Chapter 6

Asuncion-Lande, N. C. (1990). Intercultural communication. In G. L. Dahnke and G. W. Clatterbuck (Eds.), *Human communication: Theory and research* (pp. 208–226). Belmont, CA: Wadsworth

Bochner, S. (1982). The social psychology of cross-cultural relations. In S. Bochner (Ed.), *Cultures in contact: Studies in cross-cultural interaction* (pp. 5–44). Oxford: Pergamon.

Brislin, R. W., Landis, D., and Brandt, M. E. (1983). Conceptualizations of intercultural behavior and training. In D. Landis and R. W. Brislin (Eds.), *Handbook of intercultural training (Vol. 1): Issues in theory and design,* (pp. 1–35). New York: Pergamon.

Ervin, S. M. (1964). Language and the TAT content in bilinguals. *Journal of Abnormal and Social Psychology, 68,* 500–567.

Furnham, A., and Bochner, S. (1982). Social difficulty in a foreign culture: An empirical analysis of culture shock. In S. Bochner (Ed.), *Cultures in contact: Studies in cross-cultural interaction* (pp. 161–198). Oxford: Pergamon.

Furnham, A., and Bochner, S. (1986). *Culture shock: Psychological reactions to unfamiliar environments.* London: Methuen.

Giles, H., and Franklyn-Stokes, A. (1989). Communicator characteristics. In M. K. Asante and W. B. Gudykunst (Eds.), *Handbook of international and intercultural communication* (pp. 117–144). Newbury Park, CA: Sage.

Gudykunst, W. B. (1987). Cross-cultural comparisons. In C. Berger and S. Chaffee (Eds.), *Handbook of communication science* (pp. 847–889). Newbury Park, CA: Sage.

Gudykunst, W. B., and Ting-Toomey, S. (1988). *Culture and interpersonal communication theory.* Newbury Park, CA: Sage.

Infante, D. A., Rancer, A. S., and Womack, D. F. (1990> *Building communication theory.* Prospect Heights, IL: Waveland.

Leonard, R., & Locke, D. C. (1993). Communication stereotypes: Is interracial communication possible? *Journal of Black Studies, 23*(3), 332–343.

Oberg, K. (1960). Cultural shock: Adjustment to new cultural environments. *Practical Anthropology, 7,* 177–182.

Porter, R. E., and Samovar, L. A. (1976). Communicating interculturally. In L. Samovar and R. Porter (Eds.), *Intercultural communication: A reader* (2nd ed.. pp. 4–24). Belmont, CA: Wadsworth.

Rheingold, H. (1988). *They have a word for it: A lighthearted lexicon of untranslatable words and phrases.* Los Angeles: Tarcher.

Schofield, J. W. (1986). Black-White contact in desegregated schools. In M. Hewstone and R. Brown (Eds), *Contact and conflict in intergroup encounters* (pp. 79–92). New York: Basil Blackwell.

Tannen, D. (1990). *You just don't understand: Women and men in conversation.* New York: William Marrow.

Ting-Toomey, S. (1985). Toward a theory of conflict and culture. In. W. B. Gudykunst, L. Stewart, and S. Ting-Toomey (Eds.), *Communication, culture, and organizational processes.* (pp. 71–86). Beverly Hills, CA: Sage.

Ting-Toomey, S. (1980). Talk as a cultural resource in the Chinese-American speech community. *Communication, 9,* 193–203.

Whiting, R. (1989). *You gotta have wa: When two cultures collide on the baseball diamond.* New York: Macmillan.

Chapter 7

Altman, I., and Taylor, D. (1973). *Social penetration: The development of interpersonal relationships.* New York: Holt, Rinehart and Winston.

Berger, C. R., and Calabrese, R. J. (1975). Some explorations in initial interaction and beyond: Toward a developmental theory of interpersonal communication. *Human Communication Research, 1,* 99–112.

Berger, C. R., and Bradac, J. J. (1982). *Language and social knowledge: Uncertainty in interpersonal relations.* London: E. E. Arnold.

Bochner, A. P. (1984). The functions of human communication in interpersonal bonding. In C. C. Arnold and J. W. Bowers (Eds.). *Handbook of rhetorical and communication theory* (pp. 544–621). Boston: Allyn & Bacon.

Coulthard, M. (1977). *An introduction to discourse analysis.* London: Longman.

Craig, R. T., and Tracy, K. (1983) (Eds.). *Conversational coherence: Form, structure and strategy.* Beverly Hills, CA: Sage.

Dascal, M., and Katriel, T. (1979). Digressions: A study in conversational coherence. *PTL: A Journal for Descriptive Poetics and Theory of Literature, 4,* 203–232.

Frentz, T. S., and Farrell, T. B. (1976). Language-action: A paradigm for communication. *Quarterly Journal of Speech, 62,* 333–349.

Gilbert, S. J. (1976). Empirical and theoretical extensions of self-disclosure. In G. R. Miller (Ed.), *Explorations in interpersonal communication* (pp. 197–215). Beverly Hills, CA: Sage.

Goffman, E. (1967). *Interaction ritual: Essays on face-to-face behavior.* Garden City, NY: Doubleday.

Grove, T. G. (1991). *Dyadic interaction: Choice and change in conversations and relationships.* Dubuque, IA: W. C. Brown.

Jourard, S. (1968). *Disclosing man to himself.* New York: Van Nostrand.

Knapp, M. L., Hart, R. P., Friedrich, G. W., and Shulman, G. M. (1973). The rhetoric of goodbye: Verbal and nonverbal correlates of human leave-taking. *Speech Monographs, 40,* 182–198.

Krivonos, P. D., and Knapp, M. L. (1975). Initiating communication: What do you say when you say hello? *Central States Speech Journal, 26,* 115–125.

Miller, G. R. (1978). The current status of theory and research in interpersonal communication. *Human Communication Research, 4,* 164–178.

Miller, G. R. (1990). Interpersonal Communication. In G. L. Dahnke and G. W. Clatterbuck (Eds.), *Human communication: Theory and research* (pp. 91–122). Belmont, CA: Wadsworth.

Miller, G. R., and Steinberg, M. (1975). *Between people: A new analysis of interpersonal communication.* Chicago: Science Research Associates.

Nofsinger, R. E., Jr. (1975). The demand ticket: A conversational device for getting the floor. *Speech Monographs, 42,* 1–9.

Parks, M. R. (1985). Interpersonal communication and the quest for personal competence. In M. L. Knapp and G. R. Miller (Eds.). *Handbook of interpersonal communication* (pp. 171–201). Beverly Hills, CA: Sage.

Pearce, W. B., and Sharp, S. M. (1973). Self-disclosing communication. *Journal of Communication, 23,* 409–425.

Planalp, S., Graham, M., and Paulson, L. (1987). Cohesive devices in conversations. *Communication Monographs, 54,* 325–343.

Planalp, S., and Tracy, K. (1980). Not to change the topic but…: A cognitive approach to the management of conversation. In D. Nimmo (Ed.). *Communication yearbook 4* (pp. 237–258). New Brunswick, NJ: Transaction Books.

Reardon, K. K. (1987). *Interpersonal communication: Where minds meet.* Belmont, CA: Wadsworth.

Sacks, H., Schegloff, E. A., and Jefferson, G. (1974). A simplest systematics for the organization of turn taking for conversation. Language, 50, 696–735.

Spitzberg, B. H. (1988). Communication competence: Measures of perceived effectiveness. In C. H. Tardy (Ed.). *A handbook for the study of human communication: Methods and instruments for observing, measuring, and assessing communication processes* (pp. 67–105). Norwood NJ: Ablex.

Trenholm, S. (1986). *Human communication theory.* Englewood Cliffs, NJ: Prentice-Hall.

Trenholm, S., and Jensen, A. (1988). *Interpersonal communication.* Belmont, CA: Wadsworth.

Watzlawick, P., Beavin, J. H., and Jackson, D. D. (1967). *Pragmatics of human communication.* New York: Norton.

Wilmot, W. W. (1987). *Dyadic communication* (3rd ed.). New York: Random House.

Chapter 8

Baxter, L. A. (1982). Strategies for ending relationships: Two studies. *Western Journal of Speech Communication, 46,* 223–241.

Baxter, L. A. (1985). Accomplishing relationship disengagement. In S. Duck and D. Perlman (Eds.). *Understanding personal relationships: An interdisciplinary approach* (pp. 243–266). Beverly Hills, CA: Sage.

Bell, R. A., Buerkel-Rothfuss, N. L., and Gore, K. E. (1987). "Did you bring the yarmulke for the cabbage patch kid?": The idiomatic communication of young lovers. *Human Communication Research, 14,* 47–67.

Berscheid, E. (1987). Emotion and Interpersonal Communication. In M. E. Roloff and G. R. Miller (Eds.), *Interpersonal processes: New directions in communication research* (pp. 77–88). Newbury Park, CA: Sage.

Blake, R. R., and Mouton, J. S. (1973). The fifth achievement. In F. E. Jandt (Ed.). *Conflict resolution through communication* (pp. 88–102). New York: Harper & Row.

Coser, L. A. (1956). *The functions of social conflict.* New York: Free Press.

Duck, S. (1976). Interpersonal communication in developing acquaintance. In G. R. Miller (Ed.). *Explorations in interpersonal communication* (pp. 127–147). Beverly Hills, CA: Sage.

Duck, S. (1985). Social and personal relationships. In M. L. Knapp and G. R. Miller (Eds.). *Handbook of interpersonal communication* (pp. 665–686). Beverly Hills, CA: Sage.

Goldhaber, G. M. (1979). *Organizational communication* (2nd ed.). Dubuque, IA: W. C. Brown.

Hinde, R. A. (1979). *Toward understanding relationships.* London: Academic Press.

Hocker, J. L., and Wilmot, W. W. (1991). *Interpersonal conflict* (3rd ed.). Dubuque, IA: W. C. Brown.

Hopper, R., Knapp, M. L., and Scott, L. (1981). Couples' personal idioms: Exploring intimate talk. *Journal of Communication, 31,* 23–33.

Jones, E. E., and Nisbett, R. E. (1972). The actor and the observer: Divergent perceptions of the causes of behavior. In E. E. Jones, D. E. Kanouse, H. H. Kelley, R. E. Nisbett, S. Valins, and B. Weiner (Eds.). *Attribution: Perceiving the causes of behavior* (pp. 79–94). Morristown, NJ: General Learning Press.

Kelley, H. H., Berscheid, E., Christensen, A., Harvey, J. H., Huston, T. L., Levinger, G., McClintock, E., Peplau, L. A., and Peterson, D. R. (1983). Analyzing close relationships. In H. H. Kelley et al. (Eds.). *Close relationships* (pp. 20–67). New York: W. H. Freeman.

Knapp, M. L. (1978). *Social intercourse: From greeting to goodbye.* Boston: Allyn & Bacon.

Millar, F. E., and Rogers, L. E. (1976). A relational approach to interpersonal communication. In G. R. Miller (Ed.), *Explorations in interpersonal communication* (pp. 87–103). Beverly Hills, CA: Sage.

Miller, G. R., and Parks, M. R. (1982). Communication in dissolving relationships. In S. W. Duck (Ed.), *Personal relationships 4: Dissolving personal relationships* (pp. 127–154). London: Academic Press.

Reardon, K. K. (1987). *Interpersonal communication: Where minds meet.* Belmont, CA: Wadsworth.

Regan, D. T., and Totten, J. (1975). Empathy and attribution: Turning observers into actors. *Journal of Personality and Social Psychology, 32,* 850–856.

Sillars, A. L. (1980). Attributions and communication in roommate conflicts. *Communication Monographs, 47*(3), 180–200.

Wilmot, W. W. (1987). *Dyadic communication* (3rd ed.). New York: Random House.

Wilmot, W. W., Carbaugh, D. A., and Baxter, L. A. (1985). Communicative strategies used to terminate romantic relationships. *Western Journal of Speech Communication, 49,* 204–216.

Wish, M., and Kaplan, S. J. (1977). Toward an implicit theory of interpersonal communication. *Sociometry, 40,* 234–246.

Chapter 9

Amato, P. R. (1993). Children's adjustment to divorce: Theories, hypotheses, and empirical support. *Journal of Marriage and the Family, 55,* 23–38.

Bochner, A. P., and Eisenberg, E.M. (1987). Family process: System perspective. In C. Berger and S. Chaffee (Eds.), *Handbook of Communication Science* (pp. 540–563). Newbury Park, CA: Sage.

Bumpass, L. L. (1990). What's happening to the family? Interactions between demographic and institutional change. *Demography, 27*(4), 483–498.

Conn, C., and Silverman, I. (Eds.) (1991). *What counts: The complete Harper's index.* New York: Holt.

Crispell, D. (1992). Myths of the 1950s. *American Demographics,* August, 38–43.

Cuber, J. F., and Harroff, P. B. (1985). Five types of marriage. In J. Henslin (Ed.), *Marriage and family in a changing society* (2nd ed., pp. 289–297). New York: Free Press.

Curran, D. (1983). *Traits of a healthy family.* Minneapolis: Winston Press.

Dunn, J. (1992). Sisters and brothers: Current issues in developmental research. In F. Boer and J. Dunn (Eds.), *Children's sibling relationships: Developmental and clinical issues* (pp. 1–17). Hillsdale, NJ: Lawrence Erlbaum.

Ferree, M. M. (1991). The gender division of labor in two-earner marriages: Dimensions of variability and change. *Journal of Family Issues, 12*(2), 158–180.

Fitzpatrick, M. A., and Badzinski, D. M. (1985). All in the family: Interpersonal communication in kin relationships. In M. Knapp and G. Miller (Eds), *Handbook of interpersonal communication* (pp. 687–736). Beverly Hills, CA: Sage.

Fitzpatrick, M. A., and Best, P. (1979). Dyadic adjustment in relational types: Consensus, cohesion, affectional expression, and satisfaction in enduring relationships. *Communication Monographs, 46*(3), 167–178.

Fitzpatrick, M. A., and Wamboldt, F. S. (1990). Where is all said and done? Toward an integration of intrapersonal and interpersonal models of marital and family communication. *Communication Research, 17*(4), 421–430.

French, J. R. P., Jr., and Raven, B. H. (1962). The bases of social power. In D. Cartwright and A. Zander (Eds.), *Group dynamics* (pp. 607–623). Evanston, IL: Row Peterson.

Galvin, K. M., and Brommel, B. J. (1986). *Family communication: Cohesion and change.* Glenview, IL: Scott, Foresman.

Gilbert, D. A. (1988) *Compendium of American public opinion.* New York: Facts on File.

Hochschild, A. (1989). *The second shift.* New York: Viking.

Kamo, Y. (1988). Determinants of household division of labor: Resources, power, ideology. *Journal of Family Issues, 9*(2), 177–200.

McGoldrick, M., and Carter, E. A. (1985). The stages of the family life cycle. In J. Henslin (Ed.), *Marriage and family in a changing society* (2nd ed., pp. 43–54). New York: Free Press.

Robinson, J. P. (1988). Who's doing the housework? *American Demographics,* December, 24–28.

Schutz, W. C. (1966). *The interpersonal underworld.* Palo Alto, CA: Science & Behavior Books.

Trenholm, S., and Jensen, A. (1988). *Interpersonal communication.* Belmont, CA: Wadsworth.

Turner, R. H. (1970). *Family interaction.* New York: Wiley.

Vangelisti, A. L. (1993). Communication in the family: The influence of time, relational prototypes, and irrationality. *Communication Monographs, 60,* 42–54.

Vaughan, D. (1985). Uncoupling: The social construction of divorce. In J. Henslin (Ed.), *Marriage and family in a changing society* (2nd ed., pp. 429–439). New York: Free Press.

Wallerstein, J. S., and Kelly, J. B. (1985). Effects of parental divorce. In J. Henslin (Ed.), *Marriage and family in a changing society* (2nd ed., pp. 440–452). New York: Free Press.

Chapter 10

Bolles, R. N. (1990). *What color is your parachute? A practical manual for job-hunters and career changers.* Berkeley, CA: Ten Speed Press.

Gifford, R., Ng, C. F., and Wilkinson, M. (1985). Nonverbal cues in the employment interview: Links between applicant qualities and interviewer judgments. *Journal of Applied Psychology, 70,* 729–736.

Haldane, B. (1988). *Career satisfaction and success: How to know and manage your strengths.* Seattle, WA: Wellness Behavior.

Hellman, P. (1986). *Ready, aim, you're hired!: How to job-interview successfully anytime, anywhere with anyone.* New York: AMACOM.

Kahn, R. L., and Cannell, C. F. (1983). *The dynamics of interviewing: Theory, technique, and cases.* Malabar, FL: Malabar.

Lahiff, J. M. (1977). Interviewing for Results. In R. C. Huseman, C. M. Logue, and D. L. Freshley (Eds.). *Readings in interpersonal and organizational communication* (pp. 395–414). Boston: Allyn & Bacon.

Medley, H. A. (1978). *Sweaty palms: The neglected art of being interviewed.* Berkeley, CA: Ten Speed Press.

Miller, A. F., and Mattson, R. T. (1977). *The truth about you: Discover what you should be doing with your life.* Simsbury, CT: People Management Incorporated.

Rowe, P. M. (1989). Unfavorable information and interview decisions. In R. W. Eder and G. R. Ferris (Eds.), *The employment interview: Theory, research, and practice* (pp. 77–89). Newbury Park, CA: Sage.

Snyder, M., and Swan, W. B. (1978). Hypothesis testing

processes in social interaction. *Journal of Personality and Social Psychology, 36*(11), 1202–1212.

Snyder, M. (1981). Seek and ye shall find: Hypothesis testing about other people. In E. T. Higgins, C. P. Hieman, and M. P. Zanna (Eds.). *Social cognition: The Ontario symposium on personality and social psychology.* Hillsdale, NJ: Lawrence Erlbaum.

Stewart, C. J., and Cash, W. B. (1978). Interviewing: Principles and Practices (2nd ed.). Dubuque, IA: W. C. Brown.

Chapter 11

Aronson, E. (1988). *The social animal* (5th ed.) New York: W. H. Freeman.

Biddle, B. J., and Thomas, E. J. (Eds.) (1966). *Role theory: Concepts and research.* New York: Wiley.

Bormann, E. G. (1990). *Small group communication: Theory and practice* (3rd ed.). New York: Harper & Row.

Burgoon, J. K. (1988). Spatial relationships in small groups. In R. S. Cathcart and L. A. Samovar (Eds.), *Small group communication: A reader* (5th ed., pp. 351–366). Dubuque, IA: William C. Brown.

Delbecq, C., Van de Ven, A. H., and Gustafsen, D. (1975). *Group techniques for program planning.* Glenview, IL: Scott, Foresman.

Dewey, J. (1910). *How we think.* Boston: Heath.

Gouran, D. S., and Geonetta, S. C. (1977). Patterns of interaction as a function of leadership centralization in decision-making groups. *Central States Speech Journal, 28,* 47–53.

Gouran, D. S., Hirokawa, R. Y., and Martz, A. E. (1986). A critical analysis of factors related to decisional processes involved in the *Challenger* disaster. *Central States Speech Journal, 37,* 119–135.

Hill, T. A. (1976). An experimental study of the relationship between opinionated leadership and small group consensus. *Communication Monographs, 43,* 246–257.

Janis, I. L. (1982). *Groupthink* (2nd ed.). Boston: Houghton Mifflin.

Janis, I. L. (1989). *Crucial decisions: Leadership in policy making and crisis management.* New York: Free Press.

Osborn, A. F. (1957). *Applied imagination.* New York: Scribner's.

Ouchi, W. (1981). *Theory z.* Reading, MA: Addison-Wesley.

Palazzolo (1988). The social group: Definitions. In R. S. Cathcart and L. A. Samovar (Eds.), *Small group communication: A reader* (5th ed., pp. 6–19). Dubuque, IA: William C. Brown.

Peters, T. J., and Waterman, R. H., Jr. (1982). *In search of excellence: Lessons from America's best run companies.* New York: Harper & Row.

Poole, M. S. (1992). Group communication and the structuring process. In R. S. Cathcart and L. A. Samovar (Eds.). *Small group communication: A reader* (6th ed., pp. 147–157). Dubuque, IA: W. C. Brown.

Schacter, S. (1951). Deviation, communication, and rejection. *Journal of Abnormal and Social Psychology, 46,* 190–207.

Shaw, M. E. (1981). *Group dynamics: The psychology of small group behavior* (3rd ed.). New York: McGraw-Hill.

Shaw, M. E., and Gouran, D. S. (1990). Group dynamics and communication. In G. L. Dahnke and G. W. Clatterbuck (Eds.), *Human communication: Theory and research* (pp. 123–155). Belmont, CA: Wadsworth.

Shimanoff, S. B. (1980). *Communication rules: Theory and research.* Beverly Hills, CA: Sage.

Zander, A. (1971). *Motives and goals in groups.* New York: Academic Press.

Chapter 12

Aronson, E. (1980). *The social animal* (3rd ed.). San Francisco: W. H. Freeman.

Bass, B. M. (1990). *Bass and Stogdill's handbook of leadership: Theory, research, and managerial applications* (3rd ed.). New York: Free Press.

Bettinghaus, E. P., and Cody, M. J. (1987). *Persuasive communication* (4th ed.). New York: Holt, Rinehart and Winston.

Burns, J. M. (1978). *Leadership.* New York: Harper & Row.

Cattell, R. B. (1951). New concepts for measuring leadership, in terms of group syntality. *Human Relations, 4,* 161–184.

Chemers, M. M. (1987). Leadership processes: Intrapersonal, interpersonal, and societal influences. In C. Hendrick (Ed.), *Group processes* (pp. 252–277). Beverly Hills, CA: Sage.

Fiedler, F. E. (1967). A theory of leadership effectiveness. New York: McGraw-Hill.

Fisher, B. A. (1970). The process of decision modification in small discussion groups. *Journal of Communication, 20,* 51–64.

Fisher, B. A. (1985). Leadership as medium: Treating complexity in group communication research. *Small Group Behavior, 16,* 167–196.

Fisher, B. A. (1986). Leadership: When does the difference make a difference? In R. Y. Hirokawa and M. S. Poole (Eds.), *Communication and group decision-making* (pp. 197–215). Beverly Hills, CA: Sage.

Gibson, J. W., and Hodgetts, R. M. (1986). *Organizational communication: A managerial perspective.* New York: Academic Press.

Gouran, D. S. (1970). Conceptual and methodological approaches to the study of leadership. *Central States Speech Journal, 21,* 217–223.

Hackman, M. Z., and Johnson, C. E. (1991). *Leadership: A communication perspective.* Prospect Heights, IL: Waveland.

Haiman, F. S. (1951). *Group leadership and democratic action.* Boston: Houghton Mifflin.

Hemphill, J. K. (1955). Leadership behavior associated with the administrative reputations of college departments. *Journal of Educational Psychology, 46,* 385–401.

Hollander, E. P., and Julian, J. W. (1969). Contemporary trends in the analysis of leadership processes. *Psychological Bulletin, 71,* 387–397.

Klimoski, R. J., and Hayes, N. J. (1980). Leader behavior and subordinate motivation. *Personnel Psychology, 33,* 543–555.

Nash, J. B. (1929). Leadership. *Phi Delta Kappan, 12,* 24–25.

Nixon, H. L., II. (1979). *The small group.* Englewood Cliffs, NJ: Prentice-Hall.

Pruitt, D. G., and Rubin, J. Z. (1986). *Social conflict: Escalation, stalemate, and settlement.* New York: Random House.

Report of the President's special review board (1988). Washington, DC: U. S. Government Printing Office.

Riecken, H. W. (1958). The effect of talkativeness on ability to influence group solutions of problems. *Sociometry, 21,* 309–321.

Shaw, M. E. (1981). *Group dynamics: The psychology of small group behavior* (3rd ed.). New York: McGraw-Hill.

Sherif, M., and Sherif, C. W. (1953). *Groups in harmony and tension.* New York: Harper & Row.

Stogdill, R. M. (1950). Leadership, membership, and organization. *Psychological Bulletin, 47,* 1–14.

Stogdill, R. M. (1974). *Handbook of leadership: A survey of theory and research.* New York: Free Press.

Tannenbaum, R., Weschler, I. R., and Massarik, F. (1961). *Leadership and organization.* New York: McGraw-Hill.

White, R., and Lippitt, R. (1960). *Autocracy and democracy.* New York: Harper & Brothers.

Chapter 13

Benderly, B. L., Gallagher, M. F., and Young, J. M. (1977). *Discovering culture: An introduction to anthropology.* New York: Van Nostrand Company.

Mitchell, A. (1983). *The nine American lifestyles: Who we are and where we're going.* New York: Macmillan.

Weisberg, H. F., and Bowen, B. D. (1977). *An introduction to survey research and data analysis.* San Francisco: W. H. Freeman.

Chapter 16

DeVito, J. A. (1969). Some psycholinguistic aspects of active and passive sentences. *Quarterly Journal of Speech, 55,* 401–406.

Flesch, R. (1949). *The art of readable writing.* New York: Harper & Brothers. As cited in D. J. Ochs and A. C. Winkler, *A brief introduction to speech.* (2nd ed., p. 149). New York: Harcourt Brace Jovanovich, 1989.

Gunning, R. (1968). *The technique of clear writing.* New York: McGraw-Hill.

Kibler, R. J., and Barker, L. L. (1968). An experimental study to assess the effects of three levels of mispronunciation on comprehension for three different populations. *Speech Monographs, 35,* 26–38.

Kibler, R. J., and Barker, L. L. (1972). Effects of selected levels of misspelling and mispronunciation on comprehension and retention. *Southern Speech Communication Journal, 37,* 387–401.

Petrie, C. R., Jr. (1963). Informative speaking: A summary and bibliography of related research. *Speech Monographs, 30,* 79–91.

Chapter 17

Auer, J. J. (1989, February 15). Prime Minister Margaret Thatcher—Political and communications modes. *Vital Speeches of the Day,* 276–282.

Deutsch, J. A., and Deutsch, D. (1970). Attention: Some theoretical considerations. *Psychological Review, 70,* 80–90.

Frandsen, K. D., and Clement, D. E. (1984). The functions of human communication in informing: communicating and processing information. In C. C. Arnold and J. W. Bowers (Eds.). *Handbook of rhetorical and communication theory.* Boston: Allyn & Bacon.

Taylor, S. E., and Thompson, S. C. (1982). Stalking the elusive "vividness" effect. *Psychological Review, 89,* 155–181.

Chapter 18

Boorstin, D. J. (1978). *The image: A guide to pseudo-events in America.* New York: Atheneum.

Boulding, K. E. (1961). *The image.* Ann Arbor: University of Michigan Press.

Maslow, A. (1970). *Motivation and Personality* (2nd ed.). New York: Harper & Row.

Miller, G. R., Burgoon, M., and Burgoon, J. K. (1984). The functions of human communication in changing attitudes and gaining compliance. In C. C. Arnold and J. W. Bowers (Eds.). *Handbook of rhetorical and communication theory* (pp. 400–474). Boston: Allyn & Bacon.

Solomon, R. C. (1976). The passions. Garden City, NY: Anchor Press.

Index

Chapter 4: Page 80, *Double Poke in the Eye* by Bruce Nauman. © 1993 Bruce Nauman/ARS, New York; Page 89, Johnny Horne/Picture Group; Page 96, Peter Menzel/Stock, Boston.

Chapter 5: Page 112, *Retrospect* by Keith Haring. © 1994 The Estate of Keith Haring; Page 115, Rob Crandall/Stock, Boston; Page 119, Richard Luria/Photo Researchers; Page 131, Robert Azzi/Woodfin Camp & Associates.

Chapter 6: Page 144, *Sunday After the Sermon* by Romare Bearden. Art Resource/Thyssen-Bornemisza Collection; Page 147, Richard Pasley/Stock, Boston; Page 156, David Austin/Stock, Boston; Page 171, Stephen Marks.

Chapter 7: Page 178, *Evening* by Alex Katz. © Alex Katz/VAGA, New York, 1993. Courtesy Marlborough Gallery, NY; Page 188, Janeart Ltd./The Image Bank; Page 194, David Lawrence/The Image Bank; Page 203, Ben Barnhart/Offshoot.

Chapter 8: Page 212, *The Screen Porch* by Fairfield Porter, 1964. Oil on Canvas, 79 1/2 x 79 1/2. Collection of Whitney Museum of American Art: Laurence H. Bloedel Bequest; Page 215, David Dempster/Offshoot; Page 230, Mieke Maas/The Image Bank.

Chapter 9: Page 240, *Portrait of the Family Siensky* by Piotr Konchalovsky. Scala/Art Resource/Trejakov Gallery, Moscow; Page 246, Dorothy Littell/Stock, Boston; Page 258, Bob Daemmrich/Stock, Boston; Page 260, Stephen Marks.

Chapter 10: Page 268, *Mural from the Temple of Longing* by Paul Klee. The Metropolitan Museum of Art: The Berggruen Klee Collection, 1984. (1984.313.33); Page 273, Margaret Kois/The Stock Market; Page 274, David Dempster/Offshoot.

Chapter 11: Page 292, *Flight Accomplished* by James Brooks. Port Authority of New York & New Jersey; Page 296, Jim Pickerell/Stock, Boston; Page 301, Gerd Ludwig/Woodfin Camp & Associates; Page 305, David Brownell/The Image Bank.

Chapter 12: Page 316, *Conjectures*, 1964 by Jean Dubuffet. © 1993 ARS, New York/ADAGP, Paris; Page 322, Jim Pickerell/Stock, Boston; Page 326, SYGMA.

Chapter 13: Page 338, *Politics, Farming, and the Law* by Thomas Hart Benton. © T.H. Benton and Rita P. Benton Testamentary Trusts/VAGA, New York, 1993. Courtesy Missouri Department of Natural Resources; Page 340, Warner Bros.; Page 346, Craig Blouin/Offshoot; Page 353, Alon Reininger/Contact Stock Images.

Chapter 14: Page 372, *These Libraries are Appreciated* by Jacob Lawrence. Philadelphia Museum of Art: The Louis E. Stern Collection; Page 374, Patrick Pfister/Stock, Boston; Page 377, Elizabeth Crews/Stock, Boston; Page 382, Doug Bryant/Offshoot.

Chapter 15: Page 396, *The Desk*, July 1st 1984, Photographic Collage by David Hockney, 48 1/2 x 46 1/2. © David Hockney; Page 408, Mark Abramson/Woodfin Camp & Associates; Page 415, Michael Kienitz/Picture Group.

Chapter 16: Page 428, *Webster-Hayne Debate* by G.P.A. Healy, City of Boston Art Commission; Page 430, Lester Sloan/Woodfin Camp & Associates; Page 439, Black Star; Page 445, C.L. Chryslin/The Image Bank; Page 446, Terry Madison/The Image Bank; Page 455, Bob Daemmrich/Stock, Boston.

Chapter 17: Page 462, *The Country School* by Winslow Homer. Oil on Canvas, 21 3/8 x 38 3/8. The Saint Louis Art Museum; Page 464, Pamela Price/Picture Group; Page 466, Greg Heisler/The Image Bank; Page 479, David Shopper/Stock, Boston.

Chapter 18: Page 486, *Trial by Jury* by Thomas Hart Benton. The Nelson-Atkins Museum of Art, Kansas City, Missouri (Bequest of the Artist) F75-21/11; Page 497, Ray Scioscia /Habitat for Humanity International.